Accounting:
A direct
approach

Accounting:
A direct approach

J. Kellock, C.A., F.C.C.A., F.A.A.I., M.B.I.M.,
Senior Lecturer in Accounting,
Robert Gordon's Institute of Technology
Aberdeen

J. Harrison, B.EC. (ADEL.), A.A.S.A.

J. Horrocks, B.A., B.COM. (N.Z.), M.EC. (ADEL.),
F.C.A. (N.Z.), F.A.S.A.
Formerly Principal Lecturer, School of Accountancy,
Southern Australian Institute of Technology

R. L. Newman, B.COM. (MELB.), M.B.M. (ADEL.),
F.A.S.A., C.P.A., A.F.A.I.M.
Reader, Department of Commerce,
University of Adelaide

PITMAN
150
YEARS

PITMAN PUBLISHING
128 Long Acre London WC2E 9AN

© J. Kellock, J. Harrison, J. Horrocks and P.L. Newman, 1987

First published in Great Britain 1987

British Library Cataloguing in Publication Data

Accounting: a direct approach
  1. Accounting
  I. Kellock, J. (John b. 1932)
  657 HF5635

ISBN 0-273-02731-X

Printed and bound in Great Britain at the Bath Press, Avon

Contents

Preface

Accounting: A Direct Approach has been based on the widely recognised book on accounting written by Australian authors Jack Harrison, Jack Horrocks and Robert Newman. It has been in existence for more than twenty years and is used widely in Australia by colleges of advanced education and universities as a standard text.

This book incorporates to some extent the format, style and approach used by the Australian authors. However, the content has been altered, where necessary, to include the relevant text appropriate to the needs of students studying in the United Kingdom.

Objectives of this book

The text is directed primarily towards the needs of students undertaking an accounting diploma, degree or an accounting qualification. It is considered that such students need a thorough grounding in basic accounting processes which lead to the production of general purpose accounting reports. At the same time, they need to be introduced to areas of both financial and management accounting, which will be dealt with in greater depth in later-year courses. Thus, while the bulk of the text is devoted to the 'elements of accounting', some sections probe the boundaries of more advanced issues (Chapters 13, 17, 18, 19, 20 and 21 contain this type of material).

It is considered that an appropriate balance between accounting procedures and the conceptual issues which underlie those procedures and practices has been maintained. First-year accounting students need to understand and have experience with ledger accounts, journal entries, reconciliation statements, worksheets, profit and loss statements, balance sheets, etc. At the same time they need to see these processes not as ends in themselves, but in terms of the relevance and usefulness of the information produced.

The first-year accounting student also needs to become familiar with the environment within which a professional accountant must operate. It is important to recognise that this environment is subject to continuous change. Perhaps the three areas of greatest change in recent years are:

1. technological changes affecting the collection and processing of accounting data;
2. the effects of changing levels of inflation on the relevance of accounting information produced on a historic basis;
3. greater recognition of accountants' responsibilities to users of accounting information as evidenced by the growing importance of Accounting Standards.

These three areas are discussed briefly below.

Technological changes

Computers, in their various forms and sizes, continue to have a tremendous impact on the accounting process and their mode of use has changed quite dramatically over the last few years. In the face of this rapid technological change a more general and less specialised approach to the use of computers in accounting has been adopted. In Chapter 5, the student is given a basic introduction to modern recording methods and, in subsequent chapters, accounting and control procedures are dealt with in the context of both manual and computerised methods. Because of the wide variety of computing equipment in use both in educational institutions and in practice, there are no exercises which are specifically written for computer application included in the book. However, many of the exercises set can be adapted for solution by computer.

Effects of inflation

In the face of continuing criticism of the capacity of historical cost-based accounting information to provide relevant information in periods of rapid inflation, the Accounting Standards Committee which is a joint committee of the six-member professional accounting bodies, has issued Statements of Standard Accounting Practice on Current Cost Accounting. The current statement is referred to as Statement of Standard Accounting Practice (SSAP)16. Although the Accounting Standards Committee suspended the mandatory status of this Standard with effect from 6 June 1985 it still remains an authoritative reference on accounting under the current cost convention. The basic objective of current cost accounts is to provide more useful information than that available from historical cost accounts alone for guidance of the management of the business, the shareholders and others on such matters as:

> the financial viability of the business;
> return on investment;
> pricing policy, cost control and distribution decisions; and
> gearing

While retaining conventional historical cost accounting as the basis of the text, there are outlined in Chapters 10 and 11 the measurement techniques necessary to determine current costs and in Chapter 21 it is demonstrated how current costs can be incorporated into the financial statements.

Accounting Standards

During the last fifteen years there has been considerable activity both in the UK and overseas in defining what are acceptable standards of accounting reporting. Currently, in the UK, there are over twenty-three separate Accounting Standards which have been issued by the Accounting Steering Committee. Chapter 17 outlines the background to the Accounting Standard setting process and gives a brief review of the Standards currently in use.

Where appropriate in this text, reference is made to the fact that an Accounting Standard exists on a particular topic and the major thrust of the Standard is described. However, the specific content of the current Standard is not discussed in detail. It is felt that accounting students, particularly in the early years of their studies, should not be restricted to what is currently recommended practice. Accounting practices will and should change over time as the needs and demands of the users of accounting information change.

Discussion questions, exercises and problems

Three distinct classes of questions are given at the end of each chapter.

1. *Discussion questions* – These may form the basis for discussion by students in groups or be set in written assignment work. Students should not expect to find the complete answers to some of the questions from the preceding textual material. Many questions are designed to force students to think about accounting issues, to draw on their own experiences and to read other material.

2. *Exercises* – These are designed to provide the student with applications of the concepts and processes which have been dealt with in the text.

3. *Problems* – In general these are larger and/or more complex than the Exercises. Some problems include issues which are not dealt with in detail in the text, and others require

knowledge drawn from other chapters of the text. In some problems, the student is required to make assumptions, and, in these a number of alternative solutions must be regarded as acceptable.

A solutions manual is available directly from the publishers.

Acknowledgements
In the preparation of this text thanks are extended to

The Directors of William Low plc for permission to reproduce extracts from their Annual Report in Chapter 18.

JOHN KELLOCK

Chapter 1
Objectives and influences on accounting

What is accounting? ☐ Historical perspectives ☐ Forms of business owner-ship ☐ Financial accounting and management accounting ☐ The accounting profession ☐ Development of Accounting Standards

What is accounting?

This question suggests the need to frame a definition and, indeed, many accounting texts commence with an attempt to give a precise definition of accounting. However, trying to arrive at a satisfactory definition is often a time-consuming and frustrating exercise. It is probably more fruitful, at this stage, to outline some of the major features of the tasks which accountants and, under their direction, accounting systems perform.

Central to the work of an accountant is the provision of *information*. The information may consist of sales figures for a day, a week or a month; a statement showing that profits or losses have been made by the enterprise; an analysis of costs; a forecast of the amount of finance that will be needed in the immediate future, and so on. It may relate to past performance, a present position, or future prospects. It may extend to examination of business records in order that an opinion may be expressed as to the correctness of such records; or as to the value of a share in a business; or as to the value of the assets possessed by a business.

Generally, accounting information is provided for, and disseminated to, interested parties to assist them in making *decisions*. Managers of enterprises need to make decisions about how to finance the activities of the enterprise; how the capital is to be invested in various types of resources; what products or services are to be produced or provided; how these products and services are to be priced and marketed; and so on. Owners or shareholders and prospective owners or shareholders make decisions about the acquisition of an interest in a particular business or, if an interest is already held, whether that interest should be increased, decreased or retained at its present level. Creditors and lenders want to decide whether or not to grant a loan or supply goods to a particular business, and want to form an opinion as to the likelihood of the firm being able to pay its debts as they fall due. Governments and government departments make decisions on the amount of tax which should be levied on businesses and individuals and on the extent to which the business activities of these enterprises should be controlled or assisted. Customers, employees and their unions, and the general public make a variety of decisions about the activities of business enterprises. Accounting information is a necessary ingredient of all these types of decisions.

Accountants and accounting systems generally focus on the activities of one *enterprise* operating in the overall economic and business environment. The particular enterprise about which information is required and about which decisions need to be made may be a retail store, a manufacturer, a farm, a doctor's or a dentist's practice, an educational institution, a charitable organisation, a sporting club, a government department, a television station; many other examples could be given. The enterprise may be owned by one person, by thousands of people, or, in the case of government departments and authorities, by the whole population of a country.

Note that we have used the word 'enterprise' to cover all types of organisations, not just those which operate to earn profits. Note also that accounting systems may also focus on sections of an enterprise. We will return later to discuss the concept of an accounting entity. Each enterprise is continuously interacting with individuals and other enterprises: buying and selling goods, incurring and granting indebtedness, receiving and paying cash, raising capital, employing labour, paying wages, dividends and taxes, and so on. These activities may be referred to as *economic events*.

One of the first tasks of the accountant, or the accounting system, is to observe these economic events and to identify or *select* those events which are relevant to the information needs of the enterprise's decision makers. These selected events may be termed *accounting transactions*. *Data* concerning these transactions have to be collected, and these represent the raw material upon which the accounting system operates. This ingestion of raw data is often termed the 'recording' phase of accounting. It is followed by the *processing* phase in which the data are classified and summarised. Finally, the resultant information (that is, processed data) is transmitted to decision makers in what is usually called the *reporting* phase. This sequence of events is presented diagrammatically in Fig. 1.1.

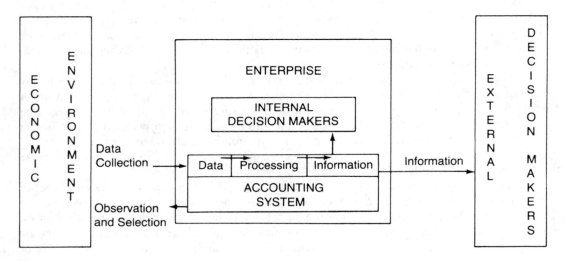

Fig. 1.1   The role of accounting.

Historical perspectives

It is important for the student of accounting to recognise that the nature of accounting has changed greatly over time and that this change is an ongoing process. Because accounting informs decision makers about the economic activities of particular enterprises, it follows that accounting systems and processes have to adapt to meet changes in the nature of economic activities and institutions, in the structure of business enterprises or in the information needs of decision makers.

Accounting is a very old profession and was well known in the early civilisations of the Egyptians, the Greeks and the Romans. In ancient times, it was mainly concerned with records of stewardship; that is, with recording the various transfers and dealings of a master. Perhaps this 'accounting' is better described as 'bookkeeping'. The records were a simple, single entry account of what had occurred, and there was little attempt to summarise the overall implications of a series of transactions.

Double entry bookkeeping was developed in Italy in the twelfth and thirteenth centuries. The Italian city states were the centres for trading with the East, and Italian merchants invested their wealth in productive resources such as ships and were entitled to a share of the profits of the trading ventures. A system was needed to calculate the shares to be apportioned. The first printed book describing double entry bookkeeping was written by a Franciscan monk, Luca Pacioli, and was published in 1494. During the fifteenth and sixteenth centuries, knowledge of the Italian method spread throughout Europe, and the first known accounting book in English was published in 1543.

While business enterprises were small in size and while owners generally maintained direct control over the management of these businesses, the role of accounting was restricted primarily to the recording of basic transactions and the consequent indebtedness. This role changed dramatically following the Industrial Revolution, when businesses became larger and more complex and a new form of business ownership developed.

The innovations of the Revolution led to enormous increases in production. Large factories were needed to accommodate machinery and larger and more permanent outlets were needed for the goods produced. To effect these changes, huge amounts of capital were needed; single organisers or 'inventors' rarely had the necessary wealth. It thus became essential that other people be persuaded to invest their savings. However, it is a difficult matter to persuade sensible people to finance a risky proposition. Not only were lenders likely to lose their money, but they could also be required to meet the debts of the enterprise. Because of the deficiencies of this type of collective ownership (company), various Acts of Parliament were introduced last century conferring *limited liability* on the members of such companies. These Acts provided for each member to hold a definite share in the enterprise and be liable only for the amount of the sum originally agreed upon if not already paid. No further claim could be made on a member for the debts of the company, which was by law given a separate legal identity quite apart from the shareholders. Prudent persons could therefore spread their savings over many companies, and, in each case, be aware of the full extent of their liability.

The development of the joint-stock company, usually with limited liability, increased tremendously the need for accounting information to be reported to owners (shareholders), who did not have direct access to knowledge of the day-to-day operations of their companies. The need for financial statements showing the results of operations for a period of time and the financial position of a company at a particular point in time was soon recognised, and the provision of such financial statements gradually became mandatory under government legislation controlling joint-stock companies. The specific nature of the company law requirements governing the published financial statements of companies has changed considerably over time, and changes are still occurring. Currently the Companies Act 1985 consolidates the greater part of all the previous Companies Acts.

Changes in the nature of ownership and control of business enterprise are only a part of the total changes which have occurred in the economic environment within which accounting operates. The major developments which have occurred in the twentieth century and which have influenced accounting thought and accounting practice can be summarised as follows:

1. *The emergence of management as a profession.* The development of large joint-stock companies, as described above, meant that the owners or shareholders could not always directly control the day-to-day operations of the enterprise. The control is delegated, through boards of directors, to professional managers who may or may not own shares in the company. Some of the accounting information which managers require for their decisions is quite different from the accounting information required by the shareholders. The distinction often drawn between *management accounting* and *financial accounting* is explained later in this chapter.

2. *Changing methods of financing business activities.* First, there has been a dramatic increase in

the number of organisations which provide the finance used in business transactions. The traditional providers of finance, such as banks, insurance companies, etc., have been supplemented by merchant banks, building societies, government agencies and others. Second, the methods of providing finance have been expanded. A variety of forms of consumer credit have been developed, and the mounting use of various forms of credit cards heralds the advent of a 'cashless society'. Both of these changes have had a significant influence on accounting practices.

3. *Increasing government influence over business activities.* This takes many forms. The most obvious is the increasing size and complexity of the taxes and duties collected by governments from businesses and individuals. Government legislation controlling joint-stock companies has been mentioned above. Other forms of government control which affect businesses, and thus accountants, are in the areas of trade practices, industrial relations (including wages determination), consumer protection, the licensing of some types of activity and the protection of environmental resources.

4. *Technological change.* There has been a tremendous advance in technology in the twentieth century. The processes of accounting, as distinct from the underlying principles, have been revolutionised by the advent and development of computers and their associated technologies.

5. *Continuing high levels of inflation.* Moderate to high rates of inflation have existed in most countries since the end of the Second World War. Methods of reporting accounting information may present a misleading picture when the prices of specific goods and services and the purchasing power of the monetary unit are changing significantly.

6. *International investment and ownership.* The emergence of multinational companies has led to a need to try to make accounting practices more uniform on a world-wide basis.

7. *The development of the accounting profession.* The organisation of the accounting profession and its role in setting accounting standards is discussed later in this chapter.

8. *Attitude and criticism of the public.* This has led to professional persons, such as accountants and auditors, being sued for negligence.

Forms of business ownership

As we have said, accounting is concerned specifically with the activities of a single enterprise. We have also noted the importance to accounting of the development of joint-stock companies. However, not all business enterprises are owned by companies, and many of the older forms of ownership persist. There are, for example, chemist shops owned by one person as well as some owned by partners or companies. Factories making furniture may be owned by one person (sole trader), or several. It is rare to find anything but companies operating large steel mills, motor car manufacturing plants, or other production units involving the use of valuable and costly plant and machinery. On the other hand, the making of 'exclusive' hats or hand-tailored suits is almost entirely restricted to sole traders and partnerships; other examples are the professions – dentists, doctors, architects. Also note that there are new types of ownership emerging. These include joint ventures between companies, trusts, and limited partnerships. Students should not regard the joint-stock company as the final stage of the development. There are six main types of ownership:

1. *Sole proprietor* (*or sole trader*) – where ownership is vested in one person only, although, of course, there may be many employees.

2. *Partnership* – where two or more owners carry on a business with a common view to profit.

Each partner is liable to the full extent of his private estate for the debts of the partnership, this being similar to the early 'companies'.

3. *Limited-liability companies* – enterprises incorporated under the Companies Act and operating as limited-liability companies. Capital is contributed by shareholders.

4. *Non-trading enterprises* – where the motive for formation is not primarily that of making profit, but of providing sport, entertainment, religion, culture, etc. Examples are football clubs, the YMCA and church groups. Some of them are incorporated under an Act of Parliament which gives members protection from debts similar to that provided by the limited-liability company. Others are unincorporated.

5. *Government and semi-government ownership* – where the 'owners' are an elected or nominated body (e.g., power-supply authorities, local councils, water boards).

6. *Co-operatives* – Sometimes a group of people with similar interests (fishermen, local residents, farmers) group together to form a co-operative, either as a limited-liability company, as an incorporated body, or as an unincorporated association. The purpose may be to get things done (erect a bridge or hall) or to eliminate the profits of a middleman by combining their resources to fix prices and sell direct to customers. Any profits made by co-operatives are usually 'ploughed back', or used for further developmental works, or are divided among the members under an agreed plan.

This does not exhaust all the possibilities of types of ownership. Certain owners are created by legal process: an executor or trustee may 'own' the property of a deceased person while carrying out the latter's wishes; a trustee in bankruptcy 'owns' the property of the bankrupt for the purpose of dividing it among the creditors, and so on. In recent years, there has been a significant increase in the creation of family trusts and trading trusts. However, these raise rather specialised accounting problems which are outside the scope of this text.

Financial accounting and management accounting

It is often useful to distinguish between two types of accounting information, the distinction being based on the group of decision makers for whom the information is prepared.

Financial accounting information is directed primarily at the needs of decision makers *external* to the business, such as shareholders, potential investors, creditors, government agencies, employees, customers and the general public. Such information generally relates to the firm as a whole, since most of the decisions of these external users concern the firm as an economic unit. Financial accounting information is often presented as part of an annual report. There are three major types of general-purpose, whole-enterprise financial statements:

1. *A balance sheet* – provides information on the enterprise's financial position as at a given date.

2. *A profit and loss statement* – shows the results of operations, profitable or otherwise, for a given period of time.

3. *A funds statement* – details sources of funds and their application for that period of time; that is, as between two successive balance sheets.

Management accounting information is prepared for use by *internal* decision makers. Because many management decisions relate to segments of the firm (particular products, branches, activities), some management accounting information concerns only part of the whole enterprise. Its primary purpose is to assist management at all levels in controlling, co-ordinating and planning the firm's activities.

Management accounting, unlike financial accounting, does not need to comply with legal and other regulatory requirements, since it is exclusively or mainly for internal use. Therefore, the design of a management accounting system or, indeed, whether such a system exists at all, is entirely at the discretion of the management of a particular firm. Thus, the form and content of management accounting reports cannot be described or summarised easily. Diversity, timeliness and usefulness are among the keynotes of effective management accounting.

On the other hand, there are strong arguments for requiring some degree of uniformity in the financial accounting reports of different businesses. External users want to make comparisons between different enterprises. These comparisons cannot be made if different rules or different principles have been used to prepare the financial statements.

The above discussion may have led the reader to believe that in a given business there are two distinct accounting systems, one for management information and one for financial statement purposes. This is not the case. Management is, of course, extremely interested in whole-enterprise financial accounting information. Also, much raw data is common to both financial and management reporting. A well-designed accounting system will integrate both types of accounting information and therefore provide for the needs of both internal and external users.

This text provides an introduction to both financial and management accounting. In early chapters, the major emphasis is placed on concepts and procedures, leading to the production of the basic general purpose financial accounting reports. At the same time, the usefulness of this information for management control is discussed. Chapter 20 deals with more specific management accounting issues.

The accounting profession

As is the case with law, architecture, medicine, etc., the accounting profession has members who practise in an independent professional capacity for the public generally, as well as those who are employed in a private capacity by industry, commerce, local authorities and government departments. The former are quite independent of owners and management. They render services to members of the public who request them and are governed solely by legal consideration and the existing requirements of the profession regarding standards of performance and ethical conduct. Throughout the world, various names are used to describe the independent accountant - chartered accountant, certified accountant, public accountant, and so on. The second group of accountants is employed by the owners of enterprises in both the private and public sectors, and they are primarily responsible for performing a wide range of financial duties. Services provided by members of the accountancy profession in private practice include auditing, business investigations, systems installation, taxation advice, trustee work, financial services and so on, for a wide range of clients. The accountant employed by an organisation often has specific responsibilities and is given a title such as financial accountant, cost accountant, controller, internal auditor or secretary, or a dual responsibility, such as accountant and secretary.

Accountants have formed associations for the advancement of their profession and themselves, and for the setting of standards of performance, ethical conduct, admission of new members, etc.

In the United Kingdom and Ireland there are six important professional accountancy bodies. Three of the accountancy bodies are the Institute of Chartered Accountants of Scotland, the Institute of Chartered Accountants in England and Wales and the Institute of Chartered Accountants in Ireland. They are quite independent, each having their own council, members, rules and regulations, examination syllabuses and student members. The oldest is the Institute of Chartered Accountants of Scotland, with origins dating back to 1854. The members of these bodies are designated Chartered Accountants and in the main control the practising aspects of accounting, although many of them hold positions in industry and commerce.

Another important body of accountants is the Association of Certified Accountants whose members are engaged principally in industry and commerce with a number engaged in professional practice. Again, the Association is separately governed by its own elected council and its members controlled by agreed rules and regulations. Like Chartered Accountants, members of the Association of Certified Accountants are to be found in many different countries in the world working as professional accountants.

The Institute of Cost and Management Accountants forms another body of accountants whose members are almost exclusively employed in industry, principally in the field of management accounting.

The final body of accountants is the Chartered Institute of Public Finance and Accountancy which was formed in 1885 and in many ways stands apart from the other professional accountancy bodies in that its members are employed predominantly in the public sector with local authorities and government agencies.

Attempts have been made in recent years to amalgamate the six main accountancy bodies but to date they have been unsuccessful. Nevertheless, the separate bodies work together closely in a number of areas. They liaise in promoting the image of the profession, in submissions to government and in particular in international activities of the accountancy profession. They also act together on a number of matters through the Consultative Committee for the Accountancy Bodies (CCAB). One of the important functions of the CCAB concerns the setting up of accounting standards through its Accounting Standards Committee and the Auditing Practices Committee.

In addition to the main six bodies, there is a further set of accountants listed in a separate set of secondary registers which include the Society of Company and Commercial Accountants, the Institute of Administrative Accountants and the Association of International Accountants. Again, their members are to be found in financial positions in business not only in the United Kingdom but in many other countries also.

Because of the improved standards of education and qualifications of professional accountants, the need has arisen for a trained support staff in this area. This has led to the formation of the Association of Accounting Technicians to train persons to provide skilled assistance to accountancy and related professions. The Association conducts its own examinations and operates within its own objectives, rules and regulations and is currently fulfilling a much-needed role as support staff to members of the profession.

Development of accounting standards

Earlier, mention was made of the desirability of ensuring some degree of uniformity in the financial accounting reports of different companies so that external decision makers are able to make comparisons between the performance and financial positions of those companies.

The Companies Act, in attempting to regulate financial reporting, has adopted the policy of stipulating in the Act, or the accompanying Regulations, specific items which must be shown in the published financial statements of companies. This is supported by the Act requiring the directors and auditors to provide an opinion that the financial statements show 'a true and fair view' of the state of the company's affairs.

More recently in many countries attempts have been made by the professional accounting bodies to spell out more precisely what are acceptable standards of financial accounting reporting. In the United Kingdom accounting standards were introduced in the early 1970s and since then over twenty Statements of Standard Accounting Practice have been issued by the Accounting Standards Committee. The policy generally has been to prepare and issue standards on specific areas of financial reporting, giving priority to those areas where it is felt there is an urgent need to achieve greater uniformity of treatment.

In recent years, professional accounting bodies on a world-wide basis have co-operated to develop and issue International Accounting Standards. The emergence of large numbers of multinational companies has contributed to the need for such standards.

Accounting standards are referred to as they affect different topics discussed throughout the book and a separate section is included later in the text where they are considered in greater detail.

Summary

1. Accounting provides information about a particular enterprise to interested parties to assist them in making decisions.

2. The collection of data on selected economic events is the first step in the accounting process. These data are classified and summarised, and the resultant information reported to users.

3. The nature of accounting has changed significantly over time and continues to change. Events which have influenced accounting include the Industrial Revolution, the development of joint-stock companies and the technological advances of the twentieth century.

4. It is useful to distinguish between management accounting information for internal use and financial accounting information for external use.

5. A member of the accounting profession may be in a public practice or employed as a commercial accountant for a particular enterprise.

6. In the United Kingdom attempts have been made to develop and promulgate standards of financial accounting reporting by the introduction of Statements of Standard Accounting Practice referred to as SSAPs.

Discussion questions

1.1 Distinguish between the terms 'data' and 'information' as used in accounting.

1.2 Accounting provides information for management decisions. Give examples of some decisions requiring accounting information, made by a factory manager, a personnel manager, a credit manager, a board of directors, the management committee of a sporting club. Indicate, in general terms, the type of accounting information required for each decision.

1.3 Explain the factors which led to the formation of 'limited-liability companies'. Discuss why it is necesary to have government control over the activities of limited-liability companies.

1.4 Explain why the performance of accounting processes has been one of the major areas of application for electronic computers.

1.5 Discuss the alternative forms of business 'ownership'. Give any commonsense reasons you can think of why it may be appropriate to operate a business enterprise as a:

(a) limited company instead of a partnership or sole trader;

(b) partnership instead of a sole trader;

(c) sole trader;

(d) co-operative.

1.6 Discuss the major classes of external users of accounting information. What are the main types of information that these external users generally require.

1.7 Why is 'uniformity' more important in financial accounting than in management accounting?

1.8 Discuss the major functions which professional accounting bodies such as the institutes of chartered accountants perform.

1.9 State, and explain the nature of, the major services provided by a firm of chartered accountants.

1.10 Discuss the reasons why the United Kingdom has developed and issued Statements of Standard Accounting Practice. Why is it often difficult to obtain agreement among accountants and users of accounting information on the precise nature of Accounting Standards?

Note: Since this chapter has been descriptive and introductory in nature, no exercises or problems, as provided in all other chapters, are necessary.

Chapter 2
Financial accounting reports

Financial accounting objectives ☐ Accounting entities ☐ The accounting equation ☐ Balance sheets ☐ Transactions and the accounting equation ☐ Nature and measurement of profit ☐ Revenue recognition ☐ Expenses ☐ Profit and loss statements ☐ Other financial accounting reports

Financial accounting objectives

Where accounting information is prepared primarily for the needs of external users, it was described in the previous chapter as financial accounting information. The three basic financial accounting reports were stated to be balance sheets, profit and loss statements and funds statements.

Before describing what is, or should be, contained in these general-purpose financial statements, it is desirable to try to set down the major objectives underlying their preparation. This is easier said than done. The formulation of a set of objectives for financial reporting has occupied countless hours of the time of accountants and committees of accountants for many years. It is also true that, judging by the lack of unanimity of acceptance, these efforts to date have not been as successful as was hoped.

A noteworthy attempt to state financial reporting objectives was undertaken by the Accounting Standards Steering Committee of the various professional accountancy bodies in the United Kingdom who produced the *Corporate Report* in 1975.[1] In that report it was stated that 'The fundamental objective of corporate reports is to communicate economic measurements of and information about the resources and performance of the reporting entity useful to those having reasonable rights to such information.' If such reports are to be useful and fulfil their fundamental objective they must possess the following characteristics: they must be relevant, understandable, reliable, complete, objective, timely and comparable.

The importance of this report is that it is the first occasion in the United Kingdom when a re-examination of the scope and aims of published financial reports in the light of modern needs and conditions took place by an official working party.

Some of the main matters discussed in the Report are discussed later in this book in Chapter 19.

No attempt is made here to try to analyse these objectives in detail or to compare them with objectives formulated by other authorities. Instead, it is submitted that the following propositions relevant to the objectives of financial reporting are generally accepted.

1. Two primary objectives of every business enterprise are profitability and solvency. In order to survive, a firm must generate reasonable earnings and also meet its debts as they fall due.

2. The cash flows of an enterprise have a consequential effect on the cash flows of its owners and creditors.

---

1 Accounting Standards Steering Committee (1975), *Corporate Report*.

3. Information about the past performance of an enterprise is one, but not the only, basis of predicting its future performance.

4. External users of accounting information seek to assess the value of an enterprise, evaluate the performance of its management and estimate its further earning power. Financial statements can and should provide some, but not all, of the information relevant to those judgments.

These general conclusions will be referred to from time to time, as methods of financial reporting are described and analysed.

Accounting entities

Any accounting system concerns itself with the events occurring in the life of one particular business enterprise. The commercial and industrial world is made up of a multitude of separate enterprises, varying greatly in size and nature. The accountant interprets the effects of a particular transaction from the point of view of the particular business for which the accounting is being done. For instance, if business A sells goods to business B, this is regarded as a *sale* in the books of business A, while in the books of business B, the same transaction is regarded as a *purchase*. When B pays for the goods, it is considered a *cash receipt* from the point of view of business A, and as a *cash payment* from the point of view of business B.

The emphasis on the effect of the transaction on the business enterprise is particularly important when applied to transactions between a business and its owner or owners. If Smith, the owner of a business, pays cash into the business bank account to increase the capital of the enterprise, then, from the point of view of the business this is a cash receipt, whereas from the point of view of Smith it is a cash payment. In accounting for any enterprise, we regard the business as an entity separate from its owner or owners. This is done irrespective of the type of ownership, whether it is a sole trader, a partnership, a company or a non-trading organisation. In the case of a sole trader or a partnership, the law does not regard the owner or owners as separate. Thus, the accounting entity sometimes differs from the legal entity. From an accounting viewpoint, however, when the business has dealings with the owner or partners, the amounts owing to or by the owners should be recorded in the same way as for other persons or firms in the books of the business. Where a person owns or partly owns more than one enterprise, it is highly desirable that separate sets of books be kept for each. In large enterprises it is often desirable, from an accounting point of view, to recognise accounting entities within one legal entity. This is discussed later in Chapter 14.

The fact that we regard the enterprise as a separate accounting entity leads us to the fundamental relationship which may be established between the assets, liabilities and proprietorship of any enterprise.

Assets may be defined, at this stage, as items of value owned by a business. (We will extend and modify this definition later.) Accepting the business as a separate entity, we may regard it as owning the property and resources of which it consists. A business's assets comprise such things as cash, stock, plant, land, buildings, debts owing to it, and so on.

Liabilities are amounts owing by the business. They include amounts owing as a result of the purchase of goods or services (usually termed accounts payable or creditors), a bank overdraft or other loans of money to the business.

Proprietorship may be defined as the interests of the owner or owners in the business. The concept of proprietorship (also referred to as owners' equity) follows directly from the recognition of a separate accounting entity. If we regard the business of A. Smith Grocer as separate from A. Smith the individual then in accounting from the point of view of business we must recognise the business's indebtedness to Smith for the capital which was contributed to establish the business.

Also, since the purpose of the business is to accumulate wealth for the owners, any profit that it makes is made from Smith and increases Smith's total claims on the business.

The accounting equation

The relationship between these three elements – assets, liabilities and proprietorship – can best be seen at the commencement of a business. A supply of funds is necessary to enable the business activity to be commenced. Often the funds are provided in cash, but they may consist of other assets; for example, a member of a tennis club may transfer ownership of a tennis court to the club, or a person may use a private car to commence a taxi business. In these cases, the funds enter the business in the form of the asset 'property' in the one case and the asset 'taxi' in the other.

Thus, when an entity comes into being, it is possible to note two aspects: the source of funds provided to start the enterprise, and the assets which represent those funds.

Since the funds provided are represented by assets of equal value, we can state this in the form of an equation as follows:

$$\text{Funds provided} = \text{Assets of the business.}$$

Where the funds are all provided by the owner we can record this as:

$$\text{Proprietorship} = \text{Assets.}$$

In the same way, if all the funds come from outsiders, the equation will be:

$$\text{Liabilities} = \text{Assets.}$$

Usually, however, the funds are provided partly by the owner and partly from outsiders. From this we get the usual accounting equation:

$$\text{Proprietorship} + \text{Liabilities} = \text{Assets.}$$

or

$$P + L = A.$$

Here are two illustrations:

1. Richard Jones began a carrying business by buying a motor vehicle from Utilities Ltd for £16 000. He paid £10 000 from his private resources and promised to pay the balance over a period of six months.

Proprietorship	— R. Jones contributed £10 000	$(P = £10\ 000)$
Liabilities	— The business owes Utilities Ltd £6000	$(L = £6000)$
Assets	— The business owns a motor vehicle £16 000	$(A = £16\ 000)$

that is, P (£10 000) + L (£6000) = A (£16 000).

2. Dorothy Black commenced practice as a dentist. She borrowed £10 000 from her sister and provided £30 000 in cash herself. She paid £35 000 for an existing business consisting of the following: furniture £1000, equipment £4000 and premises £30 000.

Proprietorship	— D. Black contributed £30 000	$(P = £30\ 000)$
Liabilities	— The business owes Black's sister £10 000	$(L = £10\ 000)$

Assets — The business owns
        Furniture   £ 1 000
        Equipment   £ 4 000
        Premises   £30 000
        Cash   £ 5 000   (A = £40 000)

that is, P (£30 000) + L (£10 000) = A (£40 000).

Balance sheets

The use of the accounting equation is limited because it expresses the asset, liability and proprietorship relationship in terms of *total A*, *total L* and *total P*. In the second example above, there were four individual assets involved in the total figure of £40 000.

If in our expression of the relationship we want to include the amounts of *individual* asset, liability and proprietorship items then this can be achieved in the form of a balance sheet. The balance sheet – a list of assets, liabilities and proprietorship suitably arranged and classified – is one of the most commonly used and accepted accounting reports.

Simple balance sheets prepared on the basis of the above two illustrations would be:

1.

Balance Sheet of R. Jones, Carrier
(at commencement of business)

Proprietorship		**Assets**	
R. Jones – Capital	£10 000	Motor vehicle	£16 000
Liabilities			
Creditors[1]	6 000		
	£16 000		£16 000

2.

Balance Sheet of D. Black, Dentist
(at commencement of business)

Proprietorship		**Assets**	
D. Black – Capital	£30 000	Premises	£30 000
Liabilities		Furniture	1 000
Loan account	10 000	Equipment	4 000
		Cash in hand	5 000
	£40 000		£40 000

1 It is not usual to detail in a balance sheet the individual names of persons who are creditors of the business.

Both of the above balance sheets have used the accounting equation in the form

$$P + L = A,$$

emphasising, on the one hand, the sources from which the enterprise's funds have been derived, and, on the other, the forms of resources in which those funds are at present residing.

If we wish to emphasise the claims of the owners to the resources of the business then we may use the equation in the form

$$P = A - L.$$

(Mathematically, we have transposed L from one side of the equation to the other and consequently have altered its sign.)

The use of the balance sheet in this form often coincides with the use of the narrative (or statement) form of presentation. In the narrative form, the items are added and subtracted down the page; they are not balanced on opposite sides of a line drawn down the centre of the page, as in the traditional form of balance sheet (often called the account form).

Dorothy Black's balance sheet, presented in narrative form, appears as follows:

Balance Sheet of D. Black, Dentist
(at commencement of business)

Proprietorship		
D. Black - Capital		£30 000
Represented by		———
Assets		
Premises	£30 000	
Furniture	1 000	
Equipment	4 000	
Cash in hand	5 000	40 000
Less **Liabilities-**Loan account		10 000
		£30 000

In recent years there has been a trend towards increasing use of the narrative form of presentation. Some of the advantages claimed by its supporters are:

1. For the layman, the addition and subtraction processes are easier to understand than the balancing of two sides of a divided page.

2. It is much easier to insert the figures of the previous year if the narrative form is used. The Companies Act requires such comparative figures.

3. It highlights the interest of the proprietor in terms of net assets, that is, assets *less* liabilities.

Students are advised to become familiar with both forms of presentation.

Transactions and the accounting equation

Until now we have shown the accounting equation as applying only on the date of commencement of business of the enterprise. In fact, it is possible at any stage of the life of a business to show that the same kind of relationship exists.

If the proprietor decides to pay in another £100 to the business and buys furniture on credit for £100 then both L and P will be increased by £100. At the same time, £100 in cash and £100 furniture will have been added to the assets, so that the equation will now read:

$$(P + £100) + (L + £100) = (A + £100 + £100).$$

The proprietor's funds have been increased by £100, and the funds supplied by creditors have increased by £100. These extra funds are represented by £100 in cash and £100 in furniture. A little further thought on the subject will show that transactions may result in:

1. An increase on one side of the equation (P or L or both) and a corresponding increase in A.

2. A decrease in one side (P or L or both) and a corresponding decrease in A.

3. An increase in P and a decrease of an equal amount in L.

4. An increase in L and a decrease in P.

5. An internal change in the nature of one of the elements without any change in the total, for example, one liability created to pay off another; one asset exchanged for another.

Table 2.1 Effects of transactions on accounting equation

Transaction	Detailed effect	Effect on equation		
		A	P	L
1. Bought van on credit	Asset (vans) increased	+		
	Liability (creditors) increased			+
2. Paid off loan or creditors in cash	Asset (cash) decreased	−		
	Liability (loan) decreased			−
3. Proprietor paid in extra capital	Asset (cash) increased	+		
	Proprietorship increased		+	
4. One partner received part of his proprietorship in cash	Asset (cash) decreased	−		
	Proprietorship (of that partner) decreased		−	
5. Arranged bank overdraft and repaid part of one partner's proprietorship	Liability (bank overdraft) increased			+
	Proprietorship (of that partner) decreased		−	
6. A sole trader paid off business debts from private resources	Liabilities (creditors) decreased			−
	Proprietorship increased		+	
7. Bought plant for cash	Asset (cash) decreased	−		
	Asset (plant) increased	+		
8. Raised mortgage to repay other loans	Liability (mortgage) increased			+
	Liability (loans) decreased			−
9. One partner sold a share of the business to another partner	Proprietorship (of one partner) increased		+	
	Proprietorship (of another partner) decreased		−	
10. A debtor paid his account	Asset (cash) increased	+		
	Asset (debtors) decreased	−		

Table 2.1 analyses the effects of a few transactions on the individual assets, liabilities and proprietorship and on the total A, total L and total P in the accounting equation.

While the analysis of the effect of separate transactions on the balance sheet is useful in developing an understanding of accounting, it cannot be seriously considered as a practical method of recording the transactions. With a large number of varied transactions occurring simultaneously, it would be impossible to draft a new balance sheet after each transaction or even at the end of each day. It becomes necessary, therefore, to use other methods of recording the many transactions that occur between the times of drawing up successive balance sheets. These methods are discussed in Chapter 3.

Another factor ignored in the above analysis is the profit element associated with many transactions. The buying and selling of goods, the incurring of wages, rent and other expenses and many other types of transactions result in a profit or loss being made by the business. We will now look at the nature and measurement of profit.

Nature and measurement of profit

Earlier in this chapter, we stated that profitability is one of the primary objectives of most enterprises. Therefore, one of the basic requirements of the accounting system of a business enterprise, as distinct from enterprises where profitability is not the major motive, is that it should be able to report profit periodically to the owners and other interested parties.

Transactions which result in a profit or loss could be analysed in terms of their effect on the elements of the accounting equation in the same way we analysed other types of transactions. If goods costing £20 are sold for £30 cash, then three changes can be isolated from this transaction: the asset 'cash' has been increased by £30; the asset 'stock' has been decreased by £20; and a 'profit' of £10 has been made. Since any profit belongs to the owners of the business, then proprietorship has been increased by £10, that is, profits increase proprietorship and losses decrease proprietorship.

However, profits and losses are rarely determined for each transaction in this way for two reasons: first, it would be tedious and unnecessary, and, second, it would be impossible to determine accurately the profit or loss resulting from each transaction. For instance, the 'profit' of £10 calculated above would not necessarily be all profit. There would be expenses such as rent, advertising, salaries, etc., part of which should be subtracted from the £30, as well as the expense represented by the actual cost of the goods themselves (£20). It is usually impossible to say what proportion of total advertising costs, for instance, should be identified with a particular sale. Therefore, instead of determining profit on a transaction basis, it is more usual to determine profit on a time basis.

It is usual to divide the continuing life of a business into arbitrary periods of time, often called 'accounting periods'. A commonly used accounting period is twelve months. The determination of profit on an annual basis is necessary to satisfy taxation requirements and, in the case of companies, to satisfy the requirements of the Companies Acts. Also, a share of the profits is often distributed to owners on an annual basis. However, sometimes the determination of profit more frequently than once every twelve months is both necessary and desirable. The issue of half-yearly or quarterly financial statements has become common in recent years and is necessary under the listing requirements of some stock exchanges. For internal decision-making purposes, the management of large organisations needs to be informed of trends in profitability far more frequently than once a year.

It is important to note that there are many terms used to qualify the general meaning of profit. Several different types of accounting profit may be recognised: gross profit, net profit, operating profit, profit before income tax, retained profit, distributable profit, departmental profit, etc. Consequently, any profit figures must be interpreted within the framework of the definitions and assumptions on which its determination was based.

When considering the methods by which periodical profit may be determined, it is possible to distinguish between two broad approaches:

1. The 'comparison of values' approach – where profit is the difference between the value of the business at the end of the period and its value at the beginning of that period.

2. The matching approach – where profit is the difference between the inflows and outflows of resources resulting from all the transactions of the period.

The 'comparison of values' approach is closely related to the economists' concept of income – defined broadly as the 'maximum value which can be consumed during a period, leaving the enterprise as well-off at the end of the period, as it was at the beginning'. The idea of a person or firm being as well-off at the end of a period as at the beginning necessarily involves a valuation process to determine 'well-offness'. This valuation of assets and liabilities enables proprietorship to be determined. However, a change in proprietorship will result from increased capital contributions or proprietorship withdrawals as well as from profits or losses.

Thus the profit (I) of a period can be calculated as:

$$I = (P_1 + D - C) - P_0,$$

where P_0 = proprietorship at the beginning, } both values for P (i.e., $A - L$) being estab-
$\quad P_1$ = proprietorship at the end, } lished at their points of time
$\quad C$ = new capital contributions,
$\quad D$ = withdrawals by owner or owners.

The economists' approach to profit determination is not generally accepted by accountants. Such a process yields a single profit or loss figure only; there is no supporting detail about what caused this profit or loss, and accountants believe that such information is important. Also there are significant difficulties involved in the valuation of assets and these difficulties, explained in later chapters, have brought about a tendency in accountants to avoid direct valuation of assets.

The second and the conventional method of determining profit is that of matching revenues and expenses on a time or period basis. *Revenue* is the gross inflow of resources (and thus the gross increase in proprietorship) resulting from the firm supplying goods or services to its customers or clients. *Expense* is the consumption or the outflow of resources (and thus the decrease in proprietorship) that is necessarily associated with the firm engaging in revenue-producing activities. It is distinguished from a payment, which may be made before or after or at the same time the expense is recognised. A more detailed consideration of revenue and expense follows later in this chapter.

Thus, we can formulate another equation.

$$\text{Profit } (I) = \text{Revenues} - \text{Expenses}$$

or

$$I = R - E.$$

However, the expression of the matching process in the form of an equation may convey an impression of precise measurement. Such is not the case. Only on rare occasions can profit be calculated with a fine degree of accuracy. One of the major factors causing this is the selection of an arbitrary accounting period. Some revenue and expense items are easily identifiable with a particular accounting period, but for others the identification is far more difficult. It is not so much a matter of when the return resulting from a revenue item is received, as when that revenue was really earned. Similarly, the date of payment of a particular expense is not important; it is necessary to try to link the expense with a particular period of time or a particular item of revenue.

More fundamentally, the profit determined by this method depends on the criteria which are adopted to define and to recognise revenue and expenses. Thus, it is necessary to examine more fully the nature of revenue and expense.

Revenue recognition

The process of earning revenue by selling particular goods or by performing particular services may take place over a lengthy period of time and may be considered to involve as many as five stages:

1. The acquisition of the necessary resources (building, plant, raw materials, etc.).
2. The receipt of the customer's order.
3. The process of producing the goods or performing the services.
4. The delivery of the goods or completion of the services.
5. The collection of cash from the customer.

These stages do not always occur in the above sequence, nor at separate points of time. For instance, when goods are sold for cash in a retail store, stages 2, 4 and 5 occur simultaneously.

The economist regards the profit as being earned gradually over all these various stages, but in the accountant's approach it is necessary to select one of these points as the point at which revenue is deemed to have been earned so that this revenue can be recorded. The most usual one selected is stage 4: the delivery of goods or completion of the services. At this stage, the profit is said to have been realised, whether the cash has been received or not. The selection of this point of realisation has been influenced by the fact that at this stage there is usually a legal obligation imposed on the recipient of the goods or services.

However, this rule may be too rigid in some cases. If we are producing for a customer an order or a job which may take a long time to complete, for example, a building contract, it is logical and permissible to recognise a proportion of the revenue before the actual final performance of the contract. This is usually done by a percentage or proportionate calculation. However, several companies which have done this have subsequently experienced financial disaster through failure to collect the actual cash. This has been a matter for criticism, not so much of the point at which revenue was recognised, as of the initial failure to assess the creditworthiness of the customer, or at least recognise the potential expense in the valuation of the sum to be ultimately received.

Where a departure from the principle of recognising revenue at the delivery or completion of contract is contemplated, the most important factor to take into account is the degree of certainty. A conventional accounting doctrine demonstrates a tendency towards caution in the processes involving measurement and valuation. As will be seen in later chapters, conservatism is applied in a number of ways, all of which tend to minimise reported profit. It defers all profits or gains in the absence of a reasonable degree of certainty, but attempts to recognise all expenses or losses. If there is doubt about the ability to perform the contract, or collect the amount due, or make an accurate estimate of expenses still to be incurred in connection with the revenue, then accountants generally defer recognition, or at least estimate it conservatively. Acceptance of the need for reasonable conservatism should not be taken as a general endorsement of all cases of conservative accounting. Excessive use of conservatism destroys the validity and usefulness of the profit figures thus derived.

Before leaving the subject of revenue recognition, we would like to make the point that in most cases it is a stage prior to the ultimate collection of cash which is chosen as the time at which revenue is recognised. *Rights* to the collection of cash are deemed to 'accrue'. Thus most accounting for revenue is on an *accrual* basis rather than a *cash* basis.

Expenses

We have previously defined expense as the consumption or outflow of resources resulting from the firm supplying goods or services to its customers. The problem is to identify for any given period the expenses which are to be associated with the revenue of that period. It does not matter whether the outflow of the resources connected with the revenue takes place before, within, or after the accounting period. This is consistent with the accrual (as distinct from cash) basis of accounting mentioned above. Some outflows can clearly be matched with particular inflows, for example the purchase price of goods sold. Others are much less obvious, for example the resources consumed in repairing a delivery vehicle. Before we consider some examples of this matching process, we should mention that there is a generally held view in accounting which is relevant to our present discussion. This is the commonsense attitude that, in the ascertaining of profit and in the reporting of that profit, certain transactions or events are so insignificant, relative to the total resource movements and structure of the business, that they do not warrant reporting separately.

Thus, while certain outflows may result in the exchange of one asset for another, for example cash to acquire postage stamps or a minor item such as a pencil, assets of this nature are so relatively immaterial and/or are consumed so quickly that usually they are recorded from the outset as an expense. Belief in such practice in accounting is described as the *doctrine of materiality* and is discernible in a number of areas. In the present context, it results in the recording of certain outflows as expenses, even though they may have some residual value at the end of the period, simply because to apportion their cost between one accounting period and the next is not worth the trouble.

There are a number of resource outflows that clearly do affect several accounting periods, for example the purchase of a substantial asset such as a building, which will last several years. On the other hand, there are some expenses which clearly do relate to a single period and probably would not carry forward a benefit to a subsequent period, for example the delivery expenses on a specific item of goods sold.

However, there are also a great many resource outflows which are not identifiable with any particular item of revenue and which may also relate to more than one accounting period. These include rents, rates and taxes, insurance, and many others. How they will be recorded within the accounting system requires that they be considered individually.

The following are some common examples where decisions have to be made as to the amount of revenue or the amount of expense to be reported for a particular period (assume in all these examples that the accounting period is one of twelve months ending 30 June):

1. A customer orders goods from us on 28 June. The goods are obtained and delivered to the customer on 2 July and the goods are paid for on 3 August. The revenue item 'sales' is deemed to be earned on 2 July.

2. On 15 August we receive interest of £600. The interest is for the six months ended 15 August. Of the £600 revenue 'interest received', £450 is deemed to have been earned in the period ended 30 June, and £150 to have been earned in the next period.

3. On 1 May we pay £360 insurance on motor vehicles for the next twelve months. Of this, £60 relates to the period in which the expense is paid, £300 to the following period.

4. During this period we purchase stationery for £400. If at 30 June one-fifth of this remains unused then £320 should be brought into this period as an expense and £80 carried forward as an asset into the next period.

5. On 1 April we sign an advertising contract and make a payment on it. If the benefit of this is not to be felt until after 30 June then none of this outlay ought to be charged against the revenue of this period. All of it should be carried forward to the next period. However, it may be very difficult to assess the period in which sales were directly affected by advertising. Conservatism often applies to record the outflow as expenses in the period in which it was paid.

6. A delivery vehicle costing £12 400 is purchased on 1 January. Here it is a question of estimating the life of the vehicle and allocating its cost to successive periods. The expense for a particular period is usually termed 'depreciation'.

7. On 1 March we sublet premises and receive £600 for six months' rent in advance. Of this, £400 is revenue for the period and £200 is carried forward to the following period.

8. Many times during the period, amounts are expended on petrol and oil for the motor vehicles used by a firm, which carries no supplies of its own. Some petrol and oil is unused at balance date. Here the expense of petrol and oil may be substantial for the whole period, but the unused portion at balance date hardly warrants measuring and carrying forward as a resource. The outflow is recorded from the outset as an expense, with no intention to report the unconsumed petrol and oil as an asset.

Profit and loss statements

The profit and loss statement, like the balance sheet, is one of the basic general-purpose, whole-enterprise, financial accounting reports. However, whereas the balance sheet shows the position of an enterprise at one point of time, the profit and loss statement shows the operations of the enterprise over a period of time.

The profit and loss statement is based on the equation previously given:

$$I = R - E.$$

If I is positive, it is usually termed 'net profit'; if I is negative, it is usually termed a 'net loss'. An example of a simple profit and loss statement for a motor-vehicle repair firm is given below.

Ace Auto Repairs
Profit and Loss Statement for the year ended 30 June 19X6

Revenues		
Service charges	£125 000	
Interest on investments	2 600	£127 600
Less **Expenses**		
Wages	52 300	
Materials	28 600	
Rent	6 800	
Power and lighting	1 360	
Advertising	940	
Office expenses	3 250	93 250
Net profit		£34 350

In a trading business where goods are bought and sold, it is usual to report *gross profit* as well as *net profit*. Gross profit is the difference between the sales value of the goods sold and the expense incurred in obtaining those goods and putting them into a condition ready for sale. Net profit is the excess of all revenues and gains of the period over all expenses and losses.

The concept of gross profit as the margin between sale price and cost price is a useful one. It is probably more useful when expressed as a percentage of the sales figure because the management of the enterprise is then able to compare the actual gross profit percentage (or rate) with the expected percentage, or with the percentage in previous periods or with the percentage achieved by similar businesses.

An example of a profit and loss statement for a trading business is given below.

Wonder Trading Co.
Profit and Loss Statement for the three months ended 30 September 19X6

Sales	£24 600
Less Cost of goods sold	16 800
Gross profit (31.7% of sales)	7 800
Add Commission received	50
	7 850

	b/fwd	£7 850
Less **Expenses**		
Rent	680	
Salaries	1 680	
Advertising	230	
Delivery expenses	830	
Power and lighting	140	
Office expenses	510	
Interest on overdraft	80	4 150
Net profit (15.0% of sales)		£3 700

Other financial accounting reports

There are two other types of financial reports which supplement and complement the information provided in balance sheets and profit and loss statements.

The first, which has been termed a 'statement of retained earnings', shows the changes in the amount of earnings which have been retained in the business over an accounting period. One of the main ways in which businesses gain funds to expand their operations is by not paying all profits out as dividends or drawings, and by keeping some of these profits in the business. It is usual to distinguish clearly between the two major components of proprietorship (or owners' equity) – contributed capital, on the one hand, and retained earnings, on the other.

A simple example of a statement of retained earnings is given below:

Bird's Stores Ltd
Statement of Retained Earnings for the year ended 30 June 19X6

Balance of retained earnings (1/7/X5)	£33 350	
Add Net profit for year	21 600	£54 950
Less Dividends		
Interim dividend	5 200	
Final dividend	10 400	15 600
Balance of retained earnings (30/6/X6)		£39 350

Note that the amount of retained earnings at the end of the accounting period (£39 350 in the above example) will be shown in the proprietorship section of the balance sheet drawn up as at the end of the period. Thus, the statement of retained earnings serves as one of the links between the balance sheet and the profit and loss statement and also serves as a link between two successive balance sheets. Note also that in published financial statements the information given above is usually incorporated in the profit and loss statement after the calculation of the net profit figure.

The other type of financial accounting report which should be discussed briefly at this stage is the 'funds statement' (or 'statement of changes in financial position'). As stated earlier in this chapter, business survival depends on two factors: the generation of earnings and the ability to meet commitments. Whereas the profit and loss statement focuses on the first factor, the funds statement helps in the assessment of the second. The balance sheet gives information on financial position at one point in time; the funds statement attempts to show changes in financial position over a period of time. These changes are usually presented in two groups: changes which increase a firm's resources (sources of funds) and those which consume the firm's resources (applications of funds).

There are a number of factors which influence the form and content of a funds statement. In particular, the choice of an appropriate definition of 'funds' is a cause of some concern. It is felt that these factors are better understood by students after they have studied accounting principles and processes in more detail. Thus we will not be concerned with the preparation of funds statements until we review financial accounting reports in Chapter 16. Meanwhile, a very simple version of a funds statement is given below:

Hawke Advertising Agency
Funds Statement for the year ended 30 June 19X6

Sources of funds		
1. From profitable operations	£26 500	
2. New capital contributions by partners	20 000	
3. Sale of obsolete furniture	1 800	
4. Loan from finance company	10 000	£58 300
Applications of funds		
1. Purchase of new motor vehicles	22 300	
2. Purchase of computing equipment	24 200	
3. Increase in debtors	8 300	
4. Increase in bank balances	3 500	£58 300

Summary

1. Accountants and users of accounting information disagree on the major objectives of financial accounting reporting but some general conclusions can be stated.

2. It is essential in accounting to consider the enterprise as a separate accounting entity, distinct from its owner or owners.

3. This gives rise to the notion of proprietorship: the interest or claims of the owners on the resources of the enterprise.

4. It then becomes possible to postulate a basic relationship between total assets, total liabilities and total proprietorship. This is called the 'accounting equation' and may be expressed as $P + L = A$.

5. A balance sheet is a list of individual asset, liability and proprietorship items.

6. The effects of all business transactions can be traced both on the totals in the accounting equation, and on the individual asset, liability or proprietorship items in the balance sheet. However, large numbers of transactions make this impracticable as a method of accounting.

7. The accounting equation may be rewritten in terms of proprietorship (i.e., $P = A - L$). This is often represented in the narrative (or statement) form of the balance sheet.

8. Profit must be determined on a *periodical* basis, not on a transaction basis.

9. Of the two possible approaches to profit determination - the 'comparison of values' approach and the 'matching' approach - accountants have adopted the latter.

10. The adoption of periodical profit determination leads to a process of the 'matching of revenues and expenses':

$$Profit = Revenues - Expenses$$

or

$$Loss = Expenses - Revenues.$$

Where revenue is the gross inflow of resources and expense is the consumption or outflow of resources.

11. There are often several distinct steps in the process of earning revenue. The accountant is forced to choose one of these steps as the time at which revenue is deemed to have been earned.

12. The most common time for revenue recognition is when the goods have been delivered or when the provision of services has been completed.

13. The major problem with accounting for expenses is to identify the period in which the revenue, associated with the expenses, has been earned.

14. The matching of revenues and expenses for a particular period is reported in a statement generally called a profit and loss statement.

15. For a trading business, profit determination is usually performed in two stages, giving at least two profit figures, gross profit and net profit.

16. It is usual to distinguish between two components of proprietorship – contributed capital and retained earnings. Changes in retained earnings during an accounting period are often reported in a statement of retained earnings.

17. A further useful financial accounting report is the funds statement, which shows the increases and decreases in a firm's resources during an accounting period.

Discussion questions

2.1 'Two primary objectives of every business enterprise are profitability and solvency.' Explain the meaning of this statement.

2.2 Discuss the limitations of using information about the past performance of an enterprise as the sole basis for predicting future performance.

2.3 (a) Explain what is meant by 'the accounting entity concept'.

(b) Explain the relationship often described as 'the accounting equation'.

(c) Briefly discuss the link which exists between the two concepts.

2.4 John S. Pryde owns a grocery store and half-share in a garage. Explain the effect and the necessity of applying the accounting entity theory to Mr Pryde's business activities.

2.5 (a) Explain the meanings of these terms: assets, liabilities, proprietorship.

(b) Explain what is meant by the 'accounting equation' and express the equation in two different forms.

2.6 What do you consider would be the main differences between the balance sheet of a corner store owned by one person, S. Bloggs, and that of a multi-million-pound mining concern operated by a limited-liability company?

2.7 Discuss the usefulness of the method of analysis used in this chapter – where the effects of each transaction on items in the balance sheet are identified.

2.8 Why do accountants choose to determine profit on a 'period' basis rather than on a 'transaction' basis?

2.9 Explain the importance of the concepts of

(a) the accounting period, and

(b) the matching of revenues and expenses
in the preparation of profit and loss statements.

2.10 Economists generally define income as 'the maximum value which can be consumed during a period leaving the enterprise as well-off at the end of the period as it was at the beginning'. Explain how this definition could be used as the basis for determining periodical profit.

2.11 What is the normal method used by accountants to determine profit often referred to as an 'accrual basis' as opposed to a 'cash basis'?

2.12 Explain the significance of 'materiality' in determining whether a particular outlay is an expense or an asset. Give examples.

2.13 Discuss why in a trading business it is often considered useful to report 'gross profit' as well as 'net profit'.

2.14 (a) What do you understand by the term 'retained earnings'?

(b) Discuss the usefulness to investors and creditors of a statement of retained earnings.

2.15 Both the balance sheet and the funds statement are concerned with information on the financial position of an enterprise. Explain the differences between the two reports and discuss why it is useful to present both to external users of accounting information.

Exercises

2.16 Arrange the following items from the books of Lucy Black, Grocer, under the correct column heading: assets, liabilities or proprietorship.

(a) Equipment.

(b) Joan Stevens (a customer to whom the business sold goods on credit).

(c) Brown & Co. (a warehouse from whom the business has bought merchandise on credit).

(d) Cash at bank.

(e) Furniture.

(f) Drawings – Lucy Black.

(g) Mortgage on land and buildings.

(h) Land and buildings.

2.17 The following are (a) the liabilities and (b) the assets of Racko Lamb, Butcher:

(a)		(b)	
Browns Abattoirs	£5 100	Cash at bank	£8 000
Blatt's Smallgoods Co.	2 710	Stock	500
		Plant and machinery	9 500
		Van	10 000

Prepare a balance sheet:

(i) in account form of presentation;

(ii) in narrative form.

2.18 Prepare a balance sheet for Clyno Garage, taking into account the following:

(a) One item is missing (which?).

(b) What is the amount of this item?

Debtors	£8 000
Creditors	1 700
Stock	6 000
Plant and equipment	38 000
Premises	42 000
Loan from Oil Co.	50 000
Interest owing on loan	600

2.19 Complete the following table:

Transaction	Effect on Accounting Equation		
	P	*L*	*A*
Example Bought furniture for cash	No effect	No effect	Increase asset 'furniture' Decrease asset 'cash'

1. Received payment from a debtor
2. Bought furniture on credit
3. Owner withdrew some cash for personal use
4. Paid a creditor's account
5. Owner paid in more capital

2.20 The balance sheet of Amos Corn as at 30 June was:

Liabilities		
Bank overdraft	£6 800	
Creditors	12 500	
Mortgage on building	20 000	£39 300
Proprietorship		
Amos Corn Capital		46 500
		£85 800
Assets		
Cash in hand	£200	
Debtors	14 600	
Stock	15 000	
Plant and equipment	18 000	
Land and buildings	38 000	£85 800
		£85 800

During the next week the following transactions occurred:

July 1 The proprietor made out a cheque for £300 for private use.
July 2 Cash received (and banked) from debtors, £800.
July 3 Bought goods on credit, £1200.
July 4 Repaid part of mortgage by cheque, £200.
July 5 Bought new item of equipment for £3000.
      Paid £500 by cheque, balance to be paid in one month.

(a) List for each day the changed totals of the balance sheet items affected.
(b) Draw up a balance sheet as at 5 July.

2.21 From the following information, prepare the balance sheet of the Juicy Pie and Pasty Co. (Bernice Stake, Proprietor) as at 30 June.

(a) There is £179 cash in the bank and £10 change on hand in the office.

(b) The following amounts are owed by shopkeepers: Colin Cake £18, Fiona Fudge £25, and Gordon Fritz £21.

(c) The business owns a delivery van £1000, machinery £700 and office furniture £80.

(d) The business owes F. Miller £40 for flour, R. Butcher £60 for meat, and D. Landlord £75 for arrears of rent.

(e) There is £25 worth of flour still on hand.

   Use the narrative form of presentation.

2.22 For each of the following items which relate to the business of Wool and Cotton, retailers of men's wear:

(a) select a short name which you consider suitable and unambiguous to describe each item;

(b) classify the item as an asset, liability or proprietorship.

  (i) Amounts owing by customers who have purchased goods.
  (ii) Tables and racks used to display goods for sale.
  (iii) The amounts which B. Wool (a partner) paid in to commence the business.
  (iv) Amounts owing by the firm to manufacturers who have supplied goods.
  (v) Change kept in cash registers.
  (vi) The amount by which, under arrangement with the bank, the firm has overdrawn its account with the bank.
  (vii) The amount that C. Cotton (a partner) has withdrawn from the business in anticipation of profits.
  (viii) A loan to the firm by B. Nylon (a friend).
  (ix) Insurance premiums on the firm's equipment which have been paid for the next twelve months in advance.
  (x) Rent on the premises occupied by the firm which should have been paid two months ago.
  (xi) Goods which are held for future sale.

2.23 For each of the following unrelated transactions, explain the effect (if any) on proprietorship which would result directly from the transaction.

(a) A partner withdraws £300 cash for his household expenses.

(b) The firm borrows £10 000 from a finance company.

(c) The sale of office equipment for £600 cash. It had cost £350.

(d) The payment of a salary to sales person, £650.

(e) The receipt of £500 from a debtor (the total amount due).

2.24 A business which balances its accounts on 30 June met the following problems in the preparation of its profit and loss statement. State in each case the amount at which you consider the item should appear in the final statement. Give your reason, or basis of calculation, in each case.

(a) New premises were occupied as from 1 September last. The rent is payable in advance at the start of each quarter and total rentals of £1800 have been paid.

(b) The only salesman employed is paid 5 per cent commission on sales. The commission is calculated each quarter and is paid at the end of the month following the end of the quarter.

Payments of commission were:

July	31	£1 600
October	31	1 420
January	31	2 100
April	30	1 850

The sales for the quarter ended 30 June this year were £34 440.

(c) An account from an electrician for £1400 was paid during the year; £650 of this was for repairs to existing electrical installations, the remainder was for the installation of new refrigeration equipment.

(d) Solicitors' fees paid for the year totalled £350; £150 of this was incurred in the collection of overdue accounts, and £200 was associated with the acquisition of a block of land on which it is proposed to erect a new factory.

2.25 Use all of the following items to prepare a profit and loss statement of Colin Goon, Merchant.

Advertising	£3 100
Carriage on purchases	3 240
Delivery expenses	2 460
Interest paid	850
Light and power	920
Postage and stationery	1 240
Purchases	61 930
Rent received	2 240
Salaries	16 200
Sales	150 700
Stock (1/7/X5)	21 200
Stock (30/6/X6)	23 400

2.26 On 1 July 19X2, Helen Cook commenced business as a travel agent and consultant. She used £12 000 from her personal savings and borrowed an additional £8000 from a finance company in order to buy an existing agency. During the first three years of operations, the earnings generated by the business were as follows:

Year ended 30 June	Net profits	Ms Cook's withdrawals
19X3	£28 500	£20 000
19X4	30 600	21 000
19X5	32 400	22 000

During the year ended 30 June 19X6, the net profit was £35 800 and the proprietor withdrew £24 000 for personal use.

(a) Prepare a statement of retained earnings for the year ended 30 June 19X6.

(b) Show the items which would appear under the heading of 'proprietorship' in a balance sheet prepared as at 30 June 19X6. (State any assumptions you have made.)

Problems

2.27 From the following information relating to Darren Lodge, dentist, prepare a profit and loss statement for the year ended 30 June 19X6 and a balance sheet as at that date.

(a) Capital as at 1 July 19X5   £12 760

    Represented by:

Cash at bank	£4 420	
Equipment	10 500	
	£14 920	
Less Creditors	2 160	
		£12 760

(b) Transactions for year

Fees received in cash	£39 300
Assistant's salary	12 400
Rent of premises	5 200
Cost of materials used	2 400
Postage, stationery, telephone	1 800
New equipment purchased	2 000
Repairs to equipment	400
Cash withdrawn for private use	12 600

(c) At 30 June 19X6

Cash at bank	£7 610
Creditors	2 850
Owing by patients for fees	4 200

(There were no fees owing at 1/7/X5)

2.28 Jane Smith tells you: 'My cousin Fred died recently and left me his business in Downtown. Bill Jones has been looking at the books for me. You know he is an efficient and dependable fellow and meticulously accurate.... Unfortunately for me he'd booked for a holiday in Australia and has just gone off for three months leaving me to cope. I don't understand accounts. My cousin always seemed prosperous and Bill says the business made a good profit last year. All I can see is a stack of bills and no money to pay them with. My cousin drew only £500 out of the business last year and was clearly living off his other income, the lucky chap. Bill Jones left me what he called a couple of trial balances, though they don't help me much. He said they were complete, at the dates indicated. Would you have a look at them for me?'

	Balances at	
	30 June 19X6	**30 June 19X5**
Trade creditors	£30 000	£21 000
Trade debtors	13 750	10 000
Sales for the year	450 000	347 000
Wages, rent and other expenses	70 000	48 100
Depreciation expense on plant	8 750	7 500
Bank overdraft	9 600	—
Stock at end of year	150 000	130 000
Fred's capital		
Balance at 1 July 19X4	—	167 550
Balance at 1 July 19X5	166 150	—
Cost of goods sold during the year	350 000	276 400
Plant at cost	94 000	75 000

Plant accumulated depreciation	£31 250	£22 500
Loan from J. Wayne	—	15 000
Cash at bank (favourable)		9 650
Fred's drawings	500	16 400

(a) From the data provided, and without further adjustment, you are required to prepare a profit and loss statement for the year ended 30 June 19X6 and a balance sheet at 30 June 19X6.

(b) Prepare a short statement explaining to Jane Smith what has caused the change in the cash position of the business.

2.29 B. Smart has asked for your advice. He is at present employed at an annual salary of £20 000. He is just 55 and, if he retired now, would receive a pension of half his salary until his 60th birthday. If he stays in his job until he is 60, he will be paid a lump sum of £50 000. Smart has invented a burglar alarm after spending £8000 developing his ideas. He has been offered £120 000 for the patent by Auto Co. Ltd. However, he is proposing retiring from his present position to manufacture the alarms himself with the help of his wife, who would leave her present part-time job which pays £6000 p.a. The two have estimated the following:

Production and sale for each of the first 5 years – 4000 alarms at £40 each.
Cost of materials – £19 per unit.
The work would all be done at home using the garage as a workshop, and the couple do all the work themselves with the assistance of machinery costing £16 000.
Packing and transport would cost £1 per unit.
Other overheads – light, power, etc. would total £2000 p.a.

(a) You are required to prepare figures which will assist Smart in deciding on the most favourable course of action in accordance with the above estimated data.

(b) List any other factors that you consider should affect his decision.

Chapter 3
Accounting processes

Processing methods ☐ The need for accounts ☐ Forms of accounts ☐ What accounts are required? ☐ Entries in accounts ☐ Double entry analysis ☐ Analysing sales transactions ☐ Balancing accounts ☐ Ledgers ☐ The trial balance ☐ Capturing accounting data ☐ Use of journals ☐ Example of a manual accounting system

Processing methods

In Chapter 1, we described accounting as the collection of data on transactions affecting an enterprise, the subsequent processing (i.e., classifying and summarising) of that data and the reporting of the resultant information to decision makers. Chapter 2 was primarily concerned with the nature of financial accounting reports and with the major types of information which are useful to external users. In this chapter we concentrate on the data collection and data-processing operations which are necessary to the production of these reports.

A major difficulty in discussing accounting processes is that the methods used vary greatly from one accounting system to another. In particular, there is a stark contrast between traditional manual methods and modern computer-based accounting systems. There is also a vast difference between the 'hands-on' computer systems of today and the batch-processing computer systems of, say, ten or fifteen years ago. Again there is the added problem that much of today's technology and techniques may well be superseded in another five years' time.

Given these dilemmas, we believe that a first-year textbook in accounting should not become too involved in detailed descriptions of processing techniques. Instead, it should concentrate more on the role of the accountant in determining what kind of data should be collected and how it should be analysed to provide meaningful information. Furthermore, we believe that because manual methods are more easily seen and understood than operations performed inside a computer, it is desirable at first to deal with accounting processes in terms of a manual system and then later to examine the adaptations which need to be made when these processing tasks are given to a computer-based system.

The need for accounts

We have seen that every business transaction has an effect on the elements of the accounting equation. We have studied the effects of some typical transactions both on the totals (A, L and P) and on the individual asset, liability and proprietorship items in the balance sheet. It is obvious however that it is neither desirable nor practicable to draw up a new balance sheet after each transaction. Other procedures must be adopted to record and summarise the effects resulting from business transactions.

In considering the tools required to record the occurrence of each transaction, we must come back again to the major purposes in accounting: to assist management in its control over the enterprise's assets and activities, and to provide relevant information to internal and external decision makers. Neither management nor other users are as interested in the changes in total assets, total liabilities and total proprietorship as they are in the changes in the individual *items* which make up or affect these totals. Therefore, it is necessary to have some mechanism to record the changes in each of these individual items.

This mechanism is the *account*, which in its simplest form is a page, sheet or card for each item for which detailed recording of changes is deemed necessary. In computer-based systems the records may be in the form of magnetic tapes or disks.

Forms of accounts

Since the changes that occur will either *increase* or *decrease* an account, it usually has two sides or two columns to record these increases or decreases. The traditional form of account has two sides, the left-hand side being called the debit, the right-hand side, the credit – as follows:

Name of Account

Date	Particulars	£	Date	Particulars	£
	(Debit side)			(Credit side)	

An alternative is to record the increases and decreases in adjacent columns:

Name of account

Date	Particulars	Debit	Credit
		£ (Debit)	£ (Credit)

Another variation includes a third column for the resultant balance of the account after each change or after a number of changes:

Name of Account

Date	Particulars	Debit	Credit	Balance
		£ (Debit)	£ (Credit)	£

Other rulings will be seen, since the form of account used by a business depends largely on the manner in which the recording is performed in that particular business. With increasing technology, the trend has been towards forms of accounts which have the money columns adjacent, as this is more convenient. The traditional two-sided 'T' form of account still has its uses, particularly with handwritten records. It is also useful in teaching and analysing the entering into accounts, the two sides (and consequently the two effects 'increase' and 'decrease') being more widely separated and thus more easily distinguishable. For this reason, we will use this form in most of our examples and illustrations.

What accounts are required?

It is impossible to set down the number or the names of the accounts needed to satisfy all accounting systems. Both vary greatly from one enterprise to another and depend on such factors as the size of the business, the activities carried on, the type of ownership, and, above all, the nature of the information that the management of the business want collected and presented to them. All the assets of the enterprise could be included in one account but, as we have seen, it is usual to supply more detail of individual assets, such as cash, furniture, machinery, and so on. If still more detail is required, separate accounts may be written up for office furniture, store furniture, or for drapery equipment, hardware equipment, grocery equipment, etc. In the same way, there may be one wages and salaries account or several, for example factory wages, sales salaries, office salaries and so on.

It is, however, possible to distinguish certain basic types of accounts needed in every enterprise. From our discussion of the balance sheet and the profit and loss statement in Chapter 2, it is clear that in order to produce those financial statements, an accounting system has to consist of five basic groups of accounts:

1. Asset accounts.

2. Liability accounts.

3. Proprietorship accounts.

4. Revenue accounts.

5. Expense accounts.

Entries in accounts

The usual system of making entries in the accounts depends on two factors:

1. Differences in the fundamental *nature* of the accounts – as shown by the five main groups listed above. These were based on the elements of the accounting equation. This factor is important if we want to carry into the accounts the 'natural agreement' which was present in the accounting equation.

2. The use of debit and credit sides in each account. This enables us to recognise in terms of debits and credits the distinction between items appearing on opposite sides of the accounting equation.

In the development of the system, one assumption is necessary: that 'all *asset* accounts are of a *debit* nature'. This is a purely arbitrary decision. It would be possible to justify a completely reversed set of rules for entry into accounts based on the opposite assumption whereby assets were deemed to be of a credit nature.

Once the decision has been made to consider all asset accounts as debits, however, the bases of entry in all other accounts can be deduced directly from it, thus:

1. Basic assumption: i.e., *Increases* in *assets* are *debit* entries.
   Asset accounts, Debit nature   *Decreases* in *assets* are *credit* entries.

Since liabilities and proprietorship in the equation are opposite to assets it follows that:

2. **Liability accounts, Credit nature**   i.e., *Increases* in *liabilities* are *credit* entries.
   Decreases in *liabilities* are *debit* entries.

and

3. **Proprietorship accounts, Credit nature**   i.e., *Increases* in *proprietorship* are *credit* entries.
   Decreases in *proprietorship* are *debit* entries.

and since by definition revenue items increase proprietorship and expenses decrease proprietorship, therefore:

4.   **Revenue accounts** are of a **Credit nature.**

and:

5.   **Expense accounts** are of a **Debit nature.**

We can summarise the position as follows:

Type of account	Basic nature of account	Entry to record an increase	Entry to record a decrease
Asset	Debit	Debit	Credit
Liability	Credit	Credit	Debit
Proprietorship	Credit	Credit	Debit
Revenue	Credit	Credit	Debit
Expense	Debit	Debit	Credit

Double entry analysis

Having formulated the above rules linking entry in the accounts with the accounting equation, any transaction occurring in a business and requiring to be recorded may be analysed as follows:

Step 1 What accounts have been affected by the transactions?

Step 2 For each of the accounts affected,
(a) What type of account is it? (asset, liability, proprietorship, revenue or expense)
(b) Has the account to be increased or decreased as a result of the transaction?

Step 3 Based on the answers given to these questions and the rules for entry developed above, what account has to be debited and what account has to be credited?

To illustrate this approach to an isolated transaction, suppose that shop fittings costing £500 are bought on credit:

Step 1 The two accounts affected are 'shop fittings' and 'creditors'.

Step 2 Shop fittings – (a) is an asset, (b) has been increased
– (a) is a liability, (b) has been increased.

Step 3 Shop fittings account to be *debited* (increase of an asset) £500.
account to be *credited* (increase of a liability) £500.

The above procedure and example illustrate the significance of the term 'double entry bookkeeping'. Under this system, the two-sided effect of every transaction is recognised and recorded in the accounts, carrying into the accounts the 'natural balance' which was apparent in the accounting equation. The value of the double entry approach has been recognised by accountants for centuries and it underlies many of the accounting control techniques to which reference will be made later.

While the effects of most transactions can be traced to two accounts, it is worthwhile remembering that there are some transactions which are of a more complex nature and which affect more than two accounts. For instance, if an item of office furniture is bought costing £4000, and a deposit of £1000 cash is paid now, with the balance to be paid in three months time, then there are three accounts affected:

The asset	'office furniture'	is increased by £4000
The asset	'cash'	is decreased by £1000
The liability	'creditor'	is increased by £3000
thus the account	'office furniture'	is debited with £4000
the account	'cash'	is credited with £1000
the account	'creditor'	is credited with £3000

i.e.,

Office furniture		Cash		Creditors account	
£4000			£1000		£3000

(Notice, however, that the *total* amount debited still equals the *total* amount credited.)

Now let us consider a simple example involving a series of transactions:

June 1 G. Rich commenced business as a retailer of television sets by depositing £8000 in a business bank account. He decided that he would deposit in the bank account all cash as received and would make all payments through the bank account.

June 2 Paid one week's rent of premises £250.
Purchased twenty television sets costing £500 each on credit.

June 3 Bought shop fittings for £2000 each.
Sold four sets on credit for £750 each.

June 4 Paid £4000 on account to suppliers of sets.

June 5 Sold four sets for cash for £700 each.
Paid for newspaper advertisements £150.

June 6 Withdrew cash for personal use £250.

The steps involved in analysing these transactions prior to entry into accounts are summarised as follows:

Transaction		Accounts affected	Type of account	Increased or decreased	Type of entry
Deposit of capital	£8000	Cash at bank	*Asset*	Increased	*Debit*
		G. Rich, capital	*Proprietorship*	Increased	*Credit*
Payment of rent	£250	Rent paid	*Expense*	Increased	*Debit*
		Cash at bank	*Asset*	Decreased	*Credit*
Purchase of goods		Stock	*Asset*	Increased	*Debit*
	£10 000	Creditors	*Liability*	Increased	*Credit*
Purchase of shop fittings	£2000	Shop fittings	*Asset*	Increased	*Debit*
		Cash at bank	*Asset*	Decreased	*Credit*
Sale of goods: (a) the revenue aspect	£3000	Debtors	*Asset*	Increased	*Debit*
		Sales	*Revenue*	Increased	*Credit*
(b) the expense aspect	2000	Cost of goods sold	*Expense*	Increased	*Debit*
		Stock	*Asset*	Decreased	*Credit*
Payment to creditor	£4000	Creditor	*Liability*	Decreased	*Debit*
		Cash at bank	*Asset*	Decreased	*Credit*

Transaction		Accounts affected	Type of account	Increased or decreased	Type of entry
Sale of goods:					
(a) the revenue		Cash at bank	*Asset*	Increased	*Debit*
aspect	£2800	Sales	*Revenue*	Increased	*Credit*
(b) the expense		Cost of goods sold	*Expense*	Increased	*Debit*
aspect	£2000	Stock	*Asset*	Decreased	*Credit*
Payment of		Advertising	*Expense*	Increased	*Debit*
advertising	£150	Cash at bank	*Asset*	Decreased	*Credit*
Withdrawals by		G. Rich, drawings	*Proprietorship*	Decreased	*Debit*
proprietor	£250	Cash at bank	*Asset*	Decreased	*Credit*

The subsequent entries into the account would result in:

Asset Accounts

Cash at Bank

June 1 G. Rich - Capital	£8 000	June 2 Rent paid	£250
June 5 Sales	2 800	June 3 Shop fittings	2 000
		June 4 Creditor	4 000
		June 5 Advertising	150
		June 6 G. Rich - Drawings	250

Stock

June 2 Creditor	£10 000	June 3 Cost of goods sold	£2 000
		June 5 Cost of goods sold	2 000

Shop Fittings

June 3 Cash at bank	£2 000

Debtors Account

June 3 Sales	£3 000

Liability Accounts

Creditors Account

June 4 Cash at bank	£4 000	June 2 Stock	£10 000

Proprietorship Accounts

G. Rich - Capital

	June 1 Cash at bank £8 000

G. Rich - Drawings

June 6 Cash at bank	£250

Revenue Accounts

Sales

	June 3 Debtors account	£3 000
	June 5 Cash at bank	2 800

Expense Accounts

Cost of Goods Sold

June 3 Stock	£2 000
June 5 Stock	2 000

Rent Paid

June 2 Cash at bank	£250

Advertising

June 5 Cash at bank	£150

Note that to make the ready identification of the other (or contra) side of the double entry easier, we have used the technique of entering the name of the contra account affected. For instance, for the first transaction on 1 June, when we debited the cash at bank account with £8000 we described it as 'G. Rich – Capital' (the name of the other account affected). Similarly, when we credited G. Rich's capital account with £8000, we used the explanation 'Cash at bank'. Other methods of cross-referencing (e.g., account numbers) can be used. Cross-referencing should not be regarded as being of paramount importance except as a means of tracing a double entry.

Analysing sales transactions

In the simple example of G. Rich above, because only one type of goods was handled and because all purchases were made at the same price it was possible each time a sale was made to identify the actual expense of the goods sold, that is, the purchase price of each item. (Note, however, that there may have been other expenses, for example, delivery expenses, advertising, associated with obtaining the sale.) The initial purchase of the goods was not regarded as an expense but as a cost – the acquisition of an asset (stock). Because we know how much of this asset was consumed for each individual sale, we were able to debit an expense account – cost of goods sold, and credit the asset account – stock. Our end-of-period stock or closing stock was readily known (at cost price) by the balance reflected in the stock account, and the cost of goods sold expense from the account of that name. That is,

Opening stock + Purchases − Cost of goods sold = Closing stock.

There are many businesses where this detailed identification and recording of movements in goods is not possible or practicable. Where many different lines are being handled, and where the purchase price is subject to variations, it becomes a major clerical problem to attempt detailed stock recording. Thus in many accounting systems the determination of cost of goods sold is postponed until the end of the period of time for which it is desired to determine profit. It is then deduced by assuming that the difference between total goods purchased and those remaining on hand at the end of the period represents the goods sold during the period. Note that this assumption is not always valid: some goods may have been wasted, damaged or stolen during the period.

Where this approach is adopted, it will not be possible to have a ledger account which will show continuously the movements in goods as the stock account did in the above example. If cost of goods sold cannot be ascertained at the time of sale and entered in this account, there is not much significance in entering the purchases of goods in the account which contains the total stock on hand at the beginning of the period. Thus it is usual to have a stock account into which entries are made only at the beginning and the end of the period, and to build up purchases for the period in a separate 'purchases' account. Then, at the end of the period, cost of goods sold is ascertained on the method of:

Opening stock + Purchases − Closing stock = Cost of goods sold.

The two methods may be contrasted as follows:

A   *Perpetual stock system* – The cost of each sale is recorded and the total of these costs is deducted from the total of goods on hand and goods purchased. The difference represents what ought to be the closing stock.

B   *Physical stock system* – The final physical stock is deducted from the total goods on hand and goods purchased. The difference is deemed to represent the cost of goods sold.

To illustrate the two different approaches, consider the following example:

On 1 July, the stock (at cost) of a wholesaler was £4500.

The following transactions relating to goods for resale occurred during the first week of July:

July 2 Purchased goods on credit	£200
July 3 Sold goods for cash	180
July 4 Sold goods on credit	150
July 5 Returned damaged goods to supplier	30
July 6 Purchased goods on credit	340

System A – where identification of cost of goods sold is possible

Suppose that in both the sales transacted, the cost price of the goods is 66⅔ per cent of the sale price (i.e., the goods are priced to give a profit margin of 50 per cent on cost); then a continuous record of goods at cost price can be maintained. An analysis of the transactions will be shown as follows;

Transaction	Accounts affected	Type of account	Increased or decreased	Type of entry
July 2 (for the purchase of goods of £200)	Stock Creditor	*Asset* *Liability*	Increase Increase	*Debit* *Credit*
July 3 (for the sale price of £180)	Cash at bank Sales	*Asset* *Revenue*	Increase Increase	*Debit* *Credit*
July 3 (for the expense of £120)	Cost of goods sold Stock	*Expense* *Asset*	Increase Increase	*Debit* *Credit*
July 4 (for the sale price of £150)	Debtor's account Sales	*Asset* *Revenue*	Increase Increase	*Debit* *Credit*

Transaction	Accounts affected	Type of account	Increased or decreased	Type of entry
July 4 (for the expense of of £100)	Cost of goods sold Stock	*Expense* *Asset*	Increase Decrease	*Debit* *Credit*
July 5 (for the return of goods purchased)	Creditors account Stock	*Liability* *Asset*	Decrease Decrease	*Debit* *Credit*
July 6 (for the purchase of goods)	Stock Creditors account	*Asset* *Liability*	Increase Increase	*Debit* *Credit*

The resultant position in the ledger will be:

Stock

July 1 Balance	£4 500	July 3 Cost of goods sold	£120
July 2 Creditors account	200	July 4 Cost of goods sold	100
July 6 Creditors account	340	July 5 Creditors account	30

Cash at Bank

July 3 Sales   £180

Debtors account

July 4 Sales   £150

Creditors account

July 5 Stock	£30	July 2 Stock	£200
		July 6 Stock	340

Sales

	July 3 Cash at bank	£180
	July 4 Debtors account	150

Cost of Goods Sold

July 3 Stock	£120
July 4 Stock	100

System B – where identification of cost of goods sold is not possible (The system most commonly used)

The analysis of the transactions will be as follows:

Transactions	Accounts affected	Type of account	Increased or decreased	Type of entry
July 2	Purchases Creditors account	*Expense* *Liability*	Increase Increase	*Debit* *Credit*
July 3	Cash at bank Sales	*Asset* *Revenue*	Increase Increase	*Debit* *Credit*

Transaction	Accounts affected	Type of account	Increased or decreased	Type of entry
July 4	Debtors account Sales	*Asset* *Revenue*	Increase Increase	*Debit* *Credit*
July 5	Creditors account Purchases returns[1]	*Liability* *Expense*	Decrease Decrease	*Debit* *Credit*
July 6	Purchases Creditors account	*Expense* *Liability*	Increase Increase	*Debit* *Credit*

[1] *Note*: An alternative to opening a separate purchases returns account was to credit the purchases account. Where returns of purchases and sales are frequent, it is preferable to have separate purchases returns (or returns outwards) and sales returns (or returns inwards) accounts, thus having such detail immediately available if required by management.

The resultant position in the ledger will be:

Stock

July 1 Balance £4500

Cash at Bank

July 3 Sales £180

Debtors Account

July 4 Sales £150

Creditors Account

July 5 Purchases returns £30   July 2 Purchases £200

July 6 Purchases 340

Sales

July 3 Bank £180

July 4 Debtors account 150

Purchases

July 2 Creditors account £200

July 6 Creditors account 340

Purchases Returns

July 5 Creditors account £30

The continuous system of stock recording illustrated in System A is usually known as *perpetual* stock. Records are kept of each addition and disposal of stock and thus it should be possible to calculate the stock which should be on hand at any time.

System B is usually termed *physical or periodic* stock. Cost of goods sold can only be determined after the balance of stock on hand has been obtained by a physical stocktaking (i.e., the identification, counting and listing of all stocks on hand). Suppose, in the above example, a physical stocktaking on 6 July indicates stock on hand of £4790; cost of goods sold can be calculated by using the following formula:

$$\text{Cost of goods sold} = \text{Opening stock (£4500)} + \text{Net purchases (£510)}$$
$$- \text{Closing stock (£4790)}$$
$$= \text{£220.}$$

An error in the calculation of opening or closing stock will result in an incorrect cost of goods sold and thus an incorrect determination of profit (or loss).

Balancing accounts

We now look at the need to ascertain the net results of all the increases and decreases in a particular account. The state of an account at a point of time is known as the *balance*. Accounts may be balanced at any time, for example annually, monthly, weekly or after each entry. The three-column form of account described earlier provides for a balance to be calculated after each entry. When a balance is required in a two-sided form of account, it is necessary to compare the total effect of the debit entries with the total effect of the credit entries. Sometimes, where only one entry has been made, no calculation is required. For instance, in the shop fittings account in the G. Rich example, the balance is obvious by observation – a debit balance of £2000.

	Shop Fittings	
June 3 Cash at bank	£2000	

Where all the entries are on one side of the account then the process of determining the balance is purely one of addition. In the sales account in that example, if the accounts are balanced on 6 June:

	Sales		
June 6 Balance	£5 800	June 3 Debtors account	£3 000
		June 5 Bank	2 800
	£5 800		£5 800
		June 7 Balance	£5 800

the credit balance of £5800 being carried down to commence the next period of recording.

Where entries are all on one side, it is common to enter the total in pencil on that side instead of inking in the balance and bringing it down below the totals. However, at the end of the trading period, it is usual to balance off as shown above.

Where there are entries on both sides of an account then the steps in balancing the account are as follows:

1. Add up the side with the greater value and enter this total on both sides, allowing enough space on the side with the smaller value for the entry of the balancing figure.

2. Add up (but do not enter) the side with the smaller value.

3. Subtract (2) from (1) to get the balance. Enter it on the side with the smaller value so that both sides now agree, and bring the balance down ready to commence the next period's entries.

In the cash at bank account for G. Rich:

Cash at Bank			
June 1 G. Rich	£8 000	June 2 Rent paid	£250
June 5 Sales	2 800	June 3 Shop fittings	2 000
		June 4 Creditors account	4 000
		June 5 Advertising	150
		June 6 G. Rich, Drawings	250
		June 6 Balance	4 150
	£10 800		£10 800
June 7 Balance	£4 150		

The balance calculated by subtracting the total credits of £6650 from the total debits of £10 800 is a debit balance of £4150. Here, again, except at the end of the period, it is common practice to total both sides in pencil only, and show the pencilled balance in the particulars column.

Ledgers

Accounts are kept together in a *ledger*. Businesses usually have more than one ledger. In addition to the main ledger, one ledger contains the accounts of all the firm's debtors; another contains the accounts of all the creditors, and so on. These can be called the 'accounts receivable' or 'debtors ledger' and 'accounts payable' or 'creditors ledger' respectively.

The accounts themselves should be given a clear title to indicate the type of transaction recorded, for example, 'Purchases, Wages, J. Jones, Plant and Machinery', and so on. They may be recorded on the pages of a bound book; on loose leaves kept in place by a mechanical binder; on small cards; or be part of a computer system. The type of ledger used depends on the nature of the entries. Individual debtors' accounts are often entered on loose leaves or cards so that strict alphabetical order can be maintained. Furthermore, accounts which have been closed because customers have died or ceased to deal with the firm may be removed from such a ledger. Clubs and societies often use cards to record financial details of members' subscriptions and fees, etc. However, where in a main ledger the accounts are of a permanent nature, the use of a bound book will have the advantage of being more protected from the loss of pages or from the fraudulent alteration of entries. In this case, however, there is difficulty in maintaining correct sequence of accounts. The use of bound books as ledgers has, of course, declined considerably with the increasing use of computer-based accounting systems.

The trial balance

If within a particular ledger the double entry system outlined above has been consistently followed, it follows that at any time the total of the debit entries should equal the total of the credit entries. Another way of expressing this is to say that after all accounts have been balanced off as described above, the total debit balances should equal the total of the credit balances. A check to ensure that this is so is usually made at the close of each convenient period (e.g. month, half-year, year). A list of balances prepared in this way is termed a 'trial balance'. It is a check on the arithmetical accuracy of the work but not, by any means, a complete check of the accounting entries. However, if the trial balance figures do not agree, it is obvious an error has been made. The trial balance is thus a form of control over the recording process.

A trial balance taken from the example on page 35 is shown in the following:

G. Rich, Trial Balance
(as at 6 June)

	Debit	Credit
Cash at bank	£4 150	
Stock	6 000	
Shop fittings	2 000	
Debtors accounts	3 000	
Creditors accounts		£6 000
G. Rich - Capital		8 000
G. Rich - Drawings	250	
Sales		5 800
Cost of goods sold	4 000	
Rent paid	250	
Advertising	150	
	£19 800	£19 800

As stated previously, the mere fact that a trial balance has been successfully prepared does not guarantee the accuracy of the accounting. Even if the two totals do correspond, there may still be one or more of the following mistakes:

1. Entries could have been made in the wrong accounts but on the correct sides, for example, a debit in the stock account instead of in the shop fittings account.

2. Wrong amounts may have been entered on both sides, for example, cash sales £300 entered as £30 in the sales account (credit side) and £30 in the cash account (debit side).

3. Two errors have been made, one compensating for the other; for example, the debit side of an account under-added by £100, and the credit side of another account similarly under-added.

4. Transactions may have been omitted entirely; for example, if there were twenty transactions, the trial balance would still agree if only fifteen of sixteen of them had been entered correctly and the others left out altogether.

Nevertheless, the trial balance is a valuable check and, as will be seen in the next chapter, it is also a useful summary of the accounts and may form the basis of preparing informative reports.

Capturing accounting data

In the examples given above, the various accounting transactions analysed were supplied as given data; for example, paid one week's rent of premises £250; bought shop fittings for £2000 cash; sold goods on credit £500, and so on. In practice, the accountant has to arrange for the collection of the originating data in the first place. Often documentary evidence (invoices, receipts, credit notes, etc.) is prepared transaction by transaction. In other cases, manual or electronic devices are used to capture basic details of the transaction.

Here we are primarily concerned with source documents, or similar evidence, as forming the first step in the accounting process. However, it must be remembered that they are often also required as legal proof that a transaction has occurred and as evidence for an auditor verifying the accuracy of the accounting records and reports.

In the case of manual accounting systems there is usually a time lag between the occurrence of the transaction and the subsequent entry in the accounting records. Even with many computer-based accounting systems, documentary evidence is collected in batches prior to being processed. However, there is a strong trend towards 'on-line' processing systems, where electronic equipment allows the transaction to be processed at the time of its occurrence.

Use of journals

In manual accounting systems, an additional step is usually interposed between the collection of the originating data and entry of the transaction into the relevant ledger accounts. This is a recording and summarising process involving entries in 'day books' or 'journals'.

There are two major functions of a journal:

1. It provides a medium for posting to the ledger by interpreting the accounting transactions into the double entries – debit and credit.

2. It provides a permanent record of the original transactions in a condensed and conveniently storable form, with easy reference back to the business documents and forward to the ledger accounts concerned.

A simple basic form of journal provides for two money columns (debit and credit) and treats each transaction separately, recording the basic details of the transactions and setting out clearly its debit and credit effects.

If such a journal (usually called a 'general journal') was used to record the transactions of G. Rich for the period 1 June to 6 June inclusive (given earlier in this chapter) then it would appear as follows:

G. Rich, General Journal

Date	Accounts	Folio	Debit	Credit
June 1	Bank		£8 000	
	G. Rich, Capital			£8 000
	Bank account to commence business			
June 2	Rent paid		250	
	Bank			250
	One week's rent			
June 2	Stock		10 000	
	Creditors account			10 000
	Purchase of 20 TV sets			
June 3	Shop fittings		2 000	
	Bank			2 000
	Purchase of shop fittings			
June 3	Debtors account		1 500	
	Sales			1 500
	Cost of goods sold		1 000	
	Stock			1 000
	Sale of 4 TV sets			
June 4	Creditors account		4 000	
	Bank			4 000
	Payment on account			
June 5	Bank		1 400	
	Sales			1 400
	Cost of goods sold		1 000	
	Stock			1 000
	Sale of 4 TV sets			

Date	Accounts	Folio	Debit	Credit
June 5	Advertising		£150	
	Bank			£150
	Newspaper advertisements			
June 6	G. Rich – Drawings		250	
	Bank			250
	Cash for personal use			

Notes:

1. The narrations (or explanations) of each entry are not always given.

2. The folio column would be used to cross-reference the number of the ledger account for each posting.

The use of the journal in facilitating posting of transactions into the ledger is often extended by having a number of specialised books for common types of transactions.

Thus, in a trading business we may find the following books in use:

Cash book (*receipts side*) – to record and summarise receipts of cash from *all* sources.

Cash book (*payments side*) – to record and summarise payments by cheque or by cash for *all* purposes.

Sales day book (*or journal*) – to record and summarise sales of goods which will be paid for later, that is, *credit sales*. It will not include sales of assets other than stock, nor sales of goods for cash (cash sales are recorded in the cash book).

Sales returns book (*or journal*) – to record and summarise returns of goods or allowances in respect of goods previously entered in the Sales Day Book.

Purchases day book (*or journal*) – to record and summarise purchases of goods which will be paid for later, that is, *credit purchases*. It will not include purchases of assets other than stock, nor purchases for cash (cash payments are recorded in the cash book).

Purchases returns book (*or journal*) – to record and summarise returns of goods or allowances in respect of goods previously entered in the Purchases Day Book.

The above journals and books therefore summarise information for similar transactions. (They are referred to as books of original entry. The general journal is also included in this classification.) All cheques drawn may be recorded in the cash book; all invoices received from suppliers for goods purchased may be entered in a purchases day book, and so on. It should be obvious that when a separate journal or book is used for a common group of transactions, the very nature of that journal signals the ultimate double entry to be made in the ledger. Thus, all cheques drawn have the physical effect of reducing the asset cash at bank. The *total* of the cash book is therefore a credit to that account. The *individual* payments may be a debit to a number of various accounts – creditors' account (reducing a liability), wages (expenses), plant (increase in asset), etc.

Where such specialised books are in use, it is still necessary to maintain a general journal to handle transactions which do not fit into these common categories. Here are some of the types of transactions which would be entered in a general journal:

1. Adjustments to ledger accounts, for example, to correct errors.

2. Sales or purchases of assets other than stock, for example, office furniture, plant, etc., bought on credit.

3. Transfers from one account to another, for example, net profit to capital.

4. Provision for expenses for which no charge has yet been made, for example, dividends.

Example of a manual accounting system

The following example illustrates the use of simple specialised books.

On 1 February 19X6, S. Burton commenced business with the following assets and liabilities:

Assets: Cash £1000; stock £7500; shop premises £12 000; delivery van £2200; furniture and equipment £520.

Liabilities: Creditors – T. Ralph £750; K. Roberts £1500.

During the month of February, the following data were collected:

1. Cash sales records

Feb.	1	£500
	21	500
	28	1 300

2. Invoices for credit sales

Feb.	2	S. Watson	£2 500
	8	W. Nichols	1 500
	20	T. Ralph	1 100
	26	W. Nichols	650

3. Invoices from suppliers

Feb.	1	K. Roberts	£1 200
	12	K. Roberts	950
	20	J. Walker (office desk)	200
	20	T. Redman	1 300

4. Amounts received from debtors

Feb.	4	S. Watson	£750
	21	W. Nichols	1 400
	28	W. Nichols	500

5. Cheques drawn

Feb	6	New typewriter	£300
	8	Purchase of goods	650
	14	Wages	320
	18	K. Roberts	1 000
	20	T. Ralph	750
	28	T. Redman	1 300
	28	Wages	320
	28	S. Burton – personal use	500

We will now demonstrate how these data could be recorded in a simple accounting system posted to the ledger, and, at the end of the month, a trial balance extracted from the ledger.

S. Burton, General Journal
Page 1

Date	Particulars	Folio	Debit	Credit
19X6				
Feb. 1	Cash	7	£1 000	
	Stock	10	7 500	
	Shop premises	7	12 000	
	Delivery van	8	2 200	
	Furniture and equipment	9	520	
	T. Ralph	3		£750
	K. Roberts	4		1 500
	S. Burton, Capital	1		20 970
	Assets, liabilities and proprietorship on commencement of business			
Feb. 20	Furniture and equipment	9	200	
	J. Walker	5		200
	Office desk purchased on credit			

Sales Day Book
Page 4

Date	Particulars	Folio	Amount
19X6			
Feb. 2	S. Watson	13	£2 500
Feb. 8	W. Nichols	14	1 500
Feb. 20	T. Ralph	3	1 100
Feb. 26	W. Nichols	14	650
		11	£5 750

Purchases Day Book
Page 10

Date	Particulars	Folio	Amount
19X6			
Feb. 1	K. Roberts	4	£1 200
Feb. 12	K. Roberts	4	950
Feb. 20	T. Redman	6	1 300
		12	£3 450

Cash Book   Page 7   Page 8

	Receipts side				Payments side		
Date	**Particulars**	**Folio**	**Amount**	**Date**	**Particulars**	**Folio**	**Amount**
19X6				19X6			
Feb. 1	Balance	GJ1	£1 000	Feb. 6	Furniture and		
Feb. 1	Sales	11	500		Equipment	9	£300
Feb. 4	S. Watson	13	750	Feb. 8	Purchases	12	650
Feb. 21	W. Nichols	14	1 400	Feb. 14	Wages	15	320
	Sales	11	500	Feb. 18	K. Roberts	4	1 000
Feb. 28	Sales	11	1 300	Feb. 20	T. Ralph	3	750
	W. Nichols	14	500	Feb. 28	T. Redman	6	1 300
					Wages	15	320
					S. Burton –		
					drawings	2	500
					Balance	c/d	810
			£5 950				£5 950
Mar. 1	Balance	b/d	810				

Note: The receipts and payments sides of the cash book have been shown in one book referred to as the cash book. Receipts are shown on the debit side and payments on the credit side. The balancing procedure is similar to that of a ledger account.

Ledger

S. Burton – Capital   Account 1

				19X6			
				Feb. 1	Balance	GJ1	£20 970

S. Burton – Drawings   Account 2

19X6			
Feb. 1	Cash	8	£500

T. Ralph   Account 3

19X6				19X6			
Feb. 20	Cash	8	£750	Feb. 1	Balance	GJ1	£750
	Sales	4	1 100	Feb. 28	Balance	c/d	1 100
			£1 850				£1 850
Mar. 1	Balance	b/d	£1 100				

K. Roberts   Account 4

19X6				19X6			
Feb. 18	Cash	8	£1 000	Feb. 1	Balance	GJ1	£1 500
Feb. 28	Balance	c/d	2 650		Purchases	10	1 200
				Feb. 12	Purchases	10	950
			£3 650				£3 650
				Mar. 1	Balance	b/d	2 650

J. Walker   Account 5

	19X6		
	Feb. 20 Furniture and		
	equipment	GJ1	£200

T. Redman   Account 6

19X6				19X6			
Feb. 28	Cash	8	£1 300	Feb. 20	Purchases	10	£1 300

Shop Premises   Account 7

19X6			
Feb. 1	Balance	GJ1	£12 000

Delivery Van   Account 8

19X6			
Feb. 1	Balance	GJ1	£2 200

Furniture and Equipment   Account 9

19X6				19X6			
Feb. 1	Balance	GJ1	£520	Feb. 28	Balance	c/d	£1 020
Feb. 6	Cash	8	300				
Feb. 20	J. Walker	GJ1	200				
			£1 020				£1 020
Mar. 1	Balance	b/d	£1 020				

Stock   Account 10

19X6			
Feb. 1	Balance	GJ1	£7 500

Sales   Account 11

19X6				19X6			
Feb. 28	Balance	c/d	£8 050	Feb. 1	Cash	7	£500
				Feb. 21	Cash	7	500
				Feb. 28	Cash	7	1 300
					Sales day book	4	5 750
			£8 050				£8 050
				Mar. 1	Balance	b/d	£8 050

Purchases   Account 12

19X6				19X6			
Feb. 8	Cash	8	£650	Feb. 28	Balance	c/d	£4 100
Feb. 28	Purchases day						
	book	10	3 450				
			£4 100				£4 100
Mar. 1	Balance	c/d	4 100				

S. Watson   Account 13

19X6				19X6			
Feb. 2	Sales	4	£2 500	Feb. 4	Cash	7	£750
				Feb. 28	Balance	c/d	1 750
			£2 500				£2 500
Mar. 1	Balance	b/d	£1 750				

W. Nichols   Account 14

19X6				19X6			
Feb. 8	Sales	4	£1 500	Feb. 21	Cash	7	£1 400
Feb. 26	Sales	4	650	Feb. 28	Cash	7	500
					Balance	c/d	250
			£2 150				£2 150
Mar. 1	Balance	b/d	£250				

Wages   Account 15

19X6				19X6			
Feb. 14	Cash	8	£320	Feb. 28	Balance	c/d	£640
Feb. 28	Cash	8	320				
			£640				£640
Mar. 1	Balance	b/d	£640				

S. Burton, Trial Balance as at 28 February 19X6

	Folio	Debit	Credit
S. Burton – Capital	1		£20 970
S. Burton – Drawings	2	£500	
T. Ralph	3	1 100	
K. Roberts	4		2 650
J. Walker	5		200
Cash	7	810	
Shop premises	7	12 000	
Delivery van	8	2 200	
Furniture and equipment	9	1 020	
Stock (at 1/2/X6)	10	7 500	
Sales	11		8 050
Purchases	12	4 100	
S. Watson	13	1 750	
W. Nichols	14	250	
Wages	15	640	
		£31 870	£31 870

Notes
1. The ruling off and balancing of the ledger accounts in this example has been done in a formal manner. In practice, a trial balance may be prepared say, monthly, by simply totalling in pencil certain of the accounts, and allowing a cumulative total for a longer period (say a year) to build up. Particularly with the revenue and expense accounts there is no need to rule off and carry

down the balances because, as will be shown later (Chapter 4), the balances in these accounts are ultimately transferred to the profit and loss account on a yearly basis. When this is done, we do want the cumulative totals of the revenue and expense items for the purpose of profit determination. It is necessary to balance the accounts of debtors and creditors formally where they contain entries on both sides. Here we are not so interested in cumulative totals as in the monthly balances, since statements are prepared from these.

Remember that having prepared a trial balance as above, we are able to compile a profit and loss statement for management *outside* the ledger, that is, *without the actual transfer of ledger balances*, providing a closing stock figure is available.

2. For the purpose of this illustration, hypothetical but unrealistic numbers have been given to the pages of the journals and the ledger accounts.

Other than the general journal, the page number of the book concerned is sufficient in the ledger folio column because the particulars column in the ledger tells us which book the entry has come from. However, for the general journal postings, it is usual to indicate in the ledger folio that the entry has originated from the general journal, for example, GJ1. Naturally, in practice, each book will contain many numbered pages – hence the use of the particular page number for quick cross-reference. It will be seen later that the books may also contain a reference to the original documents prepared at the time the transaction took place. This makes it relatively easy to investigate queries that may arise concerning any ledger account.

Summary

1. In technical terms, there is a vast difference between traditional manual methods of accounting and modern computer-based methods. However, the underlying functions of data collection and analysis remain basically the same.

2. The mechanism used in accounting to record changes in an item is called an *account*.

3. The form of account used varies according to the method of recording adopted, but the basic form consists of two sides or two columns (debit and credit).

4. There are five basic *groups* of accounts required in any system – assets, liabilities, proprietorship, revenue and expenses.

5. The decision as to whether to *debit* or *credit* a particular account as a result of a particular transaction depends on two factors:

(a) the nature of the account (i.e., A, L, P, R or E); and

(b) whether it is increased or decreased as a result of the transaction.

6. For each transaction, it is possible to analyse and record a *double entry* – that is, equal debit and credit effects in two or more accounts.

7. In a trading business, if continuous records of movements of trading stocks are to be maintained, it is necessary to be able to identify or determine cost of goods sold. If this is not possible, the method adopted to determine cost of goods sold is one of calculation.

Cost of goods sold = Opening stock + Purchases – Closing stock.

Under this latter method closing stock must be physically identified and counted.

8. The resultant position of a particular account following a series of transactions is termed the *balance* of the account. Usually accounts are balanced off (i.e., the balance determined) at regular intervals.

9. From accounts in a ledger kept on the double entry principle a *trial balance* (a list of all account balances) may be prepared. The fact that the total of the debit balances is equal to the total of the credit balances is a test of arithmetical accuracy, but not necessarily a check on the correctness of the accounting entries.

10. The first step in the accounting is the capture of data – by means of documentary or other evidence – that a transaction has occurred.

11. The general journal, cash book, day books and returns books are used to record, summarise and analyse accounting data. They provide a basis for posting to ledger accounts.

Discussion questions

3.1 How would you describe 'a ledger account' to a person with no knowledge or experience in accounting?

3.2 Explain the links between 'the accounting equation' and the 'rules of double entry accounting'.

3.3 Compare and contrast the alternative systems of perpetual stock and periodic stock. What factors influence the choice between the two systems?

3.4 What is the balance of an account? How would you 'balance an account'?

3.5 'My accounting records must be perfectly correct. I have taken out a trial balance and it balances.' Comment on this statement.

3.6 What is involved in 'capturing accounting data'?

3.7 The derivation of the term 'journal' is the French word 'jour' meaning 'day'. Does this help us in our understanding of the function of journals in accounting?

3.8 Distinguish between the use of day books and a general journal.

Exercises

3.9 For each of the following ledger account titles,

(a) classify the account as either an asset, liability, proprietorship, revenue or expense account;

(b) state the type of balance (i.e., debit or credit) that you would expect to find in such an account.

> (i) B. Sly (a debtor).
> (ii) Cash in hand.
> (iii) Purchases of goods for resale (in a ledger where cost of goods sold is not recorded).
> (iv) Sales.
> (v) Bank overdraft.
> (vi) Stock.
> (vii) J. Owner – Capital.
> (viii) Office salaries.
> (ix) Land and buildings.
> (x) J. Owner – Drawings.
> (xi) Loan from Finance Co.
> (xii) Postage and stationery.

    (xiii) Sales returns.
    (xiv) Advertising.
    (xv) C. Clear (a creditor).

3.10 The cash account of a certain enterprise had a debit balance of £1100 as at 1 March. The following transactions affecting cash occurred during the next week (the enterprise did not keep a cost of goods sold account):

March 2	Bought goods for cash	£280
March 3	Paid wages	360
March 4	Cash sales	520
March 5	Received payment of J. Bloom's account	400
March 6	Proprietor (C. Carr) withdrew for personal use	250
March 7	Cash sales	440

(a) Show the cash account in the traditional two-sided form and balance the account as at 7 March.

(b) Show the same account in the form using three money columns (showing a running balance).

3.11 The following accounts appear (with other accounts) in the ledger of G. Green, Retailer:

Cash at Bank

May 1	Balance	£1 750	May 2	G. Green – Drawings	£200
May 2	Sales	480	May 4	Purchases	560
May 3	B. Bloom	240	May 6	Furniture	350
May 6	Sales	580	May 7	Wages	270

B. Bloom (a debtor)

May 1	Balance	£500	May 3	Bank	£240
May 4	Sales	170	May 5	Sales returns	70
May 6	Sales	270			

(a) Describe clearly the position or transaction represented by each of the above entries. In doing so, list your answer in chronological (date) order and answer once only for entries common to both accounts.

(b) Give the balances of each of the above accounts as at 7 May.

3.12 Head a sheet of paper as follows:

	Debit entry		Credit entry	
Transaction	Name of account	Reason	Name of account	Reason
e.g., Bought office furniture for cash	Office furniture	Increase of asset	Cash at bank	Decrease of asset

For each of the following transactions show the double entry that should be made:

(a) cash sales;

(b) paid wages;

(c) made a loan to J. Day;

(d) received rent from sub-tenant;

(e) proprietor paid in extra capital;

(f) bought goods on credit from Gray & Co. (assume perpetual stock system);

(g) returned damaged goods to Gray & Co.;

(h) bought furniture for cash from D. Black.

3.13 (a) Enter the following transactions in the ledger of D. Owner using the following accounts – cash at bank; sales; purchases; furniture; wages; advertising; Creditors Ltd; D. Friend; D. Owner Capital.

(b) Balance the accounts.

(c) Prepare a trial balance at 8 June.

June 1	D. Owner commenced business as a grocer by paying £1000 cash into a business bank account.	
June 3	Bought goods on credit from Creditors Ltd	£8 000
	Bought furniture for cash	750
June 5	Sold goods for cash	900
June 6	Cash sales	1 300
	Paid for advertising	200
	Bought furniture on credit from Creditors Ltd	350
June 7	Returned damaged furniture to Creditors Ltd and was allowed	50
June 8	Paid wages	150
	Cash sales	1 000
	Sold goods to D. Friend on credit	800
	Paid cash to Creditors Ltd	4 000

3.14 Enter the following transactions in appropriate ledger accounts for D. Black, Garage Proprietor, using the double entry system. Balance the accounts and prepare a trial balance at the end of the period.

Jan. 6	Bought spare parts on credit from Motor Supplies Ltd	£2 700
	Cash sales of petrol	6 250
Jan. 7	Charged D. Blue for repairs	500
	Sold spare parts to R. Gray on credit	150
	Paid rent	100
	Paid subscription to Motor Proprietors' Association	30
Jan. 8	Cash sales of petrol	950
	Bought two-truck on credit from Tows Ltd	15 000
	Paid cash as deposit on truck	4 500
Jan. 10	Paid Electricity Board for power and light	250
	Received fees for parking space provided	400
	Received new neon sign for roof in payment of spare parts valued at	600
	D. Blue paid his account	500

Note: Black regards spare parts as goods purchased for resale, and includes revenue from same in his general sales. However he requires a separate individual determination of revenue from other sources.

3.15 On 1 April, G. Oats had the following assets and liabilities:

Assets – cash at bank £600, K. Way (debtor) £300, G. Sims (debtor) £500, stock £1800, equipment and fittings £900.
Liabilities – G. Gray (creditor) £200, J. Smith (creditor) £400.

During the week ended 6 April, the following transactions occurred:

April 1	Sold goods costing £100 to G. Sims for £150 on credit
April 2	Received cash from K. Way £200
April 3	Bought goods from G. Gray £400 on credit
April 4	Sold goods costing £200 for £280 cash
April 5	Paid cash to J. Smith £150
April 6	Sold goods costing £150 to B. Moggs for £230 on credit

You are required to:

(a) record the above balances and transactions in appropriate ledger accounts;

(b) extract a trial balance from this ledger as at 6 April.

3.16 On 1 September, the stock balance (at cost) of a wholesaler was £8000. The following transactions relating to stock occurred during the first week of September:

Sept. 1	Sold goods on credit to L. Lane	£300	(cost £220)
Sept. 2	Bought goods on credit from Excelsior Ltd	800	
	Sold goods on credit to M. May	180	(cost £130)
Sept. 3	Bought goods for cash	400	
	L. Lane returned goods	40	(cost £30)
Sept. 4	Returned goods to Excelsior Ltd	50	
Sept. 5	Cash sales	580	(cost £480)

Record the above transactions in suitable ledger accounts:

(a) using the information available regarding cost price;

(b) using the method which would have to be used if the information regarding cost price had not been available.

3.17 From the following list of documents record the transactions in the appropriate books and post to the ledger accounts:

Sales invoices

001	May 3	A. Black	£75
002	May 3	B. Blue	154
003	May 3	C. Redd	332
004	May 3	P. Green	219
005	May 4	A. Black	199
006	May 4	Tan & Co.	290

Suppliers' invoices

May 3	D. Lily	Goods	£877
May 3	M. Rose	Office stationery	15
May 3	Daisy Ltd	Goods	855
May 3	T.S. Ltd	Typewriter	322
May 3	Gas Co.	Heating	21
May 4	D. Lily	Goods	442

Cheques written

112	May 3	Wages	200
113	May 3	Cash purchase of goods	41
114	May 4	M. Rose	15

Cash receipts from debtors

May 4	B. Blue	154
May 4	A. Black	75

Credit notes issued

222	May 4	C. Redd	47
223	May 4	P. Green	19

Cash sales

May 3	756
May 4	555

3.18 On 1 February M. Flinders had the following assets and liabilities:

Assets Cash £120; stock £800; buildings £3000; plant £1500; office furniture £280.
Debtors - S. Patrick £75; D. Thompson £185.
Liabilities *Creditors* - D. Mitchell £46; H. Fisher £134.

During the month he had the following transactions:

Feb.	1	Sold goods for cash	£180
Feb.	2	Paid H. Fisher on account	100
Feb.	3	Sold surplus plant to F. Bacon on credit (at book value)	200
Feb.	4	Bought goods from H. Fisher	166
Feb.	6	Drew cash for personal use	25
		Paid salaries	23
Feb.	8	Received rent from J. Jones	40
Feb.	9	Bought goods for cash	75
Feb.	10	Sold goods to D. Thompson	145
		Received cash on account from D. Thompson	30
Feb.	11	Purchased office chairs on credit from Furniture Co. Ltd.	50
Feb.	12	Charged S. Patrick interest on overdue account	2
Feb.	13	Paid salaries	23
Feb.	15	Paid office expenses	27
Feb.	16	Bought goods from G. Herbert	100
Feb.	17	Sold goods to S. Patrick	80
Feb.	18	Paid advertising expenses	23
Feb.	19	Bought office desk for cash	20
Feb.	20	Drew cash for personal use	25
		Paid salaries	23
Feb.	22	Paid delivery expenses on sales	14
Feb.	23	Cash sales	67
Feb.	24	Cash purchases	80
Feb.	25	Paid office expenses	6
Feb.	26	Paid D. Mitchell	30
Feb.	27	Paid salaries	25
		Cash sales	115

You are required to:

(a) frame a general journal entry to open the books of M. Flinders as at 1 February;

(b) record the above transactions in the day books and cash book and post to the ledger;

(c) extract a trial balance as at 28 February. (It is not necessary to balance off the accounts in ink.)

3.19 The following accounts appear in the ledger of A. Lincoln:

G. Washington

July	1	Balance	£385	July	4	Cash	£50
July	14	Sales	96	July	16	Sales returns	8
July	30	Interest	2	July	31	Balance	425
			£483				£483
Aug.	1	Balance	425				

B. Franklin

July 3	Cash	£542	July 1	Balance		£560
	Discount received	18	July 8	Purchases		118
July 11	Purchases returns	13				
July 31	Balance	105				
		£678				£678
				Balance		£105

For each of the transactions recorded in the above accounts you are required to:

(a) explain the nature of the transaction;

(b) name the book from which the entry would be posted;

(c) name the document that would form the original evidence for the transaction.

Note: Discuss only from the viewpoint of A. Lincoln.

Problems

3.20 The following are extracts from the books of D. Williams for April:

Sales Day Book

April 1	K. White	£750
. .	. .	. .
April 30	S. Barnett	540
		£38 400

Purchases Day Book

April 1	Epworth Ltd	£1 180
. .	. .	. .
April 30	Comcarr Ltd	4 300
		£25 200

Sales Returns Book

April 3	G. Graham	£150
. .	. .	. .
April 28	D. Driver	380
		£2 850

Purchases Returns Book

April 8	Epworth Ltd	£200
. .	. .	. .
April 25	G.W.D. Ltd	£150
		£1 900

Cash Book (Receipts)

April	1	Sales	£650
. .	. .		. .
April	30	K. White	500
		G. Graham	720
			£43 850

Cash Book (Payments)

April	1 Office salaries	£820
	D. Williams, Drawing	400
. .	. .	. .
April	30 Comcarr Ltd	3 000
		£39 700

General Journal

April	8	Motor vehicles	£12 350	
		Supreme Motors		£12 350
		Purchase of a new vehicle on credit		
April	30	Cost of goods sold	£22 200	
		Stock		£22 200
		Total cost of net sales		
		(i.e., sales − sales returns) for April		

Show the posting into the ledger of all amounts shown above (including totals).

Note: As indicated by the last general journal entry, Williams is able to determine cost of goods sold from his stock records.

3.21 The assets and liabilities of a business at the beginning and end of 19X7 are listed below:

	1 January 19X7	**31 December 19X7**
Cash	£2 000	£5 000
Merchandise stock	17 400	20 500
Debtors	12 500	9 500
Creditors for merchandise	13 000	14 100
Equipment (net after deducting depreciation)	8 000	7 000

All purchases of merchandise and all expenses except depreciation were paid in cash during 19X7. Amounts received from customers during the year totalled £80 000, while payments to suppliers of merchandise amounted to £55 000. No other receipts or payments occurred during 19X7.

Calculate the following for 19X7:

(a) sales revenue;

(b) purchases of merchandise;

(c) cost of goods sold;

(d) other expenses;

(e) net profit.

Chapter 4
End-of-period procedures

Accounts and reports ☐ The accounting period ☐ End-of-period adjustments ☐ Adjusting, closing and reversing entries ☐ Revenue adjustments ☐ Expense adjustments ☐ Report preparation techniques ☐ Profit and loss statement formats ☐ Balance sheet formats ☐ Bills of exchange

Accounts and reports

In Chapter 2, we discussed the basic objectives and described the basic elements of the two most important financial accounting reports - the profit and loss statement and the balance sheet. In Chapter 3, we were concerned with accounting processes - that is, the interpretation of transactions, the capture of data and the subsequent recording and summarising of that data in the 'books of account'.

This chapter provides the link between the two previous chapters. We will demonstrate that the data which have been accumulated over a period of time can be further refined and processed to provide useful and meaningful financial statements. In doing so, we will touch briefly on such problem areas of accounting measurement as depreciation and stock valuation. These problems will be treated in greater depth later in this text.

The accounting period

Period refers to the length of time covered by the profit and loss statement. It may be of any length, for example, a month, six months or a year. There are a number of reasons why it is desirable and necessary to divide the continuing life of a business into accounting periods:

1. As an indication to managers and owners of the efficiency of the enterprise.

2. To determine what profit (if any) is available for distribution to the owners. This is important to the sole trader but more so when ownership is shared.

3. As a guide to future profits. This is important to management in the planning of future actions and to investors in their decisions on buying or selling interests in the firm.

4. To satisfy legal requirements. The Companies Act stipulates that directors shall periodically lay before the company in general meeting a profit and loss account. Income tax legislation requires the submission of periodical returns by all types of business, and even though accounting profit and taxable income are rarely identical, the fact that such returns are required is a factor contributing to the keeping of accounting records and the periodic review of such records.

As we pointed out in Chapter 2, the decision to divide the continuing life of a business into separate accounting periods leads to a variety of problems which the accountant has to face in trying to determine as accurately as possible the revenues and expenses, match these and thus determine the resultant profit of the enterprise for an arbitrary period of time. If accountants chose to measure profit on a cash basis rather than the accrual basis then they would avoid many of the measurement problems which are dealt with in this and later chapters. On the other hand, of course, it must be stressed that profit measured on a cash basis would be far less useful for decision makers than profit measured on an accrual basis. For example, if a long-term construction contract provided for payment only when construction was completed then a cash basis of accounting would report losses in periods prior to the completion of the contract.

The criteria which accountants use to determine the date on which particular items of revenue should be recognised and recorded in the accounts were discussed in Chapter 2. The necessity to identify, for any given period, the expenses which should be matched against the revenue of that period was also stressed. A number of examples were given to illustrate some of the decisions which have to be made so that revenues and expenses are matched accurately for a particular period.

End-of-period adjustments

We return now to questions of revenue and expense recognition in the context of the adjustments to ledger accounts necessary at the end of each accounting period. Underlying the discussion which follows is the assumption that all of the routine accounting work for the period has been completed. In terms of a manual accounting system, this implies that documentary evidence relating to the period has been prepared and filed, resultant data have been recorded and summarised in the books of the business and a trial balance has been extracted from the ledger.

Why then is it necessary for the accountant to make end-of-the period adjustments to the figures contained in the ledger and in the trial balance? The major reason is that many accountable events are, in effect, continuous transactions. For example, an investment is earning interest revenue continuously, but this interest is only received and recorded at intervals of, say, six months. Insurance premiums are normally paid and recorded annually, but the expense of insurance can be viewed as a continuous outflow of resources. Wages may be paid weekly or fortnightly, but it is possible to calculate the expense of wages on a daily basis. Thus, because of the choice of arbitrary accounting periods these revenues and expenses often overrun from one period into another, and an adjustment is needed to determine how much belongs to each period. When we acquire an asset for use over several periods (for example, motor vehicles, furniture, equipment), we record the cost of the asset in the accounts on the date on which it was acquired. Subsequently, we have to apportion part of that cost as an expense (depreciation) in each of the periods in which the asset is used to earn revenue.

Decisions about which items need to be adjusted and by what amount often require perception and judgment on the part of the accountant. Some apportionments as between the relevant accounting periods, such as insurance or interest, are obvious and can be incorporated in the regular accounting procedures. Others, such as depreciation or the amount of customers' accounts likely to be uncollectable, may be more complex, are often subject to estimate and opinion, and require careful consideration by the accountant.

Adjusting, closing and reversing entries

In a manual accounting system, end-of-period adjustments are normally initiated by means of general journal entries. In discussing the general journal entries required for common end-of-period adjustments, we need to bear in mind the subsequent effects of such adjusting entries on:

1. Items in the profit and loss statement.
2. Items in the balance sheet.

3. The revenue or expenses of the next period.

The basic function of most adjustments is to amend the recorded amount (that is, the ledger balance) of some profit and loss statement item and at the same time to amend the recorded amount of some item which will appear in the balance sheet.

For example, let us consider the adjustment often required to deal with accrued wages or salaries due to employees. We will assume that a particular firm has paid and recorded a total amount of £48 340 for sales staff's salaries up to and including the last pay day in the accounting period. We will further assume that an additional £558 is owing for the days between the last pay day and the end of the accounting period.

We require an adjusting entry which will result in the expense item 'sales staff's salaries' in the profit and loss statement reflecting the total expense for the period (that is, £48 340 + £558 = £48 898) and in the liability item 'accrued wages and salaries' in the balance sheet including in its total the £558 owing.

Thus the adjusting general journal entry required is:

		Dr.	Cr.
June 30	Sales staff's salaries (old period)	£558	
	Sales staff's salaries (new period)		£558

and the resultant effect in the ledger is:

Sales Staff's Salaries

June 30	Balance	£48 340			
	Balance (accrual)	558			
			July 1	Balance (accrual)	£558

As explained above, the amended amount for the expense item 'sales staff's salaries' in the profit and loss statement is £48 898, the new balance in the sales staff's salaries account in the ledger. The effect on the balance sheet is that £558, together with any other accrued wages and salaries, will be shown as a liability item.

It is appropriate, at this stage, to discuss the nature of closing entries. After all adjusting entries have been made and these entries posted to the appropriate ledger accounts, the revenue and expense accounts reflect the totals for all revenues and expenses for the period just completed. There are two tasks which need to be accomplished in the ledger:

1. To close off all the balances of revenue and expense accounts and, thus, to remove from them all information relating to the accounting period just completed. Then the accounts are ready to receive the entries relating to revenues and expenses of the new accounting period.

2. To transfer the net result of matching the period's revenues and expenses (that is, the profit or loss) to the relevant proprietorship account or accounts. This is on the basis already discussed that the profit or loss earned by the enterprise has the effect of increasing or decreasing proprietorship.

These ends may be achieved by having in the ledger an account (usually termed the 'profit and loss account') in which the totals of all the revenue and expense accounts are collected. This ledger account contains the same information as is reported in more clarified form, in the profit and loss statement. The revenue items are entered on the credit side of this account and the expense items on the debit side. The consequent balance of the profit and loss account, if a credit, represents the net profit of the period and, if a debit, represents a net loss. This balance is then transferred to the appropriate proprietorship account or accounts.

The general journal entries which initiate these postings to and from the profit and loss account are termed 'closing entries'. The entry required for the salaries example given immediately above is:

		Dr.	Cr.
June 30	Profit and loss	£48 898	
	Sales staff's salaries		£48 898
	Closing entry		

[Note that, in practice, it is usual to combine all the closing journal entries into one journal entry.]

In the next period the first salary payment represents in part an expense of the previous period. The apportionment of the first payment between the accrued salaries account and the expense account may be achieved by means of a general journal entry.

Let us again examine the previous example and incorporate the transfer of the sales staff's salaries to profit and loss account.

The expense account 'sales staff's salaries' following the adjustment of accrued salaries of £558 and the transfer of the total charge for salaries to the profit and loss account is shown below:

Sales Staff's Salaries

June 30	Balance	£48 340	June 30	Profit and loss	£48 898
	Balance (accrual)	558			
		£48 898			£48 898
			July 1	Balance (accrual)	£558

Note: The credit balance of £558 in the above account will be shown as an accrued charge (liability) in the balance sheet as follows:

Balance Sheet (extract)

Current liabilities
Accrued charge (salaries)   £558

Revenue adjustments

We will discuss here three common types of adjustments which relate to revenue items. Other adjustments to revenue will be dealt with in later chapters.

1. Inclusion of revenue earned but not yet received or recorded. This may be termed 'accrued revenue'.

2. Elimination of revenue received but which will not be earned until some future period – 'revenue received in advance' or 'unearned revenue'.

3. Reduction of recorded revenue by the amount estimated to be uncollectable – 'provisions for doubtful debts'.

We will deal briefly with each of these in turn.

Accrued revenue

This problem arises with those revenue items which are recorded only when received: typical examples are interest earned and commission earned. The effect of the adjusting entry must be to increase the recorded revenue by the amount not yet received, and to bring to account the asset represented by the revenue still to be received; that is, the revenue account will be credited and the amount brought down to the new period.

Example: Commission earned and received for the year ended 30 June was £4000. In addition, at 30 June there was £450 commission which had been earned but which had not yet been received or brought to account. The adjusting journal entry required is:

		Dr.	Cr.
June 30	Commission earned (new period)	£450	
	Commission earned (old period)		£450
	Commission earned but not yet received		

Commission earned will appear in the profit and loss statement as £4450 (the total revenue from this source for the period) and the closing journal entry will debit the commission earned account with £4450.

Accrued revenue of £450 will appear as a current asset in the balance sheet. The closing entry is:

		Dr.	Cr.
June 30	Commission earned	£4 450	
	Profit and loss account		£4 450
	Closing entry		

The relevant accounts in the ledger following the posting of the above entries will appear as follows:

Commission Earned

June 30	Profit and loss Account[3]	£4 450	June 30	Balance	£4 000
				Accrued Revenue[1]	£450
		£4 450			£4 450
July 1	Accrued Revenue[2]	£450			

Profit and Loss Account

			June 30	Commission earned[3]	£4 450

[1] Entry in old period.
[2] Entry in new period.
[3] Transfer to profit and loss account.

Note: The debit balance of £450 on the commission earned account will appear as a current asset in the Balance Sheet.

Revenue received in advance

Here the revenue that has been received and recorded relates partly to the next period. To adjust this it will be necessary to reduce the amount as recorded in the revenue account, and to create a temporary liability at balance date for the part which relates to next period.

Example: Rent from a subtenant is received quarterly in advance. In considering the position at 30 June we ascertain that the balance recorded in the rent from subtenant account is £1800, and this includes an amount of £600 received on 1 May for the period 1 May to 31 July. Adjustment is required – of the £600 received for three months, one month's rent (£200) relates to the next accounting period. Therefore the adjusting entry is:

		Dr.	Cr.
		£200	
June 30	Rent from subtenant (old period)		
	Rent from subtenant (new period)		£200
	One month's rent in advance		

Rent from subtenant will appear in the profit and loss statement as £1600 (£1800 − £200) and the closing entry will debit this revenue account with £1600. In the balance sheet there will be a current liability 'rent received in advance' £200. The required closing entry is:

		Dr.	Cr.
		£1 600	
July 1	Rent from subtenant		
	Profit and loss account		£1 600
	Closing entry		

The relevant accounts in the ledger following the posting of the above entries will appear as follows:

Rent from Subtenant

June 30	Received in advance[1]	£200	June 30	Balance	£1 800
	Profit and loss account[3]	£1 600			
		£1 800			£1 800
			July 1	Received in advance[2]	£200

Profit and Loss Account

			June 30	Rent from subtenant[3]	£1 600

[1] Entry in old period.
[2] Entry in new period.
[3] Transfer to profit and loss account.

Note: Balance of £200 in 'rent from subtenant' will appear as a current liability in the balance sheet.

Provisions for doubtful debts

The debits due by customers who have received goods or services represent an asset in the form of a future claim to cash. It is inevitable in most businesses that from time to time some debtors will fail to pay their accounts. Such failure gives rise to a 'bad debt', which decreases the amount of profit the business has earned. The asset 'debtors' is decreased by the same amount.

An accounting problem that arises in connection with bad debts is that debts are often found to be bad in an accounting period subsequent to the period in which the goods or services were supplied and in which the revenue was recognised and recorded. The effect of this is to distort the accounting profit of both the periods concerned, the profit being overstated in the period in which the revenue was recorded and understated in the period in which the bad debt occurred. Thus it is customary, in the period in which the revenue is recognised, to estimate on the basis of past experience the amount of debts which it is expected will not be collected and to make an entry to record that amount. They are termed 'doubtful debts'.

The way in which this estimate is made and recorded will depend upon the accounting system in operation, and particularly upon the frequency with which profit and loss statements are prepared. Alternative methods of measuring and recording doubtful debts are discussed in detail in Chapter 6. The example which follows assumes that the problem of doubtful debts is dealt with only at the end of each annual accounting period.

Example: In the first year of operations, a firm had credit sales totalling £240 000. At the end of that year, the balance in the debtors account was £35 300. Experience with similar types of businesses led management to believe that £2350 of those debts would prove to be uncollectable. The adjusting entry required is:

	Dr.	Cr.
June 30 Bad and doubtful debts	£2 350	
Provision for doubtful debts		£2 350
Accounts estimated to be uncollectable		

The ledger accounts would appear as follows:

Provision for Doubtful Debts

	June 30 Bad and doubtful debts	£2 350

Bad and Doubtful Debts

June 30 Provision for doubtful debts	£2 350

Notes

1. The balance on the bad and doubtful debts accounts will be written off as an expense to the profit and loss account.

2. The provision for doubtful debts account is shown in the balance sheet as a deduction from the gross amount of debtors. In the above example, the balance sheet would show:

Debtors	£35 300	
Less Provision for doubtful debts	£2 350	£32 950

As demonstrated in Chapter 6, the provision for doubtful debts account is adjusted in subsequent periods in the light of the bad debts which have actually occurred.

Expense adjustments

We will discuss here the following common types of adjustments which relate to expense items:

1. Inclusion of expenses incurred but not yet paid or recorded - *accrued expenses*.

2. Allocations between assets and expenses. We saw in Chapter 2 that many costs incurred involve services or benefits that are consumed in more than a single accounting period. That part of the cost which related to benefits of the current period should be treated as an expense of the current period, and that part of the cost which related to benefits in future periods should be treated as an asset and thus carried forward into future periods.

We will discuss three examples of such allocations:

1. Allocations involving *pre-paid expenses*, such as insurance, rent, hire of equipment and supplies such as fuel, stationery, etc.

2. Adjustments to the expense of *cost of goods sold* resultant upon a reassessment of stock.

3. *Depreciation* of long-lived assets such as furniture, equipment, motor vehicles, buildings, etc.

Accrued expenses

Earlier in this chapter we dealt with accrued salaries as a general example of end-of-period adjustments. There are other expenses, such as interest, electricity and gas, which should be dealt with in the same manner. They all represent expenses which have not been paid or recorded at balance date. The appropriate expense has to be brought in to the profit and loss statement of the current period and the corresponding liability shown in the balance sheet as at the end of the period.

Another example: A firm borrowed £60 000 from a finance company on 1 October last year. Interest was charged at the rate of 14 per cent per annum and is payable twice yearly at the end of March and the end of September. Thus, at 30 June, interest expense of £4200 would have already been paid and recorded. In addition, there is a further three months' interest (£2100) accrued.

The adjusting journal entry is:

		Dr.	Cr.
July 1	Interest expense (old period)	£2 100	
	Interest expense (new period)		£2 100
	Three months accrued interest on loan		

Interest expense will appear in the profit and loss statement at £6300 (£4200 + £2100) and the closing entry will credit the expense account with £6300. In the balance sheet there will be a current liability, interest payable, £2100. The closing entry is:

		Dr.	Cr,
June 30	Profit and loss account	£6 300	
	Interest expense		£6 300
	Closing entry		

The relevant accounts in the ledger following the posting of the above entries will appear as follows:

Interest Expense

June 30	Balance	£4 200	June 30	Profit and loss[3]	£6 300
30	Interest payable (accrued)[1]	£2 100			
		£6 300			£6 300
			July 1	Interest payable (accrued)[2]	£2 100

Profit and Loss Account

June 30	Interest expense[3]	£6 300

[1] Entry in old period.
[2] Entry in new period.
[3] Transfer to profit and loss account.

Note: The balance of £2100 on the interest expense account will appear as a current liability in the balance sheet.

Prepaid expenses

Where insurance, rent and similar types of expenses are paid in advance, it is usual to record the payment as an expense when it is made and then adjust the expense for the amount prepaid at the end of the period.

The method is demonstrated with the following example.

Example: On 30 June the balance of the insurance expense account is £2400. This includes premiums relating to the next period totalling £1400.

The adjusting general journal entry required is:

		Dr.	Cr.
June 30	Insurance (new period)	£1 400	
	Insurance (old period)		£1 400
	Insurance paid in advance		

Insurance expense appears in the profit and loss statement as £1000 (£2400 − £1400), and the closing journal entry will credit this account with £1000. The balance sheet will show £1400 as 'prepaid insurance'. Where there are several similar prepaid expense items a single 'prepaid expenses' account is often used.

The closing entry required is:

		Dr.	Cr.
June 30	Profit and loss	£1 000	
	Insurance		£1 000
	Closing entry		

The relevant account in the ledger following the posting of the above entries will appear as follows:

Insurance Expense

June 30	Balance	£2 400	June 30	Prepaid insurance[1]	£1 400
				Profit and loss[3]	£1 000
		£2 400			£2 400
July 1	Prepaid insurance[2]	£1 400			

Profit and Loss Account

June 30	Insurance[3]	£1 000			

[1] Entry in old period.
[2] Entry in new period.
[3] Transfer to profit and loss account.

Note: The balance of £1400 on the insurance expense account will appear as a current asset (prepaid insurance) in the balance sheet.

Cost of goods sold and stock

In Chapter 3, we distinguished between the *perpetual stock* system, where continuous records are maintained of all additions and disposals of stock, and the *periodic stock* systems, where the level of stock can be ascertained only by means of a physical stocktake. It was stressed that the perpetual stock system enabled the expense of cost of goods to be determined at any time, whereas, with the periodic stock system, cost of goods sold was normally only determined at the end of an accounting period and following a physical stocktake.

It follows that an end-of-period adjustment will always be necessary if the periodic system is in use. This adjustment will introduce the effect on the ledger account balances of the amount of stock on hand at the end of the period. What is not so obvious is that an end-of-period adjustment is also often made where the perpetual system is in use. Most firms which use the perpetual method attempt at least once a year to check by means of physical stocktaking the levels of stock shown in the stock records. Where there is a discrepancy between the *theoretical* stock, as shown by the stock records, and the *actual* stock, as revealed by the stocktake, an adjusting entry is necessary.

We will now give an example of end-of-period adjustments for stock for each of the two methods.

Example (where periodic stock is in use): At 1 July 19X5, a firm's merchandise stock account showed a balance of £82 000. During the ensuing year, purchases totalling £457 000 were recorded. A physical stocktake at 30 June 19X6 showed total inventories of £88 200.

When the periodic stock system is used the expense of cost of goods sold is calculated using the formula:

$$\text{Cost of goods sold} = \text{Opening stock} + \text{Purchases} - \text{Closing stock}$$

$$= £82\,000 + £457\,000 - £88\,200 = £450\,800.$$

We need a general journal entry (or entries) which will achieve the following:

1. Record the expense, cost of goods sold, at £450 800.

2. Close off the balance of £457 000 in the purchases account.

3. Adjust the asset, merchandise stock, from its opening balance of £82 000 to an end of the year figure of £88 200.

This may be done by two journal entries:

	Dr.	*Cr.*
June 30 Cost of goods sold	£539 000	
Merchandise stock		£82 000
Purchases		457 000
Closing off existing balances		

then

		Dr.	Cr.
June 30	Merchandise stock	£88 200	
	Cost of goods sold		£88 200
	Stock as per physical stocktake		

or using a composite journal entry

		Dr.	Cr.
June 30	Cost of goods sold	£450 800	
	Merchandise stock	6 200	
	Purchases		£457 000
	Recording of goods sold and adjusting stock to £88 200		

Assuming that the single composite entry was used, the relevant accounts in the ledger following the posting of the adjusting entry would appear thus:

Merchandise Stock

19X5			19X6		
July 1	Balance	£82 000	June 30	Balance	£88 200
19X6					
June 30	Cost of goods sold	6 200			
		£88 200			£88 200
19X6					
July 1	Balance	£88 200			

Purchases

19X6			19X6		
June 30	Balance	£457 000	June 30	Cost of goods sold	£457 000

Cost of Goods Sold

19X6			19X6		
June 30	Purchases	£457 000	June 30	Merchandise stock	£6 200

Notes

1. An entry to close the cost of goods sold account off to the profit and loss account is still required.

2. No reversing entries are required.

Example (where perpetual stock is in use): At 1 July 19X5, a firm's merchandise stock account showed a balance of £82 000. During the ensuing year, purchases totalling £457 000 were recorded, and the perpetual stock records showed cost of goods sold of £449 000. A physical stocktake as at 30 June 19X6 showed stock on hand of £88 200.

The theoretical balance of stock as shown in the merchandise stock account prior to any adjustment is calculated as:

$$\text{Closing inventory} = \text{Opening stock} + \text{Purchases} - \text{Cost of goods sold}$$
$$= £82\ 000 + £457\ 000 - £449\ 000$$
$$= £90\ 000$$

Comparison of the theoretical balance of £90 000 with the actual balance of £88 200 shows a deficiency of £1800. This represents the cost of goods stolen, lost or damaged, or errors in recording.

A general journal entry to record this deficiency will be:

		Dr.	Cr.
19X6			
June 30	Stock shortage	£1 800	
	Merchandise stock		£1 800
	Difference between account balance (£90 000) and physical stocktake (£88 200)		

The relevant accounts in the ledger following the posting of this adjusting entry will appear thus:

Merchandise Stock

19X5			19X6		
July 1	Balance	£82 000	June 30	Cost of goods sold (the total of regular postings of cost of goods sold for the year)	£449 000
19X6			30	Stock shortage	1 800
June 30	Creditors (the total of regular postings of purchases for the year)	457 000	30	Balance	88 200
		£539 000			£539 000
19X6					
July 1	Balance	£88 200			

Cost of Goods Sold

19X6		
June 30	Merchandise stock (total postings for the year)	£449 000

Stock Shortage

19X6		
June 30	Merchandise stock	£1 800

Notes

1. A closing journal entry would include credits to both the cost of goods sold and the stock shortage accounts. The stock shortage account is, like cost of goods sold, an expense account, but preferably shown separately from cost of goods sold.

2. No reversing entries are required.

Depreciation of long-lived assets

We are dealing here with assets which have been acquired for use rather than sale and assets which will clearly be of benefit to the firm over more than one accounting period. Common examples include furniture, plant and equipment, motor vehicles and buildings.

The purpose of the end-of-period adjustment for depreciation is to record as an expense of the period an appropriate portion of the cost of the asset. This amount should reflect the benefits accruing from the firm having the use of the asset during the current period. In Chapter 11, the nature and measurement of depreciation will be discussed in more detail. It is sufficient, at this stage, to note that four factors influence the calculation of the amount to be charged as depreciation expense in a particular period:

1. The original cost of the asset.

2. The expected useful life.

3. The estimated residual, or scrap, value at the end of its useful life.

4. Assumptions as to how the total benefits accruing from the use of the asset are spread over the respective period of its use.

A simple example of the calculation of depreciation follows.

Example: On 1 July 19X3 (that is, at the beginning of an accounting period), a firm purchased equipment at a cost of £10 000. Its estimated useful life was five years and its estimated scrap or residual value was £2000. The firm believed that the equipment would be equally useful in each of the five years.

The estimated effective cost of the asset over the five years is equal to the original cost (£10 000) less the estimated residual value (£2000), that is, £8000. If this cost is spread equally over the five years, the depreciation expense for each of those five years will be £8000 ÷ 5, that is £1600.

In determining the general journal entry needed to record depreciation, it is necessary to consider the significance of the asset account concerned. When a depreciable asset is first acquired, the cost of that asset may be viewed as the cost of the future benefits resulting from the asset's use. These benefits are progressively consumed or used up over the life of the asset, and the asset account needs to be adjusted to reflect the cost of the benefits yet to be consumed.

Thus the debit side of the adjusting entry represents the expense to be charged against revenue for the period and the credit side represents the decrease of the asset's unconsumed benefits. We could make an adjusting entry of the following form:

  Dr.   Depreciation expense
  Cr.   Asset

But as the calculation of depreciation is only an estimate of the expense, it is customary to retain in the ledger the original cost of the asset and we normally credit an account commonly termed 'provision for depreciation'. (An alternative title is 'accumulated depreciation'.)

In the example given above, the adjusting general journal entry at the end of each accounting period would be:

		Dr.	*Cr.*
June 30	Depreciation of equipment	£1 600	
	Provision for depreciation of equipment		£1 600
	Annual depreciation charge		

As an expense account, 'depreciation of equipment' is closed off each year to the profit and loss account. The 'provision for depreciation of equipment' accumulates each year and the balance, at any time, represents the consumed portion of the original cost.

We may illustrate this using the figures from the example above. Assume that the equipment referred to in that example is the only equipment owned by the firm. The relevant accounts in the ledger at 30 June 19X6 (that is, the end of the third year of the life of the equipment), after adjusting and closing entries had been posted, would appear thus:

Depreciation of Equipment

19X6			19X6		
June 30	Provision for dep. of equip.	£1 600	June 30	Profit and loss	£1 600

Equipment

19X3		
July 1	Bank	£10 000

Provision for Depreciation of Equipment

			19X4		
			June 30	Dep. of equipment	£1 600
			19X5		
			June 30	Dep. of equipment	1 600
			19X6		
			June 30	Dep. of equipment	1 600
					£4 800

In the balance sheet as at 30 June 19X6 the asset would be shown:

Equipment (at cost)	£10 000	
Less Provision for dep.	4 800	5 200

The net value of the asset (£5200) is often termed the 'book value'. As explained above, it represents the cost of unconsumed benefits.

Note that no reversing entry is required for depreciation adjustments.

Report preparation techniques

Given the situation where a firm has completed all of its routine recording for the period, extracted a trial balance from the ledger and identified all of the necessary end-of-period adjustments, there are two major ways in which it may proceed to produce a profit and loss statement and a balance sheet:

1. Make and post adjusting and closing general journal entries as described above; extract from the profit and loss account in the ledger the figures required for the profit and loss statement; use the balances remaining in the ledger to prepare the balance sheet.

2. Take the trial balance and use it as the basis of worksheets which will provide the figures required for the profit and loss statement and balance sheet; make and post the adjusting and closing general journal entries at leisure.

The second approach is commonly adopted because it enables the reports to be available more promptly and because it gathers in the one place all the data necessary to prepare the reports. There are many alternative forms of worksheets used. A common form is sometimes referred to as a 'ten-column trial balance'. It consists of five pairs of debit and credit columns:

Columns 1 and 2 — the original trial balance figures

3 and 4 — the adjusting entries in debit and credit form

5 and 6 — an adjusted trial balance

7 and 8 — the items for the profit and loss statement with the net profit (or loss) as the balancing figure

9 and 10 — the balance sheet items with the net profit (or loss) figures carried across from column 7 (or 8)

Variations on this format include an 'eight-column trial balance' which dispenses with the adjusted trial balance columns and which adjusts and extends the original trial balance figures in the one step.

The following example illustrates a range of end-of-period adjustments and the use of the worksheet technique:

Example: A trial balance extracted from the ledger of the Killarney General Store (R. Casey, proprietor) as at 30 June 19X6 is shown below.

Killarney General Store
Trial Balance as at 30 June 19X6

	Dr.	Cr.
Sales revenue		£319 930
Sales returns and allowances	£3 830	
Rent revenue		5 870
Purchases	207 170	
Purchases returns and allowances		2 140
Advertising	2 820	
Sales salaries	37 590	
Delivery expenses	2 350	
Office salaries	14 190	
Administrative expenses	3 770	
Interest on mortgage	5 650	
Cash at bank	5 700	
Debtors	36 640	
Provision for doubtful debts		930
Stock (1/7/X5)	21 230	
Insurance	3 320	
Fittings and equipment	28 300	
Prov. for dep. of fittings & equip.		6 770
Buildings	118 400	
Prov. for dep. of buildings		29 140
Land	62 500	
Creditors		22 930
Mortgage		52 300
R. Casey, Capital		140 050
R. Casey, Drawings	26 600	
	£580 060	£580 060

The following information is also available:

1. Stock on hand, 30 June 19X6 £23 560
2. Accrued interest on mortgage 750

3. The provision for doubtful debts is to be raised to   £1 530
4. Fittings and equipment is to be depreciated at the rate of 10 per cent p.a. on cost
5. Buildings are to be depreciated at the rate of 2.5 per cent p.a. on cost
6. Insurance prepaid now amounts to   630
7. Salaries owing - Sales   1 010
          - Office   440
8. Rent from tenant received in advance   570

The adjustments necessary as a result of this additional information could be entered in the general journal thus:

	Dr.	Cr.
19X6		
June 30 Cost of goods sold	£202 700	
Purchases returns and allowances	2 140	
Stock (£23 560 − £21 230)	2 330	
Purchases		£207 170
Recording cost of goods sold and adjusting stock to £23 560		
June 30 Interest on mortgage (old period)	£750	
Interest on mortgage (new period)		£750
Interest owing		
June 30 Bad and doubtful debts	£600	
Provision for doubtful debts		£600
Increasing provision to £1 530		
June 30 Depreciation of fittings and equipment	£2 830	
Provision for depreciation of fittings and equip.		£2 830
Annual depreciation at 10% on cost		
June 30 Depreciation of buildings	£2 960	
Provision for depreciation of buildings		£2 960
Annual depreciation at 2.5% on cost		
June 30 Insurance (new period)	£630	
Insurance (old period)		£630
Prepaid at end of year		
June 30 Sales salaries (old period)	£1 010	
Office salaries (old period)	440	
Sales salaries (new period)		£1 010
Office salaries (new period)		440
Salaries owing at end of year		
June 30 Rent (old period)	£570	
Rent (new period)		£570
Rent from tenant in advance		

As stated above in the text, there are two ways in which we could proceed to the preparation of the profit and loss statement and the balance sheet:

1. By posting the adjusting entries to ledger accounts, using closing entries to obtain a profit and loss account in the ledger and using the ledger accounts as the basis to prepare the accounting reports. (Students may find it useful to perform these steps for this example.)

2. By using a worksheet technique.

Worksheet

	Original Trial Balance		Adjustments		Adjusted Trial Balance		Profit & Loss Statement		Balance Sheet	
	Debit	Credit	Debit	Credit	Debit	Credit	Debit	Credit	Debit	Credit
Sales revenue		319 930				319 930		319 930		
Sales return & allowance	3 830				3 830		3 830			
Rent revenue		5 870	570			5 300		5 300		
Purchases	207 170			207 170						
Purchases returns and allowances		2 140	2 140							
Advertising	2 820				2 820		2 820			
Sales salaries	37 590		1 010		38 600		38 600			
Delivery expenses	2 350				2 350		2 350			
Office salaries	14 190		440		14 630		14 630			
Administrative expenses	3 770				3 770		3 770			
Interest on mortgage	5 650		750		6 400		6 400			
Cash at bank	5 700				5 700				5 700	
Debtors	36 640				36 640				36 640	
Provision for doubtful debts		930		600		1 530				1 530
Stock	21 230		2 330		23 560				23 560	
Insurance	3 320			630	2 690		2 690			
Fittings and equip.	28 300				28 300				28 300	
Provision for depreciation of fittings and equip.		6 770		2 830		9 600				9 600
Buildings	118 400				118 400				118 400	
Provision for depreciation of buildings		29 140		2 960		32 100				32 100
Land	62 500				62 500				62 500	
Creditors		22 930				22 930				22 930
Mortgage		52 300				52 300				52 300
	553 460	440 010	7 240	214 190	350 190	443 690	75 090	325 230	275 100	118 460

	Original Trial Balance		Adjustments		Adjusted Trial Balance		Profit & Loss Statement		Balance Sheet	
	Debit	Credit	Debit	Credit	Debit	Credit	Debit	Credit	Debit	Credit
b/fwd	553 460	440 010	7 240	214 190	350 190	443 690	75 090	325 230	275 100	118 460
R. Casey - Capital		140 050				140 050				140 050
R. Casey - Drawings	26 600				26 600				26 600	
Cost of goods sold			202 700		202 700		202 700			
Int. on mortgage - accrued				750		750				750
Bad & doubtful debts			600		600		600			
Depreciation of fittings and equipment			2 830		2 830		2 830			
Depreciation of buildings			2 960		2 960		2 960			
Insurance prepaid			630		630				630	
Sales salaries - accrued				1 010		1 010				1 010
Office salaries - accrued				440		440				440
Rent received in advance				570		570				570
Net profit							41 050			41 050
	580 060	580 060	216 960	216 960	586 510	586 510	325 230	325 230	302 330	302 330

The use of a ten-column trial balance for the above example is shown on pages 74 and 75. The figures obtained in the last four columns are those which will be used to prepare the profit and loss statement for the period and the balance sheet as at the end of the period. Before we show those statements for the above example, it is desirable to discuss briefly the factors which affect the form in which such statements are presented.

Profit and loss statement formats

Basically the profit and loss statement consists of the major revenue items, the major expense items and the resultant profit or loss. However, there are a number of considerations which affect the precise format of such a statement:

1. The amount of detail provided – for example, it is possible to show separate accounts for expenses such as postage, stationery, telephone, office cleaning, etc. or alternatively to group all of these together under the title of 'office expenses' or 'administrative expenses'.

2. The extent to which items are classified or grouped in the statement – we may distinguish between single-step profit and loss statements where all revenue items are shown together, all expenses shown together, with a single profit or loss reported and what are often termed segmented profit and loss statements. One example of segmentation, already referred to in Chapter 2, is the matching of sales revenue against cost of goods sold, in a trading business, providing a gross profit figure. Another example of segmentation is to distinguish between 'operating' and 'non-operating' items of revenue and expense. Some accountants class as non-operating items unusual or non-recurring items, such as gains or losses on the sale of assets not acquired for resale. They put these items at the foot of the profit and loss statement and thus show an operating profit (the result of normal operations for the period) prior to showing the final net profit for the period. Other examples of segmentation include the reporting of separate profits for different branches or activities of a firm and the classification of expenses according to management responsibility. Examples of these will be given in Chapter 14.

3. Whether certain gains and losses are included in the profit and loss statement at all – where a gain or loss occurs in a particular period as a result of a change in law, a change in the accounting methods employed or a significant change in the structure of the firm, it is sometimes argued that the effect of such changes should bypass the profit and loss statement and be shown as an adjustment to retained earnings (that is, unappropriated profits). This question is particularly relevant to published financial statements and will be discussed further in Chapter 18.

In considering the various alternatives outlined above, it is important to distinguish between profit and loss statements prepared for internal (or management) use and those prepared for external publication. Obviously management is interested in information such as gross profit, separate profits for various branches or products and the total expenses of the sales department. Such information is of limited usefulness to investors or creditors.

In whatever way the expenses and revenue are treated it is essential that consistent methods be used from period to period. If this is not done, the comparison of the figures of one period with another will be made more difficult, and misleading inferences may be drawn if inconsistent comparisons are made.

The profit and loss statement for the Killarney General Store example is given below. Assuming that R. Casey is both owner and manager, full detail, as available from the ledger, is given. Consideration might be given to the further classification of 'other expenses' into *selling expenses* (advertising, sales salaries, delivery expenses and depreciation of fittings and equipment) *administrative expenses* (office salaries, administrative expenses, insurance expense and depreciation of buildings) and *finance expenses* (interest on mortgage and doubtful debts).

Killarney General Store
Profit and Loss Statement for year ended 30 June 19X6

Sales revenue			£319 930	
Less Sales returns and allowances			3 830	£316 100
Less Cost of goods sold				
Stock (1/7/X5)		£21 230		
Purchases	£207 170			
Less Purch. returns and allowances	2 140	205 030	226 260	
Less Stock (30/6/X6)			23 560	202 700
Gross profit				£113 400
Add other revenue				
Rent revenue				5 300
				£118 700
Less other expenses				
Advertising			2 820	
Sales salaries			38 600	
Delivery expenses			2 350	
Depreciation of fittings and equipment			2 830	
Office salaries			14 630	
Administrative expenses			3 770	
Insurance			2 690	
Depreciation of buildings			2 960	
Interest on mortgage			6 400	
Doubtful debts			600	77 650
Net profit				£41 050

Balance sheet formats

Again the question arises with the presentation of balance sheets as to the amount of detail which is necessary or desirable. As with profit and loss statements, it is primarily a question of the needs of particular groups of users.

Perhaps a more important issue with balance sheets is the question of classification of both assets and liabilities. We will discuss each of these in turn.

The reason why we classify assets is to give us a clearer picture of the structure of our assets, for some assets are expected to be converted into cash in the near future while others are held for lengthy periods of time – possibly until they are worn out and have little or no cash value. It would be difficult to manage an organisation successfully if we could not readily distinguish between the various classes of assets recorded in its balance sheet, or between their liquidity attributes.

The *basis of classification* is related to the practice of dividing the life of a business into short periods of time. We have already seen that this division gives rise to the need to match the expenses with the revenue of each period, arrive at a profit or loss for the period, and state a balance sheet position at the end of the period.

Thus, in preparing the balance sheet, we normally classify our assets on the basis of liquidity related to time. We distinguish between those assets which we expect will be converted into cash (for example, debtors), or will not require cash in the following accounting period, having been paid for in the current period (for example prepaid expenses); and those which will be retained for more than one accounting period. The former are described as *current* assets and the latter as fixed assets.

Current assets

First let us consider why assets are acquired by an enterprise. Retailers or wholesalers buy stock with the intention of reselling them at a profit. Usually further stocks are purchased with the proceeds thus obtained. To obtain sales they may have to allow credit to customers, and this interposes a further asset – debtors – between the stock and their realisation into cash. Bills receivable accepted by debtors may further delay the final receipt of cash. Thus, in the ordinary cycle of trading, certain assets are interchanged to enable the enterprise to earn its chief revenue.

Assets of this type are thus constantly changing form. They are acquired in the ordinary course of buying and selling for the purpose of making profit, and if not already in the form of cash, they will be converted to cash or cash value within the next accounting period. Such assets are called *current* assets. A diagram of a trading cycle is shown in Fig. 4.1.

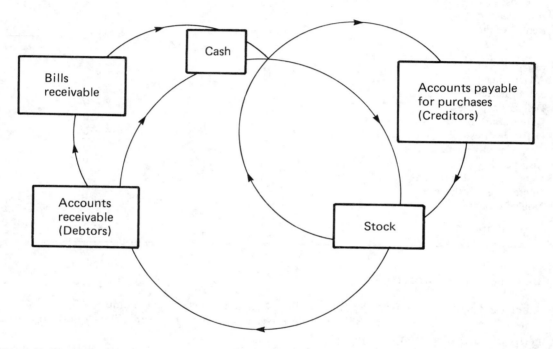

Fig. 4.1   The trading cycle.

Fixed assets

Other assets, such as premises, delivery vehicles, plant and machinery, etc., are purchased with the object of facilitating the trading cycle shown in Fig. 4.1. The intention of the enterprise is to *use* such assets in the production of revenue and not to convert them into other assets to make a profit. Shop premises are obtained to enable stock to be sold; vehicles to deliver goods sold; fixtures and fittings to help display the goods, and so on. Such assets will be retained by the enterprise for a considerably longer period than will current assets. For this reason they are referred to as fixed assets.

It should be noticed that what may be deemed current assets for one enterprise may be fixed assets for another. To distinguish between them it is necessary to examine the reason for the purchase of such assets and the intention behind the holding of the asset. For a furniture retailer, chairs and tables would be current assets, whereas for a solicitor, accountant, or college, they would be fixed assets. Although motor vehicles are usually classed as fixed assets in most enterprises, such vehicles for a car dealer would be current assets. For a motor garage examples of the two groups would be:

Current	Fixed
Cash	Cash register
Spare parts	Petrol pumps
Tyres and batteries	Tow vehicle
Debtors	Land and buildings (if owned)

It should be noted here that investments, such as shares in other companies, government securities, debentures and loans of various kinds, may be either current or fixed assets within the one enterprise, depending on the purpose for which the investments were acquired. If held with a view to resale within a short period, they would be current assets, that is, temporary investments are current assets, while long-term investments are fixed assets. Certain classifications of assets are required by the Companies Acts in the case of limited liability companies.

Tangible and intangible assets

To provide further information as to the nature of the assets, fixed assets may be considered as either *tangible* assets, that is, those having bodily substance such as plant, office equipment, fixtures and fittings, etc., or *intangible* assets, which consist of:

1. rights of various sorts (copyrights, patents, trade marks, goodwill);

2. expenditure, the benefit (and therefore the cost) of which is to be spread over several accounting periods (legal expenses of forming a company or of purchasing an existing enterprise, etc.).

It should be noted that some current assets could be regarded as intangible (for example, debts owing by customers), but the division is usually applied in connection with fixed assets only.

Note: Goodwill at this stage may be regarded as the likelihood that customers will continue dealing with an established business. If the enterprise commences in, say, an empty shop, it takes some time to build up the business. On the other hand if an established shop is taken over, most customers will continue to deal with the new owners. The fact that the business is already known to the public is an asset that would have to be purchased by the new owner in just the same way as other assets, for example stock, fittings, etc. More advanced texts deal with methods of accounting for and valuing goodwill. It should be noted that because of its nature, it is extremely difficult to value and is not normally recorded in the books of account unless it is purchased. If an enterprise is still owned by its original founders then it is not usual to find any goodwill recorded. Conservatism dictates that gains are only brought to account when they are realised. Thus, the building up of goodwill is not usually considered in the profit-determining process.

Liabilities

As with assets, it is convenient and usual to classify liabilities on the basis of time as follows:

Current liabilities – those which have to be met within the short-term period. Often this is interpreted as an accounting period of twelve months. Examples of current liabilities are trade creditors, bank overdraft, short-term loans, bills payable (short term).

Long-term liabilities – those which do not have to be met within the short-term period. Examples of this group are long-term loans, mortgages and debentures.

In more advanced works, there is a further important and practical classification of liabilities. This is the distinction between a liability which is secured and one which is unsecured. Briefly, in a secured liability the creditor has some legal priority over unsecured creditors if the enterprise is unable to pay all its liabilities in full. This legal priority may be effected by a document such as a mortgage, a debenture deed, etc. In other instances, a preference or priority of one class of creditor over another is established by law. For example, the Bankruptcy Act establishes a priority for certain creditors under specified conditions. However, at this stage we are more concerned with the classification of liabilities on the basis of time. Later it will be seen that in the balance sheet of a limited company it is necessary to indicate liabilities which are secured by a charge over some or all of the assets.

Having classified assets and liabilities into groups, there is still the question of the overall form of presentation of the balance sheet. As discussed earlier in Chapter 2, there are two basic forms of expressing the accounting equation (and thus the balance sheet):

1. Assets = Liabilities + Proprietorship

2. Proprietorship = Assets − Liabilities

The second form ($P = A - L$) is sometimes modified by subtracting current liabilities directly from current assets to give a sub-total often referred to as 'working capital'. The significance of working capital is based on the assumption that current assets will be converted into cash soon enough to be able to pay the current liabilities as they fall due. Thus, working capital is regarded as a margin of safety in assessing liquidity in the short run. The working capital approach to balance sheet presentation results in the following form:

Proprietorship = Fixed assets + Current assets − Current liabilities − Long-term liabilities

We also discussed in Chapter 2 the alternatives of the account form (two sided) and the narrative form of balance sheet presentation, and we noted some claimed advantages of the narrative form.

The balance sheet for the Killarney General Store is given below. We have used the narrative form of presentation.

Killarney General Store
Balance Sheet as at 30 June 19X6

Proprietorship
R. Casey - Capital		£140 050	
Add Net profit		41 050	
		181 100	
Less Drawings		26 600	£154 500

represented by

Fixed assets
Land		62 500	
Buildings	£118 400		
Less Provision for depreciation	32 100	86 300	
Fittings and equipment	£28 300		
Less Provision for depreciation	9 600	18 700	167 500

Balance Sheet *Cont.*   b/fwd   £167 500

Current assets

Stock		£23 560	
Debtors	£36 640		
Less Provision for doubtful debts	1 530	35 110	
Prepaid insurance		630	
Cash at bank		5 700	£65 000

Less Current liabilities

Creditors	22 930		
Accrued sales salaries	1 010		
Accrued office salaries	440		
Accrued interest	750		
Rent received in advance	570	25 700	39 300
			£206 800

Long-term Liability

Mortgage		52 300
		£154 500

Bills of exchange

A bill of exchange, as defined by the Bills of Exchange Act 1882, is 'an unconditional order in writing, addressed by one person to another, signed by the person giving it, requiring the person to whom it is addressed to pay on demand or at a fixed or determinable future time a sum certain in money to or to the order of a specified person or to bearer.'

Figure 4.2 is an example of a bill of exchange.

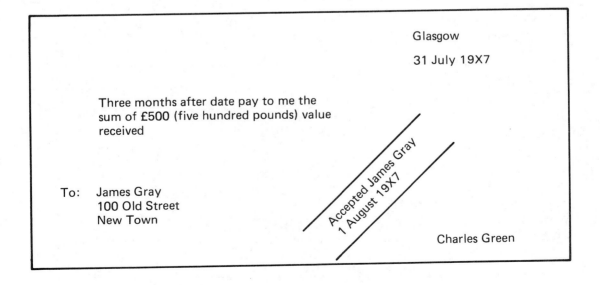

Fig. 4.2 A bill of exchange.

The following definitions relate to the principals involved in the above bill.

Drawer – Charles Green, the person who has drawn the above bill, is known as the drawer and is the person to whom it is a bill receivable.

Drawee – James Gray is the person on whom the bill is drawn and is referred to as the drawer.

Acceptor – James Gray becomes the acceptor when he signs the bill acknowledging his acceptance of it. The acceptance is made on the face of the bill although the word 'accepted' is not always included. To Gray this is a bill payable.

Discounting a bill

A bill of exchange may be discounted at a bank thus enabling a trader to obtain funds which he may immediately require for meeting financial commitments before the bill reaches maturity. In most cases, the banker will discount the bill less a sum of discount, the amount of which depends on the time the bill is payable and the discount rate ruling at that time. By discounting the bill with his banker the drawer is not relieved of his financial responsibility to the banker, in the case of the bill being dishonoured, when presented for payment. In these circumstances, he has to repay the amount of the bill to the bank plus any charges incurred by the bank.

Accounting entries to record bills of exchange

The accounting entries to record bills of exchange in the books of the acceptor and drawer, journal and ledger form, are shown below.

Journal entries for bank transactions are also included.

Entries in the books of the acceptor (James Gray) to whom it is a bill payable:

1. *On acceptance of the bill*   James Gray accepts the bill drawn on him by Charles Green at three months for £500 being the amount due to Charles Green.

Journal

Charles Green	*Dr.* £500	
To bills payable		£500
Being acceptance of bill at three months drawn by Charles Green.		

Ledger

Charles Green Account

Bills payable	£500	Balance	£500

Bills Payable Account

	Charles Green	£500

When the bill is accepted by James Gray he is required to transfer the amount of the bill from Charles Green's account to a bills payable account, thus reducing creditors and increasing bills payable.

2. *On honouring the bill*   James Gray honours the bill at maturity.

Journal

Bills payable	*Dr.* £500	
To bank		£500
Being settlement of bill drawn by Charles Green.		

3. *Discounting the bill*   If the bill is discounted by Charles Green no entries are required in the books of James Gray.

Entries in the books of the drawer (Charles Green) to whom it is a bill receivable.

1. *On acceptance of the bill*   Charles Green receives James Gray's acceptance of the bill at three months for £500 being the debt due by James Gray.

Journal

Bills receivable	*Dr.* £500	
To James Gray		£500
Being acceptance of Bill by James Gray at three weeks.		

Ledger

Bill Receivable Account

James Gray	£500	

James Gray Account

Balance	£500	Bills receivable	£500

On receipt of James Gray's acceptance of the bill, Charles Green is required to transfer the amount of the bill from James Gray's account to a bills receivable account, thus reducing debtors and increasing bills receivable.

2. *If the bill is discounted*   The bill accepted by James Gray is discounted at the bank. Bill discount charges amount to £30.

Journal

Bank	*Dr.* £470	
Bill discount	30	
To bills receivable		£500
Being bill accepted by James Gray discounted at bank.		
Discount charges amount to £30.		

Ledger

Bills Receivable Account

Balance	£500	Bank	£470
		Bill discount	30
	£500		£500

Ledger *Cont.*

Bill Discount Account

Bills receivable	£30

When a bill is discounted, the proceeds and any bill discount charges are credited to the bills receivable account. The latter account, assuming there is only one bill in existence, will be closed since the bill of exchange will be held by the bank and not by Charles Green.

3. *On honouring the bill at maturity* James Gray honours the bill at maturity.

Journal

Bank	*Dr.* £500	
To bills receivable		£500
Being settlement of bill by James Gray.		

Ledger

Bills Receivable Account

Balance	£500	Bank	£500

Bank Account

Bills receivable	£500

When the bill is met at maturity the bills receivable account is credited with the proceeds of the bill.

Summary

1. The fact that the actual basis of selection of accounting periods is an arbitrary one leads to the need to adjust recorded revenue and expenses at the end of the period (end-of-period adjustments), and to inevitable inaccuracies or deficiencies in profit measurement.

2. Common end-of-period adjustments to revenue are for accrued revenue, revenue received in advance and provisions for doubtful debts.

3. Common end-of-period adjustments to expenses are for accrued expenses, prepaid expenses, closing stock and for depreciation.

4. There are two major alternative approaches to the preparation of end-of-period reports:

(a) posting adjusting and closing entries to the ledger.

(b) using the trial balance as a basis for worksheets outside the ledger.

5. There are a variety of formats used for the profit and loss statement. Some accountants favour a single-step matching of revenue and expenses; others favour a segmented form.

6. In balance sheets it is usual to distinguish between current and fixed assets and between current and long-term liabilities.

7. A bill of exchange is an unconditional order in writing addressed by one person to another signed by the person giving it, requiring the person to whom it is addressed to pay on demand at a fixed or determinable future time a sum certain in money to or to the order of a specified person or to bearer.

Discussion questions

4.1 'Period refers to the length of time covered by the profit and loss statement. It may be a month, six months or a year.' Discuss the factors which may influence the length of period adopted by a particular enterprise.

4.2 If the routine accounting work has been done correctly during the year, why is it still necessary to make adjusting entries at the end of the year?

4.3 Explain clearly the nature and purpose of:

(a) adjusting entries;

(b) closing entries.

4.4 Explain the function of a profit and loss account in the ledger. Discuss the similarities and differences between this ledger account and the profit and loss statement.

4.5 On what grounds can you criticise the practice of recognising bad debts only when it is discovered that the debt is uncollectable?

4.6 Explain clearly the circumstances which may lead to a debit entry being made in a 'stock shortage' account.

4.7 Discuss the nature and function of the ledger account commonly termed 'provision for depreciation'.

4.8 Explain clearly how it is possible to prepare a profit and loss statement and balance sheet *before* making closing entries in the ledger. Give the reasons why this approach is frequently adopted.

4.9 Why would you expect to find the format of a profit and loss statement prepared specifically for management use different from a profit and loss statement prepared for external publication. Give examples of some of these expected differences.

4.10 (a) Discuss the basis on which assets may be classified as 'current' or 'fixed'.

(b) State, giving reasons, how you would classify each of the following:

   (i) stock

   (ii) land held for future building expansion

   (iii) a provision for depreciation

   (iv) shares in other companies held for the purpose of earning dividends

   (v) short-term investment held for the purpose of financing expected seasonal increases in stock

4.11 Explain the significance of the term 'intangible assets'. Give examples.

Exercises

4.12 X Co. commenced business on 1 February 19X6, using rented premises. The agreement with the landlord provided that rent was to be payable quarterly in advance. The initial rate was £165 per quarter but, as from 1 February 19X7, the rent was increased to £180 per quarter.

Assuming that all rent was paid when due and that the X Co. balanced its accounts on 30 June each year show:

(a) the journal entries required to adjust the expense at 30 June 19X6 and 30 June 19X7;

(b) the rent account showing all entries from 1 February 19X6 to 1 July 19X7.

4.13 (a) (i) What do you understand by 'the matching of revenue and expenses'?

(ii) Explain the importance of balance-day adjustments.

(b) Record, in journal form, for an enterprise which balances annually on 30 June, the adjustments necessitated by the following:

(i) The firm holds 12 per cent debentures of £1200 face value. Interest is payable on these debentures on 15 March and 15 September.

(ii) Rent is paid quarterly in advance. £2100 rent was paid on 1 June.

(iii) Amounts owing as at 30 June are:

Drivers' wages	£4 500
Office salaries	2 000
Delivery expenses	1 800

(iv) Estimated doubtful debts are £3500. The balance in the provision for doubtful debts account is £2800, and £2350 of bad debts written off during the period have not yet been offset against the provision.

(v) Commission earned by selling goods as agent for another firm but not yet received amounts to £800.

4.14 The MSU Co. prepares its financial statements as at 30 June each year. At 30 June 19X6, the following information became available after a trial balance had been prepared:

(a) A physical stocktaking revealed stock on hand at 30 June 19X6 as £98 500. The balance for merchandise stock in the closing trial balance was £103 200. (The company used the perpetual stock method.)

(b) An account from XL Ltd for £128 for repairs to office equipment carried out in June was received on 2 July 19X6.

(c) The firm has £20 000 invested with a building society. Interest is at the rate of 12 per cent p.a. payable half yearly. No interest has been received since 30 April 19X6.

(d) It was discovered that an uninsured item of salesroom fittings had been stolen late in June. The item had been purchased on 1 January 19X4 for £800 and was being depreciated at 20 per cent p.a.

(e) The balance of the prepaid insurance account was £1800. This represented annual premiums all paid on 1 April 19X6.

(f) A purchase of equipment for £2000 had been wrongly entered in the stock account.

Show, either by giving journal entries or by any other method, how these adjustments would affect various items in the financial statements.

4.15 Using all of the following items, prepare a skeleton profit and loss statement and balance sheet using the narrative form of presentation. (Put an X where the amount for each item would appear.)

Creditors	General office expenses
Debtors	Land
Accrued expenses	Loan on mortgage
Accrued revenue	Loss by misappropriation
Administrative salaries	Opening stock
Bank overdraft	Petty cash advance
Buildings	Postage and stationery
Closing stock	Prepaid expenses
Customs duty	Provision for depreciation of buildings
Depreciation of buildings	Provision for depreciation of furniture and
Depreciation of furniture and equipment	equipment
Discount on purchases	Provision for doubtful debts
Discount on sales	Purchases
Donations	Rates
Doubtful debts	Sales
Freight inwards	Sales promotion expenses
Freight outwards	A. Skelton – Capital
Furniture and equipment	A. Skelton – Drawings
Gain on sale of furniture	Travellers' commission.

4.16 The following are the items relevant to the profit and loss statement of the Wendy Trading Co. for the year ended 30 June 19X6 (after all adjustments have been made). Use these figures to prepare a well-presented profit and loss statement for the period.

Advertising	£11 000
Bad and doubtful debts	5 200
Buying expenses	7 500
Delivery expenses	23 200
Depreciation of office equipment	2 100
Depreciation of shop fittings	4 600
Discount on sales	10 300
Discount on purchases	4 100
General office expenses	33 500
Interest on overdraft	1 300
Stock (1/7/X5)	106 000
Stock (30/6/X6)	124 200
Lighting and power	4 300
Loss on sale of office equipment	2 400
Office salaries	23 500
Purchases	617 100
Purchases returns	8 900
Rent received	3 800
Sales	875 400
Sales staff's commission	11 400
Sales staff's salaries	49 900
Sales returns	12 400

4.17 The trial balance of the AOZ Co. at 31 March (the end of its financial year) included the following balances:

	Dr.	Cr.
Advertising	£490	
Sales staff's salaries	3 148	
Office salaries	2 900	
Rates	140	
Bad debts	380	
Interest on mortgage	280	
Rent received		£620
Revenue from repairs		1 450
Delivery vehicles	2 700	
Provision for depreciation of delivery vehicles		840
Office furniture	600	
Provision for depreciation of office furniture		280
Provision for doubtful debts		400

The following adjustments are necessary to the recorded revenue and expenses:

(a) prepaid rates £32

(b) rent received in advance £95

(c) amounts owing

Advertising	£32
Sales staff's salaries	15
Office salaries	12
Interest on mortgage	21

(d) owing by customers for repairs £280 (the practice was to record revenue from repairs only when received)

(e) depreciation on delivery vehicles at 20 per cent and on office furniture at 10 per cent (both on cost)

(f) estimated doubtful debts £450. Show journal entries for the above.

4.18 The following trial balance has been extracted from the books of J. Ray:

	Dr.	Cr.
J. Ray – Capital (1/7/X6)		£26 000
Commission received		1 250
Petty cash advance	£250	
Cash at bank	3 400	
J. Ray – Drawings	5 800	
Rent	3 300	
General office expenses	1 750	
Travellers' expenses	3 600	
Carriage on sales	850	
Creditors		19 800
Purchases	106 850	
Purchases returns		2 350
Stock (1/7/X6)	12 400	
	£138 200	£49 400
		Cont.

	Dr.	Cr.
b/fwd	£138 200	£49 400
Provision for doubtful debts		1 300
Sales		137 300
Sales returns	1 550	
Insurance	600	
Bad debts	850	
Discount allowed	2 900	
Loss on sale of motor vehicle	1 000	
Debtors	20 000	
Motor vehicles (cost)	16 000	
Provision for dep. of motor vehicles		6 400
Furniture and fixtures (cost)	4 400	
Provision for dep. of furniture and fixtures		600
Travellers' salaries	6 300	
Office salaries	3 200	
	£195 000	£195 000

Additional information:

(a) Stock (30/6/X7) £14 500.

(b) Depreciation to be charged:
Motor vehicles – 20 per cent p.a. on cost.
Furniture and fixtures – 5 per cent p.a. on cost.

(c) Provision for doubtful debts to be increased to £1500.

(d) Rent for June 19X7 (£300) unpaid.

(e) Insurance paid in advance, £150.

Prepare a profit and loss statement for the year ended 30 June 19X7, and a balance sheet at that date. Use a columnar worksheet to determine the figures for the financial statements.

4.19 (a) The following balances were extracted from the ledger of A. Trader on 30 April 19X7. You are required to consider whether each is a debit or a credit balance and to prepare a trial balance as at 30 April 19X7. Note the capital account has been omitted.

Account	Balance
Cash at bank	£1 613
Purchases	15 763
Sales	27 095
Purchases returns	197
Sales returns	153
Debtors	2 029
Creditors	1 345
Office salaries	5 162
Stock (1 May 19X6)	3 456
Insurance	75
Drawings	1 920
Power and lighting	196
Buildings	25 000

Cont.

Account	**Balance**
Rates	£90
Stationery	60
Freight on purchases	306
Carriage on sales	50
Advertising	354
Commission received	164
Loan from A. Lender	1 000
Delivery vans	2 460
Petrol and oil	560
Land	8 000

(b) Using the information in part (a) of this question as well as the other particulars listed hereunder, prepare a properly classified profit and loss statement for the year ended 30 April 19X7 and a balance sheet as at that date.

Other particulars:
   Stock 30 April 19X7 was valued at £3867 and stationery at £10.
   Rates amounting to £15 have been paid in advance.
   Delivery vans are to be depreciated at the rate of 15 per cent p.a., and buildings at 4 per cent p.a.
   Interest at 6 per cent is due on the loan from A. Lender for the whole year.

Note: Even if you are unable to complete a trial balance satisfactorily, you should make some attempt at part (b).

4.20 Because of staff shortages, the accounts of Lord and Co. for the calendar year 19X8 were prepared by a junior bookkeeper. They disclosed a profit of £38 000 and a trial balance which did not balance. You have been asked to check the accounts and in the course of your investigations you discover the following:

(a) Discounts allowed for £600 had been credited to the sales account and debited to debtors.

(b) The firm owns a motor van which had, at 1 January 19X8, a net book value of £1080 and which had originally cost £1800. The firm's policy is to depreciate vans at 20 per cent on cost but the bookkeeper had made no entry.

(c) The balance of the telephone expense account had been extracted as £69 instead of £96.

(d) A cheque for £200 received from a credit customer had been treated as a receipt from cash sales.

(e) An item of plant which had cost £10 000 and on which the accumulated depreciation at 1 January was £6000 had been sold during the year for £3200. The bookkeeper did not know how to deal with this item. He entered it correctly in the cash book but made no other entry.

(f) One of the firm's debts amounting to £30 was obviously bad at the year end but no entry had been made in recognition of this fact. (The firm does not maintain a provision against doubtful debts account.)

(g) An error had been made in the calculation of the insurance prepaid at 31 December 19X8. The amount had been calculated at £120 instead of £104. The 'incorrect amount' had been correctly treated in the books of the firm.

(h) A payment of £80 for repairs had been posted to the debit of the buildings account.

You are required to:

(i) Prepare a schedule showing the corrected profit figure, and

(ii) indicate by number which of the above errors would have caused a difference in the trial balance.

4.21 The following information summarises the transactions of the AB Business College for the year ended 31 March 19X6:

AB Business College
Trial Balance at 31 March 19X6

Bank	£2 000	
Equipment	31 000	
Accumulated depreciation of equipment		£14 000
Repairs and maintenance of equipment	2 800	
Stock of supplies (1/4/X5)	4 400	
Purchase of supplies	22 000	
Fees revenue from students		120 000
Salaries: instructors	48 000	
office	12 600	
Advertising expense	3 500	
Rent expense	5 200	
Office expenses	1 800	
Capital: AB		10 000
Drawings: AB	10 700	
	£144 000	£144 000

Additional notes
Supplies on hand at 31 March 19X6 – £5000
Depreciate equipment at 20 per cent p.a. on cost
Fees revenue includes £6400 received in advance
Salaries owing: instructors – £420; office – £105
Rent paid in advance – £400
During the year AB paid £270 rates on his private home. This was paid by cheque drawn on the business bank account and had been charged to office expenses.

From the above information you are required to prepare:

(a) a profit and loss statement for the year ended 31 March 19X6

(b) a balance sheet of the AB Business College at 31 March 19X6

Problems

4.22 An inexperienced bookkeeper has presented you with the following:

Accounts of the Lanlara Trading Co. as at 30 June 19X7

Stock (1/7/X6)	£6 400	Sales	£45 800
Purchases	36 084	Returns outwards	315
Returns inwards	435	Stock (30/6/X7)	7 680
Gross profit	10 876		
	£53 795		£53 795

Accounts of the Lanlara Trading Co. as at 30 June 19X7 *Cont.*

Store wages	1 860	Gross profit	£10 876
Shop wages	2 850	Commission received	340
Office salaries	2 240	Discount received	124
Depreciation	3 568	Accrued commission	18
Insurance	96	Prepaid insurance	20
Advertising	380	Provision for doubtful debts	
Discount allowed	210	(decrease)	50
General office expenses	468	Rent received	175
Bad debts	244	Bad debts recovered	1 028
Interest on overdraft	68	Gain on sale of land	4 000
Loss on sale of shop fittings	24		
Accrued wages and salaries	480		
Delivery expenses	560		
Rent received in advance	25		
Interest accrued	8		
Net profit	3 550		
	£16 631		£16 631

You ascertain the following information:

(a) The store is used for receiving the goods purchased and for packaging goods ready for sale.

(b) All the account balances were correct in amount.

(c) The accrued wages and salaries were made up as follows:

Store	£80
Shop	180
Office	220
	£480

(d) The bad debts recovered were written off in a previous period.

(e) Depreciation: shop fittings £568
buildings £3000

Buildings were depreciated for the first time this year (£300). The remaining £2700 represents an allowance for prior periods.

You are asked to prepare a properly presented and classified profit and loss statement. The owners of the business have requested that operating expenses be classified into four categories – cost of goods sold, selling expenses, administrative expenses and finance expenses.

4.23 The following is the balance sheet of the Harpoon Trading Company:

Harpoon Trading Company
Balance Sheet as at 30 June

Current liabilities			Current assets			
Bank overdraft	£800		Petty cash		£30	
Creditors	1 200		Debtors	£2 100		
Accrued expenses	130		*Less* Prov. doubtful debts	200	1 900	
	£2 130					

Cont.

Harpoon Trading Company
Balance Sheet as at 30 June *Cont.*

Proprietorship					
A. Harpoon – Capital	£10 700	Stock		£3 000	
		Prepaid expenses		100	£5 030
B. Harpoon – Capital	10 000				
	£20 700				
		Fixed Assets			
		Land and buildings		12 000	
		Plant and equip.	4 200		
		Less Prov. dep.	800	3 400	
		Motor vehicles	2 400		
		Less Prov. dep.	1 000	1 400	16 800
		Intangible Asset			
		Goodwill			1 000
	£22 830				£22 830

At the end of July the following information was obtained:

Sales day book	—	Total credit sales			£4 900
Perpetual stock records	—	Cost of goods sold			3 100
Purchases day book	—	Total credit purchases			3 400
Purchases returns book	—	Total credit returns			400
Cash book - payments	—	Discount	£25		
		Payments to creditors		£975	
		Motor vehicle expenses		35	
		Advertising		50	
		Office expenses		20	
		Sundries		700	
		Total cash paid			£1 780

The sundries column of the cash book - payments was made up of:

Repairs to plant			£18
Wages			660
Petty cash reimbursed:			
Tea money		£5	
Travelling expenses		2	
Stamps		15	
		22	
		£700	

A dissection of the wages sheets revealed:

	Sales staff's wages	£500
	Office wages	160
		£600

and the cash book – receipts showed:

	Discount	£45	
	Amount received from debtors		£1 500
	Sales		1 300
			£2 800

In the general journal, the only entries were as follows:

		Dr.	Cr.
July 1	Accrued expenses	£130	
	Office wages		£30
	Sales staff's wages		100
	Reversing entry		
	Insurance	£100	
	Prepaid expenses		£100
	Reversing entry		

You are required to:

(a) open up the general ledger accounts as reflected by the above balance sheet;

(b) enter into the general ledger the information recorded in the day books, journal and stock records;

(c) extract a trial balance as at 31 July;

(d) after allowing for the following unrecorded items (no entries are required in the books) as at 31 July:

(i)	Sales staff's wages accrued	£80
(ii)	Office wages accrued	24
(iii)	Insurance prepaid	50
(iv)	Depreciation plant and equipment	80
(v)	Depreciation motor vehicles	40

prepare a properly classified profit and loss statement for the month ended 31 July, and a balance sheet at that date. Profits and losses are shared equally between the two partners.

4.24 The following trial balance was extracted from the books of J. Sparkes at 31 May 19X7:

	Dr.	Cr.
Sales		£74 924
Commission received		1 100
S. Dobbs	£390	
	£390	£76 024

Cont.

	Dr.	Cr.
B/fwd	£390	£76 024
F. Granger	1 900	
G. Hughes	800	
Carriage inwards	650	
Bank		2 390
Telephone	740	
Plant and machinery	13 800	
Purchases	50 504	
Stock (at 1 July 19X6)	16 248	
Salaries and wages	21 300	
Premises	74 500	
Motor vehicles	21 450	
Mortgage on premises		18 000
Light and power (showrooms)	552	
Advertising	1 600	
S. Alberts		540
G. Croft		810
W. Phillips		1 100
Carriage outwards	600	
Insurance	1 200	
Interest paid on mortgage	1 500	
Customs duty	240	
Office furniture	3 100	
Drawings	4 000	
Capital		116 210
	£215 074	£215 074

During June 19X7, the final month of the firm's accounting period, the following transactions occurred:

19X7		
June 2	Bought goods from W. Phillips	£210
3	Paid salaries and wages	950
5	Cash sales	430
5	Owner withdrew cash for personal use	500
7	Paid advertising	150
9	Received cash from G. Hughes	430
9	Sold goods to F. Granger	184
11	Bought goods for cash	595
12	Received commission in cash	230
12	Paid G. Croft	610
14	Bought goods from S. Alberts	400
15	Received cash from S. Dobbs	90
15	Bought furniture on credit from W. Phillips	700
17	Paid salaries and wages	950
18	Paid advertising	500
20	Paid insurance	250
22	Paid for customs duty	130
22	Paid interest on mortgage	300

Cont.

June 25	Sold goods to G. Hughes	290
26	Paid cash to W. Phillips	900
28	Cash sales	650
28	Paid light and power for showrooms	148
29	Sold goods to S. Dobbs	121
30	Credit sales charged to G. Hughes on 25 June should have been charged to F. Granger.	

The following balance-day adjustments were to be accounted for at 30 June 19X7:

Stock at this date is valued at £17 006.
Salaries and wages accrued, £230.
Insurance prepaid, £150.

You are required to:

(a) Enter the balances contained in the trial balance at 31 May 19X7 into the ledger. An opening entry in the general journal is not required.

(b) Enter June's transactions into the cash book purchases and sales day book and journal. Total all day books and cash books except the general journal.

(c) Post to the ledger.

(d) Extract a trial balance at 30 June 19X7.

(e) Write general journal entries to record the balance-day adjustments.

(f) Write closing general journal entries necessary for the preparation of the profit and loss account.

(g) Prepare the profit and loss account and write the general journal entry necessary to transfer the profit and loss account result.

(h) Write the closing general journal entry necessary to transfer the drawings to capital, then total the general journal.

(i) Complete the capital account.

(j) Complete the balancing of the remaining ledger accounts.

(k) Prepare a fully classified profit and loss statement for the year ended 30 June 19X7 based on the contents of the profit and loss account.

(l) Prepare a fully classified balance sheet as at 30 June 19X7.

Chapter 5
Systems for accounting and control

Accounting and management control ☐ Fundamentals of internal control ☐ Basic accounting controls ☐ Essential features of accounting systems ☐ Computerised accounting systems ☐ Factors affecting accounting system design ☐ Charts of accounts ☐ Documenting an accounting system ☐ Accounting system cycles

Accounting and management control

The three basic functions served by accounting information comprise economic decision making, control and accountability.[1]

Let us examine briefly each of these stated functions.

1. *Decision making*. This is regarded by many as the most important function of accounting information. In Chapter 1, we highlighted the fact that accounting information is provided to interested parties, such as managers, shareholders, potential investors, creditors, government authorities and others, to assist them in making decisions. The following chapters examined the way in which accounting systems collected and processed data in order to be able to produce general purpose financial accounting reports for these decision makers. Information for decision making will continue to be stressed for the remainder of this text.

2. *Control*. Here the emphasis is on the information supplied to management for the purposes of decision making and on the protection of the firm's assets. Effective management requires the efficient use of available resources and the successful execution of plans, targets and decisions. The provision of accurate information becomes a prerequisite for the achievement of management objectives.

3. *Accountability*. The notion of accountability has developed concurrently with the emergence of the role of the professional manager. In the limited-liability company, shareholders entrust the control of their resources to directors. This is often termed stewardship. The responsibility of directors extends beyond safeguarding the resources under their control to an expectation that they will use those resources to obtain at least a reasonable return on the investment.

In the public sector, accountability holds both politicians and public servants responsible for ensuring that public resources are used for the benefit of the community, and that the community is made aware of the effect of political and bureaucratic decisions.

The three functions of decision making, control and accountability are all relevant to an understanding of the importance of 'internal control' in any accounting system.

---

[1] A.D. Barton, 'Objectives and Basic Concepts of Accounting', *Accounting Theory Monograph No. 2* (Australian Accounting Research Foundation, 1982).

Table 5.1 Internal controls

Types	Purpose	Examples
Accounting controls	Provision of accurate and reliable accounting information. (Prevention and detection of errors.)	Double-checking additions of payroll. Two officers sign each cheque.
	Assistance to management in safeguarding assets. (Prevention and detection of fraud.)	All cash banked as soon as possible. All purchase orders issued by one officer. Proper segregation of duties.
	Assistance to management in planning and attainment. (Budgetary control.)	Planning ahead for production, sales, and availability of cash and checking against results when they occur.
Administrative controls	To ensure the smooth, timely and accurate provision of data to management and to promote efficiency.	Regular reports of absentee staff, overtime worked, new employees, etc. Daily or weekly reports from outside sales staff. Systems of authorisation.
Custody controls	Assistance to management in safeguarding assets.	Regular maintenance of equipment. Installation of burglar alarms.
Other controls	Various	Employment of internal audit staff to ensure compliance with company policies. Production control and quality control. Staff control, staff training schemes.

Fundamentals of internal control

The *Auditing Standards and Guidelines*[1] defines an 'internal control system' as:

> The whole system of controls, financial and otherwise, established by the management in order to carry on the business of the enterprise in an orderly and efficient manner, ensure adherence to management policies, safeguard the assets and secure as far as possible the completeness and accuracy of the records. The individual components of an internal control system are known as 'controls' or 'internal controls'.

The definition covers a much wider scope than just ensuring that the accounting dates are accurate, and would include such items as 'custody controls' (locks on doors, high wire fences, restrictions on keys, use of safes, etc.), other protective measures such as insurance, sprinkler systems, the use of cash receipts and the employment of an internal audit staff.

---

[1] Approved by the Institute of Chartered Accountants of Scotland, the Institute of Chartered Accountants in England and Wales, the Institute of Chartered Accountants in Ireland and the Chartered Association of Certified Accountants.

Obviously, the larger the enterprise and the more remote the owners are from the actual operations, the more internal controls will be required. Table 5.1 illustrates the types of controls which may operate, although such a table cannot be exhaustive nor mutually exclusive.

Basic accounting controls

This book is mainly concerned with the *accounting controls*, particularly in the detection and prevention of errors and fraud. Efficient accounting controls result from:

1. Organisation of the staff so that the duties of each person

(a) are carefully defined;

(b) are restricted as far as possible, for example, cashier confined to receiving cash, storeman to physical custody of goods, and so on;

(c) are so arranged that errors in one section or by one officer may be discovered by another.

2. Adequate documentation including the use of

(a) charts of accounts and manuals of accounts;

(b) prenumbered documents with proper control over unused books;

(c) independent records where possible for later comparison, for example, lists of cash received in the mail separate from receipts written by cashier.

3. Established procedures such as

(a) keeping accounting records up to date;

(b) banking all cash promptly;

(c) paying by cheque wherever possible;

(d) establishing restricted authorisation, for example, for purchase of assets, hiring new staff, etc.

4. Using only staff who are adequately qualified for the duties allocated to them.

Much of the above will be considered in the following chapters. The main point to remember at this stage is that accounting controls should be an integral part of management controls.

Accounting techniques which assist in the maintenance of strong internal control include:

1. The double entry system itself with the inbuilt checks imposed by means of the trial balance.

2. Special controls over cash funds, including the use of bank reconciliation statements and the imprest system for petty cash funds. We will deal with these techniques in Chapter 7.

3. Maintenance of adequate stock records and a regular independent check of the physical quantity of goods in stock compared with the stock records.

4. The compiling of adequate records of fixed assets in the form of an assets register controlling their location, usage and general maintenance.

5. The use of control accounts together with subsidiary ledgers. These are explained briefly below and applications are provided in subsequent chapters.

There are many advantages in keeping detailed accounts in separate subsidiary ledgers, that is, a separate ledger for debtors and a separate ledger for creditors. A subsidiary ledger is a separate ledger containing accounts of a like nature which have been removed from the main or general ledger.

The information in the respective subsidiary ledgers is then represented by one total account in the general ledger. This device of using one account in the main ledger to represent the *total* of a number of detailed individual accounts in a subsidiary ledger is called a control account. Control accounts are used frequently in accounting and will be met with in later sections dealing with stock, plant, shares, etc.

The major advantages of the use of control accounts and subsidiary ledgers may be summarised as follows:

1. A trial balance may be prepared from balances in the general ledger without referring to subsidiary ledgers.

2. Voluminous detail is kept out of the general ledger.

3. The subsidiary ledgers may be distributed among different clerks. This allows for quicker and more efficient recording, and strengthens internal control.

4. Because the information comprising the control account is obtained in a different manner from that in the subsidiary ledger, it is possible to ensure the accuracy of each by comparing the balance of the control account with the total of the balances of the individual customer's accounts. These should agree before further work is undertaken, hence the name—'control account.'

5. Because of 4 above, errors are localised and are therefore easier to find and correct.

6. Responsibility for such errors can be determined.

7. The control accounts provide concise summaries of debtors and creditors for accounting report purposes, cash budgeting, etc.

Essential features of accounting systems

The major functions which any accounting system is expected to perform are as follows:

1. It must capture, record and store data on events affecting the economic results of the enterprise's operations and the enterprise's financial position.

2. It must sort and summarise this data into meaningful information.

3. As part of the sorting and summarising process, it must perform arithmetical operations on the data.

4. It must generate regular reports for a wide range of users of accounting information.

5. In addition to these regular reports, the system must be available to provide a wide range of information that may be required on an *ad hoc* basis.

The above functions represent *what* an accounting system is required to do. It is also useful to discuss *how* those functions should be performed. So far as the quality of accounting information is concerned the following are essential characteristics:

1. *Promptness.* Since reports are used as the basis of decisions, it is axiomatic that they should be reasonably up to date. Yesterday's news is stale news. In some cases, profit figures are supplied for management purposes weekly or monthly. It is no good learning six months later that the business was steadily losing money because of lower selling prices or higher costs.

2. *Accuracy.* Needless to say, if decisions are going to be made on the basis of information supplied, the figures must be as accurate as possible. At the same time, it is far better to have an

approximate position today than a meticulously accurate one in six months' time. The accountant must use judgment about how exact to be. If exact figures are needed, but definite trends can be reported now, this should be done. The doctrine of materiality is important here.

3. *Relevance*. Correct decisions can only be made on the basis of information which is truly relevant to the decisions. All information bearing on the decision should be made available, where possible, to the decision maker. Half-truths can be very misleading. On the other hand, irrelevant and immaterial information can cloud the issue and prevent the decision maker from gaining a clear view of the situation.

4. *Reliability and verifiability*. The information should represent what it purports to represent. In addition, it is desirable that the information can be checked to ensure that it does represent the situation it is meant to describe. Here the audit function is pertinent. Verifiability may be defined as the capacity of several qualified observers to come to the same conclusions.

5. *Understandability*. In order to be understood by the user, accounting information should be as simple as possible, consistent with the above requirement of relevance. Naturally, technical knowledge and competence vary significantly from one group of user to another, but, particularly in published financial reports, the needs of the lay person should be given every consideration. The use of unambiguous language, the avoidance of technical jargon, the use of descriptive headings and meaningful classification are some ways of achieving a high level of understandability.

6. *Consistency*. Reports produced should be *consistent* in form. They should be accompanied by other facts and figures so that adequate comparisons can be drawn. These latter amounts may be taken from previous results or from the budget. If they have not been consistently prepared, such comparisons could be quite misleading.

7. *Cost effectiveness*. This is probably more in the nature of a constraint than a desirable quality. Obviously the quantity of information supplied and the timeliness and accuracy of that information can be increased and improved only at some cost to the enterprise. The benefits to users of improved information are difficult to measure and the decision to incur further costs to improve an accounting system is a subjective and difficult one.

Computerised accounting systems

Given the high level of technological awareness in the community, we believe that it is now unnecessary to explain to first-year accounting students what a computer is, or to discuss the ways in which computers are programmed. The rate of technological advances in this area makes it dangerous and unprofitable to devote space to technical descriptions of computers and computer systems. Improvements in computer languages, the use of data base systems and the increasing adoption of real-time recording render obsolete any description of the current state of data processing, almost as soon as it is printed.

However, accountants have become more and more involved with electronic data-processing methods and their application to accounting systems. Professional accountants are involved in such systems (and their development) as users or as auditors; their concern is not with the technology or programming of computers. The main concern of accountants is in the provision of financial information to enable valid decisions to be made.

We believe now that it is more important to analyse why computers are so suitable and useful in an accounting system and to discuss the similarities and differences between a manual accounting system and one which uses computer technology.

The main attributes of electronic computers which have led to their widespread use in accounting systems can be summarised as follows:

1. *Speed*. Large volumes of transactions can be recorded and processed very quickly.

2. *Accuracy*. Errors in computerised systems are basically due to human error. The machine follows instructions and performs routine operations accurately and consistently.

3. *Repetitive processes*. We have seen that a large part of accounting processing consists of executing a large number of similar transactions. Computers are admirably suited to this type of processing.

4. *Storage*. Modern computers are capable of storing large quantities of data in a much smaller space than that required for written or printed records.

5. *Numerical and statistical capacity*. We have seen that mathematical calculations form part of the accounting process. Computers can be programmed to perform both simple and complex calculations. They are also capable of performing statistical analyses of the data or of constructing complex models, for example, forecasting.

6. *Communication abilities*. When linked by telecommunication networks, computers can transmit and receive data from branches, agencies, sales centres, etc., in other locations eliminating the need for the transmission of documents and records by slower and often more costly means.

7. *On-line processing*. Where terminals are located at the point at which the transaction occurs, the transaction can be recorded and analysed, the appropriate ledger accounts and documents, etc., prepared for the other party, all in the same operation. Airline reservations and computerised banking services are common examples of this.

8. *Reliability*. Where transactions are made by direct key entry, errors due to the transfer from intermediate records (such as in posting from day books to ledgers) are eliminated.

Comparison of these attributes with the suggested desirable features of accounting systems given earlier in this chapter shows why computers have been rapidly utilised to perform a large proportion of the functions of accounting.

It is important for students to recognise that the basic operations of a computerised system are the same as those of a manual system. Data processing is not a new concept. People have been processing data for centuries. No matter what data-processing method is being used, some combination of the following basic operations will be followed.

1. *Recording*. The selected data must be captured and recorded on some medium for processing, for example, a sales transaction is recorded on an invoice. It is often captured on one medium (paper) and transcribed onto another (magnetic disk). Coding is often used to condense data.

2. *Classifying*. Data having like characteristics are identified and grouped into classes, for example, all credit sales invoices are grouped together.

3. *Calculating*. Arithmetical operations are performed on the data, for example, hours worked are multiplied by a wage rate to determine gross pay.

4. *Summarising*. The classes of data are condensed so that the main points are emphasised, for example, in the sales day book all sales transactions are aggregated before posting to the general ledger.

5. *Communicating*. This refers to the transfer of data from one operation to another for further processing. This operation continues until the final information reaches the user, where communication of a different nature takes place, that is, meaning is extracted from the information rather than a simple transfer of data.

6. *Storing and retrieving*. Data, in various stages of processing, are filed on some medium for

later use. The recovery of this filed data is called retrieving. Retrieving can take many forms, depending upon how the data were stored, for example, if the data were stored in a handwritten ledger, then a clerk can find the ledger and seek the data required. On the other hand, if the ledger balances were stored on a magnetic disk, then the data may be retrieved at a computer terminal.

The basic components of a computer system performing the above functions are illustrated in Fig. 5.1.

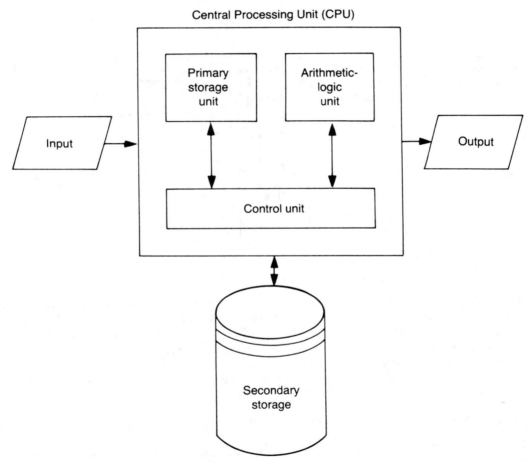

Fig. 5.1 A computer system(→ flow between the sub-systems). It should be noted that this is a very simplified description of modern computer systems.

In making comparisons between manual accounting systems and computer-based systems three points should be noted:

1. With computer-based systems, professional accounting judgment is still required in the design of the end reports and thus the determination of the accounts to be maintained; in the creation of source documents or other techniques to capture the original data; and in the unification of the necessary adjusting entries at the end of the accounting period.

2. Computer-based systems generally allow the generation of a larger number of user-oriented reports at reasonably low cost from the same basic data collected for the broad, general-purpose

financial statements. Some firms have adopted data base management systems which operate on a pool of stored information that results from processing transactions, for example, the recording of a credit sale may update all related items such as stock levels, credit rating, and purchasing in addition to the debtors account and progressive sales analysis. Transactions are set partially or completely into structures, stored in the data base, and links are created between the structures. Hence, when information in the form of reports is required, the user program (input, process and output instructions) communicates with the data management system (storage instructions) which in turn releases the required data for processing and printing (or displaying) in the required format (see Fig. 5.2).

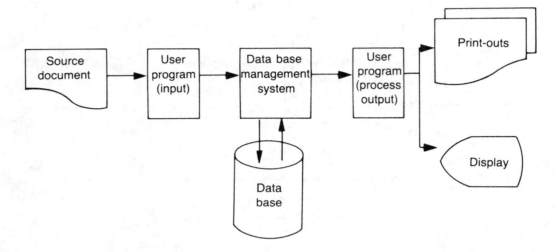

Fig. 5.2 Operation of a data base management system.

3. Computer-based systems pose additional difficulties for the auditor. In a manual system, it is possible to trace individual transactions through from the source documents to the day books and to the ledger accounts. This is often termed the 'audit trail'. In computerised systems, this trail is not as visible, and special auditing techniques are necessary to verify the accounts. Also, fraud is still possible and somewhat more difficult to detect in computer-based systems, and managers should be aware that proper controls are just as important as they are in a manual system.

Factors affecting accounting system design

We now summarise the factors which influence the selection of accounting methods and records suitable for a particular enterprise.

1 Size

The records of a business which has annual sales of £1 million will be different from those of a small business with sales of, say, £20 000 per annum. Similarly, one business may have thousands of employees, while another may have a few only. The size of a business will affect, for example, the number of accounts required in the ledger, also the manner in which the records are prepared (that is, handwritten or by mechanised methods). The fact that the business is a large one will also increase the desirability of the use of effective control techniques. In a small enterprise, the owner or manager may be able to supervise the work of all employees. In a large enterprise this is impossible.

2 Location and dispersion

If a business is a compact unit, with all its activities centred in one place, one set of accounting records covering all its activities may be the ideal arrangement. However, if for instance a business consists of a factory in one suburb and a selling centre in the city, or if it consists of a chain of stores scattered in various parts of the country, then the accounting system will have to be modified accordingly. Some of the problems associated with accounting for such an enterprise are discussed in Chapter 14.

3 Ownership

The proprietorship section of the ledger of a limited company will contain different accounts from those in the corresponding section of the ledger of a sole trader. In addition, the fact that a company has to produce annual reports for its members dictates a certain minimum of information which will have to be recorded in its books.

4 Type of product or activity

A business which manufactures motor cars will require different assets, and will have different types of revenue and expense items, from one which earns its profits by owning a television station. In addition, a particular type of product or activity often carries with it its own special problems of profit determination. Some of these problems are outlined in Chapter 15.

5 Effect of the law

As well as demanding that proper records be kept, the law (principally tax legislation and the Companies Acts) also influences the type of records an enterprise uses. In designing an accounting system, the information required to be shown in the annual reports, and the information required for taxation purposes are a 'basic' minimum on which to build.

6 Management

As we have pointed out a number of times previously, the most important factor which ought to influence accounting design is the kind of assistance the system can give to management, that is, the provision of information on which decisions may be based. In addition, the manner in which management is delegated ought to influence the design of accounts. The type of functional classification suggested for the profit and loss statement in a previous chapter (selling, administrative, finance expenses) envisages a sales manager, an office manager and, possibly, a credit manager. If we take this last factor (the requirements of management) as being the most important, the starting point in any problem in accounting design ought to be 'What kind of information is required in the reports to be presented to management?'

In other words, although during the last few chapters we have shown the accounting process in a manual system as:

Documents → Day books → Ledgers → Reports;

when we are thinking in terms of the design of an accounting system we ought to reverse this to

Reports → Ledgers → Day books → Documents.

Unfortunately, many accounting systems evolve without such logical planning. In many cases, documents are copied from other systems without much thought as to whether they will really provide the system (and consequently management) with the information it requires. Often data are recorded and never used. This involves a considerable waste of time and effort.

Planning is extremely important in converting a manual system to EDP. It is not sufficient merely to transcribe the same processes (giving the same output). A computer is more than a mere machine capable of crunching out great volumes of figures at high speed. An intelligently designed system will assist management in many ways. As an example, consider the share records. In designing the computer programs, it is wasteful merely to provide a listing of shareholders. Without much additional effort it would be simple to provide also for

1. computing the dividends;

2. sending out call notices;

3. addressing envelopes for annual reports, meetings, etc.;

4. statistics as to type, occupation, etc., of shareholders.

In the same way, a payroll system should aim to incorporate all the other relevant records, such as long-service leave entitlement, PAYE and certificates, annual leave, sick pay, etc. Time spent on proper design and integration is well worth while, whether the system is manual or not. In fact, a regular review of the accounting system often reveals wasteful or inefficient procedures, unused reports, or better methods of securing information.

Charts of accounts

While considering the essentials of good accounting systems design, it is worthwhile to consider the design of the ledger. We have stressed that the ideal in designing a system is to determine first the detail required in the reports to be presented to management, and then to implement the ledger accounts necessary to collect such detail.

  Accounting reports are usually classified in order to make them more informative and more meaningful. Therefore, the ledger account classification should correspond with the classification of items in the final reports. In addition, the order of accounts in the ledger should be such as will facilitate prompt preparation of the reports.

  Thus the five basic groups of accounts,

> assets,
> liabilities,
> proprietorship,
> revenue,
> expenses,

should be self-contained and separated from each other in the ledger. Each of these can be subdivided (for example current assets, fixed assets, non-operating expenses, etc.).

  Remember that in the recording processes it is often convenient to use an account number as a substitute for a title when indicating where items on an invoice, a goods received advice, or a costing record, etc., are to be recorded. Clerical staff become familiar with those account numbers which they know are 'proper' to their particular section, and can determine the nature of a specific item from its number. Numbers facilitate the location of accounts. Several methods may be used:

1. Straight consecutive numbers, 1, 2, 3, etc.

2. A block of numbers may be assigned to each basic ledger group, for example:

Revenue	100 to 199
Expenses	200 to 399
Assets	400 to 499
Liabilities	500 to 599
Proprietorship	600 to 699

and each basic group may be subdivided into smaller blocks, for example:

Assets	400 to 499
Current assets	400 to 449
Cash	401 to 409
Debtors	421 to 429
Stock	431 to 439
Investments	461 to 469
Fixed assets	481 to 489
Intangibles	491 to 499

This system has the advantage of simplicity and is frequently used in practice.

3. The decimal system, like the block number system, is based on the classification of accounts into groups. Under this system, a digit is allotted to each basic ledger group, for example:

Revenue	1
Expenses	2
Assets	3
Liabilities	4
Proprietorship	5

and each further step of classification brings into use another group of digits. For example, assets may be subdivided:

Assets	3
Current assets	31
Investments	32
Fixed assets	33
Intangibles	34

and then further subdivided:

Assets	3
Current assets	31
Cash	311
Cash in hand	3111
Cash at bank	3112
Debtors	312
Debtors – city	3121
Debtors – country	3122
Stock	313
Raw materials stock	3131
Work-in-progress	3132
Finished goods stock	3133
Stores stock	3134

The fact that the numbering system can be extended as above is useful in a large enterprise with a large number of accounts, particularly where it is desired to subdivide main accounts to obtain more detailed information.

Whatever the numbering system used a small problem arises with pairs of accounts of directly opposite nature which will have to be subtracted one from the other in the final reports. Examples of such accounts are:

Sales returns	which will be subtracted from	*sales.*
Provision for doubtful debts	which will be subtracted from	*debtors.*
Provision for depreciation	which will be subtracted from	the *fixed asset* to which it relates.

It is desirable that each of these 'negative' accounts be placed in the ledger next to the account from which it will be subtracted – using a further decimal or some distinguishing letter to indicate its negative nature. For example, if debtors is account No. 312, provision for doubtful debts could be numbered 312.1 or 312A.

Having arranged the ledger to facilitate recording and reporting, and having allocated a number to each account, it is logical that the preparation of a chart of accounts should follow.

A chart of accounts is a list of account titles (that is, ledger accounts) classified or grouped in accordance with a scheme of classification adapted to the needs of a particular enterprise. Its purpose is to guide those engaged in accounting and recording work in the treatment of the various transactions encountered.

The following is a simple example of a chart of accounts for a trading business owned by a sole trader. The decimal system of numbering accounts has been used.

Chart of Accounts, J. Jones

1. Revenue
    - 11 **Operating Revenue**
        - 111   Sales
        - 111A   Sales return
    - 12 **Non-operating Revenue**
        - 121   Dividends from investments
        - 122   Profit on sale of fixed assets

2. Expense
    - 21 **Cost of Goods Sold**
        - 211   Purchases
        - 211A   Purchases returns
        - 212   Carriage on purchases
    - 22 **Selling Expenses**
        - 221   Advertising
        - 222   Sales staff's salaries
        - 223   Carriage on sales
        - 224   Depreciation of delivery vehicles
    - 23 **Administrative Expenses**
        - 231   Office salaries
        - 232   Postage and stationery
        - 233   Insurance
    - 24 **Finance Expenses**
        - 241   Discount allowed
        - 241A   Discount received
        - 242   Interest
    - 25 **Non-operating Expenses**
        - 251   Donations
        - 252   Loss on sale of fixed assets

3. Assets
    31 Current Assets
        311   Cash in hand
        312   Debtors
        313   Stock
        314   Prepaid expenses
    32 Investments
        321   Shares in companies
    33 Fixed Assets
        331   Land buildings
        332   Delivery vehicles
        332A   Provision for depreciation of delivery vehicles
    34 Intangible Assets
        341   Goodwill

4. Liabilities
    41 Current Liabilities
        411   Bank overdraft
        412   Creditors
        413   Accrued expenses
    42 Long-term Liabilities
        421   Mortgage on land and buildings

5. Proprietorship
    51 Owner's Accounts
        511   J. Jones – Capital
        511A   J. Jones – Drawings
    52 Profit Determining Accounts
        521   Trading account
        522   Profit and loss account

Note that in setting up the chart of accounts, it is usual to allocate numbers to main and sub-classifications, even though there are no actual ledger accounts involved.

Also, the above items are grouped in accordance with the arrangement of the profit and loss statement and the balance sheet, which would therefore facilitate preparation of the financial statement. However, there are many other possible bases of classification, depending on the nature of the enterprise, the information required by management and the form of the accounting reports.

Documenting an accounting system

We have discussed a chart of accounts in terms of a guide to persons employed in operating an accounting system. There are other facets of an accounting system which should also be formalised and documented to ensure that the accounting controls prescribed by management are in fact enforced.

Documentation of an accounting system often takes the form of a 'manual of accounts'. It should contain all necessary instructions and explanations to the accounting staff to ensure that the system as laid down is carried out.

The contents of a typical accounting manual may be set out as follows:

1. An introduction, giving the purpose of the manual.

2. A summary of the organisation of the accounting department, with duties and responsibilities clearly defined.

3. A detailed classification and chart of ledger accounts, together with relative symbols.

4. Where necessary, specific instructions relative to certain accounts comprised in the classification.

5. Procedure to be adopted for closing accounts at balancing date.

6. The form in which financial and operating reports or statements are to be constructed; when, and by whom, they are to be presented.

7. Pro forma accounting forms, together with instructions as regards routing, filing, etc.

Documentation is perhaps even more important with computer-based accounting systems. It is vital that staff associated with the processing understand the purpose of the computer programs, and that they are fully aware of the controls which need to be exercised, particularly with respect to the data input. The procedures manual should include details of the control procedures to be exercised over input, programming, data storage and output. It should include flowcharting of the component systems.

Accounting system cycles

An accounting system may be viewed as a set of subsystems. It is useful in both the design and the operation of a system to be able to focus on one section at a time. However, it must be remembered that these subsystems are interrelated and converge within the ledger, and that data collected in one subsystem may be useful in another.

Viewing an accounting system as a number of sub-systems or 'cycles' is useful from an auditor's point of view. For example, auditors and sometimes management want to trace a purchase transaction through from the original purchase order to the receipt of the goods, the effect on stock accounts, the receipt of the supplier's invoice, the effect on creditors to the subsequent payment of the account. This is often termed the 'expenditure cycle' or the acquisition and payment cycle. A prominent international firm of public accountants uses the following four-cycles approach to the analysis of internal control and auditing procedures:

1. *Expenditure cycle* – including purchasing, receiving, creditors, personnel, payroll, capital expenditure and cash payments.

2. *Revenue cycle* – includes order entry, invoicing, shipping, debtors, sales costing and cash collection.

3. *Conversion cycle* – includes production control, cost accounting, stock and fixed assets.

4. *Treasury cycle* – includes banking, share and debenture records, investments and cash management.

These cycles are related to each other in various ways and are drawn together in what is termed the 'financial reporting cycle'.

We have used a modified cycles approach in the next few chapters of this text when dealing in detail with accounting measurement and control. The plan for these can be shown thus:

Revenue cycle	Chapter 6 – revenues and cash receipts.
Expenditure cycle	Chapters 7 and 9 – purchases, wages, payments.
Conversion cycle	Chapters 10 and 11 – stock and fixed assets.
Treasury cycle	Chapter 13 – liabilities and capital.

Summary

1. Three basic functions served by accounting information are economic decision making, control and accountability.

2. The recording processes ought to be considered in conjunction with the controls which should be instituted. These controls aim at the production of accurate and reliable accounting data and should assist in safeguarding the assets of the enterprise.

3. Accounting techniques which assist in maintaining internal control include the double entry system, bank reconciliation, imprest funds and control accounts over subsidiary ledgers.

4. Desirable characteristics of accounting information are promptness, accuracy, relevance, reliability and verifiability, understandability, consistency and cost effectiveness.

5. The ability of computers to perform routine processing at high speed with a high level of accuracy, to store large quantities of data, to perform mathematical and statistical calculations and to capture and transmit data from different locations have led to their widespread use in accounting systems.

6. The basic operations of recording, classifying, calculating, summarising, communicating, storing and retrieving are common to both manual and computer-based systems.

7. The design of an accounting system is affected by such factors as size, location, type of ownership, legal requirements and type of activity of the enterprise. The primary consideration, however, should be the requirements of management.

8. The order and classification of ledger accounts should correspond with the order and classification in the final reports.

9. A chart of accounts is a list of the titles of the accounts composing the ledger, this list being suitably classified and indexed.

10. Documentation of an accounting system, often termed a manual of accounts, is essential to ensure that the accounting controls prescribed by management are enforced.

11. The accounting system may be divided into sub-systems or cycles. This is useful in systems design, in operation and control of the system and in the auditing function.

Discussion questions

5.1 'The provision of accurate and reliable accounting information is one, but only one, aspect of an efficient system of internal control.' Explain this statement.

5.2 Much has been written in recent years about the importance of 'accountability' in the responsibilities of managers of all types of organisations. Discuss the nature of accountability as it applies to each of the following positions:

(a) the managing director of a large public company

(b) the director of a charitable organisation (e.g., a Crippled Children's Association)

(c) the vice-chancellor of a university

(d) the chief administrative officer of a city.

5.3 (a) Explain why proper segregation of staff duties is important in the maintenance of efficient internal control.

(b) Segregation of duties is not always possible in a small business. Does this necessarily mean that internal control is always weak in a small business?

5.4 We have listed the following essential characteristics of accounting information: promptness, accuracy, relevance, reliability and verifiability, understandability, consistency and cost effectiveness. However, the achievement of a high level of one characteristic may occur at the expense of not achieving a high level of another characteristic. Explain how a compromise might have to be made

(a) between promptness and accuracy;

(b) between accuracy and cost effectiveness;

(c) between relevance and understandability.

5.5 Discuss the major features of electronic computers that have resulted in their widespread use in accounting system.

5.6 'Accountants will eventually be replaced by computers.' Do you agree or disagree with this statement? Give the reasons for your view.

5.7 Discuss the ways in which the introduction of computers has made life more difficult for auditors.

5.8 Discuss why it is normally not possible to take an accounting system which has been used successfully in one enterprise and implement it in another.

5.9 Discuss the roles of a chart of accounts and a manual of accounts in:

(a) the design

(b) the operation of an accounting system

Exercises

5.10 From your observation indicate the techniques of internal control which are used

(a) in admitting patrons to a cinema;

(b) to record and collect payment in a hotel dining room;

(c) to record and collect payment in a city car park.

5.11 Draft a 'chart of accounts', with appropriate symbols, for the ledger of J. Walker, a wholesale trader, incorporating the following ledger accounts:

Creditors	Premises
Debtors	Profit and loss account
Advertising	Purchases
Carriage on purchases	Rates
Cash at bank	Returns on purchases
Discount allowed	Returns on sales
Discount received	Sales
Goodwill	Sales staff's salaries
Stock	Trading account
Mortgage on premises	Travellers' commission
Office expenses	J. Walker - Capital
Office furniture	J. Walker - Drawings
Office salaries	

Walker's ledger is arranged with balance sheet items first.

5.12 A list of accounts in the ledger of J. Taylor is given below.

Creditors	Stock, packing materials
Debtors	Lighting, office
Advertising	Lighting, warehouse
Bank overdraft	Loan from W. Gunn
Buying expenses	Office fixtures and fittings
Capital account – J. Taylor	Packing expenses
Carriage on purchases	Postage and stationery
Commission received	Profit and loss account
Commission, sales staff	Purchases
Customs duty	Rent, office
Delivery vehicles	Rent, warehouse
Delivery vehicle expenses	Returns of purchases
Discount allowed	Returns of sales
Discount received	Salaries, office
Donations	Salaries, warehouse
Goodwill	Sales
Insurance	Sundry office expenses
Interest on overdraft	Trading account
Stock merchandise	Warehouse fixtures and fittings

You are required to prepare a properly classified chart of accounts for this ledger, one which will facilitate prompt preparation of accounting reports. Use a suitable numerical system to index the chart of accounts. The warehouse is used for the display of goods.

5.13 The Dial-a-Handyman Company offers to householders services classified as painting and decorating, minor house repairs, lawn planting and maintenance, and pruning and rubbish removal. The firm operates from three different locations in a major city.

(a) How many revenue accounts are needed if the amount of revenue is to be reported for each class of service?

(b) How many revenue accounts are needed if the amount of revenue for each class of service is to be reported separately for each of the three business locations?

(c) What titles do you suggest for the revenue accounts used to classify and accumulate revenue data separately for the classes of service at the different locations?

(d) Draft the revenue section of the company's chart of accounts.

5.14 You are interested in securing a part-time job with a firm of chartered accountants. In order to test your understanding of basic financial accounting, a partner of the firm asks you to prepare hypothetical profit and loss statements and balance sheets for each of the following firms:

Jill's Hairdressing Salon
Joe's Fish and Chip Shop
Purple Cab Taxi Company

(a) Prepare the pro forma statements requested, omitting amounts.

(b) Write brief notes stating the assumptions you have made about the operations of each of the firms.

Problem

5.15 D. Armstrong has established the following block numbering scheme for his ledger accounts:

Operating revenue	100 to 149
Non-operating revenue	150 to 199
Cost of goods sold expense	200 to 249
Selling expense	250 to 299
Administrative expense	300 to 349
Finance expense	350 to 389
Non-operating expense	390 to 399
Current assets	400 to 449
Fixed assets	450 to 499
Investment assets	500 to 549
Intangible assets	550 to 599
Current liabilities	600 to 649
Long-term liabilities	650 to 699
Proprietorship – owner's accounts	700 to 749
Profit-determining accounts	750 to 799

Prepare a chart of accounts for the accounts listed below, organised according to the above scheme.

Commission received	Creditors
Insurance	Loss by theft
Donations	Advertising
Furniture	Stock
Postage	Discount allowed
Interest on mortgage	Discount received
Interest charged to customers	Machinery
Goodwill	D. Armstrong – Capital
Cash at bank	Debtors
Rent received	Shares in AGV Co. Plc
Purchases	Customs duty
Purchases returns	Sales staff's salaries
Office wages	Mortgage on buildings
Motor vehicles	Sales
Carriage inwards	Sales returns
Rates and taxes	Carriage outwards
Prepaid expenses	D. Armstrong – Drawings
Trading	Sales staff's commission
Sundry office expenses	Interest charged by suppliers
Delivery trucks	Lighting and power – office
Profit and loss	Gain on sale of furniture
Accrued expenses	Prepaid revenue
Land and buildings	Cash on hand
Government securities	Interest received on investments
Stationery	Accrued revenue
Loan from H. Bell	Shop fittings

The commission received and the rent received form part of the firm's normal operations; while the interest received from investments is considered to be outside normal operations.

Chapter 6
Revenues and cash receipts

Nature of revenues ☐ Control over credit sales and debtors ☐ Recording of credit sales ☐ Sales discounts ☐ Control over cash sales and other receipts ☐ Cash Book ☐ Debtors ledger control accounts ☐ Accounting for bad and doubtful debts

Nature of revenues

In previous chapters, we defined revenue in terms of the gross inflow of resources into an enterprise resulting from profit-earning activities. We observed that revenue has the effect of increasing proprietorship and we discussed the necessity to make adjustments to recorded revenue at the end of an accounting period in order that the accounts accurately reflected revenue earned. We also discussed problems associated with the timing of revenue recognition.

In this chapter, we are more concerned with the practical aspects of recording and measuring revenue, bearing in mind the importance of adequate controls. We will also deal with the necessity to control and record the indebtedness arising from the earning of revenue where payment is not received until some time after the revenue has been earned.

It may be useful at the outset, to summarise some of the main types of revenue-earning activity:

1. *Retail trading* – where goods are sold in a form similar to that in which they were purchased.

2. *Manufacturing* – where raw materials are converted into finished products before they are sold.

3. *Mining and other extractive industries* – producing metals, coal, oil, gas, etc.

4. *Primary production* – growing of crops and vegetables, raising of animals, supply of animal products, etc.

5. *Provision of services* – banking, insurance, professional, trade, transport, entertainment, etc.

6. *Financing* – lending and investing.

The manner in which revenue is earned affects not only the timing of the revenue recognition, but also the way in which the revenue is recorded and reported. The effect of revenue-earning transactions involves credit entries to accounts such as sales revenue, fees charged, rent revenue, subscription revenue, commission revenue, interest revenue, etc. It is in the best interests of the users of accounting reports that the sources of revenue be stated as specifically as possible.

The debit entry for revenue-earning transactions takes two major forms: either cash is received at or prior to the revenue being earned or the earning of revenue gives rise to a claim to cash commonly in the form of debtors.

In considering the controls which should be imposed in the revenue cycle, we will deal first with situations where debtors are involved and later with the receipt of cash, including that from cash sales.

Control over credit sales and debtors

Here we are using the terms 'sales' in a broad sense and to include not only the sale of goods on credit, but also the charging of fees for various types of services.

It is usual to be able to find the following features in any good system of internal control over credit sales and debtors.

1. It is desirable to investigate the creditworthiness of customers prior to allowing credit. In larger concerns, this is handled by a separate credit department under the control of a credit manager, who also has the responsibility to follow up overdue accounts, institute recovery actions, authorise special terms, write off bad debts, etc.

2. The nature of the business influences the manner in which credit sales are recorded, but whether it be a retail store, a wholesaler, or a manufacturing business, it is normal for a sales invoice with copies to be prepared. One copy is forwarded to the customer and a duplicate is used as a basis of recording credit sales. Other copies may be used for keeping a record of stock movements and to facilitate the packaging and delivery of the goods.

3. Where sales are delivered to the customer, it is necessary to prepare a delivery advice to accompany the goods. This may be a carbon copy of the sales invoice without details of prices. Many firms also use an internal form which repeats the customer's purchase order. This is a control measure to ensure that the technical description of the goods ordered is communicated accurately to the supplying departments, and copies enable an order to be divided between departments. Where a continuous or perpetual stock record is being kept, such internal forms may be the basis of recording the outgoing goods on the stock card.

4. Frequently, goods are returned or an allowance is made in connection with a previous sale. In order to adjust the customer's account and the sales figure, it is usual to raise documentary evidence with a credit note. This provides the necessary information to record the adjustment and is often printed in red. A copy is sent to the customer and a duplicate retained as the basis of recording returns of sales, and allowances in connection with sales. A credit may be given even though there is no physical return of goods. This would occur where customers have been overcharged or where breakages occurred in transit.

5. Regular statements of account should be forwarded to facilitate collection. Where large numbers of debtors are involved, the work of balancing accounts, the preparation of the statements and the collection of cash is aided by a process known as 'cycle billing'. This is achieved by spreading the balancing dates over the month. Customers are grouped alphabetically, and those whose names commence with (say) A to D are balanced on the 1st, E to G on the 6th of every month, and so on.

6. The persons handling the preparation of the debtors ledger accounts and the preparation of the statements should not have any connection with the receipt or recording of the cash received from debtors.

7. Where there is a large number of debtors, it is desirable to use a subsidiary ledger or ledgers. An important element of control is obtained by having a 'control' account or accounts in the general ledger. The use of subsidiary ledgers and control accounts for debtors is illustrated later in this chapter.

Recording of credit sales

In Chapter 3, we referred to the use of a sales day book to record and summarise credit sales where a manual system is in use. In gathering together all credit sales in the one recording mechanism, such a day book allows postings to be made, at regular intervals, of total sales to the credit side of the sales revenue account.

A simple form of sales is shown below:

Sales Day Book				Page ....
Date	Invoice No.	Customer a/c debited	Ledger folio	Sales revenue
				£

Notes:
1. Similar types of day book may be used where revenue is earned by the charging of fees for the provision of services.

2. The individual entries are posted to the debit side of customers' accounts; the total is posted at regular intervals to the credit side of the sales revenue account.

A sales returns and allowances day book may also be used where there are sufficient numbers of transactions of this type to warrant its use. A sample format is given below:

Sales Returns Day Book				Page ......
Date	Credit note No.	Customer a/c credited	Ledger folio	Sales returns
				£

Note: The individual entries are posted to the credit side of customers' accounts; the total is posted at regular intervals to the debit side of the sales returns and allowances account.

Where it is desired to analyse sales into categories – for example, sales by department or sales by product type – a columnar sales day book may be used. An example is given below:

Sales Day Book					Account credited		Page ......
Date	Invoice No.	Customer a/c debited	Ledger folio	Total debited	Sales dept A	Sales dept B	Sales dept C
					£	£	£

Note: The individual entries are posted to the debit side of customers' accounts; the totals of the three right-hand columns are posted at regular intervals to the credit sides of the three respective sales revenue accounts.

Sales discounts

Before proceeding to discuss the receipt of cash from debtors and other sources, it is necessary to discuss one factor which may affect the amount of cash actually received from a customer. This is the practice of allowing discounts. First, we need to distinguish between two different types of discounts:

1. Trade and quantity discounts.

2. Discounts for prompt payments, sometimes termed 'cash discounts'.

Trade discount

This is a discount offered to certain categories of customers and is deducted from the list price of the goods. It may be a standard term of sale because of some particular relationship between seller and buyer, for example, a manufacturer to a wholesaler, or may involve a discount in that a special price is negotiated, for example, for a larger than normal quantity. Once the trade discount is established or negotiated, the full price is not significant for accounting, the effective price being the net price which represents the legal indebtedness between the parties. It is this net price which will form the basis of the accounting entries, although the trade discount may be shown as a deduction from the list price on the supplier's invoice.

Discount for prompt payment

The frequently used term 'cash discount' is misleading because the discount is adjusted by a book entry and not by the physical transfer of cash. For example, if we sell goods to J. Jones on credit for £80, and our terms allow for 2.5 per cent cash discount for prompt payment, then J. Jones can settle within the stipulated time for £78. However, we have recorded a debit in the account of J. Jones for the sale of £80. When he pays cash £78, we must record the fact that this is in full settlement, that is, we must record the £2 allowance for discount. The £2 discount is not a cash transaction and could be treated through the general journal. Since under this method the allowance of the discount takes place concurrently with a receipt of cash, and there is a common account (the debtors account) affected by both elements of the transaction, it is found more convenient to record the allowance of the discount in the cash book. Furthermore, the same original record (the receipt) is used to supply the information for both the amount of the payment and the amount of the discount. We will illustrate the recording of discounts through the cash book later in this chapter.

It should be noted that there is a time lag between the date on which the goods are invoiced and entered in a sales day book and the date on which the account is paid and the discount recorded. If at the end of an accounting period, the amount expected to be allowed as discount on debtors' accounts is material, an end-of-period adjustment debiting sales discounts or discount allowed and crediting provision for discounts allowable should be made. Also note a basic difference between trade discounts and discounts for prompt payment: the latter are conditional, the former are not.

Control over cash sales and other receipts

Before discussing specific controls imposed over cash receipts, it is worthwhile to discuss internal control over cash in more general terms. There are two main reasons why cash is so important:

1. Many of the transactions which have to be recorded involve a movement of cash either *to* the business (a cash receipt) or *from* the business (a cash payment). In some businesses, the majority of transactions are cash receipts or payments, and in all businesses, most other transactions, such as the purchase or sale of goods or the incurring of expenses, subsequently lead to a receipt or payment at some later date.

2. The asset cash, itself, is important because cash funds present the best opportunity for people with dishonest intentions. Cash is portable, ownership is difficult to identify and it is accepted universally. It is essential that adequate controls be instituted over the asset, and that the recording procedures be such that the cash present can be checked against the amount which should be present; any deficiencies are thus revealed.

It is usual to be able to recognise the following features in any good system of internal control over cash:

1. The duties of employees are arranged so that those engaged in receiving or handling cash do not take part in the subsequent recording function. This prevents the same person being able to misappropriate cash on the one hand and subsequently make entries in the records to disguise the deficiency. A good system is such that an error made by one person will be discovered by another in the normal course of their duties, and that collusion between two or more persons would be necessary to conceal a misappropriation of cash.

2. The recording of cash receipts is arranged so that it is necessary to balance cash received against some independent record daily.

3. All cash received is banked intact at regular intervals, usually daily.

4. All payments, other than those made out of a petty cash fund kept on the imprest system (dealt with later in the next chapter), are made by cheque. A system of checking of available evidence and authorisation by a responsible officer before cheques are written ties in with this control.

5. An independent officer regularly checks the cash records against statements obtained from the bank. This is usually termed bank reconciliation.

The last three points, if adhered to, mean that the accuracy of the cash accounting is closely linked with a reliable outside check – that of the bank statement. This is a statement sent by a bank to its customers showing the deposits (amounts banked) and withdrawals (cheque drawn) by or on behalf of the customer, and the charges made by the bank, together with the balance of the account.

Control over cash payments, petty cash payments and the technique of bank reconciliation will all be dealt with in detail in Chapter 7.

The nature of controls which should be imposed over cash receipts depends on the manner in which the cash is received. Some common forms of control over cash receipts are outlined below.

1. *Cash received at the time the transaction takes place.* For example, cash sales in a retail store, fares collected on a bus, tickets sold at a cinema. Here the identity of the person from whom the cash is received is not important and this is not usually recorded. A cash docket may be written out, a ticket issued from a pre-numbered roll, a cash register or some other automatic recording device used or some combination of these methods. The important factors are:

(a) to arrive at the total amount received for the day; and

(b) to provide a means of checking the amount of cash which should be present at the end of the day.

Thus there should be a daily reconciliation of cash against tickets, cash against total of register or cash against total of sales dockets. This reconciliation should be performed or checked by an independent person.

Sometimes it will be desirable to analyse the cash received in this way into a number of different groups, for example, cash from different departments, cash from different types of goods sold, and so on. Thus, some method of indicating the nature of each item received is used on the cash register or on the cash docket.

2. *Cash received from debtors, either over the counter or through the mail.* Here either a receipt on an official prenumbered receipt form is made out for each amount received, and duplicates of receipts retained, or, more commonly, the amounts are listed. The receipt should show the date,

name of debtor, amount paid, and the amount of any discount allowed for payment within a specified period. Adequate control should be kept over the issue of receipt forms or books, and the number used at any particular time should be kept to a minimum. Mail should be opened in the presence of two officers, and the cash remittances listed in a remittances book or sheet and totalled, before being handed to the cashier. These lists should be checked against the bankings independently.

3. *Cash received from other sources.* For example, from the sale of non-trading assets (office equipment, etc.), additional capital paid in, or amounts received from an issue of shares, cash deposits received, etc. Here again, a receipt should be made out for each item and the receipt should clearly show the nature of the transaction.

4. *Cash received by the bank* (other than ordinary deposits). The bank will collect dividends, rents or interest on our behalf, and credit our bank account with the amounts received. Agents and branches, too, often pay into our bank account at different branches of the bank sums which they have collected or wish to remit. Such amounts will be evidenced in the statement of our account issued by the bank which we have explained earlier.

Cash book

The purpose of the cash book is to record receipts of money by cash and cheque and to record payments by cheque, cash payments being made through the petty cash book as explained below in Chapter 7.

The following is a simple illustration of a cash book with no analysis columns.

W. Brown
Cash Book

Date	Particulars	Folio	Amount	Date	Particulars	Folio	Amount
June 1	Balance	b/d	£150	June 10	Wages		£97
4	Cash sales		35	17	Electricity		105
8	I. Smith		201	25	W. Green		85
9	Cash Sales		55	30	Balance	c/d	154
			£441				£441
July 1	Balance	b/d	£154				

In the above example all receipts in the form of cash and cheques would be recorded in the debit side of the cash book and lodged in the bank account of the business and all cheque payments recorded in the credit side of the cash book. The posting procedure for the above would be to post the entries shown in the debit side of the cash book to the credit of the individual accounts affected and those entries shown in the credit side of the cash book to the debit of the appropriate accounts in the ledgers.

The balancing of the cash book is similar to that of a ledger account.

As can be seen the cash book consists of two sides – debit or receipts side and credit or payments side. In many businesses the cash book is divided into a cash book (receipts side) and cash book (payments side). Although many small businesses write up the cash book as one book, larger businesses tend to divide the cash book into cash book (receipts side) and cash book (payments side). This does not alter the concept of the cash book being one book but the division allows each side of the cash book to be written up by different members of staff thus speeding up the recording process. The cash book is still balanced in the normal manner at periodic intervals.

Cash book (receipts side)

In a manual recording system a cash book (receipts side) may be prepared from the original evidence of the transaction, for example, the cash register, the ticket-roll total, the duplicates of receipts issued, etc. Where machine accounting is used, it may be prepared at the same time as the receipts are being machined. The main object is to arrive at the total cash received from each of the various sources for a period, for example a month. The form of the cash book will, of course, depend on the requirements of the particular business and the number of columns used will vary considerably. It is, however, possible to distinguish between columns essential in every cash book and extra columns which may be used if required.

There are two main factors which influence the introduction of additional columns into the cash book (receipts side):

1. The first is the practice of allowing debtors a discount for prompt payment, as discussed earlier in this chapter.

2. The second factor is that it is often deemed necessary or desirable to subdivide the 'amount' column into several columns distinguishing between the main types of cash receipts. This may be looked on as a second step in the classification process referred to in Chapter 3. The first step was to classify transactions into main groups – sales, purchases, cash receipts, cash payments, etc., with a separate book for each. Now we can go further by classifying cash receipts into subgroups – cash from cash sales, cash from debtors, cash from rent received, etc. A sample ruling for a columnar cash book (receipts side) is shown below.

Cash Book (Receipts Side)								
Date	Receipt no.	Particulars	Ledger folio	Discount allowed	Amounts received from debtors	Cash sales	Rent received	Other receipts
				1	2	3	4	5

Note that the main factor influencing the selection of columns is the frequency with which the particular type of cash receipt occurs. A sundry receipts (or other receipts) column is essential for those types of receipts which do not occur often enough to warrant a separate column.

The main advantage to be gained from the use of separate columns for different types of receipts is in the elimination of unnecessary posting. If the cash book is totalled and posted monthly, there may be twenty or more entries in the cash sales column. The effect of these can be transferred to the ledger in *one* figure by posting the total of the cash sales column.

In the case of the amounts received from debtors column, the desirability of using a separate column is made a necessity if the system of control account and subsidiary ledger is being used for debtors.

A summary for the posting of the above cash book receipts side would be:

1. Total of discount column is posted to the debit of the discount allowed account and to the credit of the debtors control account. Remember that discount is in this cash book purely as a convenience.

2. Total of amounts received from debtors column is posted to the credit of the debtors control account. The individual amounts of discount allowed and cash received from individual debtors would be posted to the credit of the various debtors' accounts in the subsidiary ledger.

3. Total of cash sales column is posted to the credit of the cash sales revenue account or, if it is

not desired to have separate ledger accounts for cash and credit sales, to the credit of the sales revenue account.

4. Total of the rent received column is posted to the credit of the rent revenue account.

5. Total of other receipts column has no significance for posting purposes but is included to give a cross-check on totals. However, the individual items are posted to the credit of the various accounts involved. Where there are a number of entries in this column, it is usual to append a summary of such entries under the ruled-off total, in order to facilitate their posting. (Remember there may be several entries concerning the same account in this column, but this is still insufficient to justify a separate column.)

6. Note that all items recorded in the cash book (receipts side) must be lodged in the bank account of the business.

Debtors ledger control accounts

In Chapter 5, we explained the concept of subsidiary ledgers with control accounts in the general ledger and outlined the advantages of the use of this technique. We will now provide an example of the use of subsidiary ledgers for debtors. To keep this example reasonably compact, we will assume an enterprise with only six credit customers, but students should remember that a much larger number would be necessary before the use of a subsidiary ledger could be justified.

Example: On 1 May 19X6 the debtors control account in the general ledger of Regal Traders showed a debit balance of £18 490. A schedule extracted from the debtors subsidiary ledger at the same date showed the following debit balances:

J. Bond	£5 940
K. Davies	8 320
L. Murray	1 140
F. Pearson	2 380
G. Williams	710
	£18 490

The following are extracts from the day book, the sales returns book and the cash book (receipts side) for the month of May relevant to debtors. All other details which would be recorded in these books have been ignored.

Sales Day Book

19X6			
May	2	L. Murray	£1 230
	5	F. Pearson	1 580
	5	T. Thomas	2 640
	9	J. Bond	3 330
	10	T. Thomas	1 110
	16	K. Davies	980
	16	L. Murray	1 580
	23	F. Pearson	1 340
	26	K. Davies	1 550
			£15 340

Sales Returns Book

19X6		
May 5	K. Davies	£520
10	L. Murray	310
23	G. Williams	80
		£910

Cash Book (Receipts Side)

19X6		Discount allowed	Amount received from debtors
May 5	J. Bond	£120	£5 820
9	G. Williams	20	690
16	K. Davies	—	6 000
23	F. Pearson	40	2 100
		£180	£14 610

The recording of this information in the firm's books is illustrated below.

Cash Book (Receipts Side)

19X6		Discount allowed	Amount received from debtors
May 5	J. Bond	£120	£5 820
9	G. Williams	20	690
16	K. Davies	—	6 000
23	F. Pearson	40	2 100
		£180	£14 610

Sales Day Book

		Amount
19X6		
May 2	L. Murray	£1 230
5	F. Pearson	1 580
5	T. Thomas	2 640
9	J. Bond	3 330
10	T. Thomas	1 110
16	K. Davies	980
16	L. Murray	1 580
23	F. Pearson	1 340
26	K. Davies	1 550
		£15 340

Sales Returns Book

		Amount
19X6		
May 5	K. Davies	520
10	L. Murray	310
23	G. Williams	80
		£910

Debtors Ledger

J. Bond

19X6			19X6		
May 1	Balance	£5 940	May 5	Cash and discount	£5 940
9	Sales	3 330	31	Balance	3 330
		£9 270			£9 270
June 1	Balance	£3 330			

K. Davies

19X6			19X6		
May 1	Balance	£8 320	May 5	Sales returns	£520
16	Sales	980	16	Cash	6 000
26	Sales	1 550	31	Balance	4 330
		£10 850			£10 850
June 1	Balance	£4 330			

L. Murray

19X6			19X6		
May 1	Balance	£1 140	May 10	Sales returns	£310
2	Sales	1 230	31	Balance	3 640
16	Sales	1 580			
		£3 950			£3 950
June 1	Balance	£3 640			

F. Pearson

19X6			19X6		
May 1	Balance	£2 380	May 23	Cash and discount	£2 140
5	Sales	1 580	31	Balance	3 160
23	Sales	1 340			
		£5 300			£5 300
June 1	Balance	£3 160			

Debtors Ledger *Cont.*

T. Thomas

19X6				19X6			
May 5	Sales	2 640		May 31	Balance	£3 750	
10	Sales	1 110					
		£3 750				£3 750	
June 1	Balance	£3 750					

G. Williams

19X6				19X6			
May 1	Balance	£710		May 9	Cash and discount	£710	
31	Balance	80		23	Sales returns	80	
		£790				£790	
				June 1	Balance	£80	

General ledger

Sales

				19X6			
				May 31	Credit sales for month	£15 340	

Discount Allowed

19X6			
May 31	Discount allowed for month	£180	

Sales Returns

19X6			
May 31	Sales returns for month	£910	

Debtors' Control Account

19X6				19X6			
May 1	Balance	£18 490		May 31	Sales Returns	£910	
31	Sales	15 340			Cash and discount	14 790	
					Balance	18 130	
		£33 830				£33 830	
June 1	Balance	£18 130					

A schedule extracted from the debtors ledger at 31 May would show:

J. Bond	£3 330
K. Davies	4 330
L. Murray	3 640
F. Pearson	3 160
T. Thomas	3 750
	£18 210
Less S. Williams (credit balance)	80
	£18 130

Note: The schedule of balances does reconcile with the balance on the debtors' control account.

Points to note relating to debtors' ledger control accounts

The main purpose in preparing a debtors' ledger control account is to record in total all amounts entered in detail to the individual accounts in the debtors' ledger. The preparation of the debtors' ledger control account provides management with the total amount due from debtors in one account without the necessity of extracting a list of individual balances. It also enables errors in posting to be found and corrected more easily. The debtors' ledger control account may form part of the double entry system or the account may be prepared separately. In either method the same form of compilation is observed. It must be remembered that the control account is merely the totals of the individual entries recorded in the ledger accounts and the totals appear on the same side of the control account as they would be recorded on the ledger accounts.

Where a debtors ledger contains a very large number of customers' accounts, a subdivision of the ledger may be necessary. In that case it is usual to divide the debtors into groups, keeping each group in a separate subsidiary ledger, for example alphabetically:

A – G   in one ledger,
H – P   in another,
Q – Z   in a third.

Another way is to divide the debtors geographically, for example town debtors and country debtors. For every subsidiary ledger used in the system there must be a control account in the general ledger to record the totals representing that ledger. Thus, there would need to be for the alphabetical subdivision previously suggested:

A – G   Control account
H – P   Control account
Q – Z   Control account

This in turn will require amendments to the various journals so that these totals can be separated out. In the cash book, in place of one column headed 'Amounts received from debtors', there will have to be *three* columns headed as follows:

Cash Book (Receipts Side)

	Amounts received from debtors			
	A-G	H-P	Q-Z	

Care must be taken to ensure that amounts are entered in the correct columns. Similar extra columns will be required in other day book for example:

Sales Day Book

Date	Details	A-G	H-P	Q-Z	Total

As before, each control account should agree with the total of outstanding accounts in the relevant subsidiary ledger.

Accounting for bad and doubtful debts

In Chapter 3 we introduced the problem of accounting for bad and doubtful debts. It was pointed out that in order to produce an acceptable matching of expense with revenue for a period, an estimate should be made of the amount of debts which may ultimately be uncollectable. It was also stated that the manner of estimating and recording of these doubtful debts varies from one accounting system to another and depends particularly on the frequency of preparation of the profit and loss statement.

The approach adopted in the examples which follow is consistent with an accounting system in which profit and loss statements are prepared at frequent intervals (say, monthly). On the basis of past experience, a percentage of each month's credit sales will be considered as uncollectable and recorded as an expense by making a monthly journal entry:

Dr.   Bad and doubtful debts
Cr.   Provision for doubtful debts

Thus, for each month, it is recognised that some unidentifiable accounts will not be collectable; the estimated expense is available for the matching process in the monthly profit and loss statement, and cumulative totals are building up in the above accounts within the ledger system throughout the financial year.

Consider the following example (dealing only with the entry for a single month). During the month of May, credit sales totalling £24 000 were made. Past records reveal that, on average, $1\frac{1}{2}$ per cent of credit sales are uncollectable. Entries in the ledger after the monthly adjustment would be:

Provision for Doubtful Debts

		May 31	Bad and doubtful debts	£360

Bad and Doubtful Debts

May 31	Provision for doubtful debts	£360		

The provision for doubtful debts account is deducted from the recorded debtors total in the balance sheet. The bad and doubtful debts account records the amount of current revenue expected to be lost in the collection process. It may be regarded as an expense account.

The adequacy of the provision for doubtful debts should be regularly reviewed. One method of review used is an individual appraisal of each debtor's account, taking into account such factors as the length of time the amount has been outstanding, the debtor's previous history, correspondence, and the opinion of the credit manager. Another method often adopted is the process known as 'ageing the debtors' accounts'. In this process the total amount owing by debtors is analysed into groups according to the length of time that accounts have been outstanding. For example, we might divide the total amount owing into five groups: owing less than one month, 1–2 months, 2–3 months, 3–6 months and more than six months. Then varying percentages, based on past experience, are applied to the totals of these groups to arrive at an estimate of the desirable provision for doubtful debts. The existing provision, which has been built up during the period in a somewhat arbitrary manner based upon credit sales, may then be adjusted if necessary in the light of the additional information made available by this review. The use of EDP renders the above process a relatively simple matter.

The above review for accounting purposes is in addition to the continuous review of debtors for credit purposes by the credit manager and staff in following up overdue accounts, restricting credit, etc.

Consider the following examples to illustrate the adjustments to write off bad and doubtful debts.

Example: R. Green has been owing J. Good £20 since 1 January and is now unable to make payment of this amount due to his insolvency. Good decides to write off the balance as a bad debt at the end of his financial year which is 31 December. The entries in J. Good's books would be as follows.

Ledger

Bad and Doubtful Debts

Dec. 31	R. Green	£20	Dec. 31	Profit and Loss	£20

R. Green

Jan. 1	Balance	£20	Dec. 31	Bad and doubtful debts	£20

Profit and Loss

Dec. 31	Bad and doubtful debts	£20

Note: Some businesses maintain separate accounts for 'bad debts' and 'doubtful debts'.

Example: In the books of W. Smith on 1 January there was a balance on the provision for doubtful debts account of £500. At the end of the year it was decided to write off J. White's account of £250 as a bad debt and to increase the provision for doubtful debts to £600. The total debts at 31 December before writing off the bad debt amounted to £12 000. The entries in the books of W. Smith would be as follows:

Ledger

J. White

Jan. 1	Balance	£250	Dec. 31	Provision for doubtful debts	£250

Provision for Doubtful Debts

Dec. 31	J. White	£250	Jan. 1	Balance	£500
	Balance	600	Dec. 31	Bad and doubtful debts	350
		£850			£850
			Jan. 1	Balance	£600

Bad and Doubtful Debts

Dec. 31	Provision for doubtful debts	£350	Dec. 31	Profit and loss	£350

Profit and Loss

Dec. 31	Bad and doubtful debts	£350

Balance Sheet (Extract)

Current assets		
Debtors	£11 750	
Less Provision for doubtful debts	600	£11 150

Note: If a provision for doubtful debts account is opened any amount written off as bad is usually transferred to this account direct and not through the bad and doubtful debts account.

Bad debt recovered

It is possible that a debtor whose balance was previously written off as a bad debt may pay the amount owing later. Supposing J. Brown pays a debt of £70 which had previously been written off as bad. A receipt would be forwarded to Brown for the £70 which would be entered in the cash book (receipts side). The resultant posting would cause Brown's account to appear as follows:

	J. Brown (Debtor)			
Date	Balance	£70	Date	Prov. for doubtful debts	£70
			Date	Cash	£70

To record the fact that Brown's debt had been met, we restore the amount of the debt, and record the gain by crediting a bad debts recovered account which will appear as a revenue item (or a gain) in the profit and loss statement. An appropriate general journal entry to achieve this would be:

General Journal

		Dr.	*Cr.*
Date	J. Brown (Debtors ledger)	£70	
	Bad debts recovered		£70
	Previous bad debt now received		

Summary

1. The manner in which revenue is earned affects not only the timing of revenue recognition but also the way in which the revenue is recorded and reported.

2. Systems of internal control over credit sales generally include the investigation of creditworthiness, procedures for issuing invoices and credit notes, and procedures for billing customers and following up overdue accounts.

3. Under manual systems, the recording of credit sales involves the use of specialised sales and sales returns day books. Columnar day books can be used to analyse sales.

4. Since cash transactions are of frequent occurrence, and since cash funds are vulnerable to fraudulent intentions, it is essential that sound control measures and accurate recording techniques should be applied to this asset.

5. With cash receipts, the most important control principles are the daily banking of all cash

received and the accumulation of reliable documentary evidence in the form of receipts, remittance lists, etc.

6. Depending on the type of business activity and on the amount of secondary classification desired, the cash book (receipts side) may contain few or many columns. Columnar cash books facilitate posting to the ledger.

7. For debtors, where numbers warrant, accounting control is facilitated by the use of subsidiary ledgers with a control account in the general ledger. It is important to remember that the aggregate balances of the individual accounts in a subsidiary ledger should always equal the balance in the corresponding control account in the general ledger.

8. With debtors it is inevitable that some will not pay. Bad debts represent an expense to be written off against revenue in the profit and loss statement. As part of the matching process and to adjust debtors in the balance sheet, it is necessary to anticipate bad debts. This gives rise to a doubtful debts provision. When bad debts do occur, they are written off against the provision either immediately or at the end of the period.

Discussion questions

6.1 Where a business earns revenue from a number of different sources, why should separate revenue accounts be kept for each major source of revenue?

6.2 What is the relationship between the role of a credit manager of a retail store and the firm's accounting system?

6.3 What is the importance of a credit note

(a) to the customer,

(b) to the accounting system of the firm issuing it?

6.4 What do you understand by the term 'cycle billing'? What are the advantages of this system?

6.5 Distinguish clearly between 'trade discounts' and 'discounts for prompt payment'. Why are they treated differently in the accounts?

6.6 (a) Explain why it is important that satisfactory recording and control procedures be established for the asset 'cash'.

(b) Outline the general principles that should be followed in framing a satisfactory system of internal control over cash.

6.7 Discuss the effect on the design of a cash book (receipts side) of:

(a) the use of subsidiary ledgers for debtors;

(b) the allowance of discounts to customers who settle their accounts promptly.

6.8 (a) What is the purpose of sending out monthly statements to debtors?

(b) What do such statements actually represent?

(c) Why should the debtors' accounts be surveyed and analysed at regular intervals?

6.9 What is the purpose of a provision for doubtful debts, and how does it comply with the principle of matching revenue and expenses and the concept of the accounting period?

6.10 (a) If you were employed by a wholesale merchant and you were instructed to 'age the debtors' accounts', how would you proceed to do so?

(b) Why would this task be much easier if the customers' accounts were kept on a computerised system?

Exercises

6.11 Your control account in the general ledger shows a balance of £1756, and your schedule of debtors' balances taken from debtors' ledger cards totals £1842. On investigation you find that A.B. Smith's card balance of £14 was omitted from the list by mistake and that the sales journal was under-added £100.

(a) How do you correct these errors?

(b) How do matters stand after corrections are made?

6.12 You are accountant to a firm and wish, by drawing up a control account, to discover the total debtors at the end of the month of June. Prepare the account from the information given below.

(a)	Debtors, at 1 June	£9 746
(b)	The total of the sales day book	13 946
(c)	The total of the sales return book	348
(d)	The total of the cash received from debtors	13 301
(e)	The total of the discount allowed to debtors	297
(f)	Cheques dishonoured – charged back to debtors total	617
(g)	The journal shows you have charged to overdue debtors interest of	5

6.13 From what source has each of the following account items (including balances) been obtained?

Debtors' Control Account

June 1	Balance	£8 730	June 30	Cash	£4 300
June 30	Sales	9 416		Discount allowed	630
	Cash (retd chqs)	137		Sales returns	920
				Prov. doubtful debts	180
				Balance	12 253
		£18 283			£18 283
July 1	Balance	£12 253			

6.14 On 30 June, the general ledger of C. Wood included the following balances:

Debtors' control account	*Dr.*	£3 450
Provision for doubtful debts	*Cr.*	115

An examination of the debtors' ledger revealed the following information:

(a) The accounts of two debtors K. Cook £33 and J. Hood £22 have been outstanding for over twelve months and it is now decided to write these amounts off as bad debts. Both had been considered as doubtful at the beginning of the period.

(b) N. Doon, who had been a debtor for £40 at the beginning of the period and had been considered to be doubtful at that stage, had been declared bankrupt during the year and had paid a first and final dividend of $62\frac{1}{2}$ per cent.

(c) The following debts have been outstanding for some time and it is decided to raise the provision for doubtful debts to £180 to cover these debtors:

J. Lord	£45
M. Dean	82
L. Rowe	31
R. Park	22

These are the only debts considered to be doubtful at this date.

You are required:

(a) to frame journal entries to incorporate the above decisions;

(b) to show the ledger accounts in both the general and debtors' ledgers that would be affected by the above adjustments.

6.15 You are given the following information with respect to the books of S. Sydney:

(a) As at 1 November:

Debtors control account		*Dr.*	£1 850
Schedule of debtors' balances			
A. Allen	*Dr.*	£210	
G. Goss	*Dr.*	180	
K. Keen	*Dr.*	420	
L. Leslie	*Dr.*	370	
M. May	*Dr.*	280	
P. Potts	*Dr.*	380	
R. Rowe	*Dr.*	40	
		£1 880	
J. James	*Cr.*	30	£1 850

(b) For the month of November:

Sales Day Book

Nov. 2	L. Leslie	£40
Nov. 5	G. Goss	120
Nov. 8	W. Watson	30
Nov. 11	J. James	180
Nov. 17	Y. Young	50
Nov. 24	G. Goss	200
Nov. 26	P. Potts	130
Nov. 30	A. Allen	170
		£920

Sales Returns Book

Nov. 4	P. Potts	£30
Nov. 11	L. Leslie	10
Nov. 25	Y. Young	20
		£60

Cash Book (Receipts Side)

		Discounts	Amount received from debtors
Nov. 2	G. Goss	£5	£175
	M. May	2	88
Nov. 4	A. Allen	6	204
Nov. 5	K. Keen		100
Nov. 11	P. Potts	5	195
		£18	£762

General Journal (Extracts)

Nov. 18	Bills receivable	£150	
	J. James (debtor)		£150
	Bills receivable due 21 February		
Nov. 30	Provision for doubtful debts	40	
	R. Rowe (debtor)		40
	Irrecoverable debts written off		

You are required to show:

(a) the debtors' ledger and a schedule of debtors' balances as at 30 November;

(b) the debtors' control account in the general ledger.

6.16 X Co. recognises revenue at the time it delivers its products to its customers. Bad debts average 1 per cent of its gross sales. The following information is available for the month of June:

(a) Balances as at 1 June –

Debtors	£950 000
Provision for doubtful debts	£25 000

(b) Gross sales £500 000.

(c) Collections from customers £510 000.

(d) Bad debts specifically written off £8000.

You are required to:

(a) calculate the amount of 'doubtful debts' to be shown on the profit and loss statement for the month of June;

(b) show how the debtors account should be reported in the balance sheet as at 30 June.

6.17 A firm prepares a monthly profit and loss statement for management. This is achieved 'outside' the ledger by using the monthly trial balance data and other information. Transfers of revenue and expense account balances within the ledger are made only at 30 June (the end of the firm's financial year). At this time a major review of the adequacy of the provision for doubtful debts takes place and any adjustment deemed necessary is made.

The following information is available:

(a) Each month 2 per cent of credit sales is provided for doubtful debts.

(b)

	At 1 May	At 1 June
Debtors	£170 000	£176 892
Provision for doubtful debts	8 000	8 280
Doubtful debts	16 100	17 888

(c)

	During May	During June
Credit sales	£89 400	£90 100
Cash, discounts and allowances	81 000	87 248
Bad debts written off (no separate account used)	1 508	2 100

(d) The review of debtors at 30 June indicated that a further bad debt of £180 should be written off and that an additional sum of £800 should be added to the provision for doubtful debts.

Required are:

(a) journal entries (May and June) for:
  (i) monthly provision for doubtful debts;
  (ii) monthly write-off of bad debts;
  (iii) end-of-year additional adjustments resulting from (d) above;
  (iv) annual transfer of balances relating to debtors within the ledger.

(b) State the amount of the debit which would appear in the monthly profit and loss statement for both May and June for doubtful debts.

(c) State the balance sheet figure for debtors at 30 June.

(d) Show the following ledger accounts as they would incorporate the above entries for May and June:
  Debtors
  Provision for doubtful debts
  Doubtful debts

6.18 N. Black receives cash from three main sources, from debtors, from cash sales and from rent collections. You are asked to write up his columnar cash book (receipts side) from the following information:

(a) Receipt book duplicates

Date	No.	Name	Cash	Discount	Total
April 7	056	[1] T. Tree	£91.05	£7.05	£98.10
April 7	7	Rent	64.00		64.00
April 7	8	[1] B. Jones	178.33	6.67	185.00
April 8	9	Commission	5.00		5.00
April 8	60	[1] M. Gray	42.00		42.00
April 10	1	Rent	16.00		16.00
April 11	2	[1] D. Fend	8.32	0.68	9.00

[1] Debtors

(b) Cash register tapes

April 7	£168.32
April 8	141.91
April 9	110.19
April 10	80.68
April 11	384.34

(c) Other amounts received direct by bank on Black's behalf

April 8	Interest on mortgage	£16.00
April 10	R. Green (for rent)	24.00

Problems

6.19 N. Rockwell conducts a wholesale business. He keeps the usual accounting records and in particular uses a separate ledger for debtors (with a control account in the general ledger). He banks daily and makes all payments (other than for petty expenses) by cheque. At 30 June his balance sheet was as under:

N. Rockell
Balance Sheet as at 30 June

Creditors	£1 500	Cash at bank		£900
N. Rockwell - Capital	26 500	Petty cash advance		40
		Stock		3 200
		Debtors	£2 860	
		– Prov. for doubtful debts	60	2 800
		Land and buildings		12 000
		Plant and equipment		4 500
		Motor vehicles		3 260
		Office furniture and equipment		1 300
	£28 000			£28 000

Debtors at 30 June:

F. Ford	£200
G. Hanson	210
E. Kelly	40
Lakeside Ltd	2 200
D. Pool	110
R. River	100
	£2 860

Creditors were:

Suppliers Ltd	£1 250
P. Proud	250
	£1 500

During July the following transactions occurred:

July 1	Paid Suppliers Ltd – Cheque	£682.50	
	Discount	17.50	
			£700
	Sold goods for cash		120
July 5	Received from Lakeside Ltd – Cheque	£975.00	
	Discount	25.00	
			1000
	Sold goods for cash		22
July 6	Received cash for commission		40
	Received from F. Ford – Cheque	£195.00	
	Discount	5.00	
			200
July 8	Purchased goods on credit from Suppliers Ltd		350
	Paid Wages		60
July 11	Sold goods for cash		30
	Received from G. Hanson – Cheque	£205.00	
	– Discount	5.00	
			210
July 12	Paid for carriage on sales		15
July 14	Sold goods for cash		10
	Sold goods on credit to Lakeside Ltd		220
	Sold goods on credit to F. Ford		80
July 15	Paid office expenses		12
July 18	Purchased goods on credit from P. Proud		400
July 19	Purchased goods for cash		50
July 21	Sold goods on credit to F. Ford		100
	Sold goods on credit to G. Hanson		70
	Received from D. Pool – a bill of exchange dated 19 July at six months (bill includes interest £5)		115

July 22	Paid wages		£60
July 25	Purchased new plant on credit from Machines Ltd		500
	Sold old plant on credit to R. Rivers (at book value)		50
July 26	Gave a bill of exchange to Machines Ltd at two months		500
July 27	Cash sales		52
	Received cash from B. Masters for debt previously written off		30
	Drew cheque for cash sales returned		12
	Received from R. Rivers – Cheque	£97.50	
	Discount	2.50	
			100
July 29	Paid P. Proud – Cheque	£242.50	
	– Discount	7.50	
			250
	Drew cheque for personal use		100
July 31	Reimbursed petty cashier for:		
	Travelling expenses	£8.50	
	Advertising	5.00	
	Stamps and stationery	12.00	
	Cash sale returns	13.50	
			39
	Wrote off E. Kelly's debt as bad		40
	Made entries for items appearing on the bank statement:		
	Bank charges		4.00
	R. Rivers (cheque dishonoured)		97.50

You are required to:

(a) enter the transactions for the month into the appropriate books;

(b) enter the opening balances into the ledgers;

(c) post all day books and cash books to the ledger accounts;

(d) write off 1 per cent of credit sales to doubtful debts provisions;

(e) prepare a trial balance as at 31 July;

(f) prepare a schedule of balances from the debtors' ledger.

Notes:
1. The only ledger accounts you need formally rule off and balance are those for the debtors and creditors.
2. Folio cross references are *not* required.

6.20 The following relate to the business of R. A. Cross:

(a) Cash book (receipts side)

Date	Particulars	Discount allowed	Received from Debtors	Sundries	Bank
March 2	Commission			£80.00	£80.00
March 4	Sales			164.45	
	H. Bell	£1.26	£65.74		230.19
March 12	Bills receivable			24.00	24.00
March 14	Sales			21.00	
	B. Cann	3.30	128.70		149.70
March 18	Commission			109.77	109.77
March 21	M. Dent	2.43	95.07		95.07
	Bills receivable			99.00	99.00
March 26	Sales			100.00	100.00
March 31	S. Elvin	3.86	150.14		150.14
		£10.85	£439.65	£598.22	1037.87

(b) Sales day book

Date	Particulars	Amount
March 3	S. Elvin	£145.05
March 10	H. Bell	88.32
March 13	F. Frank	53.73
March 19	M. Dent	78.96
March 20	B. Cann	125.28
		£491.34

(c) Assets at beginning of March (there were no liabilities)

Cash at bank		£10 000.00
Debtors	H. Bell	67.00
	B. Cann	132.10
	M. Dent	97.50
	S. Elvin	154.00

(d) Payments made during March totalled £1034.00, made up of:

Cash purchases	£800.00
Wages	200.00
Sundry expenses	34.00

You are required to: (a) open ledger accounts in a debtors ledger with the balances from (c) above; (b) open a general ledger (including a control account) at 1 March; (c) assuming there were no transactions during March other than those listed above, enter the items in (a) (b) (c) (d) (e) in appropriate accounts in the general ledger and in the debtors ledger; balance the accounts and prepare a trial balance for the general ledger at 31 March, and a schedule of debtors' balances to be agreed with the control account in the general ledger.

Note: Journal entries are *not* required.

Chapter 7
Purchases and cash payments

The expenditure cycle ☐ Control over purchases ☐ Recording of purchases ☐
Control over creditors ☐ Control and recording of cash payments ☐ Discount
received ☐ Creditors control accounts ☐ Petty cash payments ☐ Bank accounts
and bank reconciliation

The expenditure cycle

This chapter and Chapter 9 deal with what is variously termed the acquisition cycle, the expenditure cycle or the purchases cycle.

First, we will examine the differences in meaning between the four terms 'costs', 'expenditures', 'expenses' and 'payments' and we will also examine the inter-relationships between these terms. All are generally associated with the acquisition of goods or services.

Normally goods or services can be acquired only by the purchasing firm giving up or agreeing to give up some of its resources. This giving up of resources is often termed 'expenditure'. The measurement of the account of resources given up is generally referred to as the 'cost' of the goods or services acquired.

Expenditure transactions, like all other accounting transactions, can be analysed in terms of their double-entry effect. The 'credit' effect of an expenditure transaction falls into one of the following three categories:

1. A decrease in cash or bank balances where the goods or services are paid for when they are acquired.

2. The creation or the increase of a liability where payment is to be made at some future date.

3. The decrease of an asset where goods are exchanged for other goods or services; for example, the trading-in of old vehicles and equipment.

The 'debit' effect of an expenditure transaction takes one of two forms:

1. The incurring of an expense where the benefits from the goods or services acquired are all likely to be enjoyed during the accounting period in which the expenditure has occurred.

2. The creation or increase of assets where the benefits from the goods or services acquired are likely to be enjoyed in future accounting periods instead of, or as well as, the period in which they are acquired.

The relationships which may exist between 'expenditures' and 'expenses' may be summarised as follows (assuming an accounting period in one year):

1. Expenditures which are expenses within the same year in which the acquisition of goods or services takes place. This is the case where the goods or services are totally consumed within the accounting period.

2. Expenditures made prior to this year which become expenses, either totally or partially,

during this year. Items which fall in this category include the sale or use of stock held at the beginning of the period, the depreciation of fixed assets and the consumption of prepaid expenses, such as insurance.

3. Expenditures made during this year which do not become expenses *until some future year of years*. This category includes not only the acquisition of stock and depreciable fixed assets, but also costs (product costs) associated with the manufacture of goods which have not yet been completed or not yet sold.

4. Expenditures made during this year which will not or may not ever become expenses. Here we include the acquisition of land which is normally not depreciable, the acquisition of investments and the payment of drawings or dividends to the owners of an enterprise.

In this chapter, we will discuss the controls and accounting techniques necessary to deal with the acquisition of goods for resale (that is, purchases in a narrow sense) and later extend and in Chapter 9 modify these to cover all the types of expenditure discussed above.

Control over purchases

Most business firms purchase goods and pay for them later. An order is forwarded to the supplier and duplicates of the order may be sent to the accounting section (for comparison with the supplier's invoice when it arrives) and to the receiving section (for the purpose of admitting and checking the goods as they arrive).

Many firms find it convenient and desirable to have a separate receiving section through which all incoming goods must pass. In that case, the officer in charge of this section raises a 'goods inwards' report or advice. A copy is forwarded to the accounting department.

An adequate system of internal control over purchases will ensure:

1. that, where possible, buying is restricted to one separate department or person, and all incoming goods pass through one point of entry;

2. that adequate records of the goods ordered are kept so that incoming goods can be properly checked;

3. that goods are purchased in the proper quantities from the suppliers at the best price available.

The usual sequence in purchasing goods is as follows:

1. The manager of the department requiring the goods writes out a standard requisition form with full details. This is sent to the purchasing department for approval. (Sometimes a member of the department – 'the buyer' – has full authority to make certain purchases.)

2. If approved, a standard prenumbered order form is completed. Details of suppliers, prices, etc. are kept filed in the purchasing department. No goods will be acknowledged unless on the firm's official order form, and all numbered forms must be accounted for regularly. Copies of the order are sent to the supplier, the accounting department and the receiving department. One copy should be retained.

3. All goods delivered must pass through the receiving department where they can be checked against the copy of the order and a goods received slip will be raised. A copy of this is sent to the accounting section and to the purchasing department after the goods have been passed. In some enterprises, there is a separate inspection section which examines the goods more carefully before issuing a satisfactory inspection report.

4. When the invoice is received from the supplier, it is checked against the purchase order and

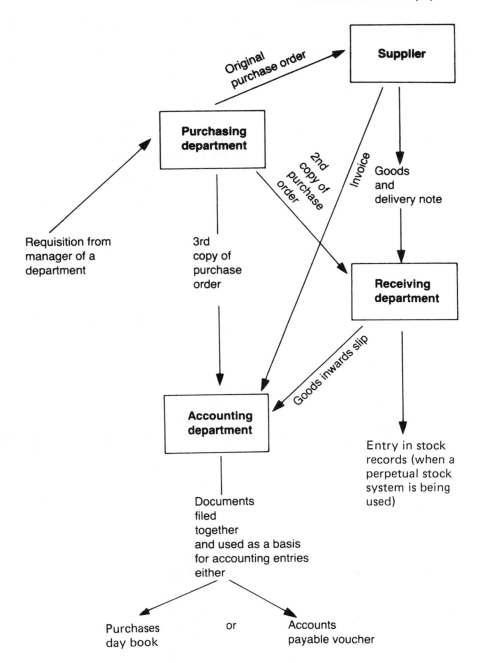

Fig. 7.1 Purchasing stock - documents and control.

goods received slip. Prices, extensions, additions, etc. are also carefully checked and initialled by those responsible.

5. Invoices are then carefully filed. They form the basis for entry into the accounting records. If a purchases day book is used, they will be summarised and entered as shown below.

The flow of documents and information as outlined in the above system of controls is illustrated in Fig. 7.1. Where goods are to be returned or an adjustment to the supplier's invoice is necessary, an advice slip (claim on supplier or debit note) should be prepared. One copy will be sent to the supplier and one will be retained as a check against the credit note when received.

Recording of purchases

As indicated previously, in a manual system, a purchases day book may be used to collect and summarise data related to the purchase of goods on credit. If the volume of transactions is sufficient to warrant it, a purchases returns day book may be also used. If it is desired to analyse purchases into departments or types of merchandise or some other basis, these day books may be of the columnar type.

The format of such day books usually follows that given in the previous chapter to record credit sales and returns and allowances on those sales. For example, a columnar purchases journal can take the form shown below:

Purchases Day Book						Page.	
Date		Supplier	Ledger Folio	Total	Dept A	Dept B	Dept C
				£ 1. 2.	£ 3.	£ 3.	£ 3.

Notes

1. Individual entries in the total column are posted to the credit of suppliers' accounts in the creditors ledger.
2. The total of the total credit column is posted to the credit of the control account in the general ledger.
3. The totals of the analysed purchases columns are posted to the debit of (a) departmental purchases accounts, if a periodic system of stock is in use; or (b) departmental stock accounts, if a perpetual system of stock is in use.

Control over creditors

The following points are relevant to the consideration of controls which should be instituted for accounts payable:

1. The main aspect of control over creditors is that settlement should be made to the correct creditor, for the correct amount, and within the time limits stipulated, in order to take advantage of discounts and maintain trade reputation.

2. To achieve this, a well-defined system of preparation, certification and authorisation of the documents connected with the transaction should be instituted and observed.

3. Clerical staff recording creditors' transactions should not have any connection with the actual payment procedures.

4. As with debtors, it is desirable to institute loose leaves or cards as subsidiary ledgers.

Discount received

It is the practice in certain businesses to encourage customers to pay promptly by allowing them a discount on the sum due if they pay within a defined time limit. This discount is referred to as a cash discount since it is calculated as a percentage of the amount of the debt. The creditor will treat this deduction from the sum due as discount received and will record it in a separate column on the payments side of the cash book. The creditor's account will be debited with the amount of discount received. The total of the discount received column in the cash book is posted to the credit of discount received account in the general ledger.

Example: W. Gray owes T. White £200 and settled this debt by paying a cheque for the amount due less 5 per cent discount.

Cash Book (Payments side)

	Discount received	Amount Paid to Creditors
T. White	£10	£190

T. White

Cash	£190	Balance	£200
Discount	10		
	£200		£200

Discount Received

Profit and loss	£10	Total from cash book	£10

Profit and Loss

		Discount received	£10

Like the cash book (receipts side), this book may be either simple or complex, depending on the amount of analysis that is desired to be carried out. A simple ruling for cash book (payments side) which includes a column for discount received is shown below.

Cash Book (Payments Side)					Page. . . . .
Date	Cheque No.	Particulars	Ledger folio	Discount received	Amount
				£	£

In the case of cheque payments the link with the bank statement is with each cheque drawn. An entry is made in the bank column of the cash book (payments side) for each cheque drawn, whereas in the cash book (receipts side), the governing factor for the entry is the total amount deposited.

If a creditors' control account and subsidiary ledger was being used for creditors, and if more classification was desired with cheque payments, then a columnar cash book (payments side) might be used as shown below. (The choice of columns, of course, would depend upon the type of payments which occur frequently enough to warrant the use of a separate column.)

Cash Book (Payments Side)								Page. . . . .
Date	Cheque No.	Particulars	Ledger Folio	Discount Received (1)	Amounts Paid to Creditors (2)	Salaries (3)	Office Expenses (4)	Other Payments (5)

Here is a summary of the posting of the above columnar cash book.

1. Total of discount received column is posted to the credit of discount received account and to the debit of the creditors' control account in the general ledger.

2. Total of amounts paid to creditors is posted to the creditors' control account. The individual amounts of discount received and amounts paid to individual creditors would be posted to the debit of the individual creditors' accounts in the creditors' ledger.

3. and 4. Totals of salaries and office expenses columns are posted to the debit sides of the respective expense accounts.

5. The total of this column is not posted to any one account. However, the individual items are posted to the debit of the various accounts involved. Where there are a number of entries in this column, it is usual to append a summary of such entries under the ruled-off total in order to facilitate their posting. (Remember that there may be several entries concerning the same account in this column, but this is still insufficient to probably justify a separate column.)

Control and recording of cash payments

In Chapter 6, we discussed the importance of adequate controls over cash transactions and cash funds, outlined essential features of control over cash, and dealt specifically with the control and recording of cash receipts.

The main concern with cash payments is that all payments should be identified with cheques drawn on the bank, after adequate steps have been taken to ensure that the payment is authorised, regular and correct. This does not mean that each individual sum has to be paid by cheque. In most businesses, there are payments which are too small to warrant the writing of a cheque, or circumstances which demand payment in cash. This necessitates the use of a petty cash fund. If this fund is kept on the imprest system, a number of petty cash payments may be covered by one cheque drawn at the end of the period during which those payments were made. However, the general rule of control is to pay by cheque whenever possible.

The original evidence record which is retained within the business is, in a simple system of payments, on the cheque stub or counterfoil. Other systems demand the preparation of a standard disbursement slip for each payment. The information contained on the stub or disbursement slip is then transferred to the cash book (payments side).

Creditors control accounts

It may appear from working through accounting problems in a theoretical context that any form of control over the accuracy of the posting of accounting entries is not of great importance, since it is quite a simple matter to check through the postings if an error is revealed in the trial balance and discover the difference. In practice, the discovery of posting errors may take a considerable time if the number of postings is numerous. In some businesses there are over ten thousand accounts in the creditors ledger alone, with perhaps an average of twenty entries in each account. If errors occur in an accounting system of that size then obviously it can take a long time to find and rectify them without the aid of some control system. It is primarily for this reason that some system has to be introduced to assist in the locating of errors. The technique generally adopted to surmount this problem is to introduce control accounts for both debtors and creditors ledgers. It must be appreciated that such a system of control accounts is introduced only to assist in the detection of arithmetical errors in the double entry system of accounting; it will not reveal compensating errors, errors in books of original entry, and postings to wrong accounts which have taken place in the recording of the transactions. This system can be used both for manual and machine accounting systems.

There are advantages of incorporating a system of control accounts within an accounting system. Some of the advantages are listed below.

1. A simple yet effective control can be kept on the arithmetical accuracy of the postings from the books of original entry to the creditors' ledger.

2. It is invaluable under a system of electronic recording of creditors' accounts.

3. It may serve as a check on the honesty of the accounting staff if used as part of an internal check system.

4. Total balances for creditors can be quickly ascertained with reference to the control account in the general ledger. This is useful in the preparation of monthly or quarterly financial statements, pending the extraction of complete lists of creditors.

The following is a typical creditors' control account:

Creditors' Control Account

Purchases returns[4]	£500	Balances b/d[1]	£5 300
Cash[5]	23 800	Purchases[2]	25 100
Discount[6]	320	Cash (refunds)[3]	200
Balances c/d[7]	5 980		
	£30 600		£30 600
		Balances b/d	5 980

Notes
1. The total of opening balances represent the list of individual balances extracted from the purchases ledger.
2. The total of purchases will be transferred from the purchases day book.
3. This amount represents any cash refunds received from suppliers and will be recorded in the receipts side of the cash book.
4. This amount will be obtained from the purchase returns book which is based on the credit notes from suppliers.
5. The amount of cash will be the amount shown in the amount paid to creditors in the cash book (payments side).
6. This is the amount of discount received from creditors and will be transferred from the discount received column in the cash book.
7. The balance of creditors in the control account must agree with the list of individual balances in the creditors' ledger.

A schematic plan of how a creditors' control account is prepared is shown in Fig. 7.2.

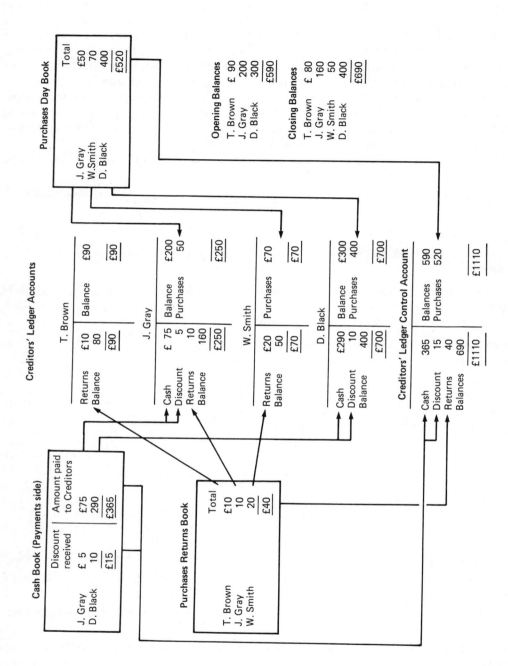

Fig. 7.2   Schematic plan of a creditors' control account

Petty cash payments

The most efficient method of operating a petty cash fund is called the 'imprest system'. Under this scheme, there is an initial amount drawn to establish the fund. At intervals, on production of adequate supporting evidence, the amount paid out is reimbursed by a further cheque drawn for the amount spent which would bring the imprest back to that initially held. For example, petty cash fund is £400, amount of expenses, etc., paid is £240, leaving £160 in the fund, with which the reimbursement of the £240 restores the original £400. As a further check, it should be noted that the amount of cash held at any time, together with the evidence of payments (vouchers), should always total £400 – the amount of the original imprest.

The size of the fund depends upon the type of business and the frequency of the demands made upon it. A fund which on the average needs to be reimbursed about once a fortnight is deemed to be satisfactory by many businesses. As a guard against fraudulent use of the fund, and against the fund being drained by large withdrawals, many firms place a maximum limit on any single withdrawal from it. Such limit may vary from £10 in a small enterprise up to £500 or more in a large business. Amounts in excess of the maximum must be paid by cheque in the normal way.

A standard petty cash voucher signed by the recipient and authorised by a senior officer should be adopted for all payments. Supporting evidence, if available, should be attached.

The fund is usually under the exclusive charge of a junior clerk who is responsible for its safety. No one else is permitted to handle the money except for the officer whose duty it is to check the fund. The accounting for the imprest system is as follows:

1 To establish the fund

A cheque is drawn and cashed. The amount is debited to the petty cash book.

2 To increase or decrease the amount of the imprest

If the amount proves insufficient and has to be reimbursed too often then a further cheque (say £200) is drawn, and the amount posted to the petty cash book.

To *reduce* the imprest amount, the petty cashier banks (or hands to the cashier for banking) the amount regarded as superfluous. The posting is made to the credit of the petty cash advance account.

3 To record and analyse the petty cash payments

The original record of each payment out of the fund is made on the voucher. A petty cash book is kept, recording the payments and analysing them into the main types of expense involved. An example of a simple type of petty cash book is shown on page 148.

4 To record the reimbursing cheque in the cash book

The petty cash book, the vouchers supporting the payments, and the balance of cash on hand having been checked, the reimbursing cheque is drawn and cashed. This cheque then forms the basis for an entry in the cash book (payments side).

At the end of an accounting period it is desirable to reimburse the petty cash, thus bringing to account all the petty cash payments for the period. This means that at balance date the petty cash fund is represented entirely by cash in hand. This amount appears as an asset in the balance sheet.

Petty Cash Book

Receipts	Date		Particulars	Voucher No.	Payment	Postage etc.	Travelling expenses	Delivery expenses	Sundry Office expenses
£ 200	April	1	Balance in fund		£	£	£	£	£
		1	Taxi fares - RLB	101	12		12		
		2	Postage - statements	102	35	35			
		2	Courier service	103	21			21	
		2	Stationery	104	18				18
		5	Stamps	105	15	15			
		5	Taxi fares - CMG	106	17		17		
		8	Donation	107	10				10
		8	Tea, Sugar, etc.	108	8				8
		8	Car expenses - JJL	109	19		19		
					£155	50	48	21	36
		8	Balance c/d		45				
£200					£200				
45		8	Balancd b/d						
155		8	Reimbursing cheque						
£200									

The reimbursing cheque is entered in the cash book (payments side), debiting the various expense accounts with the amounts as shown in the totals of the dissection columns of the petty cash book.

Bank accounts and bank reconciliation

We have stressed earlier the importance for control and accounting purposes of channelling all cash transactions through the bank account (or accounts). We now want to examine the use of the bank's records via a statement of account received from the bank.

It must be pointed out that the bank and the bank's customer (the firm for which we are accounting) are looking at the same basic set of transactions from opposite points of view. When deposits are received by the bank, the bank credits the firm's account in its records, whereas the firm, in its records, debits its cash book. Cheques drawn by the firm on the bank account result in a debit entry in the firm's accounts in the bank's records and a credit entry in the cash book.

At regular intervals, the firm should obtain a statement of account from the bank. This is, in effect, a copy of the firm's account in the bank's ledger.

At the time of the receipt of the bank statement, some cheques will not yet have been presented for payment, and if the statement is collected at the same time as a deposit is made, no entry will have been made for that deposit. Furthermore, the bank will collect or pay directly for their customers any amounts, such as rent, insurance premiums, dividends, interest, etc. which occur regularly. For these reasons, it is seldom that the balance in the cash book agrees with the statement of the ledger account prepared by the bank.

The record prepared by the bank can be an excellent control on the record kept by the firm. It follows that the two should be compared regularly, and the balances reconciled by allowing for the above-mentioned items which invariably cause them to differ – a procedure known as the bank reconciliation. The frequency with which it is done will depend on the number of transactions which take place.

The procedure for reconciling the bank statement with the records kept by the business is as follows:

1. Compare the deposits recorded in the *bank column of the cash book* (*receipts side*) with the deposits recorded by the bank in the *credit column of the bank statement*, being careful to tick each item in both records.

2. Compare the cheques drawn and recorded in *the bank column of the cash book* (*payments side*) with those presented to the bank and recorded in the *debit column of the bank statement*, being careful to tick each item in both records.

These first two steps may be termed *comparison* steps.

3. The unticked items in the credit column of the bank statement will represent such items as collections made by the bank on our behalf – dividends or interest from investments, or amounts paid directly to the bank by debtors. These should now be entered in the cash book (receipts side), completing the cash book ready for posting. The items should be ticked in the bank statement and the cash book as they are adjusted.

4. The unticked items in the debit column of the bank statement will represent payments made by the bank on our behalf, such as insurance premiums, payments to finance companies, etc., together with the charges and any interest on overdraft charged by the bank. These should now be entered in the cash book (payments side), completing it ready for posting. The items should be ticked in the bank statement and the cash book as they are adjusted.

One type of item requiring adjustment at this stage comprises cheques received by us from debtors, deposited at the bank for collection, and dishonoured when presented for payment. The bank will make a debit entry on the bank statement to offset the credit entry made when the cheque was deposited. There are two alternative ways of adjusting for these dishonoured cheques:

(a) By an entry in the cash book (payments side) offsetting the original entry in the cash book (receipts side). This is quite satisfactory where there was no discount allowed when the cheque was received. If discount was allowed, a journal entry would be necessary to reverse the discount, as the discount column of the cash book (payments side) represents discount *received*.

(b) By a journal entry. This is probably more appropriate, particularly where discount has been allowed. If a control account (with subsidiary ledger) is being used for debtors then the journal entry gives a clearer indication of the postings to the two ledgers concerned.

The third and fourth steps may be termed *adjustment* steps.

5. After adjustments have been made in the cash records for unticked items in the bank statement, the only causes of difference remaining are the unticked items in the cash book. These are of two types:

(a) The unticked items in the cash book (receipts side) representing deposits made and recorded which have not yet been credited in the bank statement. This may be caused by collecting the bank statement at the same time as the final deposit for the period was made, or by deposits being made at distant branches to the credit of a head office account.

(b) The unticked items in the cash book (payments side) representing cheques drawn, but which have not yet been presented to the bank for payment. These are, of course, quite normal, and occur more frequently than deposits not yet credited.

These two groups of items form the basis of the reconciliation statement which will appear as follows:

Bank Reconciliation Statement
as at. . . . .

Balance as per bank statement (*Cr.* or *Dr.*)		£X
Add or		
Subtract		
Deposits not yet credited		X
		£X
Subtract		
or *Add*		
Unpresented cheques		X
Balance as per cash book (*Dr.* or *Cr.*)		£X

If the account has a credit balance in the bank statement then it follows that 'deposits not yet credited' will be added and 'unpresented chqeues' will be subtracted. If the account is in overdraft (that is, a debit balance on the bank statement) then the reverse procedure will apply.

Notes

1. The process of comparing the respective records is facilitated if use is made of the previous reconciliation statement. Outstanding items on this can be checked to the bank statement at the beginning of the reconciliation process, thus eliminating any need to go through the cash book for entries prior to the current period. It follows of course that if such items still do not appear then they must be repeated in the current reconciliation statement.

    Other techniques to facilitate the reconciliation are possible, such as the numerical filing of cheque copies or vouchers. These are extracted from the file when the presented cheques are received back from the bank; those remaining constitute an unpresented file.

2. When comparing and ticking, care should be taken to see that the amounts for each item are the same. Errors located are almost invariably a mistake in the records of the firm and should be corrected.

    Step 5 may be termed the reconciliation step.

Example of bank reconciliation procedure

This example assumes that reconciliation is carried out weekly, although the number of transactions in this illustration would not warrant it so frequently.

Information available:
(a)

Bank Reconciliation Statement
as at 23 June

Balance as per bank statement (*Cr.*)		£9 833
Add Deposit not yet credited		1 683
		£11 516
Less Unpresented cheques		
Nos. 056	£270	
059	500	770
Balance as per cash book (*Dr.*)		£10 746

(b)

Cash Book (Receipts Side)

Date	Receipt No.	Details	Ledger folio	Discount allowed	Amounts received from debtors	Other receipts	Bank
June 23		Balance	b/d				£10 746
June 25	4721	J.B. Thomas		£3	£128		
	4722	C.W. Carter		6	217		
	CRS	Cash sales				£1 250	1 595
26	4723	J.T. Lamb			324		
	4724	Rent rev. (C. Bull)				500	
	CRS	Cash sales				1 051	1 875
27	CRS	Cash sales				695	695
28	4725	Interest revenue (R. Andrews)				1 000	
	4726	C.L. Black		29	851		
	4727	Loan to X. Ltd. (repayment)				4 000	
	CRS	Cash sales				1 964	7 815
29	4728	C.H. Wilson		24	966		
	4729	J.W. Wells			322		
	CRS	Cash sales				1 493	2 781
30	4730	Sale of office furn.				660	
	CRS	Cash sales				1 163	1 823
		(Pencilled totals)		(62)	(2 808)	(13 776)	(27 330)

Note: A 'bank column' has been included in the cash book. This additional column assists in the checking of the cash book with the bank statement.

(c)

Cash Book (Payments Side)

Date	Cheque No.	Details	Ledger folio	Discount received	Amounts paid to creditors	Other payments	Bank
June 25	063	Purchases				£770	£770
26	064	Salaries				3 424	3 424
	065	Office furn. (G. Bell)				2 510	2 510
27	066	Advertising				575	575
28	067	R. Stuart		48	1 400		1 400
	068	Mills and Co.		25	765		765
	069	G. Glenn		4	161		161
	070	B. Muller			900		900
							Cont.

Cash Book (Payments Side) *Cont.*

Date	Cheque No.	Details	Ledger folio	Discount received	Amounts paid to creditors	Other payments	Bank
June 30	071	Petty cash reimbursement; Delivery expenses				92	
		Travelling expenses				111	
		Postage etc.				73	
		Office expenses				58	334
		(Pencilled totals)		(77)	(3 226)	(7 613)	(10 839)

Note: Again a bank total column is included in the cash book to facilitate the checking of the cash book with the bank statement.

(d) Copy of bank statement collected on 30 June:

Baker and Co. Ltd
In account current with
The XYZ Bank, Suburbia

Date	Particulars		Debit	Credit	Balance
June 23	Balance forward				£9 833 Cr
23	C/C			£1 683	11 516 Cr
25	C/C			1 595	13 111 Cr
26	DIV			300	13 411 Cr
26	C/C			1 875	15 286 Cr
26		064	£3 424		11 862 Cr
26		059	500		11 362 Cr
27	C/C			695	12 057 Cr
27		063	770		11 287 Cr
28	C/C			7 815	19 102 Cr
28	CBK		25		19 077 Cr
28		065	2 510		16 567 Cr
29	FEE		52		16 515 Cr
29	C/C			2 781	19 296 Cr
29		066	575		18 721 Cr
30	ADT - (Dishon. chq - Andrews)		1 000		17 721 Cr
30		068	765		16 956 Cr
30		071	334		16 622 Cr

Procedure for reconciliation of the above:

Preliminary Using the last bank reconciliation statement 23 June, we can tick off in the bank statement the deposit of £1683 on 23 June and the cheque No. 059 for £500 presented on 26 June. Note that cheque No. 056 for £270 unpresented on 23 June, is still unpresented on 30 June, and will appear in the new reconciliation statement.

Step 1 Comparison of the bank column of the cash book (receipts side) with the credit column of the bank statement reveals the following differences:

Unticked in the bank statement –
Dividend of £300 collected by the bank on 26 June.

Unticked in the cash book (receipts side) –
Deposit of £1823 made on 30 June.

Step 2 Comparison of the bank column of the cash book (payments side) with the debit column of the bank statement reveals the following differences:

Unticked in the bank statement –
The bank charges of £25 (cheque book) on 28 June and the fee of £52 on 29 June.
The adjustment for the cheque dishonoured by Andrews (£1000).

Unticked in the cash payments journal –
Unpresented cheques,   Nos 067 £1400
                            069 £161
                            070 £900

Step 3 Adjustments required in the cash book (receipts side).

Date	Receipt No.	Details	Folio	Discount allowed	Amounts received from debtors	Other receipts	Bank
June 30		(Pencilled totals)		£(62)	£(2 808)	£(13 776)	£(27 330)
30	B/S	Dividend				300	300
				£62	£2 808	£14 076	£27 630

Note: Total in bank column is reconciled thus:

Opening balance	£10 746
Total receipts	16 884
	£27 630

Step 4 Adjustments required in cash book (payments side).

Date	Receipt No.	Details	Folio	Discount received	Amounts paid to creditors	Other payments	Bank
June 30		(Pencilled totals)		£(77)	£(3 226)	£(7 613)	£(10 839)
30	B/S	Bank charges				77	77
30	B/S	Interest				1 000	1 000
		(R. Andrews cheque dis- honoured)					
30		Balance	c/d				15 714
				£77	£3 226	£8 690	£27 630

Step 5 The bank reconciliation statement may now be prepared.

**Bank Reconciliation Statement
as at 30 June**

Balance as per bank statement (Cr)		£16 622
Add Deposit not yet credited		1 823
		£18 445
Subtract Unpresented cheques Nos 056	£270	
067	1 400	
069	161	
070	900	2 731
Balance as per cash book (*Dr.*)		£15 714

Summary

1. It is important to make a distinction between expenditures and expenses.

2. Control over purchases generally involves the purchasing department, the receiving department and the accounting department.

3. Control over creditors should aim to ensure that all accounts are paid, for the correct amount, within the time period stipulated in order to take advantage of discounts and maintain trade reputation.

4. A system of making all payments by cheque, linked with an imprest system of petty cash, is recommended for sound control over cash payments.

5. A creditors ledger control account should be prepared to ensure an arithmetical check is maintained on postings.

6. Regular reconciliation of the cash records with the bank statement by an independent officer completes sound control over cash recording. The reconciliation consists of comparison of the two sets of records, adjustment of the cash book and, finally, the preparation of a reconciliation statement.

Discussion questions

7.1 A businessman said 'I can't see much difference between the term 'costs', 'expenses', 'expenditures' and 'payments' – they all represent a decrease in my cash. But my accountant claims that they all have different meanings.' Discuss.

7.2 What are the major objectives of an efficient system of internal control over the purchase of goods for resale?

7.3 Outline the major steps which should be taken to ensure that settlement is made to the correct creditor, for the correct amount and within the time limits stipulated?

7.4 (a) Explain the reasons why, in most businesses, you recommend the practices of banking intact all cash received daily and drawing cheques to cover all cash payments.

(b) Explain the relationship of the imprest system of petty cash to the above rule of making all payments by cheque.

7.5 'A petty cash system should be confined to payments of less than £10.' Do you agree with this statement? Give reasons.

7.6 A delicatessen sells for cash only. Some of its purchases are for cash and some are on monthly credit terms. The proprietor wishes to know separately the sales of foodstuffs, papers and magazines, cigarettes and tobacco.

Her most common monthly payments, apart from cash purchases and payments to creditors, are for wages and rent. She banks daily all cash received and makes all payments by cheque.

(a) Design columnar cash book suitable for her use.

(b) If she kept only a cash book and no other accounting records, what information about her business would be difficult to ascertain?

7.7 Some employers of accounting graduates have complained that the 'graduates are too theoretical and don't even know how to prepare bank reconciliation'. Explain why the process of bank reconciliation is seen to be so important.

7.8 Explain why it is necessary, if bank reconciliation statements are prepared monthly, to use some information from the bank reconciliation statement prepared at the end of the previous month.

Exercises

7.9 The balance of the creditors' control account in the general ledger of A. Brook and Co. at 1 September is £1984.50, the details being as follows:

J. Smith and Co.	£378.71	
A. Brown	459.33	
C. Jones	235.38	
M. Mann	684.17	
Payne and Co.	245.18	£2 002.77
Less Debit – J. Cann and Co.		18.27
		£1 984.50

The following are the transactions relating to the creditors' accounts in September:

Sept.	4 Paid J. Smith and Co.		£150.00
	J. Cann and Co. – Goods		48.38
	A. Gray – Goods		30.55
	Paid A. Brown	£267.08	
	Discount	8.25	275.33
	11 Paid C. Jones	£169.93	
	Discount	5.25	175.18
	C. Jones – Goods		39.33
	A. Brown – Goods		75.48
	18 Goods returned to A. Brown		9.80
	Paid M. Mann		300.00
	M. Mann, Contra for goods purchased by him		89.80

Cont.

Paid Payne and Co.		£164.14	
Discount		5.08	
			£169.22
Payne and Co. – Goods			83.33
Sept. 25	A. Read – Goods		120.15
30	Allowance by A. Gray for soiled goods		3.50
	Trade discount allowed by A. Read		24.03
	(Not previously deducted from invoice)		

Open accounts in creditors ledger with balances at 1 September, and post therein the foregoing transactions. Bring down balances, list and total them. Open and write up a control account and bring down balance to agree.

7.10 Johnson and Co. have adopted the system of separate subsidiary ledgers. The balances in their control accounts at 1 January were as under:

Debtors	£9 826
Creditors	4 735

Total transactions for the year ended 31 December were as under:

Bad debts written off	£800
Discount allowed	1 389
Discount received	1 860
Sales	57 375
Returns inwards	3 260
Purchases	28 542
Returns outwards	1 560
Cash paid to creditors	25 690
Cash received from debtors	41 974
Debtors' cheques dishonoured (included originally in cash received from debtors)	574
Transfers of purchases as part payment for sales (contras)	375
Transfers of sales as part payment for purchases (contras)	566

Show the respective control accounts to record the foregoing and bring down the balances as at 31 December.

7.11 (a) Rule up a petty cash book with columns for travelling expenses, cleaning, purchases, donations, and sundry office expenses and enter the following transactions:

Sept. 1	Received and cashed cheque for £200 to commence fund	
	Bus fares	£4.50
	Cleaning	15.00
	Donation to hospital	10.50
Sept. 2	Tea and sugar	6.20
	Cash purchases	8.20
	Duty stamps	10.00
Sept. 3	Bus fares	2.80
	Typewriter ribbon	7.00
	Taxi	6.00
	Cash purchases	5.50
	Cleaning	15.00
	Milk	4.20

Sept. 5	Donation	5.00
	Bus fares	3.20
	Cash purchases	12.50
	Received reimbursing cheque	

(b) Show the entries in the cash book (payments side) resulting from the above transactions.

7.12 Prepare the petty cash book of C. Lyons for two weeks using column headings for: date, particulars, voucher number, amounts received, amounts paid, carriage, stationery, office cleaning, and sundry expenses.

19X6		
April 6	Balance brought forward from previous week	£17.55
	Received refund cheque No. 1735	32.45
	Paid office cleaning (Voucher 54)	5.00
7	Paid Norman Bros. for carriage (Voucher 55)	3.75
	Paid taxi fares (Voucher 56)	4.10
8	Paid for typing paper (Voucher 57)	1.55
9	Paid for advertisement (Voucher 58)	5.50
	Paid office cleaning (Voucher 59)	5.00
10	Paid for tea, coffee, etc. (Voucher 60)	6.16
10	Balance off the petty cash book for the first week	
13	Received refund cheque No. 1794	
	Paid bus fares (Voucher 61)	1.70
14	Paid for carbon paper and pencils (Voucher 62)	2.85
15	Paid for office cleaning (Voucher 63)	5.00
	Paid Pye & Co. for carriage (Voucher 64)	8.80
16	Paid for dry cleaning (Voucher 65)	2.50
17	Paid for telephone calls (Voucher 66)	3.30
	Paid G. Hill for carriage (Voucher 67)	5.17
17	Balance off the petty cash book for the second week	
20	Received refund cheque No. 1881.	

7.13 On 1 June, in the books of T.V. Western, the cash book showed a debit balance of £369.62. The totals of his cash book for June (not yet posted) were:

| Cash receipts | £1 291.95 |
| Cash payments | 1 163.54 |

that is, the apparent debit balance as at 30 June was £498.03.

However, his bank statement revealed a credit balance of £532.59. Comparison between the two sets of records revealed the following causes of difference:

(a) New cheque book charged to account			£2.00
(b) Interest on interest-bearing deposit, credited in bank statement			31.08
(c) Half-yearly bank charge			2.00
(d) Lodgment not yet entered in bank statement			72.92
(e) P. Mason's cheque has been returned by the paying bank marked 'insufficient funds'			142.55
(no entry has yet been made in Western's records)			
(f) Cheques drawn but not yet presented.	No. 156	£67.08	
	164	73.27	
	167	82.60	222.95

You are required to:

(a) make the necessary entries in the cash book to record transactions not previously recorded and balance the cash book.

(b) prepare a bank reconciliation statement as at 30 June.

7.14 At 1 October, the cash book of J. Winks showed a debit balance of £175.43. The cash book totals for October before adjustments were:

Cash receipts	£1 083.86
Cash payments	1 403.52

The bank statement as at 31 October showed a credit balance of £82.64. Comparison revealed the following differences:

(a) unpresented cheques totalling £184.77;

(b) deposit of £47.10 paid direct to bank by a debtor and not recorded in Winks' books;

(c) bank charges £5.00.

You are required to:

(a) adjust the books of Winks and show the closing balance in his cash book;

(b) prepare a bank reconciliation statement as at 31 October.

Problems

7.15 The following information is available to you:

(a) Cash book of G. Goss:

Cash Book

July 1	Balance	£802

(b) Transactions in cash book of G. Goss:

Cash Book (Receipts Side)

Date	Particulars	Details	Bank
July 3	H. Hill	£33	
	Cash sales	45	£78
July 8	J. Jones	52	52
July 19	Q. Queen	201	201
July 31	K. King	85	85

Cash Book (Payments Side)

Date	Particulars	Cheque No.	Details	Bank
July 3	L. Lamb	101		£63
July 5	Carriage	102		15
July 9	M. Moss	103		77
July 17	Advertising	104		25
July 27	Cash purchases	105		100
July 30	N. Norton	106		33

(c) Bank statement

G. Goss
in the account with
The Bank of XYZ

		Dr.	Cr.
July 1	Balance b/f		£802
July 3	Deposit		78
July 7	Cheque 102	£15	
July 8	Deposit		52
July 9	Cheque 101	63	
July 12	Cheque 103	77	
July 19	Deposit		201
July 24	Interest collected		50
July 27	Cheque 105	100	
July 30	Deposit (O. Oliver)		33
July 31	Bank charges	4	
	Cheque book	2	
	Balance c/d	955	
		£1 216	£1 216
	Balance b/d		£955

You are required to:

(a) compare the above records;

(b) complete the cash book;

(c) prepare a reconciliation statement as at 31 July.

7.16 The balances in the accounts in the general ledger of J. Deakin and Co., General Merchants, at 1 May, were as follows:

Sales	£34 250
Rent received	385
Purchases	24 300
Delivery expenses	760
Salaries	2 450
Postage and stationery	140
Sundry administrative expenses	220
Discount allowed	510

Discount received	£320
Interest and bank charges	345
Petty cash balance (as recorded in petty cash book)	20
Debtors	4 330
Stock (1 July)	8 450
Loan to G. Brown	250
Delivery vehicles	5 200
Office equipment	890
Freehold property	12 000
Bank overdraft	3 820
Creditors	1 840
J. Deakin – Capital	20 000
J. Deakin – Drawings	750

Note: In this exercise assume that the above accounts are the *only ones used* – no new ledger accounts are to be opened.

The following information is available for the month of May:

(a) Sales day book total   £3 650

(b) Purchases day book total   £2 280

(c) Totals of the columnar cash book (receipts side)

Discount allowed	Amounts received from debtors	Cash sales	Rent received	Sundry receipts	Bank
£48	£2 830	£880	£40	[1] £100	£3 850

[1] The £100 sundry receipts consisted entirely of part-repayment of the loan by G. Brown.

(d) The cash book (payments side) has not yet been written up but cheques drawn were as follows:

Cheque No.	Date			
023	May 2	Regal Garage – Petrol and oil for delivery vehicles		£13
024	May 3	Wells Ltd – Cash purchases		80
025	May 4	Salaries		62
026	May 8	Office Supplies – New typewriter		70
027	May 10	Regal Garage – Repairs to delivery vehicles		35
028	May 11	Salaries	£64	
		Drawings	40	
			——	104
029	May 11	Petty cash reimbursed –		
		Postage	6	
		Freight on goods sold	4	
		Sundry expenses	5	
			—	15
030	May 14	M. Reed – Refund on cash sales		15
031	May 16	Vulcan Tyre Co. – New tyres for delivery vehicles		33
032	May 16	Wells Ltd – Cash purchases		65
033	May 18	Salaries		64

Cont.

Cheque No.	Date			
034	May 23	Regal Garage – Petrol and oil		16
035	May 25	Salaries	65	
		Drawings	45	
			—	110
036	May 28	L. Thomson (£400 less £10 discount)		390
037	May 28	B. Wiseman (£360 less £9 discount)		351
038	May 28	K. Laidlaw (£160 less £4 discount)		156
039	May 28	F. McMahon (£480 less £12 discount)		468
040	May 30	Metropolitan Services – Office cleaning		8

(The cheques drawn on the 28th were the only payments for the month relating to creditors.)

(e) The bank statement as at 31 May revealed:

> (i) a debit balance of £1628,
> (ii) a fee of £1, cheque book £3, and interest on overdraft of £12 had been debited against the account;
> (iii) a deposit of £135 lodged on 31 May had not been credited;
> (iv) cheques numbered 031, 037, 038 and 040 had not been presented for payment

You are required to:

(a) design a suitable columnar cash book and to enter therein the relevant entries for the month of May;

(b) show the accounts in the *general* ledger incorporating the postings from all books for May (individual debtors' and creditors' accounts are not required);

(c) prepare a trial balance as at 31 May (ledger accounts need not be properly balanced off);

(d) prepare a bank reconciliation statement as at 31 May.

7.17 When the Western Hardware Stores reopened for business after their annual balance on 30 June the general ledger contained the following six accounts:

No.	Account	Balance
1	Stock	£3 630
2	Fittings account	1 720
3	Capital account	6 371
4	Bank account – Overdrawn	300
5	Debtors	1 916
6	Creditors	595

You are required:

(a) to open up the general ledger with the above six ledger accounts with their balances at 1 July;

(b) to complete ledger entries for the totals of the July transactions as set out below, adding extra accounts where necessary;

(c) to balance off the accounts and prepare a general ledger trial balance as at 31 July.

Summary of July transactions:

Cash transactions:

(*Note*: All receipts banked and all payments by cheque. Use No. 4 Account.)

Receipts: Total money received and banked, £1860. This was made up of cash sales £660 and cash from debtors £1200.

Payments: Total cheques paid out, £1400. This was made up of cash purchases £640, drawings £110, general expenses £320, payments to creditors £310, and fittings bought £20.

Cash discounts: Allowed to debtors £11, received from creditors £8.

Credit transactions:

Sales day book total £495. Purchases day book total £424.

General journal entries:

(a) Stock taken for private use at cost price £16.

(b) Contra accounts – debit balances in debtors' ledger transferred to the creditors' ledger £33.

7.18 The following is an outline of the recording system used by John Wells and Co. Ltd:

Day Books
Sales
Sales returns
Purchases
Purchases returns

Cash Book
Cash receipts (with columns for discount allowed, amounts received from debtors, cash sales, other sources and bank)
Cash payments (with columns for discount received, amounts paid to creditors, store wages, office salaries, delivery expenses, other payments and bank)
General journal

Ledgers
Debtors ledger
Creditors ledger
General ledger (including a control account for each of the subsidiary ledgers)

As accountant to the company you encounter the following items to be recorded:

Item 1 – An invoice is received from General Supplies Ltd. The total of £190 comprises £115 for goods for resale and £75 for a new typewriter to be used in the office.

Item 2 – The banking for a particular day consists of £211 from cash sales and a cheque for £97 from G. Grimm and Sons. The cheque is in full payment of Grimm's account of £100.

Item 3 – A cheque for £26 is drawn to reimburse the petty cash. The totals of the petty cash book reveal that the £26 comprised: delivery expenses £7, travelling expenses £6, postage and stationery £9, and sundry office expenses £4.

Item 4 – Three outstanding debtors' accounts (K. Bilson £15, D. Darke £6, and J. Waters £24) have been investigated. Darke's account represents a claim for goods returned. It is decided to allow this claim and to write the other two amounts off as irrecoverable.

Item 5 – The payroll for a particular week is as follows:

	Gross Pay	Tax Deductions	Net Pay
Store wages	£316	£35	£281
Office salaries	205	24	181
Cheque drawn for			£462

The amount owing to the Inland Revenue is not yet due for payment but the liability is to be recorded in a general ledger account.

Show, for each of the above items:

(a) Extracts from the appropriate day books and cash book.

(b) The consequent effects on all relevant ledger accounts.

Note: Deal with each of the five items in isolation.

Chapter 8
Value added tax

Introduction □ How VAT operates □ Rates of VAT □ Registration □ Duties of taxable persons □ Tax invoice □ Tax point □ Accounting entries to record transactions affected by VAT

Introduction

Value added tax was introduced on 1 April 1973 as a new form of taxation in the United Kingdom although it had been developed in some European countries over quite a long period. Value added tax or in abbreviated form VAT is in principle chargeable on all supplies of goods and services in the United Kingdom by a taxable person in the course of their business, and on the importation of goods into the United Kingdom. These goods and services are normally chargeable at the standard rate of VAT which is currently 15 per cent. In order to facilitate ease of calculation in the problems set on this topic, a standard rate of 10 per cent is assumed. You are, however, advised to be aware of the changes in the standard rate and indeed the higher rates of tax which may take place from time to time as determined by the Government.

How VAT operates

A simple example will show the basic system in operation. Consider the business of a small engineer whose purchases are subject to VAT, so that an invoice for steel may appear in abbreviated form.

INVOICE

From: The Steel Co. — To: A. N. Engineer

Date: 10 July 19X1

Supply of Steel Bolts	£100
VAT at 10%	10
Invoice Total	£110

Fig. 8.1 Simplified invoice showing VAT charge

In the above example the engineering firm is charged £100 for steel but the supplier adds 10 per cent for VAT so that the invoice total becomes £110.

Conversely, if the engineering firm invoices a customer for goods supplied then the invoice might appear as in Fig. 8.2.

```
┌─────────────────────────────────────────────────────────┐
│                        INVOICE                            │
│                                                           │
│    From:  A. N. Engineer         To:  A. Customer         │
│                                  Date:   15 August 19X1   │
│                                                           │
│                                                           │
│              Supply Steel Frame      £150                 │
│                                                           │
│              VAT at 10%                15                 │
│                                       ───                 │
│              Invoice total           £165                 │
│                                      ════                 │
└─────────────────────────────────────────────────────────┘
```

Fig. 8.2   Further invoice showing VAT charge

In this case 10 per cent VAT has been added to the selling price and consequently the customer owes £165.

However, the engineering firm is allowed to reclaim from the Customs and Excise, who administer VAT on behalf of the government, the VAT charged to the firm by the supplier. On the other hand the engineering firm is required to hand over to the Customs and Excise the VAT charged to its customer.

Again considering the earlier examples, the amount due to the Customs and Excise is arrived at as follows:

VAT charged to A. Customer	£15
Less VAT charged by The Steel Co. for goods supplied	10
The difference is paid over to the Customs and Excise	£5

The above examples give a very broad picture of how VAT operates and is illustrated in simple terms and does not take into account the various other aspects which are covered in the legislation governing the administration of VAT. Value added tax is a tax related to value added at each stage of the process of production or distribution of goods and services. The final tax is borne by the consumer.

The following illustration attempts to show how the final tax is arrived at based on the fundamental concept of 'value added'.

	Purchase price + VAT	Selling Price + VAT	Due to Customs & Excise
Supplier of raw materials	£Nil	£100 + £10	£10
Manufacturer	£100 + £10	£150 + £15	5
Wholesaler	£150 + £15	£200 + £20	5
Retailer	£200 + £20	£250 + £25	5
Consumer	£250 + £25	Nil	—
			£25

The total value added is £250 and the amount due to the Customs and Excise is £25 (10 per cent × £250).

The basic operations of VAT may be summarised like this. At each stage as illustrated above, the taxable person is charged by the suppliers to the business with VAT on the goods and services supplied. These goods and services which are supplied to the business are referred to as *inputs*, and the tax thereon as *input tax*, and are recorded in the purchasing records of the firm. When the latter business supplies goods and services to customers, then the customers are charged with VAT on the goods and services supplied and are referred to in the selling firm's sales records as *outputs* and the tax thereon as *output tax*. At intervals, usually monthly or quarterly, the firm adds up all the input and output tax for the period and deducts the smaller amount from the larger; and the difference is the sum to be remitted to or recovered from the Customs and Excise. The interval of time covered by a tax return is referred to as a tax period.

Rates of VAT

Generally, supplies of goods and services are chargeable at the standard rate of VAT, which is currently 15 per cent. Also, there are goods which are listed as zero-rated and are consequently taxed at a nil rate of tax. There are also legal provisions covering goods and services which are to be considered as exempt from VAT.

The following are the main zero-rated items:

Water and sewerage services.
Books (excluding stationery).
Drugs and medicines on prescription.
Children's clothing and footwear.
Fuel and power (with the exception of petrol).
Construction of buildings (excluding repairs, alterations, maintenance, reconstruction or extension).
Transport services (excluding hire cars and taxis).
Exports.
Food with exceptions for food supplied in the course of eating, pet food and items such as fruit drinks, crisps, etc.

The following is a list of the exempt supplies which do not attract VAT:

Health services.
Burial and cremation.
Land.
Insurance.
Postal services (excluding telephone bills).
Education.
Betting, lotteries and gaming (but not gaming machines).
Financial services.

A further point to be noted in applying the rate of VAT is that concerning the treatment of discount. If a supplier allows a customer a discount on condition that payment is made immediately or within a specified time, the tax is calculated on the discounted amount, not on the gross amount, whether or not the customer takes advantage of the discount. In the same way, if trade discount is allowed then tax is calculated on the discounted amount.

Registration

Businesses which are required to register include trades, professions and vocations and also the facilities which a club or association provides for its members.

A business is required to register if the taxable supplies exceed in value either of the following two statutory levels:

1. At the end of any quarter if the value of the taxable supplies in that quarter exceeds £7250 (for 1987) or if their value in the four quarters then ending exceeds £21 300.

2. At any time, if there are reasonable grounds for believing that the value of the taxable supplies in the period of one year from that time or from some time later, will exceed £21 300.

If a business fails to register it may result in a penalty being imposed as well as the tax due being demanded by the Customs and Excise authorities.

Duties of taxable persons

After the taxable person is registered there is a legal responsibility to perform the following tasks:

1. Record outputs and the VAT thereon.

2. Issue tax invoices showing the VAT charge, when required.

3. Record inputs and the VAT thereon.

4. Work out, for each tax period, the difference between the output tax and the deductible input tax, in order to complete the VAT form.

5. Keep records and accounts that are adequate for these purposes.

6. Keep a VAT account.

Tax invoice

Since the introduction of VAT the invoice has become an essential accounting document which provides the basic information to record transactions in the financial books of businesses. A tax invoice must be issued when a registered person supplies goods or services to another taxable person. Figure 8.3 is an example of a tax invoice showing the type of information which is required to be included in such a document.

When one registered trader supplies goods or services to another a tax invoice must be issued showing the following information:

Identifying serial number.
Tax point.
Supplier's name and address.
VAT registration number.
Customer's name and address.
Type of supply and description of goods or services.
Rate of tax and amount payable (excluding VAT).
Total amount payable excluding VAT.
Rate of cash discount offered.
Total tax chargeable.

Retailers or other persons supplying goods or services direct to the public may provide a less detailed invoice omitting the customer's name and address and the amount, but not the rate of VAT, if the tax-inclusive invoice price is £50 or less. A tax invoice is not required for an exclusively zero-rated supply.

A. N. Engineering Company,			Invoice No. 2359	
10 Steel Road,			Date 10 June 19X8	
Ironhead.				
VAT No. 267 3954 20			Tax point 10 June 19X8	

SALES INVOICE

Terms: Net 7 days

To: A. Customer,
5 Shale Road,
Anytown.

Quantity	Detail	Cost	Rate	VAT
5	Steel beams	£150. 00	10%	15. 00
	VAT	15. 00		
	Total	£165. 00		

Fig. 8.3   Tax invoice showing necessary information

Tax point

The tax on a supply of goods or services becomes chargeable at a definite time, called the tax point. The rate of tax to be charged is the rate in force at the tax point, and the supply must be accounted for in the tax period in which the tax point occurs. The basic tax point is the date when the goods are removed to give effect to the transaction, or, if they are not to be removed, the date when they are made available to the recipient.

Accounting entries to record transactions affected by VAT

There are many rulings which may be used in financial books to record VAT. This is due to the varying nature of business operations that are carried out and the method of recording these transactions adopted by each firm. The recording techniques used for VAT may vary from hand-written records to data processing systems using electronic computers. In most cases the basic principles of recording the VAT input and output tax is standard, leading through to the preparation of the VAT account. There are, however, special retail schemes introduced by the

Customs and Excise for use by retailers in relation to the recording of VAT on supplies of goods and services to their customers. As has been pointed out already, there is a necessity to record every transaction separately differentiating the VAT from the basic cost of goods or services. Most retailers cannot keep a record of that kind for all their sales, because they do not usually issue invoices at the time when a sale takes place. In these cases special schemes for retailers are available to calculate their output tax in other ways. The input tax is calculated in the normal manner.

Tables 8.1 to 8.3 show the basic rules for recording transactions where VAT is involved in the day books and returns books, the cash book and the ledgers.

Table 8.1   Recording entries involving VAT in the day books and returns books

Purchase Day Book	Purchase Returns Book	Sales Day Book	Sales Returns Book
Enter cost inc. VAT in total column.	Enter amount of credit inc. VAT in total column.	Enter amount of sale inc. VAT in total column.	Enter amount of credit note inc. VAT in total column.
Record VAT in a separate column.	Record VAT in a separate column.	Record VAT in a separate column.	Record VAT in a separate column.
Record the cost of goods or services ex VAT in the appropriate analysis columns, if any.	Record the details of credit note ex VAT in the appropriate analysis column, if any.	Record the amount of each sale ex VAT in a 'zero rated' column and a 'standard rate' column, as appropriate.	Record the details of the credit note ex VAT in a 'zero rated' column and a 'standard rate' column as appropriate.
Post the total amount of each transaction inc. VAT to the relevant personal account in the ledger.	Post the total of each transaction inc. VAT to the relevant personal account in the ledger.	Post the total of each transaction inc. VAT to the relevant personal account in the ledger.	Post the total of each transaction inc. VAT to the relevant personal account in the ledger.
At the end of each month post the VAT amount to the debit of the VAT account and the goods column total ex. VAT to the debit of the purchases account.	At the end of each month post the total of VAT to the credit of the VAT account *or* show as a deduction on the debit side of that account. Post the total of the goods column ex. VAT to the credit of purchases account or purchases returns account.	At the end of each month post the VAT amount to the credit of VAT account and the goods columns totals ex. VAT to the credit of Sales Account.	At the end of each month post the total of VAT to the debit of the VAT account *or* show as a deduction on the credit side of that account. Post the totals of the goods columns ex. VAT to the debit of sales account or sales returns account.

Table 8.2   Recording entries involving VAT in the cash book

Receipts	Payments
Enter the total amount inc. VAT in the cash or bank column.	Enter the total amount inc. VAT in the cash or bank column.
Enter the output tax in the VAT column.	Enter the input tax in the VAT column.
Enter the receipts ex. VAT in columns headed 'zero rated' and 'standard rate' or 'higher rate'.	Enter the payments ex. VAT in a separate column headed 'zero rated' and 'standard rate'.
Post the total of the VAT column to the credit of the VAT account.	Post the total of the VAT column to the debit of the VAT account.
Receipts received ex. VAT are posted to the appropriate accounts in the nominal ledger.	Payments made ex. VAT are posted to the appropriate accounts in the nominal ledger.

Note: VAT requires to be shown in the cash book if the transaction has not been recorded in a day book or in any other subsidiary book.

Table 8.3   Recording entries involving VAT in the ledgers

Personal ledger:	All amounts will be recorded including VAT as posted from the day books.
General ledger:	All amounts with the following exceptions will be entered in the accounts excluding VAT. The exceptions are private motor cars and entertainment expenses which are disallowable for income tax purposes.

VAT account

Input tax	Output tax
Totals from purchase day book	Totals from sales day book
Less Total from purchase returns book	*Less* Total from sales returns book
Totals from cash book (payments)	Totals from cash book (receipts)
Balance due to Customs and Excise	Balance due from Customs and Excise

The above account is shown in simple terms and does not take into account tax on imported goods and goods from bonded warehouses or underdeclaration or overdeclaration of tax but is shown to explain in basic terms the construction of a VAT account.

The following example illustrates the recording of transactions in the principal books of account.

Example: J. Smith commenced business on January 2 with capital of £150 which he paid into the bank. You are required to record the transactions for the month of January in the appropriate books and extract a trial balance at January 31.

Jan.	2	Bought goods on credit from J. Jones £20
	6	Sold goods on credit to R. Green £30.
	8	Bought goods on credit from W. White £50. These goods were zero-rated.
	10	Sold goods on credit to B. Black £40.
	12	R. Green paid for his goods by cheque
	14	Sold goods on credit to R. Red £56 which were zero-rated.
	15	Paid electricity by cheque £21. This is zero-rated.
	16	Returned goods to J. Jones £10.
	18	Paid wages by cheque £46. VAT is not chargeable.

Jan. 20   Purchased Machine £100. Cheque was paid on receipt of goods.
22   Cash Sales paid into bank £220 (inc. VAT) and £50 (zero-rated).
24   Paid J. Jones his bill by cheque.
26   Bought by cheque Purchases £80 which were zero-rated.
28   B. Black returned goods £10.

Note: All items are subject to VAT at 10 per cent unless otherwise stated.

Purchases Day Book

Date	Particulars	Total	VAT	Amount (ex VAT)
Jan. 2	J. Jones – Goods	£22	£2	£20
8	W. White – Goods	50		50
		£72	£2	£70

Sales Day Book

Date	Particulars	Total	VAT	Zero Rate	Standard Rate
Jan. 6	R. Green – Goods	£33	£3		£30
10	B. Black – Goods	44	4		40
14	R. Red – Goods	56		£56	
		£133	£7	£56	£70

Purchase Returns Book

Date	Particulars	Total	VAT	Amount (ex. VAT)
Jan. 16	J. Jones – Returns	£11	£1	£10

Sales Returns Book

Date	Particulars	Total	VAT	Zero Rate	Standard Rate
Jan. 28	B. Black – Returns	£11	£1		£10

Cash Book

Date	Particulars	Total	VAT	Standard Rate	Zero Rate	Date	Particulars	Total	VAT	Zero Standard Rate
Jan. 2	Capital	£150				Jan.15	Electricity	£21		£21
12	R. Green	33				18	Wages	46		
22	Sales (not through day book)	270	£20	£200	£50	20	Machine (not through day book)	110	£10	100
						24	J. Jones	11		
						26	Purchases (not through day book)	80		80
						31	Balance	185		
		£453	£20	£200	£50			£453	£10	£201
Feb. 1	Balance	£185								

Purchases Ledger

J. Jones

Jan. 16	Returns	£11	Jan. 2	Goods	£22
24	Bank	11			
		£22			£22

W. White

			Jan. 8	Goods	£50

Sales ledger

R. Green

Jan. 6	Goods	£33	Jan. 12	Bank	£33

B. Black

Jan. 10	Goods	£44	Jan. 28	Returns	£11
			31	Balance	33
		£44			£44
Feb. 1	Balance	33			

R. Red

Jan. 14	Goods	£56			

Sales Ledger *Cont.*

Electricity

Jan. 15	Bank	£21

Wages

Jan. 18	Bank	£46

Machine

Jan. 20	Bank	£100

Sales

Jan. 31	Sales Returns Book	£10	Jan. 22	Bank	£200
				do.	50
			31	Sales Day Book	56
				do.	70
					£376

Purchases

Jan. 26	Bank	£80	Jan. 31	Purchases Returns Book	£10
31	Purchases Day Book	70			
		£150			

Capital

		Jan. 2	Bank	£150

VAT

Date	Particulars	Inputs Goods	Input Tax	Date	Particulars	Outputs Standard Rate	Outputs Zero Rate	Output Tax Standard Rate
Jan. 31	Total from purchase day book	£70	£2	Jan. 31	Total from sales day book	£70	£56	£7
	Total from purchase returns book	(10)	(1)		Total from sales returns book	(10)		(1)
	Total from cash book	201	10		Total from cash book	200	50	20
	Balance		15					
		£261	£26			£260	£106	£26
				Feb. 1	Balance			£15

Trial Balance as at 31 January

Bank	£185	
Electricity	21	
Wages	46	
Machine	100	
Sales		£366
Purchases	140	
Capital		150
W. White		50
B. Black	33	
R. Red	56	
VAT		15
	£581	£581

Summary

1. Value added tax was introduced on 1 April 1973 as a new form of taxation chargeable on all supplies of goods and services.

2. Value added tax is a tax related to value added at each stage of the process of production or distribution of goods and services. The final tax is borne by the consumer.

3. Since the introduction of VAT the invoice has become an essential accounting document which provides the basic information to record transactions in the financial books of businesses.

4. The tax on a supply of goods or services becomes chargeable at a definite time, called the tax point.

Discussion questions

8.1 What are the main duties of taxable persons under the current VAT regulations?

8.2 Draft an invoice showing goods charged at standard and zero rates of VAT.

8.3 Why is the 'tax point' important on an invoice?

8.4 Explain the entries required to record a purchase invoice, involving VAT, in a trader's books.

Exercises

8.5 The following sales and purchases were made by James Grant during the month of June:

		Gross amount	VAT included
June 5	Bought goods on credit from Tom Jones	£165	£15
7	Bought goods from John Smith on credit	77	7
10	Sold goods to Bill Green on credit	88	8
15	Bought goods from Tom Jones on credit	220	20
			Cont.

		Gross amount	VAT included
June 25	Sold goods to Bob White on credit	£121	£11
28	Sold goods to Bill Green on credit	55	5
30	Bought goods on credit from James Brown	99	9

You are required to enter these transactions in the sales and purchases day book, sales and purchases ledgers and the general ledger for the month of June. You are also required to transfer the appropriate amounts to the VAT account.

8.6 You are required to record the following transactions in the books of T. Smith and extract a trial balance at 31 July:

July	1	Capital of £100 was paid into the bank
	2	Purchased goods on credit £130 from R. Green
	3	Purchased goods on credit £85 from B. Brown. Goods are zero-rated.
	4	Sold goods on credit to P. White £140.
	5	Paid R. Green his account by cheque.
	7	Paid wages by cheque £34.
	10	Returned to B. Brown goods which were faulty £10.
	15	Sold goods on credit to G. Black £88. These goods were zero-rated.
	18	P. White returned goods value £20.
	25	Goods for resale purchased by cheque £90.
	28	P. White paid his account by cheque.
	29	Sold on credit to S. Blue goods valued £30.
	30	Paid by cheque electricity £14. This is zero-rated.
	31	Cash sales paid into bank £110 (inc. VAT).

Note: VAT has to be assumed at 10 per cent. The amounts shown above are ex VAT unless otherwise stated.

8.7 Draft an invoice showing goods charged at standard and zero rates of VAT.

8.8 The High School Sports and Social Club commenced operations on 1 January 19X7 and had the following transactions during the month ended 31 January 19X7:

Subscriptions received (£10 per member)	£3 000
Bar purchases	2 500
Bar sales	2 700
Catering sales	600
Catering purchases (no VAT)	400
Golf Balls purchased	500
Golf Balls sold	650
Repairs to property (no VAT)	100
TV set purchased (no VAT)	350
Gaming machines rental	150
Gaming machines takings	400

The rate of value added tax is 10 per cent.

You are required, from the information given above, to prepare the account for value added tax for the month ended 31 January 19X7.

8.9 From the following information you are required to write up the VAT account for the month ended 31 January:

	Value (excluding VAT)
Purchases for resale (£1500 zero-rated)	£5 000
Credit sales (£1000 zero-rated)	10 000
Wages	1 700
Electricity	100
Purchase returns	30
Sales returns	150
Plant	400
Entertaining expenses (Disallowable for tax purposes)	30
Postage (exempt)	10
Cash sales (£100 zero-rated)	400

Assume VAT at 10 per cent.

Chapter 9
Costs, expenses and expenditures

Accounting for expenditures ☐ Capital and revenue expenditure ☐ Capital and revenue receipts ☐ Accounting for wages and salaries ☐ Cost flows for trading enterprises ☐ Cost flows for manufacturing enterprises ☐ Product costs and period costs ☐ Preparation of manufacturing accounts

Accounting for expenditures

This is the second of two chapters dealing with the expenditure cycle. In Chapter 7 we explained the distinctions which should be made between the terms 'costs', 'expenditures', 'expenses' and 'payments', and then proceeded to examine the accounting procedures for the purchases of goods (one type of expenditure) and the subsequent payment for these goods. In this chapter we take a much broader view of expenditures. In particular, we deal with the following:

1. The difference between capital and revenue expenditure.

2. Accounting for wages and salaries – a significant expenditure for most enterprises. In contrast to most other expenditures, the amount payable for wages and salaries is determined internally and the documentation has to be raised internally.

3. The way in which the costs recorded for expenditure transactions flow through the accounting system. We will demonstrate these cost flows, first for a trading enterprise, and then for a manufacturing enterprise.

Capital and revenue expenditure

Capital expenditure

Capital expenditure can be considered to be expenditure incurred in purchasing fixed assets of a permanent nature or spending money to increase the value of an existing fixed asset. The expenditure incurred usually benefits over one or more accounting years; in other words it is normally medium to long-term expenditure. It may be that other expenditure is incurred which should be included as an addition to the cost of the fixed asset. Examples of this are the carriage and installation costs of new machinery or the legal costs of buying property.

Example:

Cost of new machine	£10 000
Carriage costs	300
Installation costs	1 000
Total cost – Capital expenditure	£11 300

Capital expenditure is not charged to the profit and loss account but the reduction in the value of those assets having a limited life is written off by way of depreciation to the latter account. This technique is discussed later in the text.

Examples of capital expenditure:

Item	Reason for treatment
Motor car	Fixed asset
New buildings	Fixed asset
Legal costs incurred in the purchase of property	This is part of the capital cost of the fixed asset and should be added to it
Building an extension to the factory	This is an increase in the fixed assets of the business and is added to the original cost of the buildings
Patents and trade marks	These are treated as fixed assets since the business will benefit from them over a number of years
Carriage charges on new plant purchased	This is treated as part of the cost of the plant and added to it
New typewriter for office	Fixed asset
Costs of installing new machine	This is part of the cost of the machine and is added to it
Development costs of drilling an oil well	These costs are incurred in creating a fixed asset which should operate for a long period of time

Revenue expenditure

Revenue expenditure is so termed when the benefits do not extend beyond the accounting period in which the expenditure takes place. This form of expenditure is recorded in the appropriate expense accounts and written off at the end of each accounting period in the trading and profit and loss account. Such expenditure does not increase the value of the fixed assets of the business, but services and maintains them in good working condition. The costs of producing, selling and distributing the goods and services of the business, together with the administration expenses involved, are also examples of revenue expenditure. Purchases, wages, salaries, commission, rent, rates, electricity, telephone, printing and stationery are expenses of a revenue nature. In some businesses expenditure which would normally fall into the category of capital expenditure may be treated as revenue expenditure, for practical purposes, if the expenditure is relatively small, say under £50, or where there is no significant or measurable benefit accruing to a future period.

Examples of revenue expenditure:

Item	Reason for treatment
Repairs to plant	Maintenance of fixed asset
Cost of hiring a motor van	Normal recurring cost of the business
Legal fees re debt collection	Amounts expended in collection of customers' accounts. Does not add any value to a fixed asset
Repairs to property	Maintenance of buildings
Replacing new engine in delivery van	Maintenance cost. Does not increase the value of the delivery van
Annual motor insurance premiums	An expense item which only benefits the business for a year
Repainting factory	Maintenance cost. Does not increase the value of the factory

Apportionment of expenditure between capital and revenue

Some items of expenditure may require to be apportioned between capital and revenue. For example if a motor car is purchased for £6000 you may find that the cost shown on the invoice is made up as follows:

Cost of car	£5 900
Cost of motor licence disc	100
	£6 000

In this instance the cost of the car £5900 will be treated as capital expenditure and shown in the balance sheet while the licence fee of £100 will be treated as revenue expenditure and included in the profit and loss account as motor expenses.

Necessity to distinguish between capital and revenue expenditure

In general terms the distinction between capital and revenue expenditure is one of permanence. In other words, what is the duration of benefit accruing from the outlay of the expenditure? It is essential that a distinction be drawn between capital and revenue expenditure if a true and correct revenue profit or loss is to be computed. Revenue profit earned by a business is calculated by deducting the total revenue expenditure, including depreciation charges from the gross income received. If any capital expenditure is included in this calculation a false revenue profit or loss will result. Only expenditure such as the actual revenue expenses of operating the business may be charged to the profit and loss account. The diminution in the value of any of the fixed assets may be charged to the profit and loss account in the form of a depreciation provision.

Although an attempt has been made to establish rules to differentiate between capital and revenue expenditure, it does not always follow that each item of expenditure must always be classified as being capital or revenue expenditure. If a firm uses its own employees to erect an extension to its factory premises then it would be incorrect to treat the amount of wages paid to the firm's own employees engaged in this work as revenue expenditure together with the cost of any materials used in the construction of the premises. This expenditure must be treated as capital expenditure since it is not part of the cost of producing goods for resale but relates directly to the cost of acquiring a capital asset in the form of additional factory premises. Legal expenses, provided they are incurred in the collection of bad debts or for a similar reason, are written off as revenue expenditure, but if they are paid in respect of acquiring additional assets or the raising of capital they are considered to be capital expenditure and treated accordingly in the financial accounts. The title of the expense item does not of itself determine its correct allocation and consequently a careful assessment of each cost item must be made before it is classified as capital or revenue expenditure.

Example: J. Brown who is in business as a builder has produced the following financial results about his business:

Profit for year	£80 000
Total assets in balance sheet	£200 000

As you discuss his financial affairs with him you obtain the following additional information. During the year under review Mr Brown built an extension to his workshop using his own employees and raw materials from his store to build it. The extension cost £7500 made up of materials £5000 and wages of £2500. The cost of materials and wages have been charged to his profit and loss account.

It can be seen from the discussion with Mr Brown that capital expenditure in respect of the extension to his workshop has been included in the accounts as revenue expenditure. If we use the information supplied by Mr Brown the following adjustments will require to be made:

Profit for year *before* adjustment		£80 000
Add Capital expenditure treated incorrectly:		
Materials	£5 000	
Wages	2 500	7 500
Profit for year *after* adjustment		£87 500

Note from the above that the profit has now increased by £7500. The materials account will be reduced by £5000 and the wages account by £2500 since these amounts have now been transferred to the workshop account.

Total assets before adjustment	£200 000
Add Cost of new extension to workshop	7 500
	£207 500

You will see that the total assets have risen by £7500 since the workshop account will be increased by £7500 being the cost of the extension.

The above example illustrates the effect on the profit and balance sheet when an item of expenditure is incorrectly treated.

Capital and revenue receipts

Revenue receipts are those amounts received by a business which are not in respect of the sale of a fixed asset. Examples are as follows:

Sales of goods and services
Commission received
Discount received
Interest on deposit accounts

Capital receipts are those amounts received by a business in respect of fixed assets. Examples are as follows:

Proceeds of sale of property
Proceeds of sale of plant or vehicles
Proceeds of sale of investment, e.g. shares or deposit account

Accounting for wages and salaries

In many enterprises the payment of wages and salaries involves considerable recording and calculation and is important enough to be considered separately. It is common to make a distinction between 'wages', where the reward is calculated on an hourly basis, and 'salaries', where an annual amount is subdivided and paid on a weekly, fortnightly or monthly basis. In the discussion below, we deal primarily with wage payments, but students should note that many of the procedures described are also applicable to salary payments.

Wages often form a large proportion of total expense, and it is therefore essential that adequate controls are instituted over this item. In larger concerns, it is usual to separate the four functions, which are:

1. Engaging of staff and keeping of personnel records.
2. Recording of time worked.

3. Preparation of wage sheets.

4. Actual payment to employees.

While it is not intended to discuss fully the control implications of the above division, it should be noted that the final disbursement is made only after recordings have been made in several different sections of the organisation.

The following factors influence the calculation of the net amount due to the individual employee.

1. Rate of pay – this may vary according to the type of work done and whether ordinary time or overtime is involved. It is often influenced by industrial legislation.

2. Hours worked – this information may be obtained in various ways, for example,

(a) by time cards used with a time clock;

(b) by recording in a time book;

(c) by simply taking the normal hours as correct unless varied by an absentee or overtime report.

3. In some cases, employees are entitled to special incentive bonuses because of work performed at a higher than standard production. Special calculations and routines are involved here.

4. Legal provisions which require the deduction of income tax and national insurance from employees' pay on behalf of the government.

5. The common arrangement whereby the employer deducts certain amounts from the employee's earnings, for example,

(a) contributions to medical and hospital schemes;

(b) mortgage payments;

(c) social club contributions;

(d) superannuation, etc.

In view of the above factors, it follows that the preparation of the wages sheets is a major recurring clerical task for any concern with a large number of employees.

A pay section of the office staff has the task of bringing together for each employee each of the factors affecting the wage of that employee. This will involve the hours worked, rate of pay, bonuses, etc., together with the personal deductions for tax and other items. In some cases, there are extra payments for travelling time, danger money, dirt money, etc. The calculation of hours worked multiplied by the rates of pay may also have to be adjusted for overtime. It is usual to use wages sheets which are appropriately designed.

The above procedures apply largely to salary payments as well as wages. However, as salaries are more or less regular in both numbers and amounts, it is not necessary to calculate the gross amount using the hours worked and a rate, but to arrive at the figure by dividing the number of pay periods into the annual salary. There may be salary sheets separate from wages sheets.

Figure 9.1 shows an example of a wages sheet.

Payroll
Pay period week ending 7 February

No.	Name	Hours	Basic Wage	Bonus Over-time	Gross Pay	Deductions PAYE	Deductions NIC	Total	Net Pay	NIC Employer's
			£	£	£	£	£	£	£	£
1	Abel, J.	40	280	70	350	80	20	100	250	31
2	Brown, L.	40	280	—	280	75	18	93	187	26
3	Doe, J.	40	280	—	280	70	18	88	192	26
			840	70	910	225	56	281	629	83

Fig. 9.1   A wages sheet.

Note:

1. There are many possible variations to the form shown both as to design and content.

2. Many concerns use some form of mechanisation for preparing their payroll, often preparing simultaneously an employee's earnings history with taxation information, an advice of earnings (pay slip) for the employee and, in some cases, a cheque.

3. Where wages are paid in cash, a cheque is drawn for the total net amount due, cashed at the bank, and the individual pay packets are then made up and disbursed by the paymaster.

Using the totals shown, we now consider how they may be brought into the double-entry records. Before doing so, certain facts are apparent:

1. The cost of wages to the business is not the net amount due, but the gross amount.

2. The deductions for taxation, national insurance, medical funds, etc. must be paid to those bodies.

3. Tax deductions are legally payable to the Inland Revenue monthly; the other bodies may stipulate various time periods for payment.

To incorporate the amounts in the cash book and general ledger the following basic rules should be followed:

1. *Dr.*   Gross wages to wages account
   Cr.   Net wages payable to wages payable account
        PAYE and NIC (Employees') to PAYE and NIC account

2. *Dr.*   Employer's NIC to wages account
   Cr.   Employer's NIC to PAYE and NIC account

3. *Dr.*   Wages payable account with actual wages paid to employees
   Cr.   Cash book

4. *Dr.*   PAYE and NIC account with PAYE and NIC contributions for both employer and employees
   Cr.   Cash book

Example: Using the information in the illustration in Fig. 9.1, the accounts would be written up as follows:

Wages Account

Feb. 7	Wages payable and	
	PAYE and NIC[1]	£910
	PAYE and NIC[2]	83
		£993

Wages Payable Account

Feb. 7	Cash[3]	£629	Feb. 7	Wages[1]	£629

PAYE and NIC Account

Feb. 7	Cash[4]	£364	Feb. 7	Wages[1]	£281
				Wages[2]	83
		£364			£364

Cash Book (Payments side)

Date	Particulars	Folio	Total	Wages	PAYE and NIC
Feb. 7	Wages payable[3]		£629	£629	
	PAYE and NIC[4]		364		£364

Cost flows for trading enterprises

In Chapter 7 we stated that the debit (or cost) effect of an expenditure transaction takes one of two forms. Either the cost represents an *expense* (where the benefits are consumed during the current accounting period), or it represents an *asset* (where the benefits will be consumed during future accounting periods). Thus, some asset accounts (for example, stock, depreciable assets, usable supplies, prepaid insurance, etc.) may be regarded as storages or reservoirs for costs which will become expenses in future periods.

In a trading enterprise, one of the major costs is that of merchandise (that is, goods to be sold). There is a simple flow of costs through a merchandise stock account to the expense of cost of goods sold. Thus, diagrammatically:

Sometimes there may be costs associated with the goods – other than the purchase price – which should be included in cost of goods sold. Examples of such costs are carriage inwards, customs duty and costs of repackaging goods purchased in bulk into a form suitable for sale. Thus, we could extend the above diagram to include such costs as follows:

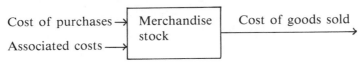

Many of the other costs of a trading enterprise, such as sales salaries, advertising, power and lighting, office salaries, interest, etc. are expenses in the period in which the expenditure occurs and in which the costs are initially recorded. However, there are other costs, such as delivery vehicles, shop fittings, insurance, office supplies, etc., which need to be stored in asset accounts and expensed only when, or to the extent to which, these accounts are consumed in the process of earning revenue.

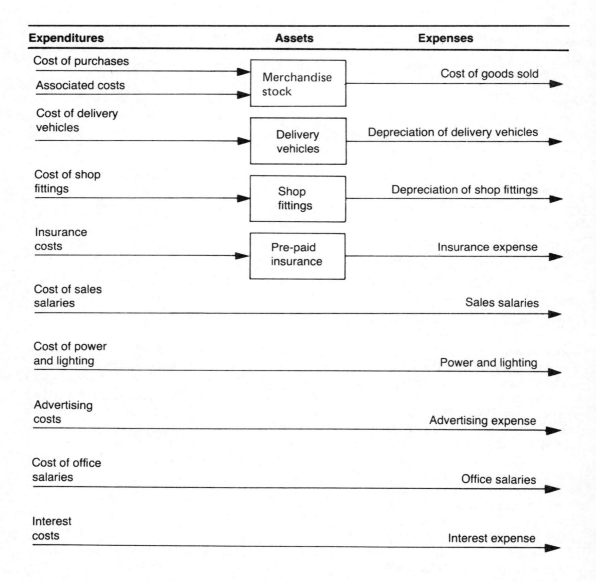

Fig. 9.2   Cost flows for a trading enterprise.

Figure 9.2 attempts to show typical cost flows for a trading enterprise. The costs specifically named are representative only and are not intended to cover the whole range.

Cost flows for manufacturing enterprises

Manufacturing involves the conversion of one type of goods or material to another through the application of labour and facilities. There are many examples of this type of activity: raw wool is converted into cloth; skyscrapers are built from steel, concrete and the like; fruit is transformed into jam; paper and ink are transformed into a book or newspaper. For the purposes of this chapter, manufacturing includes construction, manufacture, assembly and all similar forms of conversion.

For such enterprises, gross profit is still calculated as above, that is, sales minus cost of goods sold; but cost of goods sold is not so easily determined because the (finished) goods sold are not purchased but are the end product of a manufacturing process. The cost of such finished goods will include their raw-material content and some other costs of converting such raw materials into the finished goods. Because most manufacturing processes are continuous, it is likely that, at any given point of time, such as the end of an accounting period, a manufacturer will be holding several different categories of inventory, namely:

1. Raw materials which have not yet entered into production.

2. Partly finished goods (work-in-progress).

3. Finished goods held ready for sale.

4. Stocks of stores or supplies which in themselves do not enter in the final product, but are necessary to facilitate making the goods.

Thus, using one of the examples of manufacturing given above,

$$
\begin{aligned}
\text{Raw material} &= \text{Stocks of raw wool} \\
\text{Work-in-progress} &= \text{Yarn still on the machines} \\
\text{Finished goods} &= \text{Finished cloth in the finished-goods store} \\
\text{Stores and supplies} &= \text{Lubricants to service the machines}
\end{aligned}
$$

In this type of business, therefore, the accounting system has to be extended, first to obtain the data associated with the costs of conversion, and then to allow the valuation of closing stock of raw materials, work-in-progress and finished goods so that the cost of goods sold and therefore gross profit can be calculated. The accounting procedures described above form part of an area of accounting which is generally called 'cost accounting'.

Thus, the flow of costs in a manufacturing enterprise is somewhat more complex than that described above for a trading enterprise. Figure 9.3 attempts to show diagrammatically, for a manufacturing enterprise, the cost flows which eventually lead to the expense of cost of goods sold. It shows only those costs associated with factory operations and does not attempt to include the costs of the selling and administrative operations of such an enterprise. These will be basically the same as those depicted earlier in Fig. 9.2 for a trading enterprise.

Product costs and period costs

The distinction between costs which are stored in stock accounts and costs which are charged immediately to expense accounts is often referred to as the distinction between 'product costs' and 'period costs'. Product costs do not affect profit until the product has been sold, whereas period costs affect the profit of the accounting period in which they are incurred. Thus, the decision about whether to treat certain costs as product costs or period costs can affect the reported net profit of a particular period. If such costs are small relative to other costs or if stock levels do not fluctuate greatly from one period to another then the effect on reported profit may not be significant. The most important consideration, where some doubt exists about whether the costs are product costs or period costs, is that they are treated consistently as from one accounting period to another.

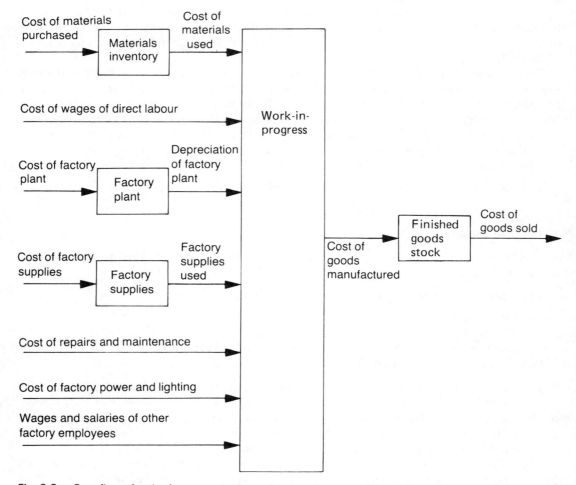

Fig. 9.3   Cost flows for the factory operations of a manufacturing enterprise.

Notes

1. This diagram is based on a common classification of manufacturing costs into three categories:

   (a) Direct materials used in production.

   (b) Direct labour – wages of employees directly involved in the production costs.

   (c) Factory overhead (costs not directly involved in production) – includes depreciation, repairs and maintenance, indirect materials, indirect labour, etc.

2. The costs specifically named in the factory overhead group are representative only and are not intended to cover the whole range.

Preparation of manufacturing accounts

The discussion which has taken place before this section relates to cost flows for the factory operations of a manufacturing enterprise. We are now considering how this information is produced for management purposes in the form of a manufacturing account.

Manufacturing accounts cannot always be drafted to a standard pattern, owing to the complexity of manufacturing operations. Each manufacturing concern must design a form of account best suited to its own requirements. It may be that in certain businesses involved in the manufacturing of several products there is a necessity to prepare a manufacturing account for each product in order to give product costs as well as total factory cost of goods produced. Although standardisation is not always possible in the design, the following elements of cost are usually shown in the manufacturing account:

1. Prime cost.

2. Factory cost.

3. Factory cost of finished goods.

Prime cost

Although different opinions are held as to the meaning of this term and what items should be included in this section of the manufacturing account it is better at least for the reader at this stage to be familiar with the usually accepted items making up this element of cost. Items to be included are:

> Opening stock of raw materials.
> Raw materials purchased (materials that enter into and become a part of the finished product).
> *Less* Closing stock of raw materials.
> Carriage on raw materials.
> Direct wages (wages paid which can be identified with manufacture).

The value of rejected materials or by-products will be credited to the cost of raw materials purchased or deleted from the prime cost.

Factory cost

Factory cost is prime cost (i.e. direct labour, material and expenses) plus all indirect expenses of manufacture, which cannot be classified as direct material, direct labour or direct expenses. These items of indirect expenditure include:

> Rent and rates of factory.
> Factory heat, light and power.
> Plant and machinery repairs and maintenance.
> Depreciation of plant and machinery used in the factory.
> Indirect wages (works manager's salary, storekeeping wages, etc.).

To prepare detailed manufacturing, trading and profit and loss accounts it is necessary to allocate costs of a similar nature between factory, warehouse and office. For example, a business may pay a rent of £10 000 per annum for a building but it is incorrect to charge the whole amount to the cost of manufacturing the goods if part of the rented premises is used for a dispatch warehouse and an office block. Obviously, an apportionment of the total rent charge would require to be made, possibly on the basis of floor space used, and a charge made on that basis to the factory cost, selling and distribution cost, and administration cost.

Factory cost of finished goods

When the total factory cost has been established an adjustment is made on this amount in respect of work-in-progress as follows:

> Factory cost
>> *Add* Work-in-progress at beginning of period.
>> *Less* Work-in-progress at end of period.

Work-in-progress is the value of incomplete work in the factory and is usually computed on the following basis:

> The cost of materials and production labour plus the proportion of indirect expenses chargeable to the work up to its present stage of manufacture.

Stock of raw materials and finished goods

Care has to be taken in dealing with stocks of raw materials and finished goods. Stocks of raw materials are shown in the manufacturing account in the prime-cost section while stocks of finished goods are recorded in the trading account in the usual way. It is important to ensure that stocks are valued on a consistent basis and that no element of profit is included in the valuation. It will be appreciated from the study of accounting so far that an incorrect valuation of stock can have a serious effect on the amount of trading profit or loss of a business.

Example: From the following information supplied by Ajax Limited we are to prepare a manufacturing, trading and profit and loss account for the year ended 31 December 19X8:

	£000
Stocks 1 January 19X8	
Raw materials	3 000
Work-in-progress	1 000
Finished goods	4 500
Stocks 31 December 19X8	
Raw materials	1 500
Work-in-progress	2 500
Finished goods	3 600
Carriage on raw materials	2 750
Sales	80 000
Factory rent and rates	250
Factory heat, light and power	1 200
Depreciation on factory plant	2 800
Travellers' salaries	5 500
Advertising	1 250
Office rent and rates	300
Office salaries	3 500
Carriage outwards	700
Purchases of raw materials	50 000
Direct wages	7 000
Plant repairs	210
Factory expenses	75

Solution

Ajax Limited
Manufacturing Account for Year ended 31 December 19X8

	£000	£000
Direct materials		
Opening stock	3 000	
Purchases	50 000	
Carriage on raw materials	2 750	
	55 750	
Less Closing stock	1 500	
Direct materials consumed		54 250
Direct labour		7 000
Prime cost		61 250
Factory overheads		
Factory rent and rates	250	
Factory heat, light and power	1 200	
Plant repairs	210	
Factory expenses	75	
Depreciation on factory plant	2 800	4 535
Factory cost		65 785
Work-in-progress		
As at 1 January 19X8	1 000	
As at 31 December 19X8	2 500	1 500
Factory cost of finished goods		64 285

Profit and Loss Account for year ended 31 December 19X8

	£000	£000	£000
Sales			80 000
Less Cost of goods sold			
Opening stock of finished goods		4 500	
Factory cost of finished goods		64 285	
		68 785	
Less Closing stock of finished goods		3 600	65 185
Gross profit			14 815
Less Administrative expenses			
Office salaries	3 500		
Office rent and rates	300	3 800	
Selling expenses			
Travellers' salaries	5 500		
Advertising	1 250		
Carriage outwards	700	7 450	11 250
Profit for year			3 565

Summary

1. It is important that a distinction is made between capital and revenue expenditure and capital and revenue receipts.

2. In many businesses, the payment of wages and salaries involves considerable recording and calculation. The four functions of personnel records, recording of time worked, payroll preparation and wage payment should be kept separate to ensure adequate control.

3. The costs of an expenditure transaction are recorded either as an expense or an asset. Costs recorded as an asset often become expenses of subsequent periods.

4. Cost flows for a manufacturing enterprise are more complex than those for a trading enterprise.

5. It is useful to distinguish between product costs and period costs. This distinction affects the reported profit of a particular accounting period.

6. In preparing a manufacturing account it is important to distinguish between prime cost, factory cost, and factory cost of finished goods.

Discussion questions

9.1 Define the terms capital and revenue expenditure and give three examples of each.

9.2 Give an example of an expense item where it may be necessary to allocate it between capital and revenue expenditure.

9.3 Give reasons why, in many firms, accounting for wages and salaries represents one of the large accounting functions to be performed.

9.4 (a) Is the distinction often drawn between wages and salaries based entirely on the jobs performed by the employees involved? Give reasons for your answer.

(b) What are accounting implications of distinguishing between wages and salaries?

9.5 As a service to employees, many organisations agree to deduct from employees' earnings amounts due to other organisations. How does such an arrangement affect the accounting procedures of the employer?

9.6 'Some asset accounts may be regarded as storages or reservoirs for costs which will become expenses in future periods.' Explain this statement. Give three examples of asset accounts which may be so viewed and three examples of assets which will never become expenses.

9.7 If an importer pays customs duties on goods purchased, should all the customs duty paid during a particular period be regarded as expenses of that period? Give reasons for your answer.

9.8 Discuss from an accounting viewpoint, the major differences between the stock of a retailer and those of a manufacturer.

9.9 What difference does it make whether repairs to factory equipment is regarded as a cost of the period rather than a cost of the product? Which treatment is more theoretically correct? Why?

9.10 Which of the following costs of the current period are also clearly expenses of the current period? Discuss reasons for your answer in each case.

(a) Factory manager's salary.

(b) Office manager's salary.

(c) Carriage on goods sold.

(d) Stationery purchased.

(e) Depreciation on sales representatives' vehicles.

(f) Depreciation on factory buildings.

(g) Payments to a security service for delivering employees' wages and salaries.

Exercises

9.11 Distinguish the following items between capital and revenue expenditure:

(a) Painting existing factory building.

(b) Commission paid to salesmen.

(c) New tyres for motor van.

(d) Cash stolen from office safe by junior clerk.

(e) Fire insurance premium.

(f) Cost of overhauling factory machinery.

9.12 Distinguish the following items between capital and revenue receipts:

(a) Proceeds of sale of buildings.

(b) Amount received on realisation of investments.

(c) Commission received.

(d) Discount received.

(e) Interest on deposit account.

9.13 On what principles would you distinguish between capital and revenue expenditure in the following cases?

(a) Replacement of a motor vehicle which originally cost £750 but which has been depreciated 20 per cent per annum on cost for four years and eventually sold for £20 by a new vehicle costing £5000.

(b) Repairs and extension of premises.

(c) Loss of stock by fire amounting to £4000 and a receipt of £3200 in full settlement from the insurance company.

9.14 Enter the following information in the appropriate ledger accounts of Starport Transport Company for the four weeks ended 29 September 19X6 at which date the deduction authorities are to be paid the amount due to them:

	Week ending 8/9/X6	Week ending 15/9/X6	Week ending 22/9/X6	Week ending 29/9/X6
Net wages paid weekly	£13 944	£14 291	£13 906	£13 887
PAYE	2 961	3 082	2 931	2 920
NIC - Employees	490	490	490	490
Pension Fund	375	375	375	390
NIC - Employer's	305	305	305	305

9.15 Top Hole Manufacturing Company had the following stock and work-in-progress on 1 May and 31 May:

	1 May	31 May
Raw materials	£40 000	£50 000
Work-in-progress	60 000	40 000
Finished goods	24 000	40 000

During the month of May the cost of raw materials purchased was £120 000, labour costs were £160 000 and other manufacturing costs totalled £60 000. Prepare a diagram showing the flow of costs through the stock accounts for the month of May. Determine cost of goods sold for the month.

9.16 The following data is available from the books of a manufacturing company:

(a) From the balance sheet

	Beginning of Year	End of Year
Raw materials	£2 410	£2 850
Work-in-progress	1 280	2 710
Finished goods	870	1 720
Factory equipment (net)	5 380	5 270

(b) From the records

Purchases of raw materials	£12 800
Purchases of factory equipment (none sold)	650
Factory wages	5 880
Factory overheads (not including depreciation)	23 460

   Calculate the cost of goods manufactured and the cost of goods sold for the year. (Show workings.)

Problems

9.17 The Dyplex Company are in business as mechanical engineers. In their general ledger they maintain the usual accounts for fixed assets and also repairs equalisation accounts for buildings and plant, to which annual charges of £150 and £1000 respectively are credited.
   The undernoted balances appear in these accounts at 1 June:

Land and Buildings	£10 720
Plant and Equipment	17 800
Motor vehicles	3 600
Building repairs equalisation account	412 (Cr)
Plant etc. repairs equalisation account	27 (Dr)

(a) You are required to complete the above ledger accounts for the year ended 31 May and include such of the following items as are appropriate:

(i) Purchase of additional land and buildings at 5 Main Street		
Purchase price	£6 750	
Legal charges	104	
Rates paid in advance by vendor	200	£7 054
(ii) Purchase of motor van ABC 106		
Basic cost	6 000	
Delivery charge	100	
Number plates	50	
Road fund tax	100	6 250
(iii) Lettering the firm's name on van ABC 106		150
(iv) Partial demolition of 5 Main Street		1 200
(v) Builder and decorator's account for 5 Main Street		
Erection of new office block	10 000	
Alterations to the original structure	1 250	
Painting and general repairs	450	11 700
(vi) Purchase of water heater for new office		120
(vii) Installation of water heater in new office		55
(viii) Purchase of lathe on hire purchase terms:		
Cash price of lathe	6 700	
Deposit	1 000	
Interest charges over two years	1 710	9 410
(ix) Cost of installing lathe		370
(x) Costs of repositioning existing lathe to accommodate new lathe		580
Other expenditure during the year was:		
Plant repairs	847	
Building repairs	214	

(b) If you consider that the correct treatments of any of the items are debatable then add brief notes supporting the methods you suggest.

9.18 The following schedule of balances was extracted from the accounting records of OK Manufacturing Company, as at 31 August 19X8:

Stocks at 1 September 19X7	
Raw materials	£13 550
Work-in-progress	6 500
Finished goods	12 800
Purchases and expenses for year to 31 August 19X8	
Raw materials	237 650
Indirect materials	1 850
Direct wages	53 230
Factory power	4 550
Factory heating and lighting	1 975
Office heating and lighting	930
Printing and stationery	1 264
Postage and telephone	520
Factory salaries	11 500
Office salaries	9 900
Factory insurances	1 210
Other insurances	450
Depreciation: factory equipment and machinery	5 000
Office equipment and machinery	650
Office expenses	1 680
Advertising	850
Sales of manufactured products to 31 August 19X8	378 150

The following additional information is relevant to the above accounting period:

(a) Stocks at 31 August 19X8:	
Raw materials	£24 000
Work-in-progress	7 987
Finished goods	18 050
(b) Prepayment at 31 August 19X8:	
Factory insurances	£116
Other insurances	45
(c) Accruals at 31 August 19X8:	
Direct wages	£1 342
Factory heating and lighting	197
Office heating and lighting	43
Factory power	350

You are required to prepare, for the year ending 31 August 19X8,

(i) manufacturing accounts;

(ii) trading account; and

(iii) profit and loss account.

Chapter 10
Stock

Nature and importance of stock ☐ Control over stock ☐ Physical stocktaking ☐ Stock valuation ☐ Perpetual stock records ☐ Retail stocks ☐ SSAP 9: Stocks and Work-in-Progress

Nature and importance of stock

In the previous chapter, we identified stock as one of those assets where the costs are stored in the asset account until the goods have been sold or until the materials or supplies have been used. In this chapter, we are more concerned with the procedures employed to ensure that such goods are adequately controlled and are accurately recorded and reported.

For a wholesaler or retailer, stocks are generally finished goods in a fully completed and saleable state. For a manufacturer, they are more varied, and normally consist of some finished goods (which may be later sold to a wholesaler or retailer), partly finished goods known as work-in-progress, and raw materials used to make the finished goods. All business enterprises usually carry 'stocks' of other things, such as packaging materials, fuel, spare parts for machines, office stationery, etc.

In considering the importance of accounting for stock the following points are relevant:

1. Since stock is the goods which the business hopes to resell at a profit, it is only natural that it is very interested in the quantity and quality of the goods in stock. It is anxious to have the right goods in the right place at the right time. Thus if they are of poor quality, in bad condition, the wrong colour or size, or out of date then sales suffer and this materially affects profit. It is therefore necessary that constant vigilance is exercised to see that the stocks are examined regularly for deterioration, poor storage or obsolescence.

2. Stocks are valuable assets, and in many businesses represent a large proportion of all assets. It is therefore essential that adequate controls are instituted so that pilfering and other stock losses are cut to a minimum.

3. Also important are the costs associated with holding the stock: storage costs, insurance, supervision and clerical costs and the interest on the capital sum invested. Another cost, one which does not lend itself to precise measurement, is the cost of stock-outs. Delay in supplying a customer may result in lost revenue in relation to both the item requested and future business dealings with the customer.

Naturally, a lot of thought has gone into these problems, and a number of sophisticated models have been developed which attempt to optimise the investment in stock by solving the problems of how much to order (economic order quantity) and when to reorder (reorder point). However, these questions lie outside the scope of this text.

4. Another important factor is the rate at which the stocks are sold. Given that the profit margin remains unchanged, the quicker the stock turnover, the higher will be the profits.

The rate of stock turnover for an enterprise is calculated as follows:

$$\frac{\text{Cost of goods sold}}{\text{Average stock carried}}.$$

If the stock figures are determined monthly then the average stock figure will be found to be more accurate than when only the opening and closing balances of each year are known. The rate is expressed either as a number of times per year, for example the stock is sold on the average 8.6 times annually, or as a period, for example assuming that there are 300 business days in the year, the entire stock is sold on the average every 34.9 days (35 days approx.)

Example: Two companies, X and Y, both purchase £1000 of the same goods. X sells all of them within a week for £1200. Y charges £1400 and takes four weeks to sell them. If X replaces the original goods as soon as they are sold it will have made four amounts of £200 (£800) at the end of the four weeks. In the same time Y will have made only £400. In this case X has a stock turnover four times as fast as that of Y.

Control over stock

In Chapter 7, we discussed control over purchases – that is, the ordering, the receipt of the goods and the checking of the suppliers' invoices prior to payment. Here we are more concerned with controls which should operate while the goods are being stored. The following factors are important in this connection:

1. The goods should be stored in separate, numbered bins or bays so that it is possible to locate them quickly.

2. They must be protected from damage, deterioration and theft.

3. The store must be locked when not in use and only store staff should have access to it.

4. Goods must be insured under an adequate insurance cover.

5. Old stocks must not be left at the bottom of bins but should be used before new stocks, particularly if subject to deterioration.

6. Constant checks should be made of the condition of goods in the store.

Physical stocktaking

In Chapter 3, under the heading 'Analysing sales transactions', we distinguished between two alternative methods of accounting for stock: the physical stock method and the perpetual stock method. We observed that some businesses are able to isolate and record the cost of goods sold. Where this is impossible or impracticable, the cost of goods sold is inferred from a calculation involving a figure obtained by actual stocktaking. Thus, in many businesses, stocktaking is a necessary preliminary to periodical profit determination. Even where the cost of goods sold has been obtained by a continuous recording of stock movements, a physical stock is desirable as a check on the accuracy of stock records. In some cases, such checks are maintained continuously; that is, a different section of the stock is checked each week or month.

Stocktaking, therefore, is an important phase of the accounting cycle, and it is important that the results obtained from it are as accurate as possible. It should be a well-planned and well-controlled operation. The following precautions are normally taken:

1. Stock is arranged in a manner suitable for counting.

2. Great care has to be taken that proper adjustments are made in respect of purchases and sales taking place just before or just after the cut-off point to ensure that goods are not counted double or omitted altogether. Whenever a physical count of stock is to be made then a point of time has to be decided upon to establish the stock owned by the firm. This is known as the cut-off point and, for an annual end-of-year stocktake, normally coincides with the balance date.

3. Numbered tags are attached to the shelves beforehand. When goods have been counted they are entered on the tags. The prenumbering of the tags ensures that all are accounted for when collected.

4. In the same way, numbered stock sheets are used for entries from the tags. This ensures that no sheets are lost or forgotten.

5. All work from the actual counting to the final addition of the stock sheets should be double-checked and signed for. In many businesses, the stocktaking is a long and tedious job. It is often begun well before balance date and may, in large enterprises, occupy several weeks. It should be under the supervision of an officer other than the normal stores officer.

However, there are limitations where a firm relies *solely* upon the periodic or physical method of stock control:

1. Errors can occur in the physical count in the values applied, the arithmetical calculations, etc., hence the precautions in the stocktaking procedures listed above.

2. Because of the time taken for the stocktaking process, it is difficult to obtain a short-term (for example, monthly or quarterly) profit and loss statement. This makes it more difficult to follow the progress of the enterprise during the year and to correct any harmful trends that show up.

3. The process of stocktaking involves a disturbance and interruption to normal business routines and this also prevents stocktaking being done more frequently than, say, twice a year.

4. There is very little control over the asset, as no attempt is made to keep a continuous record of what stocks *ought* to be present. This means there is no way of pinpointing stock losses or discrepancies; also too much or too little of some items may be carried. The former may cause excessive or wasteful capital outlay, while the latter may cause delays in delivery of sales to customers, and therefore lost profits.

These limitations may be compared with the advantages of a perpetual system:

1. Short-term (say monthly) profit determination can be achieved without the necessity of a physical stocktake.

2. Better control can be achieved over stock by having knowledge of what items *should* be present at any time.

3. The detailed records assist in keeping stock levels within acceptable limits – thus minimising the danger of stock-outs or overinvestment. They also facilitate analysis of sales by product lines, etc.

A disadvantage of the perpetual system is that it is more expensive to operate. However, computers have enabled many firms to change to the perpetual system. Computerised stock systems have enabled management to have detailed information about stocks (location, age, condition, reordering points) available on a day-to-day basis.

Stock valuation

The normal basis of measurement for stock is 'cost'. There are a number of problems associated with this seemingly simple proposition.

Cost in relation to stock includes the purchase price of the goods and all expenditure which has been incurred in the normal course of business – of bringing them to a location and a condition where they can be productively used. It includes carriage and handling costs, customs or excise duties, taxes, insurance in transit, etc. For a wholesaler or a retailer dealing in finished goods, and also for the *raw materials* stock of a manufacturer, this may be reasonably simple. However, as we saw in Chapter 9, for the type of business which produces goods from raw materials, the cost of its closing stock of work-in-progress and its finished goods can vary, depending upon the costing methods adopted. While the alternative methods will be explained briefly in Chapter 20, a detailed consideration of their effects upon stock valuation is outside the scope of first-year accounting studies. It suffices here to say that the two major alternative costing methods are absorption costing (which includes a proportionate part of the fixed costs of the period as well as the variable costs of the period) and direct or variable costing (which includes only variable costs, with the fixed costs being expensed (charged) against the revenue in the accounting period in which they are incurred). There is also the possibility that a standard costing system may be used and 'standard' costs applied to stock valuation.

A more fundamental problem is whether to use original (that is, historic) cost or current cost for determining cost of goods sold and to value closing stock. The conventional approach, still generally practised, is to use historic cost modified by the use of the 'lower of cost or market value rule' (explained later in this chapter). However, for many years the use of historic-cost-based methods in times of rapidly changing prices has been severely criticised by some accountants and other interested parties. It has been argued that current cost more fairly measures both cost of goods sold (and thus profit) and the value of stock on hand.

If historical cost is used, there is a further difficulty associated with the movement of stock which flows in and out of a business during an accounting period. During any period, prices tend to change. Assuming that stock is homogeneous and store staff make random issues, it is impossible under most circumstances to identify which cost price was paid for the unsold stock at balance date. Consider the following example:

During an accounting period, a firm purchased for resale 2000 litres of a special fluid. Three separate purchases were made:

Lot 1	500 litres at £10 per litre
Lot 2	1000 litres at £8 per litre
Lot 3	500 litres at £12 per litre

It stored the fluid in one large container. If 1700 litres were sold during the period what are

1. The cost of the goods sold?

2. The cost of the remaining stock of 300 litres?

Before considering the possible answers we should explain that while in this example we deliberately chose a fluid to illustrate the manner by which individual purchases may lose their 'cost identity', it is nevertheless typical of practically all other stock items. Many stock lines are homogeneous, for example bags of cement, tins of soup, spark plugs (of any given specification) and so on. An overwhelming proportion of stock carried by businesses using a perpetual system fit this description. They are simply stored in racks, bins, etc., and it matters little which particular item store staff may select for any given issue.

In practice, it is possible to select one of several different methods in order to measure the cost flows associated with the issues or sales. These are now explained using the above example.

1. *Actual (or identifiable) cost.* This first method is the exception to the general proposition that the original cost figure cannot be ascertained. In our example, actual cost cannot be used because we cannot identify which 300 litres do remain unsold. However, actual cost may be possible for, say, a large dealer in motor vehicles. Each vehicle would be readily identifiable by the engine and chassis number, or for second-hand vehicles, by the registration plate. The actual cost method will often be found where more costly items of stock are involved.

2. *Weighted average cost* – where the goods have lost their identity but it is assumed that the items sold (and remaining) are a proportionate sample of the purchases. The average should not be the arithmetical average (for example, £10) but should be weighted by the quantity of goods bought, that is:

	500 litres @ £10	=	£5 000	
	1 000 litres @ £8	=	8 000	
	500 litres @ £12	=	6 000	
	2 000		£19 000	
Average	=	$\dfrac{£19\,000}{2\,000}$	=	£9.50.

Thus, if average cost is used:

Cost of goods sold = 1700 × £9.50 = £16 150.
Closing stock   = 300 × £9.50 = £2850.

3. *First-in, first-out (FIFO)* – where the assumption is made that the goods received first are sold first, and that the unsold goods are those most recently purchased. The effect is to value the unsold stock at later prices in the balance sheet and use the earlier prices to calculate cost of goods sold.
    Thus if FIFO cost is applied:

Cost of goods sold = (500 × £10) + (1000 × £8) + (200 × £12)
                   = £5000 + £8000 + £2400
                   = £15 400.
Closing stock   = 300 × £12 = £3600.

4. *Last-in, first-out (LIFO)* – where it is assumed that the most recently purchased goods are used first. This results in the earlier prices being used in the balance sheet for unsold stock and the later (current) prices to calculate cost of goods sold.
    Thus, if LIFO cost is applied:

Cost of goods sold = (500 × £12) + (1000 × £8) + (200 × £10)
                   = £6000 + £8000 + £2000 = £16 000.
Closing stock   = 300 × £10 = £3000.

5. *Standard cost* – where a predetermined cost is taken and applied to all goods whether sold or unsold. For the above example, the standard cost could be, say, £10.50 per litre. Any gain or loss on purchasing at prices above or below this figure would be dealt with separately.

If standard cost of £10.50 is applied:

Cost of goods sold = 1700 × £10.50
                   = £17 850.
Closing stock   = 300 × £10.50
                   = £3150.

We do not intend to discuss the merits and weaknesses of the above methods. However, it should be observed that when prices are rising:

FIFO will minimise cost of goods sold, and maximise profit and closing stocks.

LIFO will maximise cost of goods sold, and minimise profit and closing stocks.

Weighted average will produce a result between FIFO and LIFO.

There are situations for which each may be considered to be the most appropriate solution to the problem; the decision to adopt a particular method is more likely to be a policy decision taken in the light of its effect upon profit rather than an attempt to choose a method which simulates the physical flows.

Whatever method is chosen, it will affect the cost of each sale or issue and the balance sheet figure for the remaining stock, hence consistent methods are essential.

Perpetual stock records

As we stated earlier, the perpetual stock method depends on some method of continuous stock recording. Computers are, of course, admirably suited to this function. In a manual system, the stock movements are entered on loose leaves or cards, with one for each separate type of commodity. On this appears a description of the item and what it is used for (in the case of a factory), the quantity and value of both the goods received and the goods sold or issued, and a running balance of stocks held. Some manufacturers use a 'standard' price for all raw materials used and provide for losses or gains at the time the goods are purchased. In this case, there is no need to record the value of the items, and the cards in such instances record only quantities. The storekeeper may keep a rough record in the form of bin or rack cards on which is maintained a running total of the quantities of each item in stock. This provides a further check against stocks held.

There are, of course, considerable differences in the methods and forms used, but the basic system depends on a card similar to that shown in Fig. 10.1.

Fig. 10.1   A stock card.

Item						Location	
Code No.							
Date	Reference	In		Out		Balance	
		Qty	Value	Qty	Value	Qty	Value

The values for both inwards and outwards movements entered on the cards are made at 'cost' and would be obtained from the copies of the goods inwards slips (for purchases) and from the copies of the materials requisitions (for sales or issues). Reference to the diagram for purchasing (given in Chapter 7) will show how the copies are obtained by the clerk in charge of the stock records.

From the cards it is possible to obtain:

1. the cost of goods sold and hence the value of the current stocks as they ought to be;

2. some indication of the types of sales.

It is still necessary, however, to make periodical physical counts of goods held. This provides a check on how far the theoretical or book value of the stock deviates from the actual stocks held. Such a deviation will occur if stock is misappropriated or lost, or if there are errors in the entries on the cards. However, such a count need not be done at the one point of time but may be carried out throughout the year so that variations will be picked up quickly. This will also have a restraining effect on any person with dishonest tendencies, and will ensure prompt detection of deterioration or damage, or outdated lines. The amounts shown on the cards will be used for interim monthly profit figures, but the physical stocktaking will be used for the annual accounts. Where physical stocks differ from the stock card, the card must be corrected. The point at which such adjustment takes place depends upon the system being followed by the individual firm. However, at the end of the financial year, it is essential that the total of all cards agrees with the total in the stock account. You should note that perpetual stock records are basically subsidiary ledgers similar in function to subsidiary ledgers for debtors and creditors.

A simple example involving the use of stock cards is given below.

Example: On 30 June 19X6 the balance on hand of a certain item of stock was 60 units at £30 each. Purchases were made on the first day of every month and goods inwards records showed the following:

July 1	120 units	£32 each
August 1	80 units	£35 each
September 1	100 units	£34 each

Sales invoices showed the following sales:

July	90 units
August	110 units
September	80 units

Figure 10.2 shows a stock card using a FIFO assumption, and Fig. 10.3 shows a stock card using a weighted-average-cost assumption.

Date	In			Out			Balance		
	Qty	Unit	Value	Qty	Unit	Value	Qty	Unit	Value
June 30							60	30	1 800
July 1	120	32	3 840				{ 60	30	1 800
							{ 120	32	3 840
				60	30	1 800			
July 31				30	32	960	90	32	2 880
							{ 90	32	2 880
Aug. 1	80	35	2 800				{ 80	35	2 800
				90	32	2 880			
Aug. 31				20	35	700	60	35	2 100
							{ 60	35	2 100
Sept. 1	100	34	3 400				{ 100	34	3 400
				60	35	2 100			
Sept. 30				20	34	680	80	34	2 720
				Cost of goods sold		9 120	Stock on hand		2 720

Fig. 10.2   Stock card - FIFO assumption.

Date	In			Out			Balance		
	Qty	Unit	Value	Qty	Unit	Value	Qty	Unit*	Value
June 30							60	30	1 800
July 1	120	32	3 840				180	31.3	5 640
July 31				90	31.3	2 820	90	31.3	2 820
Aug. 1	80	35	2 800				170	33.0	5 620
Aug. 31				110	33.0	3 630	60	33.0	1 990
Sept. 1	100	34	3 400				160	33.7	5 390
Sept. 30				80	33.7	2 695	80	33.7	2 695
				Cost of goods sold		9 145	Stock on hand		2 695

* Approximate values only.

Fig. 10.3   Stock card – average-cost assumption.

Retail stocks

Earlier we stated that retailers may use other methods in order to control and value stocks. A variety of methods may be used.

1. Where the articles sold are large and easily identifiable (cars, pianos, tractors), it is usual to keep a stock book of some sort. In this is entered the date the article was taken into stock, the supplier and the cost price. When the goods are sold, similar details are entered on the opposite page. This way there is no difficulty in working out the value of unsold stock. Constant checks are made to ensure that the book balance agrees with a physical count.

2. In the case of some manufactured goods (for example, refrigerators, washing machines, mowers), a serial ticket accompanies each article. As the goods are brought into the store, a record is made of each of these serial numbers. When a sale is made, the serial ticket is torn off and retained by the salesperson so that an appropriate entry can be made alongside the serial number in the book. Control is therefore maintained over the unsold goods.

3. A simpler form of stock record is seen in shops selling rolls of carpet, lino or fabrics. The original length of the roll is marked on a ticket securely attached to the centre of the roll. As each sale is made an entry is made on the ticket. From these figures it is easy to work out how much of the roll is unsold.

4. In some stores, price tickets are made out as soon as the goods arrive. On the price ticket is entered a coded symbol representing the cost price. The usual method is to choose a ten-letter word which has no letter repeated in it. The position of the letter then indicates the figures 1 to 0. Thus, if, say, *introduces* were the chosen word, then a cost price of £2.68 is shown as *n/dc* since *n* is the second, *d* is the sixth and *c* the eighth letter. This makes it possible to ascertain the cost price of the unsold stock, and, in some cases, tickets may be taken from the articles sold to give the figure for cost of goods sold. The ready accessibility of the cost price also allows for a quick decision on whether the selling price can be reduced. The cost basis in such circumstances is 'actual' cost.

5. In retail stores, it is essential that some records of at least staple items, such as white sheets, plain handkerchiefs, pillow cases, etc., are kept. Should customers find the store is 'out' of such goods, the reputation of the store will suffer. Usually one member of the staff of each department

is given the task of looking after these. That person constantly checks the stocks held of such staple articles and is responsible for maintaining sufficient stocks. Here again, the stock records kept are simple and refer to quantities and type only.

6. The larger retail stores, faced with the difficulties of many stock lines and high rates of turnover, find it impossible to maintain the perpetual records (described earlier) for much of their stock. However, management may wish to prepare short-term (say monthly) profit statements and of course to do this the cost of sales must be known. A complete physical stocktake each month is not feasible. Thus, neither the perpetual nor the physical stock method is suitable. To overcome the problem, a method known as the *retail stock method* may be used. This calculates both the cost of the goods sold and the closing stock. It is based on the 'mark-up' added to the cost price to cover expenses and profit. This mark-up is very often a standard addition, for example, 25 per cent, $33\frac{1}{3}$ per cent, etc. There are normally some variations from this standard, but such extra 'mark-ups' or 'mark-downs' can be noted and allowed for. This involves the following factors:

(a) The division of the stocks handled into convenient groups with all items within one group having the same gross profit mark-up.

(b) The conversion of opening stocks and purchases figures to selling price.

(c) The recording of any subsequent alterations to selling price, that is, mark-ups and mark-downs.

Then, if the sales figures for each particular group are known, an estimate of closing stock and cost of goods sold for the period may be made.

The retail stock method embraces the fact that it is always possible to calculate the relationship between cost price and selling price, given that we know the percentage mark-up on cost.

Example: A mark-up of $33\frac{1}{3}$ per cent is added to goods costing £100.

Therefore   cost price = £100,   selling price = £$133\frac{1}{3}$,   nominal profit = £$33\frac{1}{3}$.

Therefore the percentage relationship of profit to selling price = $\dfrac{£33\frac{1}{3}}{£133\frac{1}{3}} \times 100 = 25$ per cent.

Therefore the percentage relationship of cost of goods sold to sales = $\dfrac{100}{133\frac{1}{3}} \times 100 = 75$ per cent.

In other words, a mark-up of $33\frac{1}{3}$ per cent on cost represents a cost of sales of 75 per cent and a profit on sales of 25 per cent.

If there have been no variations to the standard mark-up, we can readily calculate the cost price of goods sold, the profit and the cost price of unsold stock. In the above circumstances, assume opening stock costing £100 and various sales as follows:

	Sales	Cost of goods sold (75%) (£)	Profit (£)	Closing Stock (£) =	Opening stock less cost of goods sold (£)
(1)	60	45	15	55	(100 − 45)
(2)	70	52.50	17.50	47.50	(100 − 52.50)
(3)	80	60	20	40	(100 − 60)

As sales are readily known from sales records (at selling price), all we need to do is to apply the percentage established between the cost and selling price to calculate cost of goods sold. Naturally, such a procedure does not allow for the possibility that shortages caused by error or theft may exist.

However, as noted above, there are normally some variations from the standard percentage mark-up because of a number of factors; for example, in any one department, some goods carried may justify a higher or lower mark-up; prices may be reduced for special sales; employees may get store discount, etc. Provided a record of such variations is kept, the retail method can still be applied.

Example: A particular department in a retail store marks all goods for sale at $33\frac{1}{3}$ per cent above cost price. The following information is available for the month of April.

Stock (April 1st) at cost	£5 400
Purchases (at cost)	3 420
Additional mark-ups	580
Mark-downs	340
Sales	4 400

Estimate the cost of the stocks on hand at 30 April and the cost of goods sold for the month.

Calculation:

	Cost	Selling Price
Stock (April 1)	£5 400	£7 200
Purchases	3 420	4 560
	8 820	11 760
Add Mark-ups (above normal)		580
		12 340
Less Mark-downs (below normal mark-up)		340
	£8 820	£12 000

The relationship thus established between cost price and selling price is $\dfrac{£8\ 820}{£12\ 000}$, and the cost price of the actual sales (£4400) can be calculated:

$$\text{Cost of goods sold } \frac{8\ 820}{12\ 000} \times \frac{4\ 400}{1} = £3\ 234.$$

$$\text{Closing stock } 8820 - 3234 = £5586.$$

A number of variations are possible in the retail stock calculation, depending upon the assumption made. The above example assumes that a proportion of the goods have their prices varied from the standard mark-up are sold, and that a proportion still remain in the closing stock. A different assumption could have been that all such articles are sold and none remain unsold. To ascertain the cost of goods sold under this latter assumption, it is necessary to adjust the recorded sales figure by the net mark-up. This is because we are using the same sterling sales figure as before, namely, £4400, but this now includes additional sales revenue of £240 (£580 − £340), which means a lesser quantity of physical goods were sold. Thus, the normal selling price would have been £4400 less £240 = £4160. Applying the same procedure as in the original calculation:

The relationship established between cost price and normal selling price is $\dfrac{£8\ 820}{£11\ 760}$, and the cost price of the actual physical sales (£4160) can be calculated:

$$\text{Cost of goods sold } \frac{8\ 820}{11\ 760} \times \frac{4\ 160}{1} = \pounds 3\ 120.$$

Closing stock $8820 - 3120 = \pounds 5700$.

Compared with the first assumption, the second assumption produces a lower cost of goods sold, a higher profit and higher closing stock. This is only true for this example where there is a net *increase* of prices above standard. A net decrease will reverse these effects.

The management of stores which use the retail method would be aware of which assumption or combination of assumptions will best adjust for the variations to standard mark-up. The method does give retail managers the ability to approximate cost of goods sold to enable the preparation of monthly or short-term financial statements in a situation where perpetual records or a physical count of all stocks carried are impracticable. However, it is usual for retailers to check the physical quantities of stock in order to compare them with the approximated amounts that should be present under the retail method. The comparison is normally made at selling prices and carried out at least annually, but for some departments is much more frequent.

SSAP 9: Stocks and Work-in-Progress

We stated earlier that conventional accounting uses historical cost as the primary basis for reporting stock as an asset in the balance sheet. Generally, the use of historic cost is modified by the application of what is known as 'the lower of cost and net realisable value'.

The basic rule contained in Statement of Standard Accounting Practice 9 (Stocks and Work-in-Progress) for the valuation of stock and work-in-progress is that the value adopted should be the lower of cost and net realisable value. The comparison of cost and net realisable value needs to be made in respect of each item of stock separately.

In order to match costs and revenue, cost is defined as 'that expenditure which has been incurred in the normal course of business in bringing the product or service to its present location and condition'. Also, such costs should include all related production overheads, even though these may accrue on a time basis. Production overheads are considered to be those incurred in respect of labour or services for production, based on the normal level of activity taking one year with another.

The standard defines net realisable value as the actual or estimated selling price after deducting trade discount and less all further costs to completion and all costs to be incurred in marketing, selling and distributing.

Methods of determining cost

In accordance with SSAP 9, the determination of the nearest approximation to cost gives rise to two problems:

1. The selection of an appropriate method of relating costs to stock and work-in-progress. Examples include, job costing, batch costing, process costing, standard costing.

2. The selection of an appropriate method for calculating the related cost where a number of identical items have been purchased or made at different times. Examples include unit cost, average cost or FIFO.

In one of the appendices to SSAP the following definitions are given relating to the method of determining cost:

1. *Unit cost* – The cost of purchasing or manufacturing identifiable units of stock.

2. *Average cost* – The calculation of the cost of stocks and work-in-progress on the basis of the

application to the unit of stocks on hand of an average price computed by dividing the total costs of units by the total number of such units. This average price may be arrived at by means of a continuous calculation, a periodic calculation or a moving periodic calculation.

3. *FIFO* (*first in, first out*) – The calculation of the cost of stocks and work-in-progress on the basis that the quantities in hand represent the latest purchases or production.

4. *LIFO* (*last in, first out*) – The calculation of the cost of stocks and work-in-progress on the basis that the quantities in hand represent the earliest purchases or production.

5. *Base stock* – The calculation of the cost of stocks and work-in-progress on the basis that a fixed unit value is ascribed to a predetermined number of units of stock, any excess of this number being valued on the basis of some other method. If the number of units in stock is less than the predetermined minimum, the fixed unit value is applied to the number in stock.

6. *Replacement stock* – The cost at which an identical asset could be purchased or manufactured.

7. *Standard cost* – The calculation of the cost of stocks and work-in-progress on the basis of periodically predetermined costs calculated from management's estimates of expected levels of cost and of operations and operational efficiency and the related expenditure.

Other methods of valuation include:

8. *Latest invoice price* – In this method the latest invoice price is applied to the total volume of stocks held. This is only an acceptable method where it can be shown that price fluctuations during the period when stock is held have been insignificant and that the result is a reasonable approximation of cost.

9. *Retail method* – In this method, which is used mainly by retailers, the total stock on hand is valued at current selling price and then reduced to approximate cost by deducting the normal gross margin.

Summary

1. Stocks are important, because:

(a) They are a valuable asset, often a significant proportion of total assets.

(b) Most trading businesses rely primarily on their stocks to make a profit.

(c) Losses can arise through over-investment, obsolescence, poor storage, or stock-outs.

2. The speed with which the stocks are turned over is as important as the size of stocks carried.

3. Adequate controls need to be exercised over stocks in storage to ensure protection against damage, deterioration and theft.

4. Adequate supervision and control over stocktaking procedures is essential, especially where the business relies solely on a physical stocktaking for profit determination.

5. Reliance on physical stocktaking alone fails to reveal stock shortages and losses. It only tells what are actually present, and there is no means of knowing what ought to be there. Furthermore, such reliance makes short-term profit determination almost impossible.

6. There is an endless variety of systems of perpetual stock recording. Computers are ideal for this.

7. To ensure the maximum control from the use of perpetual stock records, it is advisable that:

(a) The duties of recording and custodianship of the goods be kept separate.

(b) The figures for the stock records be regularly compared with the actual stocks held (this ought to be done by a third person).

(c) Control accounts be maintained in the ledger so that losses of stocks can be revealed.

8. The 'retail stock method' enables cost of goods sold to be estimated where uniform mark-ups are applied.

9. When stocks are valued at historical cost, and actual cost cannot be identified, then one of a number of possible assumptions (LIFO, FIFO, average cost, standard cost, etc.) must be chosen. The choice should be adhered to consistently from one period to another.

10. In conventional accounting, the use of historic cost as the basis of measurement for stock is modified by the application of the lower of cost and net realisable.

Discussion questions

10.1 Many firms install and operate costly computerised systems to control and account for stock. Why are they prepared to incur these costs?

10.2 'An efficient system of stock control and recording eliminates the need for a physical stocktaking.' Do you agree with this statement? Give reasons for your answer.

10.3 Explain the term 'historic cost' as it applies to stock. Discuss why the use of historic cost for stock has been subjected to criticism.

10.4 A firm buys and sells a single homogeneous commodity. During a particular accounting period it made a number of purchases of the commodity at different prices. Explain how assumptions made regarding which units were sold will affect the firm's reported profit for the period.

10.5 Give examples of where the use of the 'actual' or 'identifiable' cost method is appropriate.

10.6 (a) What is meant by 'the lower of cost and net realisable value'?

(b) On what grounds can the application of this rule be criticised?

10.7 A number of alternative methods may be used in determining cost of goods sold and the cost of stock on hand. Why is it important to be consistent in the use of one of these methods?

10.8 (a) What is meant by the 'stock turnover rate'?

(b) Does a higher stock turnover rate increase or decrease the difference between cost of goods sold using current cost' and 'cost of goods sold using FIFO historic cost'? Why?

Exercises

10.9 Assuming that stock account is a control account for the stock cards, and that cost is the basis of all stock card records, prepare from the following information a stock account, a cost of goods sold account, showing clearly the amount of the stock shortage.

Trading Statement for the six months ended 31 December 19X6

Sales			£42 000
Stock (1/7/X6)	£6 000		
Purchases	30 000		
	36 000		
Stock 31/12/X6 as per physical stocktaking	7 000		29 000
Gross profit			£13 000

Perpetual stock records

Sales for the six months ended 31 December 19X6 were represented by goods which had cost	£28 500
Stock at 31 December 19X6	7 500

10.10 The following information is available from the books of a retailer:
Stock (at 1 January) at cost £8200 (by physical stocktaking)

Totals of Day Books

	Purchases	Purchases returns	Sales	Sales returns
January	£2 549	£230	£3 400	£310
February	1 820	105	2 800	120
March	1 600	90	2 800	110
April	2 050	110	2 650	130
May	1 920	135	2 220	110
June	1 540	80	2 500	120

Stock (at 30 June) at cost £7150 (by physical stocktaking)

(a) Show the method of recording this information in the ledger where no attempt is made to keep a continuous record of stock movements.

(b) If the following figures are available as to the cost of net sales (i.e., sales minus sales returns) for each month.

January	£2 330
February	2 095
March	2 110
April	1 780
May	1 595
June	1 750

(i) Show the stock account and the cost of goods sold account in the ledger.

(ii) Prepare a trading statement showing profit for the six-month period.

10.11 The ledger of a wholesale grocer included the following accounts with balances given as at 1 April.

Sales				£22 500 *Cr.*
Sales returns				1 850 *Dr.*
Stock				1 200 *Dr.*
Cost of goods sold				15 400 *Dr.*

The following information is available for the three months ended 30 June:

From Stock Cards

Month	Sales Day Book Totals	Sales Returns Totals	Cost of Goods Sold	Sales Returns at Cost	Purchases Day Book Totals
April	£1 500	£200	£1 000	£150	£1 400
May	2 000	250	1 600	200	2 000
June	3 000	350	2 200	250	2 000

A physical stocktake at 30 June revealed stock of £2100.

You are required to:

(a) record the above information in ledger accounts;

(b) prepare a trading statement for the three-month period.

10.12 Determine the cost of goods sold from the following data using:

(a) the last-in, first-out method

(b) the first-in, first-out method

(c) the weighted-average-cost method

Nov. 1 Stock balance	400 units at £2.00 per unit
Nov. 12 Purchases	300 units at £2.50 per unit
Nov. 19 Purchases	100 units at £3.00 per unit
Nov. 26 Purchases	200 units at £3.00 per unit
Nov. 28 Sold to X	700 units at £5.00 per unit

10.13 A company, which keeps a record of stock movements throughout the year and in addition takes physical stock at the end of the financial year, reveals the following trading results:

Sales for the year ended 30/6/X6	£100 000
Stock 1/7/X5	15 000
Purchases for the year	78 000
Stock at 30/6/X6 as per physical stocktake	13 000

On first calculation, the stock cards, showing values based on the FIFO method, revealed an amount of £78 600 for cost of goods sold. However, on second check, it was found that a stock card for one item had been omitted in the above calculation.

A listing of the information that appeared on this stock card showed the following:

19X5		
July 1	Balance	400 units @ £1.00 per unit
September	Purchases	600 units @ £1.25 per unit
November	Sales	500 units
19X6		
January	Purchases	200 units @ £1.25 per unit
March	Sales	300 units

You are required to:

(a) record the appropriate information in a properly constructed stock card for the item omitted;

(b) prepare a stock account, cost of goods sold account and trading statement, showing clearly any discrepancies in stock that may have arisen.

10.14 (a) Explain the nature and purpose of the method of 'retail stock'.

(b) A retailer supplies the following figures:

Stock (1 April) at cost	£14 100
Purchases for April	8 100
Standard mark-up	$33\frac{1}{3}\%$ on cost
Special mark-ups for April	800
Special mark-downs for April	400
Sales for April	10 000

Estimate the cost value of stock as at 30 April assuming a proportionate part of the specially adjusted goods was unsold at the end of April.

10.15 W. Cook sells office furniture. His selling prices are calculated to give him a gross profit of 40 per cent on sales. He requires you to prepare monthly profit and loss statements but does not desire to carry out a physical stocktake each month.

His figures for the month of July were as follows:

Stock at 1 July (at cost)	£5 000
Purchases (at cost)	15 000
Additional mark-ups	4 000
Mark-downs	5 000
Sales	25 000
Purchases returns (at cost)	1 000
Sales returns (at selling price)	2 000

(a) Estimate the value of closing stock at cost.

(b) Prepare a statement showing estimated gross profit for July (work to the nearest pound).

(c) Assume only a proportionate part of the additional mark-ups and mark-downs was sold during the month.

Problems

10.16 Goodwill Stores carried out stocktaking on 30 June 19X6. Subsequent checking of the stock sheets revealed the following items:

(a) An invoice dated 15 July 19X6 (£1650) and recorded on that date was found to relate to goods received before the end of the financial year and they had been included in the stock sheets.

(b) A purchase of goods from overseas (£2800) had been paid in advance and recorded in the purchases account early in May 19X6, but the goods had not yet been received.

(c) Two pages of the stock sheets had accidentally stuck together during the addition process. The total of the page unrecorded was £9122.

(d) 100 units of part #A44 had been priced at £16.50 each in the stock sheets at 30 June 19X6. The correct price should have been £30 each. Similarly it was found that in the June 19X5 stocktake, 300 units of #A44 had been wrongly priced at £16.50. There had been no alteration in the price of #A44 during the year.

You are required to indicate the effect of the above items on:

(i) stock at June 30 19X5

(ii) stock at June 30 19X6

(iii) gross and net profit for year ended 30/6/X6

(iv) balance sheet at 30 June 19X6

10.17 A check of the books of a firm for the past five years has revealed that stock has been valued inconsistently. Proper valuation methods have revealed the following errors:

30 June 19X0	Stocktake correct	
30 June 19X1	Stocktake overvalued by £400	(end of first year)
30 June 19X2	Stocktake overvalued by £670	(end of second year)
30 June 19X3	Stocktake undervalued by £200	(end of third year)
30 June 19X4	Stocktake correct	(end of fourth year)
30 June 19X5	Stocktake overvalued by £550	(end of fifth year)

(a) Calculate the effect on profit at the end of each of the five years.

(b) Write the correction to the error at 30 June 19X5.

10.18 A firm trades in two different products, product X and product Y. From the transactions listed below, you are required to:

(a) prepare the perpetual stock card for product X, using the first-in, first-out method of costing;

(b) prepare the perpetual stock card for product Y, using the weighted averaged cost method of costing;

(c) prepare the stock control account, including shortages if necessary;

(d) prepare the trading account.

Oct.1	1	Balance of product X: 100 units at £1.55 each
		Balance of product Y: 70 units at £12.30 each
	4	Purchased 30 units of product X for £1.70 each
	10	Sold 20 units of product Y for £19.90 each
	12	Bought 40 units of product Y at £12.60 each
	17	Sold 80 units of product X for £3.00 each
	20	Bought 40 units of product X at £1.75 each
	24	Bought 30 units of Product Y at £13.00 each

Cont.

Oct.	28	Sold 30 units of Product X for £3.00 each
	30	Sold 70 units of product Y for £20.00 each
	31	Total both stock cards then correct each card (if necessary) to take into account the physical stock results which reveal that there are 60 units of product X and 45 units of product Y at the end of the month.

Chapter 11
Fixed assets

Types of fixed assets ☐ Control over fixed assets ☐ Determination of acquisition cost ☐ Nature of depreciation ☐ Factors affecting depreciation ☐ Methods of calculating depreciation ☐ Maintenance, betterments and disposal ☐ Revaluation of fixed assets ☐ SSAP 12: Accounting for Depreciation ☐ Fixed asset registers ☐ Accounting for goodwill

Types of fixed assets

In Chapter 4, we observed that assets are normally classified into current assets and fixed assets on the basis of the time for which they were expected to be held. Current assets are those assets already in a cash form, assets likely to be converted into cash within one accounting period or assets likely to be used up within one accounting period. Fixed assets are those intended to be retained for more than one accounting period.

Within this group of fixed assets we may recognise further subgroups. In Chapter 4, we made brief reference to the distinction which may be drawn between *tangible* assets (that is, those having a physical substance) and *intangible* assets. Common examples of tangible assets are land, buildings, plant and equipment, motor vehicles, furniture, and natural resources such as mineral deposits, oil wells, etc. Examples of intangible assets are goodwill, copyrights, patents, trademarks and investments.

A different way of classifying fixed assets is to distinguish between those which are depreciated (or amortised) and those which are not. The tangible asset land normally does not have a determinable limit to its useful life and therefore, unlike other tangible assets such as buildings, plant, vehicles, etc., does not have to be depreciated. With intangible assets the process of expensing is usually termed amortisation. Some intangible assets, such as copyrights and patents, are amortised while others, such as investments, do not require amortisation. It is problematical as to whether the intangible asset 'goodwill' should be amortised but, as we shall see later in this chapter, normal practice is to do so.

Control over fixed assets

In previous chapters, we have dealt with control over the current assets cash, debtors and stock. Although many of the controls will be similar to those used for current assets, there are some differences in the control of fixed assets because of the nature of the assets and the differences in the recording methods. An ideal system of control would ensure the following:

1. Proper authority for the purchase, and, where an asset is to be replaced, supervision of its disposal.

2. The procedure for the purchase and sale will follow similar lines to those for the purchase and sale of merchandise.

3. Documents of title, for example investments, motor vehicles, land, etc., should be kept in safe custody.

4. That each asset is properly accounted for. Special registers should be kept incorporating details such as description, purchase price, repairs and maintenance, etc. This is particularly important for such assets as plant and machinery and motor vehicles. These registers will be described in more detail later in this chapter.

5. Adequate insurance cover must be maintained over all assets.

6. Periodic checking of physical existence against registers, amount of insurance cover, condition of assets, etc. must be regularly carried out.

7. Marking and identification of the assets, proper housing and supervision, and proper maintenance.

Determination of acquisition cost

We saw in Chapters 7 and 9 that costs of expenditures could be treated either as assets or as expenses, the determining factor being whether or not some or all of the benefits would accrue in future accounting periods. The decision to treat an expenditure as an asset is often termed 'capitalisation'.

With fixed assets, the question of whether to capitalise or expense arises with some of the costs incurred when the asset is acquired. The question also arises after the date of acquisition if the asset requires further expenditure. Post-acquisition expenditure is considered later in this chapter.

With costs associated with the acquisition of a fixed asset, the basic principle is that the capitalised cost should include all expenditures necessary to make the asset suitable and ready for its intended use. Costs of installation, the expenses of getting the asset working properly, legal or valuation fees in connection with the purchase, and so on, should be added to the invoice price of the asset. For example, a machine is purchased in the United Kingdom for £5000 for use by an Australian firm. Freight, insurance costs, etc. are £650, customs duty amounts to £420, materials used in installation totalled £75, and wages paid to the firm's own workers to install the machine are £80. The entry in the machine account (if a separate account were kept) shows:

Machine Account		
Date	UK supplier	£5 000
	Freight etc.	650
	Customs duty	420
	Materials (installation)	75
	Wages (installation)	80

With some expenditures associated with the acquisition of fixed assets, the decision as to whether the cost should be capitalised or expensed is not always as straightforward as in the example given above. For instance, the costs of staff training for a new computer installation could theoretically be capitalised on the grounds that it will benefit future periods. However, in practice, such costs are normally expensed, it being argued that it is not certain whether the retrained staff will remain with the firm. There is also considerable debate on whether interest incurred during the period in which a new plant was being constructed should be treated as part of the cost of the new plant or whether it should be expensed.

Where there is some doubt about whether a particular expenditure should be capitalised or expensed, certain factors often combine to influence the decision in favour of expensing. The first is the previously mentioned tendency towards conservatism. Expensing will result in the understating rather than overstating of profit in the period in which the expenditure is incurred. Second, there is the question of convenience. Once an expenditure has been expensed it does not require any further treatment. If however it is capitalised then decisions have to be made as to the way in which it will be depreciated or amortised. Finally, management will wish to try to expense the outlay for tax purposes. Although, as stated previously, tax considerations should not, in theory, be allowed to influence accounting practices, there is some pressure on management to deal with an outlay in the accounts in a manner consistent with that adopted in the tax return.

You should remember that two very important considerations affecting decisions of expensing versus capitalising are those of materiality (that is, the size of the effect on reported profits) and consistency (that is, how such items were treated in previous periods).

There are three other problems which are sometimes associated with the determination of the capitalised cost of a fixed asset. They are the joint acquisition of two or more assets, the acquisition of an asset for a consideration other than cash and the question of how many asset accounts should be raised.

Two or more assets are sometimes acquired for a single purchase price. For example, land and buildings may be acquired or a business comprising a number of different assets may be purchased as a going concern. Because the separate assets require different treatment so far as depreciation is concerned, it is necessary to enter them separately, each with a specific cost amount, in the accounts. Independent valuation is the most common and appropriate method of arriving at these separate costs. For example, if land and buildings are jointly acquired for £2 million then an independent valuation may lead to the land being capitalised at, say, £1.3 million and the buildings at £0.7 million. If the total independent valuation is different from the purchase price, say, £1.5 million for land and £1 million for buildings (that is, a total of £2.5 million) then allocation may be made on the basis of relative values. Thus the land will be capitalised at £1.2 million and the buildings at £0.8 million.

When fixed assets are acquired for a consideration which is either totally or partially in a form other than cash (or credit) then the question arises as to whether the book value or the market value of the asset given in exchange should be used in determining the cost of the newly acquired asset. For example, suppose a used motor vehicle with a book value of £4000 is traded in at its fair market value of £5000 on a new motor vehicle and a further £8000 cash is paid to complete the deal. Theoretically, it can be argued that the new vehicle should be capitalised at £13 000 and a gain of £1000 on the sale of the old vehicle should be recorded. In practice, conservatism and taxation implications often lead to the new vehicle being capitalised at £12 000 and no gain being recorded. If however the trade-in value is less than book value then the loss on disposal of the old vehicle would be recorded.

Sometimes when a complex fixed asset is acquired a decision has to be made as to whether it is capitalised in one account or in two or more separate accounts. This is referred to as the 'unit of account' problem. For example, an airline may capitalise a passenger aircraft (at first sight, a single asset) in, say, three separate accounts – the airframe, the engines and the interior fittings. The justification for such treatment is that the separate components have significantly different lengths of expected useful life and therefore require different depreciation schedules.

Nature of depreciation

Many definitions of the term 'depreciation' have been suggested, but none seems completely satisfactory. Even when the word is used in an accounting sense it means different things to different people. This is because there are several aspects involved, and it seems that it is only satisfactory to define the term in a qualified manner, or perhaps to use different terms for each of the aspects. The fact is that each is inextricably connected.

Perhaps we can examine what are generally agreed upon as the main aspects, together with simplified historical cost examples, in order to make the implications of depreciation a little clearer.

The first and probably the most important aspect is that of cost allocation. Most fixed assets are deferred charges to revenue, that is, they are recorded as assets when acquired but become charges or expenses in subsequent accounting periods. It follows that there is a cost which must be allocated. Thus, in determining periodical profit, the total expenses for a period in which a fixed asset is partly consumed should include some part of the cost of that fixed asset.

Example: Plant costing £1000 is purchased. Its estimated useful life is five years and its estimated scrap or residual value is nil. Assume that each year gets equal benefit from using the plant. Thus, for each of the five successive accounting periods there is a depreciation expense of £200 per period, and in this sense the accounting emphasis is on cost allocation. This can be represented in the following diagram:

←─────────────	Estimated life 5 years	─────────────→		
Year 1	**Year 2**	**Year 3**	**Year 4**	**Year 5**
Expense	*Expense*	*Expense*	*Expense*	*Expense*
← £200 →	← £200 →	← £200 →	← £200 →	← £200 →
Original cost £1000				Residual Value £0
←───────────	Total allocation £1000	───────────→		

The second aspect is that the asset is being used up over its lifetime and the balance sheet should reflect this fact. Using the same example as before, it can be seen that at the *date of purchase* the plant can be shown in the balance sheet at its *full* cost; at the *end* of the first year at £800; at the end of the second at £600; at the end of the third at £400; the fourth £200; and, ultimately, at the end of the fifth year, it would not appear at all.

This reduction in the amount at which the asset appears in the balance sheet is sometimes referred to as the 'valuation aspect of depreciation'. The use of this term is dangerous as it implies that the amount appearing in the balance sheet represents a realistic assessment of the market value of the asset and depreciation based on the allocation of historic cost makes no attempt to do this. The use of the term 'book value' (that is, original cost less depreciation to date) to describe the balance sheet figure is more acceptable, provided it is clearly recognised that there is no intended relationship between 'book value' and 'market value'.

The third aspect of depreciation which warrants discussion is the widely held but falsely based view that depreciation provides funds for the replacement of the asset. This view stems from an unjustified extension of the fact that depreciation may have the effect of retaining funds within a business.

To illustrate this we will use the simple example given above but with the added assumptions that:

1. for each of the five years, total revenue is constant at £500 per annum, and

2. expenses (other than depreciation) are constant at £300 per annum, and that

3. plant is the *only* asset at the beginning of the first year.

It is obvious that if total revenue is £500 p.a. and the total expense is £500 p.a. (300 + £200), then profit p.a. is nil. The important point is that at the end of each year the balance sheet figure for plant is reduced by £200 and other assets are increased by £200. This will be readily appreciated if all the revenue (£500) has been received in cash and the expenses (£300) have been paid in cash. Then there will be a balance of cash at the end of the first year of £200, the second year £400, and so on. However, it is more realistic to regard the £200 as being represented by other assets generally. There is no outlay of cash each year for the depreciation – this is an allocation, by a book entry only, of the deferred cost of plant which was paid for at the time it was acquired. Thus, the effect of accounting for depreciation is to retain within the net asset structure an amount equal to the depreciation written off, or, in other words, to maintain intact the original capital invested in the plant.

However, although depreciation can have the effect of retaining funds, we must be very careful to avoid the error of thinking that it actually provides funds. If in the example above no revenue was generated then it is likely that depreciation would still be necesssary. Such depreciation would cause losses to be reported and the book value of the plant in the balance sheet to be decreased. But this decrease would not be offset by an inflow of other assets. Funds are generated by profitable operations, not by a book entry recording depreciation as an allocation of original cost.

Depreciation does not even ensure that funds generated by profitable operations will be available in a usable form when the asset needs to be replaced. Only a specific action of setting aside a fund will achieve this. It is still true that depreciation has the effect of retaining funds, but management seldom wants such funds kept separate in some investment or bank account bearing little or no interest. They can usually be more profitably employed in the general conduct of the business or applied to reduce liabilities; also, it is very likely that the cost of the new asset will be greater than the cost of the asset it replaces.

Factors affecting depreciation

There are four factors which determine the amount of cost allocation:

1. The original cost price of the asset.

2. The effective life of the asset.

3. The residual value of the asset.

4. The method of allocating the 'cost' between the several periods involved.

Of these only the original cost is known with any certainty. The original cost and the method of computing and recording it have already been discussed.

In considering the effective life of an asset it is possible to classify assets into three groups.

1. Where the exact life of an asset is known in advance, for example a lease for ten years, patents and copyrights which lapse at the end of a certain number of years, and so on.

In this group the asset diminishes with the effluxion of time.

2. Where an estimate has to be made, for example, motor vehicles, plant and machinery, buildings, etc.

In this group there are many factors reducing the effective life of the asset:

(a) Wear and tear or physical deterioration.

(b) Extraordinary wear, accident or destruction.

(c) Obsolescence – that is, the asset may still be capable of producing, but because of technological progress, it is no longer economic to operate. In manufacturing plants particularly, because of intense competition, the effective life planned for most machinery is often shorter than its expected physical life. Even when such machines are comparatively new, they may be replaced by improved models which result in larger production, more efficient operation or require less operating expenditure.

(d) In the case of wasting assets such as a mine, a forest or a quarry, the asset becomes exhausted or depleted.

3. Where it is possible that assets could last the whole lifetime of the enterprise, for example, land, goodwill.

The estimation of residual value involves two assessments:

(a) The effective life of the asset as shown above.

(b) The return anticipated from the disposal.

Methods of calculating depreciation

Since the cost of the asset is to be allocated to the periods in which the asset is in use, it follows that the total amount to be allocated will be the original cost less the residual value of the asset. This amount, when estimated, has to be allocated to the periods of effective use. There are several ways of doing this, but before we examine the ways they are calculated and applied, we must point out in general terms how difficult it is to determine a method of depreciation which adequately reflects the pattern of services which an asset may contribute to the earning of revenue over the several years of its useful life. With very few assets can the depreciation be spread in a completely rational pattern, for while their contribution in earning revenue comes primarily from their use, for many assets this is often an indirect association, for example, the boiler plant in a factory which services several departments. Furthermore, it usually requires a combination of assets to produce a product or effectively complete a sale. Also the using up of assets is conditional upon the intensity of their use, for example the number of shifts worked, which may vary with changes in economic conditions, and with technological changes causing obsolescence, all of which are difficult to forecast. Additionally, the longer the predicted life of an asset the greater the degree of uncertainty as to its service pattern, particularly in the later years, and its scrap value. For many assets, their effective life can be prolonged with given levels of repairs and maintenance, although there usually comes a point of time when it is economical to replace them. Many of the above factors are related. Suffice it to say that the choice of a method which could be claimed to allow for all of such factors is virtually impossible. What businesses tend to do is to select one of the more established methods, particularly when it coincides with a method acceptable to the Inland Revenue. In most cases, these are based on a function of time rather than on actual usage and are thus somewhat arbitrary. Five methods of depreciation are now explained.

1   Units of use method

Under this scheme the effective life of the asset is deemed to depend mainly on the use to which it is put. Motor vehicles may be held until such time as they have travelled, say, 80 000 miles, whereupon they will be sold. The amount of the depreciation will then be determined by the number of miles travelled in a particular accounting period. For example, a truck costs £20 000. Its resale value after 80 000 miles is estimated to be £4000. The cost to be allocated will therefore be £16 000 to be spread over the distance travelled. Thus, for each mile, depreciation will be assessed at 5p. In the same way, depreciation on any type of plant or machinery could be computed on the number of hours it is in use. This would apply particularly where machines operate three shifts daily. At the same time it must be pointed out that there are disadvantages in this method:

(a) If the motor vehicle referred to stays in the garage for a lengthy period, for example, three years, no depreciation would be charged, despite the effect of age and obsolescence, and its consequent expense to the enterprise.

(b) A more serious disadvantage is that the scheme can be applied only to certain assets. It would be difficult to calculate depreciation on the use made of buildings, furniture, fittings, etc.

(c) Accelerated or excessive use may necessitate a more than normal rate of depreciation. This is an area which has had little serious attention given it by accountants. Consequently it is much more useful to allocate the cost on a time basis rather than on a use basis. Depreciation rates are often established without the technical or physical behaviour of the asset under alternative methods of use being fully investigated.

2 Straight-line method

In this case, the cost to be allocated is spread evenly over the accounting periods during which it is effectively used. That is, if the effective life of the asset is five years, the total cost to be allocated is divided so that one-fifth is charged to each accounting period. This method assumes that the cost *should* be expensed evenly over the life of the asset. Hence, it overlooks the fact that more of the service potential of the asset may be used up in one year than in another, and therefore more of the cost should be charged against the revenue of that year; for example, if a machine is used for three shifts daily for one accounting period, and is only sporadically used in another accounting period then there will be no differentiation in the amount of the cost allocated in the two periods.

Example: A machine is purchased on 1 July for £3000. Its estimated life is five years, and the residual value is anticipated to be £700. Under the straight-line method the amount of depreciation to be charged in each of the five years ending each 30 June is calculated as follows:

$$\frac{£3\,000 - £700}{5} = £460 \text{ p.a.}$$

3 Diminishing-balance method

In some cases, an asset is regarded as more efficient when it is new, so that a larger part of the cost should be allocated in the earlier periods than in the later, when it will be breaking down and out of use for repairs, etc. Furthermore, it is thought that under the influence of conservatism it is better to recoup the major portions of the cost in the earlier periods, in case the asset becomes obsolete before the full cost has been allocated. Calculation is done by applying a constant percentage against the diminished balance of the asset as it stands at the start of each period. Using the same example as for the straight-line method above, the cost (£3000 − £700) is divided, assuming 25 per cent as the necessary percentage, as follows:

Year	Basis	Depn	Diminishing balance
1	25% original cost	£750	(£3000 − £750) = £2250
2	25% bal. of cost (£2 250)	£563	(£2250 − £563) = £1687
3	25% bal. of cost (£1 687)	£422	(£1687 − £422) = £1265
4	25% bal. of cost (£1 265)	£316	(£1265 − £316) = £949
5	25% bal. of cost (£949) (adjusted to absorb whole £2 300)	£249	(£949 − £249) = £700
		£2 300	

The required percentage D can be obtained from the formula:

$$D = 100 - 100\, \frac{\sqrt[n]{s}}{c},$$

where n = estimated years
s = estimated scrap value
c = original cost.

Obviously, the percentage used with the diminishing balance method has to be considerably higher than under the straight-line method if the net cost of the asset is to be written off over the same life.

4 Sum-of digits method

This is similar in its effects to the diminishing-balance methods, but has certain advantages over that method:

(a) It is easier to calculate.

(b) It writes off exactly the desired amount without any adjustment being necessary in the final year.

Assuming the same example as previously, the calculations would be as follows:

In the first year the asset will last for	5 years	
In the second year the asset will last for	4 years	
In the third year the asset will last for	3 years	
In the fourth year the asset will last for	2 years	
In the fifth year the asset will last for	1 year	
Sum of these digits =	15	
1st year 5/15ths of £2300 must be allocated	=	£767
2nd year 4/15ths of £2300 must be allocated	=	£613
3rd year 3/15ths of £2300 must be allocated	=	£460
4th year 2/15ths of £2300 must be allocated	=	£307
5th year 1/15th of £2300 must be allocated	=	£153
		£2 300

Comparison of three of the above methods

Year	Str. Line (2)	Dim. Bal. (3)	Sum of Digits (4)
1	£460	£750	£767
2	£460	£563	£613
3	£460	£422	£460
4	£460	£316	£307
5	£460	£249	£153
	£2 300	£2 300	£2 300

You will notice in this particular example:

(a) that the total amount allocated over the five-year period is the same in each case;

(b) that the range of method 3 is not as wide as that of 4, that is, £750 to £249 compared with £767 to £153;

(c) that the method chosen will affect the profit in each of the five years, although the total effect for the five-year period will be the same under all three methods.

5 Appraisal or revaluation

Where it is impossible to calculate the cost of an asset in any other way, as in the case of loose tools in a foundry or crockery and cutlery in a tearoom, or glasses in a hotel bar, it may be necessary to treat the asset in the same way as for stock. This means that a physical inventory has to be taken at the end of the year and the cost calculated as follows:

Opening value of asset	£250
Purchases during period	400
	£650
Value of asset at end of period (by physical inventory)	300
Allocation of depreciation	£350

Once the amount of depreciation to be charged has been calculated, the action to record this in the accounts is relatively straightforward. As explained in Chapter 4, the amount is debited to an expense account labelled 'Depreciation of_____' account and credited to a 'Provision for Depreciation of_____' account. Thus, the total amount provided accumulates in the provision for depreciation of_____ account. The use of a provision for depreciation account is preferable to reducing the value of the asset account, because the amount allocated annually is only an estimate which will not be confirmed until the asset is discarded or sold. Furthermore, this system preserves the asset account at its original cost or its restated amount. In the balance sheet, the asset will be shown at its cost, but will be reduced by the amount of the provision for depreciation on that asset.

Maintenance, betterments and disposal

When additional costs are incurred relating to a fixed asset after it has been placed in service, a decision has to be made as to when the additional costs should be treated as 'repairs and maintenance' and when as a 'betterment'. Repairs and maintenance represent work done to keep an asset in an operating condition and to ensure that the service originally expected of the asset is obtained. These costs are treated as expenses of the current period. Where costs improve the condition of the asset they are classed as 'betterments' and are capitalised. Betterments may increase the asset's productive capacity, extend the economic life of the asset beyond that originally expected or reduce the level of operating costs.

When the time comes for an asset to be discarded, it is very rarely that the estimate of either the useful life of the asset or the disposal price is exactly correct. In some cases, the asset has to be retained longer because of the difficulty or delay in replacement. In other cases, technological improvements may render it obsolete at an earlier date, and so on. In these cases, the 'cost' allocated to the various revenue periods will be either greater or less than the recorded cost. To enable the proper accounting result to be shown, it is necessary to bring together the provision for depreciation of the asset (that is, the cost already allocated), the recorded cost and the amount recovered on disposal of the asset. This is best done in a separate disposal of _____ account.

Example: A machine is purchased for cash on 1 January 19X6 for £1400. Its life is estimated at four years and 'scrap' value at £200. The machine is sold for cash on 31 December 19X9 for £350. (Assume that the accounting period is a calendar year, the straight-line method of depreciation is used and this is the only machine owned.)

Ledger

Machine

19X6			19X9		
Jan. 1	Cash	£1 400	Dec. 31	Disposal of machine	£1 400

Provision for Depreciation of machine

19X9			19X6		
Dec. 31	Disposal of machine	£1 200	Dec. 31	Depreciation of machine	£300
			19X7		
			Dec. 31	Depreciation of machine	300
			19X8		
			Dec. 31	Depreciation of machine	300
			19X9		
			Dec. 31	Depreciation of machine	300
		£1 200			£1 200

Disposal of Machine

19X9			19X9		
Dec. 31	Machine	£1 400	Dec. 31	Prov. for depn	£1 200
	Profit and loss			Cash	350
	(profit)	150			
		£1 550			£1 550

Cash

19X9		
Dec. 31	Disposal of machine	£350

Notes

1. If the sale of the asset had realised exactly £200, there would have been no surplus in the disposal account.

2. If the price obtained had been less than £200, there would have been a loss of the amount by which it fell short of £200. Profits or losses on disposal are due to the over- or under-depreciation of the asset during its lifetime.

3. If the estimated life is seen to be shorter or longer than four years, the rate of depreciation should be adjusted as soon as it becomes apparent.

4. If the asset had been disposed of during the year (instead of at the end), it is a matter of contention whether an allocation of ordinary depreciation should be made for that portion of the year before the calculation of the 'profit' or 'loss' on disposal; that is, if the above asset had been sold on 31 October 19X9 for £350, the position on disposal would have been as follows (both methods shown):

If depreciation is charged for part of the year:

		Disposal of Machine				
19X9			19X9			
Oct. 31	Machine	£1 400	Oct. 31	Prov. for depn		£1 150
	Profit and loss (profit)	100		($900 + \frac{5}{6}$ of 300)		
				Cash		350
		£1 500				£1 500

That is, £250 debited to profit and loss account as depreciation. £100 credited to profit and loss account as profit on sale.

If depreciation is not charged for part of a year:

19X9			19X9			
Oct. 31	Machine	£1 400	Oct. 31	Prov. for depn		£900
				Cash		350
				Profit and loss (loss)		150
		£1 400				£1 400

That is, £150 debit to profit and loss as loss on sale of machine.

Whichever method is used, it is essential that it be applied consistently to the disposal of all assets. In our opinion the first method more accurately reflects the true position and is to be preferred.

5. Although it is better to open a separate disposal of asset account, it is possible to make the entries in the asset account itself. However, where the asset account is a control account representing several items of a similar nature, the position is not revealed as clearly as is the case when a separate disposal account is used.

Revaluation of fixed assets

In recent years a number of companies have increased the value of certain of their fixed assets, particularly land and buildings, and to a lesser extent long-lived items of plant, etc. Some of the reasons for such revaluations are as follows:

1. A more realistic figure can be shown in the balance sheet. The original cost of land purchased a number of years ago is unlikely to represent a realistic value, taking into account changes in demand and the effects of inflation.

2. By increasing the value of assets subject to depreciation a firm is able to match against its current revenues a higher depreciation charge, one that is more representative of the present replacement costs of using the asset. This also assists the firm to maintain its operating capacity.

3. To discourage takeover bids. In recent years a number of firms have been subjected to takeover bids, which have in some cases been prompted by a knowledge on the part of the offerer that the offeree's assets, shown at historical cost, were substantially undervalued.

Note that here we are discussing 'ad hoc' or 'one every few years' revaluations, which should be distinguished from annual adjustments of fixed assets to a current cost basis, as discussed later in this chapter. The practice of irregular revaluations is open to criticism in that it is contrary to the doctrine of consistency and thus makes comparisons between the financial statements of a particular firm over a number of years more difficult to comprehend.

SSAP 12: Accounting for Depreciation

This summarises to a large extent the concepts explained earlier in this chapter. It does not mention in detail the different methods used to depreciate fixed assets but states that 'the management of a business has a duty to allocate depreciation as fairly as possible to the periods expected to benefit from the use of the asset and should select the method regarded as most appropriate to the type of asset and its use in the business'.

SSAP 12 identifies three factors relating to the assessment of depreciation and its allocation to accounting periods as follows:

1. Cost or valuation.

2. Nature of the asset and length of its expected life to the business having due regard to the incidence of obsolescence.

3. Estimated residual value.

The standard states that the precise assessment of residual value is a difficult matter and considers that if it is likely to be small in relation to cost it should be regarded as having a nil value.

Since the introduction of the standard, buildings should be depreciated having regard to the same criteria as in the case of other fixed assets. Prior to SSAP 12 being introduced buildings were usually not depreciated as it was normally the case that this asset increased rather than diminished in value. Freehold land, on the other hand, does not normally require to be depreciated unless subject to depletion, e.g. mines, quarries.

Fixed asset registers

To ensure that each item of plant, motor vehicles, etc. is properly accounted for, it is usual in the larger enterprises at least to keep adequate individual records in a register. Each machine etc. would be plainly identified with a number, and a separate sheet or card in the register would be allocated to it. On this would be recorded information (as required) concerning:

1. Description and location of machine.

2. Whether purchased new or second-hand.

3. The total purchase and installation cost.

4. Date installed or first operated.

5. Details of depreciation and calculation thereof.

6. How disposed of.

As well as depreciation calculated on a historical cost basis for accounting purposes, it may also be useful to record the depreciation allowable for tax purposes and depreciation calculated in terms of current cost.

Many firms also record the details of repairs and maintenance within such registers. The actual form of the register depends on the amount of detail desired and on the method of recording used, that is, handwritten or computerised.

The functions of registers for fixed assets are:

1. to provide information for inventory purposes – for control over assets;

2. to provide a detailed history of each item so that appropriate entries can be made when the asset is dispensed with;

3. to enable the proper calculation of depreciation to be made:

4. to guide management in respect of future purchases of assets.

You should note that such registers really constitute a subsidiary ledger. The corresponding control accounts in the general ledger are the fixed asset account (for example, delivery vehicles) and the relevant provision for depreciation account.

Accounting for goodwill

In Chapter 4 the concept of goodwill was introduced. It was stated that goodwill was the likelihood of customers being likely to continue dealing with the established business. A distinction was drawn between 'purchased goodwill', which can be identified when a business changes ownership, and 'internally generated goodwill' where the business is still owned by its founders.

The controversial topic has been the subject of discussion in the accountancy profession for many years and an attempt was made in 1984 by the introduction of SSAP 22: Accounting for Goodwill to clarify the situation and to determine rules for dealing with this intangible asset.

In the standard it is stated that it is usual for the value of a business as a whole to differ from the value of its separable net assets. The difference, which may be positive or negative, is described as goodwill.

It is further stated that goodwill is therefore by definition incapable of realisation separately from the business as a whole; this characteristic of goodwill distinguishes it from all other items in the accounts. Its other characteristics are as follows:

1. The value of goodwill has no reliable or predictable relationship to any costs which may have been incurred.

2. Individual intangible factors which may contribute to goodwill cannot be valued.

3. The value of goodwill may fluctuate widely according to internal and external circumstances.

4. The assessment of the value of goodwill is highly subjective.

Thus any amount attributed to goodwill is unique to the valuer and to the specific point in time at which it is measured, and is valid only at that time, and in the circumstances then prevailing.

The following policies must be adopted in respect of the treatment of goodwill in the financial accounts.

Amounts representing goodwill can be included only to the extent that the goodwill was acquired for valuable consideration. No amount should be attributed to non-purchased goodwill in the balance sheet.

Purchased goodwill should not be carried in the balance sheet as a permanent item. Purchased goodwill (other than negative goodwill) should normally be eliminated from the accounts immediately on acquisition against reserves, but may be eliminated by amortisation through the profit and loss account on a systematic basis over its useful economic life. Negative goodwill should be credited directly to reserves.

Summary

1. Fixed assets may be distinguished by

(a) being tangible or intangible

(b) needing to be depreciated or not.

2. Proper controls should be instituted over the acquisition, custody and disposal of fixed assets. Such controls should include the use of asset registers.

3. The capitalised cost of a fixed asset should include all expenditures necessary to make the asset suitable and ready for its intended use.

4. Depreciation accounting is primarily concerned with the allocation of deferred costs over the useful life of the asset.

5. The calculation of depreciation requires the assessment of

(a) original cost;

(b) effective life;

(c) residual value;

(d) pattern of use.

6. There are a number of methods used for assessing depreciation.

7. Post-acquisition expenditures on fixed assets may be treated as

(a) maintenance, and thus expensed, or

(b) betterments, and thus capitalised.

8. Revaluations of fixed assets may be made

(a) on an *ad hoc* basis (that is, irregularly);

(b) regularly in terms of current cost.

9. Internally generated goodwill is not normally brought to account. Purchased goodwill is normally capitalised as an asset and amortised over the period of its expected benefits.

Discussion questions

11.1 Do all fixed assets need to be depreciated? Give reasons for your answer.

11.2 Explain the role of 'fixed asset registers' in an effective system of internal control over fixed assets.

11.3 Discuss the types of expenditures which should be added to the purchase price of an item in order to arrive at its capitalised cost.

11.4 List and explain the reasons why in borderline cases a firm may decide to expense certain costs associated with the acquisition of an asset rather than capitalising those costs.

11.5 (a) Explain what is meant by the 'unit of account' problem.

(b) Explain how the selection of the unit of account affects the treatment of subsequent expenditures on the asset.

11.6 Comment on the statement that depreciation represents the sum set aside out of profits for the purpose of providing a fund to replace worn-out and obsolete fixed assets.

11.7 (a) Outline the factors which may influence the choice of a particular method and rate of depreciation for a fixed asset.

(b) Why is it difficult for an auditor to decide whether a firm's depreciation policy is 'correct' or not?

11.8 (a) Distinguish between the terms 'maintenance' and 'betterments' as they apply to fixed assets.

(b) What factors affect the decision about whether to treat a particular outlay as maintenance or a betterment?

11.9 On what ground may the practice of irregular revaluations of fixed assets be criticised?

Exercises

11.10 A trading firm purchases a motor vehicle for £11 000 cash on 1 July 19X3. The life of the vehicle is estimated at 100 000 miles and the resale value at the end of it is estimated to be £3000. It is decided to charge depreciation on the vehicle on the basis of miles travelled. The distance covered by the vehicle is as follows:

1st year	25 000 miles
2nd year	32 000 miles
3rd year	28 000 miles

On 1 July 19X6, the vehicle is sold for £4750 cash. Prepare ledger accounts to record the above information. Charge depreciation at 30 June each year.

11.11 The following assets appear in the balance sheet of the CA Co as at 30 June 19X5:

Plant and machinery (at cost)	£32 000	
Less Provision for depreciation	8 000	
		£24 000
Office furniture and equipment (at cost)	8 500	
Less Provision for depreciation	3 200	
		5 300

The only change in these assets during the following year is the acquisition of a new copier for £800.

The depreciation policy of the company is to charge depreciation on the balances of the fixed asset accounts as at the end of each financial year at the following rates:

Plant and machinery - 20 per cent on the diminishing balance
Office furniture and equipment - 10 per cent on cost

Show the items which would appear

(a) in the profit and loss statement for year ended 30 June 19X6;

(b) in the balance sheet as at 30 June 19X6;
in relation to the above assets.

11.12 The following are extracts from successive balance sheets of Gee and Tee Ltd:

	30 June 19X5		30 June 19X6	
Motor vehicles	£147 200		£156 400	
Less Provision for depreciation	52 800		53 600	
		£94 400		£102 800

You ascertain that, during the year, vehicles which cost £52 000 and which have been depreciated by £35 200 have been sold for £19 500.

Reconstruct in the general ledger the accounts relating to motor vehicles, their depreciation and their disposal.

11.13 On 1 July 19X6, a new firm purchases three motor vehicles at a cost of £12 000 each. It is decided to depreciate vehicles at the rate of 20 per cent p.a. on the straight-line method.

On 1 October 19X7 one of these vehicles is replaced by a larger van costing £15 000. The trade-in value of the vehicle replaced is £8200.

Show (for the period from 1 July 19X6 to 30 June 19X8) the following accounts in the ledger:

(a) Motor vehicles.

(b) Provision for depreciation of motor vehicles.

(c) Depreciation of motor vehicles.

(d) Disposal of motor vehicles.

(Assume that the accounting year ends on 30 June and that, where relevant, depreciation is charged for part of a year.)

11.14 The following transactions occurred with respect to a delivery van owned by Acme Wholesale Tobacconists Ltd:

19X4	
July 1	Van purchased from Marvel Motors Ltd for £13 650. This price includes £350 insurance and registration for twelve months.
July 2	Paid Signwriters Ltd £200 for painting new van.
Sept.30	Paid repairs to van £320.
19X5	
June 30	Charged depreciation on van at the rate of 20 per cent on cost.
July 1	Paid insurance and registration £300.
	Paid Star Radio £750 for installation of two-way radio in delivery van.
19X6	
June 30	Charged depreciation at the rate of 20 per cent on cost.

You are required:

(a) to show entries in the journal and cash book (payments side) to record the above transactions;

(b) to show how the above asset would appear in the balance sheet:

(i) as at 30 June 19X5;

(ii) as at 30 June 19X6.

11.15 AZ Ltd purchased machinery on 1 January 19X4 at a cost of £64 000. It was decided to depreciate the asset by the straight-line method over ten years with no residual value being anticipated.

On 1 April 19X7, the asset was replaced by a more modern machine costing £80 000, which was to be depreciated on the reducing-balance method at the rate of 25 per cent p.a. The trade-in value of the old machine was £40 000.

Show how the above should be recorded in the general ledger for the period from 1 January 19X4 to 30 June 19X8. Assume that the financial period ends on 30 June each year and that, where relevant, depreciation is to be calculated in months for that part of the year for which the particular machine has been used.

11.16 A wholesaler runs a small fleet of delivery vans. Each van is used for a maximum of five years and then replaced; depreciation is written off yearly at 15 per cent of cost, the balance at the end of five years being considered as the approximate resale or trade-in value.

At 30 June 19X6, the cost of vans then in service was £180 000, and the balance of the provision for depreciation of vans account was £70 000.

On 31 December 19X7 a van which had been purchased on 1 July 19X5 for £10 000 was traded in, £6000 being allowed against the cost, £14 000, of a larger van acquired on that date.

On 1 July 19X8, capital improvements were made to the vehicle purchased the previous year, the cost of alterations being £5000. These alterations do not affect the policy of replacing vans after five years' service, nor the expected resale value of these vans.

No other purchases or sales of vans took place.

Write up:

(a) for each year from 1 July 19X6 to 30 June 19X9:

(i) the vans account, and

(ii) the provision for depreciation of vans account;

(b) for the year ended 30 June 19X8, the disposal of vans account.

11.17 On 1 July 19X4 a company bought factory plant for £25 000 and depreciated it at the rate of 20 per cent p.a. on reducing balance for three years to 30 June 19X7, when, after a reorganisation of the accounting system, it was decided to depreciate all factory plant on the straight-line method, the rate being fixed at 15 per cent p.a. and made retrospective. This adjustment was made after the normal entries for depreciation had been made.

Present the relevant ledger accounts as they would appear in the books of the company from 1 July 19X4 to 30 June 19X9, and show how the asset would appear in the balance sheet of the company as at 30 June 19X9. Calculate depreciation on a yearly basis.

Problems

11.18 The accountant of the Classy Hire Car Service has been investigating the depreciation of the firm's cars for the past eight years. Company policy is to dispose of the hire cars at the end of the fourth year in each case. The accountant has calculated that, on average, the trade-in value of the vehicles (as a percentage of the original cost) for each of the four years is as follows:

Year	Miles driven	Trade-in value as % original cost
1	15 000	70
2	30 000	55
3	22 400	35
4	15 000	25

(a) Calculate the depreciation expense for each of the four years for a car costing £8240 using each of the following methods:

(i) straight-line;

(ii) mileage driven;

(iii) sum-of-digits.

(b) Prepare a table showing the effect on profit of the different methods of depreciation for each of the four years.

11.19 X Manufacturers Ltd purchases a machine overseas for £15 000 on 1 July 19X5. Freight charges on the machine amount to £2000 and customs duty and landing charges total £1300. Installation costs are £840 and a further sum of £860 is spent on trial production runs. The machine has an estimated useful life of five years and a scrap value of £1500. While waiting for the machine, the company renews the cement flooring and repairs and repaints the machine shop walls at a cost of £4000. On 1 July 19X7, improvements are made to the machine's performance at a cost of £2000, and it is estimated this will increase the machine's useful life by two years. The residual value is not expected to change. Depreciation is charged using the straight-line method.

You are required to prepare the appropriate ledger accounts for the three years ending 30 June 19X8 to record the above transactions.

11.20 Company A and Company B are identical in almost every respect; both began business on July 1 19X6 with store plant and equipment costing £80 000, estimated to have a ten-year life with no residual value. Neither company added to plant and equipment during the year.

Both companies purchased identical goods as follows:

July	1000 units at £25 each
Sept.	3000 units at £24 each
Dec.	2000 units at £27 each
Mar.	2000 units at £28 each
June	1000 units at £30 each

Furthermore, at the end of the financial year, before recording depreciation, both ledgers showed the following:

	Company A	Company B	
Sales	£350 000	£350 000	Both companies ended the year
Salaries	£50 000	£50 000	with 1100 units of stock
Rent	£12 000	£12 000	
Other expenses	£3 000	£3 000	

However, for the depreciation of plant and equipment, Company A chose the diminishing value method using twice the straight-line rate. Company B elected to use the straight-line method. In valuing stock, Company A adopted the LIFO basis, while Company B preferred the FIFO method. Company A also provided an amount equal to 2 per cent of sales as a provision for doubtful debts. Company B made no such provision.

You are required to prepare:

(a) a statement of profit and loss for each company showing the results for the year ended 30 June 19X7;

(b) a schedule accounting for the difference in their net profits.

Chapter 12
Partnership accounts

Introduction ☐ Relations of partners to one another ☐ Accounting requirements ☐ Admission of a new partner ☐ Goodwill ☐ Revaluation of assets ☐ Death or retirement of a partner ☐ Dissolution of partnership ☐ Conversion or sale of a business to a limited company

Introduction

Partnership as defined by the Partnership Act 1890 is the relation which subsists between persons carrying on a business in common with a view of profit. The Partnership Act 1890 codified the law relating to partnership but the exact relationship between the partners is still governed by common law except for such modifications as mutually agreed upon between the partners. Such modifications are usually included in the partnership agreement. Partnership is a common mode of trading in this country since it has some advantages over a sole trader. Additional capital may be raised on the introduction of new partners and expansion of the business can take place more easily. The principal disadvantage to general partnership is that partners are liable to the full extent of their private resources for all debts incurred by the partnership and are not in any way protected by the limited liability provisions of the Companies Act.

Relations of partners to one another

Partnership may be entered into on a verbal arrangement or constituted by a formal deed. While it is based on mutual trust and confidence it is a wise precaution, in the event of a dispute, to have the rights and duties of the partners incorporated in a written partnership agreement rather than a verbal one. In the partnership agreement, reference should be made to the name of the business under which it is to be carried on, the terms of the partnership, division of profits and losses, capital contributions of partners, interest on capital, partners' salaries, books of account to be kept, and the name of an arbiter in case of dispute.

It is usual for partners to exercise their freedom in regulating their rights and duties but if there is insufficient verbal or written evidence of these then recourse has to be made to the provision of S. 24 of the Partnership Act 1890 which states the following:

1. All the partners are entitled to share equally in the capital and profits of the business and must contribute equally towards the losses whether of capital or otherwise sustained by the firm.

2. The firm must indemnify every partner in respect of payments made and personal liabilities incurred by him.

3. Any payment or advance beyond the amount of capital each partner has agreed to subscribe is entitled to interest at the rate of 5 per cent per annum from the date of payment or advance.

4. A partner is not entitled before the ascertainment of profits to interest on the capital subscribed by him.

5. Every partner may take part in the management of the partnership business.

6. No partner is entitled to remuneration for acting in the partnership business.

7. No person may be introduced as a partner without the consent of all existing partners.

8. Any difference arising in the ordinary matters connected with the partnership business may be decided by a majority of the partners, but no change may be made in the nature of the partnership business without the consent of all existing partners.

9. The partnership books are to be kept at the principal place of business of the partnership and every partner may, when he thinks fit, have access to and inspect and copy any of them.

Accounting requirements

Partners enter into partnership with the intention of earning profits. Although careful consideration must be taken in the constitution of the partnership from a legal point of view, it is also essential that profit or loss can be measured accurately so that it may be distributed to the partners in accordance with the terms of the partnership agreement, or the Partnership Act 1890 should there be no partnership agreement in existence. The form of accounts used in partnership trading is in essence similar to that of the sole trader. The only significant changes are those affecting the partners' capital accounts and the introduction of an additional account referred to as the profit and loss appropriation account. Those changes are required to record transactions affecting the distribution of profit.

Fixed capital account

In this account is recorded the capital subscribed by a partner on entry into partnership. A fixed capital account is opened for each partner in the firm. Any additional capital contributions or withdrawals of capital are shown in this account. No other entries are recorded in this account, unlike the instance of a sole trader where only one capital account is opened and adjustments for profit and drawings are made therein.

Current account

Since no adjustments in respect of share of profits or losses, partners' salaries, interest on capital, interest on drawings, private drawings, are shown in the fixed capital account, a separate account known as the current account is opened to record these matters. A current account is opened for each partner and appears in the balance sheet separately below the fixed capital accounts. If a current account shows a credit balance this indicates that a partner has not fully withdrawn his share of profits. On the other hand if the balance on this account is at debit this signifies that a partner has overdrawn and the balance is deducted from the fixed capital account in the balance sheet. The debit balance, however, is not transferred to his capital account in the ledger but carried forward to the next trading period.

Interest on capital

Since the permanent capital of a firm is contributed by the partners it is usual to compensate them by allowing interest on the amount of capital so subscribed. Provision in the partnership agreement is normally made for this and the interest is credited to each partner's current account. The rate of interest allowed varies from firm to firm but is usually related to the normal interest rates for borrowing ruling at the time the provision is made. Conversely, many firms fix the rate nominally at 5 per cent per annum without considering the general level of interest rates. The entries to record this allowance are as follows:

Partnership salaries

In some firms the partnership agreement provides for a salary to be paid to one or more partners. The payment of partnership salary may be made to compensate a partner for extra work he has undertaken over and above his normal duties as a partner of the firm. The salary may be paid directly to the partner concerned or, if not paid in this way, credited to the partner's current account. In both cases it will be shown in the profit and loss appropriation account before the final division of the balance of profit takes place. The accounting entries are:

Dr. Partnership salaries
Cr. Partner's current account or bank

The balance on partnership salaries account is transferred to the profit and loss appropriation account at the end of the accounting period.

Interest on drawings

Partnership agreements sometimes provide for interest to be charged on partners' drawings. Such interest is charged on the principle that if interest is allowed on sums invested in the business then interest should be charged on sums withdrawn from the business. In this way benefit is given to the partner who restricts his drawings and the partner who withdraws from the firm to excess is penalised. The accounting entries are as follows:

Dr. Partner's current account
Cr. Interest on drawings

The balance on interest on drawings account is transferred to the credit of the profit and loss appropriation account at the end of the accounting period.

Profit and loss appropriation accounts

In partnership accounts the trading profit or loss is calculated in a similar fashion as in the accounts of a sole trader. The only difference is that in the accounts of a sole trader the balance of profit or loss is transferred to the profit and loss appropriation account. In this latter account are shown the entries recording the division of the trading and profit or loss between the partners in accordance with the terms of the partnership agreement such as interest on capital, interest on drawings, partnership salaries, and the allocation of the residual balance of profit or loss between the partners. Those items appear in the appropriation section of the final accounts and not in the normal profit and loss account, as they are not charges against the trading profit but appropriations from profit provided in terms of the partnership agreement.

Balance sheet

There are no statutory requirements to satisfy in the preparation of a balance sheet of a partnership and the presentation does not vary essentially from that of a sole trader. Obviously separate accounts have to be kept for each partner, distinguishing between fixed capital accounts and current accounts. It is occasionally found that this distinction is not drawn and all necessary adjustments for share of profit, drawings, etc. are made on the capital account in which event no current account is opened. This form is not recommended unless the problem specifically requests the solution to be so presented.

Example: Gray and Black are in partnership sharing profits and losses equally. The balances on their capital accounts at 1 January are Gray £10 000 and Black £9000. On 1 July Gray introduces £2000 as additional capital. The drawings for the year were Gray £1200 drawn out on 1 October and Black £1000 drawn out on 1 July. Black is to be credited with a salary of

£500. Interest is to be allowed on capital at the rate of 5 per cent per annum and charged on drawings at the same rate. The profit for the year ended 31 December amounts to £5000. The partnership agreement states that the capital subscribed by the partners has to remain fixed and any adjustments for amounts debited or credited to the partners have to be shown in separate accounts. To record the above transactions, the profit and loss appropriation account and the balance sheet of the partnership are prepared as follows:

Gray and Black
Profit and Loss Appropriation Account for year ended 31 December

Profit for year				£5 000
Add Interest on drawings				
Gray		£15		
Black		25		40
				£5 040
Less Interest on capital				
Gray		£550		
Black		450	1 000	
Partner's salary				
Black			500	
Balance of profit				
Gray		1 770		
Black		1 770	3 540	5 040

Balance Sheet as at 31 December (extracts only)

Capital accounts			
Gray		£12 000	
Black		9 000	£21 000

	Current accounts	_Gray_		_Black_	
Share of profit		£1 770		£1 770	
Interest on capital		550		450	
Salary				500	
		2 320		2 720	
Less Drawings	£1 200		£1 000		
Interest on drawings	15	1 215	25	1 025	
		£1 105		£1 695	£2 800

Notes to accounts

1. Calculation of interest on Capital:

Gray £10 000 at 5% for 1 year	£500
£2000 at 5% for 6 months	50
	£550
Black £9000 at 5% for 1 year	£450

2. Calculation of interest on drawings:

Gray £1200 at 5% for 3 months	£15
Black £1000 at 5% for 6 months	£25

Example: From a trial balance the partnership final accounts, with additional notes, are prepared as follows:

Below is a list of balances appearing in the nominal ledger of Thomson and Charles as at 31 December 19X8:

Thomson – Capital account		£7 000
Charles – Capital account		4 000
Thomson – Drawings account	£720	
Charles – Drawings account	380	
Sales		22 611
Returns inwards	120	
Returns outwards		260
Stock on hand 1 January 19X8	5 939	
Debtors	5 010	
Creditors		2 779
Bank overdraft		750
Cash in hand	45	
Furniture and fittings (cost £6500, depreciation £3000)	3 500	
Office equipment – at cost	190	
Discount allowed	140	
Staff salaries	6 700	
Commission to agents	820	
Purchases	9 468	
Carriage inwards	260	
General expenses	180	
Buildings – at cost	4 500	
Mortgage over buildings		3 000
Provision for bad debts		90
Advertising	175	
Bank – Deposit account	260	
Mortgage interest	108	
Rates	113	
Insurance	70	
Electricity	400	
Telephone	100	
Carriage outwards	550	
Repairs	142	
Thomson – Current account	400	
Charles – Current account	200	
	£40 490	£40 490

You are given the following additional information:

1. Stock on hand at 31 December Year 19X8 – £6090.

2. It is ascertained that the balances of debtors and creditors should be:

Debtors	£5 000
Creditors	£2 774

The differences are to be written off.

3. Depreciate furniture and fittings at the rate of 10 per cent per annum on the reducing balance method.

4. Accrue staff salaries £225 and mortgage interest £14.

5. Rates have been paid in advance to amount of £36 and insurance to £43.

6. Provide for partners' salaries: Thomson   £250
                                 Charles   £400

7. Interest on capital is to be provided at 5 per cent per annum.

8. Provision for bad debts is to be $2\frac{1}{2}$ per cent of debtors.

9. The partners share profits and losses equally.

The trading and profit and loss accounts for the year ended 31 December 19X8, and a balance sheet as at that date, are set out thus:

Thomson and Charles
Trading and Profit and Loss Account for year ended 31 December 19X8

Sales, less returns			£22 481
Less Cost of sales			
Purchases, less returns		£9 203	
Add Stock 1 January 19X8		5 939	
		15 142	
Less Stock 31 December 19X8		6 090	
		9 052	
Carriage inwards		260	9 312
Gross Profit			£13 169
Less Staff salaries		6 925	
Commission paid to agents		820	
Discount allowed		140	
Advertising		175	
Mortgage interest		122	
Rates		77	
Insurance		27	
Electricity		400	
Telephone		100	
Carriage outwards		550	
Repairs		142	
Bad and doubtful debts		35	
General expenses		180	
Depreciation on furniture and fittings		350	10 043
Profit for year			£3 126

Profit and Loss Appropriation Account for year ended 31 December 19X8

Profit for year			£3 126
Less Interest on capital			
Thomson		£350	
Charles		200	£550

Cont.

Profit and Loss Appropriation Account for year ended 31 December 19X8 *Cont.*

	b/fwd	£550	£3 126
Partners' salaries			
Thomson	250		
Charles	400	650	
Balance of profit			
Thomson	963		
Charles	963	1 926	£3 126

Balance Sheet as at 31 December 19X8

Fixed assets

Buildings – at cost			4 500
Furniture and fittings – at cost		6 500	
Less Depreciation		3 350	3 150
Office equipment – at cost			190
			7 840

Current assets

Stock		6 090	
Debtors	5 000		
Less Provision for bad debts	125	4 875	
Prepaid charges		79	
Bank – Deposit account		260	
Cash in hand		45	
		£11 349	

Less Current liabilities

Creditors	2 774		
Bank overdraft	750		
Accrued charges	239	3 763	7 586
			£15 426

Represented by:

Capital accounts

Thomson	7 000	
Charles	4 000	11 000

Current accounts

	Thomson		Charles		
As at 1 January 19X8	*Dr.*	£400	*Dr.*	£200	
Share of profit		963		963	
Interest on capital		350		200	
Salaries		250		400	
		1 563		1 563	
Less Drawings		720		380	
		843		1 183	
	Cr.	£443	*Cr.*	£983	1 426
Mortgage on buildings					3 000
					£15 426

Additional notes

1. Calculation of purchases

Purchases for trial balance		£9 468
Less Returns	£260	
Difference in creditors (2779 − 2774)	5	265
		£9 203

2. Calculation of sales

Sales per trial balance		£22 611
Less Returns	£120	
Difference in debtors (5010 − 5000)	10	130
		£22 481

3. Bad and doubtful debts

Bad debts provision at 31 December 19X8	£125
Less Bad debts provision at 1 January 19X8	90
	£35

4. Note the presentation of current accounts when the opening balances are at debit.

Admission of a new partner

Prior to admission to partnership the existing partners negotiate with the proposed new partner the terms and conditions on which he is to be admitted. The terms and conditions when agreed by all concerned are incorporated into the partnership agreement. The important amendments to the partnership agreement will be those referring to the new profit sharing ratio and the amount of capital contributed by the new partner. The admission of a new partner also raises certain accounting problems since he is in effect purchasing a share of a business. Before the purchase price can be established it is normal practice to review the valuation of the assets and liabilities and if necessary revise them so that the redrafted balance sheet may reflect a satisfactory valuation of the whole business. These adjustments, if any, are recorded prior to the admission of the new partner. When the sum to be subscribed as capital by the incoming partner is paid by him it is credited to his capital account in the firm. The capital contribution need not be settled wholly in cash but may be made by the introduction of other assets such as plant, stock, etc. The basic accounting entries on admission of a new partner are as follows:

> *Dr.* Bank or other assets with amount of capital subscribed.
> *Cr.* Incoming partner's capital account.

Goodwill

Mention has been made to the effect that a partner on admission purchases a share of a business and consequently every effort is made to ensure that a satisfactory valuation of the business is made on which to compute the amount to be paid by·him. It has been seen that certain assets and liabilities may require to be revalued in an attempt to reach a fair valuation of the business. By far the most complex asset to value accurately is goodwill. The valuation of most businesses is bound up to a large extent with the interpretation, consideration, and subsequent valuation of the asset goodwill. Lord Eldon defined goodwill most aptly as 'the probability that the old customers will resort to the old place'. In 1901 Lord Mcnaughton stated that 'Goodwill is the benefit and advantage of the good name, reputation and connection of a business. It is the attractive force which brings in custom. It is the one thing which distinguishes an old established from a new business at its first start. Goodwill is composed of a variety of elements. It differs in its composition in different trades and in different businesses in the same trade. One element may preponderate here, and another there.' Both these definitions have attempted to elucidate the meaning of this term goodwill but have also illustrated that goodwill by its nature is difficult to value owing to the complexities and imponderables involved in its assessment. The elements of goodwill may be summarised as sound management both in administration, purchasing and marketing, good labour and customer relationships, valuable trade marks and franchises. It is suggested by some businessmen that goodwill under normal circumstances should not be recorded as an asset in the balance sheet since it has a unique characteristic among assets in that it can hold value only provided it can be sold along with the business as a whole. This suggestion certainly has some merit if the balance sheet does not represent or intend to represent a true valuation of the business. But it certainly has little merit if the balance sheet is drawn up for the purpose of a valuation required for the introduction of a new partner, the death or retirement of a partner, or the sale of a business, since the value attached to goodwill is usually a significant amount in the overall valuation figure.

Methods used to evaluate goodwill

With all the academic theorising and practical complexities which beset the valuer of goodwill he must have some formula to use as a basis to calculate the worth of goodwill. There are many formulae in use today to determine a realistic appraisal of this asset. Below are illustrated two formulae which show the techniques adopted in some methods to establish such an appraisal.

Method A

Assume a partnership with net assets (i.e. assets less liabilities) of £100 000 and average annual profits over the last five years of £18 000, before the deduction of partners' salaries which amount to £7000, is being sold as a going concern. Calculate the value of goodwill if the purchaser requires a minimum return of 10 per cent on capital invested in the business.

Calculation of goodwill

Average annual profits	£18 000
Less Partnership salaries	7 000
Average annual profit after charging partnership salaries	£11 000

Applying the required minimum return of 10 per cent to the average annual profit of £11 000, it is capitalised at £110 000. The purchaser would be prepared, on this basis, to pay £110 000 for the business whose net assets are valued at £100 000. The difference between the two amounts is attributed to goodwill, viz. £10 000.

Method B

A partnership earned the following profits for the five years ended 31 December Year 8 (after deduction of partnership salaries):

Year 4	£3000
Year 5	4000
Year 6	7000

Year 7   £5000
Year 8   6000

Assume that the net assets are valued at £40 000 and that 10 per cent is considered a reasonable return on capital invested. Calculate the value of goodwill on the basis of 'super profits'.

Calculation of goodwill

Average annual profit	£5 000
Less Interest on capital paid for net assets at 10 per cent	4 000
Annual 'super profits'	£1 000

Goodwill to be valued at five years' purchase price of average 'super profits' = £5 000.

Additional note: 'Super profits' may be described simply as those profits earned in excess of the normal return expected from a particular business. In the above problem the super profits were arrived at by deducting from the annual average profit the return of 10 per cent of capital invested being the normal return anticipated from this type of business. Goodwill is finally evaluated by applying a number of years' purchase price on the annual 'super profits'. This can never be fixed for all businesses as it varies with the custom of each particular trade or profession.

The above examples are only two of the methods used to assess the valuation of goodwill. They are illustrated not because they necessarily give a more realistic evaluation of goodwill than other methods but rather to demonstrate the controversial nature of such formulae and how entirely different valuations for goodwill can be arrived at by applying alternative treatments.

Treatment of goodwill when it is to appear in the books on the admission of a new partner

In this method a goodwill account is created or adjusted to record the valuation of this asset. The old partners are given credit for this amount in their capital accounts in the old profit sharing ratio. The incoming partner is credited with the amount of capital introduced including any payment for goodwill.

Example: A and B are in partnership sharing profits and losses in the proportion of two-thirds and one-third respectively. They agree to admit C into partnership giving him one-fifth share of profits. It was agreed that goodwill be valued at £3000. C introduced £2000 as his capital contribution to the partnership. The journal entries to record the above, and also the revised profit sharing ratio, assuming that A and B still share profits in the same ratio in the new partnership, are as follows:

Journal

Goodwill	*Dr.*	£3 000	
To A Capital			£2 000
B Capital			1 000
Being creation of goodwill at date of admission of C into partnership credited to the partners in the old profit sharing ratio.			
Bank	*Dr.*	£2 000	
To C Capital			£2 000
Being capital introduced by C.			

New profit sharing ratio:

If C has to receive one-fifth of the profits then the balance of four-fifths will be shared between A and B in the ratio of 2 : 1:

$$A \quad \frac{2}{3} \times \frac{4}{5} = \frac{8}{15};$$
$$B \quad \frac{1}{3} \times \frac{4}{5} = \frac{4}{15};$$
$$C \qquad\quad \frac{1}{5} = \frac{3}{15}.$$

The new profit sharing ratio will be 8 : 4 : 3.

Treatment of goodwill where it is not to be shown in the books on the admission of a new partner

Under this method the value of goodwill or the increase in valuation is credited to the old partners in their old profit sharing ratio and debited to the partners in the new profit sharing ratio. As in the previous method the capital introduced by the new partner is, including any payment for goodwill, credited to his capital account.

Example: With the same information as in the previous example, the journal entries to record the transactions where goodwill is not to remain in the books will read thus:

Journal

Goodwill	*Dr.* £3 000	
To A Capital		£2 000
B Capital		1 000
Being value of goodwill at date of admission of C into partnership credited to the partners in their old profit sharing ratio.		
A Capital	*Dr.* £1 600	
B Capital	800	
C Capital	600	
To Goodwill		£3 000
Being goodwill eliminated from the books and debited to the partners' capital accounts in their new profit sharing ratio (viz 8 : 4 : 3).		
Bank	*Dr.* £2 000	
To C Capital		£2 000
Being capital introduced by C.		

Example: In the foregoing method a goodwill account was opened temporarily to record the necessary adjustments and then closed so that no amount for goodwill remains in the books of the firm. It may be, however, that the partners decide that no account for goodwill has to be opened even on a temporary basis, in which case the following method may be adopted:

Allocation of goodwill of £3000 among the partners:

	A	B	C
Profit sharing proportions	(*Cr.*) $\frac{2}{3}$	(*Cr.*) $\frac{1}{3}$	—
New profit sharing proportions	(*Dr.*) $\frac{8}{15}$	(*Dr.*) $\frac{4}{15}$	(*Dr.*) $\frac{3}{15}$
Difference	(*Cr.*) $\frac{2}{15}$	(*Cr.*) $\frac{1}{15}$	(*Dr.*) $\frac{3}{15}$
	($\frac{2}{15} \times 3000$)	($\frac{1}{15} \times 3000$)	($\frac{3}{15} \times 3000$)
	(*Cr.*) £400	(*Cr.*) £200	(*Dr.*) £600

Journal

C Capital	*Dr.* £600	
To A Capital		£400
B Capital		200
Being adjustment for goodwill valuation on admission of C as partner.		

Bank	*Dr.* £2 000	
To C Capital		£2 000
Being Capital introduced by C.		

Note: By using this alternative method the resulting balances on the capital accounts of the partners will be the same as before.

Revaluation of assets

There are many instances where the balance sheet does not reflect a satisfactory valuation of a business thus necessitating a revaluation of some or all of the assets and liabilities before a new partner is admitted. The differences between the book values of assets and liabilities and the values to which they are to be adjusted for the change in partnership are transferred to a revaluation account. This account will reveal the profit or loss on revaluation which is then transferred to the partners' capital accounts in their profit sharing ratio prior to the change.

On revaluation of the assets and liabilities the method of recording the adjustments, in journal form, is as follows:

1. *Dr.* Any increases in revaluation of assets to the appropriate asset accounts.
   Cr. Revaluation account.
2. *Dr.* Revaluation account.
   Cr. Any decreases in revaluation of assets to the appropriate asset accounts.
3. *Dr.* Any decreases in the values of liabilities to the relevant liability account.
   Cr. Revaluation account.

Note: If any increase occurs then the journal entry is reversed.

4. *Dr.* Revaluation account with any reserve for bad debts.
   Cr. Bad debts reserve account.
5. *Dr,* Revaluation account with the difference on the account after all revaluations of assets and liabilities have been completed.
   Cr. Partners' capital accounts in profit sharing ratio.

Note: If there is any excess of debits over credits on the revaluation account then the partners' capital accounts are debited and the revaluation account credited with the difference.

Example: A and B are in partnership sharing profits and losses equally. Their balance sheet at 31 December was as follows:

Balance Sheet as at 31 December

Capital accounts			Fixed assets		
A	£4 000		Premises		£3 000
B	3 000		Machinery		2 000
	£7 000				5 000
Current Liabilities					
Creditors		3 000			
			Current assets		
			Stock	£2 400	
			Debtors	1 600	
			Bank	1 000	5 000
		£10 000			£10 000

It was agreed to admit C into partnership on 1 January and to give him a one-third share of profits. He is to bring in as his capital £3000.

The partners decided to value goodwill at £1200 and to revalue the premises at £4000 and stock at £2000. It was also agreed that goodwill was to appear as an account in the balance sheet. The partners share profits and losses A, $\frac{1}{2}$; B, $\frac{1}{6}$; C, $\frac{1}{3}$. The following need to be prepared:

1. Journal entries (including bank transactions) to record the above.

2. Balance sheet of the new firm.

3. Revaluation account.

This is done as below:

Journal

Jan. 1	Goodwill	*Dr.*	£1 200	
	Premises		1 000	
	To revaluation			£2 200
	Being appreciation in value of assets on admission of C as partner.			
	Revaluation	*Dr.*	£400	
	To stock			£400
	Being reduction in value of stock on admission of C as partner.			
	Revaluation	*Dr.*	£1 800	
	To A – Capital			£900
	B – Capital			900
	Being gain on revaluation transferred.			
	Bank	*Dr.*	£3 000	
	To C – Capital			£3 000
	Being capital subscribed by C on his admission to partnership.			

4.   **Balance Sheet** (after admission of C as partner)

Capital accounts			Fixed assets		
A	£4 900		Goodwill		£1 200
B	3 900		Premises		4 000
C	3 000		Machinery		2 000
		£11 800		7 200	7 200
Current liabilities			**Current assets**		
Creditors		3 000	Stock	£2 000	
			Debtors	1 600	
			Bank	4 000	
					7 600
		£14 800			£14 800

5.   **Revaluation Account**

Jan. 1	Stock	£400	Jan. 1	Goodwill	£1 200
	A – Capital	900		Premises	1 000
	B – Capital	900			
		£2 200			£2 200

Death or retirement of a partner

It is essential to realise that when a partner dies or retires from a partnership then the partnership ceases and a new one is constituted. One of the first considerations on the death or retirement of a partner is to ascertain how much is due to the outgoing partner. Reference to the partnership agreement will have to be made to examine the provisions relating to such an occurrence. The partnership agreement often states that the assets and liabilities have to be revalued and any increase or decrease on revaluation passed through the books in a similar manner to that on the admission of a new partner. If this is the case then the outgoing partner or his executors will receive a share of the profit or loss on such a revaluation. Provision is sometimes made to allow the outgoing partner or his executors a certain percentage based on the balance of his capital account in lieu of profits if the death or retirement does not coincide with the balancing date. Alternatively, the proportion of profits may be calculated on a time basis using the normal trading accounts covering the date of death or retirement. In the event of the remaining partners in the firm not being in a position to repay immediately the retiring partner or his executors then the balance due will be transferred to an interest bearing loan account to be repaid by instalments. The interest allowed on the loan will be debited to an interest account and credited to the loan account. The following examples consider some of the accounting adjustments required to deal with this situation.

Example: A, B, and C are in partnership sharing profits and losses in the ratio 4 : 3 : 3. At 31 December the balance sheet was as follows:

Capital accounts			Fixed assets		
A	£10 000		Freehold buildings		£10 000
B	8 000		Machinery		5 000
C	4 000	£22 000			———
					15 000
Current liabilities			**Current assets**		
Creditors		£7 000	Stock	£4 000	
			Debtors	6 000	
			Bank	4 000	
				———	14 000
		£29 000			£29 000

At this date A decided to retire from the partnership and in order to ascertain the amount due to him the following revaluations were made.

Goodwill was valued at £2000 and was to be recorded in the balance sheet. Freehold buildings were revalued at £15 000. Stock was to be written down to £3000.

It was decided that a sum of £3000 should be paid immediately to A and the balance to be settled at the end of six months. The following should be prepared:

1. Revaluation account, bank account, loan account, and capital accounts.

2. The Opening balance sheet of B and C.

This is done as follows:

1. Revaluation Account etc.

Revaluation Account

Dr.   Cr.

Stock	£1 000	Goodwill	£2 000
A – Capital	2 400	Freehold buildings	5 000
B – Capital	1 800		
C – Capital	1 800		
	£7 000		£7 000

Capital Accounts

	A	B	C		A	B	C
A – Loan	£12 400			Balances	£10 000	8 000	4 000
Balances		£9 800	£5 800	Revaluation	2 400	1 800	1 800
	£12 400	£9 800	£5 800		£12 400	£9 800	£5 800
				Balances		£9 800	£5 800

Bank Account

Balance	£4 000	A – Loan	£3 000
		Balance	1 000
	£4 000		£4 000
Balance	£1 000		

A. Loan Account

Dr.			*Cr.*
Bank	£3 000	A – Capital	£12 400
Balance	9 400		
	£12 400		£12 400
		Balance	£9 400

2. Balance Sheet of B and C at 1 January

Capital accounts			Fixed assets		
B	£9 800		Goodwill		£2 000
C	5 800		Freehold buildings		15 000
		£15 600	Machinery		5 000
					22 000
Current liabilities					
Creditors	7 000				
A – Loan	9 400	16 400	Current assets		
			Stock	£3 000	
			Debtors	6 000	
			Bank	1 000	
					10 000
		£32 000			£32 000

Dissolution of partnership

Reasons for dissolution of partnership

The most common reasons for dissolving partnership are as follows:

1. Death, bankruptcy, or lunacy of a partner.

2. Resignation of a partner.

3. If a partnership has been entered into for a fixed period, at the expiration of that period.

Distribution of assets

When it has been decided by the partners to dissolve a partnership, the assets of the firm have to be realised to settle outstanding liabilities and to repay to the partners their capital contributions together with any surplus on realisation.

Section 44 of the Partnership Act 1890 states that in settling accounts between the partners after a dissolution of partnership the following rules shall, subject to any agreement, be observed:

1. Losses, including losses and deficiencies of capital, shall be paid first out of profits, next out of capital, and lastly, if necessary, by the partners individually in the proportion in which they were entitled to share profits:

2. The assets of the firm, including the sums, if any, contributed by the partners to make up losses or deficiencies of capital, shall be applied in the following manner and order:

(a) In paying the debts and liabilities of the firm to persons who are not partners therein.

(b) In paying to each partner rateably what is due from the firm to him for advances as distinguished from capital.

(c) In paying to each partner rateably what is due from the firm to him in respect of capital.

(d) The ultimate residue, if any, shall be divided among the partners in the proportion in which profits are divisible.

Accounting entries in closing the books of a partnership on dissolution

On dissolution the partnership books require to be closed. To close off the books the following procedure may be adopted:

1. Open a realisation account and transfer all asset accounts at their book amounts (with exception of cash or bank) to the debit of that account.

2. Debit cash or bank and credit realisation account with the proceeds from the sale of these accounts.

3. Debit costs of realisation to the debit of realisation account and credit cash or bank.

4. If an asset or assets are taken over by a partner of the firm then the partner's capital account is debited with the value of the asset or assets taken over and realisation account credited.

5. Creditors are settled by crediting cash or bank and debiting the creditors' accounts. If any discount is received from the on settlement then debit creditors' accounts and credit realisation account.

6. Transfer balances on partners' current accounts (if any) to the respective capital accounts.

7. The balance on realisation account will represent the profit or loss on realisation and is transferred to the partner's capital account in their profit sharing ratio.

8. In the event of a partner's capital account being overdrawn a payment requires to be made by him to make good the deficiency, the entries being debit cash or bank and credit partner's capital account.

9. After any partners' loans are settled the remaining balances in the books will only be the capital accounts of the partners and the cash or bank accounts. The final distribution of cash amongst the partners in relation to the outstanding balances on their capital accounts will close the firm's books.

Example: A and B are in partnership, sharing profits and losses equally. They agree to dissolve the partnership at the date of the undernoted balance sheet.

Balance Sheet as at 31 December

Capital			Fixed assets		
A	6 000		Premises		£2 000
B	4 000		Plant		3 000
		£10 000			£5 000
Current liabilities			**Current assets**		
Creditors		1 000	Stock	£1 500	
			Debtors	3 500	
			Cash at Bank	1 000	
					6 000
		£11 000			£11 000

The expenses of realisation amounted to £250. The creditors were paid less a 5 per cent discount. Assets realised the following amounts:

Premises	£4 000
Plant	2 500
Stock	1 000
Debtors	3 300

The realisation account, bank account, and the partners' capital accounts are as follows:

In the Ledger of A and B

Realisation Account

Premises	£2 000	Bank (Proceeds of Sale)		
Plant	3 000	Premises	£4 000	
Stock	1 500	Plant	2 500	
Debtors	3 500	Stock	1 000	
Bank (Expenses of		Debtors	3 300	
Realisation)	250		———	£10 800
Capital accounts (gain		Creditors (Discount)		50
on realisation)				
A	£300			
B	300			
	———			
	600			
	£10 850			£10 850

Bank Account

Balance	£1 000	Realisation (Expenses)		£250
Realisation (proceeds		Creditors		950
of Sale of assets)	10 800	Capital – A	£6 300	
		B	4 300	
			———	10 600
	£11 800			£11 800

Capital Accounts

	A	B		A	B
Bank	£6 300	£4 300	Balances	£6 000	£4 000
			Realisation	300	300
	£6 300	£4 300		£6 300	£4 300

Example (*more difficult*): White and Green, who had been in partnership for a number of years sharing profits and losses in the ratio of 3 : 2, decided to terminate the partnership at 31 December. From the following balance sheet drawn up on cessation of trading and the supplementary notes we are required to calculate the amount due to be paid to or by each partner; we must also verify the correctness of our solution by preparing a summary of the cash transactions.

White and Green

Balance Sheet as at 31 December

Partners' capital			Motor Car		
accounts			Written down value		£300
White	£425		Furniture and fittings		
Green	225		Written down value		120
	———	£650	Stock in trade		330
Sundry creditors		300	Sundry debtors		450
Bank overdraft		250			
		———			———
		£1 200			£1 200

Notes:

1. In settling the sundry creditors, £15 discount was taken.

2. The following further charges were incurred; accountancy fee, £50; overdraft interest, £25.

3. All debts were collected in full with the exception of a debt of £52 which proved to be bad.

4. White took over the firm's car at a valuation of £260.

5. Green took over the stock in trade at balance sheet value.

6. Furniture and fittings were sold by auction realising £82 after the auctioneer's charges.

7. White and Green agreed that gains and losses on the dissolution be allocated on the same basis as profits were shared.

Solution

In the Ledger of White and Green

Realisation Account

Motor car		£300	Creditors – Discount		£15
Furniture and fittings		120	Bank (proceeds of		
Stock		330	Sale):		
Debtors		450	Furniture and		
Accountancy fee		50	fittings	£82	
Overdraft Interest		25	Debtors	398	
				———	480
			White – Capital (car)		260
			Green – Capital (stock)		330
			Loss on realisation:		
			White – Capital	£114	
			Green – Capital	76	
				———	190
		———			———
		£1 275			£1 275

Partners' capital accounts

	White	Green		White	Green
Realisation (loss)	£114	£76	Balances	£425	£225
Realisation (assets			Bank		181
taken over)	260	330			
Bank	51				
	£425	£406		£425	£406

Bank account

Realisation (proceeds of sale)		£480	Balance		£250
Green – Capital		181	Creditors		285
			Accountancy fee		50
			Overdraft Interest		25
			White – Capital		51
		£661			£661

Garner v. Murray

It is necessary if a partner's capital account is at debit that he must contribute in cash a sum sufficient to discharge his liability so that the remaining partner or partners may receive in full the amounts standing to their credit. If a partner is unable to meet his indebtedness to the firm then it will not be possible to repay the remaining partners their capital contributions in full. The loss arising in such a situation is not shared by the solvent partners in their normal profit sharing ratio but according to the rule decided in the case of *Garner* v. *Murray* unless anything to the contrary is stated in the partnership agreement. In this case the judge held that the assets remaining, after discharging the firm's obligations, must be divided between the solvent partners in proportion to their capitals. A distinction was made, in this case, between a trading loss and a loss caused by a deficiency in assets due to a partner being unable to meet his indebtedness to the firm. This decision has caused great debate in the accountancy profession resulting in different opinions being held as to the interpretation and application of the rule established in this case. An interpretation of this rule which may be used for examination purposes is that the loss arising from the insolvency of a partner must be shared by the remaining solvent partners in the ratio of their last agreed capital accounts as shown in the last normal balance sheet of the firm prepared prior to dissolution. The balances on current accounts are ignored in calculating the proportion in which the loss is to be shared by the solvent partners.

This simple illustration shows the application of the *Garner* v. *Murray* rule.

Example: A, B, and C are in partnership sharing profits and losses equally. At the last normal balance sheet the balances on the respective partners' capital accounts were as follows:

A	Credit	£3 000
B	Credit	£2 000
C	Debit	£500

C was insolvent and unable to contribute any cash to the firm. There was a loss on realisation of £600 which is to be debited to the partners in their profit sharing ratio. We will now calculate the allocation of the deficiency in C's capital account between the solvent partners.

The total deficiency in C's capital account is as follows:

Balance on capital account at debit per last balance sheet	£500
Share of loss on realisation ($\frac{1}{3}$ × £600)	200
	£700

Allocated thus:

$$A \left(\frac{3000}{5000} \times 700 \right) \qquad\qquad = \text{£420}$$

$$B \left(\frac{2000}{5000} \times 700 \right) \qquad\qquad = 280$$

$$\phantom{B \left(\frac{2000}{5000} \times 700 \right) \qquad\qquad =\ } \text{£700}$$

Note: The ratio in which the loss has to be shared between A and B is arrived at before debiting the share of the loss on realisation to their capital accounts.

Conversion or sale of a business to a limited company

Introduction

The securing of limited liability has often encouraged partners to convert their firms into limited companies. The principal benefit accruing from such a change is that the personal liability of members of a company is limited to the amount of their shareholdings in the company. There may also be certain other legal and taxation considerations which may influence such a conversion. In these circumstances it is usual for the partners to become owners of the newly constituted company by issuing the shares to themselves in discharge of the balances of their capital accounts in the partnership. They will also assume the role of directors in the newly formed company and business will be conducted in the same manner as before but with the added protection of limited liability. The purchase price, in this type of conversion, is usually based on the position disclosed by the balance sheet at the date of conversion, the assets and liabilities being taken over by the company at their book value and the partners' capital accounts discharged by the issue of shares in the new company.

Conversely, it may happen that the existing partners desire to sell out to a limited company, but do not wish to participate in the running of the purchasing company's affairs. In this type of sale there will require to be, first of all, agreement on the assets and liabilities to be taken over by the company and, secondly, a valuation placed on them before a purchase price can be fixed. The purchase consideration may be settled either wholly in shares or cash or partly in shares or cash, depending on the terms of sale agreed between the partners and the directors of the company.

Accounting entries to record the conversion or sale of the business and to close off the books of the partnership

1. *Dr.*   Realisation account with the book value of the assets taken over by the purchasing company.
   Cr.   Appropriate asset accounts in the ledger.

Note: If the purchasing company takes over the cash or bank balances they will require to be transferred to the debit of the realisation account.

2. *Dr.*   Liability accounts at book value which are being taken over by purchasing company.
    Cr.   Realisation account.

3. *Dr.*   Purchasing company's account with amount of the purchase consideration of the firm's assets less liabilities being taken over.
    Cr.   Realisation account.

4. *Dr.*   Partners' capital accounts with any asset or assets taken over by the partners.
    Cr.   Realisation account with the agreed price of the assets taken over.

5. *Dr.*   Realisation account with any expenses of dissolution.
    Cr.   Cash or bank accounts.

6. *Dr.*   Realisation account with any gain on realisation.
    Cr.   Partners' capital accounts in profit sharing ratio with gain.

Note: If a loss in realisation is incurred then the above entries will be reversed.

7. *Dr.*   Relevant asset accounts making up the purchase consideration (shares, bank, cash, etc.)
    Cr.   Purchasing company's account.

8. *Dr.*   Partners' current accounts with any balance outstanding in those accounts.
    Cr.   Partners' capital accounts.

Note: If the balance is a debit on the current account then the entries will be reversed.

9. *Dr.*   Liability accounts which are not being taken over by purchasing company.
    Cr.   Cash or bank accounts.

10. *Dr.*   Partners' capital accounts with shares allotted to them, if any, by purchasing company.
    Cr.   Shares in purchasing company account.

Note: If the purchase consideration is partly settled by shares then it is sometimes convenient, although not obligatory, to allocate the shares to the partners in their profit sharing ratio.

11. *Dr.*   Partners' capital accounts with the sum required to repay the amount due to them by the firm.
    Cr.   Cash or bank accounts.

Example: A and B who have been in partnership for many years decide to convert their business into a limited company at the date of the undernoted balance sheet.

Balance sheet as at 31 December 19X8

Capital accounts			Fixed assets		
A	£10 000		Machinery	£4 000	
B	6 000		Fixtures	2 000	
		£16 000			£6 000
Current liabilities			**Current assets**		
Creditors		3 500	Stock	5 000	
			Debtors	6 000	
			Bank	2 500	
					13 500
		£19 500			£19 500

The Company, AB Ltd, takes over all the assets and liabilities with the exception of the bank balance. The purchase price is fixed at £20 000, to be settled by the issue of 20 000 ordinary shares of £1 each. The firm has to pay the expenses of dissolution which amount to £200. A and B are to be allocated the ordinary shares in the new company in their profit sharing ratio which is 3 : 2.

To enter the above transactions and to close off the books of the firm, proceed as follows:

In the Books of A and B

Realisation Account

Dec. 31	Machinery	£4 000	Dec. 31	Creditors	£3 500
	Fixtures	2 000		AB Ltd – Purchase Price	20 000
	Stock	5 000			
	Debtors	6 000			
	Bank (dissolution				
	expenses)	200			
	A – Capital	3 780			
	B – Capital	2 520			
		£23 500			£23 500

AB Limited Account

Dec. 31	Realisation (purchase		Dec. 31	Shares in AB Ltd	
	price)	£20 000			£20 000

Shares in AB Limited Account

Dec. 31	AB Ltd	£20 000	Dec. 31	A – Capital	£12 000
				B – Capital	8 000
		£20 000			£20 000

Bank Account

Dec. 31	Balance	£2 500	Dec. 31	Realisation –	
				(dissolution expenses)	£200
				A – Capital	1 780
				B – Capital	520
		£2 500			£2 500

Capital Accounts

Dec. 31	Shares in AB			Dec. 31	Balances	£10 000	£6 000
	Ltd	£12 000	£8 000		Realisation		
	Bank	1 780	520		(gain)	3 780	2 520
		£13 780	£8 520			£13 780	£8 520

Accounting entries to record the purchase of the business in the books of the purchasing company

1. *Dr.*   Business purchase account with the agreed purchase price.
      Cr.   Vendor's account.

2. *Dr.*   Appropriate asset accounts taken over from the firm at the company's valuation of these assets.
      Cr.   Business purchase account.

3. *Dr.*   Business purchase account with any liabilities taken over from the firm at the company's valuation of these liabilities.
   Cr.   Appropriate liability accounts.

4. *Dr.*   Goodwill being the difference between the purchase price and the value of the assets less liabilities.
   Cr.   Business purchase account.

Note: If the purchase price is less than the net assets of the business then the difference (being a capital profit) will be debited to the business purchase account and credited to capital reserve account.

5. *Dr.*   Vendor's account with the breakdown of the purchase price (shares, bank, cash, etc.)
   Cr.   Share capital account and/or bank and cash accounts.

Note: If the shares have been issued at a premium, only the nominal value of the shares will be posted to share capital account, the premium being entered at the credit of a share premium account.

Example: Jack and Jones, who are in partnership sharing profits and losses equally, decide to convert their business to a limited company at the date of the balance sheet shown below.

Balance Sheet as at 31 December

Capital accounts			Fixed assets		
Jack	£8 000		Motor car	£1 100	
Jones	7 000		Fixtures	1 500	
		£15 000			£2 600
Current liabilities			Current assets		
Creditors		2 500	Stock	8 000	
			Debtors	6 000	
			Bank	900	
					14 900
		£17 500			£17 500

The company, Jack & Jones Ltd, takes over all the assets and liabilities, with the exception of the bank balance, for a purchase price of £16 000 to be settled by the issue of 16 000 ordinary shares of £1 each. The expenses of dissolution amounting to £100 are to be met by the partnership.

The company decides to revalue the stock at £7500 and to create a bad debts provision of £300.

We record the opening entries in the company's journal and prepare the opening balance sheet of the company as follows:

In the Journal of Jack & Jones Ltd

Dec. 31	Business purchase		*Dr.*	£16 000	
	To Vendors – Jack & Jones				£16 000
	Being agreed purchase price for the business of Jack & Jones.				
	Motor car		*Dr.*	£1 100	
	Fixtures			1 500	
	Stock			7 500	
	Debtors			6 000	
	To Business purchase				£16 100
	Being assets taken over from the business of Jack & Jones.				

In the Journal of Jack & Jones Ltd *Cont.*

Dec. 31	Business purchase	*Dr.*	£2 800	
	To Creditors			£2 500
	Bad debts provision			300
	Being liabilities taken over from the business of Jack & Jones.			
	Goodwill	*Dr.*	£2 700	
	To Business purchase			£2 700
	Being Goodwill arising on the purchase of the business of Jack & Jones.			
	Vendors – Jack & Jones	*Dr.*	£16 000	
	To share capital			£16 000
	Being satisfaction or purchase consideration by issue of ordinary shares.			

Jack & Jones Ltd
Balance Sheet as at 31 December

Share capital			**Fixed assets**			
Authorised and issued			Goodwill		£2 700	
16 000 ordinary shares of			Motor car		1 100	
£1 each		£16 000	Fixtures		1 500	£5 300
			Current assets			
Current liabilities			Stock		7 500	
Creditors		2 500	Debtors	£6 000		
			Less Bad debts			
			provision	300	5 700	13 200
		£18 500				£18 500

Summary

1. Partnership as defined by the Partnership Act 1890 is the relation which subsists between persons carrying on a business with a view of profit.

2. Capital accounts of partners are usually split between fixed and current accounts.

3. The profit and loss appropriation account records the division of the trading profit or loss between the partners in accordance with the terms of the partnership agreement.

4. On the admission of a new partner it is normal practice to review the valuation of the assets and liabilities and if necessary revise them so that the redrafted balance sheet may reflect a satisfactory valuation of the whole business.

5. The valuation of goodwill usually arises on the admission of a new partner. It is normally the most complex asset to value.

6. When the assets and liabilities of a partnership are revalued the gain or loss is transferred from the revaluation account to the capital accounts of the partners.

7. When a partner dies or retires from a partnership it is necessary to calculate the amount due to be paid to the outgoing partner. There may need to be a revaluation of all the assets and liabilities of the business to determine this amount.

8. When it has been decided by the partners to dissolve the partnership the assets of the firm have to be realised to settle outstanding liabilities and to repay the partners their capital contributions together with any surplus on realisation.

9. The *Garner* v. *Murray* ruling is important when a partner is unable to meet his indebtedness to the firm.

10. It is quite usual for the partners to decide to convert the partnership to a limited company and either to become directors of the newly formed company or alternatively sell the business to other directors.

11. The realisation account is the key account when a partnership is converted or sold to a limited company. This account enables the gain or loss on sale to be calculated and transferred to the existing partners in the agreed proportions.

Discussion questions

12.1 What is the purpose of separating the capital accounts of partners into fixed and current? In your opinion, what is the best way of presenting the proprietorship section of the balance sheet of a partnership with two partners?

12.2 State what matters should be included in a partnership agreement and explain why you consider that they should be incorporated in such a document.

12.3 Do you agree with the *Garner* v. *Murray* ruling? Discuss.

12.4 'Although goodwill is an important asset when there is a change in the partnership, little importance is attached to this asset at other times in the life of the firm.' Comment.

12.5 Explain the methods which may be used to value goodwill in a partnership.

12.6 What are the main differences which affect accounting for a sole trader and a partnership?

12.7 Explain the difference between a realisation account and a revaluation account.

Exercises

12.8 A, B and C are partners in the Woodworks Trading Company. Their partnership agreement provides for:

(a) Profits and losses to be divided according to original capital which is to remain 'fixed'.

(b) Interest to be allowed on fixed capital at 6 per cent per annum, credited yearly.

(c) Interest is to be allowed on advances at 8 per cent per annum.

(d) Drawings for each partner to be limited to £100 per month and to be charged interest at 6 per cent on the daily balance.

(e) A to be paid a weekly salary of £20.

   You are required to:

(i) explain the meaning of 'partnership agreement';

(ii) state the provisions of the Partnership Act relating to the above points;

(iii) name the personal ledger accounts it would be desirable to keep for each partner, explaining:
(A) the nature and function of each account;
(B) what classification (if any) it would appear under in the balance sheet.

12.9 Slick, Smart and Howe are in partnership as painters and panelbeaters, Slick being in charge of the paint shop and Smart the panelbeating. Howe is an inactive partner. At 1 January their capitals were £4000, £6000 and £8000 respectively.

After making adjustments as provided for in the partnership agreement, the profits and losses were shared equally among the partners. Features of the partnership agreement were:

(a) Partners were entitled to interest on their fixed capitals at the rate of $7\frac{1}{2}$ per cent p.a.

(b) The two working partners were to be credited with £1500 each as annual salary for running the business.

(c) All partners were entitled to make drawings in anticipation of salary or profits, but a charge of 10 per cent was to be made on all drawings in excess of £2000.

The following information is available for the year ended 31 December:

Gross profit		£9 400
Administrative expenses (not including any of the above items)		1 860
Finance expenses (not including any of the above items)		840
Drawings: Slick	£1 400	
Smart	500	
Howe	3 600	
		£5 500

You are required:

(i) to prepare, in narrative form, a brief statement of profit and loss, and a statement of the appropriation of profit for year ended 31 December;

(ii) to show the capital and current accounts of the partners as they would appear in the ledger as at 31 December.

12.10 Brown and Green are partners who share profits and losses in the proportion of three-fifths and two-fifths respectively. They commenced business on 1 October 19X7 when they introduced into their business the following assets:

Brown: cash £900; van £400; office furniture £100.
Green: cash £500; stock £450.

Apart from the receipt of cash by the business these items had not been recorded in the partnership books.

The following trial balance was extracted from their books at the close of business on 30 September 19X8:

	Dr.	Cr.
Cash received from Brown		£900
Cash received from Green		500
Purchases and sales	£7 380	12 370
Debtors and creditors	2 760	1 350
	£10 140	£15 120
		Cont.

	Dr.	Cr.
b/fwd	£10 140	£15 120
Drawings – Brown	800	
Green	660	
Rent and rates	380	
Wages and salaries	2 030	
Discount	290	140
Bank	360	
Cash	20	
Bad debts	110	
General expenses	140	
Van running expenses	330	
	£15 260	£15 260

From the above and from the notes given below, you are required to prepare the trading and profit and loss accounts of the partnership for the year ended 30 September 19X8, together with a balance sheet as on that date:

(a) Stock at 30 September 19X8 £1080.

(b) Rent accrued at 30 September 19X8 £30.

(c) Rates prepaid at 30 September 19X8 £50.

(d) Ignore depreciation of van and office furniture.

(c) Interest is not to be allowed on capital accounts.

12.11 The following balances were extracted from the books of White and Green at 31 December 19X7:

Purchases	£21 290	Salaries	£930
Manufacturing wages	3 180	Office expenses	710
Sales	32 160	Premium on lease	3 000
White – Capital	7 000	Sundry creditors	22 080
Drawings	1 200	Loan on mortgage	5 000
Green – Capital	6 000	Freehold land and buildings	10 000
Drawings	1 000	Machinery and plant	6 000
Stock 1 January 19X7	4 170	Provision for bad debts as at	
Rates and taxes	500	1 January 19X7	700
Sundry debtors	19 180	Cash at bank	1 780

You are requested to prepare therefrom a trading and profit and loss account for the year ended 31 December 19X7 and a balance sheet at that date, taking into account the following information:

(a) White and Green share profits and losses equally.

(b) Stock at 31 December 19X7 is valued at £4320.

(c) Before ascertaining profits interest is to be allowed on partners' capital at 6 per cent per annum.

(d) Depreciate Land and Buildings by 5 per cent and Machinery and Plant by 10 per cent.

(e) The lease has five years unexpired at 1 January 19X7.

(f) Provision for bad debts to be 5 per cent of sundry debtors.

(g) Interest at 7 per cent is due on the mortgage and has not yet been entered in the books.

(h) Rates are outstanding amounting to £125.

(i) Salaries of £90 are unpaid.

12.12 Tom, Charles, and John are in partnership sharing profits and losses in the ratio 2 : 2 : 1 respectively. From the information below you are required to make the necessary adjustment of the partnership books without reopening the profit and loss account.

The profit for the year ended 31 December 19X8 was £3000, having been allocated, the balances on their capital accounts then became:

Tom £10 400; Charles £5 300; John £2 600.

When the books had been closed it was noticed that interest on capital at the rate of 5 per cent per annum and interest on drawings should have been brought into account.

The drawings and relative interest for the year were as follows:

	Drawings	Interest
Tom	£800	£30
Charles	900	20
John	1 000	25

12.13 Black and White are in partnership and carry on an agency business on a commission basis.

From the following information, prepare the profit and loss account for the year ended 31 March 19X8 and balance sheet as at that date, and also the journal entries necessary to adjust and close the books.

The trial balance as at 31 March 19X8 was as follows:

Balances in bank	£5 080	
Business expenses paid during year	3 370	
Business expenses accrued at 31 March 19X7		£80
Capital accounts at 31 March 19X7 – Black		2 800
White		1 800
Cash in hand	26	
Commissions received during year		6 836
Commissions due at 31 March 19X7	410	
Drawings account – Black	1 370	
White	840	
Office furniture and fittings – value at 31 March 19X7	420	
	£11 516	£11 516

Additional information:

(a) Provide for commissions due at 31 March 19X8, £480; and for business expenses due and unpaid at that date, £95.

(b) The office furniture and fittings have to be depreciated at 5 per cent.

(c) The partnership deed provides that:

   (i) Interest at 5 per cent per annum is to be credited to each partner on the amount at credit of his capital account at the beginning of the year.

   (ii) White is to be credited with salary of £1200 per annum.

   (iii) After charging interest on capital and salary to White, the balance of profit or loss is to be divided five-ninths to Black and four-ninths to White.

12.14 JD and PM are partners sharing profits and losses in the proportions JD two-thirds and PM one-third. Their agreement provides that interest should be allowed on partners' capitals (calculated on the balances at 1 January in each year) at 5 per cent per annum, and charged on drawings.

The following trial balance was extracted as on 31 December 19X8:

Current accounts – JD		£70
PM		30
Capital accounts – JD		9 000
PM		8 000
Drawings – JD	£4 600	
PM	2 100	
Stock in trade, 1 January 19X8	8 100	
Trade debtors and trade creditors	8 938	6 230
Purchases	72 320	
Sales		95 630
Wages and salaries	8 740	
Rent and rates	675	
Bad debts	912	
Provision for bad debts, 1 January 19X8		470
Lease of premises	400	
General expenses	5 608	
Furniture and fittings	3 200	
Discount received		1 620
Discounts allowed	1 825	
Balance at bank	3 632	
	£121 050	£121 050

You are given the following information:

(a) Stock in trade at 31 December 19X8, £10 070.

(b) Wages outstanding at 31 December 19X8, £215.

(c) Rates paid in advance at 31 December 19X8, £30.

(d) The provision for bad debts is to be increased to £550.

(e) The lease of the premises will expire on 31 December 19X9.

(f) A purchase invoice for £120 had been entered twice in the purchases journal and posted twice to the supplier's account. Two cheques for £118 (allowing £2 for discount) were sent to the supplier, and at 31 December 19X8, the balance on the personal account of the supplier was nil.

(g) A cheque for £105 received from a customer, correctly entered in the books was dishonoured on 31 December 19X8. No entry has been made to record the dishonour. It is expected that the cheque will be honoured on re-presentation.

(h) Provide for depreciation of furniture and fittings, £160.

(i) Interest on drawings for 19X8 amounts to £115 for JD and £73 for PM.

You are required to prepare the trading and profit and loss account for 19X8, and the balance sheet as on 31 December 19X8.

12.15 Hector and Alfred are in partnership sharing profits and losses equally. Their balance sheet at 31 December was as follows:

Capital			Property	£1 500
Hector	£2 000		Plant	1 000
Alfred	1 500		Stock	1 200
		£3 500	Debtors	800
Creditors		1 500	Cash at bank	500
		£5 000		£5 000

It was agreed to admit David into partnership on 1 January and to allow him a one-third share of profits. He is to bring in as his capital £1 000.

The partners decided to value goodwill at £1200 and to revalue the property at £2000 and stock at £1100. It was also agreed that goodwill was to appear as an account in the balance sheet. The partners share profits and losses: Hector, $\frac{1}{2}$; Alfred $\frac{1}{6}$; David, $\frac{1}{3}$.

You are required to prepare the necessary ledger accounts to record the above and the balance sheet of the new firm.

12.16 Hawthorn and Privet have carried on business in partnership for a number of years sharing profits in the ratio of 4 : 3, after charging interest on capital at 4 per cent per annum. Holly was admitted into partnership on 1 October 19X8 and the terms of the partnership from then were agreed as follows:

(a) Partners' annual salaries to be: Hawthorn £1800, Privet £1200, Holly £1100.

(b) Interest on capital to be charged at 4 per cent per annum.

(c) Profit to be shared: Hawthorn four-ninths, Privet three-ninths, Holly two-ninths.

On 1 October 19X8 Holly paid £7000 into the partnership bank account and of this amount £2100 was in respect of the share of Goodwill acquired by him. Since the partnership has never created, and does not intend to create, a Goodwill account, the full amount of £7000 was credited for the time being to Holly's capital account at 1 October 19X8.

12.17 Harris and Johnson are in partnership sharing profits in the proportion of three-fifths to Harris and two-fifths to Johnson. They decide at 31 December 19X8 to dissolve partnership and wind up the business.

Their balance sheet at that date was as follows:

Liabilities			**Assets**	
Capital accounts:			Cash at bank	£900
Harris	£3 200		Sundry debtors	2 400
Johnson	2 700		Other assets	3 600
		£5 900	Goodwill	1 200
Sundry creditors		2 200		
		£8 100		£8 100

Sundry debtors realised £2200 and the other assets £3100 while Goodwill was sold for £900. The sundry creditors were finally settled for £2000 and the expenses of winding up the business amounted to £90.

You are requested to show the ledger accounts for the dissolution.

12.18 Graham, Ross, and Stewart are in partnership sharing profits and losses 4 : 3 : 1. The balance sheet prepared at the date of dissolution was as follows:

Capital accounts:			Property	£8 000
Graham	£12 000		Motor vehicles	5 000
Ross	3 000		Stock	1 000
		£15 000	Debtors	3 000
			Cash at bank	1 000
Creditors		5 000	Capital account overdrawn –	
			Stewart	2 000
		£20 000		£20 000

On dissolution of the partnership it was discovered that Stewart was bankrupt and can only pay £0.50 in the £.

The assets realised:

Property	£7 000
Motor vehicles	4 500
Stock	850
Debtors	2 550

Discount received on settlement of creditors amounted to £100 and the expenses of dissolution are £200.

The original capital introduced by the partners was:

Graham	£6 000
Ross	3 000
Stewart	1000

You are required to show the necessary ledger accounts to record the dissolution.

12.19 From the following information you are required to close the books of the partnership Right and Left and to prepare the opening Balance Sheet of Centre Ltd as at 1 January 19X8.

Right and Left who are in partnership share profits and losses equally.

The balance sheet of the partnership as at 31 December 19X7, was as follows:

Capital accounts			Freehold premises	£2 000
Right	£5 000		Motor vehicles	1 500
Left	3 000		Stock	3 800
		£8 000	Debtors	2 200
Creditors		2 500	Bank	1 000
		£10 500		£10 500

It was agreed that a limited company, Centre Ltd, is formed with an authorised capital of £14 000 in ordinary shares of £1 each. The company was incorporated on 1 January 19X8 and took over the assets and liabilities at book value with the exception of motor vehicles which were revalued at £1200.

Goodwill is to be paid for and was valued at £3000. The purchase price is to be settled by issue of £1 ordinary shares at par in Centre Ltd.

12.20 Hopeful Ltd was incorporated with a view to acquiring as on 1 June 19X8 the business previously carried on by I. Maiditt. The authorised capital of the company was £116 000 divided into 81 000 ordinary shares of £1 each and 35 000 8 per cent preference shares of £1 each. The balance sheet of I. Maiditt as on 31 May 19X8 was as follows:

Capital account	£41 900	Freehold land and buildings	£22 000
Trade creditors and accrued		Plant and machinery	14 200
expenses	9 950	Stock on hand	8 000
Bank overdraft	5 150	Sundry debtors	12 800
	£57 000		£57 000

The company took over all the assets and assumed all the liabilities, with the exception of the bank overdraft, the purchase consideration being fixed at £54 300. In arriving at this figure freehold land and buildings were valued at £27 000, plant and machinery at £12 800, stock on hand at £7500 and the debtors at book value after a deduction of 5 per cent to cover doubtful debts. The bank overdraft was settled by I. Maiditt.

In settlement of the purchase consideration, 23 000 ordinary shares and 16 000 preference shares were issued at par to I. Maiditt, fully paid, the balance being paid in cash. Bright Hopes Ltd had agreed to take up 58 000 ordinary shares in Hopeful Ltd at par and these were issued to it on 1 June 19X8, the cash being paid to Hopeful Ltd on the same day. The formation expenses amounting to £1360 were paid by Hopeful Ltd.

You are required to prepare:

(a) Journal entries, including those relating to cash, to close the books of I. Maiditt, and

(b) The balance sheet of Hopeful Ltd immediately after the completion of the above-mentioned transactions.

12.21 Street and Lane were in partnership sharing profits and losses in the proportion of three-fifths and two fifths respectively. The business consisted of two shops, one situated at Rosemount and the other at Mastrick. It was decided to dissolve the partnership as at 30 June 19X8, at which date the balance sheet of the business was as follows:

Liabilities			**Assets**		
Sundry creditors			Buildings		
Rosemount	£2 034		Rosemount	£5 675	
Mastrick	1 167		Mastrick	3 283	
		£3 201			£8 958
Overdrawn on bank –			Fittings		
current account		3 434	Rosemount	1 350	
			Mastrick	975	
Capital accounts					2 325
Street	8 902		Trade investment		
Lane	1 744		at cost		511
		10 646	Stock		
			Rosemount	2 946	
			Mastrick	1 761	
					4 707
			Debtors – Rosemount	880	
			Deduct Reserve for		
			doubtful debts	100	
					780
		£17 281			£17 281

The two shop properties and the fittings, stock, and debtors of the Rosemount shop were sold to B. Alley Ltd for £14 000, the purchase price being satisfied by the issue to Street of 7500 ordinary shares of £1 each in B. Alley Ltd at £0.10 premium and the balance in cash.

Lane, who is to lease the Mastrick buildings, took over the fittings, stock, and creditors of that shop at their book value.

Of the trade investment of 500 ordinary shares of £1 each in Close Ltd, 200 shares were taken over by Street at £0.75 per share and the remainder sold for £237.

The creditors of the Rosemount shop were settled, cash discount of £43 being received. Expenses of realisation amounted to £275.

You are required to prepare the following:

(a) The realisation account.

(b) The cash account.

(c) The partners' capital accounts after the balances on these have been settled.

Problems

12.22 V. Ford and A. Holden are in partnership as merchants. The partnership agreement provides (among other things) for the following:

(a) Ford is to receive a salary of £1500 per annum together with a bonus (to the nearest £1) of 1 per cent on net sales. These amounts are not withdrawn but are credited to his current account at the end of the year.

(b) Interest on loans made by partners is calculated at 8 per cent on the final balance. This interest is to be credited to the current account of the partner.

(c) No interest is allowed on capital and no interest is charged on drawings.

(d) Profits or losses are to be shared in the proportions – Ford two-fifths, Holden three-fifths.

The trial balance of the partnership at 30 June 19X6 was as follows:

	Dr.	Cr.
Creditors		£33 377
Debtors	£62 000	
Advertising	3 379	
Bad debts	1 875	
Bank overdraft		5 580
Carriage inwards	315	
Customs duties	1 200	
Cash in hand	50	
Delivery vehicles (cost)	10 250	
Delivery vehicles expenses	2 200	
Discount allowed	4 556	
Discount received		4 000
V. Ford, fixed capital		25 000
V. Ford, current account	3 772	
Furniture and fittings (cost)	1 350	
A. Holden, loan account		10 000
A. Holden, fixed capital		40 000
A. Holden, current account		750
c/fwd	£90 947	£118 707

	Dr.	Cr.
b/fwd	£90 947	£118 707
Insurance of delivery vehicles	658	
Insurance of furniture and fittings	44	
Stocks (1 July 19X7)	14 986	
Land and buildings (cost)	48 391	
Office salaries	6 056	
Office expenses	2 895	
Profit on sale of delivery vehicles		442
Provision for depreciation of delivery vehicles		3 456
Provision for depreciation of furniture and fittings		350
Provision for doubtful debts		1 240
Purchases	141 879	
Purchases returns		1 879
Sales		195 775
Sales returns and allowances	4 889	
Shop wages	9 552	
Wrapping materials	1 552	
	£321 849	£321 849

Adjustments:

1. The following expenses are outstanding on 30 June 19X6:

Shop wages	£450
Office salaries	320
Office expenses	56

2. An amount of £431 has been earned by the partnership for commission due for work done in connection with the ordinary business of the enterprise, but no cash has yet been received.

3. Insurance on delivery vehicles has been prepaid £123.

4. The provision for doubtful debts is to be increased to 3 per cent of sundry debtors.

5. Depreciation is to be provided for at the following rates:

on furniture and fittings at 20 per cent of the reduced balance
on delivery vehicles at 20 per cent on the original cost

6. Stocks at 30 June 19X6 were valued at £16 881.

You are required to prepare (in narrative form):

(i) the profit and loss statement and appropriation statement for the year ended 30 June 19X6;

(ii) the balance sheet at 30 June 19X6.

Chapter 13
Specific issues in company accounting

Introduction to limited companies ☐ Principal differences between a partnership and a limited company ☐ Formation of a limited company ☐ Types of shares ☐ Accounting for contributed capital ☐ Issue of shares ☐ Debentures ☐ Further issues of shares ☐ Redeemable shares ☐ Purchases of own shares ☐ Redemption or purchase of own shares out of capital by a private company

Introduction to limited companies

The most common type of company is that with limited liability. The name of such enterprises must have the word 'Limited' if a private company or 'Plc' if a public limited company, as the last word in their name. A member undertakes to subscribe for shares in the company and agrees to take, say, one hundred £1 shares. The effect of this is that the maximum amount that can be demanded from the member of the company is £100. Once that amount has been paid the member is not liable for any further amounts irrespective of how much of the company's debts remains unpaid. In contrast to this, it should be pointed out that if an enterprise owned by a sole trader or a partnership cannot meet its debts from the assets of the enterprise, then the sole trader or the partners are liable for the full amount of the deficit which would have to be met from their own private resources; that is, such types of ownership involve unlimited liability. It is this limit of the liability of members which has proved such an attraction to investors in companies. It is also the reason why some partnerships prefer to re-form themselves into companies, particularly where there is a great risk of loss.

In most cases, companies are limited by shares; that is, members are liable only for the face value of their share holdings. There is, however, provision for companies to be limited by guarantee whereby members guarantee to pay a certain fixed amount to the company on demand. Such companies are sometimes floated to run community or charity efforts and are also used by some sporting and education bodies. There is a further distinction which affects the legal side more than the accounting records – limited companies may be classed as public or private companies. The main distinguishing feature is that a public company may invite the public to subscribe for shares in the company by issuing a prospectus, whereas private companies are prohibited from so doing. There is also provision for what is known as 'unlimited liability' which does not limit its members' liability.

The Companies Act lays down certain provisions with which all companies must comply. Each company must have prepared a document called the memorandum of association which is the constitution of the company. It contains the name by which the company is to be known and the capital with which it is to be initially registered, and includes the objects for which it has been formed. This document must be signed by the minimum number of members required for that particular type of company and each of them must undertake the number of shares signed for. A further document – the articles of association – giving the rules or regulations of the company is usually prepared which provides for the rights and duties of members among other things. It would include such items as when meetings are to be held, the method of voting and election of directors, appointment of the auditor, method of transfer of shares, etc. There is a model set of articles in the Companies Act known as Table A and a company if it so wishes can adopt such a set. The Act also lays down the procedure for registering a company. At the conclusion of these legal steps, a certificate of incorporation is issued to the company.

Members of a company are called shareholders and they elect a board of directors to act on their behalf in matters of policy. It is usual for the latter to approach one of their number to carry out their policy and he is usually termed the managing director. A company must also have a secretary and appoint an auditor.

Definition of a company

An incorporated company is a separate legal entity consisting of an association of persons who contribute money or its equivalent and use it for the purposes of earning profit in a trade or business. The capital, which is the money or money's worth subscribed by the members, is divided into shares and allotted to them in proportion to their capital contributions. The members receive a share of any profit earned by the company by way of dividend, normally based as a rate per cent on the subscribed capital. The liability of the members is limited and the shares are transferable subject to conditions contained in the company's articles of association.

Types of companies

The two main types of companies are public companies and private companies.

Public companies

A public company must fulfil the following requirements:

1. It must have a minimum allotted share capital of £50 000.

2. It must have not less than two members and two directors.

3. The legal provisions relating to the registration of a public company must be met.

4. The fact that the company is a public company must be stated in the memorandum of association.

5. The name of the company must end with the words 'public limited company' or the abbreviation 'plc'.

6. It must be limited by shares.

Private companies

A private company is any company which is not a public company. It includes all unlimited companies and any company limited by guarantee which does not have a share capital.

The distinguishing features of a private company are:

1. The minimum number of directors is one, but a sole director cannot also act as secretary of the company.

2. It is easier to give financial assistance for the purchase of its own shares.

3. It is authorised to purchase or redeem its own shares out of capital rather than out of distributable profits.

4. The age limit provisions for directors do not apply.

5. It cannot offer its shares or debentures to the public.

6. Less stringent conditions apply to the determination of distributable profits.

Principal differences between a partnership and a limited company

Table 13.1   Comparison of partnership and limited company

Partnership	Limited company
1. Not a legal entity separate from its partners.	1. Legal entity in its own right.
2. Partners liable for the debts of the firm.	2. In a company the liability is limited.
3. Regulated by Partnership Act 1890.	3. Regulated by Companies Act 1985.
4. Rules governing the conduct of the partnership are usually contained in the partnership agreement.	4. Rules and regulations other than those contained in the Companies Act are included in the memorandum and articles of association.
5. Number of partners limited to twenty with certain exceptions.	5. In a public company the only limit is the number of shares authorised and issued to shareholders.
6. No obligation to reveal information about its financial affairs to the public.	6. Must submit certain information about its financial position to the Registrar of Companies.
7. No legal requirement to appoint an auditor and keep proper books of account.	7. Must appoint an auditor and maintain adequate accounting records.
8. Profits are distributed to the partners in agreed proportions.	8. Profits are distributed by way of dividend based on the issued share capital.
9. Capital is contributed by the partners in agreed amounts. Also a reduction in the capital can take place if agreed by the existing partners.	9. Capital is contributed by shareholders up to a maximum authorised amount. Any reduction in capital must be approved by the court.

Formation of a limited company

The formation of a limited company necessitates the completion of certain documents and payment of fees and duties to the Registrar of Companies in Cardiff for English and Welsh companies and in Edinburgh for Scottish companies.

The principal documents to be lodged are:

1. The memorandum and articles of association.

2. A statement of the nominal capital of the company.

3. Notification of particulars of directors, secretary and registered office.

4. A statutory declaration that the requirements of the Acts have been complied with.

One of the main constituting documents, namely the memorandum of association, defines the objects and powers of the company and contains the following information:

1. The name of the company ending with 'limited' or 'public limited company'.

2. The fact that the company is a 'public limited company' if appropriate.

3. Whether the registered office of the company is to be situated in England, Wales or Scotland.

4. The objects of the company.

5. A statement intimating that the liability of the members is limited.

6. The amount of share capital with which the company proposes to be registered and the shares into which it is divided.

7. A declaration has to be made by the subscribers that they wish to be formed into a limited company in accordance with the memorandum and agree to take up the number of shares shown opposite their names.

The other main constituting document is the articles of association which defines the powers and duties of the members among themselves.

Most companies adopt Table A, with some slight modifications, as their articles of association. The principal clauses relate to:

1. Issue and transfer of shares.

2. General meetings.

3. Use of the company seal.

4. Voting powers of members.

5. Appointment and duties of directors and secretary.

6. Keeping of books and audit.

Types of shares

Each class of share may have different rights attached to it as laid down in the memorandum and articles of association. The shares issued may also be of different amounts or denominations. The following are the principal classes of shares to use at present.

Ordinary shares

These are the most common form of share issued by limited companies and constitute the majority of a normal company's share capital. Ordinary shareholders are the ultimate owners of a company. Ordinary shares carry no special rights and the ordinary shareholders are entitled to share in the profits available for dividend after corporation tax and the payment of dividends on other classes of shares. The dividend paid on this type of share is not fixed and can vary from year to year, depending on the level of profits earned by the company and the dividend policy of the directors. It is usual for companies only to declare a section of the net profit as dividends and to retain the balance of undistributed profit to provide further capital for the conduct of the activities of the business.

Ordinary shares may be issued fully or partly paid and the company may not issue all the shares authorised in the memorandum of association.

Preference shares

Preference shareholders are entitled to certain preferential rights over other classes of shareholders. Preference shares always carry the right to a fixed rate of dividend, which is usually based on a percentage on the nominal amount paid before the ordinary dividend. The dividend may be cumulative or non-cumulative, depending on the terms and conditions of the issue. If the dividends are cumulative then unpaid dividends must be carried forward and made up out of future profits, together with current dividends and before payment of any ordinary dividends. Most preference shares are also given priority of repayment of capital on liquidation. Occasionally, participating preference shares are issued which entitle the holder to the right of a further dividend once the ordinary dividend has exceeded a specific amount.

Some types of preference shares are redeemable, which means that the capital can be repaid by the company to the shareholders. There are special rules which apply to the redemption of preference shares which are discussed later. By issuing this type of share it allows the company to obtain capital of a semipermanent nature at a fixed rate of dividend which can be repaid when the capital is no longer required.

Deferred shares

These are not a common type of share; they are sometimes referred to as management, or founders' shares. They rank after ordinary shares in respect of dividend payments and repayment of capital. They are principally held by vendors or promoters of a business in consideration of the amounts of expenses and other costs in forming the company. Deferred shares are generally of small nominal value and of a highly speculative nature.

Accounting for contributed capital

For a sole trader, one account is basically necessary to record contributed capital. As discussed earlier, it is desirable to record withdrawals by the owner in a separate account.

In a partnership, particularly where the agreement between the partners provides for a certain 'fixed capital' for each partner, it is desirable to distinguish between capital accounts (showing the respective fixed amounts) and current accounts (which record the fluctuations of each partner's interest caused by profits or losses or drawings). It is possible, however, that a partner may make an advance to the partnership which is quite distinct from his or her capital; it is, in effect, either a temporary or permanent loan to the firm. The distinction between such advances and the ordinary capital of the partner must be clearly shown in the records so that in the event of a dissolution of the partnership such advances will be repaid before ordinary capital. This could be very important if assets are sufficient to pay outside debts but insufficient to meet the total of partners' capital and advances.

Accounting for the contributed capital of a company is more complex. In this chapter we will discuss the basic structure of a company's share capital and the problems associated with accounting for share issues. A company on receipt of its certificate of incorporation becomes a separate legal entity with the amount of capital stated in its memorandum of association. This is known as its authorised capital and consists of a number of shares which it can issue to prospective members. The face value of each share will also be stated in the memorandum. Thus, when the company is registered, it has a potential asset (the unissued shares) equal to the amount of its authorised capital. Of course, if nobody wants the shares, the asset is worthless. The directors may not offer all shares for subscription but issue some shares only. Thus, in their financial statements, companies must distinguish between authorised and issued capital. When shares are allotted to the applicants, the total of these represent the issued share capital and the balance the unissued capital.

In practice, the majority of share issues are made on the basis that the full price payable for the shares is required on application. However, some issues of shares are made payable by instalments. In these cases, there is always a proportion of the price payable on *application*. The remainder may be demanded by the company on *allotment* (that is, when the shareholder is notified of the acceptance in full or in part of the number of shares applied for) or at one or more subsequent dates when a *call* is made on the shares. Thus, we may distinguish between issued and called-up capital. At any point in time there may be unpaid calls and a further distinction can be made between called-up capital and paid-up capital.

Example: Pamillian Ltd has a registered capital of £10 000 divided into £1 ordinary shares. 4000 shares were offered to the public on the following terms:

25p per share on application.
25p per share on allotment.
25p first call, three months after allotment.
The balance when called for.

Applications were received for exactly 4000 shares and these were allotted by the directors. All moneys were received as arranged, except that holders of 600 shares failed to pay the amount of the first call on the due date.
The position at the end of three months would be as follows:

Authorised capital £10 000 (10 000 £1 shares)

Issued capital £4000 (4000 £1 shares)	Unissued capital £6000 (6000 £1 shares)

Issued capital £4000

Called-up capital £3000 (4000 shares called) to 75p	Uncalled capital £1000 (4000 shares at 25p)

Called-up capital

Paid-up capital £2850 (3400 shares paid to 75p + 600 shares paid to 50p)	The shaded portion represents *unpaid calls* or *calls in arrear* £150 (600 shares at 25p per share)

Fig. 13.1   Position of Pamilian Ltd after three months.

In the balance sheet the position may be stated as follows:

Shareholders' equity

Authorised capital		
10 000 ordinary shares of £1 each		£10 000
Issued capital		
3000 ordinary shares of £1 each		
75p called up	£3 000	
Less Calls in arrear	150	2 850

Note: £2850 is referred to as the paid-up capital.

We have seen the capital of a company as stated in the memorandum of association is divided into portions called shares. As has been stated earlier in the chapter, these shares may be of different classes, however, some of which may have special rights. Authority for their issue usually is included in the provisions of the articles of association. For example, preference shares may have first claim to a certain proportion of the dividends (that is, payments made by the company out of profits), or they may have priority for the return of their capital in the event of the company being wound up, or they may have both such rights. Those without any special rights are called ordinary shares. Thus, the holders of 6 per cent preference shares would have to receive a dividend of 6 per cent before the holders of ordinary shares received any. If there were insufficient profits to pay more than 6 per cent needed for preference dividends, the ordinary shareholders would receive nothing. On the other hand, no matter how much profit was available for dividend, the preference shareholders would usually receive no more than 6 per cent, even if the ordinary shareholders were paid, say, 50 per cent dividend. In some cases such shares are issued to restrict the amount of dividends paid to newer members, while in others they are issued in this form because the preference of a fixed amount of dividend in priority to ordinary shareholders acts as an inducement to invest in the company. The major point in recording various classes of shares in the books of account is that the accounts relating to each class must be kept separate.

We have already seen that shares may be issued either payable in full on application or payable by instalments over a period of time. In addition, they may be issued either:

1. at par or nominal amount, that is a £1.00 share for £1.00; or

2. at a premium, that is, a £1.00 share for, say, £1.50.

Shares may in rare cases be issued at a discount (that is, below par) and are usually subject to court approval. The entries to record this type of issue are discussed later in the chapter.

Issue of shares

The following are some of the main methods of issuing shares.

Prospectus issue

This method involves the issuing of a prospectus to the public inviting them to offer for a fixed number of shares at a fixed price. The matters which are to be included in the prospectus are detailed in the Companies Act 1985. This method of issuing shares is usually adopted where fairly large issues are being launched since it is a costly way of raising capital.

Tender issue

In this form of issue the prospectus or offer for sale states a minimum amount at or above which applicants are invited to price their applications. After receiving the applications the company fixes the price and shares are allotted to all subscribers who offered at or above the fixed price. The main advantage of this method is that it allows market demand to be more accurately assessed and ensures that there is less risk of speculators offering for the shares and selling them immediately at a profit.

Rights issue

By using this system the existing shareholders of a company are circularised advising them that they are given the right to subscribe for additional shares in proportion to their holdings at an advantageous price. They are then able to take up the offer and subscribe for the shares or sell their rights on the stock exchange.

Placement

This technique of raising capital can be adopted by private companies or by public companies with a quotation on the stock exchange. The shares are usually placed with a number of investors by an issuing house. In the instance of a small issue this may be done by a broker who has contact with a number of prospective investors and so is able to place the shares.

Offer for sale

An offer for sale is occcasionally used as an alternative to an issue of shares by means of a prospectus. Under this method the issue is sold directly to an issuing house at an agreed price. The issuing house will then offer the shares for sale to the public at a fixed price. Although it can be an expensive method of issuing shares it is a useful technique when the issue is too small to be made by a prospectus issue or where it is considered safer to allow a reputable issuing house to make the offer to the public to ensure a successful issue is made.

Accounting for share capital

Earlier in this chapter we discussed the need for a company to be able to determine the respective amounts of authorised, issued, called-up and paid-up capital for each class of share issued. Now we will discuss the accounting records and entries required to provide such information.

Example: Pamillian Ltd has an authorised capital of £10 000 divided into £1 shares. 4000 shares were offered to the public at par on the following terms:

> 25p per share on application.
> 25p per share on allotment.
> 25p per share on first call, three months after allotment.
> The balance when called for.

Applications were received for exactly 4000 shares, and these were allotted by the directors. All moneys were received as arranged, except that holders of 600 shares failed to pay the amount of the first call on the due date. The above issue of shares by Pamillian Ltd would be recorded as follows:

1. *Dr.* Share application account with amount *due* on application. *Cr.* Share capital.

2. *Dr.* Bank account with amount *actually* received from applicants. *Cr.* Share application account.

3. *Dr.* Share allotment account with amount *due* on allotment. *Cr.* Share capital account.

4. *Dr.* Bank account with amount *actually received*. *Cr.* Share allotment account.

5. *Dr.*   Share Call account. *Cr.*   Share Capital account.

6. *Dr.*   Bank account with amount received. *Cr.*   Share Call account.

7. *Dr.*   Calls in arrear with amount of calls unpaid. *Cr.*   Appropriate share call account.

In ledger form the entries would be as follows:

Share Application Account

Share capital	£1 000	Bank	£1 000

Share Allotment Account

Share capital	£1 000	Bank	£1 000

First Call Account

Share capital	£1 000	Bank	£850
		Calls in arrear	150
	£1 000		£1 000

Share Capital Account

	Share application	£1 000
	Share allotment	1 000
	Share call	1 000
		£3 000

Calls in Arrear Account

First call	£150

Bank Account

Share application	£1 000
Share allotment	1 000
First call	850
	£2 850

A balance sheet of the company at this stage (assuming no other transactions) would be as follows:

Pamillian Ltd
Balance Sheet as at................

Share capital		
Authorised		
10 000 ordinary shares of £1 each	£10 000	
Issued		
4000 ordinary shares of £1 each 75p called	3 000	
Less Calls in arrear	150	£2 850
Represented by:		
Current assets		
Cash at bank		£2 850

Note: Called-up capital = £3 000
      Paid-up capital   = £2 850

In the example quoted above, it has been assumed that the number of shares applied for was exactly equal to the number available for issue. In practice, this is often not the case, and it is common for more to be applied for than can be issued. This is known as oversubscription. The entries to record this situation are as follows:

> *Dr.*   Share application account with the amount of money returned, if any, to the applicants who have not been allocated shares.
> *Cr.*   Bank account.

Or, if appropriate,

> *Dr.*   Share application account with the excess money sent by applicants who have been allotted only a proportion of the shares for which they applied.
> *Cr.*   Share allotment account.

If the excess money is transferred to the share allotment account in this way then the applicants who have been allotted shares will have this amount deducted from the sum due by them on allotment.

Calls in advance

Calls in advance arise when a shareholder pays an amount to the company in respect of a future call to be made by the directors but before the due time for payment.

Accounting entries where calls in advance arise are:

1. *Dr.*   Bank with the amount paid in advance.
   Cr.   Calls in advance account.

2. *Dr.*   Calls in advance with the amount to be transferred to the appropriate share call account when it becomes due and payable.
   Cr.   Appropriate share call account.

Shares issued at a premium

A company may issue shares at a premium if the directors of the company are of the opinion that the investing public will be sufficiently attracted by the terms of the offer and the future prospects of the company that they will be prepared to pay a higher price than the nominal value of the shares offered. In the case of a share with a nominal value of £1 being offered to the public at £1.25 the difference between the two amounts, viz £0.25, is known as the premium.

Accounting entries where shares issued at a premium arise are:

1. *Dr.*   Share application with the amount due on application in respect of capital element.
   Cr.   Share capital.

2. *Dr.*   Share application (if premium is included in application amount) in respect of amount of share premium.
   Cr.   Share premium account.

3. *Dr.*   Bank account with amount actually received including premium.
   Cr.   Share application account.

Shares issued at a discount

When the price at which shares are issued is lower than the nominal value of the shares, these shares are being issued at a discount.

Accounting entries where shares are issued at a discount:

Dr.   Discount on shares account with the amount of discount allowed on the issue.
Cr.   Share capital account.

Forfeiture of shares

If a member fails to pay any call on the due date then the directors may decide to forfeit the shares. On forfeiture of the shares the shareholder ceases to be a member of the company and is not entitled to recover any amounts previously paid on the shares as those funds now belong to the company. When shares are forfeited they are not cancelled but become the property of the company and the directors have power to reissue them.

Accounting entries required on forfeiture of shares are:

1. *Dr.*   Share capital with the nominal amount of the shares which has become *due and payable* at the date of forfeiture and has been credited to the share capital account.
   Cr.   Forfeited shares account.

2. *Dr.*   Forfeited shares account.
   Cr.   Call account or calls in arrear account with the amount remaining unpaid on the shares forfeited. If more than one call was unpaid and no calls in arrear account was opened then each call account will be credited with the unpaid balance.

Example: Orion Ltd, which had an authorised capital of £20 000 issued 10 000 ordinary shares of £1 each at par. All shareholders had paid the first and final call of 25p with the exception of one shareholder who failed to pay the amount due on call on 200 shares issued to him. The directors resolved that the shares should be forfeited.

In the ledger of Orion Ltd

First and Final Call Account

| Balance | £50 | Forfeited shares | £50 |

Share Capital Account

Forfeited shares	£200	Balance (shares already issued)	£10 000
Balance	9 800		
	£10 000		£10 000
		Balance	£9 800

Forfeited Shares Account

First and final call	£50	Share capital	£200
Balance	150		
	£200		£200
		Balance	£150

Balance Sheet (after shares have been forfeited)

Share capital
Authorised
20 000 ordinary shares of £1 each — £20 000

Issued
| 10 000 ordinary shares of £1 each fully called | 10 000 | |
| *Less* 200 shares forfeited per resolution of directors | 200 | £9 800 |

Forfeited shares account — 150

Note: The opening balance shown in the first and final call account will represent the amount unpaid by the defaulting shareholder, viz 200 shares at 25p = £50.

Reissue of forfeited shares

Since the shares forfeited are not cancelled the directors may reissue the shares at a price which will at least make they fully paid.

Accounting entries on reissue of forfeited shares are:

1. *Dr.* Forfeited shares account with the paid up amount at which the shares are being issued.
   Cr. Share capital account.

2. *Dr.* Shareholder's account in ledger with the price agreed to be paid for the shares.
   Cr. Forfeited shares account.

3. *Dr.* Bank with the amount paid by the shareholder.
   Cr. Shareholder's account in the ledger.

4. *Dr.* Forfeited shares account with the amount of premium, if any, on the reissue of the shares.
   Cr. Share premium account.

Example: Given the information in the previous question you are advised that the 200 shares forfeited by the directors have now been reissued to Adam Scott for £140. Adam Scott pays this amount to the company immediately.

In the Ledger of Orion Ltd

Forfeited Share Account

Ordinary share capital	£200	Balance	£150
Share premium	90	Adam Scott	140
	£290		£290

Share Capital Account

Balance	£10 000	Balance	£9 800
		Forfeited shares	200
	£10 000		£10 000
		Balance	£10 000

Adam Scott Account

Forfeited shares	£140	Bank	£140

Bank Account

Adam Scott	£140

Share Premium Account

	Forfeited shares	£90

Note: The calculation of the premium on the reissue of the shares can be proved thus:

Nominal value of shares issued	£200
Less Amount previously paid on shares	150
Balance unpaid	50
Amount paid by Adam Scott on reissue of shares	140
Capital profit on reissue treated as a premium	£90

We have described the share capital structure of a company and the issue of shares in terms of the total amounts involved. The accounts in the general ledger such as share capital, application, allotment, call accounts, share premium, forfeited shares, etc. record totals only. The interests of individual shareholders are recorded outside the general ledger. The Companies Act provides that each company shall maintain a register of members containing such detailed information as the Act requires in relation to each individual member. The register of members (or share register as it is sometimes called) is in reality a subsidiary ledger controlled by the various capital accounts in the general ledger.

Debentures

An important method by which limited companies may obtain finance from the general public is by the issue of debentures of various types. Debentures are documents which evidence the fact that the holder has lent the company the amount stated in the instrument. The terms of repayment and payment of interest on the loan are stated in the debenture itself or in a trust deed. Where the owner's name is registered in the register of debentureholders, it will be necessary for subsequent holders to notify the alteration to the company.

It is usual for debentures to be secured over some or all of the company's assets. In fact, the tendency today is to restrict the use of the term 'debenture' solely to those loans which are based on some security. Where no charge is created over the assets of the company, it is usual to use the term 'unsecured notes'. The notes are documents which evidence the loan in just the same way as debentures; they are entered in a special register at the office of the company and appear in the long-term liabilities section of the balance sheet. The methods described below for the issue of debentures may also be applied to the issue of such unsecured notes. If the security is given over a particular asset or assets, the debentures create a 'fixed charge' over such assets. In the event of non-compliance with the terms of the debentures, the holders may dispose of the assets named and recoup their loans from that sum. Where the charge is given over a group of general assets, the security is called a floating charge. A trustee for the debenture holders is appointed to protect their interests.

On default, the holder of a debenture which is secured by a charge on the company's assets may:

1. Sue for repayment of the principal and any interest owing.

2. Petition for the winding up of the company.

3. Prove for the debt in the winding up.

4. Appoint a receiver of the company. This is the usual procedure.

The receiver often steers the company through its difficulties and enables it to carry on again successfully. A receiver who carries on the business in this way instead of selling up the assets is called a 'receiver and manager'.

Every mortgage and charge created by a company must be fully recorded in its own register of mortgages and charges. Details of such charges must also be filed with the registrar of companies. The register of debenture holders and the register of mortgages and charges are two of the records which the Companies Act requires a company to keep.

Theoretically, debentures and notes may be issued at par (that is, face value) at a premium (greater than face value) or at a discount (less than face value).

In the United States, for borrowing of this type, 'bonds', as they are called, are frequently issued at a premium or at a discount. American textbooks spend significant time discussing the use of the 'effective interest rate' in accounting for such borrowing.

However, it is proposed that only issues at par are considered at this stage. The procedure adopted to record the entries to issue debentures is similar to that used in the issue of shares.

Example: A company decides to issue 500 £100 12 per cent debentures at par payable in full on application.

1. When the debentures are issued:

	Dr.	Cr.
Debentureholders	£50 000	
To 12% debenture account		£50 000

Being issue of 500 £100 12% debentures at par per directors' resolution No. ....

2. When payment is received:

	Dr.	Cr.
Bank	£50 000	
To Debentureholders		£50 000

Amount received from debentureholders.

If the debentures are redeemable there are several methods which can be used to provide for their repayment. Most debentures are redeemable as they are considered to be loan capital compared to ordinary and preference shares which form the permanent equity capital of the company. The repayment of debentures does not constitute a reduction in capital and consequently no court agreement is required.

The following are the main methods in use to redeem or repay the debentures:

1. Out of capital. This is the most common method and only requires the following journal entries to make the necessary adjustment to the ledger accounts:

Dr.   Debenture account
Cr.   Debenture holders account

Dr.   Debenture holders account
Cr.   Bank

2. Out of profits.

3. Redemption through purchases in the open market.

4. Redemption by accumulating a sinking fund.

At this stage in the introductory treatment of the structure of company share capital, it may be useful to point out some fundamental differences between the share capital on the one hand and debentures on the other.

1. Holders of debentures are *not* shareholders and usually have no right to attend company meetings or vote. They are *creditors* of the company.

2. The funds contributed by members for their shares appear in the balance sheet under the shareholders' funds or proprietorship section. The amounts of outstanding debentures appear in the creditors: amounts falling due after more than one year section of the balance sheet.

3. The debentureholders are entitled to payment of their *interest*, whether the company makes a profit or not. Shareholders receive *dividends* only when there are available profits. Interest on debentures is an expense appearing in the revenue statement, but dividends on shares are an appropriation after profits have been determined. The debenture interest is deductible for tax purposes.

4. As mentioned previously, in almost all cases, the company may redeem the debenture, that is, repay the loans, but a company cannot repay the capital contributed by shareholders, except in the special cases known as redeemable preference shares.

5. In the event of the winding up of the company, holders of secured debentures have priority

over the assets charged, whereas shareholders cannot be repaid their capital until all outside claims have been satisfied in full.

Further issues of shares

The above discussion has concentrated primarily on share issues made at par (face value) when a company is first incorporated. Established companies, when they wish to expand their operations, have as one of their options the opportunity to issue shares to raise the necessary funds. As mentioned earlier in the chapter, this is the situation where a company may choose to issue shares at a premium (that is, above face value).

Factors affecting the decision to issue at a premium include:

1. The demand expected for the shares – which is influenced by the dividend and other rights attaching to the shares and the future prospects of the company.

2. The current market price of similar shares – there may have been an earlier issue of the same shares which are already quoted above par on the stock exchange.

3. The protection of the existing shareholders – if the same class of shares is already above par then it will not be appreciated by existing shareholders if further shares are issued at a lower price. However, many factors affect the decision: the size of the new issue compared with the existing issue; whether the past dividends can be maintained; whether the existing shareholders will be given first rights to the new issue; and so on.

4. The gain to the company – the issue at a premium gives rise to a 'capital' gain to the company. This gain is usually termed 'share premium account' or 'premium on shares' and is treated as a capital reserve in the shareholders' equity section of the balance sheet.

Example: The directors of Oscar Ltd decide to make a share bonus issue of ordinary shares of two new shares for every five shares held and to charge £1.80 per share for the new shares. At the date of the new issue the shareholders' equity section of Oscar Ltd's balance sheet was as follows:

Shareholders' equity	
Authorised capital - 200 000 £1 ordinary shares	£200 000
Issued capital - 100 000 £1 ordinary shares fully paid	£100 000
General reserve	60 000
Profit and loss account	55 000
	£215 000

All shareholders took up their entitlement and paid for the new shares by the due date.

The shareholders' equity section of Oscar Ltd's balance sheet following the new issue would appear as follows:

Shareholders' equity	
Authorised capital - 200 000 £1 ordinary shares	£200 000
Issued capital - 140 000 £1 ordinary shares fully paid	140 000
Share premium account	32 000
General reserve	60 000
Profit and loss account	55 000
	£287 000

Note that the net assets would have increased by £72 000, which is the amount of cash received for the new issue (that is, 40 000 shares at £1.80 per share).

New issues of shares to existing shareholders of the type illustrated above often contain provisions for the sale of rights to the new shares by shareholders not wishing to increase their shareholding. In the Oscar Ltd example above, if the current value of Oscar's shares was significantly more than £1.80 then it is likely that potential investors would be willing to pay something for the right to acquire new shares at £1.80 per share.

Sometimes the directors of a company will decide to make a free or 'bonus issue' of shares. This may be done to compensate shareholders for a relatively low cash dividend or simply to give shareholders what may be a tax-free benefit as a result of the company's growth. Bonus shares may be based on unappropriated profits, general reserves or reserves created by the sale or revaluation of some of the company's assets.

Example: The directors of Percy Ltd decide to make a one-for-five bonus issue of ordinary shares based on part of the reserve created by a recent revaluation of the company's land and buildings. At the date of the bonus issue the shareholders' equity section of Percy Ltd's balance sheet is as follows:

Shareholders' equity	
Authorised capital - 200 000 £1 ordinary shares	£200 000
Issued capital - 100 000 £1 ordinary shares fully paid	£100 000
Asset revaluation reserve	55 000
General reserve	40 000
Profit and loss account	38 000
	£233 000

After the bonus shares had been issued, the shareholders' section of Percy Ltd balance sheet would appear as follows:

Shareholders' equity	
Authorised capital - 200 000 £1 ordinary shares	£200 000
Issued capital - 120 000 £1 ordinary shares fully paid	£120 000
Asset revaluation reserve	35 000
General reserve	40 000
Profit and loss account	38 000
	£233 000

Note that the net assets have not increased at all as a result of the bonus issue. The value of the bonus issue in the hands of shareholders would depend on how the share market reacted to the bonus issue. That the number of shares has increased by 20 per cent will be a factor in market assessment. Provided that the market price does not drop by sixteen and two-thirds per cent or more, shareholders will be better off in terms of the market value of their shares. For instance, if the market price was £2.00 per share before and £1.95 per share after the bonus issue, a shareholder who previously held 100 shares (and now holds 120 shares) will see the market value of the holding rise from £200 to £234.

Redeemable shares

A company may issue shares which are to be redeemed or may be redeemed at the option of the company or the shareholder. These shares can be preference or equity shares. The appropriate legislation is in S. 159 Companies Act 1985 which states:

1. Authorisation to issue redeemable shares must be contained in the articles of association.

2. No redeemable shares may be issued unless there are some non-redeemable shares in issue.

3. On redemption of the shares they are to be treated as cancelled.

4. The shares must be fully paid.

5. The shares can only be redeemed out of distributable profits or out of the proceeds of a fresh issue of shares made for the purposes of redemption.

6. Any premium payable on redemption must be paid out of distributable profits of the company except where the redeemable shares were originally issued at a premium; in which case the premium on redemption must be paid out of the proceeds of a fresh issue of shares made for the purpose. In the latter case the provision on redemption may be provided out of share premium account provided it does not exceed the lesser of premiums received on the issue of the shares being redeemed and the balance on the share premium account.

The following example illustrates a company redeeming its preference shares at par, wholly out of profits.

Example:

Balance Sheet of Redeem Plc before redemption of its preference share capital

Share capital		
90 000 ordinary shares of £1 each fully paid		£90 000
50 000 redeemable preference shares of £1 each fully paid		50 000
		140 000
Reserves		
Share premium account – non-distributable	£10 000	
Profit and loss account	70 000	80 000
		£220 000

Balance Sheet of Redeem Plc after redemption of its preference share capital

Share capital		
90 000 ordinary shares of £1 each fully paid		£90 000
Reserves		
Share premium account – non-distributable	£10 000	
Capital redemption reserve – non-distributable	50 000	
Profit and loss	20 000	80 000
		£170 000

If we compare the capital before and after the redemption then:

Before	Ordinary shares	£90 000
	Redeemable preference shares	50 000
	Share premium account	10 000
		£150 000
After	Ordinary shares	£90 000
	Share premium account	10 000
	Capital redemption reserve	50 000
		£150 000

From the above it can be seen that the non-distributable capital is intact after redemption has taken place.

The next example illustrates the redemption of shares at a premium out of the proceeds of a new issue. (The preference shares were issued at par.)

Example:

Balance sheet of Repay Ltd before redemption

Share Capital

100 000 ordinary shares of £1 each, fully paid		£100 000
50 000 redeemable preference shares of £1 each fully paid		50 000
		150 000
Reserves		
Share premium account – non-distributable	£20 000	
Profit and loss account	40 000	60 000
		£210 000

The preference shares are to be redeemed at a premium of 10 per cent out of the proceeds of a fresh issue of shares, viz 40 000 £1 ordinary shares at a premium of £10 000.

Balance Sheet of Repay Ltd after redemption

Share capital

140 000 ordinary shares of £1 each, fully paid		£140 000
Reserves		
Share premium account (20 000 + 10 000)	30 000	
Profit and loss account (40 000 − 5000)	35 000	65 000
		£205 000

If we compare the capital before and after the redemption then:

Before	Ordinary shares	£100 000
	Redeemable preference shares	50 000
	Share premium account	20 000
		£170 000

After	Ordinary shares	£140 000
	Share premium account	30 000
		£170 000

Again it can be seen that the non-distributable capital is intact after redemption has taken place.

Purchase of own shares

It is now permissible for a company to purchase its own shares, including redeemable shares. However, the Companies Act 1985 contains the following conditions which must be satisfied before such a transaction can take place:

1. It must be authorised by its own articles.

2. After purchase, the company must have other unredeemable shares in issue.

3. After purchase, the company must have at least two shareholders.

4. A public company cannot reduce its capital below the minimum (currently £50 000).

5. The shares purchased must be fully paid.

6. Any shares purchased other than out of a fresh issue of shares must be out of distributable profits. In other words, a transfer must be made from the distributable profits to capital redemption reserve.

7. If shares are purchased at a premium then the premium must be out of profits or from the lower of the share premium on the issue of the shares being purchased or the current amount of the share premium account.

8. The purchase of a company's own shares on the stock exchange must be authorised by special resolution in general meeting. The maximum number of shares to be acquired together with the maximum and minimum prices to be paid must be stated.

9. Where a company wishes to purchase its own shares otherwise than on the stock exchange it must obtain a special resolution approving the proposed off market purchase contract.

Redemption or purchase of own shares out of capital by a private company

Private companies are now permitted to make payments out of capital to finance the redemption or purchase of its own shares. The following conditions, however, must be satisfied:

1. The articles must authorise such a purchase.

2. The purchase must be authorised by the company in general meeting by a special resolution.

3. The directors must make a statutory declaration stating that the company will continue as a going concern and be able to pay its debts.

4. The auditors are required to make a satisfactory report to the directors.

A company is only allowed to make payment out of capital referred to as 'permissible capital payment' to the extent that it is equal to the costs of redemption or purchase after deducting the distributable profits of the company and the proceeds of any fresh issue of shares made for the purposes of the redemption or purchase.

Notes

1. Calculation of 'permissible capital payment' is cost of redemption or purchase less distributable profits balance less proceeds of fresh issue.

2. If the cost of redemption or purchase less the distributable profits balance is less than the nominal value of shares cancelled then the latter are deducted from the issued capital and the shortfall is credited to capital redemption reserve.

3. If the cost of redemption or purchase less the distributable profits balance is greater than the nominal value of shares cancelled then the latter is deducted from the issued capital and the excess is deducted from other capital and revaluation reserves or the remaining issued share capital.

The following example illustrates the redemption or purchase of shares out of capital.

Example:

Balance Sheet of Strong Ltd before redemption takes place	
Non-redeemable share capital fully paid in £1 shares	£50 000
Redeemable share capital fully paid in £1 shares	20 000
	£70 000
Distributable profits	8 000
	£78 000

Strong Ltd redeems its redeemable share capital for £25 000 of which £10 000 is financed from the proceeds of a fresh issue of ordinary shares.

Balance Sheet of Strong Ltd after redemption of shares	
Non-redeemable share capital fully paid in £1 shares	£60 000
(50 000 + 10 000 new issue)	
Capital redemption reserve	3 000
	£63 000

Working notes

1. Calculation of 'permissible capital payment'

Cost of purchase of shares		£25 000
Less Proceeds of fresh issue	£10 000	
Distributable profits	8 000	18 000
Permissible capital payment		£7 000

2. Calculation of transfer to capital redemption reserve

Cost of purchase of shares	£25 000
Less Available distributable profits	8 000
	17 000
Nominal value of shares cancelled	20 000
Difference to capital redemption reserve	£3 000

Summary

1. This chapter has attempted to provide a basic introduction to some of the problem areas of company accounting.

2. The legal differences between private companies and public companies are important in understanding this topic.

3. Some types of ownership (notably limited companies and to a lesser extent partnerships) are more affected by legal provisions than others.

4. The formation of a business enterprise with any particular form of ownership should not be proceeded with until after the legal requirements have been fulfilled.

5. The capital structure of a limited company is necessarily more complex than that of a partnership or a sole trader. It should be possible to determine the respective amounts of authorised, issued, called-up, paid-up capital for each class of share issued.

6. A company can adopt different methods of raising capital when it requires additional finance to expand its operations.

7. The usual method of recording a share issue in the ledger of a company involves the use of accounts which record the amount due and received on application, allotment, call and also any calls in arrear or in advance.

8. A company has a right to forfeit shares for non-payment of call and also to reissue the shares forfeited.

9. The detailed share records of a company, as contained in the register of members, represent a subsidiary ledger controlled by the total capital accounts in the general ledger.

10. A common method used by companies to raise funds is the issue of debentures or unsecured notes.

11. Established companies may choose to issue shares at a premium. The difference between issue price and face value is credited to a share premium reserve account.

12. Some companies issue bonus shares based on past profits or on reserves created by the sale or revaluation of assets.

13. A company may issue preference or equity shares which can be redeemed at the option of the company or the shareholder.

14. It is now permissible for a company to purchase its own shares.

15. Private companies are now permitted to make payments out of capital to finance the redemption or purchase of their own shares.

Discussion questions

13.1 There are differences in the way in which the Companies Act applies to companies as compared with the operation of the Partnership Act on partnerships. Explain these differences.

13.2 Jane Doe has decided to open her own beauty salon and has the opportunity of renting a shop in the suburbs. Her brother Bob owns and operates a business as a builder and contractor. The business is operated as a limited company and he advises his sister that that would be the best type of ownership for her salon. She is not too sure whether to form a company or to operate as a sole trader and comes to you to help her decision. What should be your advice to Jane?

13.3 'The detailed share records of a limited company are an application of the "Control account – subsidiary ledger" principle.' Explain this statement.

13.4 Compare and contrast the issue of preference shares with that of debentures as a means of raising funds.

13.5 What is the nature and purpose of:

(a) a bonus share issue,

(b) a rights issue?

13.6 Compare and contrast the issue of shares with the issue of debentures covering the following aspects:

(a) Rights of the holder.
(b) Treatment of the issue in the company's ledger.

(c) Methods of repayment.

13.7 Explain the main differences between private and public limited companies.

13.8 Describe and explain the main clauses which should appear in the articles of association of a limited company.

13.9 What is the difference between a prospectus issue and offer for sale of shares in a company?

13.10 In what circumstances may a company purchase its own shares?

Exercises

13.11 Jones Ltd was registered with a capital of 100 000 ordinary shares of £1 each. The amount payable was as follows:

20p per share on application.
30p per share on allotment.
Balance three months later.

Applications were received for 150 000 shares. The excess money received on application was refunded to unsuccessful applicants. Amounts due on allotment and call were received in full.
You are required to show the journal entries to record the above (including bank transactions).

13.12 Hope Ltd has an authorised capital of £100 000 divided into 100 000 ordinary shares of £1 each. The amount payable on issue of these shares was as follows:

20p on application	1 January
50p on allotment	1 March (inc. premium)
60p on call	1 May

All money due was received by the company on the due date.
You are required to record the above transactions in the journal of the company and show the capital and share premium accounts in the company's balance sheet after the issue is completed.

13.13 The directors of Wine Ltd decided on 1 December 19X7 to forfeit 100 ordinary shares of £1 each issued to B. Grape for non-payment of the final call of £25 due by him. The directors reissued the shares to W. Cider on 20 January 19X8 as fully paid shares at 80p per share.

W. Cider paid for the shares immediately. You are required to show the journal entries to record the above transactions in the books of Wine Ltd.

13.14 Applications were invited by Growth Ltd for 150 000 of its £1 ordinary shares at £1.15 per share payable as follows:

On application on 1 April 19X7	75p per share
On allotment on 30 April 19X7 (including the premium of 15p per share)	20p per share
On first and final call on 31 May 19X7	20p per share

Applications were received for 180 000 shares and it was decided to deal with these as follows:

(a) To refuse allotment to applicants for 8000 shares

(b) To give full allotment to applicants for 22 000 shares

(c) To allot the remainder of the available shares pro rata among the other applicants

(d) To utilise the surplus received on application in part payment of amounts due on allotment

An applicant to whom 400 shares had been allotted failed to pay the amount due on the first and final call and his shares were declared forfeited on 31 July 19X7. These shares were reissued on 3 September 19X7 as fully paid at 90p per share to Arthur White.

Show how these transactions would be recorded in the ledger accounts of Growth Ltd.

13.15 The registered capital of ABC Co. Ltd consisted of 100 000 ordinary shares of £1 each, and 50 000 preference shares of £2 each. The company issued 40 000 of the ordinary shares at a premium of 25p per share under the following terms:

50p on application (including the premium)
50p on allotment
25p on the first and final call

All of the preference shares were issued on the following terms:

60p on application
60p on allotment
40p on first call
40p on the second and final call

Applications were received for 60 000 of the ordinary shares and 80 000 of the preference shares. One applicant for preference shares paid for 3000 shares in full. The directors decided to allot these shares to the applicant. Application money on 20 000 ordinary shares was refunded while surplus application money on the preference shares was applied to the cost of allotment. Later, the first call was made on both categories of shares and all money due was received with the exception of that due on 1000 ordinary shares and 500 preference shares.

Enter the above information in the journal of the company, and present the balance sheet.

13.16 The Kiwi Cement Co. Ltd. was registered with a nominal capital of £100 000 comprising 80 000 ordinary shares of £1 each and 20 000 8 per cent preference shares of £1 each.

The company decided to offer to the public:

(a) 50 000 of the ordinary shares at a premium of £0.50 per share

(b) all the preference shares at par

The terms of issue were:

Ordinary shares   – £0.75 (including premium) on application, £0.50 on allotment and £0.25 in one call.
Preference shares   – £0.50 on application and the balance on allotment.

(c) one thousand £10 8 per cent debentures at par, payable in full on application

Applications were received as follows:

(i) Ordinary shares – 100 000 shares (10 000 of these applications were accompanied by payment in full of £1.50 per share).
(ii) Preference shares – 20 000 shares.
(iii) Debentures – 800 debentures.

The directors allotted the preference shares and the debentures in accordance with the applications. With the ordinary shares they decided:

(A) to issue shares to the 10 000 applicants who paid the full £1.50 per share on application,

(B) to refuse applications for 10 000 shares; and

(C) to allot one share for every two applied for to the remaining applicants, the surplus application money being applied towards that due on allotment and call.

All money due on allotment was received. The calls were duly made and all call moneys owing were received.

You are required to show by means of general journal entries and extracts from the cash book how you would record the above. (No ledger accounts are required.)

13.17 The Express Transport Co. Ltd offered 100 000 £2 shares for public subscription on the following terms:

25p per share on application.
75p per share on allotment.
£1 per share to be called up later.

Applications were received for 160 000 shares, including an application for 20 000 shares accompanied by a cheque for £40 000.

The directors decided to allot shares as follows:

(a) The applicant for 20 000 shares who paid in full on application was allotted 20 000 shares.

(b) Applications for 40 000 shares were rejected and the application money refunded.

(c) The remaining shares were allotted on a pro-rata basis, i.e., four shares for every five applied for.

You are required to:

(i) calculate the amount of application money received;

(ii) show how the application account in the general ledger would appear after the above transactions;

(iii) calculate the amount of cash which would now be due to be paid on allotment of the shares (show all your workings).

13.18 The following is a summarised balance sheet of Repay Ltd at 31 December 19X8:

Share capital issued fully paid		**Sundry assets**	£200 000
100 000 ordinary shares of £1 each	£100 000	**Bank**	85 000
50 000 redeemable preference shares of £1 each	50 000		
Reserves			
Profit and loss account	60 000		
Liabilities – Sundry creditors	75 000		
	£285 000		£285 000

It is resolved that preference shares are to be redeemed out of profits at a premium of 10 per cent.

You are required to show the balance sheet of the company after redemption has taken place.

13.19 The following is the balance sheet of Redeem Ltd at 31 December 19X8:

Share capital – issued and fully paid		**Fixed assets**		£20 000
25 000 ordinary shares of £1 each	£25 000	**Current assets**		
10 000 6½% redeemable preference shares of £1 each	10 000	Stock	£20 000	
	35 000	Debtors	15 000	
		Investment	5 000	
Reserves		Bank	5 000	45 000
Profit and loss account	20 000			
Current liabilities				
Creditors	10 000			
	£65 000			£65 000

The company agreed to redeem the preference shares at a premium of 5 per cent.

The directors gave the required notice and redemption is to take place on 31 December 19X8 as follows:

(a) to issue 3000 ordinary shares of £1 each at par;

(b) the balance out of profits.

It was also decided to sell the investments to realise cash to pay the preference shareholders the amount due to them. The investments realised £6000.

The new issue of shares was fully subscribed.

You are required to show the balance sheet of Redeem Ltd after redemption has taken place.

Problem

13.20 The following is the balance sheet of K. Gillis & Co. Ltd as at 30 June 19X6. You are required to enter the given transactions in the ledger and cash book of the company, and present a balance sheet in narrative form at 30 June 19X7.

Balance Sheet of K. Gillis & Co. Ltd as at 30 June 19X6

Shareholders' funds

Authorised capital consisting of 200 000 shares at £1 each		£200 000
Called-up capital 80 000 shares of £1 each 75p called	£60 000	
Less Calls in arrears	500	
Paid-up capital		£59 500
Share premium reserve		5 000
Calls in advance		5 000
Total shareholders' funds		£69 500
represented by		
Fixed assets		
Furniture	£10 000	
Motor vehicles	27 000	£37 000
Current assets		
Cash at bank		31 500
Intangible asset		
Costs of issue		1 000
		£69 500

On 1 July 19X6 the company made the second and final call on the issued shares, and by the end of July all the money due had been received except that due on 1000 shares. On 31 July the company purchased furniture for cash £3500 and motor vehicles on credit from Gluer Motors Ltd for £12 000.

On 1 September 19X6, the company issued to the public a further 50 000 shares payable at the following rate:

Application	50p (including a premium of 20p per share).
Allotment	30p.
First Call	20p.
Second Call	20p.

By 30 September, applications had been received for a total of 80 000 shares. Of this number, 4000 had been paid for in full on application and 10 000 had been paid for at £1 per share. In consequence of the oversubscription, the directors made the following decisions:

(a) Allot 4000 shares to the fully paid application.

(b) Allot 8000 shares to the application paying £1 per share. Sufficient money was to be retained to cover the full cost of the shares allotted, and any surplus was to be refunded.

(c) Refund application money on 9000 shares.

(d) Allot the remaining shares to successful remaining applications on a proportional basis of two allotted for every three applied for, with surplus application to be applied towards allotment and calls in advance if necessary.

All money due on allotment had been received by 15 October 19X6. On 1 December 19X6 the company issued 500 debentures at a par value of £100 each. These debentures were to be paid for in instalments as follows:

      Debenture application   £50.
      Debenture allotment   £30.
      Debenture call   £20.

All of the debenture application money had been received by 31 December 19X6. On 14 January 19X7 the company bought business premises costing £75 000 and paid for them in the following way:

      35 000 shares issued at par value.
      200 debentures issued at par value of £100 each.
      Balance in cash.

All debenture allotment money due on the 500 public-issue debentures was received in full by 31 January 19X7. On this day, the company bought land for cash costing £25 000.

On 1 March 19X7, the company made the first call on the shares issued on 1 September 19X6. This call was received in full by the end of that month. The money due on the debenture call was collected in full by 1 April 19X7. On the same day, the company received all of the calls in arrears money in full (see balance sheet at 30 June 19X6).

On 1 June 19X7 the second call was made on the issued shares and at 30 June 19X7 all of the call money had been received except that due on 3000 shares.

Chapter 14
Accounting for sectional division

Sectional division ☐ Accounting problems of sectional division ☐ Division into selling departments ☐ Joint ventures ☐ Branch organisations ☐ Consignment accounts

Sectional division

In Chapter 2, we defined the accounting entity as that particular business enterprise about which accounting information was required. In recording and reporting for the enterprise as a whole, however, we have found it convenient to divide the accounting system into sections. For example, we discussed separately the recording and control methods adopted for such natural accounting areas as cash, stocks, debtors, creditors, fixed assets, etc. Again we divided the profit and loss statement into three main sections in order to determine gross profit, operating profit and net profit.

It is only the facilitation of the accounting processes that prompts these divisions. They are made also with the object of strengthening management control; for example, separate consideration of assets, such as stocks, cash, debtors, etc., highlights the protection and control necessary over these assets; the division of expenses into cost of goods sold, selling, administrative and finance expenses may well be associated with the separate responsibilities of the purchasing officer, the sales manager, the office manager (or accountant) and the credit manager.

A further benefit of breaking the accounting entity into segments comes from the more efficient forecasting of profit if the contributions from different product lines, departments or divisions can be ascertained. If the value of the investment in each segment is also available, rates of return on investment can then be compared.

In this chapter we examine other ways in which an enterprise and its accounting system may be segmented. In doing so, we want to emphasise the objectives of such divisions of the accounting system, that is:

1. The determination of separate sectional profit.

2. The more efficient controlling of activities of the various sections and the assisting of management in decision making.

The three basic managerial functions necessary to achieve the above objectives of assisting both internal and external users are:

1. *Planning* - such as establishing a profit target for each section.

2. *Adequate supervision* - to ensure that the plans are carried out. This implies a clear indication of individual duties and responsibilities for such activities as purchasing, selling, warehousing, etc.

3. *Revision of plans* - in the light of an analysis of the results achieved. An example could be an alteration to the profit plan because of the imposition of new taxes, the lifting of important duties or a shortage of materials.

It is essential that there is an adequate feedback of data in the form of regular reports from the various accounting sections and from the officers responsible for various functions (purchasing, employment, advertising).

The common bases adopted for the division of an enterprise into sections are summarised in Table 14.1, although the examples given are by no means exhaustive.

Table 14.1   Common bases of sectional division.

Basis of division	Examples
1 By activities or products	
(a) as normal continuing activities	(i) retail store with several departments
	(ii) manufacturer of different products
	(iii) business organised into production, merchandising, financing divisions
	(iv) insurance company with different types of policies
	(v) mixed farm with wool, crops, beef, etc.
	(vi) construction company with different projects
(b) as sporadic or special activities	(i) dances, concerts or other special functions of clubs or societies
	(ii) special consignment sales
	(iii) joint ventures such as property development by land agent and builder
	(iv) manufacture or assembly of items of plant for own use
2 By geographical location, as branches or agencies	(i) banks, chain stores, supermarkets, shipping companies, cinemas, some public accounting practices
3 By separation of legal entities	(i) holding companies and subsidiaries
	(ii) partnership of companies as for the development of oil production
	(iii) multinational companies
4 By legislation	(i) trust account transactions

Accounting problems of sectional division

There are three major aspects involved in accounting for sections of an enterprise:

1. *The effects of the sectional division on the statement of profit and loss.* In some cases, the net sectional profit figures will be sufficient. In other cases, details of sectional revenue and expense items will be desirable. The value of the determination of a separate profit for each section is that it enables management to assess the effectiveness of each particular section. Where the sectional division is linked with delegation of responsibility – for example, to departmental or to branch managers – then profit determination becomes itself an element of control. At the same time it must be remembered that some expenses (such as directors' fees, donations, etc.) and some revenue (dividends on investments, interest on loans, etc.) cannot be divided among the various sections satisfactorily. Consequently, the sectional 'profit' is usually considered as a 'contribution' by the section towards the total profit or loss of the whole enterprise. While the total profit for the enterprise would not change, whether or not it is subdivided into smaller units,

the effect of subdivision is to enable management to evaluate the profitability of each section.

Consider, for example, the operation of a bar by a club or society. This is a continuing activity, and there should be little difficulty in obtaining the figures relating to sales and purchases exclusively for the bar. Furthermore, it should not be difficult to assess the wages of the bar staff, providing they work solely in the bar. Problems will arise where the employees have other duties, such as acting as general cashier, answering telephone calls, or assisting with the cleaning or with general office tasks. It would be even more difficult to calculate the expense of heat, light, caretaking and cleaning, and other building space costs and so on, for the bar. The problem of allocation of costs and expenses is an extremely vexatious one. It should be done only where the results are meaningful, that is, where the allocation can be carried out on some logical basis so that the proportion of the expense matches as closely as possible the separate activity. Even with proper allocations it is possible to measure only the contribution towards the total profit made by that separate activity, rather than its actual sectional profit. The difficulty of allocation becomes more evident in the consideration of isolated activities such as club social functions, for example, the annual dance. Here it is almost impossible to evaluate the cost of the time spent by paid officials in preparation for the event, of telephone calls, or of the cost of the use of the club's buildings and other facilities in the preparation, holding and review of the results of the dance.

2. *The effects of the sectional division on the books of account.* The new ledger accounts necessitated by sectional division may be considered in two main groups:

(a) Separate revenue, expense, and profit-determining accounts required to ascertain separate profits for each section.

(b) Accounts designed to provide some form of control over a particular section, or over the assets and liabilities of a particular section. Separate columns may be used for each section. The subsidiary records (day books, etc.) need to be designed to reflect these.

3. *Co-ordination of accounts.* It is necessary to co-ordinate the accounts involving particular sections of an enterprise with the accounts of the enterprise as a whole. While recognising the importance of sectionalisation for the purposes of management control, we must remember also that the reports of the whole enterprise will still be required for the purpose of reporting to ownership.

The two major problems in connection with sectional division are

1. the difficulty of *allocation* of revenue and expenses where transactions are common to more than one segment; and

2. the valuation of inter-segment transfers.

These problems prevent an accurate calculation of sectional profit, but the use of common sense enables a reasonable result to be obtained.

Before considering any detail connected with sectional activity, we should recall the alternatives regarding accounting for stocks. We have seen that a business may institute a system of perpetual stock recording or rely entirely upon physical stocktaking. In some of the examples we use in this present chapter, movements of stock are involved. It is unnecessary to complicate each of them by introducing both alternatives of physical or perpetual stock. Therefore, for the sake of simplicity, we have assumed that physical stock applies throughout the whole of the examples and exercises of Chapter 14. However, students should note that if perpetual stock were being used, some differences would occur, for in such case the stocks account would be progressively entered for stock movements.

Obviously it would be impossible to describe in detail the accounting implications of all the examples of sectional division. We will deal with the following representative samples:

1. The selling departments of a retail store (to illustrate a continuity activity).

2. A trading business undertaking a joint venture with another business (to illustrate an isolated activity).

3. A retail trading organisation with branches at different locations (to illustrate the variety of branch operations).

4. A trading business undertaking the consignment of goods to an agent (to illustrate a specialised trading activity).

Further examples of sectional accounting occur in Chapter 20 in connection with the establishment of cost centres in cost accounting, in the identification of separate jobs, departments or processes for accounting purposes, and in determining the contribution made by different products or divisions.

Division into selling departments

The retail store with its various departments (for example, drapery, hardware, footwear, furniture, etc.) has been quoted above as an example of the sectionalisation of a business according to products or activities. It is a division which operates continuously, and therefore the whole accounting system can be geared to accounting for the activities of the various separate departments.

Effects on the profit and loss statement

The extent of the effects of the division of a business into departments depends on the extent to which management desires the determination of the separate profits to be attempted. It must again be stated at the outset that problems of determining separate profit are often difficult. In fact, some retail departmental stores do not attempt it at all. They use departmental division *solely* to facilitate management control.

Where a departmental profit and loss statement is desired, the first decision must be one of selecting those revenue and expense items which can be divided among the various departments. In this respect it is usually possible to distinguish between three main groups of revenue and expense items:

1. *Direct items* – those which can be divided naturally and directly between the departments. Common examples are sales, purchases, stocks, salaries, and depreciation of fittings (providing separate asset totals for each department are available).

2. *Indirect items* – those which may be apportioned according to some objective or relevant basis (such as delivery expenses, occupancy expenses).

3. *Items not allocated* – those which concern the business as a whole or for which no logical basis of apportionment may be found (for example, legal expenses, bank fees, interest receivable).

The items in groups 1 and 2 may be used to prepare the departmental section of the revenue statement (that is, to make the departmental contribution calculation) and the items in group 3 may be used in the general section of the statement (in arriving at net profit for the business as a whole).

The basis of allocation

In determining the allocation of costs and expenses in group 2 above, various common bases are used. In making the appropriate choice of base, we must consider the benefits accruing to each department or the relation of such expense to the revenue earned; for example, staff amenities costs are affected by the number of employees; light and heat depend on space occupied or kilowatt hours used; and so on.

Some of the common bases adopted to allocate items which cannot be directly attributed to particular departments are as follows:

Rent, and other occupancy expenses such as lighting, cleaning and maintenance costs may be allocated *according to floor space*.

Insurance on stock *according to value of stocks carried*.

Expenses such as advertising, delivery costs, discounts allowed, *according to sales*.

Carriage on purchases, discounts received, *according to purchases*.

All of the above bases (and the many others it is possible to use) can be criticised. For example, floor space for rent may be quite inequitable because a department with a ground-floor location has a decided advantage over a department with similar space on, say, the sixth floor of a retail store. Similarly, to allocate delivery costs according to sales figures will be inequitable if one department sells expensive but compact articles and another a much cheaper but bulkier product – compare the jewellery department with the furniture department.

A method sometimes used is to allocate an item on an agreed percentage basis, taking into account the various factors involved. However, this method, too, is open to criticism.

Our view is that items should be apportioned between departments only where there is some reasonable and logical basis for doing so. Many enterprises attempt to carry the division of revenue and expense items past this stage. Such a policy tends to destroy the meaning and usefulness of the profit figures ascertained. It is also possible that management will make incorrect decisions based on the figures produced. Consider the following simple example:

	Total	Dept A	Dept B	Dept C
Sales	300	100	100	100
- Cost of sales	200	50	75	75
Gross profit	100	50	25	25
- Allocated expenses	90	60	15	15
Dept contribution	10	− 10	10	10

The importance of the allocation of expenses in the above instance is obvious. At first examination, management will consider that Dept A has 'lost' £10 while the other two departments had 'gained' a similar amount each. If the allocation is made on a basis other than of benefits derived or of direct relationship of the expenditure then different results are obtained. A further point is that if the expenses allocated are unavoidable in the future (for example, rent of building) then the discontinuing of the 'loss' department will result in heavier imposts on the two remaining departments, and the store as a whole will suffer even more.

Effects on the accounting records

We may summarise these as follows:

1. For revenue and expense items which can be identified directly with the departments concerned, the ledger accounts will be duplicated, that is furniture sales, hardware sales, drapery sales, etc. These accounts may be kept in tabular form.

Sales Account

Date	Particulars	Fol.	Dept A	Dept B	Dept C	Dept D	Dept E	Total
July 31	Sales day book		9 300	7 100	5 652	4 909	1 209	28 170
Aug. 31	Sales day book		7 750	6 900	5 420	6 100	950	27 120

Where the number of departments exceeds the number that can be accommodated on one ledger sheet, it may be desirable to allow the general ledger to contain a sales control account which records the *total* sales, and to institute a subsidiary ledger for the detail.

Such a division of ledger accounts entails dissecting the information into departments in the day books and other primary records. For example, sales may be dissected in the sales day book, purchases in the purchases day book, returns in the returns day book, salaries and wages in the payroll. The use of different-coloured documents for each department will facilitate this division.

2. The accounts for assets directly associated with a separate activity need to be divided. For example, stock accounts have to be departmentalised so that separate cost of goods sold figures could be obtained for each department. Shop fixtures and fittings, similarly, can be divided so that the separate depreciation expense for each department can be calculated.

3. The profit-determining accounts in the ledger (that is, the trading account and profit and loss account) may be kept in tabular departmental form if desired. However this is not necessary – the apportionment of revenue and expense items for inclusion in the profit and loss statement may be performed entirely outside the ledger.

Co-ordination of the accounts of the whole enterprise

As mentioned above, some revenue and expense items may be departmentalised and others may not. The complete revenue statement will therefore consist of a departmental section and also of a general section, that is, net profit (for the enterprise as a whole) will equal contribution of Department A plus contribution of Department B plus contribution of Department C, etc., plus general revenue items (if any) minus general expense items.

As an illustration, the following information has been used in the preparation of the profit and loss statement shown below for an enterprise divided into three selling departments.

Information available (for the year ended 30 June 19X6):

1. Items which have been recorded directly:

	Dept A	Dept B	Dept C
Sales	£80 000	£50 000	£30 000
Purchases	50 000	30 000	20 000
Sales staff's salaries	5 000	4 000	2 000
Stocks (1/7/X5)	12 000	9 000	8 000
Stocks (30/6/X6)	18 000	11 000	12 000
Shop fittings	6 000	3 000	2 000
(to be depreciated at the rate of 10% p.a.)			

2. Items to be apportioned on an agreed basis:

Carriage on purchases £2000	(according to purchases)
Delivery expenses £3200	(according to sales)
Cleaning and maintenance expenses £2500	(according to floor space)
Insurance on stock £1400	(according to average stocks held)

The floor space occupied was in the ratio of Dept A, three-fifths; Dept B one-fifth; Dept C one-fifth.

3. Items not to be apportioned:

Advertising	£2 400
Postages	800
Office salaries	4 200
Office expenses	1 200
Interest received	600
Discount allowed	400

4. Method of stock recording is physical stocktaking.

Note that in the profit and loss statement below, we did not attempt any classification of expenses into selling, administrative and finance. This could have been achieved by the use of additional columns for this purpose in the above statement. In our opinion, this would make the report too involved and confusing. If the emphasis is on departmental responsibility, then functional responsibility is probably not in evidence. If the latter classification is desired then it can best be achieved by another copy of the profit and loss statement taking the total column only of the above statement and classifying the information on a functional basis. The former may be the better method for management and the latter for shareholders and others.

Statement of Profit and Loss
for the year ended 30 June 19X6

	Dept A	**Dept B**	**Dept C**	**Total**
Stock (1/7/X5)	£12 000	£9 000	£8 000	£29 000
Purchases	50 000	30 000	20 000	100 000
Carriage purchases	1 000	600	400	2 000
	63 000	39 600	28 400	131 000
Less Stocks (30/6/X6)	18 000	11 000	12 000	41 000
Cost of Goods Sold	45 000	28 600	16 400	90 000
Sales	80 000	50 000	30 000	160 000
Gross profit	35 000	21 400	13 600	70 000
Less **Departmental Expenses**				
Sales staff's salaries	5 000	4 000	2 000	11 000
Depreciation on shop fittings	600	300	200	1 100
Delivery expenses	1 600	1 000	600	3 200
Cleaning and maintenance expenses	1 500	500	500	2 500
Insurance on stocks	600	400	400	1 400
	9 300	6 200	3 700	19 200
Departmental Contribution	25 700	15 200	9 900	50 800
Add Interest received				600
				51 400

Cont.

	Dept A	Dept B	Dept C	Total
Less **General Expenses**				
Advertising				2 400
Postages				800
Office salaries				4 200
Office expenses				1 200
Discount allowed				400
				9 000
Net Profit				**£42 400**

Joint ventures

This example of sectional activity is one of isolated or sporadic activity. Joint ventures may be defined as trading ventures entered into with another business entity or person for the purpose of a single transaction or a series of transactions, for example acquiring an area of land with a view to subdivision and sale. They can be likened to a temporary partnership, and in law may be deemed as such. Joint venture arrangements differ from partnerships, however, because of their temporary nature, and the fact that they are usually confined to a single activity. Usually the reason why such arrangements are made is that each party may have special attributes which, when combined, make for success. One may have the capital, the other the technical ability, trade connections, etc. It is becoming increasingly common in oil or mining exploration for companies to combine in such joint ventures in order to spread the risk and to operate in more areas.

The accounting for such a venture may be recorded by using either of the following methods.

1. *The transactions of the venture are entered in a separate set of accounting records.* Where the venture is on a relatively large scale it is prudent to open a joint banking account and record the transactions of the venture in a separate set of books. The books will be written up in the same way as those of a partnership and at the end of the venture a profit and loss account will be prepared showing the allocation of the profit or loss on the venture among the parties to it.

2. *No joint banking account is opened and a memorandum account is prepared from the entries in the books of all parties to the venture.* This is probably the most common approach for examination purposes. If the venture is on a relatively small scale the parties may decide that there is no necessity to maintain a separate set of accounting records and that each party should keep a record of his personal transactions on behalf of the venture in his own books. No joint banking account will require to be opened.

3. *No joint bank account is opened and in each party's books appears a record of all transactions to the venture.* This method differs from the previous one since no memorandum account is prepared at the termination of the venture and a record of all transactions of the venture is shown in each party's books in the joint venture account. This account when balanced represents the profit or loss on the venture.

Effects on the profit and loss statement

Since a joint venture is, by nature, a non-recurring activity, it follows that the enterprise's share of the net gain or loss is the only item required for inclusion in the revenue statement. If the detailed revenue and expense items relating to the joint venture were included, they would have no significance when the profit statements of successive years were being compared. On the other hand, the details of the joint venture may prove of value to the parties to it where further similar operations are contemplated.

Effects on the accounting records

Using the second method described above, the following accounting procedure to record the transactions of the venture would be as follows:

1. Each party to the venture will open in their books a joint venture account with the other party.

2. All payments on behalf of the venture made by each party and allowances made to each party for services to the venture will be debited and all receipts or income credited to the joint venture account.

3. If any balance of stock remains unsold at the end of the venture the party taking over the stock will credit the joint venture account and debit the appropriate ledger accounts in his own books.

4. From the information recorded in each party's books a memorandum joint venture account is prepared. It is termed a memorandum account since it does not form part of the double entry accounting system of each party but is drawn up to calculate the profit or loss at the end of the venture. This account is similar in form to a normal profit and loss account since all the items of expenditure incurred by all parties are debited and all amounts of income credited. The resulting difference between the two sides will be the profit or loss of the venture and will be divided among the parties in the agreed profit sharing ratio.

5. When the profit on the venture has been calculated all parties will debit the joint venture account with the amount of their respective shares of the profit and credit their own general profit and loss accounts. If a loss was incurred then the entries will be reversed.

6. The remaining balance on each of the joint venture accounts will be the amount due to or by one party to the other which will require to be settled to terminate the venture.

The following illustration considers the method in which a memorandum account is opened to record the transactions of the venture.

Example: A and B enter into a joint venture with the object of buying and selling machines. Profits and losses are to be shared equally. A buys two machines at £1000 each and pays storage rent of £20.

B purchases four machines at £750 each and pays the following expenses:

Travelling	£50
Interest	15
Advertising	100
General Expenses	25

All the machines were sold on a cash basis and A received £4000, being the proceeds of sale of two machines, and B collected £6000 for the sale of the remaining machines. A sent a cheque value £1000 to assist B in paying the expenses of the venture. B pays the balance due to A.

Required are: the memorandum joint venture account and the accounts in the ledgers of A and B.

When recorded in A's books:

Joint Venture with B Account

Bank – Purchase of machines	£2 000	Bank – Sale of machines	£4 000
Storage rent	20	Balance received from B	1 415
Cheque to B	1 000		
Profit and loss – share of profit	2 395		
	£5 415		£5 415

Cash Book (Bank Account)

Joint venture with B (sale of machines)	£4 000	Joint venture with B (purchase of machines)	£2 000
(cheque from B)	1 415	(storage rent)	20
		(cheque to B)	1 000

Profit and Loss Account

	Joint venture with B (profit)	£2 395

When recorded in B's books:

Joint Venture with A Account

Bank – Purchase of machines	£3 000	Bank – Cheque from A	£1 000
Travelling expenses	50	Sale of machines	6 000
Interest	15		
Advertising	100		
General expenses	25		
Profit and loss – share of profit	2 395		
Bank – Balance paid to A	1 415		
	£7 000		£7 000

Memorandum Joint Venture Account

Purchase of machines		£5 000	Sale of machines	£10 000
Storage rent		20		
Travelling expenses		50		
Interest		15		
Advertising		100		
General expenses		25		
Profit A	£2 395			
Profit B	2 395	4 790		
		£10 000		£10 000

Note: The above account which is prepared from the information recorded in the joint venture accounts does not form part of the double entry system in either party's books.

Branch organisations

In dealing with division into branches as an example of sectional division, we encounter a problem caused by the fact that there are wide variations between different branch organisations. Some of these variations are caused by the nature of the enterprise's activities. We can simplify this by concentrating only on branch organisations which sell goods (ignoring such branch activities as banking, insurance, the provision of services, etc.). Dismissing also the variations caused by size and the number of branches involved, we may come to the conclusion that most of the other variations are caused by the differences in the relationship existing between the head office and the several branches. These are variations in the degree of *control* exercised by the head office over the activities of the branches.

It has been traditional in dealing with branch accounting to draw a clear distinction between two types of branch relationship:

1. Centrally controlled branches with all major decisions and directions emanating from the head office.

2. Locally controlled (or autonomous) branches operating with the utmost degree of independence.

While such a distinction has some merit, it must be recognised that these are really the two extreme situations. In the large majority of branch organisations, the degree of control possessed by the head office lies somewhere between the two extremes. It is a mistake to think that there are two set formulae for designing a branch accounting system. As with any problem of accounting design, there are a number of factors which influence the choice of the most suitable methods and records.

The degree of control does, however, have one very important influence. This is in determining the location (or division of location) of the accounting records. This is a similar problem to that of parties to a joint venture where the records may be kept by one party or the other.

In a branch organisation (with its division on a geographical basis), the accounting records of the one accounting entity may be spread over several different locations. There is no set pattern as to the amount of accounting done at the branches or the amount done at the head office. Many factors, such as the availability of accounting staff at the branches, will influence this distribution. There is, however, almost invariably, a strong correlation between the control delegated to the branch and the amount of accounting performed at the branch. A branch which is subject to rigid control from head office will usually have very few accounting records. On the other hand, one possessing a high degree of independence will probably have a complete accounting system at the branch. One of the main functions of accounting is to provide information on which management decisions may be based. It seems logical, therefore, to have the system producing such information located at the place where the decisions are to be made.

Thus, aware of the strong influence exerted by the degree of head office control over the location of the branch accounting records, we may proceed to analyse the effects of division into branches along the same lines used for the other examples of sectional division.

Effects on the profit and loss statement

Since the division in branches is continuous and not sporadic, the profit determination for each branch should be detailed and regular. It is desirable to be able to ascertain main items of branch revenue and of branch expenses. This virtually means the preparation of separate profit and loss statements for each branch (though of course they may be presented in columnar form in the one statement). The need to consolidate these individual branch profit and loss statements into a profit and loss statement for the enterprise as a whole is discussed later.

The method of preparation of the branch profit and loss statements depends on the location of the branch's accounting records. For a branch subject to very close control from head office, the revenue and expense information is accumulated in the head office records in much the same way as departmental revenue and expense data. There are many similarities between centrally controlled branches and the departments of a sole-location enterprise. Sometimes there will be a need to apportion administrative expenses between the expenses of the several branches concerned, in the same way as some expenses are apportioned in the preparation of a departmental profit and loss statement.

At the other extreme, a branch with a high degree of autonomy and possessing a complete double entry accounting system will generally prepare its own profit and loss statement. The only task then remaining for the head office accounting system will be the consolidation or amalgamation of the several branch profit and loss statements in order to arrive at the overall result.

Effects on the accounting records

Broadly speaking, the systems of branch accounting may be divided into the following categories:

1. Branches which do not maintain full accounting records at the branch. In this case the branch accounting forms part of the head office accounting system.

2. Branches which maintain full accounting records at the branch.

Branch accounting records kept at head office

This system is adopted generally by retail branches where goods for resale are supplied by head office.

These goods sent by head office to the branch are usually charged on the undernoted bases:

1. At cost price

2. At selling price or at cost price plus a percentage

Goods invoiced to branch at cost price

As the accounting records are kept at head office the branch forwards to head office daily or weekly a branch return showing cash sales, credit sales, cash received from debtors, cash remitted to head office, goods received from head office and, if any, goods returned to head office. From this information and the additional information kept at head office, the branch accounts are written up. The branch may keep only a petty cash book to record small items paid at the branch and a memorandum stock book to show movements of stock. If the branch sells on credit, a day book and a sales ledger may also be kept but full details of transactions entered in these books are also recorded in the head office books. Expenses of the branch, except those paid out of the branch petty cash, are paid by head office.

The following accounts are kept in the head office books:

Branch stock account

The head office records the following entries in this account:

Debits:
Branch stock at beginning of period at cost price.
Goods sent to branch by head office at cost price.
Returns by or allowances made to customers.

Credits:
Credit sales at branch.
Cash sales at branch.
Goods returned to head office at cost.
Branch stock at end of period at cost price.

Assuming that the stock has been valued at cost price and the goods sent by and returned to the head office are also valued on the same basis then the balance on the account will be the trading profit of the branch and it is transferred to the credit of the branch profit and loss account. The branch stock account is sometimes known as the branch trading account.

Goods sent to branch account
The entries in this account are as follows:

Debit:
Goods returned to head office at cost price.

Credit:
Goods sent to branch by head office at cost price.

The balance on this account is transferred to head office purchases account at the end of the trading period.

Branch debtors' account
If the branch sells goods on credit, the head office enters up a branch debtors' account which shows the following information:

Debit:
Total balance of debtors' accounts at beginning of period.
Branch credit sales.

Credit:
Cash paid by debtors.
Goods returned by debtors.
Bad debts written off.
Discount allowed to debtors.
Total balance of debtors' accounts at end of period.

Branch expenses account
This account gives particulars of the branch expenses such as:

Debit:
Branch wages.
Branch rent and rates.
Branch selling expenses, etc.

The debits shown above are in respect of branch expenses paid by the head office and credited in the head office cash book. In solutions to questions on this topic it is advisable to open a branch expenses account and enter all branch expenses in that account and transfer the total of the account to branch profit and loss account. In practice, however, it is probable that the head office will open an account for each item.

Branch profit and loss account
The items appearing on this account are as follows:

Debit:
Total of branch expenses.

Credit:
Trading profit for period from branch stock account.

The balance on this account represents the profit of the branch for the period under review and is transferred to the head office profit and loss account.

Asset accounts
If the branch has assets in addition to stock and debtors there are separate accounts opened to record these assets in the head office books.

Advantages and disadvantage of this method

This method achieves one of the objectives of branch accounting and that is that the trading profit and the 'net' profit of the branch can be ascertained with reasonable accuracy.

While the first objective is attained the second one cannot be fulfilled since the accounting system does not permit a reconciliation between the balance of stock shown in the branch stock account and the actual stock held at the branch. The stock figure in the branch stock account is the actual stock on hand at a particular date. Thus head office is unable to use this system as a method of stock control for the branch.

Example: A. Green of Glasgow has a branch shop in Edinburgh. All goods are supplied to the branch by head office at cost. The expenses are paid by head office; the branch only maintains a sales day book and sales ledger. Cash received by the branch is remitted to head office daily.

Below are the figures relating to the year ended 31 December 19X8 which have been extracted from the branch returns and from the books at head office:

Stock at branch 1 January 19X8	£4 400
Sales for cash	9 142
Sales returns and allowances	172
Cash received from customers	18 700
Bad debts written off	264
Sales on credit	19 228
Goods sent to branch by head office	17 894
Rent	928
Stock at branch 31 December 19X8	5 040
Wages and sundry expenses	4 830
Debtors at 1 January 19X8	6 380

From the above information we can prepare the necessary accounts in the head office books to show the trading results of the branch for the year ended 31 December 19X8 as follows:

A. Green

Branch Trading or Stock Account

19X8			19X8		
Jan. 1	Balance (stock)	£4 400	Dec. 31	Branch debtors (credit sales)	£19 228
Dec. 31	Goods to branch	17 894		Cash (cash sales)	9 142
	Branch debtors	172		Balance (stock)	5 040
	Branch profit and loss	10 944			
		£33 410			£33 410

19X9		
Jan. 1	Balance (stock)	£5 040

Goods to Branch Account

19X8			19X8		
Dec. 31	(HO) purchases	£17 894	Dec. 31	Branch stock	£17 894

Branch Debtors Account

19X8			19X8		
Jan. 1	Balance	£6 380	Dec. 31	Branch Stock	£172
Dec. 31	Branch stock	19 228		Cash	18 700
				Branch expenses (bad debts)	264
				Balance	6 472
		£25 608			£25 608
19X9					
Jan. 1	Balance	£6 472			

Branch Expenses Account

19X8			19X8		
Dec. 31	Branch debtors (bad debts)	£264	Dec. 31	Branch profit and loss	£6 022
	Cash (rent)	928			
	Cash (wages and sundry expenses)	4 830			
		£6 022			£6 022

Branch Profit and Loss Account

19X8			19X8		
Dec. 31	Branch expenses (HO) profit and loss	£6 022	Dec. 31	Branch trading	£10 944
		4 922			
		£10 944			£10 944

Goods invoiced to branch at selling price or at cost price plus a percentage

By using this method it is possible to keep a check on stock at the branch and at the same time find out the trading profit and 'net' profit of the branch. The branch stock account, in this system, is not used as a trading account but as a branch stock control account.

Branch stock account

All items appearing in this account are entered at selling price as follows:

Debit:
Branch stock at beginning of period at selling price.
Goods sent to branch by head office at selling price.
Returns by or allowances made to customers at actual amount.

Credit:
Credit sales at branch.
Cash sales at branch.
Goods returned to head office at selling price.
Branch stock at end of period at selling price.

The balance appearing in this account at the end of the trading period should equal the total stock on hand at the branch. If there is any difference between these figures it means that a gain or loss of stock has taken place during the period. Provided this surplus or shortage is within reason no action is taken by head office since a small difference in stock can reasonably be expected in most businesses. On the other hand, if the difference is large then an investigation of the stock position is made by head office. Any difference arising in this account is transferred to the branch stock adjustment account described later.

Goods sent to branch account

The entries in this account are as follows:

Debit:
Goods returned to head office at *cost price*.

Credit:
Goods sent to branch by head office at *cost price*.

Although the items are posted from the branch stock account only the cost price of the goods is entered in the goods sent to branch account. The 'profit loading', i.e. the difference between selling price and cost price, is credited to the branch stock adjustment account. As in the previous method the balance on this account is transferred to head office purchases account.

Branch stock adjustment account

The following entries appear in this account:

Debit:
'Profit loading' on goods returned to head office.
'Profit loading' on balance of stock at end of period.
Shortage or deficit in branch stock transferred from branch stock account.

Credit:
'Profit loading' on balance of stock at beginning of period.
'Profit loading' on goods sent to branch by head office.
Surplus in branch stock transferred from branch stock account.

Since the branch stock account under this method does not act as a trading account, an additional account has to be opened called a branch stock adjustment account. To this account is posted the 'profit loading' on the opening and closing stocks, the goods sent to and returned by the branch. The gross profit of the branch is the difference between the credit and debit sides of this account after allowing for any surplus or deficit in stock. This balance is transferred to the branch profit and loss account.

The branch debtors account, the branch expenses account and the branch profit and loss account are written up in the same way as under the first method.

Restriction in the use of this method

While this method achieves both objectives of branch accounting, it is restricted in its application. If the branch sells similar lines at fixed selling prices then this method is purposeful but in some businesses, owing to the perishable nature of the goods or by reason of variations in selling prices, it would be quite impracticable to adopt this system, in which case the previous method may be used.

Example: Baker & Son have a branch in Manchester. Goods are invoiced to the branch at cost plus $33\frac{1}{3}$ per cent being the selling price of the goods. The Manchester branch keeps only a sales ledger and sends all cash to head office daily. All expenses of the branch are paid by head office.

The following transactions relate to the year ended 31 December 19X8:

Debtors at 1 January 19X8	£2 000
Cash sales	3 500
Credit sales	9 000

Goods invoiced from head office		£13 400
Goods returned to head office at invoice price		400
Bad debt		70
Cash received from debtors		4 200
General expenses of branch		1 000

Stocks which are valued at invoice price at the beginning of the year amounted to £1200 and at the end of the year to £1600.

The accounts for the branch as they would appear in the head office books for the year ended 31 December 19X8 are as follows:

Baker & Son

Manchester Branch Stock Account

19X8			19X8		
Jan. 1	Balance (stock)	£1 200	Dec. 31	Cash - (cash sales)	£3 500
Dec. 31	Goods to branch	13 400		Branch debtors (credit sales)	9 000
				Goods to branch (returns to head office)	400
				Balance (stock)	1 600
				Branch stock adjustment (deficit)	100
		£14 600			£14 600
19X9					
Jan. 1	Balance	£1 600			

Manchester Branch
Stock Adjustment Account

19X8			19X8		
Dec. 31	Branch stock	£100	Jan. 1	Balance	£300
	Balance	400	Dec. 31	Branch stock	3 350
	Branch stock - (deficit)	100			
	Branch profit and loss	3 050			
		£3 650			£3 650
			19X9		
			Jan. 1	Balance	£400

Manchester Branch Debtors Account

19X8			19X8		
Jan. 1	Balance	£2 000	Dec. 31	Branch expenses (bad debts)	£70
Dec. 31	Branch stock	9 000		Cash	4 200
				Balance	6 730
		£11 000			£11 000
19X9					
Jan. 1	Balance	£6 730			

Goods Sent to Branch Account

19X8			19X8		
Dec. 31	Branch stock	£300	Dec. 31	Branch stock	£10 050
	(HO) purchases	9 750			
		£10 050			£10 050

Branch Expenses Account

19X8			19X8		
Dec. 31	Branch debtors – (bad debts)	£70	Dec. 31	Branch profit and loss	£1 070
	Cash – (general expenses)	1 000			
		£1 070			£1 070

Manchester Branch
Profit and Loss Account

19X8			19X8		
Dec. 31	Branch expenses	£1 070	Dec. 31	Branch stock adjustment	£3 050
	(HO) profit and loss	1 980			
		£3 050			£3 050

Notes

1. As the branch stock account is a stock control account the difference of £100 is a stock shortage and is transferred to the branch stock adjustment account.
2. In this question the 'profit loading' is a quarter of the selling price since the goods are invoiced at cost plus $33\frac{1}{3}$ per cent.

   The calculation of the 'profit loading' on the opening stock is as follows:

   £1200 (s. price) $= 133\frac{1}{3}$ per cent
   Cost price $\qquad = 100$ per cent.
   Then cost price is $\dfrac{1200 \times 100}{133\frac{1}{3}} = \dfrac{1200 \times 300}{400} = £900.$
   'Profit loading' is (£1200 − £900) = £300.

   It can now be seen that the 'profit loading' is a quarter of the selling price, viz $300/1200 = \frac{1}{4}$. The other calculations are as follows:

   Goods sent to Branch ($\frac{1}{4} \times$ £13 400) $\qquad = £3 350$

   Goods returned by branch ($\frac{1}{4} \times$ £400) $\qquad = \quad£100$

   Balance of stock at end ($\frac{1}{4} \times$ £1600) = £400

3. The amounts shown in this account have to be entered at cost price. The calculations are as follows:

Goods sent to branch	£13 400
Less 'Profit loading' (see note 2)	3 350
	£10 050
Goods returned by branch	£400
Less 'Profit loading' (see note 2)	100
	£300

An alternative presentation of these accounts is as follows:

Manchester Branch Stock and Trading Account

19X8		Trading	Stock	19X8		Trading	Stock
Jan. 1	Balance	£900	£1 200	Dec. 31	Cash – (cash sales	£3 500	£3 500
Dec. 31	Goods to branch	10 050	13 400		Branch debtors (credit sales)	9 000	9 000
	Branch profit and loss	3 050			Goods to branch	300	400
					Balance (stock)	1 200	1 600
					Deficit		100
		£14 000	£14 600			£14 000	£14 600
19X9							
Jan. 1	Balance	£1 200	£1 600				

Manchester Branch Profit and Loss Account

19X8			19X8		
Dec. 31	Branch expenses	£1 070	Dec. 31	Branch trading	£3 050
	(HO) profit and loss	1 980			
		£3 050			£3 050

Additional notes: This method is used if a branch stock adjustment account is not required. The branch stock and trading account serves a dual purpose. The first column acts as a 'trading column' and the resulting balance is the branch trading profit. Stock is shown at cost and goods sent to branch and returned by branch are also valued at cost. The entries in this column form part of the double entry principle in the head office books.

The second column acts as a stock control column, the figures being similar to those in the branch stock account in the first solution to this question but having no corresponding entries to complete the double entry. The purpose of this column is to control the branch stock and find the gain or loss on stock. All the entries in this column are shown at selling price.

The branch expenses account, branch debtors account, and goods to branch account are similar to those shown in the first part of the solution to this question.

The preparation of trading and profit and loss accounts and balance sheets where full accounting records are kept by the branch

We have stressed previously the importance of the results of the whole enterprise as well as the results of particular sections. The problem of consolidating the revenue statements of all the branches is one we must now consider.

The tabular form of presentation, as demonstrated with departmental revenue statements, is most useful. The only complication is that any transfers of goods between head office and branches must be eliminated in arriving at the total results of the whole enterprise. The following example illustrates this approach.

The following trial balances have been extracted from the ledgers of a head office and its branch as at 30 June 19X6.

	Head office ledger		Branch ledger	
	Debit	**Credit**	**Debit**	**Credit**
Capital		£15 000		
Bank	£743		£84	
Debtors	17 650		682	
Stock (1/7/X5)	10 750		808	
Furniture and equipment	3 800		1 825	
Provision for depreciation of furniture and equipment		840		£250
Branch account	6 422			
Creditors		13 285		215
Head office account				6 422
Selling expenses	2 009		581	
Discount allowed	514		72	
Rent, rates and insurance	1 363		192	
Salaries	5 038		1 005	
Bad debts	845			
Depreciation of furniture and equipment	180		57	
Sales		35 965		8 704
Purchases	29 995			
Goods sent to branch		5 525		
Goods received from head office			5 525	
Appropriation account		3 934		
Remittances from branch		4 760		
Remittances to head office			4 760	
	£79 309	£79 309	£15 591	£15 591
Stocks (30/6/X6)				
Head office	£10 325			
Branch	710			

Combined Profit and Loss Statement for the year ended 30 June 19X6

	Head office	Branch	Total
Sales	£35 965	£8 704	£44 669
Stocks (1/7/X5)	10 750	808	11 558
Purchases	29 995	—	29 995
Goods received from head office	—	5 525	—
	40 745	6 333	
Less Goods sent to branch	5 525	—	—
	35 220	6 333	41 553
Less Stocks (30/6/X6)	10 325	710	11 035
Cost of Goods Sold	24 895	5 623	30 518
Gross Profit	11 070	3 081	14 151

Cont.

	Head office	Branch	Total
Less **Expenses**			
Selling expenses	£2 009	£581	£2 590
Salaries	5 038	1 005	6 043
Depreciation of furniture and equipment	180	57	237
Rent, rates and insurance	1 363	192	1 555
Discount allowed	514	72	586
Bad debts	845	—	845
	9 949	1 907	11 856
Net Profit	£1 121	£1 174	£2 295

Note: The transfer of goods of £5525 has been eliminated in arriving at the combined profit and loss statement figures.

   Some authorities on branch accounting suggest that this combination of results should be carried into the ledger itself. In the case where the branch has its own ledger, this means the incorporation of the figures from the branch trial balance into the head office ledger at balance date. This may have some merit where the branch (through lack of qualified staff) is unable to carry out the profit determination in its own ledger. However, even in these circumstances, we believe the determination of branch profit, and the amalgamation of whole enterprise results, may be performed outside the ledger, as above. Therefore, we do not propose to illustrate the incorporation of branch trial balance figures into the head office ledger.
   Instead, where branch profit has not been determined in the head office ledger (as is done with centrally controlled branches), we will assume that the results of the branch are brought into the head office accounts in one figure (the net profit of the branch).
   For example, in the above illustration, the following entries only will be necessary:

Head Office Journal

		Dr.	Cr.
June 30	Branch account	£1 174	
	Head office profit and loss account		£1 174
	Incorporating the branch net profit		
	Remittances from branch	4 760	
	Branch account		4 760
	Closing off remittances account		

Head Office Ledger

Branch Account

Balance (1/7/X5)	£897[1]	Remittances from branch	£4 760
Goods sent to branch	5 525[1]	Balance (30/6/X6)	2 836
Head office P & L (net profit)	1 174		
	£7 596		£7 596
Balance	£2 836		

[1] Comprising the trial balance figure of £6422

   The closing balance may be reconciled with branch assets less liabilities.

Balance – Bank	£84	
Debtors	682	
Stocks	710	
Furniture and equipment	1 575	
		£3 051
Creditors		215
		£2 836

One final complication, which may affect the consolidation of branch results, is that at balance date there may be goods sent by head office which have not yet reached the branch (goods in transit), or cash remitted by the branch which has not yet reached the head office bank (remittances in transit). These items will have to be adjusted in the head office ledger before the branch results are brought in.

For example, the *branch* trial balance shows goods received from head office as a debit balance of £2280, and there are goods costing and invoiced at £350 in transit from the head office to the branch. We can expect to find the following balance in the *head office* books:

Goods sent to branch account – a credit balance of £2630 (that is, £2280 + £350).

The adjusting entry in the head office books will be:

	Dr.	Cr.
Stock in transit (or goods in transit)	£350	
Branch account		£350

Similarly, if there is cash of £180 in transit from the branch, and a debit balance of £3260 in the remittances to head office account in the *branch* books, then there should be a credit balance of £3080 in the remittances from branch account in the *head office* books. (Note that one of the main advantages of having separate remittances accounts is that transit items are more easily revealed.) The adjustment of the above item and the closing off of the remittances account in the head office books can be achieved by either:

	Dr.	Cr.
Remittances in transit account (or cash in transit)	£180	
Remittances from branch		£180
Adjusting the remittances account		

followed by

Remittances from branch account	£3 260	
Branch account		£3 260
Closing off remittances account		

or, in one entry:

Remittances from branch account	£3 080	
Remittances in transit account (or cash in transit)	180	
Branch account		£3 260

Note that in the head office balance sheet, the transit items appear as current assets, as shown in the following example.

Example: A. Black has a business in Glasgow with a branch in London. The branch keeps its own books and the balances at 31 December in the head office books and the branch books are listed below:

	Glasgow	**London**
Debits		
Furniture and fittings	£1 500	£1 000
Stock	2 000	2 600
Debtors	4 500	3 500
Property	5 000	
London Branch Account	3 200	
Cash at bank	1 700	300
	£17 900	£7 400
Credits		
Profit for year	£7 500	£3 300
Creditors	750	1 300
Head Office Account		2 800
Capital - A. Black	9 650	
	£17 900	£7 400

Goods which cost £300 were sent by head office to the branch on 31 December but were not received by the branch until after that date. On 31 December there was cash in transit from the branch to head office amounting to £100.

From this information the balance sheet of A. Black's business at 31 December is prepared as follows:

Working notes:

In Head Office Books

London Branch Account

Balance	£3 200	Cash in transit	£100
Profit and loss - branch profit	3 300	Goods in transit	300
		Balance	6 100
	£6 500		£6 500
Balance	£6 100		

In Branch Books

Head Office Account

Balance	£6 100	Balance	£2 800
		Profit and loss - branch profit	3 300
	£6 100		£6 100
		Balance	£6 100

Balance Sheet as at 31 December

Fixed Assets

Property – head office			£5 000
Furniture and fittings			
Head office		£1 500	
Branch		1 000	2 500
			7 500

Current assets

Stock			
Head office	£2 000		
Branch	2 600		
Goods in transit	300	4 900	
Debtors			
Head office	4 500		
Branch	3 500	8 000	
Cash at bank			
Head office	1 700		
Branch	300	2 000	
Cash in transit		100	
		£15 000	

Less **Current liabilities**

Creditors			
Head office	750		
Branch	1 300	2 050	12 950
			£20 450

Represented by:		
Capital – A. Black		
As at 1 January	9 650	
Add Profit of year	10 800	£20 450

Notes

1. The branch account balance is represented in the balance sheet by the net assets of the branch:

Furniture and fittings	£1 000
Stock	2 600
Debtors	3 500
Cash at bank	300
	£7 400
Less Creditors	1 300
	£6 100

2. The difference between the balance on the head office account and the branch account is reconciled in this way:

Balance on branch account per head office books		£3 200
Less Goods in transit	£300	
Cash in transit	100	400
Head office account balance in branch books		£2 800

3. The profit of the branch is transferred to the head office profit and loss account. The profit for the year added to the capital account in the balance sheet is calculated thus:

Profit - Head office	£7 500
Branch	3 300
	£10 800

4. Usually the amounts shown for assets and liabilities in the balance sheet would be consolidated and not shown separately for the head office and branch.

Consignment accounts

Nature of consignments

When goods are sent by a trader or merchant as the consignor to an agent referred to as the consignee who undertakes to sell the goods on behalf of the consignor, the transaction is known as a consignment.

The basic difference between a sale and a consignment is that in a sale the title to the goods passes on delivery to the buyer, while in a consignment legal title does not coincide with the delivery of the goods to the consignee but only when they are sold to a third party. When goods are sent by the consignor to the consignee the latter is not invoiced in the normal way with the cost of the goods but merely receives a pro forma invoice notifying him of the dispatch of the goods.

The following points must be remembered in the treatment of consignment transactions:

1. Goods on consignment should be included in the stock inventory of the consignor only.

2. The consignor is responsible to the consignee for all costs incurred on the goods from the date of shipment to the time the goods are sold to a third party unless any agreement to the contrary has been made.

3. No profit should be taken on goods on consignment until they are sold to a third party.

4. The consignee has to exercise due care of the goods held on consignment and to maintain a record of stock movements. The consignee must also exert reasonable effort to sell the goods in accordance with the terms of the consignment contract.

Account sales

It is the responsibility of the consignee to send periodic reports for consignment transactions to the consignor. These reports may be sent on a quarterly, monthly, or even weekly basis depending on the number of transactions taking place and the conditions stated in the consignment contract. The report is referred to as an 'account sales' and specifies the quantity of goods sold and the proceeds therefrom, the related expenses, commission, the amount due to the consignor, and the amount, if any, remitted. The balance of stock held by the consignor may also be incorporated in the account sales.

An example of an account sales is given in Fig. 14.1.

Account sales of 100 cases of machine parts received from Ajax Ltd, of London per Airfreight

Marks			
	50 cases of machine parts @ £1000		£5 000
	50 cases of machine parts @ £800		4 000
			£9 000
Less	Charges		
	Insurance	£200	
	Freight	800	
	Airport charges	100	
	Commission @ 5%	450	
	Del credere @ 2½%	225	1 775
	Net proceeds – sight draft herewith		£7 225

E&OE,
10 High Street,
Delhi,
India.

20 March 19....   Bazaar & Co.

Fig. 14.1 Example of account sales.

Del credere commission

Under the terms of the consignment contract the agent may be responsible for collecting the proceeds of the sales, thus indemnifying the consignee against any bad debts which may arise in the course of trading. An agent agreeing to undertake this financial responsibility is paid an additional commission known as *del credere* commission as compensation for the additional risk assumed. The consignee becomes a *del credere* agent and deducts the additional commission in the account sales in the same way as the normal commission on sales.

Consignment outwards

The consignment from the point of view of the consignor is a consignment outwards and the accounts opened in the consignor's books would be as follows:

1. *Consignment account* This is an account which shows the profit or loss on the consignment. The expenses of the consignment incurred by either the consignor or the consignor's agent and entered on the debit side together with the cost of the goods sent to the agent and on the credit side the proceeds of sale and balance of stock, if any, are shown. The balance on this account represents profit or loss on the consignment and is transferred to the general profit and loss account of the consignor.

2. *Consignee or agent's account* This is a personal account and is written up from information given in the account sales. Proceeds of sales are debited to this account and expenses incurred by the agent, including commission, are credited. The balance on this account represents the amount due by the agent to the consignor.

3. *Goods on consignment account* The cost of goods consigned to the consignee is credited to this account and the balance at the end of the financial year is transferred to purchases or trading accounts.

The above accounts would form part of the double entry system in the consignor's books.

Valuation of stock

If the whole consignment of goods has not been sold at the balance sheet date then the consignor will require to make a valuation of stock at that date so that the unsold stock can be brought down as a balance on the consignment account. In valuing the stock at the end of the financial year not only is the basic cost of the unsold merchandise taken into account but also a proportion of the expenses already incurred both by the consignor and consignee in locating the goods in a saleable condition at the consignee's place of business. The expenses usually included in the valuation are freight, insurance, landing and dock charges. Selling expenses and agent's commission are excluded. The value of the stock on hand is credited in the consignment account and carried down as a balance on that account at the balancing date.

Example: 40 cases at £25 were consigned to A. Smith in New Zealand on 1 January by R. Green of London. The following expenses were incurred:

Freight	£100
Insurance	50
Landing charges	20
Agent's commission	15
Selling expenses	5

R. Green's annual balancing date is 31 July and at that date 32 cases had been sold by A. Smith in New Zealand.

The value of stock at 31 July is as follows:

Cost of goods sent to New Zealand - 40 cases @ £25	£1 000
Freight	100
Insurance	50
Landing charges	20
	£1 170
Whereof $\frac{8}{40}$ × £1170 =	£234

Notes

1. The fraction $\frac{8}{40}$ is arrived at thus:

$$\frac{\text{Balance of cases unsold}}{\text{Total number of cases consigned}}.$$

2. Agent's commission and selling expenses are not included in calculating the value of stock.

The next example illustrates the accounting entries required in the books of a consignor.

Example: From the following particulars we are required to prepare the consignment account, the goods on consignment account, and the consignee's account in the books of AB & Company. AB & Company balance their books at 30 September.

On 1 January AB & Company consigned 100 cases costing £5000 to their agent CD in New Zealand, paying freight and insurance of £40 on the cargo.

CD paid landing charges of £30 and customs duty £500. On 30 September the agent sent an account sales to AB & Company stating that half the consignment had been sold for £4000. A draft accompanied the account sales remitting the amount due after deduction of 5 per cent commission and 2 per cent *del credere* commission.

In the books of AB & Company

Consignment to CD Account

Jan. 1	Goods on consignment	£5 000	Sep. 30	CD - Sale of half of	
	Bank - freight and			consignment	£4 000
	insurance	40		Balance - Stock	2 785
Sep. 30	CD - Landing charges	30			
	Customs duty	500			
	Commission	200			
	Del credere	80			
	Profit and loss	935			
		£6 785			£6 785
Oct. 1	Balance - Stock	£2 785			

CD Account

Sep. 30	Consignment to CD -		Sept. 30	Consignment to CD -	
	Sales	£4 000		Landing charges	£30
				Customs duty	500
				Commission	200
				Del credere	80
				Bank	3 190
		£4 000			£4 000

Goods on Consignment Account

Sep. 30	Purchases	£5 000	Jan. 1	Consignment to CD	£5 000

Notes

1. Valuation of stock

Goods sent to consignee	£5 000
Freight and insurance	40
Landing charges	30
Customs duty	500
	£5 570

The balance of stock at 30 September is valued at 50% × £5570 = £2785.

2. This profit is transferred to the general profit and loss account of AB & Company.

Consignment inwards

The consignee treats the consignment as a consignment inwards. Since legal title to the consigned goods does not rest in the consignee the consignee does not make any ledger entry recording the delivery of the goods but does, however, enter a description of the goods, quantity received, etc. in a memorandum stock book ruled for that purpose. The consignee keeps a personal account for the consignor, crediting it with proceeds of sale and debiting it with expenses and commission in respect of the consignment. The balance remaining is the amount due to be remitted to the consignor.

Example: Using the same information as in the previous example the entries in the consignee's books will be as follows:

In the books of CD

AB & Company Account

Sep. 30	Bank - Landing charges	£30	Sep. 30	Bank or sundry debtors -	
	Customs duty	500		Sale of half of	
	Commission	200		consignment	£4 000
	Del credere	80			
	Bank - Remittance to				
	AB & Company	3 190			
		£4 000			£4 000

Notes

1. The consignor's account in the consignee's books is the reverse of the consignee's account in the consignor's books.

2. The entries in the above account will form part of the double entry system in CD's books.

Summary

1. There are two main accounting aspects of the division of business into sections:

(a) Determination of separate sectional profit.

(b) Assistance in controlling the activities of the various sections.

2. The common bases for sectional division are:

(a) activities or products

(b) geographical

(c) legal.

3. The division may be either continuous (for example, departments, branches) or sporadic (for example, joint ventures).

4. In profit determination of a retail store divided into departments, there is the problem of deciding what revenue and expense items should be allocated between departments, and thus included in the departmental profit and loss statement, and what items should be left to the general profit and loss statement.

5. Joint ventures with other enterprises, being non-continuous sectional activities, generally do not warrant detailed treatment in the profit and loss statement. One profit-determining account (joint venture with X account) is sufficient.

6. The degree of control by head office (which leads to the distinction between centrally controlled branches and autonomous branches) is important in branch accounting. It influences, particularly, the location of the accounting records concerning branch activities.

7. In all examples of sectional activity, the consolidation of the results of the whole enterprise should not be ignored. It is just as important as the determination of a sectional result.

8. Nature of consignments. Methods of recording goods sent on consignment.

Discussion questions

14.1 What is the connection between 'responsibility accounting' and 'segmented accounting'?

14.2 Explain the dangers of allocation of costs and expenses in decision making.

14.3 What are the problems in allocating costs and expenses to departments or branches, and how do accountants attempt to overcome these?

14.4 What factors would be considered before determining whether the accounts of a branch should be controlled by the branch or by head office?

14.5 What problems arise in a joint venture if the venture is not complete at balance date? How are such problems solved?

14.6 In what way would the addition of or the abolition of a department affect the accounts of a retail store?

14.7 The balance of the head office account at the branch does not agree with the branch account balance at head office at the annual balance date. What are the possible causes of this, and how should the balances be reconciled?

14.8 The Bucka Stores invoices its four branches for goods at cost plus 30 per cent. What precautions will need to be taken at balance date in the preparation of the combined accounts of the head office and its branches?

14.9 The Newcastle branch of Supamarkets Ltd has authority to purchase fixed assets when necessary, although the accounts are recorded in the head office books. A truck costing £14 000 has just been bought from Coal Motors by the branch. What entries will be recorded in the head office books for this purchase?

14.10 Explain the basis of valuing unsold stock in consignment accounts.

Exercises

14.11 The following information relates to a business which conducts three separate departments. All figures are in £000.

Items directly allocated:

	Dept A	Dept B	Dept C
Stocks 1 July	£2 500	£3 000	£3 500
Purchases	9 000	8 500	10 000
Sales	11 500	12 000	12 500
Stocks 31 July	1 500	3 500	3 000
Salaries	845	870	1 175
Depreciation, fittings and equipment	100	70	105

Items to be allocated:

Carriage on purchases	£110	On the basis of purchases
Carriage on sales	114	On the basis of sales
Insurance on stock	36	On the basis of opening stocks
Rent	1 152 (p.a.)	On the basis of floor space
Rates and taxes	192	On the basis of floor space

Advertising	£90	A, 40%; B, 30%; C, 30%
Lighting and power	110	A, 30%; B, 30%; C, 40%
Floor space occupied A, 120 000 sq. ft; B, 140 000 sq. ft; C, 160 000 sq. ft.		

Items to be dealt with as general revenue or expenses:

Interest on overdraft	£12
Manager's salary	100
Legal costs	23
Bad debts	40
Commission received	90

You are required to prepare:

(a) a departmental profit and loss statement (in narrative form) with a column for each department and a total column;

(b) a statement of profit and loss (in narrative form) bringing in the departmental contribution and the items not allocated to departments.

14.12 Quick and Silver, sharing profits in the ratio of three-fifths and two-fifths respectively, conduct a business with three departments. They present you with the following information relating to the year ended 30th June, and ask you to prepare:

(a) a departmental statement showing departmental net contribution and the profit for the business as a whole;

(b) a statement showing appropriation of profit;

(c) the capital accounts of the partners;

(d) a properly classified statement of the financial position after all adjustments have been made.

	Dept A	Dept B	Dept C
Floor space	1800 sq.ft	1000 sq. ft	800 sq. ft
Sales	£6 000	£4 000	£3 250
Cost of goods sold	3 500	3 000	1 500
Stock, 30 June	600	375	245

The remaining items in their ledger were:

Rent	£630
Sales staff wages	1 060
Advertising	795
Legal costs	59
Sundry costs	106
Fixed assets	4 350
Cash at bank (asset)	270
Debtors	1 480
Creditors	1 070
Capital – Quick	2 500
Silver	1 750
Drawings – Quick	350
Silver	250

The following adjustments are required:

(i) Allow for undrawn salary of Silver, £400.

(ii) Allow interest on capital at 10 per cent p.a.

The expenses are to be allocated to departments as under:

(i) Silver's salary apportioned in the ratio of cost of goods sold.

(ii) Rent according to floor space occupied.

(iii) All other items (except legal costs) according to departmental sales.

(iv) Legal costs are *not* to be apportioned to departments.

14.13 On 21 July, J.R. Paul of London purchased goods on credit for £1800 from ABC Ltd, and consigned them to H. Mark of Glasgow as a joint venture. Paul paid the freight £200 and insurance £55. On their arrival in Glasgow (30 July), Mark paid £42 to repair some of the items and sold half the balance to X and Co. on credit for £1750. Mark guaranteed payment of X and Co.'s debt. All profits were shared equally between Paul and Mark, and the accounting records of the transaction were kept by Paul. Show the accounts relating to the joint venture in Paul's books after Mark has remitted cash to settle the venture on 4 August.

14.14 A large retail organisation invoices its goods to its branches at a selling price based on a mark-up of 25 per cent on cost.

Complete the following table:

	Selling price	Cost price
Goods sent to Branch A	£5 620	
Stock on hand at beginning		£1 200
Stock on hand at end		1 480
Goods returned from Branch A	390	

14.15 The undermentioned detail regarding the activities of a branch has been obtained from the books kept at head office and from the branch memorandum records. All records of stocks and transfers of goods are kept at cost.

Stocks on hand (1 January)	£1 225
Stocks on hand (31 December)	1 175
Goods sent to branch	9 750
Returns from branch	250
Remittances from branch (all cash remitted):	
For cash sales	5 500
For debtors	6 645
Rent, rates and taxes (paid by head office)	450
Salaries (paid by head office)	950
Sundry expenses (paid by head office)	250
[1] Debtors (1 January)	1 125
[1] Debtors (31 December)	1 250
[1] Discounts allowed to debtors	220
[1] Returns from debtors	280

[1] These figures obtained from branch memorandum records.

You are required to show the following accounts as they would appear in the head office ledger: branch stock account, branch debtors account, branch trading account, branch profit and loss account.

14.16 The following figures have been taken from the head office records in respect of a branch.

This branch sells for cash and on credit. It keeps a branch debtors ledger but no other records. Head office buys all goods and pays all accounts in respect of the branch. The branch is expected to maintain a margin of 25 per cent on sales. Money received by the branch is banked, without any deductions to the credit of head office bank account.

Stock at branch (1/7/X5)	£750 (at cost)
Goods sent to branch	6 000 (at selling price)
Debtors balances (1/7/X5)	860
Cash sales	1 200
Stock (30/6/X6)	1 590 (at cost)
Debtors (30/6/X6)	700
Wages and salaries	400
Shop rent	100
Cash received from debtors	3 800

Show in the head office ledger:

(a) branch stock account

(b) branch trading account (revealing any stock gain or deficiency)

(c) branch profit and loss account

(d) branch debtors control account

14.17 (a) The following information, extracted from the stock records of a wholesaler, relates to one type of goods:

May 1	Balance	200 units at 1.20
May 10	Purchases	100 units at 1.35
May 18	Purchases	150 units at 1.50
May 28	Sales	240 units

Determine the cost of goods sold and the value of closing stock under each of the following methods of stock valuation:

(i) first-in, first-out

(ii) average cost

(b) A retail footwear firm with several branches uses a system of stock control. All goods are invoiced to the branches at selling price, which is $33\frac{1}{3}$ per cent above cost.

The following information relates to the Smalltown branch for the six months ended 30 June.

From head office records:	
Stocks on hand, Smalltown branch, 1 January (at cost)	£7 200
Goods sent to Smalltown branch (at cost)	15 600
From reports submitted by Smalltown branch:	
Cash sales	5 600
Credit sales	12 400
Returns to head office (at selling price)	1 200
Stocks on hand at 30 June (at selling price)	10 400

You are required to:

(i) calculate the stock discrepancy (if any);

(ii) submit a statement of the trading of the Smalltown branch, showing gross profit for the six months.

14.18 Superior Traders operate a city store and two suburban branches which sell for cash only and bank intact daily to the credit of head office. All expenses are paid and all accounting records are kept by head office. A trial balance of the head office ledger as at 30 June 19X6 is as follows:

	Dr.	Cr.
Cash at bank	£800	
Stocks at head office (1/7/X5)	8 800	
Branch stock, Branch A	9 000	
Branch stock, Branch B	13 300	
Shop equipment	15 000	
Land and buildings	48 000	
Creditors		£4 300
Issued capital		60 000
Profit and loss appropriation account		9 900
Head office sales		25 000
Remittances from Branch A		10 000
Remittances from Branch B		15 000
Purchases	34 800	
Goods sent to Branch A		6 800
Goods sent to Branch B		10 500
Sales staff's salaries, head office	3 300	
Sales staff's salaries, Branch A	1 700	
Sales staff's salaries, Branch B	2 400	
Office salaries	2 400	
Office expenses	2 000	
	£141 500	£141 500

Other information:

(a) Balance of branch stock accounts as at 1 July 19X5 was:

Branch A	£2 200
Branch B	2 800

(b) Stocks on hand as at 30 June 19X6 (at cost):

Head office	£9 500
Branch A	2 400
Branch B	3 600

Show the following accounts in the head office ledger:

(i) trading accounts for head office and each branch

(ii) profit and loss accounts for head office and each branch

(iii) general profit and loss account

In order to determine the branch profit, the administrative expenses are to be charged against the head office and the branches in proportion to sales.

14.19 Brown and Co. of London have a branch at Glasgow which keeps its own accounting records.

On 30 June 19X6 the trial balance of the branch was:

	Dr.	Cr.
Goods received from head office	£2 975	
Delivery vans	280	
Furniture and fittings	70	
Debtors and creditors	1 075	£250
Stocks, 1/7/X5	725	
Sales		4 125
Rent, rates and taxes	150	
General expenses	25	
Head office account		3 720
Bank	135	
Carriage	60	
Salaries	740	
Bad debts	25	
Remittances to head office	1 800	
Discount allowed	35	
	£8 095	£8 095

Stocks on hand at 30 June 19X6 were £950.

Assuming that profit determination is carried out at the branch, and that the head office does not reproduce branch ledger accounts in its own ledger, show:

(a) the journal entries necessary in the head office books;

(b) the branch account in the head office ledger.

Show all workings.

14.20 The following extracts are taken from the trial balances of a head office and its branch:

	Dr.	Cr.
Head office trial balance (extract)		
Branch account	£2 497	
Goods sent to branch		£1 120
Remittances from branch		1 845
Branch trial balance (extract)		
Head office account		2 477
Goods from head office	1 100	
Remittances to head office	1 900	

Using the above information demonstrate:

(a) that in the respective ledgers at the commencement of the period the branch account (head office books) and the head office account (branch books) were in agreement and that, after transfer of the remittances accounts and the adjustment for items in transit, their closing balances would also be reconciled;

(b) in journal form, the entries required in the head office books:

    (i) at end of the period to raise the transit accounts;

    (ii) in the new period to close the transit accounts.

14.21 The Southvic Trading Co. Ltd has its head office in Manchester and has an Aberdeen branch. The following trial balances have been extracted from the head office and branch ledgers as at 30 June 19X6:

	Head office		branch	
	Dr.	Cr.	Dr.	Cr.
Cash at bank	£3 310		£2 110	
Debtors	21 250		13 750	
Stocks on hand (1 July 19X5)	18 700		7 800	
Shop equipment	14 500		7 500	
Provision for depreciation of shop equipment		£3 150		£1 340
Freehold premises	53 000			
Aberdeen branch account	19 300			
Creditors		7 360		2 180
Head office account				18 880
Mortgage on freehold		15 000		
Issued capital (60 000 £1 ordinary shares)		60 000		
Sales		105 800		63 600
Goods sent to branch (at cost)		10 560		
Purchases	89 400		32 380	
Goods received from H.O. (at cost)			10 320	
Rent			2 860	
Sundry selling expenses	5 480		2 160	
Salaries	7 960		4 860	
Sundry administrative expenses	4 010		1 790	
Discount allowed	1 080		680	
Discount received		1 620		210
Profit and loss appropriation account		34 500		
	£237 990	£237 990	£86 210	£86 210

Other information available:

(a) Stocks on hand at 30 June 19X6:

Head office	£23 450
Branch	7 840

(b) Goods invoiced at £240, forwarded by head office and charged to the branch, have not yet been received and brought into the branch books.

(c) A cash remittance of £180, banked by the branch to the credit of head office on 30 June 19X6, has not yet been entered in the head office books.

(d) Depreciation is to be charged on all shop equipment at the rate of 10 per cent p.a. on cost.

(e) A provision for doubtful debts of 4 per cent of all debtors is to be raised.

(f) Taxation at the rate of 30 per cent on the combined profit of head office and branch is to be provided for.

(g) A dividend of 10 per cent on all issued capital is to be provided for.

You are required to prepare:

(i) A tabular statement of profit and loss revealing both the separate profits earned by the head office and branch, and the combined profit of the Southvic Trading Co. Ltd for the year ended 30 June 19X6.

(ii) A statement showing the appropriation of profits for that year.

(iii) A balance sheet of the company as at 30 June 19X6.

14.22 On 20 January Tom Forrest of Glasgow consigned 100 cases of crockery to Halid & Co. of Bombay per MV *Indian Queen*.

Halid & Co. paid the following charges:

Insurance	£70
Transport charges	90
Storage	20

By 12 April Halid & Co. had sold 50 cases of crockery for £100 a case and the balance at £90 a case. Commission was due to them at the rate of 3 per cent. In settlement of the proceeds he forwarded a sight draft to Tom Forrest.

You are required to prepare the account sales submitted by Halid & Co.

14.23 From the following particulars you are required to prepare the consignment account, the consignee's account and the relative cash entries in the books of Thames & Co. of London for the period to 31 January 19X7 and to balance the ledger accounts at that date.

On 10 November 19X6, Thames & Co. consigned 30 cases of goods valued at cost at £139 per case to W. Gomes, their agent in Gibraltar, and at the same time paid carriage, insurance and freight thereon amounting to £513.

On 21 December 19X6, Thames & Co. drew a bill on W. Gomes at 60 days for £3000 on account of the ultimate proceeds of the consignment. On the same day they discounted the bill with their London bankers, being charged £25 therefor. The bill was duly met at maturity.

On 25 January 19X7 an account sales was received from W. Gomes showing that 25 cases had been sold for £5375 and that he had paid on the whole consignment import duty £246, landing charges £143, and insurance £28; also that he had incurred selling expenses of £162 on the 25 cases sold. A bankers' draft for the balance then due, under deduction of commission of 4 per cent on gross sales, was also received.

Problems

14.24 Sweet Tooth Ltd produces three types of chocolate bar:

Plain   which sells at £1.20
Nut   which sells at £1.40
Cherry which sells at £2.00.

Sales are falling and the sales manager has proposed that photographs of famous sports personalities be included with each bar at an additional cost of 5p each. The selling price of the bars would not be altered. Current sales are estimated at *Plain* – £120 000, *Nut* – £140 000 and *Cherry* – £200 000. The sales manager expects that with the inclusion of the photos, plus a suitable advertising campaign that would add £5000 to present levels of expense, that sales would increase as follows:

Plain   50%
Nut   100%
Cherry 30%

At present the gross contribution ratio for each bar is

Plain   60%
Nut   40%
Cherry   20%

Prepare a statement comparing the present profit position with the profit based on the estimated figures of the sales manager.

14.25 Merchant commenced business on 1 January 19X6, at a head office and at one branch. Purchases were made exclusively by head office where all goods were processed before sale and there was no loss or wastage in processing. Only processed goods received from head office were handled by the branch and these were charged thereto at processed cost plus 10 per cent. All sales whether handled by head office or the branch were at a uniform gross profit of 25 per cent on the processed cost.

The following trial balances as on 31 December 19X6 were extracted from the books before adjusting any of the matters referred to below:

	Head office		Branch	
Merchant – Capital		£15 500		
Drawings	£2 750			
Purchases	98 475			
Cost of processing	2 525			
Sales		64 000		£41 000
Goods sent to/received by branch		46 200	£44 000	
Selling and general expenses	9 450		1 060	
Debtors/creditors	15 480	30 070	5 680	540
Head office/branch – Current account	19 490			13 075
Balance at bank	7 600		3 875	
	£155 770	£155 770	£54 615	£54 615

You ascertain that

(a) Goods charged by head office to the branch in December 19X6 at £2200 were not received or recorded by the branch until January 19X7, and a remittance of £4215 from the branch to head office in December 19X6 was not received or recorded at head office until January 19X7. Any necessary adjustments in respect of these items are to be made in the head office accounts.

(b) Stocktaking at the branch disclosed a shortage of goods of a selling value of £1000. There was no shortage or surplus at head office.

(c) The cost of the stock of unprocessed goods at head office on 31 December 19X6 was £5000.

You are required to prepare in columnar form for (i) the head office; (ii) the branch; and (iii) the business as a whole:

(A) trading and profit and loss account for the year ended 31 December 19X6, and

(B) balance sheets as on that date.

For the purpose of the separate trading account of the head office, stocks are to be valued at cost. In the case of the separate accounts of the branch, stocks are to be valued at the price charged by head office. Any necessary adjustments are to be made in the head office profit and loss account.

14.26 The trial balance at 30 June 19X6 of the Trouble & Sorrow Retail Store Ltd, which operates three departments, reveals the following:

		Dr.	Cr.
Rent, rates and insurance		£1 800	
Travellers' salaries and commission		5 600	
Administration salaries		1 800	
Directors' fees		1 500	
Debtors		16 400	
Furniture and fittings		1 360	
Bad debts		200	
Advertising		3 500	
Purchases (net)			
Department A	£16 500		
Department B	30 000		
Department C	12 000		
		58 500	
Stocks on hand 1/7/X5			
Department A	3 300		
Department B	7 800		
Department C	1 800		
		12 900	
Buildings		150 000	
Interest on loan		152	
Interim dividend – ordinary		1 000	
Interim dividend – pref.		750	
Uncalled ordinary capital		30 000	
Issued capital			
150 000 £1 ordinary shares			
25 000 £1 pref. shares 6% }			£175 000
Provision for taxation			250
General reserves			5 250
Profit and loss appropriation			1 250
Provision for depreciation, furniture and fittings			160
Bank			10 726
Provision for doubtful debts			480
Creditors			6 033
Sales (net)			
Department A	24 000		
Department B	42 000		
Department C	18 000		
			84 000
Loan			2 313
		£285 462	£285 462

Adjustments:

(a) An amount of £200 for rents has been paid in advance.

(b) Stocks on hand, 30 June 19X6.

Department A	£3 000	
Department B	5 400	
Department C	1 650	
		£10 050

(c) Depreciation to be provided on furniture and fittings at 10 per cent on the diminishing balance method.

(d) Provision for doubtful debts to be 2 per cent of accounts receivable.

(e) Provision for taxation to be £2500.

(f) Provision for final dividends: ordinary share capital - £1000; preference share capital - £750.

(g) General reserves to be increased by £2000.

In the determination of departmental profit the following expenses are to be apportioned:

Travellers' salaries and commission	on basis of net
Advertising	sales
Rents, rates and insurance	Department A - $\frac{1}{4}$
	Department B - $\frac{1}{2}$
	Department C - $\frac{1}{8}$
	General - $\frac{1}{8}$
Depreciation on furniture and fittings	Department A - $\frac{1}{6}$
	Department B - $\frac{1}{2}$
	Department C - $\frac{1}{6}$
	General - $\frac{1}{6}$

You are required to prepare:

 (i) A profit and loss statement for the year ended 30 June 19X6, showing the profit contributed by each of the three departments and the net profit for the whole enterprise.

 (ii) A statement of profit and loss appropriation for the year ended 30 June 19X6.

(iii) A balance sheet as at 30 June 19X6.

Chapter 15
Accounting for variations in business activity

The varied nature of activity ☐ Effects on recording and control techniques ☐ Hire purchase accounts ☐ Long-term construction and production ☐ Accounting for royalties ☐ Farming ☐ Small business ☐ Incomplete records ☐ Non-trading concerns ☐ Other types of activity

The varied nature of activity

The enterprises used as examples earlier in this book were mainly those engaged in merchandising, either as retailer or as wholesaler. In commerce, however, merchandising is only one of an infinite variety of business activities. 'Goods' may be manufactured from raw materials; they may be assembled into a different product; raw materials may be obtained from mining, agriculture, forestry or farming. The enterprise may prefer not to sell the goods outright but rather to dispose of them by means of extended credit, such as hire purchase, lease, etc. Other enterprises provide services in the form of insurance, financial or legal advice, etc., while government and local authorities provide still other types of service.

In considering the effects of such differences in the nature of activity on accounting, we must emphasise that it is neither possible nor desirable to consider the special problems of every kind of business activity or endeavour. Instead we will examine, in general terms, how the nature of activity does influence accounting, and then develop the picture in some detail for one or two particular types.

Because of the differing natures of activities in business, each individual management requires different information. To provide the necessary data, the accountant must adapt the nature, form and content of his records and reports to suit both the needs of management and the peculiarity of the type of enterprise. The type of business operations will also dictate the extent and areas of control essential to specific activities. In addition, particular problems arise in some types of activity in respect of the determination of profit. The three areas affected, therefore, by the nature of the business activity are in the *records and reports*, in the *control techniques* and in the *determination of profit*.

Effects on recording and control techniques

As we saw in the previous chapters, if management requires specific information of the diverse operations of its business then the accounting documents, the day books and the ledgers will need to be adapted. In a similar manner, where the nature of activities undertaken requires it, it will be necessary to make alterations to the types of records already studied. A few typical examples with the reasons for each amendment are illustrated below.

1. *Professional services such as public accountants, dentists, lawyers.* Here the problem is one of accounting for time charged to clients. Each member of the staff will need to maintain his or her own diary or time record indicating the name of the client to be charged and accounting

for the total time he or she is employed. These records will be accumulated each week or month to assist management in calculating both the labour cost of jobs to be charged out and the amount of time lost in travelling, training or preparation.

2. In the case of *hotels* and *banks* the problem is one of speedy production of invoices or account balances. Since guests may leave and banking customers may cash cheques without any prior notification, it is essential that such organisations should keep their debtors' accounts up to date. In both cases, the functions of the day books and the ledger account are combined in the one record. Control totals are used to ensure greater accuracy.

3. Business enterprises that engage in *overseas transactions* constantly face the problem of conversion of the currency from the country of operation to the home country. Such conversion rates are constantly changing, and large sums can be gained or lost as a result of upward or downward valuations of the currency. In many cases, an additional column relating to the rate of conversion applying at the time of the transaction is required. In others, a choice has to be made as to which rate will be used in the calculation of the profit earned or the asset acquired, and so on.

4. Solicitors, estate agents and auctioneers have to maintain separate columns or books to record the transactions which affect money received on behalf of clients, and their own (such as fees or commissions for handling the client's business). Money received in trust in this way (for example, for the sale of property) is subject to special legislation. Also, in accounting for deceased estates, it is essential that income and assets should be divided between that which increases the value of the original estate and that which should be attributed to the beneficiaries. A dividend received after death may relate to the period prior to death and must be carefully segregated from other income received after death.

While certain control techniques, such as budgetary control and responsibility accounting, are applicable to all types of enterprise, there are some cases where these become much more important because of the nature of the activities carried on by the business.

1. *Budgetary control* is critical in the case of firms engaged in construction or manufacturing. The planning of production, sales, etc. (which constitutes the budget of the enterprise) must include careful consideration of the availability of supplies of labour and materials and the finance necessary to pay for these. In addition, it is necessary to plan for the receipt and storage of both raw materials and finished goods. During the period following these estimates, regular checks are made to see that the results are in line with what was forecast. This procedure is called 'budgetary control' and enables remedial action to be taken when warranted.

2. *Responsibility accounting* aims at a division of the business into smaller units or areas over which specific officers have control and are held responsible for the production, revenues, expenses, etc. of that unit. It attempts to ensure that if there is a deficiency or a failure or an outstanding success in the business then management is immediately aware of where responsibility lies. Here again, there are certain cases where this is more important than others. Large business organisations often have huge amounts of cash which, for short periods, are surplus to requirements. Some officer will be allotted the task of investing this regularly in the short-term money market. With hundreds of thousands of pounds involved, this activity can make the difference between a satisfactory and an unsatisfactory profit result.

3. *Credit control* is most important to many types of enterprise. The huge company failures in the United Kingdom during the last twenty years drew marked attention to losses due to bad debts, particularly in wholesale and retail firms, and in the provision of loans and other forms of credit. Control involves the careful granting of credit together with adequate follow-up and collection procedures. Adequate coloured signals on the debtors' ledger cards provide a warning

for the credit officers to consider such customers more closely. Bank managers, in particular, have to ensure the receipt of regular reports on all overdrafts, both new and old.

4. *Technological controls* are particularly important in the retail trade, where it is vital that the right price is charged and the correct change given. Electronic (computer-type) cash registers may be used to indicate the amount of change to be given, while the method of bar-coding products with the description and price ensure accuracy in both respects. Other such controls of a non-accounting nature are the methods used to maintain a visual scanning of customers and staff to control and prevent theft and fraud and the introduction of automatic reorder points into a computer program to prevent stock-outs.

It would not be possible to deal with every kind of activity. Instead, we will illustrate the problems of profit determination and of management control with representative samples.

Hire purchase accounts

Trading on hire purchase terms has become increasingly popular in recent years with both large and small businesses. The reason for financing the purchase of assets in this way is certainly not one of saving on interest charges. Generally it is costlier to borrow from a hire purchase company than it is from the bank but in many cases, owing to the inability to obtain funds from a bank or other lending institutions, it is only possible to obtain finance through a hire purchase company.

In this section we do not intend to consider in detail the law relating to hire purchase but rather to explain and illustrate the accounting treatment of transactions undertaken on hire purchase terms in the books of the buyer and seller. It is, however, recommended that if the exact legal interpretation of the different types of hire purchase agreements and the various rights attached thereto is required, then an appropriate text book on the subject should be consulted.

Hire purchase agreements and payments by instalments

It is important, before considering the appropriate accounting treatment, to distinguish between a hire purchase agreement and a credit sale agreement.

Under a hire purchase agreement the owner of the goods hires them to the would-be purchaser, called the hirer, and the ownership of the goods does not vest to the hirer until the last instalment is paid and he has exercised his option to take over the goods. Very often after the final instalment has been made on the hire purchase agreement the hirer has to pay a nominal purchase fee to secure title to the goods. In the event of the hirer failing to pay any instalment due under the agreement the owner may recover the goods from the hire purchaser and so terminate the 'hiring agreement'.

Under the terms of the Consumer Credit Act 1974, if the hirer has paid not less than one-third of the total hire purchase price, the owner cannot recover the goods from the hirer without first obtaining a court order. Where the total purchase price exceeds £5000 or where the purchaser is a body corporate the act does not apply.

In an agreement to pay a credit sale by instalment system the title to the goods passes to the purchaser immediately the agreement is entered into and delivery of the goods has taken place. Under this system a sale has actually taken place. The purchaser does not hire the goods from the seller but buys them in the same manner as he would in a normal credit sale transaction. The seller has then no legal title to the goods and his only remedy, if the purchaser defaults in payment of any instalments, is to sue the purchaser for the outstanding sum.

Hire purchase price

This term is frequently used in hire purchase transactions and differs from the cash price of the goods since the owner of the goods charges interest to the hirer based on the cash price of the goods (less any deposit) and the length of the repayment period. A deposit is payable under a hire purchase agreement. Below is an example of the calculation of the hire purchase price together with the number of repayments to be made under the hire purchase agreement:

Cash price of goods	£500
Less Deposit	100
	400
Add Interest @ 20% per annum for one year	80
	£480

Payable in 12 monthly instalments of £40 each. In this example the hire purchase price is:

Cash price	£500
Hire purchase interest	80
	£580

Hire purchase transactions in the purchaser's books

From the point of view of the purchaser of goods under a hire purchase agreement, the main accounting problem is to allocate the payments made under the agreement between capital and revenue expenditure or, in other words, between principal and interest. It would be quite inaccurate to treat the hire purchase price as capital expenditure. The element of capital expenditure in the hire purchase price is that relating to the cash price of the goods purchased and the element of revenue expenditure is the interest charged under the terms of the hire purchase agreement. There are many methods in use to record transactions of this nature in the hirer's books but although differences in presentation occur there is general agreement that the full cash price of the goods purchased should be debited to the appropriate asset account at the commencement of the agreement. This practice has been adopted to show a realistic view of the transaction rather than strictly adhering to basic accounting principles. Strictly speaking, the goods should not be included in the assets section of the balance sheet until the hirer has exercised his option to purchase the goods. In practice an exception is made from the theoretical concept of this transaction since it is almost certain in every case that it is the intention of the hirer to purchase the goods and not to return them at the end of the agreement.

Depreciation of assets acquired under hire purchase terms

Although ownership of the asset does not rest in the hirer until actual purchase takes place, it is normal practice to depreciate assets acquired under hire purchase terms during the period of repayment. Deterioration through normal wear and tear and obsolescence still take place although the asset is purchased on hire purchase terms, so an allowance for depreciation is made based on the cash price of the asset in the usual way.

In journal form the entries are:

Dr. Depreciation account or profit and loss account for depreciation.
Cr. Asset account or provision for depreciation account.

Accounting entries for assets purchased on hire purchase terms

This method tends to be used when the true rate of interest is not known and the interest charges are regarded as having accrued evenly over the period of the agreement rather than related to the amount outstanding after each instalment is paid.

1. *Dr.* Asset account with cash price of goods.
   Cr. Hire purchase company account.
2. *Dr.* Hire purchase company account with deposit paid at the commencement of the hire purchase agreement.
   Cr. Bank.
3. *Dr.* Hire purchase interest suspense account with the total amount of interest under the terms of the hire purchase agreement.
   Cr. Hire purchase company account.
4. *Dr.* Hire purchase company account with any instalments paid during financial period.
   Cr. Bank.
5. *Dr.* Profit and loss account with the relevant charge for interest at the end of the financial period.
   Cr. Hire purchase interest suspense account.

Entries 4 and 5 are repeated until the expiry of the hire purchase agreement.

Example: On 1 January A Ltd purchased a motor car from the Car Trading Company on hire purchase terms as follows:

Cash price	£7 500
Less Deposit	1 500
	6 000
Add Interest charges	600
	£6 600

Repayment is to be made by 12 monthly instalments of £550 each commencing 31 January. Depreciation is to be provided at 20 per cent per annum on cost.

The record of this transaction is entered in the books of A Ltd, whose financial year ends on 31 December, as follows:

In the books of A. Ltd

Motor Car Account

Jan. 1	HP Company	£7 500	Dec. 31	Profit and loss (depreciation at 20%)	£1 500
				Balance	6 000
		£7 500			£7 500
Jan. 1	Balance	£6 000			

HP Company Account

Jan. 1	Bank (deposit)	£1 500	Jan. 1	Motor car	£7 500
Jan. 31 to Dec. 31	12 instalments of £550	6 600		Hire purchase interest suspense	600
		£8 100			£8 100

Hire Purchase Interest Suspense Account

Jan. 1	HP Company	£600	Dec. 31	Profit and loss	£600

Notes

1. If the agreement had been for a period in excess of twelve months, balances would have been brought down on the HP company account and the hire purchase interest suspense account representing the unpaid amount due to the HP company and the balance of hire purchase interest still to be written off.

2. If there had been balances on the HP company account and the hire purchase interest suspense account then the balance on the latter account would be deducted from the balance on the former account and the net amount shown as a current liability in the balance sheet.

Hire purchase transactions in the seller's books

Owing to the number of systems employed to record sales on hire purchase terms in the books of the seller it is not possible within this section to describe and illustrate each system in detail. No matter which system of recording is adopted the seller has two basic problems to resolve before any entries are made. When sales are made on hire purchase terms, in many cases the hire purchase price may be repaid over a period of years, in which the seller has to decide on the treatment of interest charges included in this price and the gross profit on the transaction. In the case of interest the seller usually apportions the interest charges over the period of repayment. With regard to the gross profit on the goods sold the seller has to decide whether to take credit for the profit when the sale is made or to apportion the profit on some basis over the terms of the hire purchase agreement. It is the problem of apportioning the gross profit which gives rise to the various systems of recording such transactions. It is found frequently in practice that a system is adopted by the seller which has the advantages of simplicity and ease of operation rather than one which follows orthodox accounting principles and is costly to install and operate.

Accounting entries in the books of the seller

If the goods sold are of relatively low value and the period over which they are to be paid varies considerably then the following system may be used: this method is suggested where the hire purchasers' accounts are kept on a memorandum basis and without the double entry accounting system.

All goods sold on hire purchase terms are entered in a hire purchase sales day book ruled as follows:

Date	Name and address of customer	Details of sale	Folio	Cost price	Hire purchase price	Number of instalments

The hire purchase price of the goods will be entered on the debit side of the ledger account opened for each customer. In this method the ledger accounts do not form part of the double entry system but are only memoranda accounts. As each instalment is paid the cash book is debited with the amount of the instalment and the customer's ledger account credited.

At the end of each financial period a stock on hire purchase account is prepared showing the calculation of gross profit for the period:

Stock on Hire Purchase Account

Dr.			Cr.
Cost of stock on hire purchase under agreements effected during the financial period (corresponding credit appears in purchases account)		Instalments received (corresponding debit in cash book) Balance carried down: Instalment due (see schedule)	
Trading account – Gross profit for period		Cost price of instalments not due (see schedule)	
	£		£

The following schedule is prepared to calculate the instalments due and the cost price of the instalments not due at the balancing date:

Customer	Amount of instalments		Number of instalments		Cost price of goods	Cost price of instalments not due
	Due	Not due	Total	Not due		

The calculation of cost price of instalments not due, if no deposit is paid, is

$$\frac{\text{Number of instalments not due}}{\text{Total number of instalments}} \times \text{Cost price.}$$

If a deposit is paid and is equal in value to an instalment this is added to the denominator in the above equation and counts as one instalment.

You will see from a study of this method that the main principle involved is to treat all goods under hire purchase terms as stock. The hire purchase sales day book and the customers' ledger accounts do not form part of the double entry accounting system. Postings are made from the purchases day book and the cash book to the stock on hire purchase account on a monthly, quarterly, or annual basis.

Example: The HP Appliance Company made the undernoted sales under hire purchase terms:

Date	Customer	Cost price	Selling price	Payments
19X7				
Aug. 31	Edwards	£400	£500	5 instalments of £100 each
Nov. 30	Franks	200	300	6 instalments of £50 each
19X8				
Feb. 29	Green	600	840	10 instalments of £84 each
May 31	Hall	300	400	8 instalments of £50 each

The firm prepares accounts on the basis that the proportion of gross profit to be taken to the credit of trading account in any year will be based on the instalments receivable during that year.

The following instalments which were receivable during the firm's financial year to 30 June 19X8 were paid with the exception of Green who paid only four instalments:

Edwards	4 instalments	Green	5 instalments
Franks	4 instalments	Hall	1 instalment

We are required to record the above transactions in the firm's books for the year ended 30 June 19X8 using the method where the hire purchaser's accounts are kept on a memoranda basis. Ledger accounts may be prepared in an abbreviated form. (Calculations to be to the nearest £.)

We proceed as follows:

Hire Purchase Sales Day Book

Date	Name of Customer	Details of sale	Cost price	Hire purchase price	Number of instalments
19X7					
Aug. 31	Edwards	Goods	£400	£500	5
Nov. 30	Franks	Goods	200	300	6
19X8					
Feb. 29	Green	Goods	600	840	10
May 31	Hall	Goods	300	400	8
			£1 500	£2 040	

Ledger Accounts

Edwards's Account

Aug. 31	Goods	£500	?		Bank	£100
					Bank	100
					Bank	100
					Bank	100
				June 30	Balance	100
		£500				£500
July 1	Balance	£100				

Franks's Account

Nov. 30	Goods	£300	?		Bank	£50
					Bank	50
					Bank	50
					Bank	50
				June 30	Balance	100
		£300				£300
July 1	Balance	£100				

Green's Account

Feb. 29	Goods	£840	?		Bank		£84
					Bank		84
					Bank		84
					Bank		84
				June 30	Balance		504
		___					___
		£840					£840
July 1	Balance	£504					

Hall's Account

May 31	Goods	£400	?		Bank		£50
				June 30	Balance		350
		___					___
		£400					£400
July 1	Balance	£350					

Note: The above ledger accounts are shown in abbreviated form in terms with the question. In practice full details of the transaction would be shown at the top of each ledger account relating to nature of goods, terms of repayment, amount of each instalment, etc.

Schedule of cost price of instalments not due at 30 June 19X8

	Amount of instalment		Number of instalments		Cost price	Cost price of instalments not due
Customer	Due	Not Due	Total	Not Due		
Edwards		£100	5	1	£400	£80
Franks		100	6	2	200	67
Green	£84	420	10	5	600	300
Hall		350	8	7	300	262
	___	___			___	___
	£84	£970			£1 500	£709

Note: Basis of calculation of cost price of instalments not due:

Edwards	$\dfrac{\text{Number of instalments not due}}{\text{Total number of instalments}} \times \text{Cost price} = \frac{1}{5} \times £400$	$= £80$
Franks	$\frac{2}{6} \times £200$	$= £67$
Green	$\frac{5}{10} \times £600$	$= £300$
Hall	$\frac{7}{8} \times £300$	$= £262$

Stock on Hire Purchase Account

Cost price of stock on hire purchase under agreements effected during year		£1 500	Instalments received		£986
			Balance carried down:		
			(a) Instalments due	£84	
Trading account – Gross profit for year		279	(b) Cost price of instalments not due	709	793
		_____			_____
		£1 779			£1 779

Calculation of instalments received:

Edwards	4 × £100	£400
Franks	4 × £50	200
Green	4 × £84	336
Hall	1 × £50	50
		£986

A proof calculation can be made of the gross profit as follows:

Edwards	$\dfrac{\text{Number of instalments due}}{\text{Total instalments}}$ × Gross profit = $\frac{4}{5}$ × £100 = £80
Franks	$\frac{4}{6}$ × £100 = 67
Green	$\frac{5}{10}$ × £240 = 120
Hall	$\frac{1}{8}$ × £100 = 12
	£279

In the above calculation the gross profit includes the normal gross profit on the sale plus interest charges, but as the total is apportioned, there is no necessity to record the interest separately.

Long-term construction and production

Profit determination for building contracts occupying a number of years presents a special problem. Say, for example, a contract price has been determined for a hospital which will take five years to build; if only realised profits are taken into account then there will be losses for four years and possibly a very large profit in the fifth year. It thus becomes necessary to calculate the cost of work completed in each year if the reports of each accounting period are to be meaningful. In some cases the value of the work in progress at the end of a period may be determined by assessing what proportion of the job is complete. In others, the estimated cost to complete may be added to the cost to date. Such estimates are usually prepared by engineers or from architects' certificates.

A similar difficulty exists in the case of, say, wineries. Since the products in this case must be retained for some years to attain their proper maturity, it is necessary to assess the value of the maturing stock, and this problem is accentuated because of the different sizes of the annual harvest and the resultant quality of the wines produced. Forestry production has similar problems.

Accounting for royalties

The term 'royalty' once meant a fee paid to a monarch for the use of land. It has since become used as the title of the fee paid to the owner of a product for the right to use that product to generate income. It can be applied to authors for books, artists for paintings, inventors for inventions and landowners for mining. The royalty cost will be one of the expenses charged against the income derived from the use of the product. In the case of mining, the royalty cost is usually based on the output of the mine, although some minimum level of payment is agreed to in case the output is not as high as expected. If the royalty cost is not sufficient to cover the minimum rent then additional payment necessary to achieve the minimum rent is called 'dead rent'.

Accounting entries in the books of the lessee or user

(assuming the payment is made to a landlord for minerals extracted from the ground)

1. *Dr.* Royalties account with the amount of the actual royalties.
   Cr. Landlord's account.

2. *Dr.* Landlord's account when payment is made.
   Cr. Cash or bank.

The balance on the royalties account at the end of the financial year will be written off to profit and loss account. Similar entries will be recorded if payment of royalties is made to a copyright owner or a patentee.

Short workings

This is another term used in royalty accounts and means the difference between the minimum rent and the output at the rate of royalty payable. In the case of a landlord, he may allow the lessee (or user) the right to recoup short workings from the increased output in later years.

Example: X enters into an agreement with Z to mine minerals on his land at a royalty of £0.05 per tonnes extracted. A minimum rent of £100 is to be paid. In the first year X extracts 500 tonnes from Z's land. The short workings are calculated as follows:

Minimum rent payable to Z	£100
500 tonnes extracted at royalty of £0.05 per tonne	25
Short workings	£75

Note: In the above example the lessee X will require to pay £100 in royalties to the landlord Z in the first year. X may have the right to recover these short workings in later years if the agreement so provides.

Additional accounting entries in lessee's books where short workings arise

1. *Dr.* Short workings account with difference between minimum rent and actual royalties payable calculated on output.
   Cr. Landlord's account with this amount.

2. *Dr.* Landlord's account with the difference between royalties payable on increased output and minimum rent, if short workings are recoverable.
   Cr. Short workings account.

Note: The lessee or user can recover only the short workings incurred. If short workings cannot be fully recouped then the balance will be written off to the profit and loss account.

Example: AB Ltd obtained the right to extract mineral deposits from the land of XY Ltd. Under the terms of the agreement AB Ltd must pay a royalty of £5 per tonne of mineral extracted and a minimum rent of £10 000 a year was imposed. XY Ltd allowed the lessee to recover short workings for a period of three years.

Tonnage extracted:	Year 1	1500 tonnes
	Year 2	2000 tonnes
	Year 3	3000 tonnes

The amounts due to XY Ltd were settled at the end of each year. Ignoring taxation, the appropriate accounts in the books of AB Ltd are written up as follows:

In the ledger of AB Ltd

Royalties Account

Year 1	XY Ltd	£7 500	Year 2	Profit and loss	£7 500
2	XY Ltd	10 000	2	Profit and loss	10 000
3	XY Ltd	15 000	3	Profit and loss	15 000

Short Workings Account

Year 1	XY Ltd	£2 500	Year 3	XY Ltd	£2 500

XY Ltd Account

Year 1	Bank	£10 000	Year 1	Royalties	£7 500
				Short workings	2 500
		£10 000			£10 000
Year 2	Bank	£10 000	Year 2	Royalties	£10 000
Year 3	Short workings	£2 500	Year 3	Royalties	£15 000
	Bank	12 500			
		£15 000			£15 000

Notes

1. Calculation of short workings Year 1

Minimum rent per royalty agreement	£10 000
1500 tonnes at a royalty of £5 per tonne	7 500
Short workings	£2 500

This balance on the short workings account will be shown as an asset on the balance sheet until it is recovered in Year 3.

2. Calculation of short workings in Year 3

3000 tonnes at a royalty of £5 per tonne	£15 000
Minimum rent per royalty agreement	10 000
Amount available for recovery of short workings	£5 000
Restricted to balance on short workings account	£2 500

Royalties receivable

In the previous section the entries have been considered only in the books of the lessee or user. The lessor or owner will also require to enter details of the royalties received in his books.

Accounting entries in lessor's books

1. *Dr.* Lessee's personal account with royalties due to be received.
   Cr. Royalties receivable account.

2. *Dr.* Cash or bank when royalties are received.
   Cr. Personal account of lessee.

Farming

The most unusual feature of this type of activity, as with all farming, is that the stock changes in form. A bag of seed becomes a wheat harvest, lambs become sheep, fruit appears on trees, and so on. Moreover, the asset is able to multiply by natural increase, at the same time as it produces a saleable commodity, such as wool, milk or eggs. Animals may also die or stray. There are, consequently, problems of recording these changes in the asset livestock, and it will be necessary to record births and deaths when profit is to be determined.

Profit determination is usually on a sectional basis, with separate profits being calculated for each class of livestock, and for wool, wheat and chaff, and so on. Arbitrary methods are necessary in determining the values of the natural increases in livestock. Accurate assessment of profit may be rendered difficult because the conventional accounting year does not coincide with the seasonal year.

In recent years, farm management accounting has adopted many of the techniques of the cost accountant in secondary industries, but controls of this type are applied only to the larger pastoral companies. Such techniques as budgetary control, division of costs into fixed and variable, etc., calculation of return per hectare for different types of farming, comparative costs, and so on are becoming commonplace in the more efficient of these companies.

Small business

Most people tend to think that the business world is mainly comprised of large companies, such as ICI plc or Marks & Spencer plc. It comes as something of a shock to realise that easily the majority of business enterprises in the United Kingdom consist of a self-employed owner or owners operating on their own or with just a few staff members. Consider the number of self-employed plumbers, hairdressers, doctors, taxi drivers and farmers, to name but a few, and it is obvious that the country's economy rests as much on the shoulders of what is called the 'small business area' as on the titans of industry. As many small businesses employ few people, it is not possible for such businesses to employ specialists for the multifarious duties that need to be carried out, so these rest on the owner or owners.

Consider the problems facing a self-employed painter, electrician or dressmaker. The owner has to arrange contracts with customers, purchase, finance and maintain a stock of materials needed for the work, cost jobs, prepare and dispatch invoices, carry out necessary banking duties, and keep sufficient records that will enable an assessment of the progress of the business. These are only some of the duties which devolve on persons who, single-handed, operate boutiques, beauty salons, garages, etc., while carrying out the normal daily operations of selling or providing services.

Businesses are run for profit, and it is this possibility of increasing one's income that induces many to attempt self-employment. There is also the advantage of being independent. However, the majority of people are content to work for wages. This spares them possible financial failure, but offers limited scope of gaining increased wealth. Starting a business is a hazardous venture, since it usually means abandoning a steady income and risking the possibility of failure and substantial monetary loss. It also involves the loss of regular paid vacations, while long hours may have to be worked without the benefit of overtime pay. There is also the recurrent danger of sickness or accident, which may mean a complete cessation of all income. Despite these handicaps, the ultimate returns may make it well worth while.

It must be clearly understood by anyone taking the plunge into business that it is not enough to be a good TV or computer hardware mechanic, a first-class cook or a fashionable designer if the financial and management sides are neglected. Adequate planning, systematic record-keeping and the provision of useful operational information is essential for survival, just as much as is the expertise of the owner-operator. Surveys have shown that most failures of small business enterprises spring from this lack of management skill rather than from lack of operational skill.

The problems in accounting for professions and trades may be listed as follows:

1. Most self-employed professional persons and tradesmen are selling their time as well as their skill. Charges are usually based on the time spent, which means that unproductive time must be kept to the minimum. It is essential that adequate records are kept of the allocation of time during the day of each member of the staff as well as the proprietor. Travelling time, telephone conversations, and planning must all be carefully noted. In most cases, there are two aspects of this time allocation. First, each person (employer and employee alike) must keep a personal time-diary which records every quarter or half-hour during each day. Second, it is essential that time spent on particular jobs or projects should be recorded so that the client, patient or customer can be charged. Unproductive time (that is, time which cannot be charged to a debtor), such as staff training sessions, attendance at technical college, and time to write up office work, job or time records will also be properly recorded in order to calculate the cost of overheads.

2. Since many owner–operators work from a home base, it is essential to segregate private expenses from business expenses. This may involve recording the distances travelled in the family car, the number of telephone calls made, and possibly a division of house occupancy costs. This would be particularly important for doctors who have set aside part of a house as a surgery, or carpenters who operate from a workshop on the dwelling premises.

3. Management accounting should be the tool of all business enterprises whether large or small. Regular budgets and budgetary control are desirable. There should be an awareness of the effects of fixed as opposed to variable costs (see Chapter 20). Shopkeepers must be aware of the care needed in calculating mark-ups to ensure all overhead expenses are covered – that larger volumes with smaller profits may bring bigger total profits as well as the advantages of cheaper purchase prices, and so on. Hotels and other lessors need to watch the occupancy rate for their accommodation.

The following variations in the accounting records may be required:

1. In addition to the daily time-keeping records mentioned above, doctors and dentists need to keep records of their patients. Accountants, solicitors, etc. also maintain client files separate from their accounting records.

2. Most professions maintain a fees journal to list the amounts invoiced to clients, and a fees account in the ledger to summarise their revenue.

3. In the case of property owners, it is usual to operate a rent journal and rent account in the same manner as with fees.

4. To relieve the onus of maintaining full accounting records on a double entry basis, many businessmen maintain their records on a single entry or incomplete record system (described later).

5. The final accounts are very little different from those already studied for retailers and wholesalers. The major differences are that there is no trading account section for those in professions, and the classification of expenses is different. Some examples of profit-determining accounts follow:

Solicitor – Profit and Loss Statement for year ended 31 March 19X7

19X6	Income			%
175 000	Gross fees		£200 000	£100.0
100.0%	*Less*			
	Labour cost			
	Professional staff	£66 000		
	Support staff	30 000		
	Temporary staff	900		
81 000	Professional indemnity insurance	3 100	100 000	50.0
(46.3%)				
	Occupancy costs			
	Rent	8 500		
	Rates and taxes	500		
9 000	Cleaning	2 000	11 000	5.5
(5.1%)				
	Finance costs			
	Bank charges	600		
	Bad debts	1 000		
4 000	Interest partners loans	400	2 000	1.0
(2.3%)				
	Office expenses			
	Postage and telephone	3 500		
	Printing and stationery	4 500		
14 000	Lease equipment	2 000	10 000	5.0
(8.0%)				
	Sundry expenses			
	Travelling	400		
	Subscriptions and donations	2 600		
	General insurance	1 500		
6 000	Sundries	500	5 000	2.5
(3.4%)			128 000	64.0
61 000(34.9%)	**Net Profit**		72 000	36.0

Plumber – Profit and Loss Statement for year ended 31 March 19X7

Work done:	on credit	£108 000		
	for cash	12 000		£120 000
Less **Expenses**				
Workshop				
Labour costs		20 000		
Heat, power and light		5 800		
Materials used		45 000		
Gas cylinders etc.		2 500	£73 300	
Vehicle expenses				
Motor van		4 500		
Private car		1 500	6 000	*Cont.*

Other operating expenses

Telephone and postages	£1 200		
Advertising	300		
Accountancy fees	800		
Printing and stationery	400	£2 700	£82 000

Net Profit   £38 000

Medical Practitioner (whose surgery occupied 500 sq. ft of his 2500 sq. ft home) –
Profit and Loss Statement for year ended 31 June 19X7

Gross fees		£103 000	
Add Bank interest		700	
			£103 700
Less **Expenses**			
Surgery supplies	£14 000		
Wages receptionist/nurse	18 000		
Insurance	1 000		
		33 000	
Home/surgery expenses			
Rates	750		
Repairs and maintenance	1 250		
Insurance	650		
Interest on mortgage	4 350		
5/25 to business	7 000	1 400	
Other expenses			
Accountancy fees	500		
Superannuation	1 200		
Interest on over draft	300		
Attendance at seminars	800		
Journals and books	1 200		
	4 000		
Total expenses			38 400
Net profit			£65 300

Incomplete records

As already stated, many small firms do not observe the principles of double entry accounting in the recording of business transactions. Lack of knowledge of accounts on the part of the owner or the failure to employ someone who is conversant with the principles of accounting are perhaps the main reasons for this situation. Many businessmen do not consider the accurate recording of business transactions an important factor in successful trading. This, of course, results in accounting entries being inadequately recorded and if records are kept they are usually in a most unorthodox form. Since variations in the methods of recording transactions occur so frequently it is quite impossible to illustrate all possible systems. The terms to embrace all systems which fall short of the conventional double entry system of accounting is 'incomplete records'. Students of accounting must be skilled in the preparation of final accounts from incomplete records as not only is this an important examination topic but examiners in accounting consider that solving problems of this type is a real test of a student's knowledge and appreciation of double entry accounting. Study of this subject will soon reveal that a sound understanding of the principles of double entry accounting is essential if one is to prepare accounts from incomplete records.

Systems of incomplete records may be broadly classified as follows:

1. Single entry accounting system.

2. Single entry accounting with the introduction of a cash book.

Single entry accounting system

Single entry accounting is, as the term suggests, basically a system which only records one aspect of each transaction, viz the personal aspect. Consequently the only necessary book required to be written up under this system is the ledger. No other books are kept.

For example, if a credit purchase is made by T. Smith from W. Day for £100 on 1 December and paid on 15 December in cash, the entries for such a transaction would only be entered in the ledger:

W. Day Account			
Dec. 15	Cash	£100	Dec. 1	Goods	£100

No other entries would be made. In other words only one entry would be recorded for each transaction. The corresponding entries in the purchases account and in the cash book would not be made.

It is apparent from such a system that the accounting information is not as comprehensive as in a system of double entry accounting. For example, it is not possible under this system to prepare trading and profit and loss accounts showing details of revenue expenditure and income since details of purchases, sales and revenue expenditure are not kept; only debtors and creditors are known. Although a detailed statement of profit or loss cannot be prepared it is still possible to determine the profit or loss of a business for a trading period with reasonable accuracy. This is achieved by compiling a balance sheet or statement of affairs at the beginning and end of the trading period under review. The term 'statement of affairs' is one commonly used in the subject of incomplete records and may be defined as a list of assets and liabilities. The difference between the net assets or capital accounts at the beginning and end of the trading period will determine the overall profit or loss for that period. This is based on the formula that the net assets or capital at the end of the period less the net assets or capital at the beginning of the period equals the profit for the period. A profit arises where the net assets or capital at the end of the trading period exceed those at the beginning of the trading period. On the other hand if the net assets at the beginning of the trading period are in excess of those at the end of the period then a loss has taken place.

This formula can only be used to calculate the profit or loss if the owner of the business has not introduced or withdrawn any amounts from the business during the trading period. If such transactions have taken place then the formula can be expanded to meet this change and becomes:

Net assets or capital at end of period		£X
Add Drawings for period	£X	
Less Capital introduced during period	X	X
		X
Less Net assets or capital at beginning of period		X
Profit or loss for period		£X

Net assets in this formula are total assets less liabilities.

Preparation of statement of affairs or balance sheet

As the ledger is the only book of account maintained under a system of single entry accounting there will be only details of debtors and creditors recorded in the business records. All other amounts required for inclusion in the balance sheet will have to be calculated or estimated at the end of the trading period. The additional information required to produce a statement of affairs or balance sheet may be listed thus:

1. Valuation of fixed assets.

2. Valuation of stock.

3. List of accrued and unexpired charges.

4. Estimate of cash and bank balances.

5. Estimated drawings of owner.

6. Amount of capital, if any, introduced by owner during year.

Those estimates and valuations have, in most cases, to be prepared by the owner of the business and supplied to his professional accountant so that a balance sheet or statement of affairs may be produced. Obviously, the accuracy of the balance sheet and the resulting computation of profit and loss depend to a large extent on the precise information given by the owner of the business. This last statement has greater practical significance than theoretical but is made to illustrate the problems arising in practice on this subject.

This is a problem illustrating the application of the formula to calculate profit from a single entry system of accounting.

Example: The following information relates to A. Carr's business:

Assets and liabilities at	1 Jan.	31 Dec.
Fixtures	£900	£810
Debtors	240	290
Stock	1 200	1 440
Creditors	400	550
Cash	38	12
Balance at bank	780	230
Loan from B. Burton	300	100
Motor vehicle		800

During the year A. Carr had sold private investments for £200 which he paid into the business account, and he had drawn out £10 weekly for private use.

We are required to prepare a statement showing the amount of the profit or loss for the year and a balance sheet at 31 December.

The first step is to prepare a statement showing the profit or loss for the year under review.

Calculation of Profit for the year ended 31 December

Net assets at 31 December	
Fixtures	£810
Motor vehicles	800
Debtors	290
Stock	1 440
Bank	230
Cash	12
	£3 582

Cont.

	b/f		£3 582	
Less Creditors	£550			
Loan – B. Burton	100	650	£2 932	
Add Drawings (52 × £10)			520	
			3 452	
Less Capital introduced – Proceeds of sale of private investment			200	
			3 252	
Less Net assets at 1 January (Note 1)			2 458	
Profit for year			£794	

The next step is to prepare a balance sheet as at 31 December showing the assets and liabilities at that date produced from the information available in the question.

Balance Sheet as at 31 December

Fixed assets			
Fixtures		£810	
Motor vehicle		800	£1 610
Current assets			
Stock		1 440	
Debtors		290	
Bank		230	
Cash		12	
		1 972	
Less **Current liabilities**			
Creditors	£550		
Loan – B. Burton	100	650	1 322
			£2 932
Represented by:			
Capital			
As at 1 January		2 458	
Add Profit for year		794	
Proceeds of sale of private investment		200	
		3 452	
Less Drawings		520	£2 932

Working note: Calculation of net assets of A. Carr at 1 January:

Fixtures		£900
Debtors		240
Stock		1 200
Bank		780
Cash		38
		3 158
Less Loan from B. Burton	£300	
Creditors	400	700
		£2 458

Notes

1. The proceeds of sale of the private investment is treated as capital introduced since this investment was not a business asset but a private one.

2. Notice the use of the formula: (Net assets at end + Drawings for period − Capital introduced during period) − Net assets at beginning = Profit for trading, in solving this problem.

3. A detailed profit and loss account cannot be prepared since no cash book entries have been recorded which are necessary to provide the information to complete such a statement.

Single entry accounting system with the introduction of a cash book

It has been stated in an earlier section that the single entry system of accounting involves only the writing up of one book, viz the personal ledger. In practice it is found that this system, because of its limitations, is very rarely used as the businessman is usually anxious to ascertain more information about the detailed composition of his profit or loss. If a business, however small, is to be efficiently conducted, certain additional information must be known such as gross profit percentage on sales and the various nominal expenses - wages and salaries, heat and light, rent, rates and insurance. Previous years' figures for income and expenditure are also required for cost comparison and to obtain these figures trading and profit and loss accounts have to be prepared. To do this the single entry records have to be converted to double entry. This is accomplished by introducing a cash book thus departing from the fundamental principle of single entry. By writing up a cash book it is possible to convert in total the single entry accounting system to double entry. This technique can be acquired by studying the illustration following this section. Possibly the best form of cash book to use in this system is a tabular one with analysis columns on the debit side for discount allowed, cash sales, amounts received from debtors, and sundry income, and on the credit side columns for discount received, payments to creditors, cash purchases, and the nominal expenses which recur frequently over the trading period. With the cash book so analysed the amounts are in a readily available form to be incorporated in the working notes, which are compiled before preparing the final accounts.

In conclusion, the requirements to convert single entry records to double entry are as undernoted:

1. Statement of affairs or balance sheet at the start of the trading period.

2. Statement of affairs or balance sheet at the end of the trading period.

3. Summary of the receipts and payments during the period.

In theoretical problems adequate information will be given to enable one to compile the above statements, if necessary, which should be shown as working notes before attempting to prepare the trading and profit and loss accounts and balance sheet.

This practical example illustrates the technique adopted to solve a problem where a cash book has been introduced to a single entry accounting system.

Example: B, a retailer, keeps his books on an incomplete records system. The summary of his cash book transactions for the year ended 31 December 19X7 is as follows:

Summary of Cash Book

Balance in bank - 1 January 19X7	£300	Payments to creditors	£11 000
Cash sales	10 000	Cash purchases	500
Received from debtors	5 000	Electricity	50
c/fwd	£15 300		£11 550
			Cont.

b/fwd	£15 300			£11 550
		Rent and rates		100
		Wages		2 000
		Advertising		10
		General expenses		40
		Balance in bank – 31 Dec. 19X7		1 600
	£15 300			£15 300

B submits the following list of his assets and liabilities:

	1 Jan. 19X7	**31 Dec. 19X7**
Stock	£1 500	£1 750
Motor van	800	700
Debtors	400	900
Creditors	1 400	1 600
Accrued charge – Wages	50	30
Prepaid charge – Rates	20	30

Discount received from creditors amounted to £100. B took goods valued at cost £200 for his own use during the year. From the above information we may prepare a trading and profit and loss account for the year ended 31 December 19X7, also a balance sheet as at that date, as follows:

Trading and profit and loss account for year ended 31 December 19X7

Sales (Note (a))		£15 500
Less Cost of sales		
Purchases (Note 1)	£11 600	
Add Stock at 1 January 19X7	1 500	
	13 100	
Less Stock at 31 December 19X7	1 750	11 350
Gross profit for year		4 150
Add Discount received		100
		4 250
Less Expenses		
Wages (Note 1)	1 980	
Rent and rates (Note 1)	90	
Electricity	50	
Advertising	10	
General expenses	40	
Depreciation on motor van (Note 3)	100	2 270
Profit for year		£1 980

Balance Sheet as at 31 December 19X7

Fixed asset		
Motor van	£800	
Less Depreciation	100	£700

Cont.

	b/fwd			£700
Current assets				
Stock			1 750	
Debtors			900	
Prepaid charge			30	
Bank			1 600	
			4 280	
Less **Current liabilities**				
Creditors		£1 600		
Accrued charge		30	1 630	2 650
				£3 350

Represented by:
Capital account

As at 1 January 19X7 (Note 4)	1 570
Add Profit for year	1 980
	3 550
Less Drawings (goods for own use) (Note 5)	200 £3 350

Additional Notes

1. Calculation of purchases, sales, rent and rates, and wages for year:

	Purchases	Sales	Rent and rates	Wages
Per cash book summary	£11 000 ⎫	£5 000 ⎫	£100	£2 000
	500 ⎭	10 000 ⎭		
Add Creditors and Accrued				
charge at 31 Dec. 19X7	1 600			30
Prepayment at				
1 Jan. 19X7			20	
Debtors at 31 Dec. 19X7		900		
Discount received	100			
	13 200	15 900	120	2 030
Less Creditors and accrued				
charge at 1 Jan. 19X7 £1 400				50
Prepayment at				
31 Dec. 19X7			30	
Debtors at 1 Jan. 19X7		400		
Goods taken by B for				
own use 200	1 600			
	£11 600	£15 500	£90	£1 980

The above presentation is in columnar form but this information may be shown in ledger form.

2. Alternative presentation in ledger form:

Creditors' Control Account

Payments to creditors	£11 000	Balance 1 January 19X7	£1 400
Cash purchases	500	Drawings (goods for own use)	200
Discount received	100	Purchases	11 600
Balance 31 December 19X7	1 600		
	£13 200		£13 200

The purchases figure of £11 600 is calculated by totalling the debit entries (£13 200) and deducting the total of the two credit entries (£1 600). The above account is similar in format to the normal creditors' control account and is useful, in this instance, to calculate the purchases amount for the year. For the purposes of simplicity cash purchases have been included in the creditors' control account.

Debtors' Control Account

Balance 1 January 19X7	£400	Received from debtors	£5 000
Sales	15 500	Cash sales	10 000
		Balance 31 December 19X7	900
	£15 900		£15 900

In the same way the sales figure of £15 500 is calculated by totalling the credit entries (£15 900) and subtracting the debit entry (£400). The layout is similar to a debtors' control account and enables the figure for sales to be calculated. Cash sales, in this example, have been included in the debtors' control account.

Rent and Rates Account

Balance 1 January 19X7	£20	Balance 31 December 19X7	£30
Paid during year	100	Profit and loss	90
	£120		£120

The calculation of the rent and rates charge for the year can also be shown in ledger form bringing out the amount to be transferred to profit and loss account.

Wages Account

Paid during year	£2 000	Balance 1 January 19X7	£50
Balance 31 December 19X7	30	Profit and loss	1 980
	£2 030		£2 030

The calculation of wages charge for year is illustrated in ledger form.

3. Calculation of depreciation written off motor van:

Valuation of motor van 1 January 19X7	£800
Less Valuation of motor van at 31 December 19X7	700
	£100

4. Calculation of net assets as at 1 January 19X7:

Assets		
Motor van		£800
Stock		1 500
Debtors		400
Prepaid charge		20
Bank		300
		3 020
Less **Liabilities**		
Creditors	£1 400	
Accrued charge	50	1 450
		£1 570

B's capital = net assets = £1 570

5. **Goods taken for B's own use** The goods taken for B's own use have been valued at cost price and therefore the amount has been adjusted in the purchases for the year. It is usual to value this item at cost price.

Non-trading concerns

This name is given to associations of members such as religious, sporting, literary and benevolent bodies formed for purposes other than profit making. Several of them do operate dining rooms, bars, fairs, sports tournaments with paying spectators, and so on. The profit from such 'trading' is used to further the objects of the group and not to bring financial gain for the members. Such bodies may be incorporated under an Act or may be unincorporated. The major advantage of being incorporated is that the members of the association incur no personal liability for the debts of the incorporated body to which they belong. They must register in the proper legal manner and have a set of rules. The incorporated body has a separate legal identity in the same way as a company. It can sue and be sued, whereas an unincorporated group could only act in the names of all the individual members.

Such a society or club does not have a capital in the way that other enterprises have. It obtains its funds from:

1. members, in the form of fees and subscriptions;

2. donations, from various sources;

3. activities, for example, fairs, gate entrance fees.

The accumulated surplus of these funds over the expenses incurred is called 'accumulated funds'. This takes the place of the proprietorship account for other forms of ownership.

Some non-trading enterprises, such as golf clubs, issue debentures to members and others to raise funds for new land, new buildings, equipment, etc. These debentures (which may be redeemable or irredeemable) are similar to those issued by limited companies. They would be classified as a liability in the balance sheet of the enterprise.

The size of such concerns range from very large bodies, for example conducting a large charity to very small, for example a small sporting body. Their accounting systems may likewise range from the sophisticated to the very simple, as may their accounting reports to members. The larger concerns would adopt the same kind of accounting records and controls as have been described throughout this text, but because the majority of non-trading concerns are quite small, and because the student of accountancy often is elected to be responsible for their financial records, it is proposed to deal briefly with such bodies.

Often a two-column cash book, or a simple columnar cash book is the only accounting record kept. If assets other than cash are required, separate records of these are desirable. A bank account in the name of the body is usually opened, with at least two signatories necessary for the signing of cheques. Properly printed receipt books are desirable, but if bought from a stationery store they should be pre-numbered in sequence. The various items of receipts and payments are then entered from the duplicate receipts and cheque stubs into the cash records under the appropriate column. The totals of the columns may then be used to prepare the financial reports. This type of system may therefore dispense with ledger accounts and is often described as single-entry or incomplete records.

However, it is desirable that a full double entry set of records be kept for larger organisations. Separate ledger accounts would be kept for each type of activity to enable a calculation of the contribution (if any) made by each function or operation towards the total surplus (or deficit) of the organisation. One type of revenue which poses special problems is that of the annual subscriptions where consideration has to be given to the amounts uncollected in any year and to those who pay their subscriptions in advance. The method of calculating the revenue from subscriptions is shown by the following example.

Example: From the receipt book of a certain club it is ascertained that cash received during 19X7 for subscriptions from members amounted to £2340. From the statement of assets and liabilities at 31 December 19X6, it was discovered that £150 was owing for 19X6, and £100 has been paid in advance for 19X7. Further checking revealed that at 31 December 19X7, arrears of subscriptions for 19X7 totalled £200, all the previous arrears had been paid, and subscriptions paid for 19X8 (in advance) amounted to £50. What amount of subscriptions should be included as revenue for 19X7?

The cash received (£2340) included £150 belonging to 19X6 and £50 of 19X8, hence, cash belonging to 19X7 totalled £2140 (£2340 − £150 − £50). To this should be added the other 19X7 subscriptions, that is, £100 received in advance last year and the £200 unpaid at the end of the year. The amount is thus calculated as £2140 + £100 + £200 = £2440. This could be set out in ledger form as follows:

	Subscriptions Account				
19X6			19X6		
Dec. 31	Balance arrears	£150	Dec. 31	Balance advance	£100
19X7			19X7		
Dec. 31	Balance advance	50	Dec. 31	Cash received	2 340
	Current subs	?		Balance arrears	200
		£2 640			£2 640
	Balance arrears	£200		Balance advance	£50

From this arrangement, it is obvious that the missing figure is the difference between the two sides as they stand, that is, £2640 − £200 = £2440. An alternative method of treating subscriptions is to consider each year's subscription as a separate ledger account. Thus, at the end of 1986 the ledger accounts would show the following:

	19X6 Subscriptions Accounts	
Balance arrears	£150	

19X7 Subscriptions Account	
Balance advance	£100

During 19X7, the £150 received in payment of arrears would close off the 19X6 account, the £2140 received for 19X7 would be posted to the credit of the 19X7 subscriptions, and the £50 paid in advance for 19X8 posted to the 19X8 account. At this stage the accounts would appear in the ledger as follows:

19X6 Subscriptions Account			
Balance arrears	£150	Cash	£150

19X7 Subscriptions Account			
		Balance advance	£100
		Cash	2 140

19X8 Subscriptions Account		
	Balance advance	£50

At the end of the current year (19X7), a check of lists of members is made to calculate arrears for that year. This is added to the cash already received for 19X7 subscriptions and the total balance is transferred to the income and expenditure account in the usual way. The account for 19X7 would then show

19X7 Subscriptions Account			
Income and expenditure account	£2 440	Balance advance	£100
		Cash	2 140
		Balance arrears	200
	£2 440		£2 440
Balance arrears	£200		

As previously stated, the profit, or surplus is not distributed to members but transferred to the accumulated funds, which is the name given to the 'capital' of the concern. The usual accounting reports which correspond with trading enterprises are the following:

1. Income and expenditure account or statement. (This compares with the profit and loss statement of a trading concern.)

2. Balance sheet or statement of affairs.

However, in addition to these two reports, because of the importance of cash transactions, it is usual to prepare a statement of receipts and payments, which is virtually a summary of the cash transactions. The distinction between the income and expenditure statement and the receipts and payments statement lies in the familiar 'matching' rule. Whereas *all* receipts and payments are included in this statement (including opening and closing balances of cash), only those items of revenue and expense appropriate to the accounting period concerned belong in the income and expenditure statement.

For example, an issue of debentures which raises funds for a building project is not revenue but is a balance sheet liability; likewise, the acquisition of an asset which will last several periods is also excluded from the income and expenditure statement (except for possible depreciation). They would, however, be included in the statement of receipts and payments if cash were received or paid. Thus, the income and expenditure statement is more significant because it reveals the surplus or deficit of the year's operations. In preparing this report, it is desirable to highlight *net* amounts attributable to separate activities, and, if separate ledger accounts are not kept, it may be necessary to prepare separate schedules or working accounts in order that these separate results may be determined. The following example will illustrate the above points.

Information: The following balance sheet sets out the position of the Savoy Social Club at 1 January:

Liabilities			Assets		
Creditors for:			Furniture and equipment		£300
Cards and materials		£10	Bank		120
Refreshments		60	Billiard table		140
Subscriptions in advance		10	Refreshments stock		70
Accumulated funds account		610	Subscriptions in arrear		40
			Cash in hand		20
		£690			£690

During the year ended 31 December, payments were:
Refreshments, £300; cards and materials, £50; furniture, £30; rent, £160; replacement of crockery, £30; socials, £60; honorarium, £100; expenses, £50.
Receipts were:
Subscriptions, £240; sales of refreshments, £430; socials, £50.

At 31 December, subscriptions in arrear amounted to £60, and subscriptions in advance to £20. The amount owing to creditors for cards was £14, and for refreshments, £56 – both being unpaid. Cash in hand was £24, and value of unsold refreshments was £80. It was decided to write 10 per cent depreciation off the value of furniture and equipment at the beginning of the year and to write down the value of the billiard table to £100.

Prepare:

1. Statement of receipts and payments for period ended 31 December.

2. Income and expenditure statement for the same period.

3. Balance sheet as at 31 December.

4. Schedule showing the detailed composition of:
(a) refreshment trading; (b) subscriptions; (c) socials.

Suggested solution:

Savoy Social Club
Receipts and Payments Statement for year ended 31 December

Cash on hand (1 January)	£20	Refreshments		£300
Cash at bank	120	Cards etc.		50
Subscriptions	240	Furniture		30
Refreshments	430	Rent		160
Socials	50	Crockery		30
		Socials		60
		Honorarium		100
c/fwd	£860			£730

b/fwd	£860		£730
		Expenses	50
		Cash in hand (31 December)	24
		Cash at bank (31 December)	[1]56
	£860		£860

Income and Expenditure Statement for year ended 31 December

Revenue from subscriptions		£250
Revenue from refreshments		144
		£394
Deduct:		
Loss on socials	£10	
Expenses of cards	54	
Rent	160	
Crockery	30	
Honorarium	100	
General expenses	50	
Depreciation, furniture and equipment	30	
Depreciation, billiard table	40	474
Excess of expenditure over income deducted from accumulated fund		£80

Balance Sheet as at 31 December

Liabilities			**Fixed assets**		
Creditors; cards	£14		Furniture and		
Creditors; refresh-			equipment	£300	
ments	56		Billiard table	100	£400
Subscription					
in advance	20	£90	**Current assets**		
Accumulated Fund	610		Subscription arrears	60	
Less Excess expend-			Refreshment stock	80	
iture over			Cash at bank	56	
revenue	80	530	Cash in hand	24	220
		£620			£620

Working schedules:

Refreshment Trading Account

Stock 1 January	£70	Sales	£430
Purchases	296	Stock 31 Dec.	80
Profit	144[1]		
	£510		£510

Socials Trading Account

Expenses	£60	Cash	£50
		Loss	10[1]
	£60		£60

Subscriptions Account

Arrears 1 January	£40	Advance 1 January	£10
Subscriptions this year	250[1]	Cash	240
Advance 31 December	20	Arrears 31 December	60
	£310		£310

Creditors for Refreshments

Cash	£300	Creditors - Balance	£60
Creditors - Balance	56	Purchases	296[1]
	£356		£356
		Balance	£56

Creditors for Cards, etc.

Cash	£50	Creditors - Balance	£10
Creditors - Balance	14	Expenses	54[1]
	£64		£64
		Balance	£14

[1] Missing information obtained through reconstruction of relevant accounts.

Alternatively, for subscriptions the schedule could be:

19X6 Subscriptions			
Balance arrears	£40	Cash	£40[2]

19X7 Subscriptions			
Income and expenditure	£250	Balance advance	£10
		Cash	180[2]
		Balance arrears	60
	£250		£250
Balance arrears	£60		

19X8 Subscriptions			
		Balance advance	£20[2]

[2] Cash received in 19X7 (£40 + £180 + £20) = £240.

Other types of activity

A summary of the types of business activity discussed in this chapter, together with the impact each makes on the accounting records and reports, is shown in Table 15.1.

Table 15.1 General effects of the nature of business activity on accounting.

Accounting areas affected	Types of activity (examples)	Accounting and managerial requirements
Nature, form and content of records and reports	(i) Rent collection, public accountancy practice.	Additional books of prime entry and/or ledgers, e.g. rent received roll, fees earned day book, etc., to record particular types of revenue or expense of a recurring nature. *Cont.*

Accounting areas affected	Types of activity (examples)	Accounting and managerial requirements
	(ii) Hotels, banks, etc.	Dual-purpose records (day book/ledger), to speed production of guests' accounts or bank statements.
	(iii) Solicitors, auctioneers, estate agents, etc.	Separate clients' ledger, bank accounts etc., to separate transactions on behalf of clients from ordinary business transactions.
	(iv) Manufacturers, builders, printers, etc.	Special cost records, to assist managerial decisions, e.g. pricing, production and control, etc.
Control techniques	(i) Manufacturing, build-refining, etc.	Budget controls, standard costing, responsibility accounting, etc. Cost control is vital to ensure adequate profit margins.
	(ii) Sales on extended credit, finance companies, etc.	Follow-up procedures for non-paying or slow-paying customers, to minimise losses.
Profit determination	(i) Long-term construction e.g. civil engineering or long-term production, e.g. wine, forestry.	Estimate of profit for each accounting period before activity completed, to avoid distortion of period profits, e.g. waiting till conclusion of activity.
	(ii) Hire purchase, loans, mortgages, finance generally.	Estimate of profit for each accounting period before payment complete. Realisation of interest revenue delayed beyond an accounting period.
	(iii) Manufacturers, builders.	Valuation of partly completed contracts or production, to enable cost of goods sold to be calculated etc.
	(iv) Mining.	Difficult to determine whether some costs should be treated as assets or expenses. Delay (and doubt) in production of revenue.
	(v) Professional services, e.g. doctors, dentists.	Revenue may be taken on *cash* basis rather than *accrual* basis. High incidence of bad debts: delayed and irregular payment.
	(vi) Livestock farming.	Incorporation of natural increase, use of animals for rations, etc., to enable valuation of closing stocks and calculation of internal expenses.

However, it should be mentioned that the types dealt with were chosen because of the difference in the nature of the accounting problem in each case and not because of their importance in the business world. In order that other unique aspects may be appreciated, the following is a list of a few other special problems which accountants have to solve in varying spheres of activity:
1. The use of a 'cash' basis rather than an accruals' basis in the case of some professional men, for example, doctors.

2. Accounting for royalties in the case of publishing, forestry, etc.

3. Accounting for building societies' contributions.

4. Accounting for dividends, bonus shares and capital gains in unit trusts.

5. Problems of accounting in government, and local authorities.

6. Accounting for the contributions and share of profits for members of a co-operative in the rural industry.

Finally, it must be remembered that neither business activity nor accounting methods and theory remains static, and one of the remarkable features of accounting development over the years has been the way it has adapted to meet the demands made upon it by changing business circumstances – be they changes in the nature of ownership, growth and subsequent sectionalisation, or in the type of activity.

Summary

1. By activity, we mean the kind of business endeavour carried on by a business.

2. There is a large variety of business activity in the world. We have considered some of the more usual kinds of activity only.

3. A particular activity may have general effects upon the form and content of records and reports, the method of profit determination or the additional control techniques involved.

4. Accounting must continually adapt itself to meet the demands caused by changes in the nature of the activities carried on in the business world.

5. Royalties are the amounts paid to the owner of a product for the right to use that product to generate income, or the term can apply to authors for books, artists for paintings, inventors for inventions and landowners for mining.

6. It is important to recognise the difference between a hire purchase agreement and payments by instalments.

7. There is a difference in the accounting treatment of hire purchase transactions in the books of the purchaser and the seller of the goods.

8. Single entry accounting is, as the term suggests, basically a system which only records one aspect of each transaction, viz the personal aspect.

9. The following formula can be used to calculate the profit or loss if the owner of the business has not introduced or withdrawn any amounts from the business during the trading period and a cash book is not maintained.

Net assets or capital at end of period		£X
Add Drawings for period	£X	
Less Capital introduced during period	X	X
		X
Less Net assets or capital at beginning of period		X
Profit or loss for period		£X

10. To convert single entry records to double entry the following information is required:

(a) Statement of affairs or balance sheet at the start of the trading period

(b) Statement of affairs or balance sheet at the end of the trading period

(c) Summary of the receipts and payments during the period

11. Non-trading concerns consists of associations of members such as religious, sporting, literary and benevolent bodies formed for purposes other than profit making.

12. In the accounting for non-trading concerns the accumulated surplus of income over expenses incurred is called 'accumulated funds' and takes the place of the proprietorship account for other forms of ownership.

Discussion questions

15.1 'The special problems that arise because of the nature of the activity require supplementary accounting knowledge rather than a change in basic accounting principles.'

(a) What is meant by the nature of the activity?

(b) Name three types of enterprise (other than those dealt with in the chapter) where the nature of the activity would require 'supplementary accounting methods'.

(c) For each of the three types of enterprise you name, state the special accounting problem(s) involved and how they would be met.

15.2 For each of the activities below:

(a) Give examples of assets, types of revenue and types of expense which result from the nature of the activity.

(b) Indicate some of the adaptations you would make in the design or in the nature of the accounting records for the following:

   a bank;

   a general medical practitioner;

   an educational institution;

   a manufacturer;

   a church.

15.3 In what ways would the accounting (a) records and (b) reports differ between a dentist and a medium-sized retail store owned by three partners?

15.4 Two major problems in accounting are valuation of inventories and the allocation of costs. Give three illustrations of each for businesses engaged in different activities, stating how accountants try to overcome these problems.

15.5 Explain the bookkeeping entries for a hire purchase transaction in the books of a trader buying an asset on hire purchase.

15.6 What do you understand by the net assets basis of calculating the profit of a business? Give two sets of circumstances in which it could be applied. Discuss the factors which limit its accuracy.

15.7 Explain the procedure you would adopt to convert single entry accounting records to double entry.

15.8 Why should the accounting reports of governments differ from those of private enterprise?

15.9 What are the main financial and accounting difficulties facing a new small business in its first few years?

15.10 Why do clubs and societies prepare both a statement of income and expenditure and one of receipts and payments?

Exercises

15.11 AB Ltd acquired plant from XY Ltd under a hire purchase agreement extending over two years from 1 April Year 19X2.

The cash price of the plant was £754 and the terms of payment were a deposit of £160 on 1 April 19X2, and thereafter four half-yearly instalments of £160 each, commencing in October 19X2. Interest was to be charged at the rate of 6 per cent per annum calculated on half-yearly balances.

AB Ltd's accounts are made up annually to 31 December and the plant was to be depreciated over 10 years on the straight-line method, allowing a residual value at the end of the period of £4.

You are required:

(a) To record the transactions in the ledger of AB Ltd until payment is complete.

(b) To give the entries relating to the transactions as they would appear in the profit and loss account for the year ended 31 December 19X5, and the balance sheet at that date.

Income tax is to be ignored. All calculations are to be made to the nearest £.

15.12 On 1 January 19X2, S. Edge purchased a lorry for £2180 and entered into a hire purchase agreement with a finance company under which he paid £440 as deposit, the balance, plus hire purchase charges of £240, being payable by equal monthly instalments over a period of 3 years commencing 1 January 19X2.

Provision for depreciation is made at 20 per cent of the cost of the lorry each year by means of a depreciation account, the asset account for the lorry showing the cost only.

The hire purchase charges are to be regarded as having accrued in equal monthly instalments over the period of the agreement.

You are required to prepare a schedule showing the figures appearing in Edge's balance sheet as at 31 March 19X2, 19X3, 19X4, 19X5, 19X6 and 19X7 for:

(a) the Lorry account

(b) the Lorry Depreciation account

(c) the Hire Purchase account

(d) the hire purchase interest charged in the profit and loss account for the year ending on those dates.

15.13 A. Dee acquired two motor vans under hire purchase agreements as follows:

Registration number	264 DE	456 FA
Date of purchase	30 June 19X7	31 January 19X8
Cash price	£850	£910
Deposit	£94	£118
Interest (assumed to accrue evenly over the period of the agreement)	£108	£144

Both agreements provided for payment to be made in thirty-six equal monthly instalments, commencing on the last day of the month following purchase.

On 1 August 19X8, Van 264 DE was totally destroyed in an accident. On 10 August 19X8:

(a) The insurance company paid £700 in settlement, and

(b) The hire-purchase company accepted £500 in full satisfaction of the agreement.

Dee made up his accounts annually to 28 February and provided depreciation on a straight-line basis at 20 per cent for these vehicles with a full year's depreciation in the year of purchase and no depreciation in the year of disposal.

All instalments were paid on the due dates.

You are asked to record the foregoing transactions in the following accounts:

(i) motor vehicles;

(ii) depreciation;

(iii) hire purchase company.

showing the balances on 28 February 19X9.

15.14 You are required to prepare the hire purchase trading account, memorandum hire purchase debtors and sales accounts, and general trading account for the year ended 31 December 19X8 in the books of Hill and Company. The company commenced trading on 1 January 19X8 and during that year purchases were £10 000 and cash sales £12 000. The following additional sales were made on hire purchase terms:

	Cost price	Selling price	Deposit paid	Monthly instalments	No. of instalments paid during 19X8
Bedroom suite	£100	£150	£30	12 × £10	9
Television set	£80	£100	£40	12 × £5	7
Lounge suite	£90	£120	£30	18 × £5	3

Stock in trade at 31 December 19X8 amounted to £1500.

15.15 The Overseas Mining Company leased mining rights from Arthur Brown on 1 November 19X5, at a royalty of £2 per tonne of ore mined subject to a minimum rent of £2000 per annum with a right to recoup short workings during the first three years.

Output (in tonnes) during the first four years was as follows:

Year ended 31 October 19X6	600
Year ended 31 October 19X7	800
Year ended 31 October 19X8	1 500
Year ended 31 October 19X9	1 800

You are required to prepare appropriate accounts in the books of the Overseas Mining Company for the four years ended 31 October 19X9. You need not write up the relevant parts of the cash book or the profit and loss account.

15.16 Excavators Ltd, a mining company, enters into a five-year lease with Jones & Co, whereby it pays £0.05 per tonne on ore raised, subject to a minimum rent of £1750 per annum.

Excavators Ltd granted a sublease for a similar period to Peters Ltd, which provided for a royalty of £0.10 per tonne. A minimum rent of £500 per annum was payable to Excavators Ltd. Excavators Ltd and Peters Ltd had the right to recoup short workings out of surplus royalties in 19X7 and 19X8 only under the terms of the lease and sublease.

In the first three years the output (in tonnes) was as follows:

	By Excavators Ltd	**By Peters Ltd**
19X6	4 000	2 000
19X7	10 000	5 000
19X8	28 000	12 000

All payments were made at the end of each financial year. You are required to show the accounts in the ledger of Excavators Ltd to record the above transactions for the years 19X6, 19X7 and 19X8.

15.17 George Humphrey keeps his books on a single entry basis and submits the following statement of his affairs at 31 December 19X8:

Statement of Affairs as at 31 December 19X8

Liabilities		**Assets**	
Capital	£7 866	Fixtures	£600
Sundry creditors	807	Stock	3 962
		Sundry debtors	3 220
		Cash at bank	891
	£8 673		£8 673

His statement of affairs at 31 December 19X7 showed his capital as £6751.

He requests you to calculate his profit for the year ended 31 December 19X8, and to redraft the statement of affairs given above.

During the year Humphrey withdrew £75 a month from the business and also took £100 worth of stock for his private use. He received during the year a legacy of £600 and he sold his private car for £210; both these amounts were paid into the business.

Fixtures are to be depreciated by 10 per cent and a provision of 5 per cent is to be made for bad and doubtful debts.

15.18 B. Towe is a medical doctor and he has asked you to prepare his annual accounts for the year to 31 March 19X2. He maintains very good records so that you ascertain that the balances on his accounts at that date are:

Creditors for medical supplies	£106
Capital	5 000
Personal drawings	2 500
Income tax to be paid	514
Stock of medical supplies at 31 March 19X2	94
Medical and surgical equipment	4 200
Depreciation of medical and surgical equipment	600
Cash at bank	6 113
Receipts from patients	4 296
Receipts from National Health Service (as adjusted for amounts due)	12 914
Salaries of staff	2 965
Rent, light and repairs	1 660
Miscellaneous expenses	437
Purchases of medical supplies (as adjusted by stock at 31 March 19X2)	516
Amounts due from patients and National Health Service	3 629
Bad debts	116

Based upon these figures you are asked to prepare the account which you would submit to Dr. B. Towe for the year to 31 March 19X2 and set out a balance sheet as at that date.

15.19 O. Versee kept some notes relating to his own personal affairs At. 1 October 19X5 he had a freehold house which cost him £4500 and at that date the amount outstanding on the mortgage on the house was £2800. He had £560 in the Trustee Savings Bank at that time and his balance on current account with his bank was £320. He also held investments at 1 October 19X5 which cost him £1400. On the other hand he owed his brother P. Versee £500.

During the year O. Versee sold all his investments and made a profit of £410. He was in employment and his salary was £1600 from which taxation and other deductions had been made amounting to £250. The interest he received on money deposited with the Trustee Savings Bank amounted to £43. In addition to his employment, he earned money by working during the evenings and at weekends but kept no records of his receipts and expenditure.

At 30 September 19X6 he still had his house but he had repaid £800 on the mortgage (he also paid interest amounting to £160 net). He repaid his brother the whole of his loan and had £900 in the Trustee Savings Bank and £436 on current account at the bank. He had purchased a motor car costing £700.

O. Versee considered that his personal expenditure during the year would amount to £1500.

You are asked to prepare a statement showing the net income made by O. Versee in respect of the work carried out by him during the evenings and at weekends for the year ended 30 September 19X6.

15.20 These two balance sheets are available in respect of the shop owned by R. Hill:

Balance sheet as at 30 June l9X1		Balance sheet as at 30 June 19X2		
Assets		**Assets**		
Cash at hand	£2 100	Cash at bank		£3 000
Stocks	1 400	Stocks		1 750
Debtors	3 005	Debtors	£3 300	
Machinery	2 000	*Less* Provision for		
Furniture	1 900	doubtful debts	200	
Delivery vehicles	9 000			
				3 100
		Machinery		3 000
		Furniture		2 400
		Delivery vehicles		11 000
	£19 405			£24 250
Liabilities		**Liabilities**		
Creditors	2 650	Creditors		2 900
HP on vehicles	5 000	HP on vehicles		5 000
Capital	11 755	Capital		16 350
	£19 405			£24 250

His payments for 19X1-2 were: furniture £500; creditors £8400; delivery vehicles £2000; advertising £400; machinery £1000; rent £700; interest £60.

His receipts for 19X1-2 were: debtors £9100; sales £4860.

Other non-cash transactions were: bad debts £220; sales returns £180.

You are requested to prepare the profit and loss statement for the year ended 30 June 19X2.

15.21 F. Graham does not keep a set of double entry books. He has asked that you prepare a profit and loss statement and a balance sheet for the year to 30 September 19X8 making use of the information set out below:

Balance sheet of F. Graham as at 30 September 19X7

Liabilities		Assets	
Creditors	£8 500	Cash at bank	£2 500
Capital		Debtors	7 500
F. Graham	38 000	Stocks	6 000
		Furniture and fittings	500
		Motor vehicles	3 000
		Freehold premises	27 000
	£46 500		£46 500

Summary of cash receipts and payments:

Receipts		Payments	
From debtors	£32 000	Wages and salaries	£7 040
Capital	3 000	Drawings	2 080
		Payments to creditors	23 000
		Sundry expenses	1 500

Other items	
Returns to suppliers	£600
Stocks on hand (30 September 19X8)	6 500
Debtors balance (30 September 19X8)	9 500
Creditors balance (30 September 19X8)	3 400
Discount allowed to debtors	550
Discount received from creditors	380

Adjustments:

1. Depreciation to be written off both motor vehicles and furniture and fittings at the rate of 10 per cent p.a.; and off freehold premises at the rate of 2 per cent p.a.

2. Create a provision for doubtful debts fund of 4 per cent of the final debtors balance.

15.22 TB purchased an existing business on 1 December 19X5 for the sum of £20 000. The assets acquired included: premises £13 000, fixtures and equipment £1400 and trading stock £3600. He did not keep any accounting records in the first year but from documents produced by him the following facts were ascertained:

(a) All payments were made by cheque and all receipts banked immediately.

(b) On 1 December 19X5 he opened a bank account in the sum of £1200 and on 31 August 19X6 he deposited a further sum of £500 as working capital.

(c) During the year he received £20 470 in respect of cash sales and payments from debtors. At 30 November 19X6 customers owed the sum of £1656.

(d) At the financial year end 30 November 19X6 he was not able to produce details of amounts paid to suppliers of goods during the year. The only information available was a file of unpaid invoices from suppliers, which produced the amount owing to suppliers at 30 November 19X6 of £1188.

(e) Payments made from his business bank account during the year included rates £260, of which £52 was prepaid, advertising £284, fixtures and equipment £220, wages £1568, general expenses £386, drawings £2080 and £164 for household expenses.

(f) At 30 November 19X6 the selling price of the trading stock was £6400. TB normally expects to sell all goods which will produce for him a gross profit of 25 per cent on selling price. His closing bank balance was £884.

(g) Fixtures and equipment are to be depreciated at 10 per cent.

(i) Prepare a summarised cash account for the year ended 30 November 19X6.

(ii) Prepare the trading and profit and loss accounts for the year, and a balance sheet as at 30 November 19X6, and

(iii) Comment on the first year of trading under the management of TB.

15.23 Prepare an income and expenditure account for the year ended 31 December and a balance sheet as at that date for the New Social Club. The following is an abstract of the cash book for the year.

Cash in hand	£42	Expenses of dance	£43
Cash at bank	100	Repairs to hall	32
Subscriptions	250	Printing	5
Sale of dance tickets	35	Stationery	10
Sale of refreshments	57	Postages	3
Entrance fees	30	Cost of refreshments	65
		New chairs purchased	75
		Sundry expenses	9
		Cash at bank	245
		Cash in hand	27
	£514		£514

On 1 January there were subscriptions in arrears amounting to £12. The corresponding figure for 31 December was £8. Subscriptions in advance on 31 December amounted to £5. There was an invoice for a repair to the hall which was due but unpaid at the end of the year amounting to £17.

You are given the following additional information:

	As at 1 January
Furniture and fittings at valuation	£200
Kitchen equipment	120

The furniture and fittings have been revalued at £250 at 31 December. Depreciation of 10 per cent has to be written off kitchen equipment.

15.24 The following statement was presented to the Annual General Meeting the University Football Club.

University Football Club Statement of Receipts and Payments Year Ended 31 December 19X3

Cash at bank 1 January 19X3		£1 256
Add Receipts for the year		
Subscriptions	£2 360	
Sports Association grant	1 800	
Sale of club ties and sweaters	1 256	
Social functions	2 043	7 459
		£8 715

Cont.

	b/fwd		£8 715
Less Payments for the year			
Purchase of football equipment		1 600	
Purchase of ties and sweaters		1 563	
Affiliation fees		2 300	
Medical equipment		818	
Match and administration expenses		642	
Social functions		1 726	8 649
Cash at bank 31 December 19X3			£66

The treasurer supplied the following additional information:

	1 January 19X3	31 December 19X3
Subscriptions in arrears	£50	£450
Subscriptions in advance	250	60
Football equipment on hand (at cost)	3 200	4 800
Accumulated depreciation: football equipment	1 600	2 100
Creditors – medical equipment	300	—
Ties and sweaters on hand	200	800

(a) Prepare a statement of income and expenditure for the year ended 31 December 19X3.

(b) Prepare a balance sheet as at 31 December 19X3.

(c) A member considers that the substantial decline in the club's bank balance indicates that a rise in subscriptions is necessary for 19X4. Comment on this suggestion in the light of your answer to (a).

15.25 On 1 April 19X5 Edward Watson bought the Prime Butchers Company for a cash price of £4000, acquiring the following assets and liabilities:

Buildings	£3 000
Plant and fittings	200
Debtors	400
Stock of meat	200
Creditors (for purchases)	600

He opened a bank account depositing a further £800 as working capital, and in addition borrowed £2000 from Roger Mitchell at 10 per cent per annum.

He did not bank all proceeds, but made a number of payments out of cash, which during his first year of trading he summarised as:

Stock purchased	£9 728
Slaughtering charges	504
Sundry expenses	872
Heating and lighting	152
Wages (to delivery boy)	164

In addition to the above cash payments, a summary of his cheque stubs discloses the following payments:

Stock purchases	£11 304
Shop wages	864
Personal drawings	1 048
Rates	780
Interest on loan	100

Watson advises that each week he pays into the bank all cash on hand (after meeting cash payments above) except a till float of £20. The total monies paid into the bank are revealed by the paying in book to be £16 140 (exclusive of capital and loan).

At 31 March 19X6, Watson was owed £296 by debtors, and owed £860 to trade creditors and £35 for wages. He considered that he wished to make a provision of 2 per cent per annum for depreciation on buildings, and 10 per cent per annum for depreciation on plant and equipment. The stock at 31 March 19X6 was valued at £580.

(a) Prepare bank and cash accounts for the year ended 31 March.

(b) Prepare a trading, profit and loss account for the year ended 31 March 19X6 and a balance sheet as at that date.

15.26 The balance sheet of the Artisan Golf Club as at 31 December was as follows:

Current liabilities			Fixed assets		
Purchases:			Plant and tools at		
Bar	£147		valuation		£75
Catering	45		Furniture and fittings at		
Light and heat	88		cost less depreciation		840
Rent	280				915
Excise duty	53				
Subscriptions in advance	206	£819	**Current assets**		
			Stock on hand:		
			Bar	£410	
Accumulated fund		1 272	Catering	25	
			Debtors for catering	12	
			Subscriptions in arrear	43	
			Rates and insurance in		
			advance	181	
			Cash at bank	505	1 176
		£2 091			£2 091

A summary of the Cash book for the year is as follows:

Balance at bank		£505	**Purchases**		
Takings:			Bar	2 720	
Bar	3 680		Catering	974	3 694
Catering	982	4 662			
Subscriptions		2 276	**Wages and salaries**		
Locker rents		64	House	826	
Green fees		373	Course	1 435	2 261
c/fwd		7 880	c/fwd		5 955

b/fwd	£7 880		£5 955
		Rent, rates and insurance	852
		Light and heat	206
		Printing and stationery	59
		Telephone and postages	81
		Course maintenance	238
		General house expenses	94
		Excise duty	53
		Balance at bank	342
	£7 880		£7 880

On 31 December:

The club was owing: bar purchases £165; catering purchases £32; rent £280; light and heat £74; Excise duty £60.
Subscriptions paid in advance amounted to £220.
Rates and insurance paid in advance amounted to £198.
Members were owing: catering accounts £16; subscriptions £40.
Stocks on hand were – bar £442; catering £34.
10 per cent is to be written off the book value of the furniture and fittings.

(a) Prepare an income and expenditure account for the year ended 31 December.

(b) Prepare a balance sheet as at that date.

Chapter 16
Funds flow statements

Need for funds statements ☐ Concepts of funds ☐ Statement of source and application of funds ☐ Statement of Standard Accounting Practice 10 ☐ Preparation of funds statements ☐ Funds statement in accordance with SSAP 10 ☐ Fund flow projections ☐ Cash flow statements ☐ Cash budgets

Need for funds statements

In Chapter 1, we said that the funds statement, together with the profit and loss statement and the balance sheet, is one of the three major types of general-purpose whole-enterprise financial accounting reports. However, apart from a brief reference in Chapter 2, we have subsequently ignored the funds statement and concentrated on the other two statements. The major reason for this is that the funds statement does not influence greatly the way in which data are recorded and processed in the accounting system. As we will see later in this chapter, the information required for a funds statement can be obtained from the other two statements.

First, we should seek the reason why users of accounting information seek this third general-purpose financial statement. What does it attempt to show which the other two do not?

The profit and loss statement discloses the profit resulting from the matching of revenue and expenses for the period. It summarises the results of operations and the consequences of such decisions as what products to market, what prices to charge, how much to produce, how much to pay for advertising, and so on.

The balance sheet attempts to show the financial position of the enterprise at a particular point of time. Unlike the profit and loss statement, which is a period statement, the balance sheet is a static statement. It summarises the resources (that is, assets) which the enterprise owns or controls and the claims upon those resources. Part of these claims (the liabilities) rests with persons and entities other than the owners of the firm. The remainder represents the claims of the owners.

Neither of these statements is very useful in attempting to answer such questions as:

> In what ways have funds generated by the operations of the period been utilised?
> How was the new building programme financed?
> Is the enterprise having difficulty in meeting its commitments? If so why?
> Why has the bank overdraft risen?
> Why was the dividend payment so small in comparison with the profits made? etc.

What is required to answer these and similar types of questions is a report which relates to the completed accounting period and one which reflects the consequences of financing decisions as opposed to decisions about operations.

Concepts of funds

The greatest area of controversy centres round the question of what constitute 'funds'. Funds mean different things to different persons at different points in time. Assume that you are stranded in a city late at night and wish to make a call from a public telephone. Your need for funds is for cash in reasonably small denominations. A five pound note, your cheque book, credit cards, and valuable personal possessions, such as a watch or a camera, are of no use to you unless you can convert these resources into funds of the form required.

Some commonly suggested definitions of funds which are capable of being applied to funds statements are:

1. *Cash*. As suggested by the example given above, funds defined as cash are relevant to a very short-term view of liquidity in the situation where other assets cannot be converted into cash quickly enough to meet pressing commitments. For business enterprises, the situation is not common and thus many accountants regard the cash definition of funds as being too narrow.

However, as we observed in Chapter 7, cash is important because a cash receipt or a cash payment is the ultimate consequence of most business transactions. Also, the ultimate test of solvency is to be able to raise cash to meet commitments when due. For these reasons, some accountants and users see merit in the presentation of a cash flow statement which shows the effects of both operating and financing activities on the cash position. We will demonstrate the preparation of a cash flow statement later in this chapter.

2. *Net current monetary assets*. This definition of funds is a slightly broader and longer-term concept of liquidity than is cash. It is calculated by subtracting from current monetary assets (cash, debtors and short-term investments) current monetary liabilities (bank overdraft, short-term accruals and short-term loans).

3. *Working capital*. As explained earlier, working capital is defined as current assets minus current liabilities. Until recently, the most common basis for a funds statement was to use the working capital concept of funds.

4. *Total resources*. In many instances of funds statements the changes in current assets and current liabilities are listed in the body of the funds statement along with the movements in other balance sheet items. No attempt is made, under this method, to summarise in one figure the net change in working capital. This approach is commonly referred to as the 'total resources approach'.

Statement of Source and application of funds

The accounting report which provides information relating to the movement of funds is a statement of source and application of funds, sometimes referred to as a funds statement. It is a technique used to disclose the individual sources and the particular application of funds within the business during the accounting period under review. Although to some extent related it has to be distinguished from a statement of cash receipts and payments since it does not reveal the total cash receipts and payments for the period but merely discloses the net changes that occur during the period under review of comparative financial statements. For example, if cash received from debtors in 19X7 was £100 000 with debtors at beginning of period amounting to £10 000 and debtors at end of period totalling £12 000 then only the sum of £2000, being the difference between the opening and closing debtors, would be treated in the statement of source and application of funds. If a statement of cash receipts and payments was being prepared then the total amount received from debtors would be recorded as an item of income in this statement with no reference being made to the change in the debtors' position during the accounting period. Both statements are valuable in the financial planning and control of a business but must not be confused as to their primary function.

Funds are often visualised by the layman to mean cash but in this context we have to consider funds in a broader sense as working capital funds. To explain the difference in terminology, examine the following transaction. A business purchases plant for use as a business asset on credit terms. No cash at this stage passes between the business and the vendor of the plant, yet there has been an increase in funds in the business by the extension of credit to the business for the purchase of this asset. The source of funds is represented by the credit allowed by the vendor which will appear as a current liability in the balance sheet and the application of funds is reflected in the increase in the fixed asset on the balance sheet by the addition to plant.

One of the most perplexing problems which face businessmen who are not skilled in accounting is why, if profits are earned by a business, is cash not increased proportionately? The question is asked when a businessman finds that he is unable to meet his creditors' accounts on the due date of payment owing to the fact that there is insufficient cash available to meet them; although profits are being earned they never seem to increase the liquidity of the business. The simple answer to this question is that profits very often are invested in assets of the business other than cash. Plant, stock or some other assets may be purchased which will denude the cash resources, so leaving less to meet the normal trade creditors and other current liabilities. This is a symptomatic problem of the business which is expanding and increasing its investment in assets of the business.

Profits do represent a source of funds but their application may be over a number of assets. A statement of source and application of funds does assist in the explanation of changes in both current assets and current liabilities and, by so doing, enables the owners of a business to realise why, for instance, dividends cannot be paid by a company, although high profits have been earned, and also the reason for the depletion in cash resources.

A funds statement also enables management to ensure that the funds obtained from retained earnings are sufficient to finance the increase in working capital and also to decide whether fresh capital is required to finance the purchase of additional fixed assets. This statement affords an early warning of 'over-trading' and allows the owners of a business to carry out the appropriate remedial action before a major financial crisis occurs. It is also a management tool for rational financial planning.

Statement of Standard Accounting Practice 10

This states that all accounts intended to give a true and fair view of the financial position and profit and loss, other than those businesses with turnover or gross income of less than £25 000 per annum, should include a statement of source and application of funds for the year under review and for the corresponding previous year.

The statement is not intended to replace the conventional profit and loss account and balance sheet but to be complementary thereto by showing the manner in which the operations of a company have been financed and in which its financial resources have been used. In this way the funds statement will provide a link between the balance sheet at the start of the period, the profit and loss account for the period and the balance sheet at the end of the period.

The statement gives details of the funds generated or absorbed by the business operations and the way in which any resulting surplus of liquid assets (cash at bank and in hand and cash equivalents) has been applied or any deficiency of such assets has been financed, distinguishing between the long and short terms. There should be a distinction drawn between the use of funds for the purchase of new fixed assets and funds used in increasing the working capital of the company.

The amounts shown in the funds statement should be identifiable from the profit and loss account, balance sheet and supporting notes.

The statement should show the profit or loss for the year under review, together with adjustments required for items which did not use or provide funds in the year.

The following other sources and applications of funds should, where material, also be shown:

1. Dividends paid.

2. Acquisitions and disposals of fixed and other non-current assets.

3. Funds raised by increasing or expended in repaying or redeeming medium- or long-term loans or the issued capital of the company.

4. Increase or decrease in working capital, subdivided into its components, and movements in net liquid funds.

Where a funds statement is prepared for a holding company and subsidiaries it should be based on the group accounts.

Specimen presentation of funds statement

Althouth SSAP 10 does not prescribe a format which must be followed it does offer a specimen presentation which is shown below and is advised to be used for examination purposes. This presentation is included as an appendix to SSAP 10.

Company without Subsidiaries
Statement of Source and Application of Funds for year ended ....

Source of funds			
Profit before taxation			£X
Adjustments for items not involving the movement of funds:			
Depreciation			X
Total generated from operations			X
Funds from other sources			
Issues of shares for cash			X
			X
Application of funds			
Dividends paid		£X	
Tax paid		X	
Purchase of fixed assets		X	X
			X
Increase/decrease in working capital			
Stocks		X	
Debtors		X	
Creditors (excluding taxation and propósed dividends)		X	
Movements in net liquid funds			
Cash balances	£X		
Short-term investments	X	X	X

In limited company accounts the figures for the previous year would also be shown.

Preparation of funds statements

The basic approach to the preparation of a funds statement is the comparison, item by item, of two consecutive balance sheets and the calculation of the increases and decreases in each balance sheet item. These changes may be classified in three groups:

1. Changes which reflect the provision of funds – sources.

2. Changes which reflect the use of funds – applications.

3. Changes independent of fund movements.

As an example of 3, if a company has revalued land during the last accounting period then such action will have had the effect of increasing the fixed asset 'land' in the closing balance sheet and, at the same time, increasing a 'revaluation reserve' in the same balance sheet. However, this action has not changed the amount of resources under the company's control and should not affect the funds statement.

As well as information derived from such a comparison of consecutive balance sheets, some information available from the period's profit and loss statement and information derived directly from ledger accounts may also be useful in preparing a funds statement. This is true particularly in the calculation of the amount of funds generated from operations.

Before proceeding to an example we must attempt to summarise the major types of sources and applications of funds and the means by which comparative balance sheets and other available information may be utilised to produce the figures to be included in the funds statement. This is given in Table 16.1.

Table 16.1   Major types of fund flows.

Common sources of funds	How revealed
1 Self-generated – i.e. from profitable operations	Profits as disclosed in profit and loss statement adjusted for internal transactions as discussed below
2 New capital introduced	Increased proprietorship
3 Borrowing on long-term basis	Increased long-term liabilities
4 Borrowing on short-term basis	Increased current liabilities
5 Disposal of fixed assets	Decrease in fixed assets
6 Conversion of current assets	Decrease in current assets

Common applications of funds	How revealed
1 Loss in trading operations	Losses as disclosed in profit and loss statement adjusted for internal transactions
2 Profits withdrawn by owners	Dividends, drawings as shown in appropriation account or balance sheet
3 Repayment of long-term borrowings	Decrease in long-term liabilities
4 Reduction of short-term borrowings	Decrease in current liabilities
5 Purchase of fixed assets	Increase in fixed assets
6 Application to current assets	Increase in current assets

It is a fundamental concept in the preparation of a source and application of funds statement that a comparison is made between two balance sheets of a business, one showing the position at the beginning of the period and the other at the end of the period under review. The differences between the amounts in the two balance sheets represent the changes in the accounts which require to be interpreted as to their precise meaning. Such comparisons facilitate the discovery of the major sources and applications of funds and also indicate the efficient stewardship or otherwise of the funds of the business by its management.

Before attempting to prepare a source and application of funds statement, consider the following abridged balance sheets for years 19X3 and 19X4 which are shown in columnar form with the net change in each account recorded in the end column.

Ace Limited
Abridged Balance Sheet and Changes for 19X3 and 19X4

	19X3	19X4		Change
Assets				
Property	£25 000	£31 000	+	£6 000
Plant	18 000	21 000	+	3 000
Stock	60 000	54 000	−	6 000
Debtors	35 000	39 000	+	4 000
Cash	1 000	2 000	+	1 000
	£139 000	£147 000	+	£8 000
Liabilities				
Share capital	£55 000	£65 000	+	£10 000
Profit and loss account	39 000	44 000	+	5 000
Debentures	10 000	8 000	−	2 000
Creditors	24 000	21 000	−	3 000
Bank overdraft	4 000	2 000	−	2 000
Current taxation	5 000	5 000		—
Proposed dividends	2 000	2 000		—
	£139 000	£147 000	+	£8 000

From this type of layout we can interpret the financial statements more easily than by examining them in the more conventional style. Changes in the accounts become more obvious. It is clear from this analysis that the issued share capital has increased by £10 000 and the debentures have been reduced by £2000. Also, there have been increases in plant of £3000 and property £6000. Significantly, there has been an increase in the profit and loss account balance amounting to £5000 which reflects the profit for the year. This basic type of information becomes readily apparent from scrutiny of this form of financial statement. It is a useful technique but it does not entirely reflect the distinction between the source of funds and the use of funds. Nevertheless it does form the basis for producing a source and application of funds statement, albeit in a crude pattern.

From the changes in the balance sheet of Ace Limited between 19X3 and 19X4 it is possible to prepare a funds statement in a simple form showing the source and application of funds during the latter period.

Statement of Changes in Balance Sheets of Ace Limited between 19X3 and 19X4

Source of Funds	
Increase in profit and loss account	£5 000
Decrease in stock	6 000
Increase in share capital	10 000
	£21 000

Cont.

Application of Funds	
Increase in property	£6 000
Increase in plant	3 000
Increase in debtors	4 000
Increase in cash	1 000
Decrease in debentures	2 000
Decrease in creditors	3 000
Decrease in bank overdraft	2 000
	£21 000

In layman's terms, this statement really shows where funds came from and to what purpose they were used and is produced by a rearrangement of the balance sheet changes.

The foregoing statement can be shown in the conventional form as a statement of source and application of funds drawn up using the format stated in SSAP 10.

Ace Limited
Statement of Source and Application of Funds for Year ended 31 December 19X4

Source of funds			
Profit for year			£5 000
Total generated from operations			5 000
Funds from other sources			
Issue of shares			10 000
			15 000
Application of funds			
Purchase of fixed assets – Property	£6 000		
Plant	3 000	£9 000	
Repayment of debentures		2 000	11 000
			4 000
Increase in working capital			
Decrease in creditors		3 000	
Increase in debtors		4 000	
		7 000	
Less Decrease in stock		6 000	
		1 000	
Movements in net liquid funds			
Decrease in bank overdraft	2 000		
Increase in cash	1 000	3 000	£4 000

Example: Following are the abridged and not fully classified financial statements of the FIB Co. Ltd.

In addition to the information contained in these statements the following other information is available.

1. During the year, motor vehicles which had cost £21 000 and which had been depreciated by £13 500 were sold. New motor vehicles costing £34 500 were purchased during the year.

2. The directors had authorised:

(a) Transfers to general reserves of £8000.

(b) A dividend of £21 000 which was paid prior to 30 June 19X6.

3. Corporation tax paid during the year was £30 000.

FIB Co. Ltd
Profit and Loss Statement for the year ended 30 June 19X6

Sales revenue		£335 000
Less Cost of goods sold		161 500
Gross margin		173 500
Add Gain on sale of motor vehicles		3 500
		177 000
Less **Other expenses**		
Advertising	£4 500	
Salaries	56 000	
Depreciation of motor vehicles	11 000	
Office expenses	9 000	
Depreciation of buildings	3 000	
Insurance	4 500	
Interest	9 000	
Amortisation of goodwill	5 000	102 000
Net profit before tax		75 000
Less Corporation tax		35 000
Net profit after tax		£40 000

We will proceed to prepare a funds statement for the FIB Co. Ltd adopting the requirements of SSAP 10. Before presenting this statement, it may be useful to explain:

1. The changes in all balance sheet items and the significance of each to the preparation of the funds statement.

2. The calculation of the amounts of funds generated by profitable operations.

3. The significance and use of the additional information given above.

FIB Co. Ltd
Balance Sheets as at 30 June 19X5 and 30 June 19X6

	19X5		19X6	
Cash at bank		£5 000		—
Debtors		30 000		£32 000
Stocks		38 000		50 000
Prepaid insurance		3 000		2 500
Motor vehicles	£81 000		£94 500	
Less Provision for depreciation	23 000	58 000	20 500	74 000
Buildings	84 000		129 000	
Less Provision for depreciation	11 000	73 000	14 000	115 000
Land		70 000		115 000
Goodwill		55 000		50 000
		£332 000		£438 500

Bank overdraft	—	£12 000
Creditors	£18 500	22 000
Accrued salaries	1 500	1 000
Accrued interest	1 000	1 500
Corporation tax payable	30 000	35 000
Debentures	30 000	50 000
Loan on mortgage	31 000	24 000
Paid-up capital (£1 shares)	150 000	180 000
Share premium account	—	24 000
General reserve	22 000	30 000
Unappropriated profits	48 000	59 000
	£332 000	£438 500

1. *Balance sheet changes* An analysis of the changes in balance sheet items appears below. Note that some of the changes affect the funds statement directly, some have no funding implications and others, while affecting the funds statement, require further analysis.

Analysis of changes in balance sheet items for funds statement purposes

	Changes		Significance to funds statement
	Increases	Decreases	
Cash at bank		5 000	Source of funds
Debtors	2 000		Application of funds
Stock	12 000		Application of funds
Prepaid insurance		500	Source of funds
Motor vehicles[1]	13 500		Application of funds[1]
Prov. for dep. – Motor vehicles[1]		2 500	Affects funds from operations[1]
Buildings	45 000		Application of funds
Prov. for dep. – Buildings	3 000		Affects funds from operations
Land	45 000		Application of funds
Goodwill		5 000	Affects funds from operations[1]
Bank overdraft	12 000		Source of funds
Creditors	3 500		Source of funds
Accrued salaries		500	Application of funds
Accrued interest	500		Source of funds
Corporation tax payable	5 000		Does not affect funds
Debentures	20 000		Source of funds
Loan on mortgage		7 000	Application of funds
Paid up capital	30 000		Source of funds
Share premium account	24 000		Source of funds
General reserve	8 000		Does not affect funds
Unappropriated profits	11 000		Does not affect funds

[1]*Note*: These items require further analysis, as vehicles were sold, as well as purchased, during the period.

2. *Funds from operations* The information necessary to calculate the amount of funds generated by profitable operations is obtained primarily from the profit and loss statement. Most revenue items and most expense items represent fund flows during the current period. For example, sales revenue results in an increase of either cash or debtors. Expenses such as wages, insurance, interest, etc. use up funds. However, there are some profit and loss statement items

for which there is no corresponding flow of funds. The most common example is the expense of depreciation on fixed assets. The depreciable asset required funds in the period in which it was acquired, but in subsequent periods the depreciation of that asset is a 'book entry' which has no effect on funds however they are defined.

Thus, in order to calculate 'funds from operations', we must scrutinise carefully the profit and loss statement for any revenue or expense items which do not reflect movements of funds.

Notes

1. These items require further analysis, as vehicles were sold as well as purchased and an amount was writte off goodwill during the period.

In the FIB Co. Ltd example given above there are three items of this nature. Although three of the expenses, 'depreciation on motor vehicles' £11 000, 'depreciation on buildings' £3000 and 'amortisation of goodwill' £5000, have not required funds they are shown separately in the first section of the funds statement and adjusted on the 'profit before tax' figure. The other item to be shown in this section is the revenue amount 'gain on sale of motor vehicles' £3500. This amount may be regarded as a recoupment of depreciation charged in previous periods and like depreciation has no funding effect. These four items are referred to as 'items not involving movement of funds' in the funds statement. It has to be noted that the amount *received* from the sale of motor vehicles is shown as a source of funds.

SSAP 10 treats 'taxation expense' as an expense not requiring funds in the current period. Therefore 'funds generated from operations' is calculated on a pre-tax basis and the amount of taxation actually *paid* for the last year is shown as an application of funds. Also the same treatment is applied to dividends; only dividends actually *paid* are shown as an application of funds.

2. Using the information given in the profit and loss statement of FIB Co. Ltd. example, the 'total funds generated from operations' is calculated thus:

Net profit before tax		£75 000
Add Depreciation of motor vehicles	£11 000	
Depreciation of buildings	3 000	
Amortisation of goodwill	5 000	19 000
		94 000
Less Gain on sale of motor vehicles		3 500
Total funds generated from operations		£90 500

This method is often used in practice, and some accountants show this calculation in the body of the funds statement. The major reason given is that it provides a link between the profit and loss statement and the funds statement, the last amount in the profit and loss statement becoming the first figure in the funds statement.

3. *Use of additional information* The additional information available regarding the fixed asset 'motor vehicles' gives a fuller picture of the funding implications than would be available from a comparison of the two consecutive balance sheets. It is often useful here to reconstruct the relevant ledger accounts.

Motor Vehicles (at cost)

19X5			19X6		
July 1	Balance	£81 000	June 30	Vehicles sold	£21 000
19X6					
June 30	New motor vehicles	34 500		Balance	94 500
		£115 500			£115 500

Provision for Depreciation of Motor Vehicles

19X6			19X5		
June 30	Depn on vehicles sold	13 500	July 1	Balance	£23 000
	Balance	20 500	June 30	Depn for year	11 000
		£34 000			£34 000

Sale of Motor Vehicles

19X6			19X6		
June 30	Motor vehicles at cost	£21 000	June 30	Provn for dep.	£13 500
	Gain on sale	3 500		Cash amount received on sale	11 000*
		£24 500			£24 500

Thus, we have been able to calculate the asterisked figure of £11 000, the proceeds from the sale of motor vehicles and a source of funds. You should note that some examples they may be given may not contain so much information as this one and other 'missing figures' may have to be calculated.

The other additional information concerns the appropriation of profits. It is often useful to reconstruct the unappropriated profits (or retained earnings) account:

Unappropriated Profits

19X6			19X5		
June 30	Dividends	£21 000	July 1	Balance	£48 000
			19X6		
	General reserve	8 000	June 30	Net profit	40 000
	Balance	59 000			
		£88 000			£88 000

In this case, the above exercise served only to confirm that all information with respect to unappropriated profits had been provided and no new information was obtained. However, you should note that in some examples, reconstruction of this account may be necessary to obtain figures not otherwise available.

We can now proceed to prepare a funds statement adopting SSAP 10.

Funds statement in accordance with SSAP 10

Before preparing a source and application of funds statement in accordance with SSAP 10 it may be useful to show a statement of net changes in the two balance sheets covering the period of the statement. By adopting this approach you will have calculated most of the amounts which have to be shown in the funds statement. As you will see from this statement, further analysis has to be carried out relating to certain of the items, viz fixed assets, corporation tax, general reserve and unappropriated profits, since we cannot simply enter the net difference in these. Nevertheless, the statement of changes in the balance sheets is a useful working note prior to preparing the funds statement.

FIB Co. Ltd
Balance Sheets as at 30 June 19X5 and 19X6 – Statement of Changes

	19X5		19X6		Change	
Cash at bank		£5 000		—	—	£5 000
Debtors		30 000		£32 000	+	2 000
Stock		38 000		50 000	+	12 000
Prepaid insurance		3 000		2 500	—	500
Motor vehicles	£81 000		£94 500			
Less Depreciation	23 000	58 000	20 500	74 000	+	16 000[1]
Buildings	84 000		129 000			
Less Depreciation	11 000	73 000	14 000	115 000	+	42 000[2]
Land		70 000		115 000	+	45 000
Goodwill		55 000		50 000	—	5 000[3]
		£332 000		£438 500		£106 500
Bank overdraft		—		£12 000	+	£12 000
Creditors		£18 500		22 000	+	3 500
Accrued salaries		1 500		1 000	—	500
Accrued interest		1 000		1 500	+	500
Corporation tax payable		30 000		35 000	+	5 000[4]
Debentures		30 000		50 000	+	20 000
Loan on mortgage		31 000		24 000	—	7 000
Paid-up capital (£1 shares)		150 000		180 000	+	30 000
Share premium account		—		24 000	+	24 000
General reserve		22 000		30 000	+	8 000[5]
Unappropriated profits		48 000		59 000	+	11 000[6]
		£332 000		£438 500		£106 500

Notes: Before preparing the funds statement an analysis of the items numbered above is required:

1. Motor vehicles
   Details of this change are shown earlier in this chapter.

2. Buildings

Cost 19X6	£129 000		
Less Cost 19X5	84 000	£45 000	Application of funds
Depreciation 19X6	14 000		
Less 19X5	11 000	30 000	Shown as an adjustment on profits
		£42 000	= Change

3. Goodwill

At 19X6	£50 000		
At 19X5	55 000	£5 000	Shown as an adjustment on profits.

4. Corporation tax payable

Taxation paid	£30 000	Application of funds.
Provision for taxation payable	35 000	Deducted in profit and loss statement
	£5 000	Change

5. General reserve

At 19X6	£30 000	
At 19X5	22 000	
	£8 000	Change – this is an appropriation of profits and does not affect the funds statement – see below

6. Unappropriated profits

At 19X6	£59 000	
At 19X5	48 000	
	£11 000	Change

Accounted for by:			
Profits before tax		£75 000	
Less Provision for tax payable		35 000	See above
		40 000	
Less Dividends paid	£21 000		Application of funds
Transfer to general reserve	8 000	29 000	See above
		£11 000	

We can now proceed to prepare a funds statement in accordance with SSAP 10 based on our calculations made earlier:

FIB Co. Ltd
Statement of Source and Application of Funds for Year Ended 30 June 19X6

Source of funds			
Profit before taxation			£75 000
Adjustments for items not involving			
the movement of funds:			
Depreciation - Motor vehicles	£11 000		
Less Gain on			
sale	3 500	7 500	
Buildings		3 000	
Amortisation of goodwill		5 000	15 500
Total generated from operations			90 500
Funds from other sources			
Issue of shares		30 000	
Share premium on issue		24 000	
Issue of debentures		20 000	
Proceeds of sale of motor vehicles		11 000	85 000
			175 500
Application of funds			
Dividends paid		21 000	
Corporation tax paid		30 000	
Purchase of motor vehicles		34 500	
Purchase of buildings		45 000	
Purchase of land		45 000	
Repayment of mortgage		7 000	182 500
			7 000
Decrease in working capital			
Increase in debtors	2 000		
Increase in stock	12 000		
Decrease in accrued salaries	500		
	14 500		
Less Decrease in prepaid insurance	500		
Increase in accrued interest	500		
Increase in creditors	3 500	4 500	10 000
Movement in net liquid funds:			
Increase in bank overdraft		12 000	
Decrease in cash at bank		5 000	17 000	7 000

Note: Since

Working capital = current assets − current liabilities,

Increase in current assets = increase in working capital,

Decrease in current assets = decrease in working capital,

Increase in current liabilities = decrease in working capital,

Decrease in current liabilities = increase in working capital.

Fund flow projections

As stated earlier in this chapter, one of the principal objectives of a funds statement is to summarise the consequences of financing decisions. In the FIB Co. Ltd example, it can be seen from the funds statements that the company decided to expand significantly its non-current assets (motor vehicles, land and buildings). This required funds of £124 500 during the 19X5–6 financial year. This expansion was financed partly by issues of both share and debenture capital and further by the retained funds generated from profitable operations. However, these sources together were not sufficient to finance all funding requirements and the company's working capital was 'run down' by £7000. (We return to this example later in Chapter 19 where we use it as an illustration of analysing and understanding financial statements.)

The usefulness, from a management point of view, of funds statements like the one illustrated above is limited by the fact that, like the other financial statements on which they are based, they are historical in nature. The financial decisions have already been taken, the funds for expansion have been committed and the new capital raisings have been undertaken. More useful for management decision-making purposes are projected or forward-looking funds statements. Management should attempt to plan what expansions it will undertake, the funding requirements of such plans and where these new funds can best be obtained. This is, of course, part of the process of budgeting, which will be further developed in this chapter and, later, in Chapter 20.

Cash flow statements

As stated in this chapter, some accountants and some users of accounting reports prefer to define funds in terms of cash and thus to present a report which shows the sources and uses of cash for the period. One way of preparing such a report is to extract from the ledger and the cash book the movements in cash for the period in terms of the major items of cash receipts and the major items of cash payments. A statement of receipts and payments is particularly important for organisations such as charities and sporting and social clubs where most of the transactions are cash transactions and where the custodianship of cash funds is important. In Chapter 15, we discussed the reports of non-trading enterprises and provided an example of a statement of receipts and payments.

For a business enterprise, it is more useful to relate movements of cash to financing decisions in the same manner in which movements in working capital are linked to such decisions in the type of funds statement illustrated earlier. Again we may start by calculating the funds (in this case cash) generated by profitable operations. For the FIB Co. Ltd example, this calculation, together with supporting explanations, is given below. We can then use the changes in fixed assets, long-term liabilities and owners' equity, as given previously, to produce the statement of cash flows given on page 389.

FIB Co. Ltd.
Calculation of Cash Provided by Operations

Collections from sales revenue[1]		£333 000
Less		
Payments to suppliers[2]	£170 000	
Advertising	4 500	
Salaries[3]	56 500	
Office expenses	9 000	
Insurance[4]	4 000	
Interest[5]	8 500	
Corporation tax payments[6]	30 000	282 500
		£50 500

Notes

1. Collections from sales revenue = Sales revenue − Increase in debtors.

   = £335 000 − £2000 = £333 000

2. Purchases = Cost of goods sold + Increase in stock

   = £161 500 + £12 000 = £173 500

   Payments to suppliers = Purchases − Increase in creditors

   = £173 500 − £3500 = £170 000

3. Salary payments = Salaries expense + Decrease in accrued salaries

   = £56 000 + £500 = £56 500

4. Insurance premiums = Insurance expense − Decrease in prepaid insurance

   = £4500 − £500 = £4000

5. Interest payments = Interest expense − Increase in accrued interest

   = £9000 − £500 = £8500

6. Corporation tax payments = £35 000 − £5000 = £30 000.

Cash budgets

Again, from a management point of view, historical cash flow statements are of limited usefulness. The best use of available cash funds is made possible only after careful consideration of the enterprise's future requirements.

The need for predictive or 'forward-looking' accounting arises not only with cash but with all areas of the accounting system. Thus, a cash budget (a list of estimated future cash receipts, estimated future cash payments and the estimated future cash position) is usually only a part of an integrated set of budgets for the business as a whole. Some of the more important budgets usually prepared are the sales budget, the production budget (for a manufacturer), the stock budget, the expense budget, the capital expenditure budget, the budgeted profit and loss statement and the budgeted balance sheet. Brief reference will be made to some of these budgets in Chapter 20.

Some of the factors which make the preparation of a cash budget desirable are:

1. An enterprise's reputation and goodwill depend to some extent on its ability to meet its commitments in cash when they fall due.

FIB Co. Ltd
Statement of Cash flows for the year ended 30 June 19X6

Sources of Cash

1. Cash provided by operations	£50 500
2. New issue of shares – 30 000 £1 shares at £1.80 per share	54 000
3. Issue of debentures	20 000
4. Sale of fixed assets – Motor vehicles	11 000
5. Decrease in bank balance	17 000
	£152 500

Cont.

Applications of Cash

1. Dividends paid		£21 000
2. Reduction of long-term liability – Loan on mortgage		7 000
3. Acquisition of fixed assets		
Motor vehicles	£34 500	
Buildings	45 000	
Land	45 000	124 500
		£152 500

2. There is very often a considerable time lag between the earning of revenue and its collection in cash. A healthy trading position does not always mean a healthy liquid position.

3. Many businesses depend on borrowed funds (for example, bank overdraft), and the interest payable on that finance is an important expense. It is desirable to plan so that the interest expense is minimised as far as possible.

4. Many businesses are seasonal in nature – they require large amounts of cash in one part of the year and have excess cash at others. This makes careful planning a vital factor.

5. Internally, the preparation of budgets of cash outlays helps to curtail waste and inadvisable expenditure. Those in charge of the various sections or departments of the business know the target aimed for. The preparation of a budget forces a review of the present position and future plans, and should increase the efficiency of the organisation.

6. The avoidance of funds lying idle in the bank. (Amounts in current accounts do not usually earn interest.)

In the management of its cash resources, a number of the above points may conflict: it is difficult to assess what is an optimal cash balance at any time, bearing in mind the need to pay on time but avoid idle excesses. External economic fluctuations are difficult to predict, and many profitable and otherwise financially sound enterprise have got into difficulties because of a failure to maintain sufficient liquidity following sharp changes in the economic climate. While a carefully considered cash budget is the keystone of liquidity management, it is supported by several other concepts (to be found in the literature of business finance), which are outside the scope of this text.

Cash budgeting is usually carried out on a monthly basis (sometimes divided into smaller periods) and covers a period from three to six months in advance. It is usually difficult to make accurate estimates beyond this. Here is an example of a simple cash budget:

Information:

1. It has been found in the past that credit customers pay about 60 per cent of their accounts in the month following purchase and 30 per cent of the total in the second month. The last 10 per cent is usually paid in the third month and bad debts are rare. Information obtained regarding sales:

		Cash sales	Credit sales
Actual sales	November 19X5	£20 000	£40 000
	December 19X5	10 000	15 000
	January 19X6	8 000	12 000
Estimated sales	February 19X6	18 000	30 000
	March 19X6	24 000	45 000
	April 19X6	10 500	36 000
	May 19X6	21 000	43 000

2. Purchases have to be paid for during the month following receipt of goods. Purchases information:

Actual purchases	January 19X6	£7 500
Estimated purchases	February 19X6	32 000
	March 19X6	25 000
	April 19X6	18 000

3. Wages amount to £2000 per month and other expenses to be paid in cash should total £3100 per month.

4. A payment of £48 000 has to be made to the contractor for new buildings in March and income tax of £18 500 has to be paid in April.

5. At 31 January 19X6 the business had a bank overdraft of £9500.

Prepare a cash budget for the months of February, March, April and May, 19X6.

Procedure:
The most involved step in preparing a cash budget on the basis of the above information is the calculation of estimated receipts from debtors. The following worksheet is a useful way of setting out this calculation.

		Receipts from debtors			
		Estimated to be received in –			
Credit sales in		**February**	**March**	**April**	**May**
November	£40 000	£4 000			
December	15 000	4 500	£1 500		
January	12 000	7 200	3 600	£1 200	
February	30 000		18 000	9 000	£3 000
March	45 000			27 000	13 500
April	36 000				21 600
		£15 700	£23 100	£37 200	£38 100

Then the cash budget may be set out as follows:

Cash Budget for four months February–May 19X6

	February	March	April	May
Estimated receipts				
Cash sales	£18 000	£24 000	£10 500	£21 000
Receipts from debtors	15 700	23 100	37 200	38 100
Total estimated receipts	£33 700	£47 100	£47 700	£59 100
Estimated payments				
Wages	£2 000	£2 000	£2 000	£2 000
Other expenses	3 100	3 100	3 100	3 100
Payments to creditors	7 500	32 000	25 000	18 000
Builder		48 000		
Corporation tax			18 500	
Total estimated payments	£12 600	£85 100	£48 600	£23 100

	February	**March**	**April**	**May**
Bank balance (1st of month)	£9 500 OD	£11 600 CR	£26 400 OD	£27 300 OD
Excess of receipts over payments	21 100			36 000
Excess of payments over receipts		38 000	900	
Bank balance (end of month)	£11 600 CR	£26 400 OD	£27 300 OD	£8 700 CR

From the budget it can be seen that provision will have to be made for an extended overdraft or other temporary finance to cover the deficiency in March and April.

The usefulness of a cash budget (or any other budget) does not end when the prepared plan is put into operation. Valuable knowledge is,-of course, gained in preparing and planning the means of finance. However, the concept of budgetary *control* takes on a great deal of real significance when the actual results for the period are compared with the budgeted figures for the same period. Discovering the causes for variations between the two can result in positive action by management to correct undesirable trends before it becomes too late to do so. The above example shows the estimated position. Furthermore, it is prepared for a single level of activity only. This is a fixed budget, as distinct from a flexible budget, which can estimate the position for several different levels (or a range) of activity. The latter is generally considered desirable, and introduces the need for a conceptual understanding of how changes in the level of activity affect a budget. This together with a comparison of actual results with budgeted figures is discussed in Chapter 20.

Summary

1. A funds statement is a third general-purpose, whole-enterprise accounting report, supplementary and complementary to the profit and loss statement and the balance sheet.

2. The funds statement is a period statement which attempts to show the results of the firm's financing decisions.

3. Four alternative concepts of funds are:

(a) Cash

(b) Net current monetary assets

(c) Working capital

(d) 'Total resources'

4. The basic approach to funds statement preparation is the comparison, item by item, of two consecutive balance sheets.

5. The information for the calculation of funds generated by operations is obtained primarily from the profit and loss statement. It is important to disregard revenue and expense items which do not affect funds.

6. Management is more interested in projected fund flow statements than those prepared on a historical basis.

7. Some accountants and users prefer a funds statement prepared using the cash concept of funds.

8. The preparation of cash budgets (as part of the whole system of budgetary control) enables management to plan effectively, and to ensure the best use of cash resources available.

Discussion questions

16.1 Explain the differences between the statement of profit and loss and the funds statement of an enterprise.

16.2 What different information is provided by a funds statement as compared with a cash flow statement?

16.3 'There is more to the preparation of a funds statement than the mere comparison of one item in a balance sheet with another.' Explain this statement with examples.

16.4 What is meant by 'non-fund items'? Give examples.

16.5 The two sections of the funds statement are the resources and the application of funds. To which section would you allocate the following:

(a) increase in prepaid insurance;

(b) reduction in goodwill;

(c) provision for final dividend;

(d) increased revaluation of plant;

(e) decrease in provision for depreciation of premises?

16.6 Explain the type of information produced by a funds statement which would be useful to management.

16.7 Why do some firms prepare a 'flexible budget'?

16.8 'Depreciation represents an increase in working capital.' 'Depreciation represents a source of funds.'
  Comment on these two statements.

Exercises

16.9 The following balance sheets represent the financial position of an enterprise on successive balance dates:

	30 June 19X6		30 June 19X7	
Current assets				
Cash on hand		£30		£40
Debtors		18 105		17 815
Stock on hand		6 320		7 430
Fixed assets				
Plant and machinery	£8 970		£8 970	
Less Provision for depreciation	2 450		3 010	
		6 520		5 960
		30 975		31 245

Cont.

	30 June 19X6		30 June 19X7	
b/fwd		£30 975		£31 245
Motor vehicles	£2 340		£2 340	
Less Provision for depreciation	1 200		1 400	
		1 140		940
Premises		7 850		13 700
		£39 965		£45 885
Current liabilities				
Creditors		£11 455		£13 465
Bank overdraft		6 510		8 420
Proprietorship				
J. Hudson – Capital		22 000	22 000	
Add Profit for year		—	3 000	
			25 000	
Less Drawings		—	1 000	
				24 000
		£39 965		£45 885

Prepare a statement to show the sources from which funds were derived in the year ended 30 June 19X7 and the manner in which these funds were applied.

16.10 Although A. Trader earned a satisfactory net profit for the year ended 30 June 19X7, investment in new equipment has changed materially the financial position of the business. To indicate the nature of the change, prepare a funds statement for the year, from the following information:

Balance Sheets of A. Trader as at 30 June

	19X6		19X7	
Cash		£1 200		—
Debtors		3 200		£5 050
Stock		12 500		18 000
Pre-payments		200		250
Investments, at cost		1 000		
Plant and equipment at cost	£22 000		£29 000	
Less Provision for depreciation	10 000		13 000	
		12 000		16 000
Leasehold premium, at cost	5 000		5 000	
Less Provision for depreciation	2 500		3 000	
		2 500		2 000
		£32 600		£41 300
Creditors		£2 000		£5 000
Bank overdraft		—		2 500
Capital, A. Trader		30 600		33 800
		£32 600		£41 300

During the year:

(a) the investments were sold for £900;

(b) equipment which cost £3000 and which was written down to £1800, was sold for £1600; and

(c) A. Trader drew for private purposes £2080.

16.11 The balance sheets of the Ajax Co. Ltd as at 30 June 19X6, and 30 June 19X7, were as under:

		30 June 19X6		30 June 19X7
Assets				
Cash at bank		£3 070		£2 400
Debtors		4 250		4 970
Stock		12 000		15 200
Plant and machinery	£16 500		£23 400	
Less Provision for depreciation	3 500		4 700	
		13 000		18 700
Goodwill		1 000		—
		£33 320		£41 270
Liabilities				
Creditors		£1 200		£2 600
Loan from X Co. (long-term)		4 500		3 700
Capital		20 000		25 000
Profit and loss appropriation account		2 420		3 170
Reserves		5 200		6 800
		£33 320		£41 270

Additional information:

(a) A dividend of £2000 was paid during the year.

(b) Plant and machinery which cost £1500, and which had been written down by £800, was sold for £600 cash.

You are required to prepare a statement showing the sources and application of funds for the year ended 30 June 19X7.

16.12 The balance sheets of the firm of Miller and Morris as at 30 June 19X6 and 30 June 19X7 were as follows:

		30 June 19X6		30 June 19X7
Current assets				
Cash in hand		£10		£20
Debtors		8 340		9 010
Bills receivable		520		380
Stock		5 630		6 470
Fixed assets				
Furniture and equipment	£4 200		£4 750	
Less Provision for depreciation	640	3 560	720	4 030
		18 060		19 910

	30 June 19X6		30 June 19X7	
b/fwd		£18 060		£19 910
Motor vehicles	£3 680		£2 760	
Less Provision for depreciation	820		850	
		2 860		1 910
		£20 920		£21 820
Liabilities				
Bank overdraft		2 600		430
Creditors		2 360		2 520
W. Miller - advance		1 000		1 000
Proprietorship				
W. Miller - capital		8 000		9 000
T. Morris - capital		6 000		6 500
W. Miller - current account		640		1 440
T. Morris - current account		320		930
		£20 920		£21 820

Each partner's current account had been credited with £1200 as salary, while Miller has been credited with £70 interest on his advance. During the year Miller has withdrawn £920 in cash and Morris £1040. A motor car which had cost £920, and had been depreciated to £310, was sold for £375.

You are required to prepare a statement showing sources and application of funds for the year ended 30 June 19X7.

16.13 From the following data you are required to prepare a statement showing the sources and application of working capital for the ABC Co. Ltd for the year ending 30 June 19X7. Include with your answer a worksheet showing the net change in the working capital position.

Balance Sheet Items

	30 June 19X6		30 June 19X7	
	Dr.	Cr.	Dr.	Cr.
Bank		£2 100	£1 200	
Debtors	£12 500		14 000	
Stock	17 400		19 000	
Plant	12 500		14 750	
Provision for depreciation of plant		4 150		£5 300
Buildings	4 250		15 000	
Creditors		8 250		10 850
Bills payable		800		300
Debentures (long-term)		—		10 000
Called up capital (£1 shares)		26 250		30 000
Uncalled capital			—	
Reserve		3 500		5 000
Appropriation account		1 600		2 500
	£46 650	£46 650	£63 950	£63 950

Other information:

(a) Corporation tax paid during year, £700.

(b) Dividends paid during year, £180.

(c) No depreciation is provided on buildings.

(d) An item of plant which had cost £2000, and had been depreciated to £850, was sold for £1000 cash.

16.14 Using the following information prepare a funds statement for the PRT Co. Ltd for the year ended 30 June 19X7:

(a) Balance sheet items as at:

	30 June 19X6		30 June 19X7	
	Dr.	Cr.	Dr.	Cr.
Cash in hand	£30		£50	
Bank	780			£1 850
Debtors	14 350		15 320	
Stock	16 800		17 950	
Prepaid expenses	240		200	
Shares in A.T. Ltd (at cost)	1 300		2 000	
Delivery vehicles (at cost)	6 740		9 110	
Provision for depreciation of delivery vehicles		£2 340		2 600
Land and buildings (at cost)	65 000		85 000	
Preliminary expenses	3 500		3 000	
Accrued expenses		330		210
Creditors		6 450		5 330
Proposed final dividend		3 250		4 000
Provision for taxation		6 000		6 000
Unsecured debentures		15 000		10 000
Called-up capital		35 000		50 000
Premium on shares				1 250
General reserve		25 000		30 000
Profit and loss appropriation		15 370		18 390
Asset realisation reserve				3 000
	£108 740	£108 740	£132 630	£132 630

(b) Other information available:

 (i) Net profit after providing for taxation for the year ended 30 June 19X7 was £16 520.

 (ii) Interim dividend paid during the year was £4000.

 (iii) During the year land which had cost £5000 was sold for £8000, the profit being credited to the asset realisation reserve. New buildings had been erected on the remaining land.

 (iv) During the year a delivery vehicle which had cost £1300 and which had been depreciated to £400 was sold for £550.

16.15 The following details have been extracted from the accounting reports of V. Gogh and Sons, paint and wallpaper supplies.

(a) Statement of profit and loss for year ended 30 June 19X6:

Net sales (all credit)		£220 000
Less Cost of sales		
Opening stock	£40 000	
Purchases	190 000	
	230 000	
Closing stock	50 000	180 000
Gross profit		40 000
Less Selling expenses	14 000	
Administrative expenses	2 000	
Finance expenses	2 000	18 000
Net profit		£22 000

(b) Balance sheet items as at 30 June:

	19X5	**19X6**
Cash at bank	£10 000	£6 000
Debtors	30 000	44 000
Stock	40 000	50 000
Land and buildings	50 000	54 000
Furniture and fittings (net book value)	20 000	18 000
Motor vehicles (net book value)	10 000	8 000
	£160 000	£180 000
Capital	£70 000	£90 000
Creditors	50 000	40 000
Accrued expenses	10 000	10 000
Mortgage on land and buildings	30 000	40 000
	£160 000	£180 000

Note: The owners had withdrawn £2000 in cash. Prepare a cash flow statement for the year ended 30 June 19X6.

16.16 From the following information prepare a cash budget showing the estimated bank balance as at the end of May and June:

(a) The concern pays for its credit purchases in the month following purchase.

(b) Debtors regularly settle their accounts, on average, as follows: 80 per cent in the month following sale; and 20 per cent in the second month.

(c) Expenses are paid by cash in the month incurred.

(d) At 1 May:
Debtors totalled £12 500 (this includes April sales of £10 000 and March unpaid sales of £2500. Total credit sales in March had amounted to £12 500).
Bank overdraft was £4900.

(e) Estimated figures for the months of May and June are:

	Cash sales	Credit sales	Cash purchases	Credit purchases	Expenses
May	£1 900	£6 500	£1 000	£3 900	£3 000
June	2 400	7 000	1 900	4 000	3 200

16.17 From the information below, you are required to complete a worksheet to determine expected cash receipts from customers, and a cash budget for the three months, June, July, August.

(a) The bank balance at 1 June was an overdraft of £850.

(b) Estimated cash sales for the period June to August

June	£7 600
July	4 780
August	5 830

(c) Wages normally amount to an average of £2300 per month.

(d) Actual credit sales amount to:

March	£6 300
April	4 900
May	2 700

(e) Customers normally pay off their debts at the following rate:
  80 per cent in first month after sale;
  20 per cent in second month after sale.

(f) Estimated credit sales for the period of June to August

June	£4 400
July	5 100
August	3 800

(g) Estimated cash purchases for the period June to August

June	£1 980
July	3 150
August	3 060

(h) Taxation amounting to £1500 is payable in August.

(i) Goods purchased on credit are not paid for until the month following the month of purchase. Estimated credit purchases to be made during the period June to August are

June	£5 105
July	2 175
August	4 285

(j) At the end of May accounts payable are owed a total of £2550.

Problems

16.18 Company A and Company B at the beginning of the year had almost identical amounts of issued capital. At the end of the year each produced a funds statement (in £000) as follows:

	Company A		Company B	
Source of funds				
From operations	£100		£100	
Debentures issued	400			
Shares issued			400	
		£500		£500
Application of funds				
Purchase fixed assets	100		350	
Payment of dividends	300		50	
		400		400
Increase in working capital		£100		£100

Working Capital (in £000)

	Increase	Decrease	Increase	Decrease
Current assets				
Cash at bank		£50	£100	
Debtors	£350		100	
Stocks	550		150	
	900	50	350	
Current liabilities				
Creditors		350		£50
Accrued expenses		400		200
	900	800	350	250
Increase in working capital		100		100
	£900	£900	£350	£350

Prepare a report showing the differences in the accounting and financial policies of the two companies and suggest which policy is the more viable.

16.19 The following are the balance sheets (in £000) of AN Ltd at 30 June:

	19X6		19X7	
Issued and paid-up capital	£500		£600	
General reserve	100		125	
Profit and loss appropriation	300		375	
Share premium account			25	
Bank overdraft	25		33	
Provision for depreciation	64		99	
Provision for dividend	50		50	
Provision for taxation	50	£1 089	93	£1 400
Freehold property	220		420	
Plant and machinery	350		394	
Investments Shares	170		171	
Debtors	125		140	
Cash	1		1	
Stock	200		251	
Goodwill	23	1 089	23	1 400

Profit and Loss Appropriation Account at 30 June 19X7 (£000)

Transfer general reserves	£25	Balance (30/6/X6)			£300
Interim dividend paid	25	Profit before tax	£210		
Balance (30/6/X7)	375	Prov. for tax	85		125
	£425				£425

Investigation of the books disclosed:

1. There was a private issue of 10 000 £1 shares at a premium of 25p per share.

2. Corporation tax of £42 000 was paid in March 19X7 for the 19X6 tax. This had been debited to the provision.

3. Shares in other companies recorded at £20 000 had been sold for £18 000.

4. Movements in the plant and machinery account were:

   additional purchased £60 000;
   plant (costing £16 000 and fully depreciated) was scrapped.

5. An additional £55 000 was charged to the provision for depreciation of plant and machinery.

Prepare a statement of sources and application of funds. Comment on the financial policies disclosed by the funds statement.

16.20 Tom Sparks operates a small specialised printing business. He started the business the previous year when he rented a small factory for £12 000 p.a. The lease was for a seven-year period with an option to renew at the end of the seven years. Rent was payable quarterly in advance on the first of January, April, July and October.

Before commencing production last year, the premises had to be considerably modified at a cost of £28 000. If the lease is not renewed, no compensation will be received from the owner of the property. The cost of fixtures and fittings was £30 000. These would have a useful life of fifteen years, but would have negligible salvage value.

The printing machines cost £120 000. It is estimated that they would last for ten years, but it is intended to exchange them every three years when the trade-in value would be one-quarter the original cost.

During the month of July, £8000 worth of paper and other materials was purchased on credit and the previous month's purchases of £6000 were paid. It was estimated that the value of materials on hand at the beginning and end of July was £3000 and £4000 respectively.

During July, £35 000 had been received for work done in the previous months. Invoices forwarded to customers for work done in July totalled £20 000. Other payments for expenses incurred in the month were:

Wages for assistant	£1 500
Miscellaneous expenses	£3 000
Money for own use	£4 000

From the above information prepare:

(a) A performance statement for the month of July based on the net cash flows as a measure of performance.

(b) A conventional accounting statement of profit and loss for the month of July.

(c) A report as to which statement gives the better indication of the long-run viability of the enterprise.

Chapter 17
Accounting standards

Background ☐ Accounting standards issued by ASC ☐ Statements of recommended practice ☐ Brief review of SSAPs ☐ Conclusion

Background

Although many accountancy recommendations have been made during the period from 1942 to 1969, it was not until 1971 that the first Statement of Standard Accounting Practice was issued. Those recommendations, made by the Institute of Chartered Accountants of England and Wales, were based on the collective experience of practising accountants in the United Kingdom. It was considered that useful as these recommendations were, in order to provide some form of uniformity in financial reporting there was an urgent need to set up a committee whose responsibility it would be to issue statements of standard accounting practice to deal with the inadequacy of accounting methods occurring by the late 1960s and to provide some conformity on accountancy practice.

The Accounting Standards Steering Committee was set up in January 1970 by the Council of the Institute of Chartered Accountants in England and Wales with the object of developing definitive standards of financial reporting. In 1976 it changed its name to the Accounting Standards Committee, or ASC, becoming a joint committee of the six member bodies who act collectively through the Consultative Committee of Accountancy Bodies (CCAB).

The six major accountancy bodies are:

> The Institute of Chartered Accountants in England and Wales
> The Institute of Chartered Accountants of Scotland
> The Institute of Chartered Accountants in Ireland
> The Chartered Association of Certified Accountants
> The Chartered Institute of Management Accountants
> The Chartered Institute of Public Finance and Accountancy

The Accounting Standards Committee terms of reference are to:

1. keep under review standards of financial accounting and reporting;

2. propose to the councils of the governing bodies statements of standard accounting practice and interpretation of such statements;

3. publish consultative documents, discussion papers and exposure drafts and submit to the governing bodies non-mandatory guidance notes with the object of maintaining and advancing accounting standards;

4. consult as appropriate with representatives of finance, commerce, industry and government and other bodies and persons concerned with financial reporting; and

5. maintain links with the International Accounting Standards Committee and the accountancy profession in Europe and throughout the world.

As a result of criticism of the composition of the membership of the ASC, it was decided in 1982 to alter it to the following:

In practice	7
In private and public industry and commerce	6
Users	4
Non-trading public sector	2
Academic	1
	20

In December 1969 the Institute of Chartered Accountants in England and Wales issued 'a Statement of Intent on Accounting Standards in the 1970s' in which it proposed to advance accounting standards along the following lines:

1. Narrowing the areas of differences and variety in accounting practice by publishing authoritative and where possible definitive statements of best accounting practice.

2. Disclosure of accounting bases. Where there were areas of subjectivity and when judgment had to be relied on it was established that the basis used in arriving at amounts should be fully disclosed.

3. Requiring disclosure of departures from definitive accounting standards. Where a company has departed from a standard it is required to explain fully that it has done so.

4. Introducing a system for wide exposure of draft proposals for accounting standards to appropriate representative bodies for discussion and comment.

5. A continuing programme to encourage improvements in accounting standards laid down by law and regulatory bodies.

Statements of Standard Accounting Practice are formulated by the Accounting Standards Committee and are issued on the authority of the individual CCAB bodies. Although they do not have the legal force of an Act of Parliament they are mandatory so far as the members of the participating professional bodies are concerned in their capacity as auditors or even preparers of financial accounts. The standards apply to all financial accounts which purport to present a true and fair view of the overall financial position and profit or loss of a limited company. To ensure compliance with Statements of Standard Accounting Practice the professional bodies in the United Kingdom lay down a duty on its members to observe these standards. Failure to comply with them may result in internal disciplinary procedures against the defaulting member.

The standard setting procedure involves a considerable amount of research, discussion and comment before a standard is issued. The standard procedure is summarised as follows:

1. A topic is identified.

2. A research study is commissioned to examine the topic.

3. A preliminary draft based on the research study is prepared by a working party.

4. The preliminary draft is then circulated to the technical committees for the members of the CCAB for comment.

5. After the comments have been received on the preliminary draft, an Exposure Draft (ED) is prepared and circulated for comment from any interested parties.

6. After a period of time has elapsed, usually at least six months, the working party summarises

and discusses the comments received and makes recommendations to the Accounting Standards Committee. Thereafter a final draft is prepared and if accepted by the members of the participating bodies it is then issued as a standard.

Accounting standards issued by ASC

These are listed in Table 17.1.

Table 17.1   Statements of Standard Accounting Practice and Exposure Drafts issued by the Accounting Standards Committee

Number	Title	Date of issue
SSAP 1	Accounting for Associated Companies	April 1982
SSAP 2	Disclosure of Accounting Policies	November 1971
SSAP 3	Earnings per Share	August 1974
SSAP 4	The Accounting Treatment of Government Grants	April 1974
SSAP 5	Accounting for Value Added Tax	April 1974
SSAP 6	Extraordinary Items and Prior Year Adjustments	June 1975
SSAP 7	Withdrawn	
SSAP 8	The Treatment of Taxation Under the Imputation System in the Accounts of Companies	August 1974
SSAP 9	Stocks and Work in Progress	May 1975
SSAP 10	Statements of Source and Application of Funds	July 1975
SSAP 11	Withdrawn	
SSAP 12	Accounting for Depreciation	December 1977
SSAP 13	Accounting for Research and Development	October 1977
SSAP 14	Group Accounts	September 1978
SSAP 15	Accounting for Deferred Tax	May 1985
SSAP 16	Current Cost Accounting	March 1980
SSAP 17	Accounting for Post Balance Sheet Events	August 1980
SSAP 18	Accounting for Contingencies	August 1980
SSAP 19	Accounting for Investment Properties	November 1981
SSAP 20	Foreign Currency Translation	April 1983
SSAP 21	Accounting for Leases and Hire Purchase Contracts	August 1984
SSAP 22	Accounting for Goodwill	December 1984
SSAP 23	Accounting for Acquisitions and Mergers	April 1985

The following Exposure Drafts are currently under discussion and as yet have not been made into standards:

ED 32	Disclosure of pension information in company accounts	
ED 36	Extraordinary items and prior year adjustments	
ED 37	Accounting for depreciation	
ED 38	Accounting for charities	

Statements of Recommended Practice (SORP)

The ASC consider that it is necessary from time to time to issue Statements of Recommended Practice the primary aims of which are to narrow the areas of difference and variety in the accounting treatment of the matters with which they deal and to enhance the usefulness of published accounting information. SORPs are to be issued on subjects on which it is not considered appropriate to issue an accounting standard at the time.

Unlike accounting standards SORPs are not mandatory on members of the governing bodies of the ASC.

Brief review of SSAPs

The following is a brief review of the accounting standards in force at the time of writing. The intention of this section is not to give a detailed summary of each standard but merely to highlight some of the important points included in each in an abbreviated form. In the case of several of the standards more detail appears in other parts of the book, but the reader is advised to refer to the original standard if fuller information is required.

SSAP 1: Accounting for Associated Companies

The main purpose of this standard is to provide a system of accounting for the profits of an associated company. An associated company is one in which the investing company has a substantial interest which is considered to be not less than 20 per cent or more of the shares. Under this standard the investing company records in its consolidated profit and loss account the aggregate of its share of before-tax profits of the associated company and not just the amount of dividend received from the company.

SSAP 2: Disclosure of Accounting Policies

This is an important standard as it sets out four fundamental accounting concepts which are regarded as acceptable and which are considered as the broad basic assumptions underlying the financial accounts of businesses:

1. The 'going concern' concept – the continuance of the business as an operational entity for the foreseeable future;

2. the 'accruals' concept – revenue and costs are accrued, matched with one another so far as their relationship can be established or justifiably assumed, and dealt with in the profit and loss account of the period to which they relate;

3. the 'consistency' concept – the accounting treatment of like items within which each accounting period and from one period to the next is maintained on a consistent basis;

4. the 'prudence' concept – revenue and profits are not anticipated, but are recognised by inclusion in the profit and loss account only when realised in the form either of cash or of other assets where the ultimate cash realisation can be assessed with reasonable certainty; provision is made for all known liabilities; expenses and losses whether the amount of these is known with certainty or is a best estimate in the light of information available.

SSAP 3: Earnings per Share

The purpose of this standard is to ensure that every company with a listing on a recognised stock exchange publishes its earnings per share in the profit and loss account. The detailed calculations are explained in the standard. It is usually made by dividing net profit after tax, but before extraordinary items, by the number of ordinary shares in issue.

SSAP 4: Treatment of Government Grants

Grants may be given by government to cover either revenue or capital items. Revenue grants should be credited to revenue in the same period in which the revenue expenditure to which they relate is charged. In the case of capital grants two treatments are allowed under the standard

1. reduce the cost of the fixed asset by the amount of the grant, or

2. treat the amount of the grant as a deferred credit and transfer a portion of it to revenue on an annual basis.

SSAP 5: Accounting for Value Added Tax

Turnover and expenses shown in the profit and loss account should exclude VAT if the trader is registered for value added tax. On the other hand, irrecoverable VAT in respect of certain fixed assets and other items should be included in their cost and disclosed separately in published accounts if amounts are material.

SSAP 6: Extraordinary Items and Prior Year Adjustments

To ensure that the results of any one year can be compared with those of other years it is necessary to exclude extraordinary items and prior year adjustments. Extraordinary items are those items which derive from events or transactions outside the ordinary activities of the business and which are both material and expected not to recur frequently or regularly. An example might be the costs of closing a factory.

Prior year adjustments are those material adjustments applicable to prior years arising from changes in accounting policies and from the correction of fundamental errors. They do not include the normal recurring corrections and adjustments of accounting estimates made in prior years. An example might be change in an accounting policy to depreciate a fixed asset.

SSAP 8: Treatment of Taxation under the Imputation System in the Accounts of Companies

Under this standard the following practice has to be adopted:

Profit and loss account

1. The following items should be included in the taxation charge:

(a) the charge for corporation tax for the year;

(b) tax attributed to franked investment income;

(c) irrecoverable ACT.

2. Outgoing dividends should not include either the related ACT or the attributable tax credit.

3. Incoming dividends from UK companies should be included at the amount of cash received or receivable plus the tax credit.

Balance sheet

1. Dividends proposed should be included net in current liabilities, i.e. the amount payable to the shareholders.

2. The ACT on proposed dividends should be shown as a current liability.

3. If the ACT on proposed dividends is recoverable then it should be deducted from the deferred tax account. If no deferred tax account is kept then the ACT should be shown as a deferred asset.

SSAP 9: Stocks and Work in Progress

The basic rule contained in this standard for valuation of stock and work in progress is that the value adopted should be the lower of cost and net realisable value. In order to match costs and revenue, cost is defined as 'that expenditure which has been incurred in the normal course of business in bringing the product or service to its present location and condition'.

In the case of long-term contracts, that will take more than a year to complete, there is the problem of deciding what profit, if any, should be recognised in the accounts before the contract is completed. The standard favours the matching concept here, perhaps at the expense of prudence. It allows part of the profit to be included in work-in-progress valuations, but does provide that it should be on a prudent basis. The standard is not very specific as to how this should be computed, other than on a prudent basis and that an overall profit is anticipated on the contract. If a loss is anticipated this should be accounted for immediately.

SSAP 10: Statements of Source and Application of Funds

This standard requires that any business with a turnover in excess of £25 000 per annum must publish a statement of sources and application of funds as an appendix to the accounts. The method of preparing such statements has been explained earlier in the book.

SSAP 12: Accounting for Depreciation

This standard does not advocate any specific method of depreciation to be used to depreciate fixed assets but leaves it to management to choose the most appropriate method applicable to the company's assets. The standard does state that this should be subject to annual review. However, once a system has been selected it should be used consistently. The standard also states that depreciation should be calculated and provided in respect of all assets having a finite life. If the system is changed then the unamortised value should be written off over its expected life using the new method. A note of the effect on the profit should be made in the year of change. Freehold land does not require to be depreciated unless its value has fallen as a result of a loss in its commercial value or for some other valid reason. Freehold property must be depreciated since it has a finite life.

For each major class of depreciable asset there must be disclosed:

1. the depreciation method used;

2. the useful life or depreciation rate;

3. the total depreciation for period;

4. the gross amount of depreciable assets and accumulated depreciation to date.

SSAP 13: Accounting for Research and Development

The standard seeks to establish a common treatment for expenditure on research and development.

There are three categories of research and development expenditure which are defined as:

1. *Pure research*   Original investigation undertaken in order to gain new scientific or technical knowledge and understanding. Basic research is not primarily directed towards any specific aim or application. Such costs must be written off immediately.

2. *Applied research*   Original investigation undertaken in order to gain new scientific or technical knowledge and directed towards a specific practical aim or objective. The standard states that those costs should be written off in the year of expenditure.

3. *Development*.   The use of scientific or technical knowledge in order to produce new or substantially improved materials, devices, products, processes, systems or services prior to the commencement of commercial production. This expenditure should be written off in the year of expenditure except when (a) there is a clearly defined project; (b) the project is reasonably certain to reach a successful conclusion; (c) the project will produce revenue against which the expenditure can be matched; (d) adequate resources exist to enable the project to be completed.

SSAP 14: Group Accounts

This standard deals with the presentation of group accounts for a group of companies. One or two definitions made in this standard are relevant to the contents of this book, as follows:

1. *Subsidiary company.* A company shall be deemed to be a subsidiary of another if

(a) that either

(i) is a member of it and controls the composition of its board of directors; or

(ii) holds more than half in nominal value of its equity share capital; or

(b) the first mentioned company is a subsidiary of any company which is that other's subsidiary.

2. *Holding company.* A company is a holding company of another if, but only if, that other is its subsidiary as defined above.

3. *Group.* A holding company and its subsidiaries.

In accordance with the standard of accounting practice a holding company should prepare group accounts in the form of a single set of consolidated financial statements covering the holding company and its subsidiary companies at home and overseas.

SSAP 15: Accounting for Deferred Tax

The reason for this standard is that often profit shown in the profit and loss account bears no relationship to the taxable profit. Consequently, differences between these two amounts arise which are classified into permanent differences and timing differences. These terms have been explained in a later section of the book. Deferred tax relating to the ordinary activities of the business should be shown separately as a part of the tax on the profit either on the face of the profit and loss account or in a note. The deferred tax balance should be disclosed in the balance sheet. Any transfers to and from deferred tax should be disclosed by way of note.

SSAP 16: Current Cost Accounting

As from 6 June 1985 the Accounting Standards Committee has suspended the mandatory status of this standard. However, SSAP 16 remains an authoritative reference on accounting under the current cost convention and is discussed in Chapter 21, which deals with accounting for changing prices.

SSAP 17: Accounting for post Balance Sheet Events

Post balance sheet events are those events, both favourable and unfavourable, which occur between the balance sheet date and the date on which the financial statements are approved by the directors. Adjusting events are defined as 'post balance sheet events which provide additional evidence of conditions existing at the balance sheet date'.

Examples of post balance sheet events which normally should be classified as adjusting events:

1. *Fixed assets.* The subsequent determination of the purchase price or the proceeds of sale of assets purchased or sold before the year end.

2. *Property.* A valuation which provides evidence of a permanent diminution in value.

The following are some examples of non-adjusting events:

mergers and acquisitions;
issue of shares and debentures;
purchases and sales of fixed assets and investments.

Adjusting events need to be reflected in the financial statement but non-adjusting events, if sufficiently important, only require to be shown as a note for the attention of shareholders.

SSAP 18: Accounting for Contingencies

A contingency is a condition which exists at the balance sheet date whose outcome will be determined by the occurrence or non-occurrence of some future event. If the effect of a contingency is such that a loss, although not incurred, will be incurred and the amount of the loss can be reasonably estimated then provision should be made for it. If the loss is improbable and cannot be reasonably estimated then it should only be disclosed in note form. If it is probable that a contingent gain will be realised then it should be noted in a memorandum disclosure. If it is possible that the gain will not be realised then it should not be disclosed at all.

SSAP 19: Accounting for Investment Properties

The purpose of this standard is to ensure that Investment Properties are not subject to periodic changes for depreciation on the basis set out in SSAP 12, except for properties held on loan which should be depreciated on the basis set out in SSAP 12, at least over the period when the unexpired term is twenty years or less. Investment properties should be included in the balance sheet at their open market value.

SSAP 20: Foreign Currency Translation

The main purpose of this standard is to ensure that there is some conformity of foreign transactions and investments. The standard outlines the procedures to be adopted and the various methods of translation to be used for converting foreign currencies into sterling. The basis of translation and treatment of exchange differences are to be disclosed. The following additional information is also to be disclosed:

1. net amount of exchange gains and losses on foreign currency borrowings less deposits analysed between:

(a) the amount charged/credited to profit and loss account and

(b) the amount relating to 'hedging' operations taken to reserves;

2. net movement on reserves arising from exchange differences.

SSAP 21: Accounting for Leases and Hire Purchase Contracts

This standard has been produced to standardise the accounting treatment for leases. A distinction is drawn between different types of lease. A finance lease is considered to be a lease which transfers substantially all the risks and rewards of ownership to the lessee. The other type of lease is an operating lease which is in essence a lease other than a finance lease. The standard states the accounting treatment to be adopted in dealing with these types of leases. There is also a section of the standard which states the disclosure requirements by lessees and lessors.

SSAP 22: Accounting for Goodwill

In this standard goodwill is defined as the difference between the value of a business as a whole compared with the total value of the separable assets less liabilities. It distinguishes between purchased and non-purchased goodwill. Purchased goodwill is considered to be goodwill which is established as a result of the purchase of a business accounted for as an acquisition and non-purchased goodwill is any goodwill other than purchased goodwill.

The accounting policy followed in respect of goodwill should be explained in the notes to the accounts. No amount should be attributed to non-purchased goodwill in the balance sheet. Purchased goodwill should normally be eliminated from the accounts immediately on acquisition against reserves but may be eliminated by amortisation through the profit and loss account on a systematic basis over its useful economic life. Negative goodwill should be credited to reserves.

When purchased goodwill is eliminated by amortisation it should be shown as a separate item under intangible fixed assets until fully written off. Also, the movement on the goodwill account during the year has to be disclosed showing the cost, accumulated amortisation and net book value at the beginning and end of the year and the amount of goodwill amortised through the profit and loss account during the year.

SSAP 23: Accounting for Acquisitions and Mergers

This standard deals with accounting for business combinations, which arise when one or more companies become subsidiaries of another company. It deals only with accounting in group accounts and not with the accounting to be used in individual companies' own accounts. The standard explains the two different methods which have been developed to account for business combinations: acquisition accounting and merger accounting. The detailed disclosure requirements necessary for all significant combinations, whether accounted for by acquisition or by merger accounting in the group accounts in the year of the combination, are listed in this standard.

Conclusion

The foregoing review has been produced so that you may acquire both an awareness of some of the important points included in the accounting standards issued by the Accounting Standards Committee and an appreciation of the requirements of the standards in order to assist the accounting profession to standardise some aspects of its financial reporting methods. Although the standards attempt to harmonise the treatment of many contentious areas in financial reporting there has been substantial debate within and outside the profession as to the adequacy and relevance of some of them. It is interesting to note that some standards have been withdrawn and several others revised to meet the changing demands of the accountancy profession and the users of financial information. It must be recognised, however, that at present accounting standards deal only with certain areas of accounting and do not prescribe a complete system of financial reporting. As previously mentioned, the promulgation and revision of accounting standards is an ongoing process.

Before concluding this chapter it should be mentioned that in recent years professional accountancy bodies world wide have co-operated to develop and issue international accounting standards. However, although mention is made of this fact it is considered that accounting students, particularly in the early years of their studies, should concentrate to a greater extent on those standards issued by the UK accountancy bodies and understand their relevance and importance to the financial reporting methods in this country.

Summary

1. The first accounting standard was introduced in 1971 by the Accounting Standards Steering Committee.

2. The major accountancy bodies in the UK make up the Consultative Committee of Accountancy Bodies.

3. The standard-setting procedure involves a considerable amount of research, discussion and comment before a standard is issued.

4. Before a standard is issued an exposure draft is produced to obtain comment from all interested parties.

5. The Accounting Standards Committee has agreed to issue Statements of Recommended Practice (SORP) to enhance the usefulness of published accounting information.

6. Although accounting standards have not the legal force of an Act of Parliament they are mandatory as far as the members of the participating professional bodies are concerned.

7. It is essential to be aware of the main points included in the accounting standards issued by the ASC.

8. Accounting standards deal only with certain areas of accounting and do not prescribe a complete system of financial reporting.

Discussion questions

17.1 Discuss the reasons why the accountancy profession in the United Kingdom has developed and issued accounting standards.

17.2 Why is it difficult to obtain agreement among accountants and users of accounting information on the precise nature of accounting standards?

17.3 The introduction of accounting standards has improved the quality of financial reporting? Discuss.

17.4 Differentiate between 'extraordinary items' and 'prior year adjustments'.

17.5 Describe the procedure followed by the Accounting Standards Committee in the setting of an accounting standard.

17.6 What are the main categories of research and development expenditure included in SSAP 13? How is the expenditure treated in the financial statements?

17.7 Why should accounting policies be disclosed in the financial accounts of a company?

Note: Since this chapter has been descriptive and introductory in nature, no exercises or problems, as provided in most other chapters, are necessary.

Chapter 18
Published company reports

Why study company annual reports? ☐ Accounting records ☐ Major influences on company reporting ☐ Presentation of the annual report ☐ Allocation of profits, reserves and provisions ☐ Form and content of final accounts of limited companies ☐ Directors' report ☐ Auditors and audit reports ☐ Small and medium-sized companies ☐ Taxation in company accounts ☐ Nature of consolidated statements ☐ Simple examples of consolidated statement preparation

Why study company annual reports?

It is not intended that this chapter should serve as a reference manual to accountants engaged in the preparation of an annual report for a company. To provide adequate guidance on the accounting requirements of the Companies Act would require a book rather than a chapter. It would also be necessary to explain, in some detail, the impact of the professional bodies' accounting standards on the published financial statements and, for companies listed on the stock exchange, to outline the listed requirements of the stock exchanges. Such a task is beyond the scope of a first-year accounting course and a first-year accountancy text.

The objectives here are much more modest and may be summarised as follows:

1. To illustrate how the information presented in the basic general-purpose accounting reports discussed in previous chapters may be utilised, adapted and re-expressed to provide the information required for company annual reports.

2. To assist students to understand and interpret the content of published financial statements of companies. This objective is pursued further in the chapter.

3. To provide students with a basic groundwork so that they are able to proceed to more advanced and more specialised studies in company accounting and the financial statements of companies and in auditing.

Accounting records

Section 221 of the Companies Act 1985 requires every company to keep accounting records sufficient to show and explain the company's transactions. They must be such as to:

1. disclose with reasonable accuracy, at any time, the financial position of the company at that time; and

2. enable the directors to ensure that any balance sheet and profit and loss account prepared by them comply with the 1985 Act.

The accounting records must in particular contain:

1. entries from day to day of all sums of money received and expended, and the matters in respect of which receipt and expenditure take place;

2. a record of the assets and liabilities of the company; and,

3. where the business involves dealing in goods,

(a) statements of stock held by the company at the end of each financial year of the company;

(b) all statements of stocktaking from which any such statements of stock as are mentioned in (a) have been or are to be prepared; and

(c) except in the case of goods sold by way of ordinary retail trade, statements of all goods sold and purchased, showing the goods and the buyers and sellers in sufficient detail to enable all these to be identified.

Major influences on company reporting

In broad terms, the major external factors which influence the form and content of company annual reports may be summarised as follows:

1. All registered companies must comply with the accounting provisions of the Companies Act 1985.

2. Those companies listed on the stock exchange have to comply with the accounting disclosure requirements set out by the stock exchanges.

3. Statements of Standard Accounting Practice.

Accounting principles

Companies Act 1985 requires that every balance sheet and profit and loss account give a true and fair view, and be based on certain accounting principles; the accounts must also:

1. be prepared on the basis of the four fundamental accounting concepts contained in SSAP 2, namely the going concern concept, the consistency concept, the prudence concept and the accruals concept;

2. employ appropriate accounting policies consistently applied;

3. present an overall picture that is not in any way misleading;

4. disclose all information material to a proper understanding of the accounts;

5. describe the amounts in the accounts in such a way that their true nature is explained unambiguously; and

6. strike a balance between completeness of disclosure and the summarisation necessary for clarity.

A company's directors are allowed to depart from any of the accounting principles where there are special reasons to do so. If they do so, however, the notes to the financial statements must give particulars of the departure, the directors' reasons for it and its effect.

True and fair view

The overriding requirement of all financial statements drawn up under the Act is that they must present a true and fair view. This requirement is fundamental. Where compliance of a legal rule would inhibit a true and fair view then the statutory requirement can be ignored. Details of the special circumstances where such an approach was adopted must be stated in the accounts. The interpretation of what constitutes 'a true and fair view' is left in the hands of accountants, directors and auditors and, ultimately the courts. The use of generally accepted principles and practices represents an important criteria used in this interpretation.

Obviously, accounting standards play an important role in defining more specifically what accounting methods will provide a true and fair view. In 1983 the then chairman of the National Companies and Securities Commission wrote as follows:

> It has been long recognised that it is impractical for legislation to seek to describe in detail all the requirements in order to ensure that financial statements prepared by directors give a true view. It is these considerations which have led to the promulgation of accounting standards developed principally by the accountancy profession, with the object of supplementing the legislative requirements imposed on the directors and auditors. [1]

Presentation of the annual report

Much time, thought and energy are put into the presentation of published accounts by those involved in the preparation of them. It is only right that such importance should be placed on this matter since accounts can be of value only if they present the financial results in a form which can be readily understood by those who are not trained accountants.

There are statutory obligations on the directors of every limited company to send a copy of the annual report not only to each shareholder, debenture holder and any person entitled to receive notice of general meetings but also to the Registrar of Companies to be available for inspection by any interested party. The information to be disclosed in the annual report is set out in the Companies Act 1985.

The intention in including such provisions in the Companies Act is to ensure that investing shareholders and creditors are given an opportunity of examining the company's accounts and attached reports to determine the company's financial strength or weakness. To enable this financial analysis to take place, it is necessary that the accounting data should be compiled in such a way as to facilitate this examination. Provided the statutory requirements on disclosure are observed a certain freedom is allowed in the presentation of this information to shareholders. By studying the published accounts prepared by some limited companies in this country it can be readily seen that many varied and useful techniques are employed to present the statutory information. In recent years companies have experimented with different methods of presentation in an endeavour to report the facts in as realistic and intelligible a form as the law permits. The introduction of employee accounts has greatly assisted company employees to obtain an insight into the financial affairs of their company without initially gaining the necessary technical expertise of financial analysis.

Let us look now at the various items normally found in the annual reports of companies. First, we may distinguish between two major types of information:

1. *Statutory* Information which is required to be presented in order to comply with the provisions of the Companies Act.

2. *Optional* Other information which directors feel will be useful to shareholders and other interested parties. Typical examples are information about new products and new activities, condensed financial highlights, statistical information, staff matters, etc.

---

[1] Masel, L. The future of accounting and auditing standards, *Australian Accountant*, September 1983, 543.

Second, in each of the above categories, we may distinguish between:

(a) Accounting and other financial information.

(b) Information related to activities, shareholding, production, employment, etc.

We will concern ourselves primarily with information directly related to the accounting function. Therefore, when later in this chapter we reproduce extracts from the annual report of a public limited company, we will limit it to the following:

1. Profit and loss statement.

2. Balance sheet.

3. Notes to and forming part of the accounts.

4. Statement of source and application of funds.

5. Directors' report.

6. Auditor's report.

Note that all of the above reports and statements, with one exception, are specifically required under the provisions of the Companies Act and Codes. The exception is the statement of source and application of funds, but this statement is required to be incorporated under the terms of Statement of Accounting Practice 10.

Allocation of profits, reserves and provisions

Because a company is a separate legal entity, there are several differences in the treatment and division of profits which do not arise with partnerships and sole traders, as follows:

1. In the case of partnerships and sole traders, all profits (even when retained in the business) are allocated to the various capital accounts of the owners. A company, however, is an entity quite distinct from the owners, and can therefore retain some or all of the profits in accounts termed 'reserves'. Although members own shares in the company, they have no direct claim to these reserves. In consequence, such reserves are kept separate from the amounts of capital subscribed.

2. Since no individual proprietorship accounts for the shareholders are kept in the general ledger, their separate shares of profit could not, in any case, be allocated to them, as is done for partners. After the directors have decided what part of the profits will be retained and what portion will be paid to the shareholders, the amounts due to members are paid in cash by the company. These payments are termed dividends – the profit being divided in proportion to the number and amount of the shares held. Most shareholders regard their shares as an investment, and the dividend thus becomes the income return from their investment.

3. In dividing up the profits, the directors have to ensure that their actions comply with the provisions of the Companies Act, and are in accord with the articles of association of the company. This is important because certain profits are not available for dividends, for example, premiums on share issues. Just what profits are 'available for dividends' it is difficult to decide, since there is a difference between the accounting and the legal concept in this matter. The accounting attitude is that only *realised* revenue profits arising from the normal activities of the enterprise should be distributed as cash dividends. It does, however, accept the view that other realised profits, for example profit from the sale of plant, or even unrealised profits from revaluation of land and buildings, may in certain cases be used to issue bonus shares to members.

The Companies Act states that only realised profits at the balance sheet date can be included in the profit and loss account. Realised profits are stated to be profits determined in accordance with accounting principles generally accepted. Thus profits included in the accounts in accordance with Statements of Standard Accounting Practice are realised profits. As there have been important legal decisions relating to this matter, you should refer to textbooks on company law or auditing for further information.

4. When the profit of a particular year is insufficient to support a dividend payment, it may nevertheless be possible to pay a dividend by drawing on the undistributed profits of past years.

5. Because it is a separate legal entity in law, a company is required to pay corporation tax on its profits, whether they are distributed or retained. Before the profits can be allocated it will therefore be necessary to provide for this taxation.

The division of the profits of a company is thus seen to be more complicated than is the case with partnerships, and a profit and loss appropriation account is generally regarded as essential. The elements of profits to be divided will consist of:

1. The previous balance of unappropriated profit (if any).

2. The profit (after provision for corporation tax) transferred from the profit and loss account for the year.

These amounts may be allocated to all or any of the following:

1. Transfers to reserves.

2. Payment of (or provision for) dividends to shareholders.

3. Leaving a balance of undistributed profits to be carried forward to next year.

The decision as to what portion of the profits are to be retained and what dividends are to be paid to shareholders is made by the directors after studying the profit and loss statement. Their decision is final, although the payment of the dividends must be approved by the shareholders at the annual meeting.

The amounts retained for future use are called 'reserves'. If they are to be used for a particular purpose, such as the building extensions or replacement, then they are termed specific reserves. If they are to strengthen the resources of the enterprise, or are set aside either to protect the business against a sudden loss of profits, or to help equalise the rate of dividend paid, then they are called *general* reserves. The main feature of specific reserves is that the directors have declared their explicit intention with respect to the allocation of these profits. Should the purpose for which the reserve was created not eventuate, then it may be used in the same manner as general reserves. Note also that reserves may be created other than from the appropriation of trading profits. Thus, where shares are issued at a premium, or where there is a surplus caused by asset revaluation, or where the shares are forfeited and resold at a profit, etc. then the resultant 'profit', is a *capital* reserve, and such reserves are not 'available for cash dividends'. They are usually the subject of separate direct entries and are not included in either the profit and loss or the appropriation account.

Note again, also, that profits retained in the business are represented by an increase in the net asset structure. To this extent, the increase enables the business to expand its operations, although it is not necessarily represented by an increase in cash.

In deciding what amounts will be paid by way of dividends to shareholders, the directors will need to examine the articles of association to ensure that the provisions are complied with. Usually these state that dividends are to be calculated on the paid-up value of the shares. No dividends can be paid unless there are profits of the current or prior years 'available for distribution'. Although it was stated that the accounting attitude to this was that only revenue profits should be distributed as cash dividends, it must not be inferred that non-operating revenue is never distributed. Items such as interest and rent received may be regarded as non-operating but would still be available for dividend purposes.

Where there are preference shares in addition to ordinary shares, the directors must have regard to the terms of issue. Usually the preference shares carry a fixed rate of dividend, and this must be appropriated in full before any payment can be made to the ordinary shareholders. If the preference shares carry rights to cumulative dividends, arrears of dividends (if any) must also be fully satisfied before paying any ordinary dividends.

Since the dividends will be paid after the profit determination and following approval of members at the annual meeting, it follows that the amounts to be paid will have to be provided for in the appropriation account. A provision for dividend account (or separate provisions where there are various classes of shares) will have to be created and a transfer made to this account (or accounts) from the profit and loss appropriation account. This provision is then a definite liability for the company and will have to be paid after the holding of the annual meeting. It appears in the balance sheet in the section headed 'Creditors – Amounts falling due within one year'.

In well-established companies, it is usual to distribute some of the dividend half-way through the year. This happens where profits (and dividend rates) are relatively stable. This interim dividend, as it is called, will approximate to half the regular rate paid, and will be paid in cash by the company long before the end of the financial year. The total of the interim dividend will appear in a dividends account, which will be closed off to the appropriation account at the end of the year. After the final accounts have been prepared, the directors will assess the amount of the total dividend payable for the year and provide for the net balance due as a final dividend.

A distinction must be drawn between a *provision* and a *reserve*. The expression *provision* is defined as any amount written off or retained by way of providing for depreciation, renewals or diminution in value of assets or retained by way of providing for any known liability of which the amount cannot be determined with substantial accuracy. On the other hand, the term *reserve* does not include any amount which can be classified as a provision.

Form and content of final accounts of limited companies

Introduction

Section 228 of the Companies Act 1985 contains the requirement for accounts to be prepared in a standard format. It was the Companies Act 1981 which laid down for the first time the requirement of a format for annual accounting statements. The intention of this requirement is to improve the information content for users of financial information and allow for greater comparability.

Two balance sheet formats are permitted, one being a vertical format and the other a horizontal format, although the same headings are used in both.

Four alternative formats are available for the profit and loss account. These consist of two alternative approaches; either may be adopted in a vertical or horizontal format. The principal difference between these approaches is in the classification of expense items. Formats 1 and 3 analyse expenses by function, and so disclose cost of sales, distribution costs and administrative expenses. Formats 2 and 4 analyse expenses by nature, showing raw materials purchased, staff costs and other charges.

Profit and loss account

The following is the information required to be disclosed. Format 1 is the one most commonly used in practice, and is therefore used to explain the disclosure requirements.

Format 1

1. Turnover.
2. Cost of sales.
3. Gross profit or loss.
4. Distribution costs.
5. Administrative expenses.
6. Other operating income.
7. Income from shares in group companies.
8. Income from shares in related companies.
9. Income from other fixed-asset investments.
10. Other interest receivable and similar income.
11. Amounts written off investments.
12. Interest payable and similar charges.
13. Tax on profit or loss on ordinary activities.
14. Profit or loss on ordinary activities after taxation.
15. Extraordinary income.
16. Extraordinary charges.
17. Extraordinary profit or loss.
18. Tax on extraordinary profit or loss.
19. Other taxes not shown under the above items.
20. Profit or loss for the financial year.

1. *Turnover* This amount relates to the amounts derived from the provision of goods and services by the company after deducting trade discounts and value added tax. If substantially different geographical markets have been served then the turnover attributable to each market must be shown.

2. *Cost of sales* This item will include the normal cost of sales including purchases, stocks and work-in-progress adjustments, direct labour, fixed and variable production overheads and depreciation charges relating to plant and machinery and other productive assets in the case of a manufacturing company.

3. *Gross profit or loss* The difference between turnover and cost of sales.

4. *Distribution costs* This includes all costs relating to the holding of goods for resale, selling and distribution costs. Any depreciation charge relating to the selling and distribution activities of the company must be included.

5. *Administrative expenses* These will be all other operating costs not included in cost of sales and distribution costs. Again, any charges for depreciation relating to the administrative activities of the companies must be included.

6. *Other operating income* Show any operating income under this heading but show net income from rents of land separately.

7. *Income from shares in group companies.*

8. *Income from shares in related companies.*

9. *Income from other fixed-asset investments.*

10. *Other interest receivable and similar income.*

11. *Amounts written off investments.*

12. *Interest payable and similar charges*   Distinguish between:

   (a) amounts payable to group companies;

   (b) interest on bank loans and overdrafts repayable within 5 years;

   (c) interest on all other loans.

13. *Tax on profit or loss on ordinary activities*   Show separately UK corporation tax with basis of computation.

14. *Profit or loss on ordinary activities after taxation.*

15. *Extraordinary income*   Give particulars.

16. *Extraordinary charges*   Give particulars.

17. *Extraordinary profit and loss*   This is the difference between 15 and 16.

18. *Tax on extraordinary profit or loss.*

19. *Other taxes not shown under the above items.*

20. *Profit or loss for the financial year.*

Note: Adjustments for (a) amounts transferred to or withdrawn from reserves and (b) aggregate amount of dividends paid and proposed are made from the amount shown in 20 and the retained profit for the year is transferred to the profit and loss account in the balance sheet.

   Other items are required to be disclosed in the profit and loss account usually, by way of note are as follows:

1. Amounts for redemption of share capital and of loans.

2. Staff costs:

Directors   The following information must be given in relation to directors' emoluments distinguishing between fees and other amounts:

   (a) Aggregate emoluments.

   (b) Pensions.

   (c) Compensation for loss of office.

   (d) Number of directors waiving emoluments and the aggregate amount.

   (e) Number of UK directors whose emoluments fall in each £5000 bracket.

   (f) Emoluments of the chairman and of the highest paid director if more than the chairman.

Employees   The following information must be disclosed for employees:

   (a) Average number during year.

   (b) Wages and salaries.

   (c) Social security costs.

   (d) Other pension costs.

   (e) Number of employees whose emoluments fall in each £5000 bracket from £30 000 up.

3. Depreciation – the aggregate depreciation written off fixed assets.

4. Hire of plant and machinery.

5. Effect of any prior year items.

6. Effect of any exceptional transactions.

7. Basis of translation of foreign currencies.

8. Auditors' remuneration to include fees and expenses.

9. The aggregate amount of recommended dividend.

10. Comparative figures for the previous year must be shown.

Format 2

1. Turnover.
2. Change in stocks of finished goods and in work-in-progress.
3. Own work capitalised.
4. Other operating income.
5. (a) Raw materials and consumables.
   (b) Other external charges.
6. Staff costs:
   (a) wages and salaries;
   (b) social security costs;
   (c) other pension costs.
7. (a) Depreciation and other amounts written off tangible and intangible fixed assets.
   (b) Exceptional amounts written off current assets.
8. Other operating charges.
9. Income from shares in group companies.
10. Income from shares in related companies.
11. Income from other fixed-asset investments.
12. Other interest receivable and similar income.
13. Amounts written off investments.
14. Interest payable and similar charges.
15. Tax on profit or loss on ordinary activities.
16. Profit or loss on ordinary activities after taxation.
17. Extraordinary income.
18. Extraordinary charges.
19. Extraordinary profit or loss.
20. Tax on extraordinary profit or loss.
21. Other taxes not shown under the above items.
22. Profit or loss for the financial year.

Format 3

A.   Charges.
1. Cost of sales.
2. Distribution costs.
3. Administrative expenses.
4. Amounts written off investments.
5. Interest payable and similar charges.
6. Tax on profit or loss on ordinary activities.
7. Profit or loss on ordinary activities after taxation.
8. Extraordinary charges.

9. Tax on extraordinary profit or loss.
10. Other taxes not shown under the above items.
11. Profit or loss for the financial year.

B.   Income
1. Turnover.
2. Other operating income.
3. Income from shares in group companies.
4. Income from shares in related companies.
5. Income from other fixed asset investments.
6. Other interest receivable and similar income.
7. Profit or loss on ordinary activities after taxation.
8. Extraordinary income.
9. Profit or loss for the financial year.

Format 4

A.   Charges.
1. Reduction in stocks of finished goods and in work-in-progress.
2. (a) Raw materials and consumables.
   (b) Other external charges.
3. Staff costs:
   (a) wages and salaries;
   (b) social security costs;
   (c) other pension costs.
4. (a) Depreciation and other amounts written off tangible and intangible fixed assets.
   (b) Exceptional amounts written off current assets.
5. Other operating charges.
6. Amounts written off investments.
7. Interest payable and similar charges.
8. Tax on profit or loss on ordinary activities.
9. Profit or loss on ordinary activities after taxation.
10. Extraordinary charges.
11. Tax on extraordinary profit or loss.
12. Other taxes not shown under the above items.
13. Profit or loss for the financial year.

B.   Income
1. Turnover.
2. Increase in stocks of finished goods and in work in progress.
3. Own work capitalised.
4. Other operating income.
5. Income from shares in group companies.
6. Income from shares in related companies.
7. Income from other fixed asset investments.
8. Other interest receivable and similar income.
9. Profit or loss on ordinary activities after taxation.
10. Extraordinary income.
11. Profit or loss for the financial year.

Balance sheet

The following information must be disclosed in the balance sheet or accompanying notes. Format 1 is used to explain the disclosure requirements as it is the most commonly used one in practice.

Format 1

A. Called up share capital not paid.

B. Fixed assets.

I   Intangible assets.
        1. Development costs.
        2. Concessions, patents, licences, trade marks and similar rights and assets.
        3. Goodwill.
        4. Payments on account.

II   Tangible assets.
        1. Land and buildings.
        2. Plant and machinery.
        3. Fixtures, fittings, tools and equipment.
        4. Payments on account and assets in course of construction.

III   Investments.
        1. Shares in group companies.
        2. Loans to group companies.
        3. Shares in related companies.
        4. Loans to related companies.
        5. Other investments other than loans.
        6. Other loans.
        7. Own shares.

C. Current assets.

I   Stocks.
        1. Raw materials and consumables.
        2. Work-in-progress.
        3. Finished goods and goods for resale.
        4. Payments on account.

II   Debtors.
        1. Trade debtors.
        2. Amounts owed by group companies.
        3. Amounts owed by related companies.
        4. Other debtors.
        5. Called-up share capital not paid.
        6. Prepayments and accrued income.

III   Investments.
        1. Shares in group companies.
        2. Own shares.
        3. Other investments.

IV   Cash at bank and in hand.

D. Prepayments and accrued income.

E. Creditors: amounts falling due within one year.
   1. Debenture loans.
   2. Bank loans and overdrafts.
   3. Payments received on account.
   4. Trade creditors.
   5. Bills of exchange payable.
   6. Amounts owed to group companies.
   7. Amounts owed to related companies.
   8. Other creditors including taxation and social security.
   9. Accruals and deferred income.

F. Net current assets (liabilities).

G. Total assets less current liabilities.

H. Creditors: amounts falling due after more than one year.
   1. Debenture loans.
   2. Bank loans and overdrafts.
   3. Payments received on account.
   4. Trade creditors.
   5. Bills of exchange payable.
   6. Amounts owed to group companies.
   7. Amounts owed to related companies.
   8. Other creditors including taxation and social security.
   9. Accruals and deferred income.

I. Provisions for liabilities and charges.
   1. Pensions and similar obligations.
   2. Taxation, including deferred taxation.
   3. Other provisions.

J. Accruals and deferred income.

K. Capital and reserves.

   I   Called-up share capital.

   II   Share premium account.

   III   Revaluation reserve.

   IV   Other reserves.
      1. Capital redemption reserve.
      2. Reserve for own shares.
      3. Reserves provided for by the articles of association.
      4. Other reserves.

   V   Profit and loss account.

A. *Called-up share capital not paid*   Only include in this section unless shown under CII5 below.

B. *Fixed assets.*

   I   *Intangible assets.*
      1. *Development costs*   If these costs are capitalised, the reason for such treatment must be shown, and the period of write-off given.

      2. *Concessions, patents, licences, trade marks and similar rights and assets*   These are only included if acquired for valuable consideration.

3. *Goodwill*   This should only be included if it is purchased goodwill and should be written off over its economic life.

4. *Payments on account*   These refer to payments made on account in respect of items shown under 1 to 3 above.

II   *Tangible assets.*

1. *Land and buildings.*

   (a) Amounts split between freehold and leasehold.

   (b) Amount of leasehold allocated between long (equal to or greater than 50 years) and short leases.

2. *Plant and machinery.*

3. *Fixtures, fittings, tools and equipment.*

4. *Payments on account and assets in course of construction*   See additional notes for items 2 to 4.

III   *Investments*   Included in this heading are investments which it is intended should be held for a long period of time.
   Separate headings are to be shown for:

1. *Shares in group companies.*

2. *Loans to group companies.*

3. *Shares in related companies.*

4. *Loans to related companies.*

5. *Other investments other than loans.*

6. *Other loans.*

7. *Own shares.*

The amount of listed investments must be identified together with the split between those listed in the United Kingdom and those listed in other reputable stock exchanges. The aggregate value of the listed securities must also be disclosed. If stock exchange value is less than market value then both have to be disclosed.

C. *Current assets.*

I   *Stocks*   Separate amounts must be shown for:

1. *Raw materials and consumables.*

2. *Work-in-progress.*

3. *Finished goods and goods for resale.*

4. *Payments on account.*

These should be valued at purchase price or production cost; or, if lower, at net realisable value; or at current cost.

II   *Debtors*   Separate amounts must be shown for:

1. *Trade debtors.*

2. *Amounts owed by group companies.*

3. *Amounts owed by related companies.*

    4. *Other debtors.*

    5. *Called-up share capital not paid* (unless shown under A).

    6. *Prepayments and accrued income* (unless shown under D below).

There must be separate disclosure under each head for amounts falling due after more than one year.

III   *Investments*   Separate amounts must be shown for:

    1. *Shares in group companies.*

    2. *Own shares.*

    3. *Other investments.*

Similar information has to be disclosed as in BIII.

IV   *Cash at bank and in hand.*

D. *Prepayments and accrued income* (show here unless disclosed under C II6).

E. *Creditors: Amounts falling due within one year*   Separate amounts must be shown for:

    1. *Debenture loans.*

    2. *Bank loans and overdrafts.*

    3. *Payments received on account* (if not shown as deductions from stocks and work-in-progress).

    4. *Trade creditors.*

    5. *Bills of exchange payable.*

    6. *Amounts owed to group companies.*

    7. *Amounts owed to related companies.*

    8. *Other creditors including taxation and social security.*

    9. *Accruals and deferred income* (this may be shown under J below).

Details of any debentures issued during the year together with reasons for making the issue must be shown. Particulars of redeemed debentures which the company has power to reissue must be disclosed.

F. *Net current assets (liabilities)*   This amount represents the total current assets and total current liabilities, namely $C + D - E$.

G. *Total assets less current liabilities*   This represents $A + B + F$.

H. *Creditors: amount falling due after more than one year*   The headings are similar to those under E above.

I. *Provision for liabilities and charges*   Separate amounts must be shown for:

    1. *Pensions and similar obligations.*

    2. *Taxation including deferred taxation.*

    3. *Other provisions* (give details of each provision under this heading).

J. *Accruals and deferred income*   Only required if information is not shown under E and/or H above.

K. *Capital and reserves.*

I *Called-up share capital* The following information must be disclosed:

(a) Amount of authorised capital.

(b) Number and aggregate value of nominal shares of each class allotted.

(c) Called-up amount paid.

(d) Particulars of any redeemable shares.

(e) Particulars of arrears of fixed cumulative dividends.

(f) Any allotments made during period.

(g) Conversion and other option rights.

II *Share premium account* The aggregate value of the premiums on shares issued is shown in this account.

III *Revaluation reserve* Any movements in this reserve must be disclosed.

IV *Other reserves* Separate amounts must be shown for:

1. *Capital redemption rerserve* (This is a reserve arising when a company redeems its own shares.)

2. *Reserve for own shares* (This is a reserve arising when a company acquires a holding in its own shares.)

3. *Other reserves* (Any movements in these reserves must be disclosed.)

V *Profit and loss account* (This will include the unappropriated balance brought forward together with the current year's profit retained.)

Additional information to be disclosed in the balance sheet is as follows:

1. *Movements of fixed assets* There must be disclosed all changes in the balance due to additions, disposals and transfers and also revisions in value. The effect of movements on cumulative depreciation as well as cost or valuation must be shown in the case of depreciating assets. This information must also be disclosed for investments.

The following is an example of the form of presentation required by the Companies Act to be disclosed by way of note:

	Equipment	Vehicles	Total
Cost or valuation			
As at 1 January 19X7	£100 000	£20 000	£120 000
Additions during year	25 000	3 000	28 000
Disposals during year	(10 000)	(4 000)	(14 000)
	£115 000	£19 000	£134 000
Depreciation			
As at 1 January 19X7	35 000	8 000	43 000
Charge for year	11 000	5 000	16 000
Disposals	(2 000)	(1 000)	(3 000)
	£44 000	£12 000	£56 000
Net book value			
As at 31 December 19X7	£71 000	£7 000	£78 000

2. *Movements on reserves*   All movements on reserves must be disclosed.

3. *Particulars of charges*   If there is any charge on the company's assets for the liabilities of others, particulars of these must be given.

4. *Contingent liabilities*   The amount of estimate, legal nature and whether security is given in connection with it.

5. *Capital expenditure*   Details of capital expenditure contracted for but not provided and authorised but not contracted for must be disclosed by way of note.

6. *Financial commitments*   Details of any other relevant financial commitments not provided for must be shown.

7. *Foreign currency*   Basis of translation to be shown.

8. *Comparative figures*   Previous years figures to be shown.

General notes

1. Accounting policies   The accounting policies adopted in determining the amounts to be included in respect of all material items in the balance sheet and profit and loss account must be disclosed in a note to the accounts.

    Some examples of the policies which are disclosed are as follows:

(a) The method used to translate foreign currencies.

(b) Depreciation and diminution in value of assets.

(c) Valuation of stock and work-in-progress.

(d) Basis of consolidation in respect of group accounts.

2. *True and fair view*   As a true and fair view of the financial accounts must be given, the directors are required to provide additional information not required by the standard formats or disclosure rules where failure to do so would prevent a true and fair view from being given.

Format 2
Assets

A. Called-up share capital not paid.

B. Fixed assets.

  I   Intangible assets.
        1. Development costs.
        2. Concessions, patents, licences, trade marks and similar rights and assets.
        3. Goodwill.
        4. Payments on account.

  II   Tangible assets.
        1. Land and buildings.
        2. Plant and machinery.
        3. Fixtures, fittings, tools and equipment.
        4. Payments on account and assets in course of construction.

  III   Investments.
        1. Shares in group companies.
        2. Loans to group companies.
        3. Shares in related companies.
        4. Loans to related companies.
        5. Other investments other than loans.

      6. Other loans.

      7. Own shares.

C. Current assets.

  I Stocks.

      1. Raw materials and consumables.

      2. Work in progress.

      3. Finished goods and goods for resale.

      4. Payments on account.

  II Debtors.

      1. Trade debtors.

      2. Amounts owed by group companies.

      3. Amounts owed by related companies.

      4. Other debtors.

      5. Called-up share capital not paid.

      6. Prepayments and accrued income.

  III Investments.

      1. Shares in group companies.

      2. Own shares.

      3. Other investments.

  IV Cash at bank and in hand.

D. Prepayments and accrued income.

Liabilities

A. Capital and reserves.

  I Called-up share capital.

  II Share premium account.

  III Revaluation reserve.

  IV Other reserves.

      1. Capital redemption reserve.

      2. Reserve for own shares.

      3. Reserves provided for by the articles of association.

      4. Other reserves.

  V Profit and loss account.

B. Provisions for liabilities and charges.

      1. Pensions and similar obligations.

      2. Taxation including deferred taxation.

      3. Other provisions.

C. Creditors.

      1. Debenture loans.

      2. Bank loans and overdrafts.

      3. Payments received on account.

      4. Trade creditors.

      5. Bills of exchange payable.

      6. Amounts owed to group companies.

      7. Amounts owed to related companies.

      8. Other creditors including taxation and social security.

      9. Accruals and deferred income.

D. Accruals and deferred income.

Directors' report

A directors' report is one of the principal documents which must be included in each company's annual report and accounts. The main purpose of including a directors' report is to supplement the financial information in the profit and loss account and balance sheet and so give the user of the annual report and accounts a more complete picture of the company.

The principal matters on which the directors have to report are:

1. Principal activities of the company, stating any significant changes which have taken place during the year.

2. A review of the development of the business of the company and its subsidiaries during the year.

3. Significant changes in fixed assets and the nature of these changes. Also any differences between the market value and book value of land where the directors consider that this should be of such significance as to be drawn to the attention of the shareholders and debentureholders.

4. An indication of the likely future developments in the business of the group must be given.

5. Proposed dividends and transfers to reserves are to be disclosed. Any waivers of dividends by shareholders are also to be stated.

6. If the trading results shown by the accounts differ materially from any published forecast made by the holding company then an explanation should be given.

7. Particulars of important events which have occurred between the end of the financial year and the date of approval of the accounts must be disclosed.

8. An indication of the activities, if any, in the field of research and development must be given.

9. The total of any sums given for charitable and political purposes if greater than £200 together with the names of the recipients.

10. Names of directors in office during the year.

11. Directors' interests in the shares and debentures of the company. This information may be disclosed either in the directors' report or in a note to the acccounts.

12. If the average number of employees exceeds 250, a statement relating to the company's policy as to the employment of disabled people and the continued employment and training of persons who became disabled while in employment of the company.

13. Details of shares of the company purchased by the company during the financial year.

14. Details of the company's own shares where they have been acquired by the company, its nominee, or with financial assistance from the company or acquired by forfeiture or by surrender in lieu of forfeiture.

15. A report in the case of larger companies (more than 250 employees) has to be included describing what action has been taken during the year to introduce, maintain or develop arrangements aimed at furthering employee involvement in the company's affairs.

Auditors and audit reports

In earlier chapters, we learned that accounting is not as mathematically precise as the balancing of the double-entry system would lead us to believe. The accountant not only has to decide which of several alternative methods to adopt, but of necessity must make certain estimates, assumptions and forecasts. In the case of fixed assets, for example, both the life of the asset and the anticipated residual value at the outset have to be estimated. In addition to this, different accountants may choose to depreciate using the straight-line method; others may select the units-of-use or the diminishing-value method. A choice has to be made in the valuation of stocks, in the estimated completion of work-in-progress and in the calculation of expected bad debts. Hence, different accountants would produce different accounting reports including different amounts for the key figures of net profit.

The owners of a business (whether a partnership or company) or the members of a club or society have to depend on the accounting reports to measure the financial success or failure of their enterprise and to make relevant decisions for the future. In the cases where the owners are not only separated from the management of the enterprise (as in most companies) but have no access to the accounting records other than through the published reports, an opinion from an independent expert has to be obtained. This expert (the external auditor) examines the accounting records and associated documents and reports to the owners (shareholders or members).

As stated above, however, it is hardly likely that two accountants would produce identical reports. The auditor is, therefore, not stating that the report produced by the accountant is correct, or that the auditor would have produced exactly the same report. After a careful examination of all the circumstances and evidence, the auditor gives a considered opinion whether the accounts are within the guidelines of accepted accounting practice, comply with the relevant law, present no misleading data, and fairly represent the results of operations of the period and the financial position at a particular balance date.

Under UK company law, the auditor is required to state an opinion as to whether the accounts are drawn up so as to give a 'true and fair' view, as well as being prepared in accordance with the Companies Act 1985.

Audits are compulsory for certain persons or groups by law. This includes all companies. Although partnerships are not compelled to have their accounts audited, many firms do so to gain greater credibility for the purpose of borrowing from banks and agreeing their taxation liability.

To carry out the audit, the auditor will first examine the internal controls operating, to test their effectiveness in practice. If it is considered there are weaknesses in the controls, the auditor will concentrate on areas affected and will prepare an audit programme covering all aspects of the work and a tentative timetable. This will be a list of instructions for the separate sections of the operations, for example the examination of purchases, payment of wages, etc. The auditor will specify what is to be examined – the date, the amount, the relevant documents and records, and so on. Working papers showing the results of the work carried out will be carefully prepared and filed to provide satisfactory evidence for any opinion given. The onus is on management to ensure the production of accurate accounting records, and it is for this purpose that internal controls are inaugurated. If the controls operate satisfactorily, the records should be authenticated. Hence, the auditor checks the operation of controls by checking some of the entries. If satisfied that the sample chosen has been dealt with by the established and recognised internal procedures, the auditor assumes that the rest of the records will have been dealt with in the same manner. It is obvious that the size and scope of the sample will be critical to the establishment of opinion, and many auditors now have become aware of the advantages of statistical sampling in the choice of size and type of sample. If findings are satisfactory, the auditor proceeds with the testing of other areas. If not, the auditor will take further samples, or examine every item if need be. No attempt to remedy any defects is made. Errors or omissions will be reported to management with a request that they be corrected.

The auditor may give a plain statement that the accounting reports are 'true and fair', or may qualify the opinion, giving details of objections. In rare cases, the auditor may report being unable to reach an opinion either because of the lack of proper records or because of their incompleteness. The report (in the case of companies) must be included in the published reports of the company. Before qualifying a report, however, an auditor discusses possible changes with the management. In most cases they may agree with suggestions, but, failing agreement, the auditor must report honestly. An example of an audit report is given in this chapter.

In addition to an external auditor, many institutions appoint an internal audit staff. Their duties vary widely and they are different from the external auditor in that they are not independent to the same extent, since they are employees; they are not subject to the same legal constraints; nor do they have to report externally. Internal auditors often ensure that the accounting procedures are carried out properly, check the records and therefore constitute part of the internal control organisation of the enterprise. In addition, they are used to assess the efficiency of operations and to suggest improvements in documentation, procedures or staffing etc. Usually they work in close cooperation with the external auditor, and their working papers are valuable to the latter.

Small and medium-sized companies

Companies qualify to be treated as small or medium-sized companies if, in respect of the financial year and the preceding year, they satisfy at least two of the following conditions:

	Small	Medium-sized
Turnover does not exceed	£2m.	£8m.
Balance sheet total does not exceed	£975 000	£3.9m.
The average number of employees does not exceed	50	250

Public companies are not eligible for these exemptions.

Small companies are allowed to file only an abridged balance sheet. No profit and loss account or directors' report is required to be submitted to the Registrar of Companies. Details to be included in the balance sheet are restricted to headings denoted by letters or roman numerals. The only additional information required to be disclosed relates to the following matters:

1. Accounting policies.
2. Share capital.
3. Particulars of allotments.
4. Particulars of creditor repayment periods and related security given.
5. Basis of translation of foreign currency.
6. Corresponding amounts to the items stated in the notes.

A company qualifying as medium-sized is allowed to file a modified profit and loss account. It must however file a full directors' report, balance sheet and notes, although the amount of turnover need not be disclosed.

The modified profit and loss account will be set out in the standard formats subject to the combining as one item, under the heading 'Gross profit or loss' namely in Format 1 items for turnover, cost of sales, gross profit or loss and other operating income.

Although the Companies Act 1985 allows abridged accounts to be submitted to the Registrar of Companies, small and medium-sized companies must still present unmodified accounts to its shareholders.

Taxation in company accounts

Accounting periods for corporation tax

Corporation tax is assessed on the profits in the company's accounting period. The accounting period will normally be the period for which a company makes up its accounts, but an accounting period should not exceed twelve months. If a company prepares accounts for a period of eighteen months, the first twelve months constitute an accounting period and the remaining six months are treated as a separate accounting period. Corporation tax is due to be paid nine months after the end of the accounting period for which it is assessed, or one month later after the making of the assessment, whichever is later. In the case of a company which traded before April 1965 the same interval between the company's accounting date and the tax due date is retained.

Example: A company whose financial year ended on 31 December 19X7 showed a profit of £250 000 on its ordinary activities before taxation. The corporation tax based on the profits of the year was estimated to be £100 000.

The entries in the profit and loss account and balance sheet will be as follows:

Profit and Loss Account for year ended 31 December 19X7	
Profit on ordinary activities before taxation	£250 000
Taxation on profit on ordinary activities:	
Corporation tax for the year	100 000
Profit on ordinary activities after tax	£150 000

Balance Sheet	
Creditors - Amounts falling due within one year	
Corporation tax	£100 000

Imputation system of corporation tax

Corporation tax is charged at a single rate on a company's income whether distributed or not. If no dividend is paid then the whole of the tax is payable on the due date. On the other hand, if a company makes a dividend payment to shareholders, it does not withhold income tax from the payment, but is required to make an advance payment of corporation tax (ACT). The amount of ACT will normally be set off against the company's total liability for tax on its income tax for the same accounting period.

Example: In the year ended 31 March 19X7 a company has a corporation tax profit of £60 000 and pays a dividend of £14 000 in that year.

ACT £14 000 @ $\frac{3}{7}$		£6 000
Corporation tax liability £60 000 @ 50%	£30 000	
Less ACT	6 000	
Mainstream corporation tax payable at the due date		24 000
Total corporation tax paid		£30 000

In other words:

Tax due by the company	£30 000
Less ACT	6 000
Actual payment of mainstream corporation tax (MCT)	£24 000

In effect the company has paid £6000 in respect of ACT to the Inland Revenue at an earlier date in respect of the dividend payment and then recovers it when payment of the MCT is made.

On the other hand the shareholder who is in receipt of the dividend still has a tax credit from the ACT and thus the corporation tax is said to be imputed to the shareholder.

The company's total liability for tax is as follows:

MCT	£24 000
ACT	6 000
	£30 000

Note: The rates used for MCT and ACT in the above example have been selected for ease of calculation. The reader is advised to consult tax legislation to establish the current rates of taxation.

Deferred taxation

Often the amount of taxation payable on the profits of a particular period bears little relationship to the amount of income and expenditure appearing in the profit and loss account. This results from the different basis on which profits are arrived at for the purpose of computing taxation as opposed to the amounts at which profits are stated in accounts.

The different basis of arriving at profit for tax purposes derives from two main sources:

1. Certain types of income may be tax free or certain expenditure is disallowable for tax purposes, giving rise to 'permanent differences' between taxable and book profits, e.g., entertainment expenses.

2. The existence of items included in the accounts of a period different from that in which they are dealt with for taxation, giving rise to 'timing differences' of which accelerated depreciation allowances is an example.

Deferred tax relating to the ordinary activities of the business should be shown separately as a part of the tax on profit or loss on ordinary activities, either on the face of the profit and loss account or in a note.

The deferred tax balance, and its major components, should be disclosed in the balance sheet or by way of note.

Example to illustrate the preparation of the financial accounts of a limited company

The following list of balances is prepared from the books of Grate Plc on 31 December 19X8, which is the end of the company's accounting year:

	Dr. £000	Cr. £000
Called-up capital – Ordinary shares of £1 each		500
General reserve		310
Sales		3 800
		4 610

Cont.

	Dr. £000	Cr. £000
b/fwd		4 610
Development costs	415	
Share premium		200
Stock – Raw materials	270	
Work-on-progress	83	
Stock – Finished goods	460	
Bills of exchange		15
Prepayments and accrued income	18	
Deferred taxation		175
Revaluation reserve		150
Goodwill	125	
Plant and machinery – at cost	380	
Provision for depreciation on plant and machinery		175
Motor vehicles – at cost (selling and distribution)	140	
Provision for depreciation on motor vehicles		62
Profit and loss account – Unappropriated balance		932
Land and buildings	630	
Investments – listed – at cost	183	
Amounts owed to related company in five years' time		37
Shares in related companies – at cost	175	
Debentures repayable in ten years' time		250
Debtors – Trade	442	
Creditors – Trade		247
Bank overdraft (secured over assets)		127
Royalties received during year		35
Extraordinary charge – Closure of factory	7	
Purchases	1 880	
Bank interest paid	28	
Wages – Production	630	
Hire of plant – Administrative expenses	40	
Auditors' remuneration and expenses	135	
Accrued expenditure		12
Dividends from shares in related companies		20
Selling and distribution expenses	290	
Administrative expenses	397	
Fixed overheads – Production	317	
Cash	2	
	7 047	7 047

Additional information:

1. Authorised capital of the company is £1 000 000.

2. The bills of exchange are due to be paid in three years' time. There is a contingent liability in respect of these bills amounting to £5000.

3. Closing stocks are:

Raw materials	£310 000
Finished goods	620 000
Work in progress	50 000

4. The market value of the investments is £195 000.

5. Depreciation is charged as follows:

Motor vehicles	25 per cent on cost
Plant and machinery	10 per cent on cost

6. Included in the administrative expenses are the following items:

Directors' remuneration	£100 000
Debt collection costs	2 000
Discount allowed	6 000

7. Corporation tax is to be provided for amounting to £75 000.

8. There are commitments for capital expenditure items amounting to £80 000 which have been approved by the directors but not contracted for.

9. Transfer £20 000 to general reserve.

10. A dividend of 10p per ordinary share is proposed.

Problem
From the foregoing information prepare a profit and loss account and balance sheet suitable for submission to shareholders as at 31 December 19X8 in accordance with the Companies Act 1985.

Solution:

GRATE Plc
Profit and Loss Account for year ended 31 December 19X8

	£000	£000
Turnover		3 800
Cost of sales		2 698
Gross profit		1 102
Distribution costs	325	
Administrative expenses	572	897
Operating profit		205
Royalties received		35
		240
Income from shares in related companies		20
		260
Bank interest paid		28
Profit on ordinary activities before taxation		232
Tax on profit on ordinary activities		75
Profit on ordinary activities after taxation		157
Extraordinary charge – factory closure		7
Profit for the financial year		150
Proposed dividend of 10p per share on ordinary shares	50	
Transfer to general reserve	20	70
Retained profit for year		£80

Grate Plc
Balance Sheet as at 31 December 19X8

	£000	£000	£000
Fixed assets			
Intangible assets			
Development costs	415		
Goodwill	125	540	
Tangible assets			
Land and buildings	630		
Plant and machinery	167		
Motor vehicles	43	840	
Investments			
Shares in related companies	175		
Other	183	358	1 738
Current assets			
Stocks			
Raw materials	310		
Work-in-progress	50		
Finished goods	620	980	
Debtors			
Trade	442		
Prepayments and accrued income	18	460	
Cash on hand		2	
		1 442	
Creditors Amounts falling due within one year			
Trade creditors	247		
Bank overdraft	127		
Other creditors including taxation	125		
Accrued expenditure	12	511	
Net current assets			931
Total assets less current liabilities			2 669
Creditors Amounts falling due after more than one year			
Debentures		250	
Bills of exchange payable		15	
Amount owed to related company		37	302
			2 367
Provision for liabilities and charges			
Deferred taxation			175
			£2 192
Capital and reserves			
Called-up share capital			500
Share premium account			200
Revaluation reserve			150
Other reserves			
General			330
Profit and loss account			1 012
			£2 192

Notes for Publication to Shareholders

1. *Operating profit*   Operating profit is arrived at after charging the following:

Directors' remuneration	£100 000
Auditors' remuneration and expenses	135 000
Hire of plant	40 000
Depreciation of fixed assets	73 000

2. *Tangible assets*

	Plant and machinery	Motor vehicles	Total
At cost 1 January 19X8	£380 000	£140 000	£520 000
Depreciation			
As at 1 January 19X8	175 000	62 000	237 000
Charge for year	38 000	35 000	73 000
	£213 000	£97 000	£310 000
Net book value as at 31 December 19X8	£167 000	£43 000	£210 000

3. *Other creditors including taxation*

Dividend	£50 000
Corporation tax	75 000
	£125 000

4. *Investments*

Shares in related companies at cost	£175 000
Listed investments (market value £195 000)	183 000
	£358 000

5. *Reserves*

General	
As at 1 January 19X8	£310 000
Add Transfer during year	20 000
As at 31 December 19X8	£330 000

6. *Profit and loss account*

As at 1 January 19X8	£932 000
Add Profit for year retained	80 000
	£1 012 000

7. *Share capital*

Authorised	
1 000 000 Ordinary shares of £1 each	£1 000 000
Issued and fully paid	
500 000 Ordinary shares of £1 each	£500 000

8. *Taxation*   Corporation tax charged is based on the profits of the year.

9. *Dividend* Final proposed dividend of 10p on each ordinary share.

10. *Contingent liability* There is a contingent liability in respect of bills of exchange amounting to £5000 which have been discounted.

11. *Capital expenditure commitments* Amounts authorised but not contracted for   £80 000

12. *Bank overdraft* The bank overdraft is secured over the assets of the company.

In problems of this type more information would require to be given so that the profit and loss account and balance sheet would meet the requirements of the companies. Some of this information is as follows:

1. Comparative amounts for previous year.
2. Details of directors' remuneration.
3. The redemption dates of debentures.
4. The makeup of the deferred taxation account.
5. Earnings per share.

Working notes (not for publication)

1. *Cost of sales*	£000	£000
Purchases		1 880
Stocks at 1 January 19X8		
Raw materials	270	
Finished goods	460	
Work-in-progress	83	813
		2 693
Less Stocks at 31 December 19X8		
Raw materials	310	
Finished goods	620	
Work-in-progress	50	980
		1 713
Add Wages- Production	630	
Fixed overheads	317	
Depreciation on plant and machinery	38	985
		2 698

2. *Distribution costs*	
Selling and distribution costs	290
Depreciation on motor vehicles	35
	325

3. *Administrative expenses*	
Administrative expenses	397
Auditors' remuneration and expenses	135
Hire of plant	40
	572

Nature of consolidated statements

In order that an investor company may exercise effective control over the policies and operations of the investee company, it is usually necessary for the investor company to acquire more than 50 per cent of the issued ordinary capital. There are, however, occasions on which control has been exercised with less than a majority shareholding (for example, where holding more than half of voting power).

Where effective control exists, the investor company is termed a 'holding' (or parent) company and the investee company a 'subsidiary'. The holding company in its own books accounts for its investment and for the revenue from that investment as described above, in most cases using the dividend method. But irrespective of whether the dividend or the equity method is adopted, the reports of the holding company provide very little detailed information about the subsidiary and its operations. In an attempt to remedy this deficiency, the Companies Act stipulates that the shareholders of the holding company should be provided, in addition to the financial statements of the holding company, with *consolidated financial statements* (group accounts), unless the directors (with the consent of the auditor) consider that some other presentation would be true and fair.

It is impossible, in a text of this nature, to provide a full treatment of the problems involved in the preparation of consolidated financial statements. In the remainder of this chapter, we outline the major features of the consolidation process and provide some simple examples illustrating these features.

The financial statements of a holding company normally contain only two items related to the activities of the subsidiary. These are the revenue from dividends in the profit and loss statement and the investment in the subsidiary, usually shown at cost, in the balance sheet. These amounts do not normally represent the effective earnings by the subsidiary or the effective value of the investment in the subsidiary.

In a group of companies (that is, a holding company and its subsidiaries), each of the various companies is a separate legal entity and thus has to be accounted for separately. But, from an accounting point of view, it is also possible and desirable to define an additional accounting entity – the group of companies as a whole. The group functions as an economic unit and, like any other business entity, uses resources to earn profits. Thus, in order to assess the performance of this economic entity, it is necessary to measure and report the *combined* revenues, expenses and profits of the group as a whole and to relate these profits to the group's resources as represented by the *combined* assets less liabilities. The basic function of consolidated statements is to report these combined figures.

Consolidated statements are prepared at the end of the accounting period from the separate financial statements prepared for each company in the group. Essentially, the consolidation process is one of *addition*. For example, the amounts shown for the asset 'cash at bank' in the balance sheets of each of the individual companies are added together to provide the amount to be shown as 'cash at bank' in the consolidated balance sheet. However, in order to avoid double-counting, the effects of intercompany indebtedness and intercompany transactions have to be eliminated from the addition process. For instance, sales revenue earned by one company by selling goods to another company in the group is not included in the combined 'sales revenue' shown in the consolidated profit and loss statement. The sales revenue of the group should represent only the sales made to customers outside the group.

Simple examples of consolidated statement preparation

We will illustrate the consolidation process first by an example which shows the preparation of a consolidated balance sheet at the date of the acquisition by the holding company of shares in the subsidiary company.

Example 1: On 30 June 19X6, Hut Ltd purchased all of the issued shares of Shack Ltd by paying existing shareholders £80 000 cash. The balance sheets (simplified) of the two companies prior to this transaction were as follows:

Balance Sheets as at 30 June 19X6

	Hut	Shack		Hut	Shack
Creditors	£60 000	£30 000	Cash at bank	£100 000	£30 000
Issued capital	100 000	50 000	Debtors	30 000	20 000
Profit and loss			Stocks	40 000	30 000
appropriation			Fixed assets (net)	80 000	20 000
account	90 000	20 000			
	£250 000	£100 000		£250 000	£100 000

The balance sheet of the subsidiary Shack Ltd will not be affected by the acquisition of the shares, but the balance sheet of Hut Ltd, now a holding company, will appear after the acquisition as follows:

Hut Ltd
Balance Sheet as at 1 July 19X6

Creditors	£60 000	Cash at bank	£20 000
Issued capital	100 000	Debtors	30 000
Profit and loss appropriation		Stocks	40 000
account	90 000	Shares in Shack Ltd	80 000
		Fixed assets (net)	80 000
	£250 000		£250 000

The asset 'shares in Shack Ltd' represents the investment in the net assets (that is, assets less liabilities) of Shack Ltd. The book value of these net assets in Shack's balance sheet at the date of acquisition was £70 000 (£100 000 assets less £30 000 liabilities). Hut Ltd was willing to pay £10 000 in excess of this amount in order to gain control of Shack Ltd. This £10 000 may be viewed as 'goodwill on consolidation'.

In the consolidation process, it is convenient to use a five-column worksheet – the first two columns containing the figures from the separate statements of the holding company and the subsidiary, the next two columns for elimination entries and the final column for the amounts which will appear in the consolidated statement.

A worksheet for the consolidation of Hut and Shack at the date of acquisition will be as follows:

Consolidated worksheet

	Hut	Shack	Eliminations Debit	Eliminations Credit	Consolidated statement
Cash at bank	£20 000	£30 000			£50 000
Debtors	30 000	20 000			50 000
Stocks	40 000	30 000			70 000
Shares in Shack Ltd	80 000	—		£80 000[1]	—
Fixed assets (net)	80 000	20 000			100 000
Goodwill on consolidation	—	—	£10 000[1]		10 000
	£250 000	£100 000			£280 000
Creditors	£60 000	£30 000			£90 000
Issued capital	100 000	50 000	50 000[1]		100 000
Profit and loss appropriation account	90 000	20 000	20 000[1]		90 000
	£250 000	£100 000	£80 000	£80 000	£280 000

[1] Elimination of investment in subsidiary at the date of acquisition.

In Example 1, the holding company acquired 100 per cent of the shareholding in the subsidiary. In cases where control is obtained with less than 100 per cent interest, it is necessary to show in the consolidated balance sheet the amount of equity held by minority interest shareholders. Example 2 illustrates this situation.

Example 2: Given the balance sheets of Hut Ltd and Shack Ltd at 30 June 19X6 as in Example 1, assume that Hut Ltd purchased 80 per cent of the issued shares of Shack Ltd for £50 000 cash.

In this case, Hut Ltd has acquired 80 per cent of net assets of £70 000 (that is, £56 000) for £50 000. Thus, there is a negative amount of £6000 for goodwill in consolidation. This is normally (termed as a capital reserve) and shown as part of shareholders' funds in the consolidated balance sheet.

The consolidation work sheet for Example 2 is given below:

Consolidated worksheet

	Hut	Shack	Elimination Debit	Elimination Credit	Consolidated statement
Cash at bank	£50 000	£30 000			£80 000
Debtors	30 000	20 000			50 000
Stocks	40 000	30 000			70 000
Shares in Shack Ltd	50 000	—		£50 000[1]	—
Fixed assets (net)	80 000	20 000			100 000
	£250 000	£100 000			£300 000
Creditors	£60 000	£30 000			£90 000
Minority interest	—	—		14 000[2]	14 000
Issued capital	100 000	50 000	40 000[1] 10 000[2]		100 000
Profit and loss appropriation account	90 000	20 000	16 000[1] 4 000[2]		90 000
Capital reserve	—	—		6 000[1]	6 000
	£250 000	£100 000	£70 000	£70 000	£300 000

¹ Elimination of investment in subsidiary at date of acquisition against 80 per cent of the capital and undistributed profits of the subsidiary.
² Minority interest of 20 per cent of the capital and undistributed profits of the subisidiary, calculated as follows

Net assets of Shack Ltd	£70 000
Less 80% acquired by Hut Ltd	56 000
Attributable to minority shareholders	£14 000

The item 'minority interest' is normally shown as a separate item in the consolidated balance sheet, distinct from either the liabilities or the shareholders' funds of group shareholders.

The final example in this highly simplified treatment of consolidated statements introduces five additional aspects:

1. The consolidation of the profit and loss statements and the profit and loss appropriation statements.

2. Sales from one member of the group to another member of the group.

3. Inventories held by one member of the group which have been purchased from another member of the group at a price above cost to the seller.

4. Intercompany dividends.

5. Intercompany indebtedness.

Example: Assume the acquisition of shares in Shack Ltd by Hut Ltd as given in Example 2 above. Assume that a year later, on 30 June 19X7, the two companies present financial statements as follows:

Profit and Loss Statements for year ended 30 June 19X7

	Hut Ltd	Shack Ltd
Sales	£300 000	£140 000
Less Cost of goods sold	187 000	87 000
Gross profit	113 000	53 000
Add Dividend revenue	8 000	—
	121 000	53 000
Less Selling and administrative expenses	45 000	23 000
Net profit before tax	76 000	30 000
Less Taxation	36 000	14 000
Net profit after tax	£40 000	£16 000

Profit and Loss Appropriation Statement for year ended 30 June 19X7

	Hut Ltd	Shack Ltd
Balance of profit and loss appropriation account (1/7/X6)	£90 000	£20 000
Add Net profit after tax	40 000	16 000
	130 000	36 000
Less Dividends declared (and paid)	15 000	10 000
Balance of profit and loss appropriation account (30/6/X7)	£115 000	£26 000

Balance Sheets as at 30 June 19X7

	Hut Ltd	Shack Ltd		Hut Ltd	Shack Ltd
Creditors	£40 000	£35 000	Cash at bank	£46 000	£19 000
Provision for tax	36 000	14 000	Debtors	50 000	33 000
Loan from			Stocks	55 000	45 000
Hut Ltd	—	20 000	Loan to Shack		
Issued capital	100 000	50 000	Ltd	20 000	—
Profit and loss			Shares in Shack		
appropriation			Ltd	50 000	—
account	115 000	26 000	Fixed assets (net)	70 000	48 000
	£291 000	£145 000		£291 000	£145 000

Further assume that the sales revenue for Hut Ltd given above includes goods sold to Shack Ltd for £40 000 and that the stocks held by Shack Ltd at the end of the year include goods which had been purchased from Hut Ltd for £9000 and which had cost Hut Ltd £6000.

In preparing the consolidated statements it is essential that intercompany sales and purchases be eliminated in order to avoid double-counting.

Further, it is essential to eliminate the profits earned by one member of the group where the goods on which the profits have been earned are still held at balance date by the other member of the group.

The consolidation worksheets for Example 3 are given below:

Consolidation worksheet – Profit and Loss Statement

	Hut Ltd	Shack Ltd	Eliminations Debit	Eliminations Credit	Consolidated statement
Sales	£300 000	£140 000	£40 000[1]		£400 000
Less Cost of goods sold	187 000	87 000	3 000[2]	40 000[1]	237 000
Gross profit	113 000	53 000			163 000
Add Dividend revenue	8 000		8 000[3]		—
	121 000	53 000			163 000
Less Selling and administrative expenses	45 000	23 000			68 000
Net profit before tax	76 000	30 000			95 000
Less Taxation	36 000	14 000			50 000
Net profit after tax	40 000	16 000			45 000
Less Profit due to minority interest	—	—	3 200[4]		3 200
Group net profit after tax	£40 000	£16 000	£54 200	£40 000	£41 800

[1] Elimination of intercompany sales and purchases.
[2] Elimination of profits on stocks sold by holding company to subsidiary and still held as stocks by subsidiary.
[3] Elimination of intercompany dividends.
[4] Elimination of 20 per cent of subsidiary profit – due to minority interest shareholders.

Consolidation worksheet – Profit and Loss Appropriation Statement

| | Hut Ltd | Shack Ltd | Eliminations | | Consolidated statement |
			Debit	Credit	
Balance profit and loss appropriation account (1/7/X6)	£90 000	£20 000	{ £16 000[1] 4 000[2]		£90 000
Net profit after tax	40 000	16 000	{ 3 000[3] 8 000[4] 3 200[5]		41 800
	130 000	36 000			131 800
Less Dividends declared	15 000	10 000		8 000[4] 2 000[5]	15 000
Balance profit and loss appropriation account (30/6/X7)	£115 000	£26 000	£34 200	£10 000	£116 800

[1] Elimination of 80 per cent of profit and loss appropriation account of subsidiary as at date of acquisition.
[2] Elimination of minority interest (20 per cent) of balance of profit and loss appropriation account of subsidiary at beginning of period.
[3] Elimination of profits on stocks (see profit and loss worksheet).
[4] Elimination of intercompany dividends.
[5] Elimination of 20 per cent of net profit of subsidiary and 20 per cent of dividend declared by subsidiary (minority interest share).

Consolidation worksheet – Balance Sheet

| | Hut Ltd | Shack Ltd | Eliminations | | Consolidated statement |
			Debit	Credit	
Cash at bank	£46 000	£19 000			£65 000
Debtors	50 000	33 000			83 000
Stocks	55 000	45 000		£3 000[3]	97 000
Loan to Shack Ltd	20 000	—		20 000[4]	—
Shares in Shack Ltd	50 000	—		50 000[1]	—
Fixed assets (net)	70 000	48 000			118 000
	£291 000	£145 000			£363 000
Creditors	40 000	35 000			75 000
Provision for tax	36 000	14 000			50 000
Loan from Hut Ltd	—	20 000	20 000[4]		—
Minority interest	—	—		15 200[2]	15 200
Issued capital	100 000	50 000	40 000[1] 10 000[2]		100 000
Profit and loss appropriation account	115 000	26 000	16 000[1] 5 200[2] 3 000[3]		116 800
Capital reserve	—	—		6 000[1]	6 000
	£291 000	£145 000	£94 200	£94 200	£363 000

[1] Elimination of investment in subsidiary against 80 per cent of the capital and undistributed profits of the subsidiary at date of acquisition.
[2] Minority interest of 20 per cent of the capital and undistributed profits of the subsidiary.
[3] Elimination of profits on stocks.
[4] Elimination of intercompany loan.

An illustrative example of company reporting

We are indebted to the directors of Wm Low & Company Plc for permission to reproduce extracts from their annual report as presented to an annual general meeting of the company in 1986. You are advised to study these financial statements as they will assist in your understanding of the legal requirements relating to disclosure of information to shareholders discussed earlier in this chapter.

Directors' Report

Results and Dividends

The group's net profit for the period was £3,252,000.

The directors recommend that a final dividend of 9.0p per share be paid, £1,176,000 which together with the interim dividend paid makes total dividends for the period of £1,764,000. This leaves profit retained of £1,488,000 which the directors recommend should be taken to reserves.

Review of the Business

The group's activities are the operation of retail superstores, supermarkets and freezer centres.

A review of the development of the business of the group is included in the chairman's review on pages 4 and 5.

Land and Buildings

The directors are of the opinion that the market value of freehold land and buildings is in excess of the value stated in the balance sheet.

Executive Share Option Scheme

The Wm Low Group Executive Share Option Scheme received Inland Revenue approval under the Finance Act 1984 on 7 January 1986.

On 31 January 1986 options were granted to subscribe for a total of 148,068 Ordinary 20p shares at a price of 525p per share. These options are exercisable between 31 January 1989 and 31 January 1996.

Directors and their Interests

Mr A L Leslie was appointed to the board on 16 May 1986 and in terms of the articles of association retires at the annual general meeting and, being eligible, offers himself for re-election. All other directors named below have held office throughout the period. Mr I W Stewart and Mr C C R Mitchell retire by rotation and, being eligible, offer themselves for re-election. At 6 September 1986, the unexpired period of Mr I W Stewart's service contract was 1 year 7 months and that of Mr C C R Mitchell and Mr A L Leslie was 3 years.

The interests of the directors in the shares of the company are as follows:

		6 September 1986		7 September 1985	
		Ordinary Shares	Share Options	Ordinary Shares	Share Options
C Blake	Beneficial	2,500	–	2,500	–
H L Findlay	Beneficial	345	27,038	345	–
R K Johnson	Beneficial	490	19,047	490	–
A L Leslie	Beneficial	300	15,238	(16.5.86) –	15,238
J L Millar	Beneficial	5,892	36,080	5,892	–
C C R Mitchell	Beneficial	5,850	27,809	5,850	–
P D Stevenson		–	–	–	–
I W Stewart	Beneficial	171,064	–	178,064	–
	Non Beneficial	32,830	–	36,156	–

Between 6 September 1986 and 29 October 1986 no changes occurred.

Mr P D Stevenson is a director of Noble Grossart Limited. At 6 September 1986 Noble Grossart Limited had advanced to the company an unsecured loan of £1 million which has since been repaid. Interest was payable based on short term market rates.

No other contracts in which any director was materially interested subsisted during the period.

Substantial Shareholders

So far as the directors are aware at 29 October 1986, no shareholder had an interest in 5% or more of the issued share capital.

Close Company

So far as the directors are aware the close company provisions of the Income and Corporation Taxes Act 1970 do not apply to the company.

Auditors

The auditors Arthur Young have indicated their willingness to continue in office and a resolution to reappoint them as auditors will be proposed at the annual general meeting.

Employee Involvement

The group informs all employees of changes and developments within the group by means of a quarterly newspaper and by briefing meetings held by managers and senior management.

In addition an annual Report to Staff advises employees of the financial results and progress of the group.

Consultation with employees on matters affecting them is carried out through staff committees established to represent employees in all locations throughout the group.

Employment of Disabled Persons

The group makes every endeavour to employ disabled persons where the disabilities do not handicap these persons in the performance of their duties.

Where a person already in employment becomes disabled every effort is made to resettle that person in a suitable post and appropriate training given.

Registered disabled persons, once employed, receive equal opportunities for training, career development and promotion.

Political and Charitable Contributions

During the period political contributions amounted to nil and charitable donations to £2139.

H L Findlay, Secretary
Dundee 29 October 1986

Consolidated Profit & Loss Account

For the period 8 September 1985 to 6 September 1986

	Notes	1986 £000	1985 £000
Turnover	3	233,361	206,874
Cost of sales		216,668	192,250
Gross profit		16,693	14,624
Distribution costs		5,858	4,688
Administrative expenses		3,428	2,826
Operating profit	4	7,407	7,110
Interest receivable		54	171
Gain on sales of fixed assets		16	134
		7,477	7,415
Interest payable	5	214	1,149
Profit on ordinary activities before taxation		7,263	6,266
Taxation on profit on ordinary activities	7	2,175	2,047
Profit on ordinary activities after taxation		5,088	4,219
Extraordinary item	8	1,836	–
Profit for the financial period	9	3,252	4,219
Dividends	10	1,764	1,447
Profit for period retained		1,488	2,772
Earnings per share – on stated earnings	11	38.94p	39.13p
– on earnings excluding deferred taxation credit in 1985		38.94p	32.93p

The notes on pages 12 to 16 form part of these accounts

Consolidated Balance Sheet

As at 6 September 1986

	Notes	£000	1986 £000	1985 £000
Fixed Assets				
Tangible assets	12		61,804	42,985
Current Assets				
Stocks – goods for resale		13,429		12,486
Debtors	14	1,222		1,392
Cash at bank and in hand	15	742		5,636
		15,393		19,514
Prepayments and Accrued Income				
Deferred taxation asset	21	700		625
		16,093		20,139
Creditors: Amounts falling due within one year	16	39,091		25,870
Net Current Liabilities			22,998	5,731
Total Assets less Current Liabilities			38,806	37,254
Creditors: Amounts falling due after more than one year	17		1,290	2,151
Provisions for Liabilities and Charges	18		1,805	880
			35,711	34,223
Capital and Reserves				
Called up share capital	19		2,613	2,613
Share premium account			21,425	21,425
Profit and loss account	20		11,673	10,185
			35,711	34,223

C Blake, Director
H L Findlay, Director

The notes on pages 12 to 16 form part of these accounts

Balance Sheet

As at 6 September 1986

	Notes	£000	1986 £000	1985 £000
Fixed Assets				
Tangible assets	12		49,604	36,750
Investments	13		7,105	7,105
			56,709	43,855
Current Assets				
Stocks – goods for resale		10,587		8,895
Debtors	14	13,443		9,660
Cash at bank and in hand	15	742		4,424
		24,772		22,979
Prepayments and Accrued Income				
Deferred taxation asset	21	480		35
		25,252		23,014
Creditors: Amounts falling due within one year	16	38,400		25,801
Net Current Liabilities			13,148	2,787
Total Assets less Current Liabilities			43,561	41,068
Creditors: Amounts falling due after more than one year	17		1,290	2,151
			42,271	38,917
Capital and Reserves				
Called up share capital	19		2,613	2,613
Share premium account			21,425	21,425
Profit and loss account	20		18,233	14,879
			42,271	38,917

C Blake, Director
H L Findlay, Director

The notes on pages 12 to 16 form part of these accounts

Consolidated Source & Application of Funds

For the period 8 September 1985 to 6 September 1986

	£000	1986 £000	1985 £000
Source			
Operating profit after interest received and paid	7,247		6,132
Depreciation	2,640		2,164
Extraordinary item excluding non cash items	(1,738)		–
		8,149	8,296
Proceeds of shares issued on acquisition		–	3,935
Proceeds of rights issue less expenses		–	14,939
Proceeds of disposal of tangible fixed assets		281	785
		8,430	27,955
Applied			
Purchases of tangible fixed assets		22,132	14,835
Goodwill on acquisition of subsidiary		–	5,054
Dividends paid		1,633	1,059
Corporation Tax (including ACT) paid		2,018	880
Decrease in working capital			
Increase in stocks	943		3,859
Decrease in debtors	(170)		822
Increase in creditors	(2,640)		(4,443)
		(1,867)	238
Increase in provisions for liabilities and charges		(925)	(880)
		22,991	21,186
Resultant decrease in net liquidity			
Decrease in short term deposits	(4,401)		4,401
Decrease in bank loans due after more than one year	–		2,500
Increase in bank overdrafts less cash	(10,160)		(132)
		(14,561)	6,769
		8,430	27,955

The notes on pages 12 to 16 form part of these accounts

Notes to the Accounts

As at 6 September 1986

1 Accounting Policies

(a) Basis of Consolidation
The consolidated accounts comprise the accounts of Wm Low & Company PLC and its wholly owned subsidiary Laws Stores Limited for the 52 week period ended 6 September 1986.

No profit and loss account is presented for Wm Low & Company PLC as provided by section 228(7) of the Companies Act 1985.

(b) Depreciation
The group's policy is to provide depreciation at rates which are calculated to write off the cost of the tangible fixed assets by equal annual instalments over the following estimated useful lives:
Freehold buildings – varying from 20 to 100 years
Leasehold buildings – not exceeding the period of the lease
Fixtures, fittings and equipment – varying from 3 to 10 years
No depreciation is provided on freehold land.

(c) Stocks
Stocks are valued at the lower of cost and net realisable value. For branch stocks, cost is calculated as retail price less standard margin and for warehouse stocks as the actual supplier cost.

(d) Deferred Taxation
Deferred taxation is provided on all timing differences which are expected to reverse in the foreseeable future calculated at the rate at which it is estimated that tax will be payable.

(e) Capitalisation of Interest
Interest incurred after 7 September 1985 on borrowings to finance new property developments prior to commencement of trading is capitalised. Prior periods have not been adjusted on the grounds of immateriality.

(f) Leases
Payments in respect of leases are charged against profits in the period to which they relate.

2 Accounts
These accounts were approved by the board of directors on 29 October 1986.

3 Turnover
Turnover represents total retail sales in the period exclusive of Value Added Tax.

	1986 £000	1985 £000
4 Operating Profit		
(a) Profit is stated after charging		
Depreciation	2,640	2,164
Lease rentals – plant and equipment	372	402
– land and buildings	2,029	1,725
Directors' remuneration	242	316
Auditors' remuneration	35	36
(b) Directors' Remuneration		
Directors' fees	36	33
Emoluments including pension contributions	204	191
Compensation for loss of office	–	90
Pension to widow of past director	2	2
	242	316
Emoluments of the Chairman (1985 – from 18.2.85)	11	7
Emoluments of the Chairman to 18.2.85	–	21
Emoluments of the highest paid director	49	46

The number of directors whose emoluments fell within the following ranges was

Nil to £5,000	1	1
£5,001 to £10,000	1	1
£10,001 to £15,000	1	1
£20,001 to £25,000	–	1
£30,001 to £35,000	1	1
£35,001 to £40,000	3	2
£45,001 to £50,000	1	1

5 Interest payable

	1986 £000	1985 £000
Wholly repayable within 5 years:		
Bank loans and overdrafts	841	1,119
10% unsecured loan stock	40	30
	881	1,149
Interest capitalised	(667)	–
	214	1,149

Tax relief of £253,000 (1985– nil) has been claimed on interest capitalised.

6 Employees

	1986	1985
The average weekly number of employees during the period was made up as follows:		
Branches – full time	1,547	1,448
Branches – part time	4,966	4,359
Head office – management, distribution and administration	435	367
	6,948	6,174

	1986 £000	1985 £000
Employment costs during the period amounted to:		
Wages and salaries	18,538	15,738
Social security costs	1,012	1,187
Other pension costs	616	591
	20,166	17,516

7 Taxation

	1986 £000	1985 £000
The taxation charge is made up as follows:		
Based on the profit of the period		
Corporation Tax at 37.92% (1985 – 42.92%)	2,246	2,715
Deferred Taxation	–	(668)
	2,246	2,047
Overprovided in previous periods	(71)	–
	2,175	2,047

8 Extraordinary item

	1986 £000	1985 £000
Closure and reorganisation costs of Laws branches (net of tax relief of £310,000)	1,836	–

9 Profit for the Financial Period

Of the profit for the financial period of £3,252,000 (1985 – £4,219,000) the amount dealt with in the accounts of Wm Low & Company PLC is £5,118,000 (1985 – £3,859,000).

10 Dividends	**1986** **£000**	1985 £000
Interim dividend on 13,065,143 (10,050,110) 20p shares at 4.5p (4.0p) per share	**588**	402
Proposed final dividend on 13,065,143 (13,065,143) 20p shares at 9.0p (8.0p) per share	**1,176**	1,045
	1,764	1,447

11 Earnings per share

The calculation of earnings per share is based on £5,088,000 (1985 – £4,219,000) and on 13,065,143 (1985 – weighted average of 10,782,552) ordinary 20p shares.

12 Tangible Fixed Assets

		Land and Buildings		Fixtures	Assets in course	
Group	Freehold £000	Long Leasehold £000	Short Leasehold £000	Fittings & Equipment £000	of Con- struction £000	Total £000
Cost						
7 September 1985	27,075	1,021	7,257	13,215	4,172	52,740
Additions	5,964	3	693	3,856	11,616	22,132
Transfers	2,217	–	(15)	20	(2,222)	–
Disposals	(307)	–	(228)	(982)	–	(1,517)
6 September 1986	34,949	1,024	7,707	16,109	13,566	73,355
Depreciation						
7 September 1985	1,771	121	1,307	6,556	–	9,755
Provided during period	433	17	337	1,853	–	2,640
Transfers	(43)	49	(6)	–	–	–
Disposals	(140)	–	(147)	(557)	–	(844)
6 September 1986	2,021	187	1,491	7,852	–	11,551
Net Book Amounts						
6 September 1986	32,928	837	6,216	8,257	13,566	61,804
7 September 1985	25,304	900	5,950	6,659	4,172	42,985
Company						
Cost						
7 September 1985	23,475	564	5,923	10,212	4,172	44,346
Additions	5,249	3	265	3,235	6,437	15,189
Transfers	2,202	–	–	20	(2,222)	–
Disposals	(173)	–	–	(299)	–	(472)
6 September 1986	30,753	567	6,188	13,168	8,387	59,063
Depreciation						
7 September 1985	1,357	72	947	5,220	–	7,596
Provided during period	387	11	274	1,501	–	2,173
Disposals	(37)	–	–	(273)	–	(310)
6 September 1986	1,707	83	1,221	6,448	–	9,459
Net Book Amounts						
6 September 1986	29,046	484	4,967	6,720	8,387	49,604
7 September 1985	22,118	492	4,976	4,992	4,172	36,750

Group freehold land and buildings includes £4,909,000 (1985 – £3,718,000) for land not depreciated.
Interest capitalised of £667,000 (1985 – nil) is included in group additions.

13 Investments

	Company £000
Subsidiary Companies	
Shares at cost	7,141
Less: amount written off	(36)
	7,105

Wm Low & Company PLC owns 100% of the issued share capital of Laws Stores Limited, registered in England, and 100% of the issued share capital of Lowfoods Limited, a non trading company.

14 Debtors

	Group 1986 £000	1985 £000	Company 1986 £000	1985 £000
Amounts owed by subsidiary company	–	–	12,276	8,440
Other debtors	228	693	228	549
Prepayments and accrued income	994	699	939	671
	1,222	1,392	13,443	9,660

The amounts owed by the subsidiary company are not repayable within one year.

15 Cash at Bank and In Hand

	Group 1986 £000	1985 £000	Company 1986 £000	1985 £000
Short term deposits	–	4,401	–	3,901
Other bank and cash balances	742	1,235	742	523
	742	5,636	742	4,424

16 Creditors: Amounts falling due within one year

	Group 1986 £000	1985 £000	Company 1986 £000	1985 £000
Bank loans and overdrafts	14,815	5,148	14,815	5,148
Trade creditors	14,903	13,143	14,903	13,101
Corporation Tax	2,656	1,873	2,656	1,873
Other taxes and social security costs	467	521	467	514
Proposed final dividend	1,176	1,045	1,176	1,045
10% unsecured loan stock	331	462	331	462
Other creditors	2,440	1,429	1,749	1,409
Accruals	2,303	2,249	2,303	2,249
	39,091	25,870	38,400	25,801

17 Creditors: Amounts falling due after more than one year

	Group 1986 £000	1985 £000	Company 1986 £000	1985 £000
Corporation Tax due 4 December 1987	1,290	2,151	1,290	2,151

18 Provisions for Liabilities and Charges

	Group 1986 £000	1985 £000	Company 1986 £000	1985 £000
Reorganisation costs of subsidiary company	1,805	880	–	–

19 Share Capital

	1986 £000	1985 £000
Authorised		
17,400,000 ordinary shares of 20p each	3,480	3,480
Allotted issued and fully paid		
13,065,143 ordinary shares of 20p each	2,613	2,613

20 Profit and Loss Account

	Group £000	Company £000
7 September 1985	10,185	14,879
Profit for period retained	1,488	3,354
6 September 1986	11,673	18,233

21 Deferred Taxation

	Group 1986 £000	Group 1985 £000	Company 1986 £000	Company 1985 £000
(a) Provided				
Capital allowances	–	–	–	(413)
Other timing differences	220	177	–	–
Advance Corporation Tax recoverable against future Corporation Tax	480	448	480	448
Deferred Asset	700	625	480	35
(b) Potential liability				
Capital allowances	3,769	3,315	3,769	3,315
Other timing differences	(220)	(177)	–	–
Capital gains	463	852	341	352
Advance Corporation Tax recoverable against future Corporation Tax	(480)	(448)	(480)	(448)
	3,532	3,542	3,630	3,219

22 Lease Obligations

	Group 1986 £000	Group 1985 £000	Company 1986 £000	Company 1985 £000
Operating leases: land and buildings				
Lease payments due within one year in respect of leases:				
Expiring after five years	1,913	2,047	1,563	1,569
Operating leases: plant and equipment				
Lease payments due within one year in respect of leases:				
Expiring within one year	8	11	2	2
Expiring within two to five years	118	140	116	116
	2,039	2,198	1,681	1,687
Finance leases				
Lease payments due:				
Within one year	164	289	–	–
Within two to five years	124	204	–	–
	288	493	–	–
Less: finance charges	75	127	–	–
	213	366	–	–

23 Capital Commitments

	Group 1986 £000	Group 1985 £000	Company 1986 £000	Company 1985 £000
Amounts contracted for	7,855	5,185	4,685	4,500
Amounts authorised but not contracted for	10,900	3,125	8,170	3,125

24 Pension Commitments

The group operates a retirement benefits scheme to provide pensions based upon final salaries and life assurance of twice current salary to full time staff.

Group pension fund payments during the period were £616,000 (1985 – £591,000). Based on the latest actuarial valuation, current funding levels are adequate to meet the future liabilities.

Auditors' Report

To the members of Wm Low & Company PLC

We have audited the accounts on pages 8 to 16 in accordance with approved auditing standards.

In our opinion the accounts, which have been prepared under the historical cost convention, give a true and fair view of the state of affairs of the company and the group at 6 September 1986 and of the profit and source and application of funds of the group for the period then ended and comply with the Companies Act 1985.

Arthur Young, Chartered Accountants
Dundee 29 October 1986

Five Year Financial Review

All figures in £000s	1986	1985	1984	1983	1982
Turnover	**233,361**	206,874	154,224	132,593	119,819
Profit before taxation	**7,263**	6,266	5,106	3,941	3,340
Taxation	**2,175**	2,047	2,225	651	970
Profit after taxation	**5,088**	4,219	2,881	3,290	2,370
Extraordinary item	**1,836**	–	–	–	436
Net profit for period	**3,252**	4,219	2,881	3,290	1,934
Dividends	**1,764**	1,447	925	795	691
Profit retained	**1,488**	2,772	1,956	2,495	1,243
Earnings per share	**38.94p**	39.13p	30.19p	34.48p	28.24p
Dividends per share	**13.5p**	12.0p	10.0p	8.6p	8.0p
Dividend cover	**2.88**	2.92	3.11	4.14	3.43
Fixed assets					
At start of period	**42,985**	30,965	25,754	17,186	14,460
Additions less disposals	**21,459**	14,184	6,877	9,732	3,734
Depreciation	**(2,640)**	(2,164)	(1,666)	(1,164)	(1,008)
At end of period	**61,804**	42,985	30,965	25,754	17,186
Deferred asset	**700**	625	–	242	234
Current assets	**15,393**	19,514	9,585	7,899	8,692
Current liabilities and provisions	**(40,896)**	(26,750)	(18,599)	(15,402)	(11,585)
Medium term bank loans	**–**	–	(2,500)	(2,500)	(600)
Taxation due	**(1,290)**	(2,151)	(1,433)	(318)	(747)
Deferred taxation	**–**	–	(387)	–	–
	35,711	34,223	17,631	15,675	13,180
Share capital	**2,613**	2,613	1,850	1,850	1,850
Share premium	**21,425**	21,425	3,314	3,314	3,314
Reserves	**11,673**	10,185	12,467	10,511	8,016
	35,711	34,223	17,631	15,675	13,180

Figures have been adjusted to apply current accounting policies to prior periods, where material.
Earnings per share have been adjusted for the rights issues in 1982 and 1985.

Summary

1. Section 221 Companies Act 1985 requires every company to keep accounting records sufficient to show and explain the company's transactions.

2. There is a requirement included in the Companies Act 1985 that every balance sheet and profit and loss account shall give a true and fair view.

3. There are statutory obligations on the directors of every limited company not only to send a copy of the annual report to each shareholder, debenture holder and any person entitled to receive notice of annual general meetings but also to the Registrar of Companies so that it may be available for inspection by any interested party.

4. It is important to recognise the difference between reserves and provisions.

5. The Companies Act 1985 lays down two formats which can be used for the presentation of the company's balance sheet and a choice of four formats for the profit and loss account.

6. There are a considerable number of disclosures which are required to be made in the annual report relating to financial matters. These requirements are stated in the Companies Act and the accounting standards.

7. The directors' report is an important document which must be included in each company's annual report and accounts.

8. Every limited company must appoint an auditor whose responsibility is required to state an opinion as to whether the accounts are drawn up so as to give a 'true and fair' view, as well as being prepared in accordance with the Companies Act and the appropriate accounting standards.

9. Small and medium-sized companies, as defined in the Companies Act, may publish an abridged form of annual accounts.

10. Corporation tax is assessed on the profits in the company's accounting period. The accounting period will normally be the period for which a company makes up its accounts.

11. Deferred taxation is an amount set aside to prevent undue tax charge fluctuations caused by timing differences in respect of depreciation allowances etc.

12. Consolidation statements are normally prepared where a holding company controls the activities of one or more subsidiary companies.

13. Consolidated profit and loss statements reflect the revenues, expenses and profits of the group as an economic entity, and consolidated balance sheets show the assets and equities of the group.

Discussion questions

18.1 What is the difference between a reserve and a provision in company accounting?

18.2 What are the main differences between a limited company and a partnership?

18.3 Compare and contrast the issue of preference shares with that of debentures as a means of raising funds.

18.4 'A balance sheet is an historical document.' Explain the significance of this statement.

18.5 What is meant by the expression 'true and fair'? Discuss.

18.6 Explain the role of the auditor in a limited company.

18.7 Explain whether you consider that the introduction by the 1985 Companies Act of required formats for financial statements has improved the reporting of companies' financial affairs.

18.8 What criteria determine whether a company is small or medium-sized? Do you agree that these companies should be allowed to produce abridged accounts?

18.9 'Provision for deferred tax.' How does such a provision arise and why should it be required?

18.10 When and for what reasons should inter-company sales within a group be eliminated in the consolidated statements?

18.11 'Financial statements should be so clearly stated that every shareholder of ordinary intelligence should be able to understand them.' To what extent do you agree that published company reports comply with this requirement?

Exercises

18.12 On 31 December 19X8, before providing for depreciation, directors' fees and corporation tax, but after transferring all other revenue balances to the trading and profit and loss accounts, the following balances remained in the general ledger of Traders Ltd:

	Dr.	Cr.
Land – at cost	£2 100	
Trade creditors		£4 238
Profit and loss account		10 265
Plant and machinery – at cost	12 650	
Goodwill – at cost	1 200	
Shares in subsidiary company – at cost	900	
Provision for depreciation – on plant		5 670
Provision for depreciation – on buildings		1 600
Prepaid insurance	84	
Profit and loss appropriation account		8 364
Mortgage		4 500
Buildings – at cost	18 200	
General reserve		17 500
Accrued expenses		145
Authorised and issued share capital in £1 shares		25 000
Bank (secured over assets)		1 469
Cash in hand	30	
Investments, at cost	784	
Stock	29 555	
Debtors – trade	16 398	
Capital reserve		2 500
Provision for doubtful debts		650
	£81 901	£81 901

Depreciation is to be provided for at the rate of 2 per cent on cost for buildings and 10 per cent on the reducing balance method for plant and machinery. Directors' fees for the year have not been paid, and are to be brought in at the agreed sum of £500. The estimated corporation tax on the profit for the year ended 31 December 19X8 is £4186. The directors are recommending a dividend of 5p per ordinary share and this provision is to be included in the final accounts.

You are required to prepare for submission to shareholders a profit and loss account (disclosing as much information as given in the question) for the year ended 31 December 19X8 and a balance sheet at that date.

18.13 (a) Outline the factors that you consider limit the value of the balance sheet as a statement of net worth.

(b) Rearrange the following unclassified balance sheets in a form to comply with the requirements of the Companies Act. Supply missing details where necessary.

Fern Ltd
Balance Sheets as at 30 June

	19X4	19X5		19X4	19X5
Provision for			Plant and equipment	£24 500	£29 000
doubtful debts	£2 250	£2 650	Cash at bank	9 300	8 200
Mortgage	19 500	18 200	Land and buildings	47 000	55 000
Creditors	19 450	23 900	Debtors	26 200	28 950
Provision for			Motor vehicles	8 000	10 000
depreciation on			Shares in X-Ray Ltd	24 000	28 000
motor vehicles	2 900	3 700	Stocks	21 500	28 500
Provision for depreci-			Unissued capital	120 000	100 000
ation on plant and					
equipment	5 350	6 300			
Provision for taxation	7 850	8 300			
Authorised capital	200 000	200 000			
General reserve	20 000	22 000			
Profit and loss					
appropriation	3 200	2 600			
	£280 500	£287 650		£280 500	£287 650

18.14 The bookkeeper of Lang Ltd has prepared the following balance sheet for submission to the shareholders. He has asked you to examine this statement and redraft it, where necessary, to conform with the provisions of the Companies Act and best modern methods of statement presentation.

Balance Sheet as at 30 June 19X5

Capital			Stock (at cost)		£26 880
Nominal £1 5% preference	£50 000		Cash at bank		14 250
£1 Ordinary	90 000		Calls in arrears –		
Net profit year ended			preference		620
30 June 19X7	28 100		Debtors		21 500
Total proprietorship	168 100		Appropriation		
	———		account, 1/7/X6		56 000
Creditors (trade)	43 750		Land and buildings	£72 000	
Call in advance-preference	2 000		(at cost)		
Bills payable (due 30/5/X8)	17 500		*Less* Mortgage (due	15 000	57 000
Reserves and Provisions			19X9)	———	
Depreciation – vehicles	15 000				
	£78 250				£176 250

Cont.

b/fwd	£78 250			£176 250
Depreciation – plant	37 500	Vehicles £28 000,		
Depreciation – fixtures	8 600	plant £63 000 and		
Doubtful debts	2 100	fixtures £12 100 (all		
Discounts allowable £500		at cost)		103 100
Less Discounts		£1 shares in subsid-		
receivable 420		iary (at cost)	£20 000	
	80	*Less* Loans by		
Holiday pay due to employees	3 600	subsidiary	8 000	12 000
Stock reserve	5 000			
Dividend equalisation reserve	14 000	Government stock		
Loans of subsidiary guaranteed		(at cost)		6 500
£6500		(Temporary invest-		
		ment)		
		Deposit on new		
		factory		15 000
		Unissued capital £1		
		preference		5 000
		Unissued capital £1		
		ordinary		20 000
		Uncalled capital £1		
		preference		8 000
				345 850
		Less Debentures		
		(secured by a float-		
		ing charge)		28 000
		Accrued interest on		
		debentures		620
				28 620
Total liabilities and				
proprietorship	£317 230	**Total net assets**		£317 230

From an examination of the company's records, you ascertain the following:

(a) At 1 July 19X6 preference dividends were £5000 in arrears. The directors propose to recommend to shareholders that a preference dividend of £2000 be paid from the current year's profits.

(b) Estimated tax liability on the profits for the year ended 30 June 19X7 – £8700. This has not been entered in the accounts.

(c) Debtors include loans to employees of £6000 due in 19X9.

(d) A contract was signed for the erection of a new factory. Contract price was £85 000. A deposit of £15 000 was paid on 31 May 19X4 the remainder being due on completion which is expected to be in October 19X7.

(e) The stock reserve was the amount by which the market value of stock was less than its cost price.

Problems

18.15 The following balance sheet and profit and loss account of Laceys Limited has been prepared by the secretary:

Balance Sheet as at 31 December 19X5

[1]Issued shares –		
50 000 £1 6% Cumulative preference		£50 000
400 000 £1 Ordinary, paid to 75p		300 000
[1]5% Mortgage debentures		120 000
Profit and loss account (31/12/X4)		58 000
General reserve		38 000
Doubtful debts reserve		2 600
Plant depreciation reserve		39 400
Dividend equalisation reserve		12 000
Profit for year		2 000
Provision for corporation tax		16 000
Bank overdraft		12 000
Accrued charges		5 000
Trade creditors		33 000
Bills payable		6 000
[1]Raw materials	£45 000	
[1]Finished goods	123 000	
Trade debtors	52 900	
Achilles Limited, current account	13 000	
[1]Investments	124 000	
Plant at cost	154 400	
Buildings at cost	127 500	
Trade marks at cost	8 500	
[1]Freehold land	32 500	
Preliminary and share issue expenses	11 000	
Prepaid expenses	500	
Cash on hand	200	
[1]Advance to director	1 500	
	£694 000	£694 000

Profit and loss account

Gross profit		£91 140
[1]Achilles Limited – Dividend		3 300
Ajax Limited – Dividend		5 500
Profit on sale of plant		2 000
Depreciation	£15 440	
Administrative expenses	14 500	
Director's salary	3 500	
Debenture interest	6 000	
Amount written off preliminary expenses	2 000	
Directors' fees	500	
[1]Dividends paid	27 000	
Corporation tax	16 000	
Transfer to general reserve	15 000	
Net profit per balance sheet	2 000	
	£101 940	£101 940

[1] See further details below.

The directors issued instructions for the re-drafting of the balance sheet and profit and loss account in a more presentable form. The following additional information was obtained:

(a) The authorised capital is £600 000, divided into shares of £1 each, of which 500 000 are ordinary shares.

(b) The debentures are redeemable in annual instalments of £20 000, the first repayment being due on 1 July 19X6.

(c) The stocks have been valued as follows:
Raw materials   Lower of cost or market
Finished goods   Cost of materials and labour plus an appropriate percentage to cover manu-
facturing expenses

(d) Investments, which are stated at cost, are:
Achilles Limited
60 000 fully paid ordinary shares   £75 000
This represents 70 per cent of the issued capital

Ajax Limited
56 000 £1 shares fully paid   49 000
These shares are quoted on a stock exchange and are held by the bank
as security for the overdraft.
                                                                          _____
                                                                          £124 000

(e) The land which cost £22 500, was revalued during the year by a competent valuer. The surplus on revaluation was credited to general reserve.

(f) The advance to director represents three advances, each of £500, made in March 19X4, April 19X5 and August 19X5. The total amount is repayable on 30 days' notice.

(g) Achilles Limited earned a profit of £12 000 for the year ended 30 September 19X5 after charging directors' fees of £750. This represented payments of £250 to each of three directors, two of whom are also directors of Laceys Limited.

(h) The dividends paid during the year were:
Ordinary – Final 19X4   £12 000
         – Interim 19X5   12 000
Preference 19X4   3 000
                                                                          _____
                                                                          £27 000

(i) The directors decided to recommend the payment of a final dividend on ordinary shares for the six months ended 31 December 19X5 at the rate of 10 per cent per annum on the paid-up capital, together with the yearly dividend on preference shares.

You are required to submit:

(i) A revised balance sheet at 31 December 19X5.

(ii) Revised profit and loss account for the year ended 31 December 19X5.

Your answer should conform with modern practice and comply with the requirements of the Companies Act. It should also incorporate any final adjustments that may be necessary to ensure that the balance sheet is properly drawn up so as to record a true and fair view of the state of the affairs of Laceys Limited at 31 December.

18.16 On 1 July 19X6, Hudson Ltd acquired all of the issued shares of Shaw Ltd for £90 000 cash. The balance sheets of the two companies immediately *prior* to the acquisition of the shares were as follows:

	Hudson Ltd	Shaw Ltd
Cash at bank	£110 000	10 000
Debtors	40 000	20 000
Stocks	60 000	25 000
Fixed assets (net)	90 000	45 000
	£300 000	£100 000
Creditors	£20 000	£20 000
Debentures	50 000	—
Issued capital	200 000	50 000
Profit and loss appropriation accounts	30 000	30 000
	£300 000	£100 000

Prepare a consolidated balance sheet as at the date of acquisition of the shares.

18.17 Using the balance sheets of Hudson Ltd and Shaw Ltd as given in problem 18.16 above, prepare a consolidated balance sheet on the basis that Hudson Ltd purchased 80 per cent of the issued capital of Shaw Ltd for £60 000 cash.

18.18 On 1 July 19X6, Harper Ltd acquired 75 per cent of the issued capital of Scott Ltd. The profit and loss statements for the two companies for the year ended 30 June 19X7 were as follows:

	Harper Ltd	Scott Ltd
Sales	£300 000	£120 000
Less Cost of goods sold	185 000	76 000
Gross profit	115 000	44 000
Less Expenses	62 000	23 000
Net profit before tax	53 000	21 000
Less Corporation tax	21 000	10 000
Net profit after tax	£32 000	£11 000

The sales of Harper Ltd included goods sold to Scott Ltd for £25 000 and which had cost Harper Ltd £15 000. On 30 June 19X7, the stocks of Scott Ltd included goods which it had purchased for £5000 and which had cost Harper Ltd £3000.

Prepare a consolidated profit and loss statement for the year ended 30 June 19X7.

18.19 The accounting reports of Hail Ltd and its subsidiary Snow Ltd for the year ended 30 June 19X6 are given below:

Profit and Loss Statements for the year ended 30 June 19X6

	Hail Ltd	Snow Ltd
Sales	£746 000	£375 000
Less Cost of goods sold	484 000	245 000
Gross profit	262 000	130 000
Add Dividend revenue	16 000	—
	£278 000	£130 000

Cont.

	Hail Ltd	Snow Ltd
b/fwd	£278 000	£130 000
Less Expenses	145 000	72 000
Net profit before tax	133 000	58 000
Less Corporation tax	55 000	28 000
Net profit after tax	£78 000	£30 000

Statements of Profit and Loss Appropriation for the year ended 30 June 19X6

	Hail Ltd	Snow Ltd
Balance profit and loss appropriation (1/7/X5)	£87 000	£80 000
Add Net profit after tax	78 000	30 000
	165 000	110 000
Less Dividends declared	40 000	20 000
Balance profit and loss appropriation (30/6/X6)	£125 000	£90 000

Balance Sheets as at 30 June 19X6

	Hail Ltd	Snow Ltd
Debtors	£85 000	£25 000
Stocks	88 000	23 000
Loan to Snow Ltd	15 000	—
Shares in Show Ltd (at cost)	120 000	—
Fixed assets (net)	192 000	197 000
	£500 000	£245 000
Bank overdraft	£3 000	£18 000
Creditors	32 000	22 000
Loan from Hail Ltd	—	15 000
Loan on mortgage	40 000	—
Issued capital	300 000	100 000
Profit and loss appropriation account	125 000	90 000
	£500 000	£245 000

Further information available:

(a) Hail Ltd acquired its shares in Snow Ltd several years ago when it paid £120 000 for 80 000 £1 shares (80 per cent of the issued capital of Snow Ltd). At that date, the balance in Snow Ltd's profit and loss appropriation account was £40 000.

(b) During the year ended 30 June 19X6, Hail Ltd sold to Snow Ltd for £70 000 goods which had cost Hail Ltd £42 000. At the end of the period, Snow Ltd's stocks included goods which it had purchased from Hail Ltd for £10 000 and which had cost Hail Ltd £6600.

Prepare consolidated financial statements.

18.20 The following trial balance has been extracted from the ledger of the Fantastic Manufacturing Co. Ltd, as at 30 June 19X6:

	Dr.	Cr.
[1]Creditors		£33 377
Debtors	£71 248	
Advertising	3 379	
[1]Audit fees	315	
Bad debts	1 875	
Bank		5 580
[1]Call No. 2 (ordinary shares)	1 200	
[1]Capital reserve		830
[1]Debentures 6%, repayable 19X8		50 000
Directors' fees	2 200	
Factory expenses	10 269	
Finished goods on hand (1 July 19X5)	32 125	
[1]General reserve		8 000
Goodwill and trade marks	29 900	
Corporation tax paid	4 556	
Insurance	904	
[1]Interest on debentures	3 000	
Interim dividend (ordinary shares)	4 500	
Lighting	1 936	
Office expenses	2 895	
Office furniture and equipment (cost)	16 140	
Office salaries	6 072	
Plant (cost)	88 000	
[1]Preliminary expenses	750	
Provision for depreciation of plant		17 600
[1]Provision for depreciation of office furniture and equipment		1 919
Provision for doubtful debts		1 600
Provision for corporation tax		4 000
[1]Petty cash advance	50	
Profit and loss appropriation (1 July 19X5)		4 625
Purchases of raw materials	142 798	
[1]Raw materials on hand (1 July 19X5)	34 672	
Authorised capital (150 000 £1 ordinary shares and 50 000 £1 7% preference shares)		200 000
Rent	1 620	
[1]Sales		303 875
[1]Sales staff's salaries	6 028	
[1]Uncalled ordinary capital	30 000	
Unissued ordinary capital	30 000	
Unissued preference capital	20 000	
Wages	84 974	
	£631 406	£631 406

Other information: The net profit for the period after allowing for necessary adjustments but before providing for taxation was £22 000. The directors made the following recommendations:

(a) £6000 to be provided for estimated tax on the year's profit.

(b) A final dividend of £4500 to be paid on ordinary shares.

(c) The preference dividend of 7 per cent on all preference shares issued be paid.

(d) £250 to be written off preliminary expenses and a further £2000 be transferred to the general reserve.

You are required for each of the items marked[1]

(i) to give a brief explanation of the nature of the item;

(ii) to state the classification you would give the item in the final reports.

Present the profit and loss appropriation account, and the shareholders' funds section only of the balance sheet, after these recommendations had been incorporated.

Chapter 19
Understanding financial accounting reports

User needs ☐ Qualities of accounting information ☐ Conventional assumptions and propositions ☐ Limitations of conventional accounting ☐ Analysis of financial statements ☐ Measures of profitability ☐ Measures of resource utilisation ☐ Measures of financial condition ☐ An illustrative example of financial statement analysis

User needs

In some respects, this chapter is a review chapter. We want to consider again the basic objectives of financial reporting and then to assess to what extent conventional accounting reports meet these objectives. Thus, we will be making reference to concepts and propositions introduced in earlier chapters.

In Chapter 1, we stated that 'accounting information is provided for, and disseminated to, interested parties to assist them in making decisions'. We then proceeded to identify the major users of accounting information and, in broad terms, to specify the types of decisions they made and, thus, their need for accounting information. We will now try to be more specific about the information needs of those major users.

1 Management

There are three major features of the accounting information requirements of management. First, measures of profit are required in order to evaluate the effects of management's past decisions and policies and as a guide to dividend policy. Second, management needs to know patterns of cash flows, both historical and predicted, so it can maintain liquidity and its reputation for creditworthiness. Third, a large amount of detailed information is required for control purposes: to assist in the control not only of assets and liabilities but also of the actions of employees.

Management information requirements tend to be more detailed and more frequent than the requirements of other groups of users.

2 Investors and potential investors

There are two major aspects to the information needs of investors. First, the investor wants to be able to use information on the past performance and the present position of the company in order to attempt to predict future returns on the investment. This prediction, taken together with other information, such as economic conditions and market rumours, assists the investor to place a value on the shares and thus to make a decision to sell, buy or hold on to the shares. Economists and business finance theorists have developed models of investor behaviour but these are too complex and varied to be dealt with here. A basic feature of most of these models is the concept of 'present value' (to be dealt with in Chapter 21). Sufficient to say that there is, as yet, no universally accepted model of investors' decision making.

The second use to investors of accounting information is to assist them in evaluating management performance. Investors, by electing boards of directors, have some control over the company's activities. The emergence of the investor as the most important external user of accounting information can be traced to the period when the identity of management became separated from the identity of shareholders.

3 Creditors

Prior to the divorce between ownership and management which we have just mentioned, creditors were the most important single group of external users of accounting information. This explains why, before the twentieth century, the balance sheet was regarded as more important than the profit and loss statement, and it also provides one explanation for the importance of conservatism for the preparation of financial statements. Creditors should still be regarded as important users, particularly in view of the fact that large amounts of company finance are raised by means of debentures and secured loans. The basic interest of creditors lies in the amount of security existing for their debt and in the extent and priority of other liabilities. Their interest in earning capacity is limited to the extent to which the company is able to generate funds for the payment of interest and the repayment of the principal.

4 Government and semi-government authorities

We have mentioned already the necessity for the accounting system to provide information for the purposes of taxation and to comply with the provisions of the Companies Act designed to control the activities of companies and to protect the interests of investors and others. In addition, there is an increasing use of accounting information in such other areas of government responsibility as price justification, tariffs, restrictive trade practices and foreign investment; as well as the use of aggregated accounting data in decisions related to monetary and fiscal policy.

5 Employees

Although 'the ability to pay' has not been accepted fully as a criterion for wage fixation, in recent years there has been an increasing use of company and industry profit figures in wage claims and disputes by trade unions and employee representatives.

6 Economists

Many economic researchers and advisers, employed by government, by private enterprise and by academic institutions, use accounting data as a basis for their research.

7 The general public

There is increasing interest in the effects of firms' activities on other people and on the environment. This involves such issues as monopoly profits, the quality of product, harmful or dangerous products, pollution, unfair advertising and foreign control. We are reaching the end of the era when companies need to account only to management, investors, creditors and governments and to account for their activities solely in terms of wealth and profits.

The accountant and the accounting system are faced with a dilemma in trying to provide relevant information for such a wide variety of decisions and decision makers. There are three approaches to this problem. The first is to rank users in some sort of priority and then to attempt to design general-purpose financial statements which will satisfy the decision models of the majority of the more important users. The second is to provide a number of different accounting reports, each tailored to suit the information requirements of a particular group of users. The third approach is that the accountant should not attempt to assume the decision model of any particular group of users but should concentrate on supplying a wide range of factual data from which the user can select the items relevant to the particular decision. The second and third approaches are of necessity more costly than the first, but are becoming more possible with the advances in data-processing technology.

Qualities of accounting information

In Chapter 2, we made general reference to the attempts in recent years to establish a conceptual framework for financial reporting in the form of the *corporate report*. This report was commissioned by the Accounting Standards Steering Committee, now the Accounting Standards Committee, with terms of reference which included the requirement to 're-examine the scope and aims of published reports in the light of modern needs and conditions. It is concerned with the public accountability of economic entities of all kinds, but especially business enterprises. It seeks to establish a set of working concepts as a basis for financial reporting. Its aims are to identify the persons or groups for whom published financial reports should be prepared, and the information appropriate to their interests. It considers the most suitable means of measuring and reporting the economic position, performance and prospects of undertakings for the purposes and persons identified above.' The *corporate report* identifies seven distinct groups of users of financial reports. They are:

1. The equity investor group (basically existing shareholders and potential shareholders).

2. The loan creditor group.

3. The employee group (this consists of existing, potential and past employees).

4. The analyst–adviser group (principally professional advisers, e.g., stockbrokers, investment analysts, etc.).

5. The business contact group (for example, suppliers, trade creditors and customers).

6. The government (taxation authorities, etc.).

7. The public.

Having determined the users of financial information the report identifies the fundamental objective of corporate reporting as follows:

> The fundamental objective of corporate reports is to communicate economic measurements of and information about the resources and performance of the reporting entity useful to those having reasonable rights to such information.

In this text, we have spent time on the elements of financial reporting, such as assets, liabilities, income, revenues, expenses, gains and losses, etc., but not as much on the qualitative characteristics of accounting information. If corporate reports are to be useful and to fulfil their fundamental objective they must possess the following characteristics:

1. *Relevance*   This is considered to be the capacity of information to make a difference to the decision by improving the decision maker's ability to predict or to confirm or to correct their earlier expectations. It has, however, to be recognised that the users themselves are free to define their own objectives and the information with which they wish to be supplied.

2. *Understandability*   Here it is maintained that a user's ability to gain from information provided depends upon the reader's ability to understand it. Understandability requires the provision, in the clearest possible form, of all the information which the reasonably instructed reader can make use of and the parallel presentation of the main features for the use of the less sophisticated.

3. *Reliability*   Here the information must be reasonably free from error and bias and faithfully represent what it purports to represent. Verifiability is closely associated with reliability.

4. *Completeness*   The information presented should be complete in that it provides users, as far

as possible, with a rounded picture of the economic activities of the reporting entity.

5. *Objectivity*   The information presented to the user should be unbiased. This obviously implies the necessity for reporting standards which are themselves neutral as between competing interests.

6. *Timely*   Information should be published reasonably soon after the end of the period to which it relates. This ensures that corporate reports are more useful when they contain up-to-date measures of value.

7. *Comparability*   Information is useful only when it can legitimately be compared with some benchmark. Typical examples of benchmarks are the same items in the statements of other companies in the same industry, or the same item in previous years' reports of the same firm. Uniformity is important in the case of the first example; consistency is important in the second.

As well as the above seven characteristics contained in the *corporate report*, reference must also be made to two other pervasive concepts:

1. The constraint of weighing the costs of providing certain information against the benefits to be obtained from that information.

2. The materiality or magnitude of an omission or misstatement of accounting information. Here the question is again – will it affect the decision? Materiality has been discussed earlier in this text and will be referred to again later in this chapter.

Conventional assumptions and propositions

The above discussion has tended to concern financial statements as we would like them to be in an ideal world. We do not live in an ideal world and therefore we have to come back to the usefulness of financial statements as they are normally presented. It will be useful to summarise the main assumptions and propositions which are seen to underlie the preparation and presentation of conventional financial statements. These are given different labels by different writers and there is no 'official list' of conventional accounting principles. We have referred to most of them earlier in the text, so that only a brief explanation of each is necessary here.

1 The accounting entity

It has become customary to consider the business enterprise as the accounting entity, irrespective of whether or not it is in fact a separate legal entity. The adoption of the entity concept enables us to recognise the concept of proprietorship and thus to formulate the accounting equation.

2 The accounting period

Resulting from the need to report profit for a particular, arbitrary period of time, conventional accounting determines profit by 'matching revenue with expenses'. The problems of balance-day adjustments with the need to estimate stock values, depreciation of fixed assets, doubtful debts, taxation and many other factors, all arise in the course of this matching process.

3 The realisation principle

In determining profit by matching revenue with expenses, it is necessary to choose a point in time at which the revenue is deemed to be recognised and the profit on the activity thus 'realised'. Conventionally, the 'point of sale' has almost invariably been used. We have suggested in Chapter 2 that a rule of realisation at the point of sale is too rigid to be applied in all cases and that other factors should be taken into consideration.

4 The 'going concern' (or continuity of activity) assumption

This is the assumption, underlying many decisions in the profit-determining process, that the business will continue to operate indefinitely. Conventional accounting ignores the realisable or market value of fixed assets, believing that it will be necessary to retain these assets in future periods for the purpose of earning revenue. Similarly, in many businesses, goodwill is ignored because its value will become important only when the ownership of the business changes in some significant way.

5 The monetary unit

The fact that the pound is used as the basic unit of accounting measurement brings with it two problems. First, there is the valuation problem when specific prices change. Conventional accounting adheres very largely to historical cost as the basis of valuation for stocks, investments and property, and usually ignores changes which have occurred in the cost which would be necessary to replace these assets. The second problem is caused by the fact that the value of the pound itself (in terms of its purchasing power) also changes. The accountant has usually ignored these changes in general price levels and has assumed a stable monetary unit.

6 Conservatism

This is the traditional tendency towards caution in the determination of profit. Profits are rarely brought to account unless they have been realised. On the other hand, allowance is made for all losses to the extent of trying to estimate possible future losses, such as doubtful debts or decreases in the market value of stocks held. In recent years, accountants have been criticised frequently for their overemphasis on conservatism. If carried too far, this leads to understatement of profit by such means as under-valuing stocks, over-depreciating assets, and over-providing for tax. This has often been termed the creation of 'secret reserves' – the deliberate disclosure to the shareholders of a position worse than the actual.

7 Materiality

There is the belief that it is desirable in reporting accounting information to concentrate on those matters which are relatively important to the exclusion of the less important details. An example is the rounding off to the nearest thousand pounds in the published reports of many companies. Another is the tendency with small outlays, such as postage stamps, to ignore stocks on hand at the end of the period – that is, to ignore the accurate apportionment of the expense between two accounting periods. The purpose of the report is often an important factor in determining what is material. Materiality in this sense is defined as the presence or absence of any item which would make the accounting reports misleading.

8 Disclosure

Adequate disclosure is often used as a criterion to justify or to condemn particular accounting practices. The desire to convey to the readers of accounting reports as accurate a picture as possible influences the manner of reporting unusual items, such as adjustments to depreciation, adjustments to taxation or the use of different methods from those of previous years. At times, the concepts of conservatism on the one hand and disclosure on the other are in direct opposition to one another.

9 Consistency

Accounting reports take on greater significance when they are compared with the reports of other periods. However, such comparisons are valid only when the same principles are applied consistently from one period to another or if the effects of changes are clearly disclosed.

Consistency is important in such matters as methods of stock valuation, methods of depreciation, bases of accounting report classification, etc.

Many writers have divided the above concepts into two groups – accounting conventions (the first five above), and accounting doctrines (the last four above). The term 'convention' has implied a commonly accepted concept or assumption. A 'doctrine' on the other hand is the tendency or inclination to follow a certain belief or approach. We believe that the use of these labels is not very helpful. Some of the conventions merely describe accepted practices (for example, the entity convention and the accounting period) without attempting by logical reasoning to justify their use. Other conventions (for example, the monetary convention and the 'going concern' convention) refer to assumptions, made by accountants, which are not always valid in a real situation. For instance, adherence to the monetary convention results in ignoring changes in the price level, while adherence to the 'going concern' convention overlooks the fact that owners of business are interested in realisable values of assets and do contemplate selling fixed assets, investments and even the business itself. The doctrines describe features of current accounting practice without probing the reasons which may cause conservatism, disclosure or consistency to be desirable.

The alternative to this pragmatic type of approach to accounting theory is the adoption of a deductive approach, beginning with the formulation of the objectives of financial reporting and the observation of the economic, social, political and legal factors and constraints affecting accounting. This is followed by the deduction, by the process of logical reasoning, of a set of principles. Finally, these principles are applied to specific situations to derive procedural methods and rules.

Limitations of conventional accounting

Before proceeding to examine the methods used to analyse and interpret conventional financial statements, we must reiterate the warning that the effective use of accounting information is limited by the quality of such information. Earlier in this chapter we distinguished between desirable characteristics of accounting information and the fact that all of these characteristics are not always fully achieved using conventional accounting practices. There is also the appearance of exact precision, despite the estimates and assumptions adopted in the reports as presented (because of the effect of adopting the double entry system).

Common criticisms of conventional accounting may be discussed under three headings:

1. Lack of uniformity.

2. Failure to adapt to changing conditions.

3. Problems caused by changing prices.

All of these specific areas of criticism may be linked together in a more general criticism that accountants have failed to develop a coherent, logical and generally accepted body of theory by which alternative methods can be appraised and new problems met when they arise.

1 Lack of uniformity

Items of accounting information are really useful only when they are capable of being compared either with similar items in the report of another firm or with similar items in the reports of the same firm in prior periods. Uniformity between different firms and consistency within the same firm are extremely desirable characteristics of accounting information. We have seen that in many areas of accounting, and particularly with depreciation and stock valuation, generally accepted practice allows for a wide range of alternative methods to be used. This wide freedom of choice, as well as rendering inter-firm comparisons invalid, permits some degree of manipulation of profit figures within the scope of generally accepted accounting principles.

2 Failure to adapt to changing conditions

While conventional accounting principles are open to criticism on the grounds that they are too flexible at any particular point in time, it has also been alleged that they have tended to be too inflexible over time. Because accepted accounting principles tend to be distilled through experience rather than being derived from a sound theoretical base, new situations and problems tend to be met by trial-and-error methods and by the application of existing methods not suited to the new conditions. There has often been a significant time lag before accountants have agreed on solving problems such as hire purchase, leasing, development land sales, tax allocation, investment in other companies and, of course, coping with the problems caused by significantly high rates of inflation. Too rigid adherence to the point of sale as the point at which revenue is to be recognised and rigid adherence to historical cost as the prime method of asset valuation have brought forth criticisms from theorists, some practitioners and the financial press.

3 Problems caused by changing prices

Probably the most loudly voiced and widely debated criticisms of conventional accounting stem from the effects of changing prices and price levels on the usefulness of the information provided. The whole of Chapter 21 is devoted to this issue; it includes discussion of both the criticisms and the various proposals which have been advanced.

Analysis of financial statements

The pound amounts for items in a financial statement when viewed in isolation have only limited significance. To be told that the XYZ Co. earned a net profit of £84 000 in a particular year does not really help us greatly in assessing the performance of the company. If we are able to compare the £84 000 with the profit earned in the previous year, or if we know the value of resources used to earn the £84 000, then the profit figure takes on a greater significance. Benchmarks are necessary before we are able to assess whether the performance is good, bad or indifferent.

Thus, it is common for users of financial information to perform some analysis of the figures provided so as to be in a position to make decisions based on that information. The basic ingredient of such analysis is the ratio – a percentage or decimal relationship of one number or amount with another. An example of an accounting ratio (the gross profit ratio) was introduced in Chapter 2. If sales total £80 000 and the gross profit is £28 000 then the gross profit ratio is:

$$\frac{28\ 000}{80\ 000} \times 100 = 35 \text{ per cent.}$$

The gross profit ratio is an example of what is often called 'vertical analysis'. This is where one number is expressed as a percentage of another number within the same financial statement. In profit and loss statements presented to management, it is common to find various categories of expenses and the various types of profit (gross profit, profit before tax, profit after tax) to be expressed as a percentage of sales.

Similarly, in balance sheets, we may find current assets expressed as a percentage of total equities and so on.

Other ratios require the use of amounts from both the profit and loss statement and the balance sheet. One common example is to relate the net profit figure with some measure of funds employed, shareholders' equity.

When various ratios have been calculated, they still may be relatively meaningless unless the ratios themselves are compared against some benchmark. Two types of benchmarks are commonly used:

1. Comparison of a ratio with the same ratio of the same firm in a previous period. Here it is essential that the financial statements used to calculate the ratios are prepared on a consistent basis from one period to another. Even where consistency is observed, comparisons over significant periods of time tend to be rendered invalid by inflation.

2. Comparison of a ratio with the same ratio for other firms in the same industry or with industry averages. One difficulty here is the variation in the accounting methods employed by different firms.

It is neither practicable nor desirable to try to deal with all of the various ratios that can be calculated. There are specialised texts which deal in depth with techniques of analysis and interpretation of financial statements. We attempt only to describe some of the more commonly used of these measures. In doing so, we distinguish between three major types of ratios:

1. Measures of profitability – ratios which relate to some measure of profit or return with some measure of the size of the firm or its level of activity.

2. Measures of resources – ratios which attempt to measure the efficiency with which particular assets, particular groups of assets or total assets are being utilised.

3. Measures of financial condition – ratios which assist in the assessment of a firm's ability to meet its commitments.

Measures of profitability

When investors are making decisions on becoming or remaining shareholders in a particular company, they wish to compare expected future dividends and capital gains in that company with alternative investments. To the extent that past profits may provide some indication of future earnings, ratios which are based on past profits can be of assistance.

Some of the more commonly used ratios which are based on past profit figures are:

1. *Net profit ratio*, that is, *net profit divided by net sales*. As mentioned above, this ratio is obtained by vertical analysis within the profit and loss statement. This ratio is probably more useful for predictive purposes if the effects of abnormal gains or losses are removed from the profit figure used.

2. *Return on total assets*, that is, *net profit divided by total assets*. This attempt to measure the return on total funds employed is probably more useful if the profit figure used is one calculated excluding interest charges on long-term liabilities. Total assets are supplied partly by shareholders and partly by creditors. Therefore, it is appropriate that the measure of profitability should be based on the profit before deducting the return to either group.

Total assets may be calculated as at the beginning of the year, the end of the year or an average of the two. The most commonly used base is the end of the year, but the most important consideration is to adopt one method consistently from one period to another.

3. *Return on shareholders' equity*, that is, *net profit divided by shareholders' equity*. Obviously this should be an after-interest profit figure and, if preference shareholdings are involved, preference dividends should be subtracted from the net profit figure before dividing by the equity of ordinary shareholders.

4. *Earlings per share*, that is, *net profit divided by the number of ordinary shares*. Again preference dividends, if any, should be deducted from net profit. This is a ratio widely used by analysts, particularly in making comparisons between a number of different companies. A derivative of this ratio is the 'price/earnings ratio' obtained by dividing *the market price of the share by its earnings per share*.

5. *Dividends yield*, that is, *per share divided by market price of ordinary shares*. This is a ratio which expresses the dividend as a return on the current share price.

Measures of resource utilisation

The profitability of a firm depends, to a large extent, on how effectively management is able to use the resources given to it. Three comonly used measures of efficiency are:

1. *Total-asset turnover*, that is, *total sales divided by total assets*. Note that this ratio is closely linked to two ratios discussed in the previous section – the net profit ratio and return on total assets.

Since

and

$$\text{Net profit ratio} = \frac{\text{Sales}}{\text{Net profit}},$$

$$\text{Total-asset turnover} = \frac{\text{Sales}}{\text{Total assets}},$$

$$\text{Return on total assets} = \frac{\text{Net profit}}{\text{Total assets}} = \frac{\text{Net profit ratio}}{\text{Total-asset turnover}}$$

What this means is that the same return on funds employed can be achieved by having either a high turnover at a low profit margin or a low turnover at a high profit margin.

2. *Rate of stock turnover* – calculated by dividing *cost of goods sold by the average stocks held*. As well as giving an indication of the volume of activity, this figure can assist in detecting the weakness of 'overstocking'. Often we have to be content with averaging the opening and closing stock figures. These are not always a good indication of the stock level throughout the period, and more frequent stock figures, if available, add to the usefulness of this calculation. The rate may be expressed in terms of 'x no. of times per year' or 'once every y days'.

3. *Turnover of book debts* – calculated by dividing the *average daily credit sales into the closing debtors balance*, giving the number of days' sales represented by outstanding debts. Prompt collection of debts is an important factor in maintaining financial stability and this is an attempt to measure the effectiveness of credit control. There are alternative suggestions as to how many days should be divided into the year's sales to give average daily sales. Some authorities say 365, some 300 (on the basis of a six-day week), and others 250 (for an enterprise operating on a five-day week). The main point to remember is that the results should be interpreted on the basis of whichever method is chosen, and that consistency is again important.

Measures of financial condition

We have stressed throughout this text that there are two conditions jointly necessary for the successful operation of a business enterprise. These are profitability (measures of which have been discussed above) and the ability to meet commitments as they fall due.

Some commitments are immediate or short term in nature, others emerge in the longer run.

Thus, we need measures of solvency for both of these situations. Commonly used ratios which measure the firm's ability to meet its various present and future commitments are as follows:

1. *Working capital (or current) ratio: current assets to current liabilities.* The term 'working capital' is often used to express the surplus available from current assets after meeting current liabilities. The working capital ratio is a measure of an enterprise's apparent ability to meet its short-term commitments with assets intended to be converted into cash in the short-term period. It is, of course, desirable that current assets should cover current liabilities with a margin for safety. However, arguments that the working capital ratio should always be greater than, say, 2 : 1 can be countered by quoting many cases of successful businesses which have operated with a much poorer ratio. As with other relationships, the movements (that is, increases or decreases) in the working capital ratio may indicate a strengthening of weakening of the short-term position.

2. *Quick-asset (or liquid) ratio: current assets less stock and work-in-progress) to current liabilities.* The current ratio reveals the variations and trends in working capital and is most important in determining whether a business is capable of meeting its obligations in the short term. By including stock and work-on-progress this ratio may be misleading since stocks are not, in many businesses, readily available to meet the claims of creditors, particularly if the stocks are held for long periods of time. To overcome this problem, a further ratio is used known as the quick or liquid ratio which is similar in character to the current ratio with the exception that stock and work-in-progress are excluded in the computation of current assets. Only very liquid assets such as cash in hand, cash at bank, debtors, and short-term investments are included in the grouping of current assets, which are then compared with the current liabilities. This ratio enables measurement to be made of the ability of a business to pay its immediate debts as and when they fall due.

Consistency in the basis of calculation is again important if the test is to be a reliable one. In most circumstances, the quick-asset ratio should be more than 1 : 1, but trends in the ratio are also important.

3. *Debt–equity ratio: outside liabilities divided by owners' equity.* This is sometimes called the 'leverage' ratio. It is a test of financial stability from a longer-term point of view. With liabilities, interest payments often have to be maintained; in time the principal has to be repaid; and perhaps suitable borrowing may not then be available. Thus over-reliance on external funds may be a weakness in times of economic crisis. What is a suitable relationship between owners' funds and outside funds depends on the nature of the enterprise and other circumstances. Once again movements in the ratio are important.

An illustrative example of financial statement analysis

In the example which follows, we have taken the financial statements used in Chapter 16 to illustrate the preparation of funds statements and cash flow statements. Necessary information additional to that previously given consists of:

1. The provision of profit and loss statement figures for the year ended 30 June 19X5.

2. The stock balance at 1 July 19X4 was £34 000.

The profit and loss statements for two successive years and the two successive balance sheets are given below. In each case, the more important vertical (or structural) ratios have been calculated and shown.

It is difficult to comment fully on the analysis of FIB Co. Ltd's financial statements with only two years' figures available. Also, it would be helpful if we knew the industry in which the company operates and were able to compare the various ratios and the comparative figures for other firms in the industry. However, on the basis of the information which is available the following points are worthy of comment:

1. The company is in a growth situation. Significant increases in fixed assets have been financed partly by a new share issue and partly by borrowing.

2. Increases in sales have led to higher net profits. The net profit ratio has risen from 10.9 to 11.9 per cent, despite a fall in the gross profit ratio from 53.3 per cent to 51.8 per cent.

FIB Co. Ltd
Comparative Profit and Loss Statements for the years ended 30 June

	19X5			19X6		
	£	£	% of sales	£	£	% of sales
Sales revenue		290 000	100.0		335 000	100.0
Less Cost of goods sold		135 500	46.7		161 500	48.2
Gross margin		154 500	53.3		173 500	51.8
Add gain on sale of motor vehicles		—			3 500	
		154 500			177 000	
Less **Other expenses**						
Advertising	3 000			4 500		
Salaries	52 500			56 000		
Depreciation of motor vehicles	9 500			11 000		
Office expenses	8 000			9 000		
Depreciation of buildings	2 500			3 000		
Insurance	4 000			4 500		
Interest	8 500			9 000		
Amortisation of goodwill	5 000	93 000	32.1	5 000	102 000	30.4
Net profit before tax		61 500	21.2		75 000	22.4
Corporation tax		30 000	10.3		35 000	10.4
		£31 500	10.9		£40 000	11.9

3. It would appear that the increased resources are not yet being fully utilised. There have been slight decreases in both the return on total assets and the return on shareholders' equity and a significant decrease in the total-asset turnover and the stock turnover.

4. The company has maintained the balance between debt and equity funding at about the same level as previously. It would appear that the company is not relying too heavily on borrowing and should be able to meet its long-term debt commitments.

5. However, the short-term financial position has deteriorated and gives some cause for concern. Working capital in pound terms, the working capital ratio and the quick-asset ratio have all decreased significantly. The fact that £35 000 in corporation tax will have to be paid during next year should be noted. The company appears to be dependent in the short term on being able to maintain and probably increase its bank overdraft.

FIB Co. Ltd
Comparative Balance Sheets as at 30 June

	19X5			19X6		
	£	£	% of Total assets	£	£	% of Total assets
Fixed assets						
Motor vehicles (net)	58 000			74 000		
Buildings (net)	73 000			115 000		
Land	70 000			115 000		
Goodwill	55 000	256 000	77.1	50 000	354 000	80.7
Current assets						
Cash at bank	5 000			—		
Debtors	30 000			32 000		
Stock	38 000			50 000		
Prepaid insurance	3 000	76 000	22.9	2 500	84 500	19.3
		£332 000	100.0		£438 500	100.0
Shareholders' equity						
Paid-up capital	150 000			180 000		
Premium on shares	—			24 000		
General reserve	22 000			30 000		
Unappropriated profits	48 000	220 000	66.2	59 000	293 000	66.8
Current liabilities						
Bank overdraft	—			12 000		
Creditors	18 500			22 000		
Accrued salaries	1 500			1 000		
Accrued interest	1 000			1 500		
Corporation tax	30 000	51 000	15.4	35 000	71 500	16.3
Long-term liabilities						
Debentures	30 000			50 000		
Loan on mortgage	31 000	61 000	18.4	24 000	74 000	16.9
		£332 000	100.0		£438 500	100.0

The ratios discussed previously, for each of the two years, are as follows:

FIB Co. Ltd,
Selected Financial Statement Ratios

	19X5	19X6
A. Measures of profitability		
1. Net profit ratio (after tax)	$\dfrac{£31\ 500}{£290\ 000} = 10.9\%$	$\dfrac{£40\ 000}{£335\ 000} = 11.9\%$
2. Return on total assets	$\dfrac{£70\ 000}{£332\ 000} = 21.1\%$	$\dfrac{£84\ 000}{£438\ 500} = 19.2\%$
3. Return on shareholders' equity	$\dfrac{£31\ 500}{£220\ 000} = 14.3\%$	$\dfrac{£40\ 000}{£293\ 000} = 13.7\%$

Cont.

	19X5	19X6
4. Earnings per share	$\dfrac{£31\ 500}{£150\ 000}$ = £0.21 p/s	$\dfrac{£40\ 000}{£180\ 000}$ = £0.22 p/s
B. Measures of resource utilisation		
Total-asset turnover	$\dfrac{£290\ 000}{£332\ 000}$ = 87.3%	$\dfrac{£335\ 000}{£438\ 500}$ = 76.4%
2. Rate of stock turnover	$\dfrac{£135\ 500}{£36\ 000}$ = 3.76 times	$\dfrac{£161\ 500}{£44\ 000}$ = 3.67 times
3. Turnover of book debts[1]	$\dfrac{£30\ 000}{£966.7}$ = 31.0 days	$\dfrac{£32\ 000}{£1\ 116.7}$ = 28.7 days
C. Measures of financial condition		
1. Working capital ratio	$\dfrac{£76\ 000}{£51\ 000}$ = 149.0% or 1.49:1	$\dfrac{£84\ 500}{£71\ 500}$ = 118.2% or 1.18:1
2. Quick-asset ratio	$\dfrac{£38\ 000}{£51\ 000}$ = 74.51% or 0.74:1	$\dfrac{£34\ 500}{£71\ 500}$ = 48.25% or 0.48:1
3. Debt–equity ratio	$\dfrac{£112\ 000}{£220\ 000}$ = 50.9%	$\dfrac{£145\ 500}{£293\ 000}$ = 49.7%

Note: [1] Assumed that all sales were credit sales and 300 days per year.

Summary

1. One of the problems the accountant faces is the need to supply information relevant to the decisions of a wide variety of users.

2. The major groups of users of accounting information are:

(a) Management

(b) Investors and potential investors

(c) Creditors

(d) Government and semi-government authorities

(e) Employees

(f) Economists

(g) The general public

3. The following qualitative characteristics are generally deemed to be important:

(a) Relevance

(b) Understandability

(c) Reliability

(d) Completeness

(e) Objectivity

(f) Timely

(g) Comparability

4. Conventional financial statements are based on the following assumptions and propositions:

(a) The accounting entity

(b) The accounting period

(c) The realisation principle

(d) The going concern assumption

(e) The monetary unit

(f) Conservatism

(g) Materiality

(h) Disclosure

(i) Consistency

5. Conventional accounting practices are subject to criticism on the following grounds:

(a) Lack of uniformity.

(b) Failure to adapt to changing conditions.

(c) Indirect valuation of assets, instead of direct valuation, which is more relevant.

(d) Weakness highlighted by changing prices.

6. The inherent limitations of conventional financial statements make interpretation of such reports difficult and sometimes invalid.

7. The preliminaries to intelligent interpretation of accounting reports are:

(a) The comparison of the profit and loss statements and balance sheets in successive years or within the industry.

(b) The analysis of the information by the calculation of percentages, ratios, rates, etc.

8. We should be wary of attaching too much significance to any one ratio or relationship. It is dangerous to draw conclusions without considering the effect of all relevant information.

Discussion questions

19.1 What community benefit results if the quality of accounting and financial information of business enterprises can be relied upon?

19.2 Can the results as shown by the annual financial reports of different enterprises provide a satisfactory comparison? Discuss.

19.3 Conservatism is the basis for some of the choices of options made by accountants. Give four examples of this.

19.4 Members of the annual meeting of the Pongo Cricket Club raised no questions about the annual accounts after one member said 'They must be okay because everything balances.' Comment.

19.5 Is a good profit in a particular year a certain measure of the efficiency of management? Discuss.

19.6 If historical cost accounting has grave deficiencies, what is the use of calculating ratios based on such figures?

19.7 If the figure for the stock turnover is much lower than it was last year, what aspects of operations would you examine to try to explain the reduction?

19.8 Explain the importance to management and to the shareholders of the debt–equity ratio.

19.9 If you were not so interested in the amount of dividends received, but were looking more towards long-term capital growth as a hedge against inflation, what particular aspects of the published reports of companies would you be more concerned with, and why?

Exercises

19.10 The following balances appear in the ledger of Pop Limited at the dates shown.

	31 December 19X6	31 December 19X7
Advertising	£200	£300
Bad debts	50	500
Depreciation expense	170	170
Freight and inwards charges	400	600
Interest paid	150	700
Insurance	80	80
Office expenses	250	700
Office salaries	800	850
Purchases	6 000	8 000
Rent paid	500	500
Rents received (tenanted property)	1 500	1 500
Sales (net)	12 000	18 000
Sales staff's salaries	1 000	1 800
Stock	1 400	2 000
Subsidiary company dividend received	250	1 500
Tenanted property expenses	650	200
Travelling expenses of sales staff	400	1 200
Stock at 1 January 19X6 – £1 500		

Prepare profit and loss statements for the two years in a form suitable for analysis, list ratios and submit a written report of your findings as a result of your analysis of the company's trading.

19.11 Rearrange the following unclassified balance sheets in a form suitable for purposes of analysis and show comparative group percentages and balance sheet relationships:

XYZ Co. Ltd Balance Sheet as at 30 June 19X6

Creditors	£8 250	Cash in hand	£50
Provision for doubtful debts	400	Plant	10 200
Provision for depreciation of plant	1 600	Motor vehicles	7 500
Bank	4 550	Debtors	9 600
Provision for depreciation of motor		Stock	14 750
vehicles	2 100	Premises	12 000
Provision for taxation	1 500	Unissued capital	25 000
Appropriation account	2 700	Uncalled capital	5 000
Mortgage on premises	8 000		
Authorised capital	50 000		
Reserve	5 000		
	£84 100		£84 100

as at 30 June 19X7

Provision for doubtful debts	£800	Cash in hand	£400
Bank	14 700	Stock	19 400
Provision for depreciation of plant	2 200	Debtors	12 500
Provision for depreciation of		Motor vehicles	12 800
motor vehicles	3 500	Uncalled capital	1 000
Mortgage on premises	8 000	Unisued capital	20 000
Creditors	15 900	Plant	27 400
Provision for taxation	5 400	Premises	14 000
Authorised capital	50 000		
Reserve	6 000		
Appropriation account	1 000		
	£107 500		£107 500

19.12 The following information is available from the records of Burns & Co. Limited. Balance of stock accounts at 1 January was £13 000.

	January	February	March
Purchases	£5 000	£4 000	£7 000
Purchases returns	500	—	700
Sales	10 000	11 000	8 000
Sales returns (at cost price)	300	100	400
Sales returns (at selling price)	500	200	600
Cost of goods sold (from perpetual stock records)	6 000	7 500	5 000

All purchases and sales are made on credit.

You are required to:

(a) Record the above information in relevant ledger accounts. The accounts need not be balanced off.

(b) Prepare trading statements for each month in a form to facilitate comparison.

(c) Calculate the gross profit ratio and the stock turnover for each month, and comment on the results.

19.13 The following information is available from the records of JRT Ltd:

	Year ending 30 June 19X6	Year ending 30 June 19X7
Advertising	£400	£800
Cost of goods sold	28 000	36 000
Delivery vehicle expense	900	1 650
Depreciation on delivery vehicles	500	550
Depreciation on office furniture and equipment	150	150
Discount allowed	400	600
Discount received	200	300
[1]Dividends from investments	—	400
Doubtful debts	500	700
Insurance	300	300
Loss on sale of office equipment	100	—
Office expenses	700	800
Office salaries	2 050	2 250
Profit on sale of delivery vehicles	—	200
Sales	40 000	50 000
Sales staff's salaries	2 200	3 000

[1] The receipt of dividends was not considered to be part of the normal business of the company.

You are required to:

(a) prepare comparative profit and loss statements for the above two years. Include the main profit and loss statement ratios for each year.

(b) Give brief notes on the main trends apparent to you. (A full report is not required.)

19.14 (a) Outline the factors that you consider limit the value of the balance sheet as a statement of net worth.

(b) Rearrange the following unclassified balance sheets in a form suitable for analysis and show comparative group percentages.

(c) Calculate appropriate balance sheet relationships.

(d) Comment briefly on changes in these relationships.

Fern Ltd
Balance Sheets as at 30 June

	19X6	19X7		19X6	19X7
Provision for			Plant and equipment	£24 500	£29 000
doubtful debts	£2 250	£2 650	Cash at bank	9 300	8 200
Mortgage	19 500	18 200	Land and buildings	47 000	55 000
Creditors	19 450	23 900	Debtors	26 200	28 950
Provision for			Motor vehicles	8 000	10 000
depreciation on			Shares in X-Ray Ltd	24 000	28 000
motor vehicles	2 900	3 700	Stock	21 500	28 500
Provision for			Unissued capital	120 000	100 000
depreciation on plant					
and equipment	5 350	6 300			
Provision for taxation	7 850	8 300			
Authorised capital	200 000	200 000			
General reserve	20 000	22 000			
Profit and loss					
appropriation	3 200	2 600			
	£280 500	£287 650		£280 500	£287 650

19.15 (a) In the analysis and interpretation of accounting reports, a distinction is often drawn between ratios which assist the assessment of earning capacity and ratios which assist the assessment of financial stability. Discuss the need for such a distinction and give some examples of each type of ratio.

(b) A summary of the balance sheets of a trading company which has been incurring losses revealed the following:

	19X6		19X7		19X8	
Shareholders' Funds						
Paid-up capital	£60 000		£60 000		£60 000	
Reserves	50 000		40 000		30 000	
		£110 000		£100 000		£90 000
Current Liabilities						
Bank overdraft	6 000		9 000		25 000	
Creditors	31 000		24 000		18 000	
Other current						
liabilities	3 000		2 000		2 000	
		40 000		35 000		45 000
		£150 000		£135 000		£135 000

Cont.

	19X6		19X7		19X8
Fixed Assets					
Property	£30 000		£30 000		£51 000
Plant, equipment, vehicles	10 000		10 000		9 000
		£40 000		£40 000	£60 000
Current Assets					
Stock	65 000		60 000		50 000
Debtors	45 000		35 000		25 000
		110 000		95 000	75 000
		£150 000		£135 000	£135 000

You are required to:

(i) calculate the significant ratios for each of the three years;

(ii) comment on the main trends apparent to you.

19.16 Study the following comparative balance sheets, then answer the questions below:

Kennedy Traders
Balance Sheets for 19X6 to 19X9

	19X6	19X7	19X8	19X9
Assets	£1 000	—	—	—
Cash at bank	9 000	£12 000	£16 000	£20 000
Stock	3 000	5 500	7 200	9 000
Debtors	50 000	60 000	60 000	60 000
Premises	2 000	7 000	6 000	6 000
Equipment	3 000	3 000	2 500	2 500
Furniture				
	£68 000	£87 500	£91 700	£97 500
Liabilities				
Bank overdraft	—	£2 000	£6 000	£9 000
Creditors	£3 300	4 000	6 600	8 500
Mortgage on premises	10 000	10 000	10 000	10 000
Proprietorship (at end of each year)	54 700	71 500	69 100	70 000
	£68 000	£87 500	£91 700	£97 500

Further information available is given below:

	19X6	19X7	19X8	19X9
Cash sales	£30 000	£35 000	£30 000	£40 000
Credit sales	50 000	60 000	80 000	65 000
Cost of goods sold	45 000	50 000	62 000	64 000
Net profit	6 000	7 050	6 500	5 700
(Stock at 1 January 19X6 was valued at £7 000.)				

Show in columnar form, the following ratios in respect of each year:

(a) Rate of stock turnover

(b) Gross profit ratio

(c) Working capital ratio

(d) Net profit to proprietorship ratio

(e) Rate of turnover of book debts (assuming a 300-day year)

Comment on the trend in the working capital ratio, including discussion on the causes of the trend, and the possible result to be expected in 19X0.

19.17 From the following information you are required to calculate for each of the three years:

(a) gross profit ratio

(b) rate of stock turnover

(c) current (or working capital) ratio

(d) quick-asset ratio

(e) net profit ratio

	19X6	19X7	19X8
Purchases	£34 000	£38 000	£37 000
Sales	51 000	52 000	55 000
Financial expenses	3 600	5 300	4 400
Cash at bank	2 200	—	—
Stock (start of year)	7 000	10 000	8 000
Stock (end of year)	10 000	8 000	11 000
Debtors	13 000	20 000	19 000
Bank overdraft	—	3 000	1 000
Prepaid expenses	1 200	300	2 000
Creditors	10 000	17 000	22 000
Mortgages	15 000	20 000	20 000
Selling expenses	4 200	3 000	2 700
Motor vehicles	25 000	31 000	33 000
Accrued expenses	800	2 200	2 600
Non-operating revenue	1 400	1 000	850
Provision for taxation	2 000	1 600	2 100

For the purposes of this question, assume a 300-day year.

19.18 The following information has been extracted from the records of A. Co. Ltd.

	30 June 19X6	30 June 19X7	30 June 19X8
Assets			
Freehold property	£36 000	£26 000	£26 000
Plant and machinery	54 000	75 000	88 000
Stock	60 000	86 000	108 000
Debtors	89 000	106 000	132 000
Cash at bank	32 000	8 000	—
Investments (long term)	39 000	—	—
	£310 000	£301 000	£354 000

Cont.

	30 June 19X6	30 June 19X7	30 June 19X8
Liabilities			
Paid-up capital	£56 000	£84 000	£84 000
General reserve	118 000	85 500	81 400
Profit and loss appropriation	26 000	26 500	28 600
Creditors	74 000	65 000	118 000
Bank overdraft	30 000	29 000	28 000
Accrued expenses	2 000	3 000	2 000
Provision for taxation	4 000	8 000	12 000
	£310 000	£301 000	£354 000
Opening stock 1/7/X5 – £31 000			
Sales	£254 000	£308 000	£608 000
Gross profit	60 000	45 000	200 000
Net operating profit	18 400	17 640	9 700

You are required to:

(a) Show in columnar form the following ratios in respect of each year.

    (i) working capital ratio

    (ii) debt/equity ratio

    (iii) quick-asset ratio

    (iv) stock turnover

    (v) net profit on proprietor's funds

(b) Indicate what each of these ratios can be used to test in the financial statements.

(c) Comment briefly on the apparent trends in the company;

Problems

19.19 Joe Bloggs, retired butcher, won a substantial prize in a lottery and decided to invest the money in company shares. He obtained several published financial reports of different companies but could not decide which would prove the best investment. He consulted his grandson, a first-year accountancy student, who advised him to invest in companies with the following attributes:

    The item 'cash at bank' was the biggest asset.
    The fixed assets were greater than the current liabilities.
    The balance of 'shareholders' funds' and 'debentures' were approximately equal.
    The figure for 'shareholders' funds' was much greater than the figure for total assets.
    The amounts shown as 'provision for depreciation of assets' were the largest.

You are required to:

(a) comment on each of the student's suggestions;

(b) list the weaknesses, deficiencies or ambiguities inherent in the preparation of such published financial reports which would make it difficult to decide which was the best company investment.

19.20 Listed in the left-hand column below is a series of business transactions and events. Opposite each transaction is listed a particular ratio used in financial analysis. You are required to explain the effect that each transaction or event would have on the ratio listed opposite to it;

that is, as a result of this event would the ratio increase, decrease, or remain unchanged, and why?

Transaction	Ratio
(a) Purchased stock on credit	Quick-asset ratio
(b) A larger physical volume of goods was sold at smaller unit prices	Gross profit percentage
(c) Company declared a cash dividend	Current ratio
(d) An uncollectible debt was written off against the provision for doubtful debts	Current ratio
(e) Issued additional shares and used proceeds to retire long-term debt	Rate of earnings on total assets
(f) Net operating income increased 25 per cent; interest expense increased 10 per cent	Times interest charges earned
(g) Appropriation of retained earnings to general reserve	Rate of return on shareholders' equity
(h) Purchased factory supplies on credit	Current ratio (assume that ratio is greater than 1 : 1)
(i) Issued shares in exchange for patent rights	Proprietorship ratio
(j) A debt settled by transferring goods from inventories	*Amount* of working capital

19.21 A shareholder of Electrifying Sales Ltd, an appliance retailer, has asked you to explain why the company has failed to pay a dividend for 19X8, although profit after tax is the same as for the previous year. He is also concerned as to the wisdom of retaining his shares in the company and asks you to report on the profitability and financial position of the company as shown by the published figures.

The following information has been extracted from the reports of Electrifying Sales Ltd (all amounts are expressed in £000):

(a) Balance sheet information as at 31 December:

	19X6		19X7		19X8	
Current assets						
Debtors (net)	60		80		150	
Stocks	80		130		280	
Investments	210		150		20	
		350		360		450
Fixed assets						
Premises and plant (net)	358		406		528	
Patents	2		9		22	
		360		415		550
		710		775		1 000

Cont.

	19X6		19X7		19X8	
Current liabilities						
Bank overdraft	5		20		145	
Creditors	80		110		160	
Provision for taxation	25		30		30	
		110		160		335
Shareholders' funds						
Paid-up capital	500		500		500	
Reserves	100		115		165	
		600		615		665
		710		775		1 000

(b) Additional information for year ended 31 December:

	19X6	19X7	19X8
Sales (all on credit)	£1 200	£1 600	£1 800
Cost of sales	700	1 000	1 300
Profits after tax	40	50	50
Dividends	25	35	—

You are required to prepare a report (addressed to Mr A. Shareholder and signed I. Check) stating in language that could be understood by non-accountants (that is, avoiding technical terms as far as possible) your analysis and interpretation of the above figures, including answers to the questions posed by Mr Shareholder.

Chapter 20
Introduction to cost and management accounting

Nature of cost accounting ☐ Nature of conversion costs ☐ Analysis and allocation of costs ☐ Behaviour of costs ☐ Budgets and budgetary control ☐ Methods of cost accounting ☐ Accumulation of costs ☐ Accounting for the costs of manufacture ☐ Job costing ☐ Process costing ☐ An alternative to absorption costing ☐ Standard costs ☐ Information for management decisions

Nature of cost accounting

Earlier we explained that accounting may be designed for external use (reports to shareholders, taxation authorities, etc.), or for internal use, or for both. Chapter 9 also dealt with the differences between the flow of merchandising costs as compared with those of manufacturers. This chapter will develop further the method of accounting for manufacturing costs. These are required for management to use in establishing and controlling the cost of goods produced; from this comes the setting of prices and profits. Manufacturing in this sense includes assembly (for example, of electrical goods from component parts) and construction (for example, of buildings, bridges, etc.), as well as the manufacture from raw materials (for example, plastics, steel bars, jams, etc.). Hence, cost accounting, in addition to recording the cost of purchases of raw materials, must accumulate the costs of converting this raw material to finished goods. Although this chapter is restricted to manufacturing enterprises, it must be realised that some of the techniques of cost accounting are also used in calculating the cost of the provision of services, whether professional or trades (for example, lawyers, electricians).

Cost accounting is a separate but integrated part of the overall accounting information system. It is a very important segment of the system because of the dependence of the financial profit on the calculation of cost of goods sold. It also provides other information of value to help management in the following ways:

1. establishing selling prices or the amount of a tender;

2. assisting the decisions about whether capital outlays are advisable;

3. providing control over day-to-day production;

4. developing strategic plans for the future.

As we will see, cost accounting is vitally concerned with budgeting or estimating future activities. It concerns itself with quantities as well as with pound values, and obtains great benefit from the use of various mathematical and economic techniques.

Cost accounting deals mainly with costs and expenses. 'Costs' are the prices of acquisition of goods or services, while 'expenses' cover those parts of 'costs' used up in the earning of revenue.

In the case of manufacturing, costs are regarded as unexpired until such time as the finished goods are sold. At this stage, the cost of goods sold becomes an *expense* to the business. Raw materials, unfinished goods and finished goods that are not sold are maintained in stock as unexpired *costs*, that is, assets. Let us now examine the nature of the costs and expenses involved in the term 'conversion costs'.

Nature of conversion costs

The elements required to convert raw material into finished products are labour, materials, the use of facilities (such as premises and plant) and some other costs. In most types of enterprise, different products are manufactured from the above elements. To calculate the cost of any one product, it is necessary to relate the costs and expenses to that specific product. Where materials and labour or other costs are directly related to the goods being manufactured, such items are termed *direct* costs or expenses. If no direct relationship exists then they are called *indirect*. The cost of specific doors or windows in the erection of a building would be termed *direct* costs, as would the wages of carpenters or bricklayers working exclusively on that job. On the other hand, the wages of a supervisor or the cost accountant responsible for several construction jobs would be *indirect*. In some cases, however, the amount of the direct cost cannot be easily or economically calculated (for example, glue used in an article of furniture). In such cases, the costs are usually treated as indirect. Examples of direct and indirect costs for a motor-vehicle manufacturer are as follows:

Direct costs	Indirect costs
Purchase of special dies or jigs.	Purchases of foodstuffs for a staff cafeteria.
Wages of operators actually producing the vehicles.	Wages of factory cleaners or watchmen.
Costs of the basic raw materials or components of the vehicles.	Costs of repairs and maintenance of plant and machinery.
Costs of testing the vehicles.	Factory occupancy costs (such as rates, heating, etc.).

   The distinction will be seen to be important in the allocation of costs to products. In the case of indirect costs or expenses, an arbitrary decision normally has to be made by the cost accountant as to how much of that expense should be allocated to each product or batch.

Analysis and allocation of costs

The processes of cost accounting depend on

1. accumulation

2. analysis

3. allocation

of costs and expenses. Accumulation of the costs through cost centres is dealt with later. Analysis and allocation of the costs involves such procedures as:

1. Determining the behaviour of specific costs, particularly the analysis of mixed costs into their fixed and variable components. This becomes important because of the relationship of costs to changes in volume, and is why it is often necessary to prepare a 'flexible' budget, that is, one which covers changing costs for different volumes of production.

2. In some cases, different products are subjected to the same operation or process and it becomes necessary to analyse these costs to enable a fair allocation.

3. Some sections of the enterprise (for example, repairs and maintenance, factory, office) are 'service' departments. Their costs have to be allocated fairly to the 'production' departments. This involves an analysis of the causes of the expense so that a proper base can be established (this may depend on area, horsepower, number of sales or other factors) in the same way as was done in Chapter 14 for department stores.

4. In both job and process costing, it is necessary to allocate the costs between completed and uncompleted goods, that is, the costs of conversion must be split between finished goods and work-in-progress. This involves some measure of valuation and an analysis of the stage of completion of the unfinished units. If the products or jobs are almost complete, it is usual to adopt the method of 'equivalent units' as shown later.

Behaviour of costs

A further distinction with considerable importance, both in the accumulation of cost and in its influence on management decisions, results from the different ways in which costs behave when output changes. Consider the case of telephone costs. The total annual rental for the period remains the same no matter how many calls are made during the year. On the other hand, a set fee is charged for every outward call made, irrespective of the total number. The rental is referred to as being *fixed*, whereas the cost of the calls is *variable*. Thus, a fixed cost or expense is one where the total cost or expense remains unchanged (fixed) for a period irrespective of the volume associated with it. On the other hand the total *variable* cost or expense increases with volume. (Note the differences between the terms 'volume' and 'capacity'. Capacity is the ability to produce volume. Thus, a factory working at half capacity could have produced double the volume of goods if required.) Examples of fixed and variable costs for a motor-vehicle manufacturer are as follows:

Fixed	**Variable**
Cost of licence to manufacture.	Cost of raw materials, e.g., wheels and tyres for each vehicle manufactured.
Rental of factory.	Cost of power used in pressing shop.
Fire insurance of factory.	Cost of petrol, oil and tyres for testing.
Factory manager's salary.	Wages of press operators.

In deciding into which category specific costs should be considered, it is necessary to study the relevant range of production. If production increases to the point where the existing factory is too small to cope, then additional rent (and insurance) for another factory may become necessary. Thus, such fixed costs remain so only within a 'relevant range'. Similarly, it does not mean that there can be no change in 'fixed' costs, such as the manager's salary. 'Fixed' in this instance means that the amount is not determined by changes in volume.

Again, it must be carefully noted that the terms 'fixed' and 'variable' relate to *total* costs.

If the *unit* cost is considered then it will be seen that for higher volumes of production the fixed cost *per unit* will fall. In the case of variable costs, the costs involved for each particular *unit* (for example, cost of tyres and wheels) remain virtually the same for different volumes. Since we are engaged in recording the *total* costs of conversion, the distinction of costs being fixed or variable *in total* becomes important. Obviously, not all costs fall into one or other of these categories. Some costs are partly fixed and partly variable, for example water rates are fixed to a certain minimum volume, but users are charged extra costs for quantities above that minimum. Such costs are termed semi-variable.

The relationship between the total of variable costs and the volume of production may alter. Some costs have a linear relationship, that is, the cost increases directly in relation to volume. Thus, if each unit involves a cost of £4 for material, 100 units will cost £400. Other costs rise in steps, for example if it is considered that a foreman is needed for each ten workers, an increase from, say, ten to fourteen workers will involve additional costs of a foreman. A further increase to eighteen will result in no increase in cost for supervision. Volume discounts may also affect the behaviour of variable costs. Diagrammatic representation of the behaviour of various types of costs is shown in Fig. 20.1.

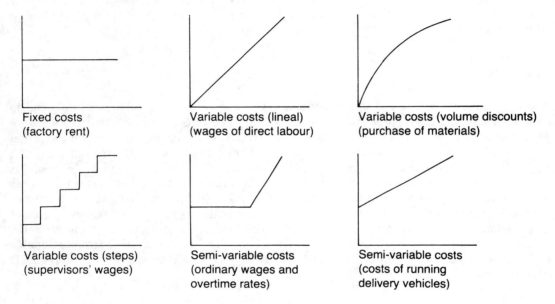

Fixed costs
(factory rent)

Variable costs (lineal)
(wages of direct labour)

Variable costs (volume discounts)
(purchase of materials)

Variable costs (steps)
(supervisors' wages)

Semi-variable costs
(ordinary wages and
overtime rates)

Semi-variable costs
(costs of running
delivery vehicles)

Fig. 20.1   The behaviour costs.

Budgets and budgetary control

The purpose of cost accounting includes 'providing control over day-to-day production' and 'developing strategic plans for the future'. In fact these two are closely associated. One valuable method in evaluating the actual achievement of an enterprise is to compare its results with those expected or hoped for. To do this involves some type of future planning or forecast. When such plans are constructed in financial terms, they are termed budgets, and the process is 'budgeting'. Budgets are, therefore, a means of control, but only if the comparison between achievement and budget is conscientiously carried out. At the same time, this budgetary control must not be permitted to become so rigid that it stifles initiative and limits profitable developments.

The budget of a manufacturer must be properly co-ordinated and involve all aspects of the business. It is useless planning to make 10 000 units if possible sales are not more than 500. It is equally wrong to consider the purchase of vast quantities of raw material if the company lacks the finance to pay for it. Hence, it is vital that those in charge of the various activities should be involved in developing a comprehensive plan that takes into account all the limiting factors. Furthermore, if the budget is to work, each of those in charge of production, sales, etc. should realise his or her responsibility for the achievement of the forecast aims. This is enhanced where those with responsibility have had a part in the construction of the budget.

Business firms usually prepare both long-term and short-term budgets. The long-range plans may involve five, ten or twenty years and would include such items as moving into the export market, increasing the number of branches, extending the factory premises, and so on. The shorter budgets would cover the next six months or a year, and provision would be made in all cases for a flexible approach to changes due to altered circumstances.

Although the compilation of the annual budget will move from one section to another, limitations at various points may require a review of earlier estimates. Thus, if a part of the machinery is unable to cope with the volume suggested then the sales and production figures may need revision. The usual sequence is:

1. Establish the *sales budget*. This will depend on management policy, the suggested selling price, elasticity of demand and the nature of competition. It may also be influenced by the advertising and promotion budget.

2. Next comes the *production budget*. This will involve ensuring the availability of labour and materials, as well as adequate facilities.

3. The *expenditure budget* will depend on both the above. Wages, advertising, selling and delivery expenses, and so on will have to be estimated in the light of sales and production figures.

4. At this stage, it will be necessary to ensure that there is sufficient finance to pay for the above and a *cash budget* (as indicated in Chapter 16) must then be produced.

5. Most budgeting systems also include a *capital investment budget*.

At the conclusion of the budget strategy planning, a master budget is compiled and each responsible officer provided with a copy.

We have dealt with budgeting in a very simple manner. In practice there would be many problems, since it is usual for many more than just one product to be manufactured. The questions of how many of each type and when planning for new models should be started, the introduction of new technology into production methods, the vagaries of competition and of fashion, all combine to make a reasonably viable budget very difficult. At the same time, the preparation of budgets of itself assists the various levels of management to understand the problems of the enterprise, and this, together with regular comparison of budget figures with those actually occurring make for a much more successful business.

Methods of cost accounting

The methods of obtaining the costs of conversion depend largely on the nature of the conversion and of the finished goods. This is similar to the need to adapt accounting methods caused by the differing nature of business activity as shown in Chapter 15. The differences in cost accounting occur in the methods of

1. Recording.

2. Valuing closing stocks.

3. Controlling the costs.

1. Where there is a fair amount of variation in each final product (often termed custom-built articles), the *job-order* costing system is used. Thus, for each building erected by a construction firm, the separate costs of each job are accumulated. For the assembly of motor cars or the production of tins of jam, because of the similarity of each final product, the costs are

accumulated by operations or processes, for example, pressing (or boiling), assembling (or canning), painting (or labelling), and so on. The total cost of each process when added to the others results in a total conversion cost for a given batch of units. From this figure an average cost of each unit can be obtained. The methods are not mutually exclusive. In some cases, for example printing, it is possible to cost the processes of setting up, printing, binding, etc., in order to accumulate the total for a specific individual printing job.

2. As will be seen later in this chapter, the valuation of the closing stocks of work-in-progress and of finished goods may include both fixed and variable costs (absorption costing), or may include variable costs only (*direct* costing).

3. When costs are accumulated as they occur, there is no check on whether production methods were or were not efficient. By using *standard* costs, an enterprise will be aware of what the costs *ought to be*, rather than what they are in fact. By establishing the standard which should be attained, management is made aware of any variances from the ideal laid down.

Accumulation of costs

Irrespective of the costing method used, it will be necessary to discover the costs of each of the three elements: materials, labour, and other costs; these other costs are usually termed 'overhead' or 'indirect manufacturing cost' (IMC). As was pointed out previously, costs which can be related directly to the finished product are termed 'direct' costs. This includes wages of production workers (direct labour), basic raw materials used (direct materials) and possibly direct costs incurred (for example, costs of using a hired crane). The remainder are 'indirect' costs. In some cases it is not economical to include the costs of materials which, although they can be directly associated with a product, are too small to be separately included, for example the cost of varnish, glue or screws in a table. Such items are classed as 'indirect' and are added to the overhead costs (or indirect manufacturing cost).

Cost of materials

These are obtained by means of stores requisitions, that is, written requests to the storeman to release materials for specific job-orders or for processes. Only authorised officers would be permitted to issue such requisitions. In some cases, a mass requisition (based on a bill of materials) may be lodged to cover a number of different components. If the amount allowed in the bill of materials is exceeded because of waste or spoilage then a further special requisition will be required for the extras, thus ensuring greater control over production. In either case, the store records would be adjusted for the issue and completed requisitions forwarded to the cost office.

There is a problem which arises when various purchases are made during the period at different prices. This problem was dealt with previously in connection with stocks in Chapter 9. The requisitions will be priced using either FIFO method or average cost, depending on management's decision, and this will need to be adhered to consistently.

Cost of labour

Two sets of records relating to the payroll must be kept. The *amounts paid* to each person depend on individual rates of pay and the time worked (obtained usually by means of time clocks). It will be necessary to keep separate records showing the *time worked* on individual jobs, machines or processes. This record is referred to as the labour costs.

Employees must therefore account for the nature of the work done as well as for the number of hours worked. The cost of holiday pay and provision for sick leave are not usually included with the payroll. Instead, they are added to the overhead costs.

Overhead (or indirect manufacturing) costs

These will be accumulated in a number of ways. Much of the cost will result from the financial records, for example, heat, light and power, fuel, building maintenance costs, and the like. In addition, there will be the costs of depreciation and defective work, together with indirect materials from requisitions and indirect labour from the payroll, and so on.

The flow of costs in production is illustrated in Fig. 20.2.

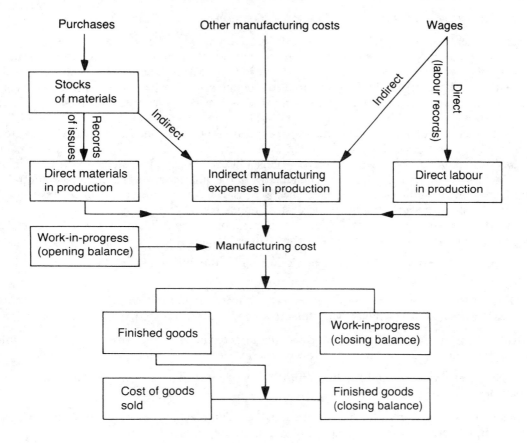

Fig. 20.2   Flow of costs in an absorption costing system.

Absorption rates

Using the system outlined in Fig. 20.2 for a job-order, the cost accountant at the end of the job would have accumulated all the direct labour and material costs, but only some of the indirect manufacturing cost or overheads. This is because the latter consists of a number of varied types of cost which occur at different or irregular intervals. Indirect labour may be paid weekly, but power, heat and light, factory rent, repairs and maintenance are charged quarterly, monthly, or as they occur. Depreciation is another cost which has to be allowed for.

It would be very difficult to establish prices for profit determination if the accountant had to wait for all the various costs to be actually advised. Instead, it is usual to attempt to estimate a rate for these at the beginning of the period by preparing a budget of such costs. This may be carried out by the establishment of different *cost centres*. These may consist of a department, a process, or a single machine. Since not all jobs or products necessarily use all cost centres, a separate predetermined rate may be established for each centre from a budget of costs related to that centre. The budget costs, as predetermined, are allocated to the jobs, products or processes by one of several methods, as follows:

1. according to the number of direct labour *hours*;

2. as a percentage of the direct labour *cost*;

3. according to the units of use, for example, pound per hour of machine use.

Management makes the choice of base in accordance with the relationship between the overheads and the nature of the jobs. Where most of the overheads involve costs related to labour, such as holiday pay, canteen costs, etc., either the labour costs or labour hours method is used. However, if the factory is highly automated, the better base may be related to the number of machine hours, and so on. Different bases may be used for different 'cost centres' within the same factory.

Assume that the total indirect manufacturing costs are expected to be £100 000 and the expected labour hours to be worked are also 100 000. To record the *total* cost of a particular job, £1 for every direct labour hour worked on the job is added. At the end of the period, the indirect manufacturing cost actually incurred is matched with the amount absorbed into production (by the £1 per hour formula), and any difference is considered as a gain or loss in the profit and loss statement, or an adjustment to the cost of goods sold.

Unfortunately there are many difficulties in the above budget calculation which cannot be resolved in an introductory text such as this. These include:

1. The problem of estimating a volume of production for the forthcoming period. Often a flexible budget for different volumes is produced.

2. The fact that some costs are associated not with production but with service departments (such as repairs and maintenance department) which, in turn, indirectly affect the production.

3. An analysis of the behaviour of the direct manufacturing costs into fixed, variable or semi-variable may not be accurate, thus affecting the budget.

4. It may be necessary to establish bases for different processes because all production may not use all processes or departments.

5. In some cases, costs may need to be allocated to a completed process or to a partial process only, as in the production of components sold as spare parts.

6. In some cases, there are joint costs which are difficult or impossible to separate.

7. Separate rates may need to be established to cover the fixed and the variable overhead costs.

Accounting for the cost of manufacture

It is almost certain that some of the goods or jobs being manufactured will not be completed by the end of the accounting period. In calculating the cost of manufacture, allowance must be made for this work-in-progress. The cost of manufacture will thus include both finished goods and unfinished goods (that is, work-in-progress).

Having gathered the necessary information, the cost accountant is in a position to report on the cost of production over a particular accounting period, and this may be done in the form of a statement such as is shown below.

Exeter Manufacturing Co. Ltd
Statement of Costs of Goods Manufactured for the month of July 19X6

Work-in-progress (1/7/X6)	£5 600
Direct materials issued	12 350
Direct labour costs	10 000
Indirect manufacturing costs (at 50% of direct labour cost)	5 000
Total manufacturing costs	32 950
Less Work-in-progress (31/7/X6)	7 000
Cost of finished goods	£25 950

The work-in-progress is in itself made up of the three cost elements and, if desired, the figure for opening and closing balances can be broken up into their component costs. The cost of finished goods, calculated as above, is transferred to the profit and loss statement. The closing balance of work-in-progress is included as part of the next month's manufacturing costs.

If work-in-progress at the end of the accounting period is valued in its components of materials, labour, and IMC rather than in a lump sum as shown above, then how is the statement prepared? There is a need to calculate the 'cost of raw materials used', 'the cost of direct labour used', and the 'indirect manufacturing expense used', with each of these calculations being based on the following pattern:

$$\text{Total cost} = \text{Opening stock} + \text{Costs} - \text{Closing stock}.$$

Exeter Manufacturing Co. Ltd
Statement of Cost of goods Manufactured for the month of October 19X6

Raw material cost			
Stock of raw materials (1/10/X6)		£12 400	
Raw materials in work-in-progress (1/10/X6)		1 600	
Purchases of raw materials		53 000	
Carriage inwards on raw materials		900	
		67 900	
Less Stock of raw materials (31/10/X6)	£11 500		
Raw materials in work-in-progress (31/10/X6)	2 000	13 500	
			£54 400
Direct labour cost			
Direct labour in work-in-progress (1/10/X6)		1 100	
Cost of direct labour		9 000	
		10 100	
Less Direct labour in work-in-progress (31/10/X6)		900	
			9 200
Prime cost			63 600
Indirect manufacturing expense			
Manufacturing expense in work-in-progress (1/10/X6)		660	
Indirect expense incurred in July		3 300	
		3 960	
Less Manufacturing expense in work-in-progress (31/10/X6)		590	
			3 370
Cost of finished goods			£66 970

Once the 'cost of finished goods' has been calculated, this cost along with the cost of purchasing finished goods (if any), is used in the determination of cost of goods sold within the profit and loss statement.

Exeter Manufacturing Co. Ltd
Profit and Loss Statement for month ended 31 October 19X6

Sales of finished goods		£133 200	
Less Sales returns		1 190	
			£132 010
Less Cost of goods sold:			
Stock of finished goods (1/10/X6)		21 400	
Cost of finished goods		66 970	
Purchases of finished goods	£37 400		
Less Purchases returns	900		
		36 500	
Carriage inwards on purchases of finished goods		1 200	
Customs duty on purchases of finished goods		800	
		126 870	
Less Stock of finished goods (31/10/X6)		23 700	
			103 170
Gross profit			£28 840

It can be seen from the manufacturing statement above that prime cost is equal to the total of raw material cost and direct labour cost. Work-in-progress may be valued in the two components of prime cost and indirect manufacturing cost, rather than in three components as illustrated in the October figures or in one lump sum as illustrated in the July figures. If work-in-progress is valued in the two components of prime cost and indirect manufacturing cost then the example given of October figures will read as follows:

Exeter Manufacturing Co. Ltd
Statement of Cost of Goods Manufactured for the month of October 19X6

Work-in-progress at prime cost (1/10/X6)		£2 700
Raw materials cost		
Stock of raw materials (1/10/X6)	£12 400	
Purchases of raw materials	53 000	
Carriage inwards on raw materials	900	
	66 300	
Less Stock of raw materials (31/10/X6)	11 500	
		54 800
Direct labour cost		9 000
		66 500
Less Work-in-progress at prime cost (31/10/X6)		2 900
Prime cost		63 600

Cont.

b/fwd		£63 600
Indirect manufacturing expense		
Manufacturing expense in work-in-progress (1/10/X6)	660	
Indirect expense incurred in July	3 300	
	3 960	
Less Manufacturing expense in work-in-progress (31/10/X6)	590	
		3 370
Cost of finished goods		£66 970

The statement of cost of goods manufactured, sometimes called a manufacturing statement, may be prepared in account form. Sometimes the finished goods are transferred from the factory to the warehouse at a fixed transfer price. This is normally higher than the cost price and enables the factory to show a 'profit' on the transfer. If for example, the transfer price of the goods costed at £66 970 in the above statement had been £72 000, then the factory profit is valued at £5030.

Exeter Manufacturing Co. Ltd
Manufacturing Account for the month of October 19X6

Cost of finished goods	£66 970	Trade price of finished goods	£72 000
Factory profit	5 030		
	£72 000		£72 000

The factory profit of £5030 is transferred from the debit of the manufacturing account to the credit of the profit and loss account, while the transfer price of finished goods is transferred from the credit of the manufacturing account to the debit of the trading account so that it forms part of the calculation of cost of goods sold. Had the trade price been used in the preparation of the profit and loss statement for October 19X6, it would take the place of 'cost of finished goods'. Since in this example the transfer price is higher than the cost of finished goods, the use of this price would cause the gross profit to be lower. This decrease in gross profit is compensated for by the existence of factory profit. The profit and loss account would thus be credited for both the gross profit from trading account and the factory profit from manufacturing account.

Job costing

A simple example of a job cost ledger for July follows:

Data	
(a) Estimates for year	
Inspection and supervision	£20 000
Depreciation of plant	4 000
Indirect labour	16 000
Factory rent	8 000
Indirect supplies	2 000
Expected indirect manufacturing expense	£50 000
Expected direct labour cost £80 000	

Cont.

(b) Balances on hand beginning of month

Work-in-progress (Control)		£4 000
made up of Job 1	£1 800	
made up of Job 2	1 000	
made up of Job 3	900	
made up of Job 4	300	
	4 000	

(c) Raw materials and supplies in hand		3 800
Materials purchases		3 000

(d) Materials and supplies requisitions

Direct: Job 1	£800	
Direct: Job 2	1 200	
Direct: Job 3	1 000	
Direct: Job 4	2 000	5 000
Indirect supplies		300

(e) Factory payroll allocation

Direct: Job 1	1 200	
Direct: Job 2	600	
Direct: Job 3	1 000	
Direct: Job 4	1 200	4 000
Indirect	£900	900

(f) Other indirect expense incurred in July		£1 600

(g) Jobs 1 and 2 were completed and invoiced out to customers.

Solution:

Calculation of rate

IMC is applied at $\dfrac{£50\ 000}{£80\ 000}$ = 0.625 of labour cost.

Cost ledger

Note: Numbers in brackets refer to double entries, including general ledger control account on page 504.

Materials and Supplies

Balance[1]	£3 800	Work-in-progress[3]	£5 000
Purchases[2]	3 000	IMC incurred[4]	300
		Balance	1 500
	£6 800		£6 800

Payroll

Cash[5]	£4 900	Work-in-progress[6]	£4 000
		IMC incurred[7]	900
	£4 900		£4 900

Cont.

IMC Incurred

Supplies [4]	£300		
Indirect labour [7]	900		
Cash [8]	1 600		

IMC Applied

		Work-in-progress [9]	£2 500

Work-in-progress

Balance [1]	£4 000	Finished jobs (Job 1) [10]	£4 550
Materials [3]	5 000	Finished jobs (Job 2) [11]	3 175
Direct labour [6]	4 000	Balance	7 775
IMC applied [9]	2 500		
	£15 500		£15 500

Cost of Finished Goods

Work-in-progress [10]	£4 550	
Work-in-progress [11]	3 175	

Subsidiary Job Cost Ledger

Job 1

Balance	£1 800	Finished jobs	£4 550
Materials	800		
Labour	1 200		
IMC (applied)	750		
	£4 550		£4 550

Job 2

Balance	£1 000	Finished goods	£3 175
Materials	1 200		
Labour	600		
IMC (applied)	375		
	£3 175		£3 175

Job 3

Balance	£900	
Materials	1 000	
Labour	1 000	
IMC (applied)	625	
Balance	£3 525	

Job 4

Balance	£300	
Materials	2 000	
Labour	1 200	
IMC (applied)	750	
Balance	£4 250	

Cont.

Work-in-progress Control Trial Balance

Job 3	£3 525
Job 4	4 250
Work-in-progress	£7 775

The following points should be noted from the above example.

1. If desired, the cost ledger can be made self-balancing by the use of a control account (general ledger control account) representing items accounted for in that ledger. This account would appear at the end of the month as:

General Ledger Control Account

	Balance[1]	£7 800
	Purchases – materials[2]	3 000
	Cash payroll[5]	4 900
	Cash IMC[8]	1 600
		£17 300

and the cost ledger trial balance would then appear as:

Cost Ledger Trial Balance

Materials and supplies	£1 500	General ledger control	£17 300
IMC incurred	2 800	IMC applied	2 500
Work-in-progress	7 775		
Cost of finished goods	7 725		
	£19 800		£19 800

2. The charging out of jobs (and the profit determination) is usually recorded in the general ledger.

3. Although it would seem that the rate for applying the IMC has proved to be low (£2800 incurred, £2500 applied), this may be due to the irregularity of the costs other than indirect labour and materials, for example, sick pay may be higher this month; repairs may have been heavier, and so on. The two accounts will be reconciled, and a balance struck at the end of the year. The IMC is then said to be over or under-absorbed by that amount.

Process costing

In process costing, costs are accumulated in each processing department and the sum of the unit costs for each process becomes the cost of the completed product. A simple example follows.

Example: Assume that a new product is to be manufactured using two processes:

    Assembly of components in the assembly department
    Painting and finishing in the finishing department

Assume further that 1050 units were commenced in the assembly department and that at the end of the period 950 were ready for transfer to the finishing department while 100 were at various stages of assembly. If the materials and labour are incurred steadily through the process then an assumption can be made that the 100 unfinished units are 50 per cent complete on average. Thus the equivalent completed units in the assembly department for the period are

950	completed and transferred	950
100	50 per cent completed equivalent to	50
	Total equivalent completed units	1 000

An absorption rate for overhead (or separate fixed and variable rates) is predetermined for the assembly department by means of a budget as previously explained, and the total costs (direct materials, direct labour and IMC applied) for the department obtained. Assume this total is £9000. From this we calculate that each of the completed units transferred from the assembly to

the finishing department has cost $\frac{£9000}{1000}$ = £9, so that the 'input' of material at the beginning

of the second process (finishing) shows a total initial cost of (950 × £9) = £8550. Assume that, at the end of the period, costs of the finishing department show:

Input from assembly dept	£8 550
Finishing – additional direct material	850
Direct labour	2 300
IMC (100% direct labour cost)	2 300
Total manufacturing cost	£14 000

If all the 950 units are finished, no further calculations need be made. Assume, however, that only 450 are completed and the other 500 are equivalent to 50 per cent complete. The total of the equivalent units for the finishing department is calculated as:

450 completed units		£450
500 (50 per cent completed) equivalent to		250
950 input	Total equivalent completed units	£700

The cost of each completed unit is then determined as:

Total manufacturing cost	£14 000
No. equivalent completed units	700
Average cost per unit	£20

From this figure is determined the value of finished units (450 × £20)	£9 000
and the value of work-in-progress in the finishing department (250 × £20)	£5 000
	£14 000

There are, of course, complications when there are

1. materials added at different stages of a process;

2. different products manufactured in the same process;

3. products which do not undergo all processes;

4. losses or spoilages during the process, and so on.

In a simplified treatment such as this, it is not possible to deal with such problems.

An alternative to absorption costing

We have seen that the total manufacturing costs are allocated either to the cost of goods sold or to separate stock accounts for finished goods or work-in-progress. Since one component of manufacturing cost is the applied overhead, it follows that both the stock accounts will include part of this indirect manufacturing cost. Some accountants argue that, for the fixed overhead cost at least, this allocation is incorrect. By definition, we showed that the total fixed cost within defined volumes of production does not alter. The rent of a factory, for instance, bears no relationship to the volume of activity within its walls. Assume a rent of £1000 for a particular period. If this cost is absorbed into manufacturing cost and 1000 articles are made, each bears a rental cost of £1. If 100 000 articles are produced, the cost of rent per unit is 1p. Such a difference will obviously cause distortion in the value placed on stocks, and such values will vary with the volume manufactured and that unsold.

A distinction is made on the grounds that such fixed costs are *period* costs, whereas variable costs (which vary with activity) are *product* costs. Users of this method (called direct costing, variable costing or marginal costing) would exclude fixed factory costs from the costs of manufacture and would charge it directly against sales for the period. This means that the only overhead costs included in either the cost of goods sold or the closing stocks are variable overhead costs. Such a system becomes important in those cases where there are violent fluctuations in the volume of goods manufactured or sold.

Example:

Direct material	£6 000	No. of units manufactured	10 000
Direct labour	4 000	No. of units sold	6 000
Overhead – Variable	5 000	Selling price per unit	£4
Fixed	5 000		
	£20 000		

Absorption method

Total manufacturing cost	£20 000
Manufacturing cost per unit	£2
Cost of good sold (6000 × £2)	£12 000
Stocks at cost (4000 × £2)	£8 000
Contribution (£24 000 − £12 000)	£12 000

Variable costing method

Variable costs (£6000 + £4000 + £5000)	£15 000
Unit cost (10 000 units manufactured)	£1.50
Cost of goods sold (6000 × £1.50)	£9 000
Stocks at cost (4000 × £1.50)	£6 000
Fixed costs	£5 000
Contribution (£24 000 − £9000 − £5000)	£10 000

From the above, it can be seen that the 'profit' under the absorption system is £12 000, while the variable system yields only £10 000. Stocks in the absorption method are valued at £8000 compared with £6000 for the variable cost method. This is because, using direct costing, the fixed costs are deducted from the sales revenue for the period instead of being divided between sales and the cost of stock. However, in the following year, the opening stock of £8000 will increase the cost of goods sold under the absorption method by £2000 more than the opening stock in the other method. If sales are greater than the number produced (that is, also selling the opening stock units) then the contribution under the variable costing system can be greater than that for the absorption method.

Standard costs

In the method described up to this point, the costs have been recorded as they were incurred (except for the predetermined applied IMC rate). These costs may include waste, inefficiency or mistakes in production without being recorded as such.

Management would prefer to know whether these costs were above or below what they *should have been*. By establishing (through engineers, industrial consultants, etc.) a *standard* cost for production, it is possible to judge the efficiency of various aspects of the manufacturing. The most valuable benefit from such a system is that the variations in cost (called *variances*) can be pinpointed, a reason for the variances adduced and steps taken to correct it for the future. This is another aspect of what is termed 'management by exception'. Management can concentrate on the items which are different from the normal expectations. Obviously, the standard costs have been based on a volume which may or may not be attained. If the number of units produced is near the estimated volume, however, it means that management can measure the 'actual' costs against the predetermined standard and discover whether the faults lie with the material, the labour, or the use of facilities. Thus, a standard cost sheet for a particular product may be:

Raw material	
3 kg of X @ £1 kg	£3.00
Direct labour	
4 hours @ £2 hour	8.00
Indirect manufacturing cost (based on direct labour hours)	
4 hours @ £3 per hour	12.00
Standard cost	£23.00

When production of a batch of units is completed, a comparison is made between the actual cost and the standard cost; for example, assume the above was based on production of 1000 units and that 1000 were actually produced with the following costs:

Raw material	3500 kg @ £0.95 kg
Direct labour	3850 hrs @ £2.02 hr
IMC labour	£11 600

Examination of these figures would enable management to discover the following *variances*:

1. An additional usage of 500 kg materials.

2. A saving of 5p per kg on material used.

3. A saving of 150 hours direct labour.

4. A loss of 2p per hour on direct labour cost.

5. A saving of £400 in IMC.

Investigation of the above results (a more complex analysis of variances is beyond the scope of this text) may show that the cheaper material resulted in more waste or damage. On the other hand, because more skilled labour was employed at a higher rate, the number of hours occupied in producing the goods was reduced. Standard costs of products are incorporated in the ledger in the stock of finished goods and in the cost of goods sold, that is, at £23 each in the above example.

Information for management decisions

1   Break-even point

In deciding the number of units to produce, management is interested in the point at which costs exactly equal the revenue from sales. This is termed the 'break-even point'. Production above the break-even point results in profit, below it in a loss.

Below is an example which assumes the following:

1. There is no opening balance of work-in-progress.

2. The period is one of three months.

Selling price per unit	£10
Expected sales and production	10 000 units
Fixed costs for quarter	£35 000
Variable costs per unit	£3

Statement of contribution to fixed costs

Sales @ £10 each (10 000 units)	£100 000
Less Variable costs @ £3 each	30 000
Contribution @ £7 each	70 000
Less Fixed costs	35 000
Net profit	£35 000

In determining at what point the contribution just covers fixed costs, it is necessary to divide the total fixed costs by the unit contribution,

that is, £35 000 ÷ 7 = 5000 units

The position at the break-even point of 5000 units is:

Sales @ £10 each (5000 units)	£50 000
Less Variable costs @ £3 each	15 000
Contribution	35 000
Less Fixed costs	35 000
Net profit	—

This may also be shown graphically as in Fig. 20.3.

From this chart management can determine the expected results of various types of decisions such as the following:

What sales are necessary to provide a profit of £15 000?
What will happen if fixed costs are increased to £60 000 and variable costs reduced to £2 per unit?
What will be the effect of increasing the selling price to £15 with the same unit sales? and so on.

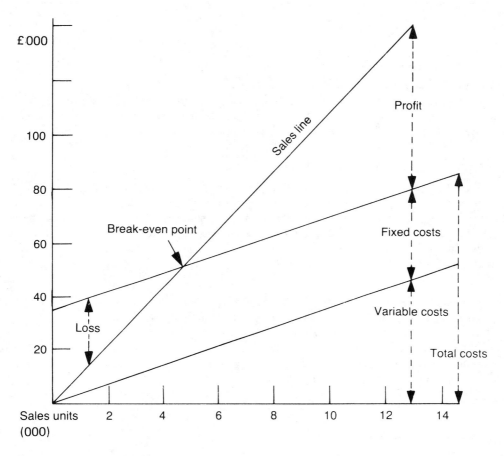

Fig. 20.3   Break-even chart.

2   Pricing variations

It can be seen from the above that the more goods sold, then the smaller is the fixed cost per unit. In the above example illustrating the break-even profit, sales of 1000 units means a fixed cost of £35 each, whereas sales of 35 000 units result in only £1 per unit for fixed costs. The variable cost (and hence the unit contribution) appears at the same figure of £3 and £7 respectively. This fact has an implication for management when considering further contracts.

Example: Data as before for fixed, variable costs and selling price. Assume sales to be normally 10 000 but that practical capacity of plant is 15 000 units.

Management have been asked to supply a further 3000 units for export at a selling price of £6.

Normal sales	10 000 @ £10	£100 000
	Variable costs 10 000 @ £3	30 000
	Contribution @ £7 each	70 000
	Fixed costs	35 000
	Profit on normal sales	£35 000

Export sales	3000 @ £6	£18 000
	Variable costs @ £3	9 000
	Profit	£9 000

The total profit becomes £44 000 for 13 000 units.

As calculated previously, a profit of £35 000 results from the normal sale of 10 000 units. At that stage, all fixed costs have been covered. Hence, there is a need to cover variable costs only for the extra production. All amounts surplus to the variable cost per unit represent profit.

3 Capital expenditure decisions

New facilities are purchased to increase or improve production (and, hopefully, profit). Here, too, management needs to accumulate, analyse and allocate costs in order to gauge whether such purchase is wise. This involves problems of the present value of future cash flows, the return on capital expected, problems of additional costs and an assessment of future potential and some non-quantitative factors. These problems involving probability and risk are somewhat advanced for a text such as this, but you should be aware of the types of problems which occur in this area such as:

Should we automate the factory, thus increasing fixed costs but reducing variable costs?
Should we buy or lease our delivery and sales vehicles?
If capacity is increased, how will this affect sales and selling prices?
Should the present plant be replaced?
Should we introduce new products?
Should we open new outlets? and so on.

Summary

1. Cost accounting is a separate but integrated part of the overall accounting system. It may be used in service organisations as well as in manufacturing, assembly, building construction and the like.

2. Future planning by means of budgets, followed by regular checks on actual results, enables more efficient operations.

3. The basic costs of manufacturing, etc. are direct labour, direct materials and indirect manufacturing cost (IMC).

4. Direct costs are those directly related to a product. Costs not so related, or which cannot be economically calculated for individual products, are termed indirect costs.

5. Fixed costs are those costs the total of which does not alter within a relevant range of activity. The total of variable costs does increase with increases in volume of production. Semi-variable costs contain elements of both fixed and variable costs.

6. There are two main systems of recording in cost accounting. Job costing is used for production of individually different items. Where the products are basically homogeneous, process costing is normally used.

7. Indirect manufacturing costs have to be estimated so that an absorption rate (or separate rates) may be applied to jobs or processes.

8. In process costing, work-in-progress has to be estimated by the use of equivalent completed units.

9. Absorption costing means that the closing stock of finished goods contains a proportion of both fixed and variable costs. In a variable costing system, the fixed costs are treated as period costs and are not included in the closing stock of finished goods. There is a greater divergence between the results of the two methods where sales and production figures fluctuate widely in different periods.

10. Standard costs are established to enable management to determine efficiency of production. Variances from the standard require explanations from those responsible. Steps may then be taken to remedy unfavourable variances in the future.

11. The break-even point is the point in the production and sales cycle where sales revenue is exactly equal to total costs. Management then knows at which stage profits begin to accumulate.

12. Cost accounting and allied techniques enable management to make proper decisions regarding pricing, production and capital investment.

Discussion questions

20.1 The purpose of installing a cost accounting system is not solely to enable the calculation of the cost of manufacture. What are the other objectives of such systems?

20.2 Give examples of (a) direct and (b) indirect expenses in the following types of enterprise: a bread baker, a dental mechanic who makes dentures, a commercial college, a house builder, a cinema.

20.3 Explain (with examples) what is meant by a 'service centre' in (a) the factory of a motor vehicle assembler and (b) a large department store.

20.4 Give examples of fixed and variable expenses in the following types of business: a radio station, a taxi owner, a medical practitioner, a public accountant, a restaurant.

20.5 List five examples of semi-variable costs and explain which parts are fixed and which are variable.

20.6 Why is it preferable to have a group of executives to prepare a budget in the case of a manufacturer rather than to leave the whole job to, say, the accountant?

20.7 This year Sorbo Ltd manufactured 10 000 sorbos but sold only 6000. Last year production was 8000 and all were sold. Explain to management the difference between absorption costing and direct costing and the effect the choice of method has upon the profit.

20.8 Which type of costing (job or process) would you expect the following to adopt:

(a) A baker who sells thousands of buns and bread rolls.

(b) A dressmaker who prepares individual exclusive garments for customers.

(c) A cabinetmaker who makes four types of kitchen adapted to the requirements of each client.

20.9 Explain the term 'cost centre' and indicate its importance to a costing system.

20.10 What kinds of variance can occur in standard cost systems?

20.11 In calculating the 'break-even point' certain assumptions have to be made. What are they?

Exercises

20.12 Indirect manufacturing cost for a particular period was estimated at £360 000. Other estimated data included:

Direct material cost	£600 000
Direct labour cost	£300 000
Direct labour hours	120 000

(a) Calculate the rate for IMC to be applied on each of the following bases:

    (i) Direct labour cost
    (ii) Direct labour hours
    (iii) Direct material cost

(b) A particular job cost £50 000 for material and £3000 for 1000 hours of direct labour. Compute the amount of IMC for each of the suggested bases.

20.13 Winkle Ltd manufactures one product only, and its capacity ranges from 500 to 2000 units annually. Its costs are

Direct labour	£24 per unit
Direct materials	£16 per unit
IMC variable	£10 per unit
Fixed costs	£20 000 p.a.
Selling price	£70 per unit

(a) Compute the break-even point.

(b) If the selling price is raised to £75 while costs remain the same, what is the new break-even point?

20.14 From the following information you are to prepare a statement showing the cost of production, revealing the separate elements of cost, for the quarter ended 30 September.

Stock at 1 July:		
Raw material		£9 000
Work-in-progress		
Material	£2 700	
Labour	1 100	
Expense	550	
		4 350
Stock at 30 September:		
Raw material		11 100
Work-in-progress		
Material	2 300	
Labour	1 000	
Expense	500	
		3 800
Purchase of raw material		9 000
Cartage on purchases of raw material		780
Productive labour		4 200
Manufacturing expenses		2 600

20.15 (a) The Moron Manufacturing Company has prepared the following operating statement for the financial year ending 30 June 19X6:

Sales		£200 000
Less Manufactured cost of goods sold		
Fixed costs	£5 000	
Depreciation of plant – calculated on a straight-line basis	4 000	
Direct materials	25 000	
Variable costs	10 000	
Direct labour	20 000	64 000
Gross margin		136 000
Less Selling expenses		
Fixed	20 000	
Sales staff's commissions (payable @ 20p in £1 of sales)	40 000	
Advertising	24 000	84 000
Trading surplus		52 000
Less Administrative expenses		
Fixed	20 000	
Variable	2 000	22 000
Net profit		£30 000

The records of the company reveal further information as follows:

(i) Sales staff are remunerated by commission only, at the rate of 20p in the £1 of gross sales.

(ii) Advertising cost comprised a fixed service fee of £1000 per annum, plus variable charges for newspaper space taken up throughout the year.

(iii) Through 19X6, the plant operated at 80 per cent capacity, producing and selling 200 000 units of product.

(A) Determine the break-even point in sales value.

(B) Given that the selling price remains constant, calculate the net profit at full production and sales capacity.

(C) The company wishes to make a net profit of £40 000 at full production and sales capacity. What selling price should it set?

(b) A company is considering the manufacture of a part for sale and has the alternative of purchasing either machine 'A', with an annual capacity of 25 000 units, annual fixed costs of £25 000 and a variable cost of £2 per unit; or machine 'B', with an annual capacity of 20 000 units, annual fixed cost of £20 000 and a variable cost of £2.50 per unit.

The selling price is £5 per unit. The firm has sufficient funds to purchase only one machine, that is, either 'A' or 'B'.

Assuming that sales would equal production in any period, at what volume level would it become more profitable to use one machine relative to the other?

20.16 W. Williamson, a manufacturer, submits the following unclassified trading account for the year ended 30 June 19X7:

Stock of raw			Sales		£63 200
materials (1/7/X6)		£8 450	Returns on purchases		
Stock of finished			(raw material)		720
goods (1/7/X6)		6 700	Stock of raw		
Work-in-progress			materials (30/6/X7)		9 210
(1/7/X6):			Stock of finished		
Raw materials	£1 500		goods (30/6/X7)		7 400
Direct labour	600		Work-in-progress		
Manufacturing			(30/6/X7):		
expense	900		Raw materials	£2 100	
			Direct labour	800	
		3 000	Manufacturing		
Stock of fuel			expense	1 100	
(1/7/X6)		420			4 000
Purchases of raw					
materials		24 250	Stock of fuel		
Returns on sales		400	(30/6/X7)		530
Purchases of fuel		4 370			
Factory lighting		830			
Depreciation of plant		3 860			
Freight on raw					
materials		1 830			
Direct wages		9 700			
Indirect wages		3 250			
Factory rent		3 500			
Gross profit		14 500			
		£85 060			£85 060

You are required to present separate manufacturing and trading statements to reveal:

(a) cost of raw materials used;

(b) manufacturing expense;

(c) cost of goods manufactured;

(d) gross profit.

20.17 The standard cost sheet for a certain product appears below.

Standard cost per unit (based on 100 units)

4 pieces material @ £5 each	=	£20
10 hours' labour @ £4 hour	=	40
IMC 200% direct labour cost	=	80
		£140

Actual production = 100 units
material cost = 430 pieces @ £4 each
labour cost = 900 hours @ £4 hour
IMC incurred £7 500.

(a) What is the actual unit cost of the 100 units produced?

(b) What is the total difference between 100 units

(i) at the actual cost, and

(ii) at standard cost?

(c) Compile a worksheet showing variances for:

  (i) materials usage;

  (ii) materials cost;

  (iii) labour efficiency;

  (iv) labour cost;

  (v) IMC.

20.18 Estimated data for the coming year for Go-Getters Ltd show:

Fixed costs	£800 000
Variable costs	70% sales
Selling price	£200 each
Sales at that price	40 000

Management is anxious to increase profit and is considering reducing the selling price to increase sales. The sales manager submits the following estimate of the effects of reductions:

Reduce selling price	Increase volume
20 per cent	20 per cent
10 per cent	15 per cent
5 per cent	10 per cent

(a) Construct a worksheet showing the effect of each change on the profit, and indicate the best alternative for management.

(b) State any problems which may arise as a result of management's decision concerning the selling price.

20.19 Estimated costs for producing units of Paulerines are as follows:

Direct material	£15
Direct labour	10
Indirect manufacturing cost: fixed	20
variable	5
	£50 per unit

These costs are based on an expected production of 4000 units, all of which are expected to be sold at £90 each. An overseas firm has offered to pay £45 each for 1000 units. No additional costs of selling or delivery would be incurred, as these will be met by the customer.

Advise management (showing your workings) as to whether the overseas order should be accepted. State any qualifications you would make in your report.

20.20 You have just been appointed manager of the Airport Hotel which has 300 available bedrooms, let at a flat rate of £20 per night. After a month you are dismayed to find that occupation of the hotel bedrooms is rarely more than 50 per cent of capacity. Examination of last year's records disclose that sales revenue from rooms was £1 000 000. The daily rate has been unchanged for 18 months. Fixed costs associated with the letting came to £500 000, while variable costs (which varied in direct proportion to room usage) totalled £200 000.

You are required to:

(a) calculate the break-even points in pounds (assuming no change since last year);

(b) assuming that the hotel operated for 365 days last year, ascertain the break-even point in the *number of rooms* occupied;

(c) You wish to increase the previous years's profit by £100 000 this year (assuming no changes in costs or rates charged).

Calculate:

   (i) The sales revenue required to achieve the higher profit.

   (ii) The *additional number of rooms* let per night beyond the average numbers occupied nightly last year.

20.21 Slide A Tray Ltd manufactures plastic trays. In the past two years, the company has been unable to work at more than half capacity because of the downturn in demand. *Variable* manufacturing and selling costs amount to £1.30 per tray, while *fixed* costs at the current production volume is equal to £1 per tray. A large hospital has offered to pay £1.20 each to take up 50 per cent idle capacity. The manager tells you, 'Sure we will lose 10p on the variable costs, but by spreading the fixed costs over twice the volume we will save 50p per tray. That should net us 40p on each one produced.'

You are required to prepare an answer to the comments of the manager showing figures that either justify or negate the manager's argument.

Problems

20.22 You have been asked to prepare the selling and distribution cost budget for the calendar year 19X8. You have been provided with last year's budget as follows:

Direct selling expenses		
Sales staff's salaries	£145 500	
Sales staff's commissions	89 000	
Sales staff's expenses	15 500	
Car expenses	105 000	£355 000
Distribution expenses		
Warehouse wages	75 000	
Warehouse occupation costs	12 500	
Delivery vehicle expenses	90 000	
General expenses	17 500	195 000
Sales office		
Salaries	100 000	
Occupation costs	20 000	
Depreciation	10 000	
Postages, telephones and stationery	40 000	
General expenses	20 000	190 000
Advertising		
Newspapers	40 000	
Television	80 000	
Promotion prizes	27 000	
Shop-window displays	13 000	160 000
		£900 000

You ascertain the following information regarding changes in 19X8:

(a) Sales are expected to be £4 450 000.

(b) Sales commissions are 2 per cent of all sales.

(c) Sales salaries are to increase by 5 per cent and office salaries 10 per cent.

(d) Sales staff's expenses, delivery vehicle expenses and car expenses are expected to rise by 10 per cent.

(e) Warehouse wages will increase by 5 per cent.

(f) An extra sales office clerk will be engaged at £250 per week.

(g) Newspaper and television advertising will rise by 10 per cent.

(h) Postage, telephone and stationery will rise by 20 per cent.

(i) Special window displays costing an additional amount of £25 000 over last year's budget will be held in August.

(j) Assume that all other expenses remain unchanged.

Prepare the budget for selling and distribution costs for 19X8.

20.23 Bilge Ltd is planning the introduction of a new product and estimates the demand at various selling prices as follows:

Price	Est. unit sales
£2.00	200 000
£2.25	180 000
£2.50	160 000
£3.00	130 000

Estimated costs:	
Fixed manufacturing costs	£30 000
Variable overhead costs	10p per unit
Direct materials	80p per unit
Direct labour	40p per unit
Selling expenses (variable)	10% of sales
Administration expenses (fixed)	£15 000

Prepare a schedule showing the selling price that Bilge Ltd should charge in order to maximise its profit on the figures supplied.

20.24 Two competing food firms were side by side at a fair. Both occupied equal space at the same rent of £1250 and charged similar prices for food. A employed three times as many employees as B. Other information was:

	A	B
Sales	£8 000	£4 500
Cost of goods sold	50% of sales	50% of sales
Wages	£2 250	£750

(a) Explain (showing detailed figures) why A is more profitable than B.

(b) By how much would B's sales have to increase in order to justify the doubling of the number of its employees at the same rate of pay if the desired net profit is £350?

20.25 Slikpaks Ltd sells two products, A and B. This year it sold 2000 of A @ £100 each. It had purchased these at a cost of £60 per unit and repackaged them at an additional cost of £10 each. It sold 2000 of B at £50 each. These were purchased for £35 and did not need repackaging. All other costs of Slikpaks Ltd were fixed. These amounted to £60 000 and were allocated to A and B in proportion to sales revenue.

(a) Prepare an income statement in which all costs are assigned to each product; and a statement showing the contribution to fixed cost of each product and the profit of the company as a whole.

(b) Discuss the differences between these two statements.

(c) If in the following year, because of competition, the sale price of Product B has to be reduced to £40, what effect would this have on income, assuming all other data is unchanged?

(d) In view of (c) above, should product B be discontinued?

20.26 Computex Ltd manufactures a standard component part (known as XL6) for computers, and supplies many of the large computer manufacturers. There is a constant excess demand for XL6 (which is sold for £525) as Computex Ltd is unable to obtain the skilled labour needed to expand production beyond its present level and so satisfy the market.

The firm's costing system has enabled the following unit cost information to be obtained:

Cost of one XL6 computer component

Direct material	£150.00
Direct labour	100.00
Variable overhead	25.00
Fixed overhead	125.00
	£400.00

Computex Ltd has received an order from a foreign computer manufacturer for 50 slightly modified XL6 parts. The modification concerns an electronic auto-switch which will have to be added to each XL6 component. These auto-switches can be: (a) brought in by Computex Ltd from another firm for £70 each; or (b) made by Computex Ltd by using skilled workers at present working on the manufacture of the conventional XL6 component part.

The estimated cost of making the auto-switch is as follows:

Direct material	£10.00
Direct labour	20.00
Variable overhead	5.00
Fixed overhead	25.00
	£60.00

Note: Established fixed overhead costs will not be affected by the decision to accept or reject the order.

The potential foreign buyer has offered a price of £30 000 for the batch of 50 modified XL6 parts.

Draft a report for the Management of Computex Ltd showing the most profitable course of action for Computex Ltd and pointing out any problem areas involved.

Chapter 21
Accounting for changing prices

Problems caused by changing prices ☐ Income measurement and asset valuation ☐ Economic income and present value ☐ Current market selling value ☐ Current cost ☐ Accounting for changes in purchasing power ☐ Relative price-change accounting ☐ SSAP 16 Current Cost Accounting ☐ Simplified example of current cost accounting

Problems caused by changing prices

The most serious and most criticised weakness of conventional accounting is its inability to cope with the problems caused by changing prices. Moderate to high rates of inflation have existed in most countries since the end of the Second World War, and the very high inflation rate experienced by the United Kingdom and many other countries in the 1970s has highlighted this problem as the major one facing the accounting profession today.

We must distinguish first between specific price changes and general price changes. Specific price changes are the movements in the price of individual commodities or services. They are the result of factors such as supply and demand, the cost of inputs and changes in technology and consumer tastes. General price changes are the movements in the prices of all goods and services, or inversely, the changes in the purchasing power of the monetary unit.

There are four major weaknesses in conventional accounting when exposed to conditions of changing prices.

1. *Distortion of net profit.* This is caused by stating depreciation expense and cost of goods sold and, to a lesser extent, some other expenses in out-of-date prices or pounds.

As an example, consider a taxi company which purchased a vehicle for £12 000. The estimated life of the vehicle was three years with an estimated residual value of £3000 at the end of that life, and the company used straight-line depreciation. In each of the three years, the taxi produced net *cash* revenues (after meeting all expenses, such as fuel, wages, repairs, etc.) of £5000. The company paid out as dividends all of its net profit each year (that is, £2000) and placed the cash surplus (that is, £3000 each year) in a bank account. At the end of the third year, it had accumulated £9000 in the bank. It sold the vehicle for £3000 as anticipated, giving it £12 000 in the bank, but found that the cost of a new vehicle with almost exactly the same technical specifications and performance was now £16 000.

In view of the fact that, ignoring interest, the company now has to find an extra £4000 to be as well-off, in terms of physical or productive capacity, as it was at the beginning of first year, can we really say that net profit was £2000 per year for three years? If net profit means anything in terms of well-offness, conventional accounting - subtracting from revenues expressed in current terms, expenses expressed in terms of historical costs - overstates net profit in times of rising prices of the specific inputs.

2. *General price-level changes.* Conventional accounting ignores the gains or losses which arise when monetary assets and liabilities are held during periods in which the general price level

changes. Monetary assets include cash in hand or at bank, debtors and fixed-interest-bearing loans and investments. Suppose a company holds £10 000 (face value) of 9 per cent government stock during a year in which the general price level rises by 15 per cent. Is the company really £900 better off at the end of the year than it was at the beginning, in terms of the purchasing power, or command over goods and services, which this investment represents?

At the end of the year, the monetary value of the stock is still £10 000 (that is, the same as it was at the beginning). However, the purchasing power of £10 000 has decreased significantly. If we restate the value of the stock at the beginning of the year in terms of pounds of end-of-the-year purchasing power (that is, £11 500) we can calculate a conceptual loss of £1500 on holding the monetary asset which more than offsets the £900 interest of £1500. Conventional accounting does not, in any way, attempt to report this loss.

Conversely, if we have liabilities in a period when the general price level is rising, there is a conceptual gain in holding those liabilities. In periods where the general price level is falling, there is a gain on holding monetary assets and a loss on holding monetary liabilities.

3. *The additivity problem.* Conventional balance sheets include assets measured in terms of different values, some contemporary and some not, and expressed in pounds of different years and thus of different purchasing power. Are we entitled to add them together? If we do, is the figure of total assets meaningful at all? Similarly, in the profit and loss statement, we had revenues expressed in current pounds, from which we attempt to subtract expenses some of which are expressed in out-of-date pounds. Isn't this rather like trying to take two apples from a plate containing six oranges?

4. *Distorted rates of return.* Many investors and analysts attempt to compare firms by calculating a rate of return. There are many forms of such calculation, but the general approach is to divide net profit by shareholders' equity or by total funds employed, or by some other base.

We have observed above that in times of rising prices, conventional accounting tends to overstate net profit. Coupled with this is the fact that the conventional balance sheet understates the values of some assets as compared with current values. Given an expression where the numerator is overstated and the denominator is understated, the resultant rate of return is being grossly overstated. There have been many instances in recent years where companies' financial statements implied a reasonable rate of return on funds invested, but if both the profit and loss statement and the balance sheet had been adjusted to reflect current values, rather than historical costs, the consequent rate of return would have been less than that obtainable from gilt-edged investments.

Income measurement and asset valuation

Before discussing specific proposals which have been advanced to try to rectify the above weaknesses, it is useful to discuss in more general terms the process of income measurement and the associated question of asset valuation. We have observed earlier that the measurement of profit or income is one of the major functions of a firm's accounting system. There are a number of generally recognised purposes for which some measure of the income of a business may be required. These may be summarised briefly as follows:

1. *A base for determining the amount of dividend to be paid to shareholders.* There are, of course, other factors, such as the firm's liquidity situation and the internal investment opportunities available, which influence the final dividend decision.

2. *A base for taxation.* Although some economists have criticised income as a measure of taxable capacity, it is the major base used for this purpose. We have stressed that rules currently used

to determine taxable income are significantly different from those currently used to determine accounting profit.

3. *To assist investors in the prediction of future returns.* There are inherent limitations to the use of historical income, however measured, as a prediction of future income. Nevertheless, the past can be of some assistance in trying to forecast the future.

4. *To assist investors in evaluating the performance of management.* Income is one of the indicators necessary to an assessment of the efficiency with which management has utilised the resources entrusted to it.

5. *To assist management in evaluating the results of its past decisions.* A rational decision maker will always attempt to learn from his past experiences.

6. *To assist economists and governments in making recommendations and decisions.* There are two main types of decisions: those concerned with the allocation of resources, and those concerned with the regulation of firms and industries.

Clearly all of these objectives cannot be fully satisfied by a single income concept, especially where that figure is suspect because of changing prices. However, while a number of different concepts of income have been developed to attempt to satisfy the objectives given above, it is possible to identify a notion common to all concepts. This is the notion of a gain in wealth. The best known definition of income is that of the economist Hicks, who said that income is 'the maximum value which a man can consume during a week, and still expect to be as well-off at the end of the week as he was at the beginning'. Hicks and many other writers since have discussed at length the problems of giving precise meaning to this definition and, in particular, the problem of measuring 'well-offness'. But at least the definition provides a general framework around which to discuss the various concepts of income.

Generally we can say that

$$I = (V_1 - V_0) + D.$$

where I = income for the period t_0 to t_1,
V_1 = value of the firm at point of time t_1,
V_0 = value of the firm at point of time t_0,
D = dividends (or drawings).

We can thus see that the problems of income measurement are very closely linked with the problems of the valuation of a firm and, in particular, the valuation of assets. This close link between income determination and asset valuation is demonstrated in conventional financial reporting by the close relationship which exists between the profit and loss statement and the balance sheet. The surplus of net profit over dividends declared is reflected in the balance sheet by the consequent increase in shareholders' equity.

There are four major bases of asset valuation which come into consideration for use in determining 'well-offness', or the measurement of income.

1. *Historic cost.* The price at which the asset was acquired.

2. *Replacement cost.* The current market buying price of similar assets or asset services.

3. *Net realisable value.* The current market selling price of the asset, less any cost necessary in converting the asset into cash.

4. *Present value.* The expected future net cash receipts (that is, receipts less payments) associated with the asset, discounted for the expected time of receipt or payment (see the explanation of the discounting process given below).

Different concepts of income have been developed using these different bases of asset valuation. The other major factor which differentiates between different income concepts is whether or not the concept attempts to recognise changes in the purchasing power of the pound, that is, general price level changes.

We will confine our discussion to six major approaches to the measurement of income.

1. *Historic cost.* In this approach, income is determined by matching revenues of the period against the expenses (some of which are expressed in historic cost). Non-monetary assets generally are valued at historic cost less depreciation where applicable. The term *accounting profit* may be used for the result obtained from this approach. Since this profit concept is the basis of conventional accounting and has been described in detail in previous chapters, no further treatment is required in this chapter.

2. *Present value.* This approach uses present value as the basis of asset valuation to determine what is generally known as *economic income* or *subjective profit*.

3. *Current value* (selling price). Net realisable value is used as the basis of asset valuation. A form of *current income* is derived.

4. *Current cost.* Replacement cost is used to determine expenses and as a basis for valuing non-monetary assets. *Current operating profit* is the most generally accepted name for the income thus derived.

5. *General price level.* Conventional accounting statements are adjusted by the use of a general price level index to reflect changes in the purchasing power of the pound. The income derived may be termed *adjusted accounting profit* or *constant pound value income*.

6. *Relative price.* In addition to using either replacement cost or net realisable value as a basis for asset valuation, an adjustment is made for the effects of changes in purchasing power. Some authors have called the results of this approach *real income*, but this title is somewhat misleading.

Economic income and present value

The ownership of an asset may be regarded as the right to future benefits accruing from that asset, and the asset may be valued in terms of the future cash flows expected to be derived from that asset. We can capitalise these expected future cash flows by using a discount rate which reflects the preference which people have for current use rather than for future use of money, and also the uncertainty which increases as we try to forecast these cash flows further into the future.

In the simplest case, the present value of a single cash receipt or payment expected at some date in the future is given by the formula:

$$V_0 = \frac{F_n}{(1 + r)^n},$$

where V_0 = present value,
F_n = amount to be received or paid,
r = discount rate,
n = number of periods involved assuming that interest is compounded each period.

Compound-interest tables giving the value of $\frac{1}{(1 + r)^n}$ are useful for performing this type of calculation.

Example: Suppose that your rich uncle gives you the choice between a gift of £10 000 now or

£12 000 in three years' time. Which would you accept? Explain the reasons for your decision.

A logical approach to this type of decision is to calculate the present value of the £12 000 and to compare this with the £10 000.

Let us assume that 8 per cent is an appropriate discount rate, that being the rate at which we could borrow or invest. We will also assume annual compounding.

Reference to appropriate compound-interest tables indicates that the present value of £1 receivable or payable in three periods from now at 8 per cent per period is £0.7938.

$$\text{Therefore } V_0 = £12\ 000 \times 0.7938$$
$$= £9525.60$$

Thus the present value of £12 000 discounted back three years at 8 per cent is less than £10 000. Therefore, it would be preferable to accept the £10 000 now rather than to wait and receive £12 000 in three years' time.

A similar decision would be reached if we compare the two alternatives at the *end* of the three-year period. If the £10 000 were invested at 8 per cent for three years, the resultant sum at the end (in future value) would be £12 597.10.

The discounting process illustrated above is a valuable tool in appraising the value of investment proposals such as the purchase of new plant, the introduction of a new product or the acquisition of an existing business. For example, suppose that an existing business is for sale and that the prospective purchaser is told that it will earn net cash returns of £25 000 p.a. for each of the next ten years with no residual value. Let us assume further that the purchaser requires a return of 12 per cent p.a. on the investment. The return of £25 000 per year may be termed an annuity (that is, an amount to be received or paid each period for a specified number of periods). The appropriate formula for calculating the present value of an annuity is:

$$V_0 = A \left[1 - \frac{\frac{1}{(1 + r)^n}}{r} \right]$$

where V_0 = present value,

A = amount of the annuity to be received or paid,

r = discount rate,

n = number of periods involved assuming that interest is compounded each period.

Compound-interest tables provide values for the expression

$$\left[\frac{1 - \frac{1}{(1 + r)^n}}{r} \right]$$

and for r = 12 per cent and n = 10 the appropriate value is 5.650. Therefore, the present value of an annuity of £25 000 for ten years discounted at 12 per cent is equal to:

$$£25\ 000 \times 5.650 = £141\ 250.$$

Thus, given the above forecasts and assumptions, the prospective purchaser would be prepared to pay no more than £141 250 for the business. We return now to the application of present value to the measurement of income. Economic income may be defined as follows:

$$I = (V_1 - V_0) + D,$$

where I = economic income for the period t_0 to t_1,

V_0 and V_1 = present value of expected future net cash receipts at points of time t_0 and t_1 respectively and

D = dividends.

Example: Suppose that a simple business consisted of a single fixed asset which would last for three years and which was capable of producing an output forecasted to yield net cash receipts of £10 000 in the first year, £8000 in the second year and £6000 in the third year. Let us further assume that no dividends were paid and that the net cash receipts were invested in securities yielding 10 per cent p.a. Assuming that 10 per cent is an appropriate rate at which to discount the expected future net cash receipts from the fixed asset, reference to compound-interest tables reveals that where $r = 10$ per cent the present value of £1 receivable or payable in n years time is

0.9091 where $n = 1$,
0.8264 where $n = 2$,
0.7513 where $n = 3$.

Thus

$$V_0 = (£10\ 000 \times 0.9091) + (£8000 \times 0.8264) + (£6000 \times 0.7513)$$
$$= £9091 + £6611 + £4508$$
$$= £20\ 210 \text{ (to the nearest pound)}$$
V_1 = the present value of the fixed asset at the end of year 1 + value of securities (£10 000).
$$= (£8000 \times 0.9091) + (£6000 \times 0.8264) + £10\ 000$$
$$= £7273 + £4958 + £10\ 000$$
$$= £22\ 231 \text{ (to the nearest pound)}.$$

Thus

$$I = V_1 - V_0$$
$$= £22\ 231 - £20\ 210$$
$$= £2021.$$

The above example illustrates, among other things, that if the expectations of future cash receipts and the appropriate discount rate do not change, economic income is equal to V_0 multiplied by the interest rate (that is, £20 210 × 10 per cent). However, where expectations and/or the discount rate do change then V_1 as calculated at point of time t_1 will be different from V_1 as anticipated in advance at point of time t_0, and therefore the amount of economic income calculated at t_1 will be different from that anticipated at t_0. In addition, the amount of net cash receipts actually received during the period may be different from the amount forecast at the beginning of the period.

Although, as pointed out earlier, present value calculations are extremely useful in assisting a variety of investment decisions, there are a number of reasons why economic income, based on present values, fails to meet most of the objectives of income measurement specified above. These reasons are summarised below:

1. The subjective nature of the present value calculation makes the verification (or auditing) of the figures an impossible task.

2. Because economic income contains unrealised as well as realised profits, it is inappropriate as a base for dividend and for taxation purposes.

3. Different investors have different risk and time preferences and, therefore, different discount rates are relevant.

4. Economic income depends very heavily on the formulation of plans; therefore variations in the extent to which different firms or the same firm over time, engage in research and development will affect the amount of economic income calculation significantly.

5. With respect to the objective of assisting the investor in evaluating managerial performance, the economic income does not distinguish between gains due to management efficiency and gains due to fortuitous circumstances.

6. Because economic income is calculated by the comparison of values at two different points of time, a statement of economic income does not provide details of the causal factors underlying a particular period's profit (that is, individual revenue and expense items). Also, because of the difficulty and, at times, impossibility of measuring the present value of individual assets (where assets are combined to produce streams of revenues), there would often be a lack of detail in a balance sheet prepared on the basis of present values.

Current-market selling value

It may be argued that 'well-offness', and thus income, may be measured more objectively by reference to the market place than by reference to the expectations of individual firms and their managers. A concept of income based on current-market selling valuation of assets may be defined as follows:

$$I = V_1 - V_0 + D,$$

where I $\quad$ = current income for the period t_0 to t_1,
V_0 and V_1 = sum of the net realisable values (or current cash equivalents) of the firm's net assets at points of time t_0 and t_1 respectively and
$\quad\quad D$ = dividends.

Some proponents of this concept of income adopt the view that all firms and individuals are adaptive and seek to convert and use their resources in the manner which will maximise their ability to command resources and thus future earnings. Thus it is argued that the appropriate valuation of a firm's assets at any particular point of time is the current monetary equivalent of those assets.

It is not intended here to examine in detail an accounting system which would give continuously the current cash equivalents of all assets and thus provide a measure of periodic current income. However, the following features of this approach should be noted.

1. The method is more objective and thus more verifiable than the use of present values.

2. All assets are consistently valued at net realisable value, thus overcoming the additivity problem referred to above.

3. Net realisable values are extremely relevant to decisions about whether to sell or retain assets. Thus, the income concept is undoubtedly relevant to an industry which is in decline. Writers are not unanimously agreed that the concept is also relevant in stable or expanding industries.

4. Current income, as defined above, includes unrealised as well as realised profits. Thus its relevance for dividend and taxation purposes may be questioned.

5. There are practical difficulties involved in the measurement of net realisable value for some types of assets, particularly work-in-progress and large integrated or unique fixed assets. In addition, it is debatable whether the selling price of a marginal unit of particular goods should be applied to all units of that good held. Therefore, such net realisable values should be calculated on the assumption of an orderly sale and not a forced liquidation. Furthermore, net realisable value may be different in different markets.

Current cost

This approach seeks to retain the realisation concept associated with conventional accounting profit but to remedy the defects of historic cost valuation referred to above. Thus, fixed assets are valued at current (or replacement) cost up to the point of realisation and current operating profit is measured as:

$$I = R - E,$$

where I = current operating profit for the period t_0 to t_1,
   R = the sum of revenues earned for that period measured in current values and
   E = the sum of expenses incurred in earning those revenues, such expenses being measured in terms of current costs.

The major difference between this concept of current operating profit and the concept of conventional accounting profit is that conventional accounting profit, in periods in which the current costs of the firm's inputs have risen, comprises in part what may be termed 'realised holding gains'. A firm's profits, in a period in which specific prices have risen, may be divided into two parts – profits from *operation* (that is, manufacturing, buying and selling) and profits from *holding* assets.

Example: At the beginning of a period, suppose a firm holds 100 units of a particular item and that these stocks cost £10 per unit. Suppose further that prior to the sale of any of these units the current (or replacement) cost rose to £12 per unit and then 60 units were sold for £15 per unit. A conventional profit and loss statement (ignoring expense other than cost of goods sold) would show a profit of £300 calculated thus:

Sales revenue (60 units @ £15)	£900
Less Cost of goods sold (HC) (60 units @ £10)	600
Net profit	£300

A profit and loss statement prepared using current cost would show a current operating profit of £180:

Sales revenue	£900
Less Cost of goods sold (CC) (60 units @ £12)	720
Current operating profit	£180

The conventional accounting profit of £300 includes a realised holding gain of £120 earned by holding 60 units of stock while the current cost rose from £10 per unit to £12 per unit. Actually, the total holding gain was £200 (£2 per unit on 100 units held). At the point of time at which the 60 units had been sold there was an *unrealised holding gain of £80*. This could be reflected in a balance sheet prepared at that point of time showing stock at current cost of £480 (rather than the historic cost of £400) and the unrealised holding gain of £80 as a reserve and thus part of shareholders' funds.

   The splitting of a firm's profit into an operating component and a holding component is often termed 'dichotomisation'. The major arguments in favour of dichotomisation of income are:

1. Current operating profit is a better base for dividend and taxation purposes than conventional accounting profit. In the above example, if the firm wished to maintain its stock level at

100 units, it could not afford to pay out all of the £300 accounting profit as dividends and still be able to replace the 60 units at the current cost of £12 per unit.

2. For a firm which intends to remain in the same industry and when technology is not changing rapidly, current operating profit may be a better predictor of future earnings than conventional accounting profit.

3. Under most circumstances current operating profit is a better indicator of management performance than conventional accounting profit. Of course some holding gains may result from deliberate speculation in stocks in anticipation of a price rise, but most holding gains and losses are outside the control of management.

Accounting for changes in purchasing power

Some accountants take the view that the major defect in the conventional accounting concept of profit is that it assumes that the purchasing power of the monetary unit is constant over time. Thus, they advocate the adoption of a concept of adjusted accounting profit sometimes termed constant pound-value income. This involves the adjustment of relevant items in conventional financial statements by the use of a single general price-level index. This approach is sometimes referred to as current purchasing power (CPP) accounting.

It must be stressed that CPP accounting deals with the effects of general price-level changes only and makes no attempt to report the current values of specific assets and cost. Most proposals for CPP accounting recommend its use as supplementary to conventional financial statements and as an end-of-period method of adjustment. Thus, the method is basically the application of a single general price-level index to all relevant individual items in profit and loss statements and balance sheets prepared in accordance with conventional accounting principles. In addition, the method involves the calculation and reporting of the net gain or loss for the period of holding monetary assets and liabilities while the general price level is changing.

The method received some support from accountants and was at one stage recommended by the Institute of Chartered Accountants in England and Wales. The major reasons for such support may be summarised as follows:

1. Once an appropriate general price-level index has been selected or recommended by some government or professional authority, the method is extremely simple and objective in its implementation and all businesses use the same index.

2. Because the method involves end-of-year adjustment only, it does not cause a significant disruption to existing accounting systems.

3. The method does not involve any major change in conventional accounting principles.

4. The method does give some recognition to the effects of changing prices. In periods of very rapid inflation where the prices of all goods and services are moving in the same direction and at roughly the same rate, the usefulness of the information provided is improved.

5. The method allows for the calculation and reporting of gains or losses on holding monetary assets and liabilities.

Two major objections have been levelled against the proposals for CPP accounting. The first is associated with the problem of finding an appropriate general price-level index. Conceptually, it is impossible to construct a price-level index which reflects satisfactorily, for all firms and individuals, the effects of changes in the purchasing power of the monetary unit. Increases in the price of beer have no effect on the purchasing power of pounds in the hands of a teetotaller;

reductions in meat prices do not affect a vegetarian, but yet these increase and decreases will be reflected in any index which purports to measure changes in the general level of prices. Proponents of CPP accounting generally recommend the use of the Gross National Product Implicit Price Deflator, which is prepared by government statisticians to convert the GNP as measured in money terms to GNP in real terms; it is thus a weighted average of all price changes occurring everywhere in the economy of a particular country.

The second, and more important, criticism of CPP accounting is directed at the relevance of the information provided. Clearly the prices of all goods and services do not move consistently in the same direction and at the same rate. Where a particular firm holds assets the prices of which are moving at a significantly different rate or in a direction different from that of the general price level, CPP accounting will not reflect accurately the impact of price changes on the position of the firm. A Committee of Inquiry appointed by the British Government reported that 'CPP accounting is unlikely to be useful to the majority of users of company accounts'.

Given that the method has received relatively little general support, we do not believe that it is necessary to give examples of its use. However, there is one aspect of the method which can and has been incorporated into other proposals – the concept of gains or losses on the holding of monetary assets and monetary liabilities. This concept was illustrated earlier in this chapter by reference to holding government stocks (a monetary asset) during a period in which the general price level rose.

The effects of holding monetary assets or monetary liabilities when general price levels are changing may be summarised thus:

Type of Item Held	Movement of General Price Level	Effect
Monetary asset	Increase	Loss
	Decrease	Gain
Monetary liability	Increase	Gain
	Decrease	Loss

Relative price-changing accounting

Methods of current value accounting, using either current exit values (net realisable value) or current entry values (replacement cost) are designed to reflect changes in the specific prices of goods and services affecting a particular firm. The general price-level approach, to which we have just made reference, reflects changes in the purchasing power of the monetary unit (that is, the prices of all goods and services). Some theorists argue that the ideal income concept should take into account changes in *both* specific prices and the general price level.

This can be achieved by first valuing assets in terms of current values (either exit or entry) and then making an adjustment for changes in the purchasing power of the pound as it affects the net equity of the firm. This second step isolates and reports the gain or loss for the period on holding net monetary assets.

SSAP 16: Current Cost Accounting

Although the Accounting Standards Committee suspended the mandatory status of SSAP 16: Current Cost Accounting with effect from 6 June 1985 it still remains an authoritative reference on accounting under the current cost convention.

The standard applies to all annual financial statements prepared by companies listed on the stock exchange and unlisted companies satisfying two or more of the following criteria:

1. Turnover more than £5 million.

2. Balance sheet assets exceeding £2.5 million.

3. Average number of employees exceed 250.

The standard requires production of separate current cost accounts in addition to the historical cost accounts.

The basic objective of current cost accounts is to provide more useful information than that available from historical cost accounts alone for the guidance of the management of the business, the shareholders and others on such matters as:

the financial viability of the business;
return on investment;
pricing policy, cost control and distribution decisions; and
gearing.

Adjustments to profit and loss account

To arrive at a current cost operating profit three major adjustments are made. These are as follows:

1. *Depreciation adjustment.*   The depreciation adjustment adjusts the current year's historical cost depreciation charge to the value to the business of the fixed assets consumed during the year. Its purpose is to enable the company to maintain the existing operating capability of the business.

2. *Cost of sales adjustment.*   The purpose of this adjustment is to alter the current year's historical value to the business of that stock. This will enable the company to maintain the existing operating capability of the business.

3. *Monetary working capital adjustment.*   Most businesses have other working capital besides stock involved in their day-to-day operating activities. For example, when sales are made on credit the business has funds tied up in debtors. Conversely, if the suppliers of goods and services allow a period of credit, the amount of funds needed to support working capital is reduced. The monetary working capital is an integral part of the net operating assets of the business. Thus the standard provides for an adjustment in respect of monetary working capital when determining current cost operating profit. This adjustment should represent the amount of additional, or reduced, finance needed for monetary working capital as a result of changes in the input prices of goods and services used and financed by the business.

The gearing adjustment

In most companies the net operating assets are financed partly by borrowings and partly by the shareholders. Where borrowings are fixed in monetary terms, any liability to repay is not affected by changes in the prices of the assets financed out of borrowings. When prices are rising this benefits the shareholders. The purpose of the gearing adjustment is to ensure that the current cost profit attributable to the shareholders reflects this benefit.

The logic behind the gearing adjustment is that the shareholders need finance the increased replacement cost only of assets whose original purchase they financed. When the purchase of assets was financed by borrowings, the shareholders need finance only the historical cost of such assets: this amount will equate to the amounts so borrowed.

The current cost reserve

The current cost balance sheet includes a reserve in addition to those included in historical cost accounts. The additional reserve may be referred to as the current cost reserve. The total reserves will include, as appropriate:

1. Unrealised revaluation. surpluses on fixed assets, stock and investments.

2. Realised amounts equal to the cumulative net total of the current cost adjustment: that is

(a) the depreciation adjustment;

(b) the working capital adjustments;

(c) the cost of sales adjustment;

(d) the gearing adjustment.

Simplified example of current cost accounting

The following simple example is intended to illustrate the main type of adjustments required to be made when current cost accounts are required to be produced.

Question

Balance Sheet as at 30 June 19X9

19X8 £000		19X9 £000	19X9 £000
200	**Fixed assets** – At cost	200	
60	*Less* Accumulated depreciation	80	120
140			
	Current assets		
40	Stocks	52	
25	Debtors	43	
5	Cash at bank	25	
70		120	
20	*Less* Current liabilities	25	
50	*Net current assets*		95
190			215
	Represented by:		
100	**Share capital**		100
40	**Reserves**		65
140			165
50	10% **Debentures**		50
190			215

Profit and Loss Account for year ended 30 June 19X9

	£000	£000
Sales		265
Less Cost of Sales		
Opening Stock	40	
Purchases	212	
	252	
Less Closing Stock	52	200
Gross profit		65
Less Expenses (including Depreciation £20 000)	35	
Interest	5	40
Retained Profit for year		25

You are given the following additional information:

1. The price index numbers for the stock at the end of each month were as follows:

March 19X8	120
April 19X8	125
June 19X8	130
December 19X8	135
March 19X9	140
April 19X9	142
June 19X9	150
Average for year ended 30 June 19X9	137

The average stock was acquired three months before the year end.

2. The calculations should be to the nearest £000.

3. The fixed assets were purchased at the beginning of the financial year ending 30 June 19X6. The replacement cost of these assets at 30 June 19X9 would be £300 000 and at 30 June 19X8 £250 000.

From the foregoing information you are required to prepare:

(a) a current cost profit and loss account for the year ended 30 June 19X9, and

(b) a current cost balance sheet at 30 June 19X9.

Working notes

1. *Calculation of cost of sales adjustment* The following formula can be used to make this calculation:

$$\frac{\text{Average index for the period}}{\text{Index at date of purchase}}.$$

		£000
Opening stock	$40 \times \dfrac{137}{120}$	46
Purchases for year		212
		258
Closing stock	$52 \times \dfrac{137}{140}$	51
Current cost of sales		207
Less Historical cost of sales		200
Cost of sales adjustment		7

Note: Since the stock is bought on average three months before the end of the year, stock turn-over period is consequently six months.

2. *Depreciation adjustment* Since the replacement cost valuations have been given in the question the calculation for the additional depreciation charge is as follows:

	£000
Depreciation charge - current cost basis $10\% \times £300\,000$	30
Less Depreciation charge - historical cost basis	20
Additional depreciation charge	10

3. *Monetary working capital adjustment* SSAP 16 defines monetary working capital (MWC) as the aggregate of:

(a) trade debtors, prepayments and trade bills receivable, plus

(b) stock not subject to a cost of sales adjustment, less

(c) trade creditors, accruals and trade bills payable, in so far as they arise from day-to-day operating activities of the business

   Calculation of net monetary working capital:

	19X8 £000	19X9 £000
Debtors	25	43
Creditors	20	25
	5	18
Net increase in MWC		13

(This represents the unadjusted changes in the volume of MWC.)

The following formula is then applied:

$$\text{Adjusted opening MWC} = \frac{\text{Opening MWC at HC}}{\text{Opening index}} \times \text{Average index}$$

$$\text{Adjusted closing MWC} = \frac{\text{Closing MWC at HC}}{\text{Closing index}} \times \text{Average index}$$

Then Opening MWC is $5 \times \dfrac{137}{130} =$		5	
Less Closing MWC $18 \times \dfrac{137}{150} =$	16	11	
Increase due to inflation MWCA			2

4. *Gearing adjustment* The purpose of this adjustment is to calculate the current cost accounting profit attributable to shareholders. This is accomplished by adding the benefit accruing to them from the extent of gearing to the current cost profit. There are three stages necessary to complete this adjustment. These are:

Calculation of average net borrowings

Calculate the gearing proportion

Calculate the gearing adjustment itself.

Calculation of average net borrowings:

	19X8 £000	19X9 £000
Debentures	50	50
Less Cash at bank	5	25
Net borrowing	45	25

Average net borrowing $\dfrac{45 + 25}{2} = 35$

Calculation of average net operating assets:

	19X8 £000	19X9 £000
Fixed assets – replacement cost	250	300
Less Depreciation (10% p.a. for 3 years)	75	
(10% p.a. for 4 years)		120
	175	180
Stocks $\quad 40 \times \dfrac{130}{120}$	43	
$52 \times \dfrac{150}{140}$		56
Net MWC	5	18
	223	254

Average $\dfrac{223 + 254}{2} = 238.5.$

Gearing proportion is $\dfrac{35}{238.5} \times 100 = 14.7\%.$

Then the gearing adjustment will be:

£000

$14.7\% \times (7 + 2 + 10) = £3$

5. *Calculation of current cost reserve* This reserve will include unrealised gains (or holding gains) on the revaluation of fixed assets, also realised surpluses, depreciation, cost of sales, monetary working capital and gearing adjustments.

	£000	£000
Surplus arising on revaluation of assets		
Net replacement cost	180	
Less Net book value	120	
	60	
Additional depreciation charge	10	70
Cost of sales adjustment		7
Monetary working capital adjustment		2
Gearing adjustment		(3)
Stock at replacement cost $52 \times \dfrac{150}{140}$	56	
Less Historical cost	52	4
		80

Current Cost Profit and Loss Account for year ended 30 June 19X9

	£000	£000
Sales		265
Historic cost trading profit		30
Less Current cost operating adjustments:		
Depreciation	10	
Cost of sales adjustment	7	
Monetary working capital adjustment	2	19
Current cost operating profit		11
Gearing adjustment	3	
Interest on borrowing	5	2
Retained current cost profit of the year		9

Current Cost Balance Sheet as at 30 June 19X9

	£000	£000
Fixed assets	300	
Less Depreciation	120	180
Current assets		
Stock	56	
Debtors	43	
Cash at bank	25	
	124	
Current liabilities		
Creditors	25	99
		279
Share capital		100
Reserves		49
Current cost reserve		80
10% debentures		50
		279

Notes

1. The index number used for cost of sales adjustment has been adopted for the debtors and creditors.
2. The depreciation adjustment has been calculated using the end of year values.

Summary

1. There are four major weaknesses of conventional accounting when exposed to changing prices:

(a) Distortion of profit when depreciation and cost of goods sold are expressed in historical cost.

(b) Failure to recognise changes in the purchasing power of monetary items.

(c) Additivity problems.

(d) Distorted rates of return.

2. There are a number of recognised objectives of income measurement and no single concept of income is capable of fully satisfying all of these objectives.

3. A notion common to all concepts of income is that income represents the amount that a person or firm can consume during a period and remain as 'well-off' at the end of the period as it was at the beginning.

4. The differences between various concepts of income are basically differences in opinion as to what constitutes 'well-offness' and thus how assets should be valued.

5. The major income concepts described in this chapter were:

(a) Accounting profit using historic cost valuation.

(b) Economic income using present values.

(c) Current income using net realisable values.

(d) Current operating profit using replacement cost.

(e) Adjusted accounting profit using a general price-level index.

(f) 'Real' income using both current values and an adjustment for changes in purchasing power.

6. Although the Accounting Standards Committee suspended the mandatory status of SSAP 16: Current Cost Accounting with effect from 6 June 1985 it still remains an authoritative reference on accounting under the current cost convention.

Discussion questions

21.1 'Inflation causes an erosion of capital.' Explain (with examples) the meaning of this sentence with reference to the accounting reports of companies.

21.2 Carefully explain the differences between the historic cost, the replacement cost and the net realisable value of a fixed asset.

21.3 What is the difference between the present value and the current value of an investment?

21.4 Assets such as business premises are sometimes revalued. Is this a contradiction of the historic cost basis of accounting? How is the surplus on revaluation treated, and why is it not included in the profit and loss statement?

21.5 Three identical blocks of land are purchased at ten-year intervals for £40 000, £60 000 and £100 000 respectively.
How would the item 'land' appear in most balance sheets? Comment.

21.6 Compare and contrast holding gain, realised holding gain, unrealised holding gain.

21.7 Discuss the weaknesses of historical cost accounts.

21.8 Will the net profit of a company calculated on a current cost basis (such as SSAP 16) always be lower than the profit calculated on a historic cost basis? Explain.

21.9 What preparatory steps would need to be taken by an accountant who is introducing current cost accounting for the first time?

21.10 What in your opinion are the major objections to the introduction of an accounting standard making the introduction of current cost accounting mandatory for all businesses?

Exercises

21.11 Assume that you can invest or borrow money at an interest rate of 9 per cent p.a. and that you are given the choice of these two proposals:

Proposal A: You may collect £20 000 now.
Proposal B: You may collect £25 000 in three instalments – £5000 one year from now, and £10 000 at the end of each of the second and third years.
Which proposal would you choose?

Reference to compound-interest tables shows that the present value of £1 at 9 per cent for *n* years from now is:

n = 1   £0.9174,
n = 2   £0.8417,
n = 3   £0.7722.

21.12 You are considering the purchase of a business, and you estimate that it will yield net cash receipts of £18 000 per annum for the next six years and then have no resale value. You require a return of 12 per cent p.a. on your investment.

(a) What is the maximum amount which you would be prepared to pay for this business? (Reference to compound-interest tables shows that the present value of an annuity of £1 for six periods is £4.111.)

(b) The balance sheet of this business shows net assets less liabilities of £65 000. Explain why you are prepared to pay more than this amount.

21.13 The Sturtwood Company began operations on 1 January 19X6. Balance sheets on that date and the 31 December 19X6 are as follows:

	1 Jan.	31 Dec.
Cash	£2 000	£8 000
Debtors	—	2 000
Stock	4 000	6 000
Plant and equipment	18 000	18 000
Accumulated depreciation	—	(2 000)
	£24 000	£32 000
Creditors	4 000	8 000
Issued shares	20 000	20 000
Retained earnings	—	4 000
	£24 000	£32 000

The profit and loss statement for the year ended 31 December 19X6 was as follows:

Sales	£30 000
Less Cost of goods sold	22 000
	8 000
Less Expenses (including depreciation)	4 000
Net profit	£4 000

During the period, the price index rose steadily from 100 to 110.

(a) Calculate the purchasing power gain or loss on net monetary assets during 19X6.

(b) Explain the nature of a purchasing power gain or loss on net monetary assets.

Index